Jewish Philosophical Politics in Germany, 1789–1848

THE TAUBER INSTITUTE SERIES FOR THE STUDY OF EUROPEAN JEWRY

Jehuda Reinharz, General Editor
Sylvia Fuks Fried, Associate Editor
Eugene R. Sheppard, Associate Editor

The Tauber Institute Series is dedicated to publishing compelling and innovative approaches to the study of modern European Jewish history, thought, culture, and society. The series features scholarly works related to the Enlightenment, modern Judaism and the struggle for emancipation, the rise of nationalism and the spread of antisemitism, the Holocaust and its aftermath, as well as the contemporary Jewish experience. The series is published under the auspices of the Tauber Institute for the Study of European Jewry—established by a gift to Brandeis University from Dr. Laszlo N. Tauber—and is supported, in part, by the Tauber Foundation and the Valya and Robert Shapiro Endowment.

For the complete list of books that are available in this series,
please see www.upne.com

Sven-Erik Rose
Jewish Philosophical Politics in Germany, 1789–1848
ChaeRan Y. Freeze and Jay M. Harris, editors
Everyday Jewish Life in Imperial Russia: Select Documents, 1772–1914
David N. Myers and Alexander Kaye, editors
The Faith of Fallen Jews: Yosef Hayim Yerushalmi and the Writing of Jewish History
Federica K. Clementi
Holocaust Mothers and Daughters: Family, History, and Trauma
*Ulrich Sieg
Germany's Prophet: Paul de Lagarde and the Origins of Modern Antisemitism
David G. Roskies and Naomi Diamant
Holocaust Literature: A History and Guide
*Mordechai Altshuler
Religion and Jewish Identity in the Soviet Union, 1941–1964
Robert Liberles
Jews Welcome Coffee: Tradition and Innovation in Early Modern Germany
Sharon Faye Koren
Forsaken: The Menstruant in Medieval Jewish Mysticism
Nils Roemer
German City, Jewish Memory: The Story of Worms
David Assaf
Untold Tales of the Hasidim: Crisis and Discontent in the History of Hasidism
Jehuda Reinharz and Yaacov Shavit
Glorious, Accursed Europe: An Essay on Jewish Ambivalence

*A Sarnat Library Book

Sven-Erik Rose

Jewish Philosophical Politics in Germany, 1789–1848

BRANDEIS UNIVERSITY PRESS
Waltham, Massachusetts

BRANDEIS UNIVERSITY PRESS
An imprint of University Press of New England
www.upne.com

Manufactured in the United States of America
Typeset in Bulmer by Integrated Publishing Solutions

University Press of New England is a member of the Green Press Initiative. The paper used in this book meets their minimum requirement for recycled paper.

Library of Congress Cataloging-in-Publication Data

Rose, Sven-Erik.
Jewish philosophical politics in Germany, 1789–1848 / Sven-Erik Rose.
p. cm.—(Tauber Institute series for the study of European Jewry)
Summary: "Fresh look at how Jewish intellectuals thought about Judaism within a German philosophical tradition"—Provided by publisher.
ISBN 978-1-61168-578-7 (cloth: alk. paper)—
ISBN 978-1-61168-579-4 (pbk.: alk. paper)—
ISBN 978-1-61168-580-0 (ebook)
1. Jewish philosophy—Germany—18th century. 2. Jewish philosophy—Germany—19th century. 3. Judaism and philosophy. 4. Judaism—Germany—History—18th century. 5. Judaism—Germany—History—19th century. I. Title.
B5800.R674 2014
181′.06094309034—dc23

2014003913

5 4 3 2 1

For Claire, Asher, and Noam

Contents

Acknowledgments

The earliest parts of this book grew out of my participation in a seminar on Kant and the Haskalah given by Christoph Schulte at the Moses Mendelssohn Center in Potsdam. At the University of Pennsylvania, Lilianne Weissberg guided the project as it developed. Her intellectual energy is an inspiration.

I wrote and rewrote this book while at Miami University (Ohio). I am deeply thankful for the rigorous level of intellectual conversation that my colleagues in Miami's Department of French and Italian maintain and for their kindness, collegiality and good humor, and their enduring support of my work—even when, as in this book, it took me far afield of French studies. As this project developed over many years, Jim Creech, Elisabeth Hodges, Anna Klosowska, Sante Matteo, Mark McKinney, and Jonathan Strauss engaged generously and probingly with it in the department's vigorous works-in-progress series. Jim and Jonathan also read portions of the manuscript and helped me tighten my thinking and my prose.

Colleagues in Miami's German studies works-in-progress group also read and discussed portions of the developing manuscript; I thank in particular Mila Ganeva, Ole Gram, Eric Jensen, and Pepper Stettler. Steve DeLue saw value in my work at a crucial time. This project has benefited from the advice and support of many other colleagues and friends in the wider Cincinnati community, in particular Susan Einbinder, Adi Gordon, Eran Kaplan, and Michael Meyer.

Miami University granted me a semester of research leave in spring 2009 that greatly facilitated the research and writing of this book. I am grateful to the Simon Dubnow Institute in Leipzig and its director, Dan Diner, for granting me a fellowship in summer 2011, which gave me the resources and time to draft chapters 2 and 3. Colleagues there—in particular, Nicolas Berg, Jörg Deventer, Lutz Fiedler, Elisabeth Gallas, Natasha Gordinsky, Omar Kamil, and Susanne Zepp—were wonderfully welcoming, and their wide-ranging interests and dedication to research energizing. My office mate Yael Almog set a standard to emulate for *Sitzfleisch*, even as our occasional coffee breaks provided a welcome distraction from things Hegelian.

I am indebted to several people and institutions for inviting me to present work related to this book: Dan Magilow, University of Tennessee, Knoxville; Julie Klein, Villanova University; Mark Raider, University of Cincinnati; David

Biale on behalf of the Posen Foundation; Dan Diner, Simon Dubnow Institute, Leipzig; and Sylvia Fried and Eugene Sheppard, Tauber Institute for the Study of European Jewry, Brandeis University. I thank the audiences at these lectures for their questions and remarks, as well as the audiences of panels on which I presented aspects of this project at the Association for Jewish Studies, the German Studies Association, and the Duke German Jewish Studies Workshop.

My research was aided by the staffs of Hebrew Union College's Klau Library in Cincinnati; the University of Cincinnati's Langsam Library; Miami University's King Library; and the Shields Library at the University of California, Davis. Thanks go also to Katharina Erbe, who transcribed several handwritten documents of the Verein für Cultur und Wissenschaft der Juden.

I am especially indebted to Eugene Sheppard for showing an interest in this project well before it was fully formulated and for encouraging me to submit it to be considered for publication in the Tauber Institute Series for the Study of European Jewry. As associate director of the Tauber Institute, Eugene read and most helpfully commented on the entire manuscript. Sylvia Fried, associate editor of the Tauber Institute series, and Phyllis Deutsch, editor-in-chief at the University Press of New England, have shared sage advice throughout the process of making final revisions, for which I am greatly appreciative. I thank Jeanne Ferris for the thoroughness with which she copy-edited my manuscript, and Michael Taber for preparing the index. I am enormously grateful to Jonathan Hess, who, as a reader for the press, could not have been more incisive in his evaluation of my project, or more intellectually generous in his suggestions for improving it. I also thank an anonymous reader for providing constructive criticism. David Biale, who read the manuscript as a reader of my tenure file at Miami University, likewise commented extensively on the project and made suggestions that have greatly improved this book.

My new colleagues in the Department of German and Russian at the University of California, Davis—in particular, Gail Finney, Jaimey Fisher, Elisabeth Krimmer, and Chunjie Zhang—have shown generous interest in my work and warmly welcomed me to my new institutional home.

An earlier version of much of chapter 1 appeared as "Lazarus Bendavid's and J. G. Fichte's Kantian Fantasies of Jewish Decapitation in 1793," *Jewish Social Studies* 13, no. 3 (2007): 73–102; I am grateful to Indiana University Press for permission to reprint material from that article here.

I could not have written this book without my family and friends. Leah Hochman kept me on track during a critical half year or more by receiving, biweekly, my latest pages and consistently encouraging me no matter how meager or rough they were. Julia Scheffer shared her insights on a couple of particularly thorny translations. My deep appreciation goes to my intellectual companions Darcy Buerkle, Eric Kligerman, Dan Magillow, and Anna Parkinson. David Bathrick's virtuosity in the genre of conversation is a keen pleasure and rich source of ideas, and his faith in my work has been an enormous support. My gratitude to John Wright and Phoebe Varinia DeMund for their enduring friendship grows with the years.

I am fortunate to have a warm, supportive, and infinitely interesting family in the United States and Europe. On the European side, special thanks go to Jaspar Jansen, a cousin who is more like my brother. My affectionate appreciation goes also to Boukje van Tulder, Ellis Galesloot, and Ton Lakeman. My warm gratitude goes as well to Birgit and Rune Palm, my aunt and uncle, and Håkan and Maria Palm, my cousins.

Stateside, special thanks go to my sister, Marta; my sister-in-law, Julie Steiner; and Trixie and Micah, my niece and nephew. The love, work ethic, and sensitivity to the challenges of academic research of my father, Jim, have sustained this project at every stage. I also thank his partner, Anne Bower, for her kindness and support. I am grateful to my mother-in-law, Athene Goldstein, for her generosity, intelligence, and patient belief in me and this project, so long in the making. The memory of two people who inspired my intellectual and human *Bildung* infuses the pages of this book: my almost uncannily insightful and infinitely kind father-in-law, Marvin Goldstein; and my mother, Beatrix Bloem Rose, who—with her huge heart, irreverence, and passion for ideas—continues to be my guiding star.

My sweet, funny, boundlessly curious and energetic, *och ibland mer än lovligt busiga* sons, Asher and Noam, brighten every day of my life. They have followed the ups and downs of my progress on this project, probably more closely than they should have had to. It is a pleasure at last to be able to answer their recurrent, exasperated questions as to whether this book would ever be finished. Claire, my companion and constant and favorite interlocutor, has heard and read (and reread) the arguments in this book at every stage and has done more than any other person to make them better. I dedicate the book with all my love to Claire, Asher, and Noam.

Jewish Philosophical Politics in Germany, 1789–1848

Introduction

From the late eighteenth century Jews gained increasing exposure to German cultural life. Possibilities for Jews to participate in politics in German lands, however, remained severely limited. Although a modest number of Jews served in city administrations in the decades before 1848, they were excluded from estates' assemblies at the state level. It was not until the tumultuous events of the Revolution of 1848–49 that Jews (briefly) experienced something approaching full political and civil rights and played a prominent role in German politics—serving in the parliaments or constitutional assemblies of numerous German states, in the Vorparlement (preliminary parliament) in Frankfurt, and later in the National Assembly—as well as fighting and dying on the barricades alongside their non-Jewish fellow revolutionaries.[1]

Jewish Philosophical Politics in Germany, 1789–1848 examines how, in the absence of more tangible possibilities for political engagement in these years, the creative explosion of German philosophy provided resources that certain intellectuals drew on to envision a place for Jews in the polity. A passionate Kantian, Lazarus Bendavid, in the early 1790s (chapter 1); an association of first-generation Jewish university students who organized themselves according to Hegelian principles into the Verein für Cultur und Wissenschaft der Juden (association for the culture and science of the Jews) around 1820 (chapters 2 and 3); the young Karl Marx, trying to overcome philosophical and political abstraction in the early 1840s (chapter 4); the popular novelist Berthold Auerbach and his friend Moses Hess, the visionary communist philosopher and political activist, each finding in his divergent interpretation of Spinoza in the late 1830s and early 1840s a way to harmonize Jews with a wider community (chapters 5 and 6)—all the thinkers this book scrutinizes creatively deployed the conceptual tools made available to them by different philosophical paradigms to imagine the potential, terms, and consequences of Jewish inclusion in the polity.

In engaging in this sort of philosophical politics, these writers performed a Jewish variation on a wider theme in German philosophical culture of the period. Although the political turmoil in France—the Revolutions of 1789 and 1830 and the Napoleonic era in between—demonstrated the possibility of radical social and political change, German intellectuals felt keenly that they were reduced to theorizing about the sort of historical transformations being enacted across the Rhine. Yet their tantalizing proximity to such political upheaval also led German intellectuals to interpret their reflections in highly politicized ways and to ascribe powers of historical agency to their theoretical interventions. As Bernard Yack has shown, the shadow cast by the Revolution of 1789 led a generation of left Kantians to interpret Kant's philosophy in a politicized key and to endeavor to realize Kantian freedom, in spite of the impossibility of such a project from Kant's own point of view.[2] Hegel, too, assigned the act of cognition privileged agency in the historical process, a tendency that Left Hegelians in the 1830s and 1840s both savaged and radicalized.

Subjectivity had been a, if not the, central focus of modern epistemology from Descartes's *Meditationes de prima philosophia* (*Meditations on First Philosophy*; 1641) to Kant's *Kritik der reinen Vernunft* (*Critique of Pure Reason*; 1781); however, the nature and demands of subjectivity took on great political urgency in the reception of Kantian thought after 1789. While the autonomous subject is the hero of Kantian moral philosophy and its politicized heirs, Hegel and Hegelians deemed Kant's formal conception of subjectivity an obstacle to ethical community. Definitions of what constituted salubrious or toxic forms of subjectivity were protean, yet subjectivity persisted as a nodal point around which philosophical and political debates crystallized in German culture between 1789 and the Vormärz. For Jewish thinkers, historical and communal bonds and commitments complicated the task of theorizing (Jewish) subjectivity and reconciling it with available political and philosophical models.

Freighting the issue further for Jewish intellectuals was the fact that "the Jew" not infrequently figured as the embodiment of deficient and socially corrosive subjectivity, whether as heteronomous rather than self-legislating, in Kant's sense; as abstract and unreconciled to objective spirit, in Hegel's sense; or as basely egoistic, in the understanding of various Young Hegelians, including Ludwig Feuerbach, Bruno Bauer, and Karl Marx. The discourse of Jewish egoism also reached beyond the philosophical Left in Germany to include a range of conservative and reactionary critics of Heinrich Heine and other Jewish writers, for example. Even as they tried to imagine narratives of Jewish history and forms of Jewish identity and community that could allow Jews to play a role within the wider polity, the thinkers and writers I study had to negotiate real or discursively constructed forms of Jewish specificity that presented obstacles to citizenship.

A substantial body of scholarship from the 1950s to the present has dealt with the way German Idealism theorizes Judaism, and more recent scholarship also explores ways that Jewish thinkers have negotiated and contested German Idealism's purported antisemitism.[3] Paul Rose and Michael Mack have each argued that antisemitism is neither a minor nor an incidental, but in fact a constitutive, component of German Idealism.[4] For Rose, Kant and Fichte (as well as Herder) laid the intellectual foundation for what Rose calls "revolutionary antisemitism," a secular form of Jew hatred that constructs Jews and Judaism as that from which both the German nation and humanity at large must be redeemed. Mack makes the similar argument that for Kant and Hegel, the Jews "embody all that which hinders the construction of a perfect body politic in the here and now," and that in German Idealism's quest to construct a "perfect, noncontingent world," "the Jews represented this detrimental difference of worldly contingency" and thus "signified that which had to be overcome."[5] This study departs from both the traditional study of German Idealism's image of Judaism and from Rose's and Mack's critiques of antisemitism's constitutive role in the German intellectual tradition by focusing primarily on Jewish intellectuals who tried to "think Jewish" not only against, but also with, conceptual models invented or reinvented during the classical age of German philosophy.

When analyzing how German Idealism constructs Jewishness as its Other we must be careful not to let our own analytic aperture complete the job. Privileging the (real) anti-Jewish strains in Kant and Hegel leads almost ineluctably to an impoverished reading of Jewish intellectuals who think in their wake as either resistant or self-hating.[6] Yet the conceptual resources these master thinkers put at their followers' disposal were enormous, and Jewish intellectuals thinking through Jewish modernity in the keys of German Idealism were not limited to or necessarily dominated by its anti-Jewish strains. Indeed, once we let go of the binary of German philosopher and Jewish Other, we discover that Jewish thinkers from the classical age of German philosophy showed themselves to be quite nimble in thinking with, not only against, the master thinkers—challenging some aspects of their thought but skillfully appropriating and deploying others in ways that allowed them to imagine a place for themselves in the philosophical community of German modernity. This book takes seriously such thinkers who tend to explode the German philosopher–Jewish Other binary by using the conceptual tools of German philosophy to think through and intervene in the situation of Jews in political modernity. It should go without saying that this is not tantamount to celebrating any of the specific postures that these thinkers adopted or programs that they advocated. My aim, rather, is to illuminate the complex, often ambivalent, and sometimes bewildering uses to which a range of Jewish thinkers put the tools that German philosophy placed at their disposal in the heady era of 1789–1848 in order to reimagine Jewish history, community, and political agency so as to accord with, and contest, the terms of political inclusion. Although both German intellectuals during this period and scholars who have studied it since widely acknowledge that philosophy served as a major arena for the negotiation of politics, few have focused on the political dimension of Jewish engagements with philosophy in Germany during its most explosive years between Kant and the Young Hegelians. This book takes this question as its central concern.

It is the variable convergence of philosophy and activism that has determined my selection of the figures and texts in this study. Criteria of inclusion are necessarily criteria of exclusion, and my interest in the compelling nexus of politics, philosophy, and negotiations of Jewish subjectivity in this period has drawn my attention away from figures who would have to figure centrally in a study of any single component of this nexus. Thus Gabriel Riesser, the most vigorous Jewish political activist of the 1830s and 1840s, makes only a fleeting appearance in the pages of this book simply because he did not imbue his political writings with philosophy. Conversely, Salomon Maimon, the most brilliant Jewish philosophical mind in the German cultural orbit in the last decades of the eighteenth century, also receives scant mention since he never intervened in or meditated in a sustained way on the political situation of Jews in Germany, despite the existence of richly suggestive moments in various of his texts.[7]

This book is informed by intellectual history but is not meant to be a history. The contextualized close readings that make up the backbone of this study probe paradigmatic attempts to engage in (or, in Marx's case, to disengage from) philosophy as a displaced politics in Germany during the emancipation era. My approach is indebted to my training in comparative literature and literary theory, a field of inquiry defined less by a common canon or corpus than by a commitment to careful reading across and at the intersections of different disciplines and modes of discourse. At the intersection of disciplines—Jewish studies, intellectual history, philosophy, and literary studies—*Jewish Philosophical Politics in Germany, 1789–1848* does not attempt, chiefly, to tell a story or trace an evolution, but rather to examine how Jewish intellectuals negotiated an abiding (if variable) constellation of concerns, aspirations, and predicaments with conceptual and rhetorical tools made available by different philosophical frameworks. Whatever stories my book tells emerge as a welcome by-product of this aim. A number of stories and connections do emerge and are worth foregrounding here.

Numerous biographical and anecdotal linkages connect the various moments of this study. Lazarus Bendavid, who popularized Kantian philosophy in the 1780s and 1790s, was a member of the Verein in the early 1820s. Though he never became reconciled to the Verein's Hegelian orientation, he contributed two articles to its short-lived journal. Heinrich Heine—philosophically interested, politically discordant, and ostentatious in his staging of ironic subjectivity—haunts several moments of this study. Like Bendavid, Heine was a member of the Verein and carried on correspondences during and after its demise with several of his Verein colleagues, whom he once characterized as his fellow *Wissenschaftsjuden* (Jews of science). Heine later became a friend of Marx and was a positive and a negative inspiration in the early careers of Hess and Auerbach, respectively. Hess and Marx were also close associates in the early 1840s. Hess wrote one of the most famous descriptions of the young Marx—then virtually unknown—in a letter to Auerbach;[8] and Marx's deployment of crude rhetoric in "Zur Judenfrage" ("On the Jewish Question") draws deeply, rhetorically and conceptually, on Hess's essay "Über das Geldwesen" ("The Essence of Money"). The Jewish deployment of Spinoza in counterpoint to Hegel links the *Vereinler* of the 1820s with Auerbach and Hess in the 1830s and 1840s. In his famous lead essay to the inaugural issue of the Verein's journal, as I read it, Immanuel Wolf appeals to Spinoza to subvert the Christian coordinates of Hegel's narrative of the development of Spirit, and Hess and Auerbach likewise look to Spinoza in part as an alternative to Hegel.

The most salient broad trajectory to emerge from my analysis of these variously interconnected moments involves the shift from a Kantian to a Hegelian—and then a Left Hegelian—paradigm. Within Bendavid's Kantian conceptual framework the obstacle to the integration of Jews into the wider polity was their purported deficit of autonomous subjectivity. Given Hegel's trenchant critique of subjectivism in general, and the subjective limits of Kantian epistemology and morality in particular, the danger that Hegel and his followers saw to an integrated polity lay not in a deficit, but in a surfeit, of (intransigent) subjectivity. Although Hegel at times depicted Jews as self-isolating and egoistic, the main targets of his critique of subjectivism, both as an epistemological and an ethical-political problem, lay elsewhere, above all with competing forms and conceptualizations of Christianity. Hegel's identification of subjectivity and its moral correlatives as insufficient and potentially disruptive of ethical life set the stage for the Young Hegelian assault on subjectivity as the linchpin of what they considered reactionary and socially atomizing Restoration politics.[9] And while Hegel did not generally privilege Jews as the embodiment of such corrosive subjectivity, several Young Hegelians did—including Ludwig Feuerbach and, above all, Bruno Bauer, to whom Marx responds in "Zur Judenfrage." The Young Hegelian figuration of the egoistic Jew provided the conceptual and rhetorical context for Marx's novel deployment of this stereotype. The Jew as embodiment of deleterious subjectivity—in Young Hegelian as well as less philosophically rigorous discourse—was also a crucial context for Auerbach's and Hess's different engagements with Spinoza as a thinker who was at once Jewish and universal, and who seemed to point the way beyond the limitations and perils of Jewish egoism, and of subjectivity *tout court*.

It is no coincidence that the thinkers I examine in this study were all marginal figures, at least at the moments with which I am chiefly concerned. The belief in the political efficacy of philosophical thought was the refuge of a new kind of intellectual who socially, professionally, and institutionally was neither here nor there. Contemporary observers during this period, as well as scholars of the history and sociology of intellectuals, have noted that the numbers of highly educated young men far outstripped the possibilities for their employment in the late eighteenth and early nineteenth centuries.[10] Young Hegelian intellectuals were excluded from university positions (and, eventually, from careers in journalism) due to their political radicalism, and they became further radicalized due to that exclusion.[11] Their intense political investment in radical critique, articulated from the social—as well as professional and institutional—periphery, not infrequently took the form of a desperate faith in the quasi-messianic leap of thought into action. Except for Marx, the intellectuals who are the focus of this study were even more marginalized than their non-Jewish counterparts due to legal restrictions on professional opportunities. Moreover, they generally found themselves on the fringes of mainstream Jewish communal, intellectual, and institutional life as well. If their precarious social and professional positions were one factor that encouraged these intellectuals to exaggerate the transformative power of thought and to engage in philosophical politics, other factors were the sheer power and novelty of the philosophical systems they took up—that is, their unprecedented, unsettled, and therefore all the more urgent quality. This is especially true in the case of Kant's thought as Bendavid deploys it in his 1793 pamphlet *Etwas zur Charackteristick der Juden* (On Jewish characteristics) and of Hegel's ideas from which the Verein (1819–24) drew inspiration. Bendavid was not only a Jewish Kantian but the first Jewish Kantian:[12] when he examined Jewish history, collectivity, and subjectivity through a Kantian lens in 1793, Kant's thought was still radically new, and its political implications were up for grabs. The Hegelians in the Verein were likewise the first Jewish Hegelians. They heard Hegel's early Berlin lectures from 1818 through the early 1820s, before his thought achieved wide acceptance. Nearly all the figures I examine here were young during the moments in question: Bendavid was thirty-one in 1793; the Hegelian *Vereinler* were in their twenties in the early 1820s; Marx was in his early to mid-twenties in the early 1840s; and Hess and Auerbach, both born in 1812, were in their mid-twenties to early thirties in the later 1830s and early 1840s. All of these figures were involved in processes of self-definition and self-positioning as intellectuals or authors. The performative dimension in their philosophical politics—the attempt to think at a threshold of political action, even to think as a political act—went hand in hand with their self-invention in and through novel intellectual and artistic postures.

Scott Spector has advocated a more profound engagement with German-Jewish subjectivity as a way of accessing areas and complexities of the German-Jewish past that have remained unexamined in the dominant strains of German-Jewish historiography.[13] He has in mind in particular unselfconscious reflections, feelings, and behaviors, which could reveal an irreducible imbrication of Germanness and Jewishness, and thus the inadequacy of thinking of these terms as being in binary opposition, or even as part of an assimilated–nonassimilated spectrum. Spector's call for attention to subjectivity in German-Jewish history and cultural studies is suggestive, yet the material I focus on complicates his conception of subjectivity as interiority in contrast to rigid external discourses.[14] The figures I examine theorized Jewish politics in the idioms and contexts of philosophical and wider cultural debates in which subjectivity, self-consciousness, and related terms figured centrally; and it is indeed with subjectivity as explicit cultural discourse, rather than as interior experience, that this book is chiefly concerned. Bendavid's project is to replace what he calls the hydra of the traditional Jewish collectivity with so many autonomous Kantian moral subjects. The *Vereinler*'s vision of *Wissenschaft des Judentums* answers Hegel's call for a *Wissenschaft der Religion* that would harmonize religious subjectivity with ethical life, rather than allowing religious subjectivity to be defined in irrational affective terms and in opposition to the rational state. Marx and Hess contribute differently to a Young Hegelian discourse that highlighted sovereign subjectivity as a theological, philosophical, and political problem. Auerbach, for his part, tries to negotiate a cultural discourse that—in large part through attacks on Heine—identified indulgent, frivolous, and corrosively ironic subjectivity with Jews and vice versa. In general, I do not seek out a level of subjective experience opposed or prior to such external discourses, yet I do try to unearth the heady experience of what it felt like to think Jewish politics in a Kantian or Hegelian vein, for example, or how Hegel's critique of subjectivity continued to inform the way erstwhile *Vereinler* Immanuel Wolf and Moses Moser (call them recovering Hegelians) experienced and evaluated themselves and each other in a correspondence spanning over a decade. For the group of thinkers I treat in this study, boundaries between external discourses of subjectivity and inner subjective experience were porous and equivocal.

Each of this book's six chapters explores an attempt to think through relations between Jewish particularity and evolving conceptions of the modern polity and state. Some thinkers attempt to harmonize Jewish subjects with the state (Bendavid, and the Hegelian *Vereinler*) or with an idealized national German community (Auerbach). Others mobilize an image of Jewish subjectivity (Marx) or an idiosyncratic interpretation of a Jewish tradition (Hess) to critique the liberal subject and the political state as harmful ideological illusions. All the thinkers I study, however, elaborate their political visions in dialogue with powerful philosophers, whose thought provides the idiom through or against which they articulate their philosophical politics.

Proceeding chronologically, *Jewish Philosophical Politics in Germany, 1789–1848* examines four paradigmatic moments in which my three key concerns—philosophy, politics, and Jewish subjectivity—confront each other in changing constellations. Chapter 1 explores Bendavid's theorization of Jewish citizenship in what I argue is a politicized appropriation of Kant's moral philosophy in the shadow of the French Revolution, which had both redefined citizenship in France and extended it to Jews. I analyze how Bendavid's attempt to conceptualize a transformation of Jews into citizens in *Etwas zur Charackteristick der Juden* leads him to a gruesome image of decapitation, which echoes an infamous scenario in a tract published by Johann Gottlieb Fichte the same year. I analyze how this surprising convergence derives from the Kantian foundation of each philosopher's conception of humanity and morality. Approaching civil rights for Jews from the standpoint of the normative Kantian moral subject, both Bendavid and Fichte conclude that only the paradoxical means of (symbolic) decapitation could fashion the new Jew fit for the civil sphere. Although Fichte's Kantian fantasy of Jewish decapitation is vehemently anti-Jewish and intended to dismiss the possibility of Jews being included in the polity, Bendavid's path to a metaphorics of Jewish decapitation is more complex and ambivalent. His historical narrative of the Jews derives in part from his interest in the genre of the case history as it was emerging in the inchoate field of popular psychology. Shortly before the appearance of *Etwas zur Charackteristick der Juden* in 1793, Bendavid published two case histories of Jewish patients in the first German-language psychology journal, *Gnothi Sauton oder Magazin zur Erfahrungsseelenkunde als ein Lesebuch für Gelehrte und Ungelehrte* (Know yourself, or journal of empirical psychology: a reader for scholars and laymen), in which he engaged on an individual level some of the same questions that would animate his collective (case) history of the Jews, such as a Jew's capacity to embrace Kantian reason or to integrate productively into society. Bendavid finally leans on Kant both to diagnose the pathologies of Jewish history and to overcome them through an aporetic cure, which would render Jews autonomous subjects and fit citizens of an idealized state through metaphorical decapitation. Bendavid's contribution, at its inception, to the corpus of Jewish Kantian thought productively highlights certain dangers in Kantian moral universalism that subsequent Jewish Kantians tended to gloss over. Although the tradition of German-Jewish Kantians culminating in Hermann Cohen recognized a profound affinity between Kantian and Jewish thought, above all in the ethical thrust of each, Bendavid stages the encounter between Kantian moral philosophy and Jewish history and collective identity in terms both of political possibility and of normative violence.

Chapters 2 and 3 look anew at the origins of academic Jewish studies: the attempt by first-generation university students in Berlin to construct a *Wissenschaft des Judentums* during the late 1810s and early 1820s. Hegelian theory provided a way for these young intellectuals to theorize—and act out—a place in "the state" (as theorized by Hegel) during precisely the pivotal years when the Prussian state was closing the doors to Jewish participation, doors that had seemed to be opening during the preceding era of reform. Against the dominant critical trend, which views the Verein für Cultur und Wissenschaft der Juden chiefly as the institutional framework out of which the new scholarly project of academic Jewish studies emerged, my reading follows the Verein's members in understanding their association chiefly as a political experiment. Inspired by Hegel's *Philosophie des Rechts* (*Philosophy of Right*; 1821) and *Vorlesungen über die Philosophie der Religion* (*Lectures on the Philosophy of Religion*; first delivered in 1821), among other works, Eduard Gans, Immanuel Wolf, and their fellow members of the Verein ascribed crucial political importance to their para-academic pursuits. Hegel closely aligned the state with *Wissenschaft* and insisted that rationality, not religious affiliation, was the true criterion on which to base inclusion in the state. In making Jews both the subjects and objects of science, the Verein's members sought to reorganize Jews according to Hegel's conception of ethical community and to integrate them into the rational totality of the Hegelian state. Feeling authorized by Hegelian theories of the state, religion, and the agency of rational discourse, they dressed up their modest society in bureaucratic trappings in an attempt to embody the role of Jewish civil servants in the state as Hegel envisioned it. At times, too, the Hegelian intellectuals of the Verein challenged aspects of the Hegelian script from which they worked—in particular, the dominant role of secularized Christianity in Hegel's philosophy of history. Eventually the disparity between Hegelian theory and Prussian realpolitik became too rude for the *Vereinler* to sustain such a politically contestatory, if finally illusory, lived Hegelianism. Yet the problem was not that the Verein's members were ultimately excluded from Hegel's state, but that it was only to Hegel's state that they could gain access. In contrast to a prevalent tendency to assume that Hegel was bad for the Jews, I take seriously the Verein's project of a Hegelian Jewish politics.

Chapter 4 focuses on the function of "the Jew" in the evolution of Marx's thought around the pivotal year 1843, when he radicalized his critique of liberalism in "Zur Judenfrage," a two-part review article responding to essays by Bruno Bauer on the Jewish Question, and in other essays. In contrast to my focus in the other chapters of this study on how Jewish thinkers draw on and sometimes contest philosophical models of subjectivity and the state and other forms of community in order to imagine new Jewish involvements in politics, I read Marx as doing nearly the opposite. He mobilizes a philosophical version of a stereotype of Jewish subjectivity—the Jew as the crude embodiment of materialistic egoism—in order to critique the institution of liberal politics per se as chimerical. Scholars interested in the evolution of Marx's thought typically pass over in silence, summarily explain away, or simply consider irrelevant Marx's antisemitic rhetoric in "Zur Judenfrage," while scholars who take Marx's antisemitic language seriously generally understand it in terms of Jewish self-hatred, without inquiring into its function within Marx's theoretical project. In a provocative rereading of Marx's infamous essay, I locate the antiheroes of part 2 of "Zur Judenfrage"—"real Jews"—at an ambivalent theoretical crossroad between two other, more viable heroes of different stages of Marx's evolving theory, the *Volk* of his 1842 political journalism and the proletariat, which Marx half discovered and half invented immediately after writing "Zur Judenfrage." Situating Marx's essay within the Left Hegelian assault on narrow subjectivity in favor of variously conceived social ontologies of the self, I argue that Marx deploys antisemitic rhetoric of the egoistic, radically "real" Jewish subject in an attempt to conjure up a social reality that he still lacked the analytical tools to theorize. On this conjured reality he could ground his critique of Hegelian and neo-Hegelian idealism (above all that of Bruno Bauer). It is a commonplace to see in Marx's diatribe against "Jewish" civil society an anticipation of his mature critique of the bourgeoisie. Through a reading of figures of social abjection in Marx's early texts, I show how in his figuration of "real Jews" Marx begins, ambivalently, to productivize social abjection, a strategy that would gain theoretical coherence as he developed his conception of the proletariat within his broader theory of production and the social relations it organizes in 1844–45.

Chapters 5 and 6 tell a tale of two Spinozas in the Germany of the 1830s and 1840s. Auerbach and Hess were close friends for a number of years in the late 1830s and early 1840s, a period when each was intensely engaged both with Spinoza and with trying to find his own political orientation and intellectual or artistic voice. Auerbach made his debut as a novelist in 1837 with *Spinoza: Ein historischer Roman* (Spinoza: a historical novel) and in 1841 published a German translation of Spinoza's complete works, to accompany which he also wrote a biography of Spinoza. Hess also made his debut in print in 1837, with *Die heilige Geschichte der Menschheit* (The Holy History of Mankind), which appeared anonymously "by a disciple of Spinoza," and Spinoza's thought continued to inspire Hess's revolutionary socialist essays of the 1840s and 1850s as well as his proto-Zionist 1862 *Rom und Jerusalem* (*Rome and Jerusalem*).

Spinoza had become the subject of keen interest in Germany during the period that my book treats, and Auerbach and Hess drew on his thought variously to critique the ethical and epistemological limitations of subjectivity against the background of a wide-ranging debate about the role of subjectivity (and related terms including egoism, individuality, and personality) in German culture and politics. For Auerbach, Spinoza embodied a paradoxically Jewish way to transcend Jewish subjectivity, which was frequently held up as the quintessence of egoism. For Hess, Spinoza's pantheism provided a universal—yet still Jewish—framework from which to elaborate a communist critique of possessive individualism. Although both Auerbach and Hess used Spinoza to engage with the complex ramifications of debates about the relationship between discrete individuals and wider communities, their interpretations and investments followed divergent paths. Auerbach would embrace a moderate liberal, national stance that idealized the *Volk* as a universal ethical community, while Hess would embrace cosmopolitan communist humanism.

A PROMINENT TENDENCY in recent scholarship on German-Jewish intellectual and cultural life, as Jonathan Hess has noted, is to celebrate a quasi-heroic Jewish subversiveness vis-à-vis hegemonic German philosophical and cultural discourses.[15] As examples of the tendency to underscore the contestatory thrust of German-Jewish culture, Hess points to Susannah Heschel's 1998 *Abraham Geiger and the Jewish Jesus* and his own 2002 *Germans, Jews, and the Claims of Modernity*, each a field-changing work. Heschel's study explores how the leading figure of nineteenth-century Reform Judaism was not—in contrast to a long-lived and widespread stereotype—motivated by a rush to assimilate but rather, in Heschel's adaptation of postcolonial theory, "reversed the gaze" of hegemonic Christian culture to establish a distinctly Jewish Jesus, with provocative consequences for how to assess Western culture and the place of Jews within it.[16] Hess, in his analysis of German-Jewish thinkers of the late eighteenth and early nineteenth centuries like Moses Mendelssohn and Saul Ascher, likewise teases dynamics of contestation and subversion out of an era of German-Jewish discourse that was conventionally taken to exemplify a Jewish preoccupation with assimilation to external norms and values. Such dynamics of Jewish contestation also animate studies such as Mack's *German Idealism and the Jew* and Todd Presner's *Mobile Modernity*. By any measure, the subversive paradigm within German-Jewish studies has been analytically powerful and has enriched, and at times dramatically altered, how we understand crucial currents within German-Jewish culture. I too tease out instances of scrappy Jewish counter-punching, for example in what I read as Immanuel Wolf's undoing of the secularized Christian supercessionism that underpins the place that Hegel assigns Spinoza in the development of Spirit. Yet to the extent that unearthing subversive tendencies in the German-Jewish tradition allows us to identify with and, at times, root for its misunderstood heroes, it should also give us pause. There is much truth in the narratives of German-Jewish subversion, but such narratives are also perhaps seductively satisfying. Although indispensable, the paradigm of subversion is not without blind spots. As Hess has shown, the nineteenth-century middlebrow German-Jewish literature that he unearths and analyzes in *Middlebrow Literature and the Making of German-Jewish Identity* resided in one such blind spot, and doing justice to it required a change of critical perspective.[17] Heroicizing narratives that pit intellectual Davids against the Goliath of the German intellectual tradition are apt to miss crucial questions that certain Jewish thinkers pose regarding the terms of Jewish and German modernity by trying to think, as Jews, not only against but also with some of the most powerful currents in the German philosophical tradition. What is significant about Bendavid, for example, is not how he might be read to subvert Kant nor how he might simply be marshaled to corroborate the verdict that Kant's philosophy is structurally antisemitic. In a more complicated picture, Bendavid highlights dangers of Kant's autonomy-heteronomy dualism even as he deploys the most hazardous edge of Kantian thought to negotiate a place for Jews in the polity. Similarly, I am not only (although I am certainly also) interested in the attempts of the members of the Verein to think their way around Hegel, but also in their attempts to think their way into Hegel's state. What possibilities and dangers did different philosophical paradigms afford Jewish intellectuals for thinking a polity in which they would have a place? How did minority groups refract and mobilize new theoretical paradigms that would eventually become foundational to philosophical and political modernity? How do we reassess Kant and Hegel in light of the philosophical politics that they inspired on the part of their Jewish adherents? These are the questions that Bendavid's and the *Vereinler*'s projects pose, projects that render it difficult to cast their authors in the role of unequivocal Jewish heroes but that (and, to some extent, that therefore) reveal a rich texture of German-Jewish self-reinvention at thresholds of philosophical and political modernity.

In *The First Modern Jew: Spinoza and the History of an Image*, Daniel Schwartz studies the evolution of the Jewish image of Spinoza from despised excommunicate to intellectual hero, a role in which he continues to be cast in contemporary Spinoza scholarship. Willi Goetschel's *Spinoza's Modernity: Mendelssohn, Lessing, and Heine* is incisive and suggestive, yet the sort of unabashedly celebratory embrace of Spinoza it exemplifies is apt to miss, for example, how Auerbach drew on Spinoza for cultural and political ends that were squarely opposed to those of his nemesis, Heine. Whereas Goetschel reads Heine as deploying Spinoza to subvert a grand narrative of German intellectual history, and Hegel's place or self-placement in this narrative in particular, Auerbach's intensive engagement with Spinoza was not only compatible with, but in many ways prepared the way for, the esthetics and political vision of the *Schwarzwälder Dorfgeschichten* (*Black Forest Village Stories*), the phenomenal success of which bestowed on Auerbach the cultural identity of a German *Volkschriftsteller*. *Jewish Philosophical Politics in Germany, 1789–1848* does not oppose or seek to supplant or coyly subvert the paradigm of subversion, which has been the most fecund development in German-Jewish studies in recent decades. It does, however, aspire to augment it and to provoke reflection both on the dangers of projection inherent in it and on the sort of cultural dynamics to which it may be ill equipped to do full justice.

Chapter One

Off with Their Heads?

Lazarus Bendavid's Vision of Kantian Subjects at the End of Jewish History

> *But to give them [the Jews] civil rights—I at least see no means of doing so other than, in one night, to cut off all their heads and replace them with others containing not a single Jewish idea.*
>
> JOHANN GOTTLIEB FICHTE, *Beitrag zur Berichtigung der Urteile des Publikums über die französische Revolution*

> *It [Judaism] is the hydra, all of whose heads must be cut off at once if two are not to grow back in place of every one severed.*
>
> LAZARUS BENDAVID, *Etwas zur Charackteristick der Juden*

The year is 1793. While the Terror rages in Paris, two German proponents of the new Kantian philosophy, Johann Gottlieb Fichte and Lazarus Bendavid, theorize the desirability, legitimacy, and possible means of incorporating Jews into the state as citizens. This issue has different stakes for the two thinkers, yet each envisions a scenario in which the very gesture that would integrate Jews into the polity also seems to threaten their existence.

Bendavid (1762–1832) is little known today, although during his lifetime he was an influential popularizer of Kant, whom he introduced to Vienna in well-attended lectures during the mid-1790s, and whose philosophy he explicated in a series of widely read books. Born in Berlin, Bendavid attended lectures at Halle and Göttingen on a wide array of subjects including mathematics and philosophy. He supported himself in a variety of occupations, including newspaper editor and accountant, and from 1806 to 1825 he served without compensation as the director of the Jewish Free School in Berlin. In addition to his publications on Kant, Bendavid wrote on mathematics and authored a number of texts on Jewish topics, generally with a polemical edge. The most famous of his Jewish writings is *Etwas zur Charackteristick der Juden* (On Jewish characteristics) of 1793.

Etwas zur Charackteristick der Juden is Bendavid's attempt to imagine a bridge leading Jews from the periphery to full integration and participation in civic life. He draws on Kantian philosophy—which he was explicating in his lectures in Vienna at the time—to diagnose modern Jews as morally deficient subjects, the products of a pathologizing history of post-Temple Judaism. Though a provocateur at the fringe of the Haskalah (Jewish Enlightenment), Bendavid devoted himself to Jewish institutions over the decades and opposed conversion —in *Etwas zur Charackteristick der Juden* and throughout his life. It is startling that he should arrive at a fantasy of cutting off Jewish heads so strikingly parallel to Fichte's famously antisemitic conclusion—also from 1793—that Jews could be rendered fit for citizenship only through decapitation. The uncanny similarities in Bendavid's and Fichte's rhetoric, I will argue, reach back to the Kantian foundation of both thinkers' conceptions of humanity and morality. Approaching the question of extending Jewish civil rights from the standpoint of the normative Kantian moral subject, both Bendavid and Fichte come to the conclusion that the only way to incorporate Jews into the civil sphere is, in fact, through the paradoxical and gruesome means of symbolic decapitation. Both Kantians come to view decapitation as the only possible cure, as it were, for Jewish wrongheadedness.[1]

I propose to read Bendavid's deployment of Kant in his diagnosis of the moral and psychic deficiencies of the modern Jew, and his vision of a cure for the affliction of Jewishness thus understood, alongside the remarks Fichte makes on a Jewish "state within a state" in *Beitrag zur Berichtigung der Urteile des Publikums über die französische Revolution* (Contribution toward the correction of the public's assessment of the French Revolution), comments that marked an important shift in anti-Jewish discourse from a theological to a purely philosophical denigration of Jewishness.[2] By doing so I try to lay bare the double bind in which the Jewish Kantian Bendavid found himself when he tried to advocate for civil emancipation for Jews from the normative foundation of Kantian universalism.

The suprahistorical Kantian moral subject provides both the implicit standard—in terms of which Bendavid plots the deviant path of Jewish (psychic) history in the diaspora—and the model for the curative dissolution of this history (or case history) of the Jews. As we know, however, the Enlightenment was not the golden age at the end of history but rather the conceptual laboratory in which many of the concepts later appropriated by nineteenth-century historical thought were fabricated. Even as Bendavid wrote, the sort of emergent nationalism we find in Fichte's text was eroding Enlightenment universalism.[3] In the aggressiveness of his assimilationist demands, and especially in his characterological understanding of the Jews, Bendavid comes very close indeed to

Fichte's equally aggressive and characterological understanding of the essential nonhumanity of Jews. Unlike Fichte, however, Bendavid politicizes Kantian moral philosophy in order ultimately to gain access to the German polity for himself and enlightened Jews like him. Although Bendavid's tract throws into relief the serious dangers inherent in Kantian universalism, it is vitally important to appreciate that it does so precisely as an articulation of a Jewish Kantian politics. What makes Bendavid's work so richly fascinating and troubling—and why it takes us beyond the mere question of whether Kant's moral philosophy is structurally antisemitic—is that Bendavid seeks to establish terms of equal participation in the polity for Jews precisely by deploying Kantian thought's most perilous edge.

Although Bendavid's implicit Kantianism guides his diagnosis of Judaism as a pathology to be overcome via a leap into a model of suprahistorical moral subjectivity, his work is also rooted in the psychological discourse that emerged at the intersection of medicine and popular philosophy in the decade prior to the publication of his treatise. To understand how Bendavid arrived at his volatile, aporetic, and highly politicized diagnosis of Jewish history and subjectivity, then, requires a threefold contextualization. In addition to the dynamics of Kantian moral philosophy at play in Bendavid's work—the crucial philosophical context—his text responds to its historical and political context of the emancipation debate in Germany during the 1780s and early 1790s. In addition, Bendavid's narrative of Jewish history emerges in dialogue with the phenomenon of a new diachronic appreciation of the disease process and the concomitant possibilities for narrating history as pathography that this temporalization of medicine opened up. Bendavid's approach to the history of the Jews grows out of and extends his earlier foray into the emerging discourse of popular psychology, which took the form of two case histories of individual Jews. In these case histories, Bendavid dramatizes questions regarding the capacity of particular Jews to embrace Kantian reason, or to reconcile their social and legal station with productive and moral participation in society. While Kantian moral philosophy figures the end of Bendavid's narrative of Jewish history as the history of a psychic pathology, it is in the genre of eighteenth-century popular psychology that this narrative has one of its origins.

The Politicization of Jewish History from Dohm to Bendavid

In *Über die bürgerliche Verbesserung der Juden* (On the civil improvement of the Jews), the Prussian civil servant Christian Wilhelm von Dohm elaborated an early version of, to use Salo Baron's famous term, the "lachrymose" theory of Jewish history.[4] He attributed the sociocultural situation of European Jews to a history of passive suffering: centuries of exile, persecution, and neglect. Dohm argued that improving the Jews' civil status would also improve the Jews themselves, rendering them fit citizens and a valuable resource for the state. Soon after the publication of Dohm's seminal treatise in September 1781 (the timing was coincidental, not causal) came the first emancipation legislation in Austria.[5]

In the dynamic discursive and political context of the 1780s and early 1790s, the task of theorizing the relationship between history, Jewish tradition, and the Jews' place in the polity became central for a number of Jewish Enlightenment intellectuals, or *maskilim*. David Sorkin notes "a subtle, albeit significant shift" that took place in the years after the deaths of Moses Mendelssohn and Frederick the Great in 1786. The early Haskalah project of cultural renewal became politicized, and "the early Haskalah's prescriptions for the intellectual renewal of Judaism were now enlisted as remedies for the affliction of the Jews."[6] The possibility of emancipation engendered debate over what involvement in the state could be extended to Jews, and to which Jews. The Enlightenment emancipation debate thus not only reconfigured the relationship between Jews and the broader society but also intensified and lent greater political stakes to differences among Jews.

Dohm's "lachrymose" history of the Jews, which so powerfully influenced the emancipation debate throughout the 1780s and 1790s, not only helped prepare the ground for this eventual shift in the Haskalah from cultural revival toward social and political issues, but also ensured that narratives of Jewish history would serve as an important medium through which Jews and non-Jews alike would articulate competing positions on Jewish emancipation.[7] Politicization and historicization went hand in hand: history, which had not been a preoccupation for Jews as long as Jews maintained a high degree of autonomy, quickly became an urgent issue as cultural and civic distinctions between Jews and non-Jews grew blurred and contested.

Such is the heady context in which Bendavid elaborated *Etwas zur Charackteristick der Juden*, one of the most controversial and confounding texts of the Jewish Enlightenment.[8] Dominique Bourel has pointed to the "quasi-messianic ecstasy" with which German-Jewish intellectuals of the 1780s and early 1790s believed in an imminent improvement in the civil status of Jews.[9] Bendavid's text appeared not only a decade after Joseph II's Edicts of Toleration but also shortly after the French National Assembly granted civil equality to the Jews in 1791, and immediately after the first naturalization of Jews in Prussia and the first admission of Jews to the Prussian civil service.[10]

Bendavid wrote his treatise in German, a language not accessible to the majority of even "German" Jews in 1793. He first submitted it—whether in earnest or as a provocation is not clear; at any rate, it was rejected—to the Haskalah journal *Ha-measef* (The gatherer),[11] and an independent publisher in Leipzig eventually published it. Bendavid does not analyze religion and Judaism, as had—however differently—Moses Mendelssohn (in *Jerusalem oder über religiöse Macht und Judentum* [Jerusalem, or on religious power and Judaism], 1783) and Saul Ascher (in *Leviathan oder über Religion in Rücksicht des Judentums* [Leviathan, or on religion in regard to Judaism], 1792), but rather the Jews.[12] His point of departure is not theological but characterological and psychological, and the foundation of his call for reform is unabashedly pragmatic. Bendavid's deployment of a certain history of the Jews constitutes a new departure in Jewish Enlightenment discourse: his aim is not to show the compatibility between Jewish law and modern enlightened sensibilities (in contrast to Mendelssohn), nor to argue for reforming the latter so as to harmonize with the former (in contrast to Ascher). Making an aggressive distinction between himself as an enlightened *Mensch* (*ich*), and backward and timorous Jews (*euch*), Bendavid argues for a quid pro quo of rehabilitation for rights, the demolition of halakhah as a prerequisite for the curative transformation of Jews into citizens. The only impediment to political emancipation, Bendavid admonishes his backward coreligionists, is the "slave mentality of bygone centuries" (*Sklavensinn voriger Jahrhunderte*).[13] A blissful life as *Bürger* (citizens) and *Menschen* (human beings) awaits the Jews if only they muster the pluck to shake off their Jewishness (*sich vom Judenthum losmachen*). Such a reform would demonstrate the Jews' willingness to meet the government halfway in becoming citizens of the enlightened state.

Bendavid apostrophizes his coreligionists in a provocative tone that blends flagrant contempt for Jewish practices with advocacy for the Jewish cause. He vigorously proselytizes for a rationalistic form of Judaism scarcely distinguishable from deism. His treatise has three parts. In the first he elaborates a diachronic evaluation of Jewish history. In the second he offers a synchronic typology of contemporary Jewish society, which he divides into four groups: traditionalists (who keep the *mitzvot*); hedonists (who do not, but only out of depravity); good-hearted Jews (who only out of weakness cling to unreformed Judaism [*ungeläuterten Judenthum*]); and Enlightened Jews (like himself, who have essentially superseded Judaism to become natural religionists). In the final section, Bendavid presents a virulent manifesto addressed to the good-hearted Jews of his third category (the first two he considers simply incorrigible), whom he urges to cast off Jewish belief and practice.

In Bendavid's narrative of Jewish history, after the destruction of the Second

Temple and failed attempts to regain their lost sovereignty, the Jews turned—as a last resort—to a moral attack, hoping to regain their homeland not by might but rather by moral improvement. Since the destruction of the Second Temple, to further summarize Bendavid's construction of post-Temple Jewish history, Jewish biblical exegesis has been overdetermined by the needs of a "slave mentality." Bendavid traces a fateful displacement from robust action to impotent piety, from praxis to superstitious belief. He erodes the theological underpinnings of Jewish history and reduces Jewish piety to a powerless people's neurotic and delusional form of warfare. Bendavid not only psychologizes but also pathologizes Jewish post-Temple existence and the entire rabbinic tradition. In Bendavid's hands, Dohm's *Leidensgeschichte* (lachrymose history) is transformed into a *Krankengeschichte* (pathography): a diagnostic case history of what Bendavid casts as an essentially pathological modern Jewish character.

In his attempt to reconcile Jews with Enlightenment reason and citizenship, Bendavid's historicization of the Jews is subtended by a normalizing universalist anthropology—specifically, the Kantian moral subject. Bendavid relies on the logic of Kantian morality in order both to construct and to dissolve his history of Jewish particularity as private pathology. Bendavid's interest in Kantian philosophy was far-reaching and provides the implicit, though never explicit, conceptual framework of *Etwas zur Charackteristick der Juden*. What a Christian theological bias had earlier cast as divine punishment of the Jews, Bendavid recasts in terms of their own subjective moral weakness, a failure of will that it has now become incumbent on them to redress through a leap out of the symptomatology of Jewish history and into the suprahistorical realm of autonomous Kantian moral subjectivity. This philosophical framework significantly contributes to the contradictions of Bendavid's unsettling discourse, and it animates the violent fantasy with which he tries to resolve these contradictions, a political fantasy with deep philosophical affinities to Fichte's. However, as I have already noted, although Bendavid's treatise owes its conceptual architecture to Kantian moral philosophy, it is also rooted in the emergent discourse of popular psychology.

Jews and the Emergent Discourse of Popular Psychology

In its psychologizing thrust, Bendavid's treatise marks an emphatic departure from a long history of early modern theologically invested ethnographies of Jews written in German by baptized Jews such as Johann Pfefferkorn (*Judenbeicht* [Jews' confession], 1508; and *Osterbüchlein* [Easter book], 1509) and Antonius Margaritha (*Der Gantz Jüdisch Glaub* [The complete Jewish belief],

1530) and by Christians like Martin Luther (*Von den Juden und ihren Lügen* [*On the Jews and Their Lies*], 1543).[14] Johann Buxtorf the Elder's expansive *Juden Schul* [The Jewish synagogue] of 1603 would remain the authoritative representative of this genre into the eighteenth century, when it would be eclipsed by such works as Andreas Eisenmenger's virulent *Entdecktes Judenthum* [Jewry revealed], which first appeared in 1700, and Johann Jacob Schudt's multivolume *Jüdische Merckwürdigkeiten* [Jewish curiosities], 1714–17.[15] The thrust of such catalogues was generally to trace Jewish behavior back to its basis in theological error. Jewish rebuttals—for example, by the seventeenth-century Italian rabbi Leone Modena in *Historia de' riti hebraici* (Account of Jewish rituals; written in 1614–15 and published in two different editions in 1637 and 1638), or the apologies for Jews and Jewish customs that the Amsterdam rabbi Menasseh ben Israel penned in the 1650s in the context of the debate over the readmission of Jews to Cromwellian England—generally emphasize the rationality of the Jewish customs they catalogue as well as their rootedness in scripture.[16]

Bendavid's approach is radically secular. He abandons religious apologetics, and although he does admonish Jews to cast off all vestiges of Jewish custom and "return" to "the pure teaching of Moses," the purportedly "Mosaic" doctrine to which Bendavid would have Jews "return" amounts to nothing more than "the doctrine of natural religion."[17] Vis-à-vis earlier accounts of "characteristics" of the Jews, Bendavid's project marks a departure from theological ethnography toward normative philosophical anthropology. He may take the critical narrative —familiar from Christian theologians like Buxtorf—of rabbinic Judaism as a history of decline and perversion, yet he detheologizes, psychologizes, and indeed pathologizes it. A temporalized and quasi-medical framework displaces the concern with essentially timeless theological truth or error. What Bendavid traces is the historical evolution of a psychic disturbance.

The temporalization of medicine and psychology that made Bendavid's diagnosis possible was part of the paradigm shift in the human and natural sciences at the turn of the eighteenth and nineteenth centuries, analyzed most influentially by Michel Foucault. Though several of Foucault's particular claims in *The Birth of the Clinic* have been contested from a range of perspectives, his insistence on a shift in what we could call the temporality of pathology is generally accepted and finds corroboration in the work of historians of science such as Wolf Lepenies.[18] Throughout the seventeenth century and most of the eighteenth, Foucault argues, diseases were understood as timeless essences, whose manifestation in any given patient entailed a kind of corruption. Subject to the contingencies of time, manifest symptoms were viewed as altogether deceptive nosographical signs. Temporality, so problematic for classical medicine, would take on a key function in the new medical discourse. Whereas the classical doctor had striven to transcend the suspect temporality of concrete pathological symptoms, now diseases came to be perceived in terms of an organic process. The doctor's task was no longer to assign a disease its proper place in an established nosographical table, but rather to observe the course of individual cases.

As Volker Roelcke argues, the conjunction between the temporalization—or, indeed, narrativization—of illness and medical discourse, on the one hand, and the modern concept of history as organic development, on the other hand, made diagnostic cultural criticism possible. At the same time that illnesses began to tell stories, history came to be seen as the cause of particular diseases. Toward the end of the eighteenth century, a certain class of illness (*Zivilisationskrankheiten*) came to be seen as the product of specifically historical development.[19] Since illness and history were now understood as operating according to basically analogous logics (temporalized causality), medicine was able to provide a potent vocabulary with which to plot the course of history. Medicine, especially psychology and psychiatry, emerged as a privileged locus of cultural critique precisely as the diagnosis of cultural illness came to imply a certain philosophy of history, and, conversely, as philosophies of history came to be articulated in terms of the movement of history toward health or illness.[20]

As diseases acquired a temporal and quasi-narrative structure, the stories they told were naturally recorded. New medical or quasi-medical genres emerged in the eighteenth century. A new medical historiography self-consciously broke with an older form of medical chronology and stressed the importance of identifying causal connections in the progress of medical history. New genres emerged, such as the individual pathography and—most importantly for Bendavid—the psychological case study. The most important periodical for the publication of case studies in the late Enlightenment was *Gnothi Sauton, oder Magazin zur Erfahrungsseelenkunde als ein Lesebuch für Gelehrte und Ungelehrte* (Know yourself, or journal of empirical psychology: a reader for scholars and laymen), a pioneering psychological journal that appeared from 1783 to 1793 under the editorship of Karl Philipp Moritz, sometimes assisted by coeditors Karl Friedrich Pockels and, in the journal's final years, Salomon Maimon.

As Martin Davies has noted, it was Moritz who first "advanced the notion of the 'case-study' as means of self-knowledge" by generalizing his own pietistic introspectiveness.[21] In programmatic essays launching the *Magazin zur Erfahrungsseelenkunde* Moritz called for accounts based on self-observation as well as case histories of others by "moralische Ärzte" (moral doctors). In one 1782 essay he underscored the need to complement conventional medicine with a science of diseases of the psyche (*Seelenkrankheitslehre*).[22] In 1786 Moritz recast traditional moral flaws such as jealousy, avarice, vengefulness, and vanity as so many psychological afflictions, or "Krankheiten der Seele," a move Bendavid would echo in *Etwas zur Charackteristick der Juden*.[23]

The *Magazin zur Erfahrungsseelenkunde* explored phenomena at the margins of rational Enlightenment culture: trauma, melancholy, paranormal experiences, and eccentric behaviors of various types. It pursued the psychology of language in studies of deaf-mutes, included studies of the blind, and so forth. The journal occupied a place at the social margins as well. Many contributors recorded the damage they and others had suffered through social forces. Moritz's magnum opus, *Anton Reiser: ein psychologischer Roman* (Anton Reiser: a psychological novel), is a searing portrait of the experience of abject poverty and social violence. The novel—parts of which first appeared as case studies in the *Magazin zur Erfahrungsseelenkunde* —is essentially an autobiography written in the third person, or a case study of the self. It is not accidental that Maimon became the first Jew to edit a German-language journal when he joined Moritz at the *Magazin zur Erfahrungsseelenkunde*. In fact, a part of Maimon's famous autobiography likewise first appeared in the journal, not as a first-person narrative by Maimon but as a third-person case study called "Fragmente aus Ben Josuas Lebensgeschichte" (Fragments from the life of Ben Joshua).

Ernst-Peter Wieckenberg has written on the large number of Jewish contributors to the *Magazin zur Erfahrungsseelenkunde*. (It was Moses Mendelssohn, for example, who convinced Moritz to organize the journal according to medical categories, and Marcus Herz—along with several other, lesser-known Jewish figures—also contributed to it.) Wieckenberg speculates plausibly that the journal was attractive to socially marginal individuals, including many Jews, in part because of its emphasis on the possibilities for self-enhancement and self-liberation through self-analysis, and especially the analysis of the socially conditioned nature of one's pain and suffering. As Wieckenberg notes, Maimon's autobiography is structured as a pursuit of truth intended to lead out of all inhibiting social entanglements. His life story takes the form of the liberation of a purely rational self from its own history.[24]

In 1792 Bendavid published a pair of case studies in the *Magazin zur Erfahrungsseelenkunde*, each dealing with psychologically disturbed Jews. The first of these, "Selbstmord aus Rechtschaffenheit und Lebensüberdruß" (Suicide out of honesty and life-weariness), describes a man who harbors a death wish and ultimately commits suicide. What makes his case noteworthy, according to Bendavid, is that his wish to die is not born of a momentary passionate impulse but rather of sustained reflection on a structural contradiction in his life.

A humble merchant by trade, he is honest by nature, yet he is driven to engage in smuggling by the need to support his wife and six children. The conflict between his responsibilities to his family and to the state erodes his self-esteem and will to live: "He had to . . . do things that conflicted with his honesty, made him despicable in his own eyes, and made the end of his life appear desirable." Bendavid presents a man who is fully conscious of the conflict by which he is torn: "'I am a harmful member of the state,' he would often say to me [Bendavid] with the deepest agitation. 'The laws of the state are sacred to me, and I transgress them, am forced to transgress them.'" The "Jewish" pathology is not personal but rather the symptom of an irreconcilable contradiction between Jews' mutually antagonistic private and public responsibilities.[25] Marginalized economically by his status as a Jew, the man nonetheless passionately affirms the state's laws in an impossible identification with the civic realm to which he is not granted full inclusion.

In the second case study, "Sonderbare Art des Trübsinnes" (Peculiar type of melancholy), Bendavid presents a Jewish "patient" who seems in many ways to suffer from Jewishness itself. This study documents the case of E. from H[amburg], who suffers a nervous breakdown while studying with Kant in K[önigsberg]. E.'s friends in Königsberg send him back to Hamburg in the hope that he will recover in the bosom of his family. Stopping in Berlin on the way to Hamburg, E. comes under Bendavid's care. Bendavid describes E.'s curious habit of standing naked for hours at a time before a mirror and regarding himself with extreme satisfaction. Bendavid later discovers the reason for this in E.'s delusion that he is the son of a famous prince: "You probably also believe that the Jew in H. is my father? I am not of Jewish parents, at any rate not sired by a Jew. I also don't bear the mark of a Jew on my body, and that safeguards me from L.—whom you know and who resembles me—being able to masquerade as me, much as he would like to."[26] E. insists that he is not circumcised and finds his claim confirmed in his mirror image, thus rejecting his Jewish paternity on the plane of fantasy.

Bendavid implies that the illness to which E. succumbs is intimately bound up with his Jewishness. It is during his studies with Kant, the Enlightenment philosopher par excellence, that E.'s pathology emerges. The Jewishness that makes E. a failed student of the Enlightenment, a failed universal subject, has both the social derivation that E. tries to overcome through a Freudian family romance and a more private origin, to which E.'s psychosis equally attests. These forces conspire to leave E. with a fractured and tormented identity.

One of Bendavid's subjects takes his own life; the other takes leave of his reason. Both men suffer from the incommensurability of their Jewish particularity and a wider society to which they passionately wish to gain access. In *Etwas zur Charackteristick der Juden*, Bendavid extends the case history of individual Jews to a more grandly conceived collective subject and writes a case history of the Jews, in which the ambivalent oscillation persists between a sociopolitical and a purely private pathogenesis of Jewishness.

Bendavid's Psychological History and the Genealogy of Nietzschean Genealogy

The lasting significance of Bendavid's treatise is frequently seen in the crude sociology of contemporary Jewry it elaborates—the way it reflects (and reflects on) the emerging stratification within German Jewry.[27] Less remarked on in Bendavid's treatise is his historical derivation of Jewish character. Bendavid's historical and psychological analysis anticipates Nietzsche's acerbic diagnosis of Jewish values in *Jenseits von Gut und Böse* (*Beyond Good and Evil,* 1886) and, especially, *Zur Genealogie der Moral* (*On the Genealogy of Morals*, 1887).[28] As I argue in the second half of this chapter, Bendavid's genealogy of Jewish morals relies on a distinctly Kantian framework for both the normative standard according to which it diagnoses the pathologies of Jewish history and for the conception of moral will that it proffers as their cure. Yet Bendavid's vehement, adversarial deployment of historicization to undercut conventional ethical values and to call for a bold leap beyond the weakness and deformation of character they dissemble and valorize marks the moment when the sort of modern critical diagnostics that would find its most famous articulation in Nietzschean genealogy first becomes possible.

Notwithstanding Nietzsche's bold claim to have been the first to interrogate the value of moral values, Bendavid was in his own way positioned—socially, historically, and philosophically—at a point when a radical critique of the value of Jewish values became both possible and, to him, urgently necessary. Although Bendavid's and Nietzsche's historical contexts, outlooks, and investments in Jewish values are fundamentally different, the affinities between their arguments are profound. Bendavid elaborates a historical and psychological understanding of Judaism as an unhealthy reaction to the loss of power, as the convoluted form of impotent revenge that Nietzsche would famously call *ressentiment*. Most saliently, Bendavid analyzes Jewish morality as a reactive psychological product: he traces the emergence of a Jewish value system as the vexed response to the loss of power. Along related lines, he analyzes the formation of a Jewish moral ego as a psychological internalization and inversion of external power relations, which inevitably leads to a contradictory and illusory relation to the self. The period in Jewish history that Bendavid diagnoses in his etiology of modern Jewish character has a clear starting point in the loss of political sovereignty with the destruction of the Second Temple, to which the elaboration of ritual observance, in Bendavid's view, is a neurotic response.[29] For Bendavid the period of Jewish history that opened in 70 CE likewise has—or should have—a clear endpoint in the Enlightenment: Jews can now free themselves of their obsolete slave mentality and at last become men and citizens.

Bendavid theorizes how submission to power eventually becomes morally validated:

> When it loses its freedom, every animal also loses its sense of freedom [*Sinn für Freyheit*]; and the man who has become accustomed to subservience [*Frohndienste*] requires but a small step in order voluntarily to accept the yoke of slavery. In the beginning, he still dares to make certain attempts to regain his freedom—attempts that are inspired by despair and thus seldom carried out with the intelligence and poise necessary for the victory of oppressed men, and that therefore generally fail, leaving in the heart [*Gemüt*] of the poor people [*des armen Volkes*], which until now had still been able to find in hope a slight comfort, nothing but a sense of remorse over the errors it has committed, the wish to be able to return to the God of its fathers, recognition of His Judgment [*Anerkennung seines Strafgerichts*], and voluntary submission to the yoke of its oppressor, the executor of divine will.[30]

The eventual internalization and acceptance of one's weakness entails the projection of a punishing God, who invests with meaning and purpose the inassimilable experience of being dominated. Only after repeated attempts to regain freedom have failed, and seem forever doomed to fail, does bad conscience emerge in a defeated people, which begins to feel "remorse over the errors it has committed." Thus an essentially sick transvaluation of weakness occurs in morality. As would Nietzsche a century later, Bendavid theorizes that the dominated deduce a punishing divine will from the experience of subjugation in order to imbue this bewildering experience with meaning.[31] Bendavid characterizes this morality born of weakness—the rabbinic reinterpretation of Jewish ritual—as a method, however deluded, of waging war.[32] All slaves (not only Jewish ones) resent their masters.[33] Yet this

> general source of envy . . . was accompanied among the Jews by another that lent the original one a different direction and, of pitiable men, not infrequently made such creatures as could not help but draw [*auspressen*] tears of

> indignation from the eye of the philanthropist. Sinful, the Pentateuch taught them, namely, they would forfeit sovereignty over their land; moral improvement would restore it to them.
>
> Now, nothing was more natural, given this premise, than that the Jews would turn with the greatest eagerness to this method of waging war [*zu dieser Art Krieg zu führen*]. They sought to appease the Eternal One through the observance of the laws of their fathers, sought in his omnipotence the God of the common people [*der Schaaren*] who would smash their enemies or restore their waning powers and give them courage to persevere. But the laws of their fathers were for the most part local and could hardly be practiced at all without property and Temple; and now they were at a loss as to how they should regain their forfeited favor [*Gnade*]. They thus culled such rituals from heathens, Greeks, Romans, and the newly arisen Christian religion as were more or less compatible with Judaism; replaced sacrifice with prayer; the practical Mosaic with ritual laws; actions with articles of faith; the old religion with a new *belief*.[34]

In Bendavid's account an impotent desire for revenge replaces healthy activity with neurotic belief. As later in Nietzsche's critique, weakness becomes productive of a system of moral values.

Bendavid describes the formation of pious Jewish "egoism" (*Egoismus*), which likewise resonates with Nietzsche's analysis of the ascetic ego divided against itself. Healthy activity in the world is disdainfully renounced and replaced by a form of egoism that seeks recognition no longer in active accomplishments but rather in ascetic piety:

> This sad mood of the soul simultaneously produces two different effects. On the one hand, the misanthrope, since he believes himself to despise men and therefore also their approval, renounces everything that might win him such approval. Every outward perfection is neglected, every concept of honor repressed, every participation in the world and humanity viewed as weakness. . . . On the other hand, however, contempt of humanity is always connected to egoism; and egoism, far more than any other temperament, requires the approval of others, even if it is under the delusion of being able to do without it. . . . Thus the Jew, his misanthropy notwithstanding, had to experience the greatest pleasure when other Jews regarded him as a pious, God-fearing man—the only thing he still valued.[35]

In Bendavid's account weakness becomes recoded as moral strength. Having become incapable of pursuing true honor by asserting himself outwardly, the pious Jewish egotist seeks self-aggrandizement and pleasure through self-abnegation and altruism.

A crucial structural contrast between history and a case history is that the latter ends, or should end, at some more or less definitive point. Bendavid frames Jewish history as the evolution of a psychic pathology, a historically determined deformation of the Jews' moral will, and in his conception the pathology of Jewish history moves always toward the moment of its ultimate resolution in suprahistorical Kantian moral autonomy. Bendavid's case history thus opens up a novel (if uncomfortable) radically secular way of looking at Jewish history, yet also forecloses the legitimacy of secular Jewish history as an ongoing process. As we will see, Kant's conception of moral autonomy and his opposition between morality and history offer Bendavid tools to reconceive Jewish history in bold ways, yet finally in order to make the Jew's pathological history disappear like a symptom.

Kantian Moral Subjectivity and Ethical Alterity

Bendavid's treatise occupies a singular position in the long and varied Jewish reception of Kant.[36] As Christoph Schulte observes, the question of why there was such a substantial engagement—at times bordering on identification—with Kant among Jewish intellectuals in the nineteenth and twentieth centuries has been "frequently and always differently answered."[37] I agree with Schulte that, given the range not only of prominent Jewish Kantian and neo-Kantian philosophers but also and especially of both Liberal and Orthodox Jewish intellectuals who appropriated Kant in philosophies of Judaism over the span of 150 years, the question admits of no single, general answer. Friedrich Niewöhner provides a thorough overview of both negative and positive factors contributing to the attraction of Kant for Jewish thinkers.[38] Aside from unmistakably Christian conceptual paradigms (Hegel) and antisemitic rhetoric (Fichte and Marx) that may have made certain alternatives even more problematic than Kant for a philosophy of Judaism, Kant was also the key figure of the German Enlightenment, with which German Jews strongly identified. Kant was a towering figure in the bourgeois institution of German *Bildung*, and one whose rationalism and commitment to political Enlightenment resisted appropriation by romantic and nationalistic movements. In the course of the nineteenth century, and certainly by the *fin de siècle*, the cultural capital and political culture that had become attached to "Kant" inevitably encouraged Jewish thinkers' perceptions of affinities between their various versions of Judaism and their various versions of Kant.

Kant's Jewish contemporaries, in contrast, tended to avoid explicit references to the philosopher when they wrote on topics of Jewish concern. In a programmatic 1783 essay in *Ha-measef* titled "The Uses of Engagement with Past Ages," Isaak Euchel "smuggles" Kant (of the first critique) into an essay on the importance of secular historical study even for the understanding of the sacred tradition. Euchel avoided mentioning Kant's name so as not to offend traditionalists, whom he was still courting as readers of the recently launched Haskalah journal.[39] As we will see Bendavid likewise smuggles Kant—poorly disguised as Mendelssohn—into his more radical discourse, which still formally addresses fellow Jews. Kant was a far more controversial figure in his day to both Jewish and non-Jewish audiences than the philosopher that nineteenth-century German cultural history would enshrine. It is worth noting that Bendavid, who effectively brought Kant to Vienna—where he lectured and published on the three critiques in the 1790s—was escorted out of the city in 1797 by the police, who found the Protestant Prussian philosopher—and probably his Jewish prophet—too revolutionary.[40]

Significantly, the Kant that Bendavid brings unnamed into *Etwas zur Charackteristick der Juden* is that of the second critique, not, as was the case with Euchel, the first. Bendavid distinguishes himself in this treatise from the long tradition of Jewish Kantians by working closely (if only implicitly) from Kant's moral philosophy. This claim will seem perverse to anyone who takes the Jewish Kantian tradition on its own terms, for that tradition celebrates purported elective affinities between Judaism and Kant above all in the area of ethics. As Niewöhner provocatively argues, however, the chorus of claims about harmonies between Kantian and Jewish ethics notwithstanding, Orthodox and Liberal Jewish Kantian philosophers alike avoid Kant's moral philosophy almost completely; and when they do, however briefly, take up Kant's central writings on ethics, they fundamentally criticize rather than concur with them.[41]

Niewöhner makes the case that it is much more Kant's epistemology than his ethics that animates Jewish Kantian writing. He argues that it was above all Kant's method of positing the thing-in-itself that seemed to parallel critiques of anthropomorphism by Jewish writers (especially Maimonides) and provided a rational basis for conceptions of God or the Law as noumenal. In short, the Jewish appropriation of Kant occurred "in the sphere of the epistemological foundation [*Begründung*] for ethics, not in the area of ethics itself."[42] Bendavid's argument is singular in the way it implicitly starts from Kantian moral philosophy and gets caught in the aporias and violence to which even, and perhaps especially, a faithful reading of Kant can lead.

Etwas zur Charackteristick der Juden is the most significant attempt by a Jewish contemporary of Kant to think the place of Jews in German politics with Kant in real time—to intervene in a highly volatile contemporary moment by mobilizing a brand-new conceptual paradigm. Bendavid's fidelity to Kantian thought sets him apart from other notable interlocutors and disseminators among Kant's Jewish contemporaries. Marcus Herz—Kant's student, correspondent, and explicator in lectures in Berlin—by his own admission did not keep up with Kant after his critical turn. The most brilliant and original Jewish philosopher of his day, Solomon Maimon, who grasped Kant's epistemology with a subtlety that Kant acknowledged, also read it skeptically and raised fundamental challenges to it.[43] Saul Ascher likewise used conceptual tools from various areas of Kantian philosophy to argue with Kant himself. In *Eisenmenger der Zweite* (Eisenmenger the second), Ascher took Fichte (of *Beitrag*) and Kant himself (of *Religion within the Boundaries of Mere Reason*, 1793) to task for their vehemently anti-Jewish appropriation of Kant's ethics. Ascher argued that Fichte's was a possible but not a necessary use of Kant.[44] This is surely true, and my claim is not that Bendavid's tract shows Kant's moral philosophy to be inherently or ineluctably either good or bad for the Jews.

Still, in contrast to Maimon and Ascher, Bendavid remained the most dutifully Kantian of the philosopher's contemporary Jewish interpreters,[45] and Bendavid's deployment of Kant in his intervention in Jewish politics can complicate in productive ways how the corpus of Jewish Kantian philosophy has understood itself. If the use he makes of Kantian ethics is by no means inevitable, it nonetheless remains close to and issues from the dynamics of Kant's own theory of practical reason. Bendavid's deployment of Kant is indeed gruesome; however, it is arguably less contrived than the many problematic appropriations of Kant's moral philosophy that circumvent its basic structure in order to proclaim it harmonic with a purported essence of Judaism. "Apparently straightforward but deeply perplexing" is how Gillian Rose aptly characterizes the culmination of this tradition, Hermann Cohen's 1910 "Inner Relations between Kant's Philosophy and Judaism."[46] By the same token, however, Bendavid's mobilization of Kant in the service of a Jewish political cause complicates assessments of Kantian moral philosophy as inherently or structurally antisemitic—that is, antisemitic at a deeper level than Kant's explicit disparagements of Judaism.[47] Although Bendavid's Kantian critique of Jews and Judaism is inexorably hostile to traditional values and practice, Bendavid is still very much thinking with Kant as a Jew about how to negotiate political modernity as a Jew.

Finding a space in the polity for Jews within a Kantian framework entailed formidable challenges, and consequently Bendavid's attempt to think Jewish with Kant is highly fraught. Fichte's philosophical antisemitism emanates from the same conceptual sources that Bendavid mines in his ambivalent vision of Jewish inclusion. The political binary of Jew versus *Bürger* is subtended in both

Bendavid and Fichte by the more fundamental binary of Jew versus *Mensch*. The significant differences in their deployments of Kant notwithstanding, a Kantian perspective leads both thinkers out of the traditional opposition between Christian and Jew into a pernicious and distinctly modern opposition between Jew and *Mensch*, where civic competence is predicated on human moral competence. Although both Bendavid and Fichte stress the fundamental misanthropy (*Menschenfeindlichkeit*) of the Jews, we must—in order to understand clearly the problem that the Jews pose to Bendavid's and Fichte's Kantian reasoning—turn the tables and ask not why the Jews, as the age-old charge has it, are misanthropic, but rather why the Kantian conception of humanity has such difficulty accommodating Judaism. As a functioning ethical community that resists assimilation to the universal ethics of Kantian humanity, the Jews mark the possibility of a limit to this would-be universalist moral project. It is precisely because the Jew resides at the periphery of Bendavid's and Fichte's Kantian understanding of the human, I would argue, that they subject the figure of the Jew to the normative force of their rhetorical violence. In Fichte's and Bendavid's fantasies of humanization through decapitation of the universal *Mensch*'s uncanny Other, the Jew, the normative (but usually self-masking) violence that constitutes the Kantian moral subject as universal becomes flagrant.

The fact that the two Kantians both resort to decapitation as the only possible means of incorporating Jews into the enlightened polity is striking. Behind this radical and paradoxical cure, which succeeds (if it succeeds) by killing the patient, looms the historical context of the Terror, in the shadow of which Bendavid and Fichte wrote.[48] The violence also stems from the way each draws on Kant's moral philosophy in his conception of humanity, the state, and the relationship between the two. An excursion into two related aspects of Kantian moral philosophy will illuminate these issues. The first aspect is the relationship, or rather the lack of relationship, between the sphere of Kantian morality and any possible alterity or exteriority—the inability of Kant's system to countenance, or even acknowledge, any form of ethical difference. The second aspect is the role violence plays in structuring the Kantian moral will. Exploring these questions will help us understand why our two Kantians cannot imagine forms of mediation between the ethical universality of the Kantian *Mensch* and the moral particularity of the Jews, and so must resort to fantasies of the Jews' radical and instantaneous erasure.

In a famous and singularly poetic passage intended to bridge the first and second parts of the *Critique of Pure Reason*, Kant offers a geographical image to help his readers envision the nature of the epistemological terrain he is mapping. He likens the phenomenal realm, the sphere of possible human knowledge, to an island that is surrounded by the waters of the noumenal world, alluring but also deceptive and treacherous because ultimately unchartable.[49] Elaborating on Kant's metaphor, we could envision the transcendental schemata, which produce the phenomenal realm of human knowledge by mediating between sensible intuitions and concepts a priori, as the island's shoreline: a boundary that touches the water yet still belongs and lends contours to the land. A space is only mappable by virtue of its limits, and the schemata set the limits to human knowledge, delineating its contours.

Kant offers no comparable image to aid in understanding the structure of practical reason. But if theoretical reason strains outward to its own limit—to the shoreline it cannot cross without losing itself in perilous waters—practical reason can be thought of as moving in the opposite direction, from its outer limit infinitely inward. Practical reason is not constrained by its limit because practical reason in fact constitutes itself in the very act of setting its own limit. Hegel was in this sense right in critiquing the categorical imperative as tautologous. Through the infinite force of its founding tautological gesture, Kantian morality constitutes itself as an absolute interiority, a space that shares no seam or border with any exteriority. (I use "interiority" in a purely spatial sense, not as a realm of human affect or sentiment.) Constituted as it is in its very universality, Kantian morality is structurally inimical to any alterity. Of course this is not to say that there is nothing other than morality (the sensible world is rigorously other than the moral). Rather, there is no possible Other that Kantian morality can recognize as moral. Anything not completely within the realm of moral reason is by definition radically incommensurable with it.[50]

No mediation between the moral and the nonmoral is possible according to the Kantian system, but neither is any mediation necessary. Kantian theoretical reason is a kind of epistemological compromise between the sensible and the intelligible and can exist only in the form of mediation between the two. In Kant's famous formulation, "thoughts without content are empty, intuitions without concepts are blind."[51] In contrast, Kantian practical reason is sui generis: were it capable of any dialogue with anything else, were it capable of maintaining a common border with something other than itself, its self-constituting hermetic circle would be broken, its infinite inward force lost.[52]

Even though, given Kant's strict dualism, no true mediation is possible between the intelligible realm of morality and that of the senses, some means of adjusting the latter to the dictates of the former is required. In *Critique of Practical Reason* and *Groundwork of the Metaphysics of Morals*, Kant theorizes this nonmediatory possibility of adjustment through the related concepts of *Willkür* (free choice) and *Nötigung* (rational compulsion). He distinguishes between the terms *Willkür* and *Wille* (will), the latter being essentially synonymous with practical reason itself. *Willkür* designates the human capacity to make choices based on pure moral reason.[53] It also encompasses, however, the possibility of choosing not to do so—in which case, Kant says, *Willkür* has been "pathologically affected" by empirical or sensuous causality.[54] Sensuous inclinations such as greed, lust, envy, and so on may cause one's *Willkür* to deviate from the rules of one's own deep (or, to use a Kantian idiom, intelligible or noumenal) moral grammar. Such pathologizing influences require a corrective force, and Kant calls this force *Nötigung*, a conscious (and therefore potentially corrective) representation of laws of practical reason. Such a representation is formalized in an imperative.

A protean concept, then, *Willkür* is both the aspect of the will that is susceptible to the pathologizing influence of the sensuous realm and the force that can overcome this influence. In casting difference in terms of pathological deviation from the noumenal norm, Kant leaves no room for forms of moral freedom whose autonomy could be said to inhere in their very incompatibility with Kant's own conception of moral reason (for Kant, this conception is not particular but universal). Traditional Jewish ethics based on the (from Kant's vantage point) heteronomous authority of the *mitzvot*, for example, can by definition claim no moral validity, no autonomy.[55] In this way, traditional Jewish practice is rendered (in a rigorous sense) unreasonable, fundamentally incompatible with practical reason. *Willkür*, then, effectively provides a buffer around the pure moral *Wille*, allowing the tautologous structure of moral reason to remain hermetically intact and immune to any form of alterity. *Willkür* does not mediate between the pure moral will and the sensuous world; rather, it interposes itself between the two. One's *Willkür* caries out any negotiations or dirty work with sensuous inclinations, permitting the *Wille* to remain pristine.

We are now in a better position to see how Kant's universalism can take the form of a kind of moral blackmail. One either wills to submit to the maxims that one's own moral autonomy generates, or one fails to will to do so and thus to correspond to one's own moral self. The only valid ethical sense must be routed through the universal autonomous subject, which is defined in its essence by the use of universally generalizable practical reason. Particularity as such—any heterogeneity between the universal laws of practical reason and an individual's ethical sensibilities—is reduced to a failure of resolve and must be corrected by *Nötigung*, the enforcer of one's own moral conscience. From the Kantian perspective, the nonuniversalizable, the particular, is by definition not in harmony with itself. The bifurcated structure of Kant's moral will (*Wille* and *Willkür*), I would argue, allows moral freedom to coexist with violent coercion because the freedom and the violence are relegated to separate spheres. The Kantian moral subject can be said to achieve autonomous freedom by submitting to (its own) norms—that is, through a form of self-inflicted violence that, because it can only take place in the space of *Willkür* and not in the pristine space of *Wille*, never taints or stains the morality it in fact founds. Nietzsche perceived the foundational violence of the Kantian moral subject keenly. In the course of elaborating his hypothesis that moral concepts like guilt, duty, and conscience originate in the act of exacting a price of violence, of *Leiden-machen*, Nietzsche suggests that the world of such concepts has "never completely lost a certain odor of blood and torture," and he adds "not even in old Kant: the categorical imperative reeks of cruelty."[56]

The Moral Law, Jewish Alterity, and the State

The constitutive violence of Kant's categorical imperative structures the way both Bendavid and Fichte theorize the possibility of incorporating Jews into the state and thus brings the two Kantians' positions perilously close to each other. The underlying similarity in how Bendavid and Fichte approach the question of extending civil rights to Jews appears most clearly in the ways they each conceive of the relation between moral *Mensch* and political *Bürger*. Each thinker treats *Mensch* and *Bürger* as fundamentally synonymous, even though they entertain different visions of what this basic unity of human being and citizen implies for the state's right to intervene in the lives of individuals.

Fichte's philosophically radical project has the effect of stripping the state as such of virtually all authority. His argument in *Beitrag zur Berichtigung der Urteile des Publikums über die französische Revolution* is that the *Mensch* is sovereign and not fundamentally dependent on the state. The state merely amounts to one particular contractual agreement (the social contract, or *Bürgervertrag*) into which autonomous *Menschen* may, or may not, choose to enter. In subordinating all political authority to inalienable rights constituted and sanctioned by the moral law (*Sittengesetz*) inherent in human beings as such, Fichte radically attenuates the authority of the state. Because Fichte's citizens receive no essential rights from the state, noncitizens (*Menschen* who have no contract with the state) should theoretically enjoy the same human rights. The moral and political, *Mensch* and *Bürger*, are essentially similar in Fichte, then, because the *Bürgervertrag* adds nothing, in moral terms, to the a priori *Sittengesetz* that humanity possesses intrinsically. What I called the "absolute interiority" of Kantian autonomous ethical subjectivity thus delimits the horizon of any politics for Fichte: no political arrangements can legitimately contradict or alter humanity's inherent moral law, and any possible political sphere can legitimately occupy only a restricted region within the sphere of human ethics itself, a region within which particular sorts of contractual arrangements, including the *Bürgervertrag*, can be freely entered into or refused.

Although Bendavid is not rigorously consistent, his most emphatic pronouncements imply a view of the legitimate authority of the state that is nearly the opposite of Fichte's. Bendavid repeatedly charges that Jews suffer from a lack of will,[57] and he closes his tract with this comment to his Jewish readers: "may the Eternal One give you strength and courage to will."[58] The will he evokes is unmistakably the Kantian moral will, the self-founding moral gesture of the universal ethical subject. Bendavid formulates the "main thesis of this treatise" as follows: "unless in the reforms that have been or are to be undertaken with them, the Jews intervene by abolishing their pointless ceremonial law, which utterly does not accord with the present times; unless they adopt a purer religion, one more worthy of the divine father—the pure teaching of Moses—they will necessarily remain, even after being baptized, indifferent and citizens harmful to the state."[59] Bendavid's rhetoric minimizes the agency of the state in the reforms to which he refers, and he locates the moral struggle within Jews instead of between Jews and the state. Jews must freely will the reform that is to be undertaken with them. In order to be a good citizen, one must first reform one's self; it becomes the moral responsibility of each Jew to give up traditional Judaism in favor of pure rational (Kantian) religion (disingenuously packaged here as "the pure teaching of Moses"). Bendavid occults the violence that the state inflicts on Jews in intervening in their value system and way of life by presenting the Jew's own moral and political will as paramount.

To be sure, Bendavid's position in *Etwas zur Charackteristick der Juden* on the extent to which the state should intervene in the lives of Jews is at times ambiguous and seemingly ambivalent. He certainly argues against the efficacy of state coercion. On Joseph II's project of enlightening the Jews, Bendavid comments that "the influence of the prince, to the extent that it consists in anything more than a removal of obstacles, effects nothing at all unless the people willingly cooperates and does what no prince can order it to do: *will* to be enlightened!"[60] Were the state to force the Jews into "the rights of humanity," their compliance would be merely external and superficial, not heartfelt. Worse, since unenlightened Jews erroneously link morality (a completely internal matter of good will) with the outward observance of Jewish law, forcing them to desist from outward observance would imperil whatever moral sensibility they possessed.[61]

Bendavid's dilemma is clear enough. Approaching the question of political rights for Jews as he does from the standpoint of the Kantian moral subject, he cannot—yet he simultaneously must—rely on the intervention of the state. On the one hand, if the Jews are coerced into enlightening themselves, such externally imposed enlightenment will remain devoid of true moral content. Enlightenment ultimately must come down to a matter of free will. On the other hand, absent coercive measures the majority of Jews would continue to practice traditional Judaism and feel no need to enlighten themselves at all. Bendavid's dilemma, then, is closely related to the problem of mediation in Kantian ethics examined above, and it can be formulated as a problem of how to get inside the moral will of the Jew when Jewish will seems to be utterly outside the sphere of pure moral reason. Bendavid is in need of a paradoxical, noncoercive form of coercion—and this is what he finds, or at least what he seeks, in decapitation, a fantasy of total violence that seems to resolve the paradox of how the state might legitimately intervene to transform the Jews' will.

The immediate context of Bendavid's comment about decapitating the Jewish hydra deals directly with the central question of his treatise, how to convert Jews into *Menschen* and *Bürger*:

> The restriction the state imposes on the happiness of these noble souls [Bendavid's fourth category of enlightened Jews] is, I hear, to be lifted. Friedrich Wilhelm the father of all upright men, also wishes, in accordance with his compassionate heart, to be the father of all upright Jews. But how long that nonsense with the shameful, senseless ceremonial law will be carried on, how long the Jew will continue to believe that the divine father will bestow upon him a special crown for observing it—only He who knows everything knows this! Certainly it can never cease if no one dares to speak loudly and earnestly to the hearts of the Jews, and makes robustly apparent to them the imprudence of the maintenance of their customs; but at the same time also asks the state for its endorsement [*Genehmigung*] of this abolition, since the maintenance [of Jewish custom] must needs have a truly harmful influence on the character of the Jew and, through him, on the state. In order to bring this about, it will, I believe, be sufficient, given the wisdom of the government, to remark that without this general abolition of the ceremonial law things will needs transpire as they unfortunately always have with every ferment that has arisen among the Jews. A portion of them, via various routes and means, get themselves free from Judaism, and the others huddle together more closely than before, abandon themselves more eagerly to their nonsense, and propagate it more prolifically. It is the hydra, all of whose heads must be cut off at once if two are not to grow back in place of every one severed.[62]

Bendavid's civic cure for *Judentum* involves an attack on two fronts. He appeals to Jews to reform themselves from within and appeals to the state to aid in a total reform from without. Bendavid's problem, clearly, is how to mediate between these two spheres, how to bring the moral Other into the absolute interiority of Kantian moral subjectivity.[63] The absolute interiority or self-referentiality of Kantian morality, however, is predicated on the impossibility of such a problem arising in the first place. The universal Kantian moral logic with which Bendavid would appeal to the Jew as moral Other is only binding, paradoxically, to the extent that there can exist no moral Other to address. In this light it is interesting to note one of Bendavid's rhetorical strategies for infiltrating the moral essence of the "good-hearted" Jews he is addressing, and thus undermining any claim they might have to moral autonomy. "You already feel like *Menschen*," Bendavid writes, sounding like a moral hypnotist, entering into and giving voice to the silent recesses of the Jews' moral will: "You already wish, secretly, to be *Menschen*." Adopting the tone of the prophet of Enlightenment, he continues: "You lack only strength. Come listen! I want to inspire you with strength. Hear the consequences of your cowardice and shudder!"[64] Bendavid attempts literally to speak the essence of a universal moral will (*Mut*, *Kraft*, *Wille*) into (*einsprechen*) the secret and silent (*im Stillen*) void of Jewish ethical Otherness, the only form—a void, nothing—that ethical alterity can take from the point of view of Kantian ethical universalism. How to address, even if only to interpolate, the moral Other when alterity is inimical to the universal morality into which the Other is to be interpolated?

It is in order to overcome this impasse that Bendavid appeals to the state. Since Jews remain beyond moral autonomy's reach, the task of accomplishing the impossible mediation between the morally Other and the morally autonomous devolves on the external power of the state. Even as it is called on to remedy the essential inability on the part of universal moral subjectivity to engage an Other, however, the state must be seen as contiguous with—not external to—the moral sphere, lest the state appear inimical to the very moral subjectivity it wishes to instill in the Jew. Thus Bendavid assumes, at least rhetorically, the political good will of Friedrich Wilhelm as he had done with Joseph II when discussing Joseph's projects for reforming the Jews in his lands. The political intentions of these heads of state accord with—are the political analogues of—the good will of Kantian ethics. There can be no fundamental discord between the moral and the political spheres because politics is predicated on, derives its legitimacy from, and should merely extend ethics. Far from overstepping its legitimate moral authority, then, the state, in a presumed preestablished harmony with the moral law, effectively becomes the agent of moral *Nötigung*. The state does not coerce Jews but rather gives them the gift of moral autonomy; it coerces them to obey only the dictates of their own moral freedom.[65]

Bendavid's harmonization of the violence of state power with the moral autonomy of the subject remains fragile at best. The problematic equation of state agency with moral agency cannot provide a satisfactory resolution of the dilemma of how to engage Kantian *Nötigung* in a Jewish subject who seems to exist outside the purportedly universal inside of Kantian ethics. In fact, this dilemma seems insoluble by any but phantasmic means. I suggest that Bendavid conjures his gruesome image of decapitation as an attempt to resolve this aporia. Easily overlooked precisely because it is, while alarming, "only" a metaphor, Bendavid's Jewish hydra is a condensation of his Kantian philosophical politics.

Arguing that only a total abolition of Jewish ceremonial practice would be effectual, Bendavid envisions a clean break from traditional Judaism, likening the state-sponsored program of eradication he proposes to the heroic task of simultaneously severing all the myriad heads of the mythical hydra. We are reminded of the violence of the categorical imperative that is, I have argued, self-inflicted at the inception of Kantian ethical subjectivity. If individual Jews can muster, from within, the will to become *Menschen*, then the state, with its paternalistic good will, surely will adopt them as *Bürger*. Should they obstinately persist in their allegiance to the collective Jewish pathology, however, the state must intervene to cut off the malignant Jewishness they lack the will to "cast off" themselves. In doing violence to Jewish collective existence, the state does not violate the basic rights of the Jews because, according to Bendavid's particular deployment of Kantian logic, it is only through this very violence that the Jews are liberated from the pathological collective Jewish body and constituted as autonomous human beings. The state's violent intervention stands in for the self-inflicted violence that inaugurates the Kantian ethical subject and thereby creates the very autonomous moral subjects with whose moral law its politics can harmonize. If, in Kant's moral philosophy, *Nötigung* is imposed by one's own moral freedom, Bendavid's coercion of his fellow Jews is of a more sociopolitical cast: Kant's practical reason, we might say, becomes Bendavid's tactical reason, as he admonishes Jews to will what is, as he sees it, practically necessary. The normalizing thrust of the last part of *Etwas zur Charackteristick der Juden* attempts to provide the *Nötigung* required to correct the historically deformed or, in Kant's term, "pathologically affected" *Willkür* of Bendavid's less enlightened coreligionists. He presents the Jews with a moral imperative to cast off their Jewishness and become universal *Menschen*.

The metaphor of decapitation seems perfectly chosen to finesse the insoluble problem that remains: how to incorporate any instance of moral alterity into the absolute interiority of Kantian ethics. In its absolute violence, decapitation provides a phantasmic resolution of this problem of the impossibility of mediation with the absolute. Decapitation figures a form of noncoercive coercion. The moral subject constructed by the absolute violence of decapitation is not scarred, as it were, by this violence and can bear no witness to it, precisely because it is instantaneous and total. As Daniel Arasse writes in his study of the guillotine, "by its instantaneous action, the guillotine sets before our eyes the invisibility of death at the very instant of its occurrence, exact and indistinguishable."[66] Just as the guillotine redefined death as a moment without history, narrative, or self-awareness, moral decapitation inflicts no violence because it eradicates the Other instantaneously. Simply put, there is no Jewish subject left who could have suffered a morally unwarranted coercion.

Further, Bendavid's metaphor engages two important oppositions: individual autonomy versus collectivity, and humanity versus monstrosity. Traditionally thought of as the key to Jewish survival, *am yisrael* (the Jewish people) now appears as a monster. It is still the key to survival; however, the survival in question is no longer that of Jewish tradition but rather that of the pathology of collective Jewishness. Unless utterly eradicated, the malignant Jewish hydra will only metastasize: two heads will grow back for every one that is severed. Decapitation of the many-headed hydra is not only a means of slaying the monster but also one of fully individuating its insufficiently autonomous heads. Bendavid's metaphor is skillfully chosen indeed: the Jewish disease can be cured only if Jewish individualization through decapitation is realized completely. The Jew's head that remains afflicted with Jewishness remains only semiautonomous and, therefore, from Bendavid's Kantian point of view, effectively only semihuman: latently and potentially human, yes, but still connected to the nonhuman monster of the Jewish collectivity. Bendavid castigates with particular vitriol the pathological vigilance (a sign of denatured individuals) with which Jews observe public ritual, the collective practices of the communal Jewish body that are patently irreducible to religion defined as a sphere of strictly individual moral conscience. Just as the morality of the Kantian human individual is universal, Jews must universally be made moral individuals in order to leave the sphere of the deformed and monstrous and become fully human. If they will not choose to be morally free individuals, they must be coerced into becoming free. They must be severed from the collective monster of the Jewish people by a force so absolute in its violence that it paradoxically obliterates any traces of itself: decapitation.

The political intentions of Fichte's assessment of the essential nonhumanity of the Jew, often taken to be a salient moment in the construction of modern philosophical antisemitism, are basically opposed to Bendavid's, yet Fichte and Bendavid are strikingly similar in rhetoric and, more importantly, in underlying conception, as an examination of Fichte's Kantian framework will show.

Fichte argues against the very possibility of Jewish inclusion in the civil community of the state. He views Jews as already constituting a state apart, a "state within a state," and thus as ineligible for inclusion in the civil contract. Fichte infamously concludes that the only means he can see for including Jews in the civil contract would be to cut off their heads and replace them with different heads totally free of Jewish ideas.[67] Not only is Fichte's statement alarming but it also—a point that has seldom been appreciated—abruptly turns against the philosophical defense of the French Revolution that the philosopher has been preparing for more than a hundred pages and that amounts essentially to a defense of the right of free individuals to form states within states. From Fichte's point of view there is no moral justification for prohibiting autonomous individuals from forming states within states.[68] This is because there can be no fundamental incompatibility between different states. The moral law defines the sphere within which all possible civil contracts, including those that found states, must exist; the space defined by the moral law—internally harmonious, by definition—is the only space that states can inhabit. Since the human *Sittengesetz* is the ultimate source of authority for all the various states in the human community, it does not so much adjudicate between as obviate the very need for adjudication between states.[69]

What, then, is so problematic about the Jewish state within a state? Although Fichte's use of the term to refer to the Jews is highly memorable and can indeed be said to inaugurate the modern, antisemitic career of this slogan (which had long been used to refer to various non-Jewish groups), it tends to obscure what is actually at stake.[70] If the issue were really one of Jewish adherence to a Jewish state, there would be no problem. Fichte's Jews are problematic not as *Bürger*, however, but as *Menschen*. If Jews pose a threat to Fichte's political philosophy—and the rhetorical violence with which he assaults them suggests that they do—it is not by constituting a state within the state but by testing the very limits of the human community on which Fichte predicates the legitimacy of all states. What is deeply troubling about Fichte's Jews is the doubt they cast on the ineluctability of the logic governing the would-be universal moral sphere.

It is not difficult to see why one must locate the problem that Fichte has with the Jews and Jewish subjectivity (and the inseparability of collective and subjective Jewish identity is indeed one way of stating the problem) in their human rather than merely civic status, for this limit is the only truly significant border in Fichte's moral and philosophical topography. As we have seen, the mere existence of a Jewish state based on a *Bürgervertrag* among Jews would present no philosophical problem to Fichte. His Jewish state, however, is not merely another example of a civil contract between freely reasoning human beings who happen to be Jewish, but rather a collectivity bound by a Jewish reasoning that seems fundamentally incommensurable with autonomous human moral reason. Jews represent the possibility of moral alterity, of being moral outside of Kantian-Fichtian ethical humanity. Fichte's Jews hover—unbearably for him—at the limit of the moral-human sphere, a limit that must exist absolutely or not at all.

It is the Jews' purported misanthropy, and not even their lack of belief in Jesus Christ, that makes them so ethically problematic: here it becomes clear that Fichte's Jews are not opposed to the Christian community—even if that is understood in essentially secular, cultural terms—but rather to the human community:[71] "May the Jews indeed not believe in Jesus Christ, may they not even believe in any God, if only they did not believe in two different moral laws and in a misanthropic God. Human rights they must have, even if they do not grant us the same; because they *are* human beings."[72] The Jews' misanthropy goes hand in hand with their adherence to an additional, incommensurable *Sittengesetz*. (Since the moral law is synonymous with ultimate respect for the freedom of all human beings, misanthropy and adherence to a different moral law imply each other mutually.) The curious italicization in the phrase "they *are* human beings" (a final determination on a hard-to-decide question? a sign of perplexity?) aptly testifies to the way the disparate Jewish *Sittengesetz* strains against the very limits of the human as Fichte understands it. And, much as in Bendavid, the only possible mediation between the *Mensch* and the Jew, the only way to incorporate the Jews into the sphere of the human whose limits they so vex, is through the absolute violence of decapitation.

A Diagnostician at the End of Jewish History

A similar Kantian framework subtends the vision of the fringe *maskil* Bendavid and the philosophical antisemitism of Fichte. Yet the two thinkers' relationships to the political status of the Jews are radically different. For Fichte, Jews and Jewish ethics are a vexing obstacle to his politicized ethical project. Bendavid faces the more poignant problem of how to take up a position in the polity as a Jew. His attempt to show fellow Jews the way to become *Menschen* and *Bürger* hinges on how successfully he can present himself before a German-language Enlightenment reading public as a human being worthy of citizenship. Kant provides Bendavid with the structural possibility, however problematic, both of narrating a certain version of Jewish history as pathological and of ultimately resolving this history into a suprahistorical model of the moral subject. Indeed, in diagnosing the sick Jewish soul Bendavid lays claim to a locus of enunciation beyond the pathologies engendered by Jewish history. Just as moral freedom, for Kant, is what remains once the causal relations of the empirical world have been transcended or stripped away, so true freedom is possible—according to Bendavid—only through a leap beyond the causal relations of Jewish history. It is incumbent on each Jew to "shake off" his pathological history and thereby enter the polity, a realm of idealized or intelligible political relations, as a universal (and German-speaking) *Mensch* and *Bürger*. The Jews' particular history should disappear like a symptom.

According to the Kantian view of the relationship between history and moral will, history can unfold only as a narrative of the progressive liberation of a latent, essentially suprahistorical, human moral freedom. History is necessary for the realization of moral freedom, yet essentially extrinsic to it. Kant's dualistic vision of the subject as both inside yet essentially outside history is implicit in his famous definition of Enlightenment as "man's emergence from his self-incurred immaturity."[73] History is the process of exiting history, understood as one's dependence on others. It is a progressive excavation and distillation of the pure suprahistorical subject from the historical forces that the subject is guilty of having suffered. A historically incurred pathology is self-incurred: to suffer history is a moral weakness.

Bendavid identifies the arrival of Mendelssohn and the Enlightenment as the promise of a new era in—or beyond—Jewish history, one that can only now be fully realized.[74] Even as Bendavid ventriloquizes his message through Mendelssohn, however, the latter serves as a Jewish stand-in for Kant, notwithstanding the incompatibility between the two philosophers' positions on religious truth. Bendavid disingenuously appropriates this modern Moses in order to admonish his contemporary coreligionists to "return" to "the pure doctrine of Moses, the doctrine of natural religion," a "doctrine" that Bendavid understands, contra Mendelssohn, according to Kantian postulates.[75] Self-styled prophet of Enlightenment or messiah of *Menschheit*, Bendavid states repeatedly in the final pages of his tract that the time of Judaism is past. The moment of truth has arrived at long last, and it is time to make the leap beyond Jewish history into the realm of *Menschheit* and its political analogue, the state.[76] Bendavid's Kantian framework permits him, then, to trace a history (or pathogenesis) that he considers constitutive of Jewish particularity while still positing a universalist human essence that both precedes and, potentially, follows the historical aberration of Judaism's pathologizing rabbinic detour. Indeed, in asserting the competence to diagnose the Jew as sick, as *Mensch manqué*, Bendavid takes up a position as precisely this universal, post-Jewish *Mensch*.

Bendavid's intervention is unsettlingly complex. Even in his advocacy of slaying the communal monster, he understands himself to be acting in the service of Jewish commitments. Unlike Fichte, Bendavid is trying to conceive, with Kant, of a universal polity that would have a place for Jews. The fact that this vision of universality is predicated on potentially violent exclusion should be clear enough from the foregoing analysis, yet Bendavid's intellectual and rhetorical self-modeling constitutes an attempt to practice a Jewish (not merely an anti-Jewish) Kantian politics. Bendavid proposes the Kantian moral will as the gateway into the enlightened polity, a gateway very much in opposition to the only existing option: conversion. He repeatedly cautions against conversion to Christianity, as conversion without inner conviction would merely aggravate, not overcome, the Jew's lack of moral will.[77] Bendavid's imperative is for the Jew to become an autonomous *Mensch*, not merely to find a socially more viable way to accommodate his lack of autonomy.

As critical as Bendavid was of traditional Jewish practices and as extreme—especially in the heady year of 1793—as may have been both his diagnosis of how history had deformed the Jewish psyche and his vision of an Enlightenment cure, he remained engaged in Jewish institutional life and in Jewish intellectual pursuits throughout his life. In 1806 he became the director of the Jewish Free School (*Jüdische Freischule*) that David Friedländer and Daniel Itzig had founded in 1778, a post he held until the school closed in 1825. He published a handful of essays on Jewish subjects and refers repeatedly to a major work on the Pentateuch, which, however, he probably never finished.[78]

Bendavid was also one of the few members of his generation (David Friedländer was another) to be invited to join the Verein für Cultur und Wissenschaft der Juden (association for the culture and science of the Jews) in Berlin. In 1823 he contributed two articles to its epochal though short-lived journal, edited by Leopold Zunz.

The Verein is the focus of the following chapter, and since it was in the context of the Verein that the young Heinrich Heine, also briefly a member, met the elder Bendavid, Heine's—typically equivocal—appreciation of Bendavid can serve as an apt bridge between the foregoing discussion of Bendavid's Kantian philosophical politics and the Jewish Hegelianism of the *Vereinler*. In a letter to Zunz dated June 27, 1823, Heine writes wryly that he "would like to apply roughly what you [Zunz] expressed at the publication of the first volumes of Jost's *History* when you refrained from all judgment, since it was after all possible that these were intentionally written so poorly so that subsequent volumes would appear that much more brilliant; in the same way, I'd like to suspect that you have arranged the essays of the *Zeitschrift* in such a way that one will some day be able to demonstrate with precision in a series of annual volumes how German style has gradually developed among us *Wissenschaft* Jews [*Wissen-*

schaftsjuden]."[79] In contrast to the timely yet impenetrable style of Hegelian contributors like Eduard Gans and Ludwig Marcus, "Ben David is clear, but what he writes suits neither the times nor the journal. These are essays that would have been appropriate for the *Theological Journal*, year 1786."[80]

But if the dyed-in-the-wool Kantian Bendavid seemed out of touch to the Hegelian *Wissenschaftsjuden* in 1823—Heine includes himself in this group, however ironically—after the Verein imploded and, more importantly, after first Heine and then Gans converted, Heine comes to see Bendavid and his fellow Kantian holdover Friedländer differently. In a letter to Moses Moser dated April 23, 1826, Heine waxes nostalgic for the days of the Verein, which he now presents as a heroic Jewish cause that he and Gans have betrayed. Heine looks longingly back at the time when Gans was "not yet baptized and wrote long addresses to the Verein and reflected on [*trug sich mit*] the motto 'Victrix causa Diis placuit, sed victa Catoni' [the victorious cause pleased the Gods, but the inferior one pleased Cato]." In the same letter Heine encourages Moser to write up and publish the "excellent" thoughts Moser had had at that time about "Judaism, the despicableness of Christian proselytizing, the despicableness of Jews who, through baptism, aimed not only at obviating difficulties but rather wanted to obtain, haggle something for themselves."[81] Heine holds up Friedländer and Bendavid as examples of courageous Jews who, throughout their long lives, rejected the expedient of conversion.[82] Heine muses that "as Solon said that one cannot call anyone happy before his death, so one can also say that no one can be called a brave man before his death. I'm happy that old Friedländer and Ben-David are old and will die soon. Then we'll have secured them [*diese haben wir dann sicher*], and no one can reproach our age with not being able to demonstrate a single scrupulous man."[83]

Finally, in an 1844 eulogy for Ludwig Marcus, which is also a reckoning of sorts with the whole Verein project, Heine describes Bendavid as "a Kantian to the bone" (*ein eingefleischter Kantianer*) out of step with the Hegelianism of his younger colleagues. Yet Heine also pays Bendavid great respect, here again stressing his commitment to the Jewish community and refusal to convert: "Bendavid was for his entire life the most fervent adherent of Kantian philosophy; in his youth, he suffered the greatest persecutions for this, and yet he never wanted to separate himself from the old community of the Mosaic confession. He never wanted to change his outer confessional badge [*äußere Glaubenskokarde*]. Even the appearance of such a denial filled him with loathing and disgust."[84]

The author of *Etwas zur Charackteristick der Juden* ended up a Heinean Jewish hero of sorts.

Chapter Two

Becoming Citizens of Hegel's State, or the Politics of *Wissenschaft des Judentums* in 1820s Germany

In Berlin on November 7, 1819, seven Jewish intellectuals, most of them students at the newly formed University of Berlin, founded a "society for the improvement of the condition of the Jews in the federated German state" that in 1821 adopted the name Verein für Cultur und Wissenschaft der Juden (association for the culture and science of the Jews).[1] The context of the Verein's formation was one of crisis. The newfound German nationalist spirit that had emerged in the campaign against Napoleon gave rise to conceptions of Germans as belonging to a *Volksgemeinschaft* (folk community). Strains of antisemitism became prevalent, notably in the student fraternity or *Burschenschaft* movement—which, especially after the 1817 Wartburgfest, became popular not only among students, many of whom were returning soldiers, but also among certain professors, such as Friedrich Rühs of the University of Berlin and Jakob Friedrich Fries of the University of Heidelberg.[2] In March 1819, the dramatist August von Kotzebue was assassinated by the militant *Burschenschaftler* Karl Sand, resulting in the issuing of the Carlsbad Decrees, which not only suppressed the *Burschenschaften* but also severely restricted freedoms of academic life and the press. The Verein was also established in no small part in response to the Hep-Hep pogroms that broke out in August 1819 in Würzburg and, targeting Jews and Jewish property, spread throughout August and September to many cities in southwestern Germany—notably, to Hamburg.

Both the *Burschenschaft* movement and the reactionary policies issued in response to the political assassination carried out by one of its most radical members were deeply troubling—and the recrudescence of anti-Jewish violence shocking—to the Verein founders, most of whom were first-generation university students who had left the traditional Jewish community behind and had good reason to hope that their future in Germany would be wide open. They had come of age in the context of the liberalizing reforms that Karl August von Hardenberg and Baron Karl vom und zum Stein had introduced in the wake of

Prussia's defeat by Napoleon at Jena in 1806, including Prussia's 1812 Jewish Emancipation Edict, which greatly expanded Jewish civil rights (though many of the advances would be rescinded in Restoration Germany). Even after the Carlsbad Decrees, Germany's political and intellectual future, and the place of Jews in each, remained very much open questions. The Jewish Emancipation Edict had been ambiguous about whether Jews would be permitted to hold academic appointments, and the question lingered until the Verein's president, Eduard Gans (1797–1839), who was seeking an appointment to Berlin University's law faculty, pressed the issue a full decade later. Friedrich Wilhelm III's cabinet order—the so-called Lex Gans of August 18, 1822—definitively excluded Jews from state teaching positions.[3]

One of the key components of the political and intellectual landscape in Berlin that infused the Verein members—or *Vereinler*—with optimism during the heady years of the late 1810s and early 1820s was the philosophy of Georg Wilhelm Friedrich Hegel. Given Hegel's great admiration for Protestantism (or, at any rate, for his philosophical version of it), negative view of Judaism's accomplishments (evident in both harsh criticism and silent disregard), and the secularized supersessionism basic to his thinking, scholars have expressed legitimate skepticism about the compatibility of Hegel's thought with Jewish commitments and historical narratives, whether religious or secular. Michael Meyer, for example, writes:

> Hegel's veneration for the state as the highest embodiment of the World Spirit created an atmosphere of political quietism, which stifled prophetic morality. For about a generation before midcentury, Hegel's influence in Germany was enormous. Jewish thinkers could not help but be affected by his grand system and its cherished goal of freedom. Yet like Spinoza, Hegel left no room in his thought for significant individual responsibility. And that was essential to any conception of Judaism, especially for the Reformers, who dwelt on Judaism's moral imperative. Although thoughtful Jews had to grapple with Hegel's philosophy, ultimately they all rejected some of its most basic elements.[4]

The lingering but erroneous view that Hegel's veneration of the state was politically quietist vis-à-vis the Prussian Restoration state, which indeed worked to roll back rather than advance gains in Jewish civil rights, has contributed to the widespread image of Hegel as bad for the Jews. One scholar has gone so far as to contend that Hegel's narrative of world spirit—with its orientalist, Eurocentric geocultural orientation and tendency to level alterity in the name of the universal—culminates in the "European, Christian State."[5] There has been a critical consensus for some time that Hegel, despite engaging in a certain amount of fearful equivocation, was a decided opponent of the German-Christian Restoration state, and it is not necessary to argue that point again here.[6] Yet Meyer's observation that aspects of Hegel's philosophy made it more of an obstacle to contend with than a source of inspiration for Jewish thinkers underscores the singularity of the Hegelians in the Verein. Many Jewish thinkers were influenced by Hegel to various degrees. Some, such as Solomon Formstecher (1808–89) were only weakly Hegelian. Nachman Krochmal (1785–1840) was clearly inspired by Hegel's concept of absolute spirit and narratives of historical development, yet his theory of Judaism as absolute spirit—essentially suprahistorical, and thus perennially reborn—is incompatible with basic tenets of Hegel's thought.[7] Noah Rosenbloom has argued that *Nineteen Letters on Judaism* (1836) by the intellectual founder of modern Orthodox Judaism, Samson Raphael Hirsch (1808–88), draws heavily on Hegel's philosophy of history.[8] As Gershon Greenberg has shown, Samuel Hirsch (1815–9) was more profoundly engaged with Hegel, yet he, too, drew on Hegel largely in order to reject him.[9] The Hegelians among the *Vereinler* were certainly the first Jewish Hegelians, and they were arguably the most faithfully Hegelian of all the nineteenth-century thinkers who interpreted and appropriated Hegel's thought to reconceive the philosophical and historical meanings of Judaism. Much as Lazarus Bendavid, as we saw in chapter 1, drew on a still new Kantian philosophical framework to theorize Judaism in ways that responded to the immediate political landscape, the Hegelian *Vereinler* shuttled between Hegel's lecture theater and their own meetings as they theorized themselves as Jewish intellectuals, and the relationship of Jews and Judaism (*Judentum*) to the state, according to Hegelian principles. And although Meyer attributes Hegel's influence on Jewish intellectuals of the 1830s and 1840s to the enormous impact he had on German academic and intellectual life in general, it is worth noting that the *Vereinler* were thinking with Hegel in Hegel's early Berlin years—when, in John Toews's characterization, "Hegel's philosophy was still struggling for recognition and acceptance."[10]

The image of Hegel as antagonistic to the Jews also derives largely (though by no means wholly) from his theological manuscripts from the 1790s, which articulate very negative stereotypical images of the Jew as egoistic and misanthropic.[11] (Since these texts were not published in Hegel's lifetime, however, they were unknown to the *Vereinler*.) Although hardly generous to Judaism, Hegel's mature work became increasingly nuanced and positive about Jewish contributions to the development of spirit, though the debate over how fundamentally Hegel's views about Jews changed is unresolved.[12] Whatever one may think about Hegel's compatibility or incompatibility with Jewish commitments (and however one defines these), the *Vereinler*'s enormous respect for and relative fidelity to Hegel stand out as unique. Although, as we will see, they sometimes deployed certain possibilities that Hegel opened up to combat other aspects of Hegel's philosophy of history that tended to belittle Jewish contributions, the *Vereinler* nonetheless remained more directly in dialogue with Hegel than several later and more weakly Hegelian Jewish thinkers. The Verein is arguably the only attempt to think Judaism in a truly Hegelian key.

The view of Hegel as bad for the Jews has led scholars sometimes to downplay the Verein's Hegelianism, or to acknowledge it with a certain embarrassment.[13] Most scholarship to date appreciates the Verein chiefly as the institutional framework for the new scholarly project that Gans famously dubbed *Wissenschaft des Judentums* (the science of Judaism, or the academic study of Judaism). The short-lived Verein—remembered by the name it adopted in 1821, Verein für Cultur und Wissenschaft der Juden—has in this way been enshrined as one origin of modern academic Jewish studies. This image of the Verein finds justification above all in the pioneering work of Leopold Zunz, and to a lesser extent in that of Isaak Markus Jost.[14] Yet it is worth recalling that Zunz inaugurated the field of *Wissenschaft des Judentums* (*avant la lettre*) in 1818, before the Verein was founded, with his seminal essay "Etwas über die rabbinische Literatur" (On rabbinic literature) and that Jost quickly became disillusioned with and left the Verein.[15] I would argue that when we write the Verein into the narrative of what we do as scholars today, we miss much of what they thought they were doing, which—although articulated largely in and through academic, and specifically Hegelian, discourse—was always thoroughly political. Accounts of the emergence of secular Jewish studies out of the Verein during the pivotal years in Berlin of the late 1810s and early 1820s may provide a satisfying tale of disciplinary origins, but they tend to gloss too quickly over the political aspirations that thoroughly saturated the *Vereinler*'s pursuit of Jewish scholarship in a new key. In the next two chapters I describe some of the ways the Verein aspired to transform the relationship of Jews to the state through the fascinating if equivocal strategies of a lived Hegelianism.

Indebted to seminal work by Sinai (Siegfried) Ucko, Hanns Reissner, Ismar Schorsch, John Toews, Rachel Livné-Freudenthal, and others, my intervention constitutes a significant shift in emphasis rather than a radically new claim, for all serious scholarship on early *Wissenschaft des Judentums* acknowledges its implication in politics and ideology.[16] Yosef Yerushalmi, for example, locates the emergence of the *Vereinler*'s ideal of *Wissenschaft* in ideology, and the ideology of *Wissenschaft* receives serious attention in the secondary literature.[17] Moreover, virtually every scholar who has written on the Verein acknowledges the Hegelian language that characterizes much Verein discourse. Nonetheless, the construction of the Verein as an origin of the discipline of modern Jewish studies, and the reticence about Hegel within this discipline, have conspired to leave unexplored much of what most profoundly animated the Verein—a Hegelian philosophical politics. The political aspirations the *Vereinler* pursued become truly legible only when viewed through the Hegelian conceptual lens that did so much to inspire, and warp, their understanding of the Verein's significance in the context of Restoration Prussia.

The Verein between Jewish Scholarship and the Spell of Hegelian Theory

Two seminal assessments of the early Jewish *Wissenschaftler* as a point of origin for the modern practice of Jewish historiography—by Yerushalmi and Schorsch—exemplify how "autobiographies" of the discipline of Jewish studies are prone to neglect the philosophical politics at the heart of the *Vereinler*'s project.[18] Yerushalmi assigns the *Vereinler* epochal importance as the first practitioners and theoreticians of modern Jewish historiography. Whereas, according to Yerushalmi, even the Haskalah continued to appreciate history primarily as an aid in the pursuit of traditionally valued learning, the *Vereinler*'s new historical sensibility marks a decisive break with the world of traditional Jewish memory: "From Weisel [or Wessely] and the Me'assef to the famous manifesto published by Immanuel Wolf in 1822 and entitled *On the Concept of a Science of Judaism* is a span of forty years, a biblical generation. Yet it represents a drastic leap into a new kind of thinking."[19] Notwithstanding the immense historical and ideological distance between nineteenth-century *Wissenschaft* and the contemporary Jewish historian, Yerushalmi sees remarkable continuity between the modern historical sensibility into which the *Vereinler* abruptly "leapt" and his own poignantly ironic self-consciousness as a "*parvenu*" Jewish historian: "As a professional Jewish historian I am a new creature in Jewish history. My lineage does not extend beyond the second decade of the nineteenth century, which makes me, if not illegitimate, at least a *parvenu* within the long history of the Jews. . . . I live within the ironic awareness that the very mode in which I delve into the Jewish past represents a decisive break with that past."[20] Although Yerushalmi considers the ideology of emancipation largely responsible for launching the new historiographical enterprise, it is the new historical sensibility as a rupture with traditional Jewish culture that commands his interest. These dimensions are salient for his beautiful reflection on his own ambivalent relationship to the historical conditions of possibility of the modern Jewish historian.

Schorsch's relationship to nineteenth-century *Wissenschaft* is more straightforwardly affirmative. He downplays the break between Jewish memory and Jewish history that is structural to Yerushalmi's essay, affirms the sustaining quality of the work of his nineteenth-century predecessors, and remains sanguine that Jewish historiography can continue to inspire Jewish identity: "In short, emancipation altered the nature of Jewish memory; it did not destroy it. Nor is the change as far-reaching as one might think. . . . Historical consciousness was always the substratum of Jewish identity."[21] Schorsch's emphasis on continuity from preemancipation Jewish culture to the historical turn in nineteenth-century *Wissenschaft* to his own scholarly practice—together with his great admiration for Zunz—predispose him to see scholarship as the Verein's raison d'être: "The decision to place a new type of Jewish scholarship at the heart of the society's agenda had been made possible by the publication of a revolutionary tract just a year before its founding. Zunz's *Etwas über die rabbinische Literatur* has long been justifiably revered as the cornerstone of the *Wissenschaft* edifice. Without it the *Verein* would have been just another Jewish fraternal or cultural organization; with it the *Verein* became the testing ground for the viability and application of rethinking Judaism historically."[22] Although it is true that, had it not produced "a new type of Jewish scholarship," the Verein would be of scant interest to contemporary scholars, it does not necessarily follow that the *Vereinler* understood their group's importance as coextensive with the production of scholarship. In circumscribing the Verein's meaningful activity within the vision of *Wissenschaft* that Zunz set forth in his epochal 1818 essay, Schorsch belittles the aspects of the Verein's project that exceeded Zunz's particular vision of *Wissenschaft*. To inscribe the Verein in a narrative of intellectual continuity leading, eventually, to practitioners of Jewish studies today virtually requires such privileging of the least Hegelian member of the Verein's thoroughly Hegelian inner circle. Zunz was indeed the one member of the group who went on, over the course of a half-century and without institutional support, to produce a substantial and enduring body of scholarship on Jewish subjects.[23] It is surely no coincidence, moreover, that the Verein's most serious scholar was among the least Hegelian of its active members.[24] Reflecting on the demise of the Verein in a letter to Immanuel Wohlwill in summer 1824, Zunz identified *Wissenschaft des Judentums* as the one lasting element to emerge from the wreckage.[25] Even as he did so, however, he effectively distinguished it from the Verein's main project of reforming *die Juden* and *das Judentum*:

> I've come to the point of nevermore believing in a reformation of the Jews [*Juden-Reformation*] . . . The Jews and Judaism that we wanted to recon-

struct are riven asunder and the prey of barbarians, fools, money-changers, idiots and *parnasim*. . . . [Jews'] own scholarship [*Die eigene Wissenschaft*] has died out among the German Jews, and they have no interest [*Sinn*] in European scholarship because they have become untrue to themselves, alienated from their Idea [*der Idee entfremdet*], and the slaves of naked self-interest. . . . After this grisly sketch of Jewry, you'll require no explanation as to why the Verein and its journal have expired [*eingeschlafen*] and are as little missed as the temple, schools and civic happiness [*das Bürgerglück*]. The Verein didn't die as a result of the special *Vereine*, which could have been called merely the consequence of an administrative error, but rather never existed in reality. Five to ten enthusiastic people found each other and, like Moses, dared to hope for the propagation of this spirit. That was delusion. The only lasting thing to emerge from this *mabul* [deluge] is the *Wissenschaft des Judenthums*; for it will live on, even if no one were to lift a finger for it for centuries. I confess that, along with surrender to God's final Judgment, the occupation with this science [*Wissenschaft*] is my comfort and security.[26]

Even as Zunz identifies *Wissenschaft des Judentums* as the sole abiding remnant of the Verein, he comes very close to opposing *Wissenschaft des Judentums* —as it remained—to the Verein's project of reforming the Jews. Whereas *Wissenschaft des Judentums* will persist, the Verein never really existed: it was grandiose illusion and self-deception (*Täuschung*). The *Wissenschaft des Judentums* that abides is clearly not synonymous with the Verein, or even with *Wissenschaft* as it was deployed in the Verein's illusory ideology, which envisioned *Wissenschaft* as part of a massive reorganization of Jewish culture and society. Post-Verein Zunzian *Wissenschaft des Judentums*, unlike that of the Verein, is not inherently transformative: it will endure even if no one contributes to it for a century. No longer aligned with the ineluctable march of world history, *Wissenschaft des Judentums* becomes the *Trost und Halt* of its solitary practitioner.[27]

Heinrich Heine describes his 1844 eulogy for his friend and fellow Verein member Ludwig Marcus as also a eulogy for the entire Verein (he comments also on Gans, Zunz, Moses Moser, and, as I discuss at the end of chapter 1, Bendavid). Like Zunz's letter, Heine's homage to Marcus distinguishes between scholarship and the Verein as a project. "We considered Marcus's participation in the Association for the Culture and Scholarly Study of Judaism more important and notable than all of his tremendous knowledge and the entirety of his scholarly contributions. The time when he gave himself over to the endeavors and illusions of that Association may have appeared also to him as the brightest halcyon days of his troubled life."[28]

What Heine remembers having been most salient about Marcus to his fellow Verein members was not his prodigious knowledge or scholarship but rather his enthusiastic participation (*Teilnahme*) itself, his devotion to the endeavors and illusions (*Bestrebungen und Illusionen*) of the Verein—which, clearly, were not reducible to the pursuit of *Wissenschaft*. Heine underscores an experiential and performative dimension of the Verein: its members felt that in it something was happening, and what was happening was not only happening in or around the production of scholarship, but also—and perhaps primarily—in the participation in the exhilarating, if ultimately illusory, collective enterprise. Heine also recalls that "the esoteric aim of this association was none other than a reconciliation [*Vermittlung*] of historical Judaism [*Judentum*] with modern *Wissenschaft*, of which one assumed that it would, in the course of time, achieve world dominance."[29] The Verein was a vehicle for *Wissenschaft*, but *Wissenschaft*, in turn, allowed the thoroughly marginalized *Vereinler* to sustain a triumphalist fantasy. *Wissenschaft* was less the humble activity that scholars actually practice, and more an imaginary means of mobilizing political power. As Gans remarked in his secretarial report to the Verein of March 11, 1820, regarding the Verein's future prospects: "In this period the Verein not only sought to organize itself organically inwardly, but the intention [*Ansicht*] was also brought forward to seek a firmer, more certain external delimitation. Should this intention be granted, as is not to be doubted [will be the case], and also supported from without, then the Verein should [*dürfte*] very soon be comparable to a state that, well ordered inwardly [*in sich durchaus gerundet*] and morally strong, has only to look where it wishes to make conquests."[30] In a similarly triumphalist idiom, Gans went on to characterize the statutes that the *Vereinler* were in the (long) process of elaborating as the "granite cliffs upon which our beginnings are erected" and as "the Magna Carta of our institutions."[31]

Hanns Reissner, Gans's biographer, characterizes Hegel's theory of science (*Wissenschaftslehre*) as an intellectual catalyst (*geistiger Katalysator*) that thrust the Verein in directions that members at the founding meeting scarcely could have anticipated.[32] As they conceived of and established the Verein, Hegel's young Jewish devotees heard him lecture in Berlin on an array of subjects. The most influential lectures for the Verein were those on the history of philosophy (summer 1819 and winter 1820/21), the philosophy of religion (summer 1821), the philosophy of world history (winter 1822–23), and the philosophy of right (winters 1818–19, 1819–20, 1821–22, and 1822–23).[33] The book version of *Philosophy of Right* also appeared in January 1821. Noteworthy, too, is Hegel's elaboration of the relationship between religion and state in his 1822 foreword to his former student Hermann Friedrich Wilhelm Hinrichs's first book, *Die Religion im Inneren Verhältnisse zur Wissenschaft* (Religion in its inner relation to science).[34] In addition to Hegel's 1817 *Encyclopedia of the Philosophical Sciences in Outline*, these are the key Hegelian texts in dialogue with which the *Vereinler* worked out their program and theorized the Verein's historical, cultural, and political significance.[35] In order to tease out the philosophical politics that the *Vereinler* pursued through their association, I propose to look less at the scholarship they produced and more at how certain aspects of Hegelian theory that imbue their programmatic writings, speeches, meeting minutes, and correspondence allowed them to understand their pursuits as a form of participation in "the state." Through recourse to a Hegelian philosophical politics, the *Vereinler* attempted to negotiate the emerging terms of Restoration Prussia and invent a place for themselves in it as Jews.

It is important, as a first step, to appreciate the extent to which Hegel's and the *Vereinler*'s political hopes were aligned, their very different positions vis-à-vis the Prussian state notwithstanding. The *Vereinler* drew on Hegelian theory to interpret and try to intervene in the political and intellectual scene in Berlin in these years, only to see their hopes disappointed; the same was largely true of Hegel. As Laurence Dickey, Terry Pinkard, and others note, Hegel came to Berlin in 1818 confident that the Prussia he had been summoned to help shape would fulfill the era of progressive reforms begun under the leadership of Hardenberg and Stein. Dickey notes that when Hegel came to Berlin there were "few signs . . . of the coming political and religious reaction."[36] And Pinkard argues that "Hegel was not coming to Berlin merely to hold a job doing something he liked; he was coming to achieve his modernist program, which hinged on philosophy's becoming the unifying element of the modern university, which was itself a necessary institution if the post-revolutionary world was to succeed in its own aspirations."[37]

Delivered on October 22, 1818, Hegel's inaugural address at the University of Berlin reflects his confidence in the basic alignment between his theoretical vision of the modern state and the trajectory he believed Prussia to be following. This address is important in relation to the Verein for at least two reasons: it exemplifies the crucial function that Hegel understood the institution of the university and the academic work pursued there, above all philosophy, to have in realizing the ethical state; and it exemplifies the way that Hegel invited his students to collaborate with him in the politically saturated project of *Wissenschaft*. Like his admirers in the Verein, Hegel in his early Berlin years believed that whatever gap yawned between his progressive liberal political vision and

Prussian realities was destined to shrink, not widen, and that his work at the university would play a key role in the process of liberalization.

The strong position Hegel took in this address against philosophical subjectivists like Jakob Fries would have been particularly inviting to Jewish students. In 1816 Fries had published a notorious anti-Jewish tract.[38] A further component of Hegel's address that must have been exhilarating to the likes of Moses Moser,[39] who attended the talk and became the first Hegelian enthusiast among the future *Vereinler*, was its—in Dickey's characterization—"call to the young people of Germany to become more engaged in public life—first through their achievements in education (*Bildung*) and then by applying what they have learned about 'the ethical power of the spirit' (*die sittliche Macht des Geistes*) to public life."[40] Hegel's call to unlock "the ethical power of the spirit" through university education and to use that *sittliche Macht* to transform public life was virtually a recipe for the Verein. Hegel invites his future students into a partnership to advance the politically saturated cause of *Wissenschaft*, concluding with rousing remarks that could only have encouraged the sort of overvaluation of the political effectuality of philosophical thought and consciousness that would so characterize the *Vereinler*'s self-conception:

> I *salute* and invoke this *dawn of a worthier spirit*[41] and *I address myself to it alone* when I *declare* that *philosophy* must *have a content* (*Gehalt*) and *when I* proceed to expound this content to you. But *in doing so*, I appeal to the *spirit of youth* in general, for youth is that fine time of life when one is not yet caught up in the *system of the limited ends of necessity* (*Not*) and is inherently (*für sich*) capable of the *freedom of disinterested scientific activity*; nor is it yet affected by the *negative spirit of vanity*, by *purely critical drudgery with no content*. A heart which is still in good health still has the *courage* to demand truth, and it is in the realm of truth that philosophy is at home, which it [itself] constructs, and which we *share in by studying it*. Whatever is true, great and divine in life is so by virtue of the *Idea*; the goal of philosophy is to grasp the Idea in its true shape and universality. Nature is confined to implementing reason only by necessity; but the realm of spirit *is the realm of freedom*. All that holds human life together, all that has value and validity, *is spiritual in nature*; and this realm of the spirit exists solely through the *consciousness* of truth and right, through the comprehension of Ideas.
>
> May I express the wish and hope that I shall manage to gain and merit your confidence on the path, which we are about to take. But first of all, the one thing I shall venture to ask of you is this: that you bring with you a trust in

> *science*, *faith* in *reason*, and *trust and faith in yourselves*. The *courage of truth* and *faith* in the *power of the spirit* is the primary condition of *philosophical study*; man should honor himself and *consider himself worthy of the highest* [things]. He cannot overestimate the greatness and power of the spirit; the closed essence of the universe *contains no force*, which could withstand the courage of cognition; it must open up before it, and afford it the spectacle and enjoyment of its riches and its depths.[42]

Hegel encourages students to understand thinking (with him) in the most grandiose, and politically grandiose, terms possible. He takes "youth" extremely seriously and considers his students—largely on the basis of their youth—to be potentially transformative intellectuals. He tells them that they are singularly poised to grasp, and thus to help finally realize, the essence of history: the principle of human freedom. Hegel paints thinking as a heroic activity ("Mut der Wahrheit," "Mut des Erkennens"). He says: the door to freedom, realized self-consciousness, and ethical community is open before you; trust in the power of reason and boldly think your way through it!

If Hegel cast his brand of philosophy as a form of transformative engagement and public service, I am suggesting that the *Vereinler* conceptualized their project of making Jews the subjects and objects of *Wissenschaft* as precisely this sort of theoretical intervention. The society met frequently in the short period between its founding in November 1819 and its collapse in January 1824. In an *Unterrichtsanstalt*, or pedagogical institute, its members tutored students, mostly from Eastern Europe, in the knowledge and skills needed to pursue studies in Germany. The society's core members comprised a *wissenschaftliches Institut*, or academic seminar. They shared papers and, under Zunz's editorship, put out the historically important, if short-lived (only three issues appeared, between spring 1822 and spring 1823) and virtually unread, *Zeitschrift für die Wissenschaft des Judenthums*. At its height the Berlin Verein had twenty-five members, but many were not active in the association, which was also true of most of the twenty-three members of a *Specialverein* founded in Hamburg in 1821. The number of members in attendance at the Berlin Verein's weekly meetings rarely exceeded ten.[43]

Gans quickly emerged as the most charismatic, energetic, and organizationally talented member of the group. He became the Verein's president on March 11, 1821, and remained so until the end. A student whom Hegel considered among his most talented, Gans—not Hegel—would go on to teach the likes of Young Hegelian upstarts David Friedrich Strauss, August von Cieszkowski, and Karl Marx the intricacies of Hegel's political philosophy.[44] He would likewise play a central role in publishing the *Jahrbücher für Wissenschaftliche Kritik* (Yearbooks for scientific critique), the central organ of Hegelianism, launched in 1826, and in editing his mentor's posthumous works. But fellow Verein members Marcus, Moser, Wolf (who adopted the name Wohlwill in 1822), and Heine also took a keen interest in Hegel and followed his lectures at the University of Berlin.[45]

Even before becoming the Verein's president, Gans largely set its agenda; from beginning to end, he was a driving force in the life of the association and its visionary interpreter. He served as its secretary in January and February 1820 and insisted on prioritizing two related goals: attaining official government recognition and working out formal statutes for the association. These twin priorities highlight the hopes the *Vereinler* invested in the institution as both a real and a symbolic political project. Although the pursuit of a novel research agenda was a central component of the Verein's project, Gans and his Hegelian colleagues subordinated that agenda, for the first eighteen months of the society's four-year existence, to the pursuit of state recognition.[46] Even later, the *Vereinler*'s increasingly strained identification with the state continued to influence to a great degree how they understood their scholarly pursuits.

The chasm between the Verein and the state opened early and only widened over time. Although they approved its pedagogical program, the Prussian authorities denied the Verein the privileges of an incorporated society.[47] The Prussian government's ruling on the Verein's petition for incorporation found that the Verein required no special recognition, "since its purpose is chiefly academic (*ein wissenschaftlicher*)."[48] The irony of the situation boded ill: although the Verein understood itself as contiguous with the state in no small part by virtue of its devotion to and prowess in *Wissenschaft*, the Prussian state declined to recognize the Verein's need to be recognized precisely because its chief purpose was *wissenschaftlich*. A further tactical maneuver also met with equivocal results: the *Vereinler* decided to submit the organization's statutes for publication in late 1821 with the thought that the censor's approval would imply de facto state sanction of the Verein's intentions. Even though the statutes had been formally adopted, however, they were permitted to be published only with *Entwurf* (draft) in the title.[49]

Even as political realities increasingly strained the *Vereinler*'s ability to identify with the Prussian state, they were able to imagine a positive relationship to "the state," largely to the extent that Hegelian theory rendered "the state" geographically, legally, and institutionally ambiguous. When the state takes up a metaphysical residence, it ceases to be coterminous in its rules of inclusion and exclusion with the literal state—from which, however, it can also never be extricated: what the state is, where it is, and who has a place in it and on what terms are all up for grabs—at least in theory, if you will. The *Vereinler* would ultimately discover that neither the Jewish community nor the reactionary Prussian state had any use for Hegelian theory. The Verein would collapse when the distance that yawned between the *Vereinler*'s Hegelian philosophy of Judaism and actual Jews, and also between their conception of the state and the real Prussia, became too wide and too existentially acute to bridge.

The Verein and Hegel's State

In "Jews and the State: The Historical Context," Richard Cohen concisely overviews Jewish relationships to the early-modern and modern state. Jews in the diaspora traditionally looked to the state or crown for permissions and protections.[50] Alliances with rulers were generally the only viable strategy for Jewish communities. Negotiating arrangements with a central state authority was certainly more effective than trying to pursue alliances with other possible entities, whether the corporations, clergy, local authorities, or—most anxiogenic of all—the unruly masses. Because absolutist rulers benefited from the high annual taxes they could levy on Jewish communities, states and Jewish communities frequently maintained marriages of convenience: the ruler received money, and the Jewish community enjoyed relative autonomy and a measure of protection.

In the heyday of absolutist centralization in Central Europe, the seventeenth and eighteenth centuries, the interests of centralizing absolutist rulers and Jews living in their territories often overlapped. Jews' position as social outsiders proved useful to rulers trying to wrest power from the estates and local authorities. During this period, a small Jewish elite moved in the highest strata of power and, as minters, tax collectors, bankers, and army purveyors, provided services that were indispensable to the project of centralization. Such "Court Jews" were often in a position to intercede on behalf of their communities, but equally often they served as convenient scapegoats for failed policies or governmental corruption. The fate of entire Jewish communities could hinge on Court Jews' precarious fortunes.[51]

In the late eighteenth century concerted efforts began to integrate Jews more fully into Central European states, a phenomenon that many *maskilim* applauded but that traditionalists looked on with well-founded skepticism. In his epochal 1782 *Divrei shalom ve'emet* (Words of peace and truth) Naphtali Herz Wessely welcomed with almost messianic excitement the first of Joseph II's Edicts of Toleration for Jews in the Habsburg territories—policies that relaxed professional and residence restrictions for Jews but also curtailed Jewish autonomy, including in education.[52] Several prominent rabbis promptly excoriated Wessely's tract. They saw a threat not only in the encroachments of the modern state but also in Wessely's unprecedented gesture of speaking as a Jew to Jews about the welfare of Jews from a position outside of, and contesting, rabbinic authority.[53] Fellow Jewish enlighteners such as David Friedländer, Herz Homberg, Moshe Hirschel, and Saul Berlin in the 1780s and early 1790s radicalized the challenge to rabbinic authority, a stance that for many of them went hand in hand with promoting Jewish integration into modern states.[54] Like the later intellectuals of the Verein, these enlighteners tended to express contempt for the common Jewish masses, who could not muster the same enthusiasm for their cultural program or embrace of the modern state.[55]

The precedent of *maskilim* looking up to the state, down at common Jews, and spoiling for a fight with the rabbis is an important one for the defiantly elitist program of the Verein, although it also highlights the *Vereinler*'s historical singularity. The interests of economically elite Jews and Jewish intellectuals had sometimes converged, as when Court Jews in Berlin, who had amassed great wealth through army provisioning during the Seven Years' War (1756–63), supported the Berlin Haskalah, which they viewed as in harmony with their goals of acculturation and removal of legal restrictions. In Sorkin's words, "as a state-dependent mercantile elite, the Court Jews served as a surrogate for the state, making it possible for some of the maskilim to function in the penumbra of the state."[56] This new relationship to the state in the form of the economic dependence of the *maskilim* on "the state's surrogates—the mercantile elite" accelerated the Haskalah's "entrance into the political realm" insofar as it led many *maskilim* to adopt aspects of their patrons' mercantilist outlook and thus to assess the value of their own projects partly in terms of utility to the state.[57] Yet neither financial dependence on the state's surrogates nor anything in the ideology of the Haskalah led its practitioners to imagine that their intellectual labors embodied the essence of the state in a way comparable to how the Hegelian *Vereinler*—with virtually no financial support and no real place in or influence on the actual Prussian state—imagined that their *wissenschaftlich* prowess empowered them to guide the wider Jewish community and effectively represent the state in matters concerning the community. What inspired the *Vereinler* to displace the terms of meaningful involvement in the workings of the state from a basis in real economic resources and political access to a power they imagined to inhere in intellection and scholarly or *wissenschaftlich* discourse? Overwhelmingly, I maintain, their engagement with Hegelian thought. Both the *Vereinler*'s continuity with and novel departure from the history of the relations between Jews and the state come into focus when we understand them as "state Jews" of the Hegelian state.

If a diachronic glance at the history of Jews and the state helps to contextualize the Verein's image of itself as a parastate institution at a transitional moment between the erosion of Jewish autonomy and the full *Verbürgerlichung* of the Jews, the political role of associational life in Germany after 1815 offers a crucial synchronic perspective. In his study of associations as a social structure in German lands in the late eighteenth and early nineteenth centuries, Thomas Nipperdey reminds us of the important way *Vereine* helped render palpable emerging identifications with abstract entities like "humanity" or "nation" ("imagined communities," in Benedict Anderson's influential term), as these began to replace the more immediate group affiliations of traditional corporate society.[58] Nipperdey draws attention to three aspects of associational life after 1815 that help contextualize the *Vereinler*'s project and self-understanding. First, associations devoted to expressly cultural pursuits such as *Kunst*, *Gesang*, and *Wissenschaft* began to proliferate after 1815.[59] Second, although such associations were devoted to an ostensibly autonomous and apolitical cultural realm, they were often political or cryptopolitical organizations. Third, there was broad cooperation between the state and civil society or, more to the point, between the liberal reform-minded state bureaucracy and the *Vereine*, civil society's increasingly popular organizational units. Thus Nipperdey sees the state-supported associations as occupying a middle position between state "bureaucracy and civil society."[60] The Verein was part of a dramatic growth in associational life in Germany in the early nineteenth century, and its devotion to *Kultur* and *Wissenschaft* was thoroughly compatible with its political aspirations. The *Vereinler*'s understanding of their contiguity with the Prussian state bureaucracy was thus not entirely outlandish, even if it ultimately proved to be illusory.

Although the history of Jewish negotiations with the state and the vitality of associational life and its mediating role between civil society and state bureaucracy go far in illuminating the *Vereinler*'s aspirations and self-conception, it was the powerful infusion of Hegelian theory into this mix that acted as the crucial intellectual catalyst (to employ again Reissner's apt phrase) that fueled the Verein's dream of itself as the hub of a thoroughgoing reorganization of Jewish life. Hegel's theory of the state provided the intellectual framework the *Vereinler* used to understand and misunderstand the political stakes of their project. Against the background of this history of Jews and the state, the Verein's relation to "the state" (that is, the gray zone between the Prussian state and Hegel's) emerges as a theory-drenched iteration of a traditional Jewish political strategy. The Verein's novel and peculiarly modern intervention was to try to deploy cognitive prowess, understood in a Hegelian key, as the paramount means of gaining access to the state. The breakdown of the traditional mode of negotiations between the Jewish community and the state, in which well-positioned Jews would negotiate financial arrangements with the state on the community's behalf, was a necessary condition for the *Vereinler*'s novel conception of their relationship to the state. But we can also see the latter as an imaginative usurpation of the traditional elite's role. The *Vereinler* tried to take over the role of a Jewish elite that could negotiate with the state by redefining the expertise required for such negotiations in terms of *wissenschaftlich* rather than financial prowess, and indeed by displacing the negotiations themselves into theoretical territory. Similarly, although the interface between associational life and the state was well established in early-nineteenth-century Germany, Hegel's emphasis on the importance of political associations, or on associational life as political, inflected and greatly enhanced the *Vereinler*'s interpretation of their modest institution.

The *Vereinler* responded to and appropriated both performative and substantive aspects of Hegel's thought. Although much in Hegel's style of thought, theorization of the role of *Wissenschaft*, and understanding of the function of specific institutions and forms of social and political mediation encouraged the Verein's members dramatically to overestimate the association's significance and agency, we must not forget that Hegel's political vision—including his position on Jewish civil rights—was decidedly on the progressive end of the spectrum. Hegel intervened in the political culture of Prussia with a conception of the state based on principles of universal rationality and constitutionalism. He spoke out against antisemitism, adamantly rejected *völkisch* conceptions of ethical community, and took on the romantic nationalism of his academic rivals in the historical school. Moreover, as Friedrich Wilhelm III reneged on promises of constitutional reform and began to consolidate the alliance between throne and altar, Hegel's political theory provided a secular countermodel to the emerging Christian-German state.[61] Hegel's deep appeal to the young Jewish students of the Verein—in Schorsch's apt description, "immersed in the best of German culture, alienated from traditional Judaism, and vulnerable to the counter-attack of the resurgent Right"—is entirely understandable.[62] The *Vereinler* explored Hegel's thought because it theorized modern politics and institutions in ways they found suggestive for their own attempts to theorize politics and reinterpret the nature of the Jewish community in ways that would enable Jews, as Jews, to become fully integrated into the modern state. We should take this seriously.

For all the many ways it made good sense for the *Vereinler* to turn to Hegel to conceptualize and navigate their self-consciously modern relationship to the state, however, Hegelian theory was also a heady and seductive discourse. As

I showed in the case of Bendavid in chapter 1, Kantian universalism provided some of the more radical *maskilim* with a powerful tool to attack rabbinic authority and reconceive the Jews' place in the polity. Hegel did this and considerably more for the *Vereinler*. His assertion that history and politics culminate in cognitive comprehension and self-awareness extended to them an invitation to inflate the political importance and transformative potential of their *wissenschaftlich* endeavors. In tandem with this effective ascription of political agency to "scientific" thought, Hegel's idealization of the Prussian *Beamtentum*, or civil service, also provided the *Vereinler* with a powerful mirror in which to see—or into which to project—themselves.[63]

Bureaucrats play a crucial role in Hegel's theory of the state, as mediators between the private interests of civil society and the higher substantive unity of the state. Hegel understands civil society as a Hobbesian *bellum omnium contra omnes*. Yet this sphere of unbridled egoism has both internal checks and complex mediations with the universality of the state. The complementarity of private interests tends to coalesce into an ironically balanced system of needs: everyone's attempt to exploit everyone else works to the advantage of all. There are also important supra-individual institutions—the family and corporations—in civil society that check its egoism. Most important, it is the essential function of the state to reconcile the uninhibited subjectivity of civil society with a higher substantive unity. The state accomplishes this through three institutions: the monarchy, the bureaucracy, and the diets (*Stände*), in which representatives of the estates confer with representatives of the monarchy and bureaucracy.

Of these three mediating institutions, the bureaucracy alone constitutes itself as universal solely by virtue of expertise. The monarch transcends private interests by virtue of his hereditary position. The institution of primogeniture among the landed nobility similarly lends first-born sons a stable position above the vicissitudes of personal interest. The corporations of the third estate also introduce a more universal, supra-individual ethical perspective among its members. But the universality of professional bureaucrats derives solely from their competence and integrity of character.[64] In contrast to actual Prussian practices, Hegel conceived of the bureaucracy as a pure meritocracy in which appointments should be open to all—including Jews—and made solely on the basis of the "objective" factors of knowledge and ability.[65] It is not hard to see the attraction for Gans and his colleagues of imagining themselves as Hegelian civil servants. For Hegel, intellectual merit and "objective" knowledge alone constitute the universality of the universal class of bureaucrats. Surely not every member of the Verein understood prowess in the new Jewish *Wissenschaft* to legitimate a claim to a universal status as Jewish civil servants, but there is ample evidence that the Hegelians in the group thought along precisely these lines. Their self-conception as arbiters of universal *Wissenschaft* seemed to authorize them to claim a position in Hegel's idealized bureaucracy. Their "objective" expertise in Jewish history and culture permitted them to speak from a universal perspective and, in this way, to achieve contiguity with the universal state bureaucracy. The *Vereinler* understood their function to be very much like that of Hegelian Jewish bureaucrats: they would use their rational expertise to mediate between the private interests of the Jewish community and the universal state.[66]

The pioneering Jewish historian Isaak Markus Jost derides the narcissism and hubris of the young *Wissenschaftler* in a letter to Samuel Meyer Ehrenberg in August 1822. A founding member of the Verein, Jost withdrew from the organization in May 1820 after Gans prevailed in his efforts to make drawing up formal statutes for the Verein and gaining official state recognition paramount priorities.[67] Jost's rancor is still evident in the letter he wrote to Ehrenberg two years later: "[The Association] is a product of the wildest conceit, the stupidest arrogance of a few young people who imagine themselves sufficiently grandiose to change an entire nation that is unknown to them. As the foundation, so its effectiveness. To this the ludicrously pretentious statutes, the childish censoriousness about all that exists, and the mindless (*verstandlose*) Journal bear witness."[68] Jost ridicules the *Vereinler*'s assumption that they possess expertise about Jews and the capacity to change them, both of which he feels they woefully lack. He takes particular aim at the Verein's preöccupation with its governance statutes, which he describes as risibly self-important (*prahlerisch lächerlich*). Jost diagnoses a void at the heart of the Verein: it is sustained by nothing but empty, self-indulgent gestures like formal statues, pseudo-rigorous academic rhetoric, and captious criticism. Jost views participation in the Verein as so much playacting, a hall of mirrors that serves no purpose other than to sustain the *Vereinler*'s pretentious self-image. The very bureaucratic trappings that Jost found such a laughable distraction from the task of research, however, crucially facilitated the *Vereinler*'s identification with the state.

Jost was also brutally lucid about the disparity between the overdrawn rhetoric of his Hegelian colleagues and existing Prussian political realities. Since the Prussian authorities had not approved the Verein, he notes, it in fact existed illegally:

> Moreover, such boasting is altogether out of place in our state; they let (*man lässt*) everyone say what he wants, and then continue to act according to the existing laws. Furthermore, this Association has so far *not* been approved

> by the authorities; it thus exists *illegally*. I have nothing against an organization of Jewish scholars for the *Bildung* of their erring brothers, but they first must demonstrate *Bildung* themselves. This is unfortunately what they lack most of all. Their entire practice (*Thun*) until now has been costly, without, however, yielding a payoff, and a great deal better could have been accomplished with more modest sacrifices. Therefore I am keeping my distance from something to whose founding I enthusiastically contributed. . . . It is better, where the sum of reason (*Vernunft*) cannot be added up, for each smaller portion to work alone. For the rest, the Jews now stand at the culmination point of embarrassment. The scholarly among them have absolutely no career possibilities, and only baptism saves them for humanity. If we do not promote the trades, our entire next generation will turn to Christianity. And with good reason; what should bind them to the religion of their fathers?[69]

Jost faults the Verein for investing inordinate amounts of time and energy in the quixotic pursuit of official state sanction, at the expense of research. In Jost's hostile estimation, the group squanders its energies on empty pursuits that not only fail to advance, but actually inhibit, serious scholarship. He considers it wiser to work alone than in such a counterproductive group. Jost also cogently exposes the wishful thinking in the *Vereinler*'s belief that *Wissenschaft* would bring about a grand human reconciliation. Jews with a passion for scholarship (*die Wissenschaftlichen* among the Jews) could in reality hope for viable professional futures only at the price of conversion. Only an interpretation of Jewish *Wissenschaft* that radically abstracted from the predicament of actual Jewish scholars, let alone nonscholars (the need to promote trades), and invested "science" with purely symbolic if not phantasmagorical meanings, could sustain such grand hopes.[70]

Hegel enabled just such a self-interpretation. At the inaugural meeting of the Verein on November 7, 1819, Moser read a memorandum proposing that the association should strive to assume the role of, or act in the place of, the state (*diesen [den Staat] nach Kräften zu ersetzen*) in an effort to bring the cultural *niveau* of German Jews into accord with that of the state ("*dem Staat*").[71] In the preamble to the published Verein statutes, the *Vereinler* describe themselves as an elite group of highly educated Jews, distinctly qualified to lead their coreligionists into the modern European world, the age, and the state. In the formal document that centrally preoccupied them for eighteen months, and through which they hoped to achieve official integration into the state, the *Vereinler* cast themselves unmistakably in the role of Jewish civil servants with the competence to help overcome the disparity between the Jewish community, on the one hand, and the state and contemporary European world, on the other.

> The incongruity between the entire internal condition of the Jews and their outward position among the nations, existing for centuries but emerging more starkly than ever in the modern age which, through a mighty revolution in ideas (*Ideenumschwung*) everywhere gave rise, including among the Jews, to altered ambitions that daily render more universal the oppressiveness of the contradiction, urgently requires totally reworking (*Umarbeitung*) the particular education and purpose in life (*Lebensbestimmung*) that have obtained among the Jews until now, and guiding them to the standpoint at which the rest of the European world has arrived. If this reworking can essentially issue only immediately from the Jews themselves, still it cannot be the work of the totality, but rather must have the like-minded more cultured ones as its authors. To be efficacious in these aims is the intention of an Association, which accordingly proposes (*vorstellt*): an alliance of those men who feel within themselves the power and the calling for the enterprise of bringing the Jews, through an educational process to unfold from within, into harmony with the age and with the states in which they live. As comprehensive as is the indicated purpose of the Association, just as comprehensively must its law-governed activity be conceived.[72]

In the preamble to the Verein's statutes, the *Vereinler* further propose to pursue their work of harmonizing the Jews with the state both "from above," through scholarly pursuits and educational reforms, and "from below," by strategies of making the Jews productive, through which "every particularity recalcitrant to the whole will eventually be surmounted (*bezwungen*)."[73] It is important to bear in mind that Hegel uses the term "state" both more narrowly, to designate a legal and political framework, and more expansively, as incorporating—in Joseph McCarney's words—"a range of spiritual phenomena, including religion and, it seems, science and art too."[74] The slippage in the claim advanced in the preamble to theVerein's statutes that an inner process of *Bildung* among the Jews will lead to harmony between them and the *Zeitalter*, and between them and the actual *Staate* in which they reside, exemplifies the ambiguous way the lens of Hegelian theory could refract the concept of the state. To take one further example, the statutes define the Verein's pursuits as an "activity, governed by laws, for the highest aims of humanity and the state, relevant to the Jews."[75] This formulation casts the Verein's engagement with Jews as serving the ends of "humanity" and "the state," reducing these entities to a point of virtual indistinction.

Although the Verein could never achieve more than a fraction of the grand plan it drafted for itself, the important point is that the role the *Vereinler* wrote for themselves was that of Jewish civil servants. They envisioned themselves using expertise—universal *Bildung* and *Wissenschaft*—to mediate between Jewish particularity and the presumed universality of the state. Hegel's conception of the bureaucracy as a universal class provided a key theoretical ingredient of the *Vereinler*'s self-image. Their expertise as producers of universal *Wissenschaft* could legitimize, if not simply double as, administrative competence. With hypertrophied faith in *Wissenschaft*, the *Vereinler* envisioned themselves as universal Jewish civil servants, mediating between the Jewish community and a nebulous entity that was, certainly, the state but was also, at times, the fatherland, Europe, or the age.

Jewish and Other Hegelians: A Comparative Perspective

The Verein's Jewish Hegelians tried to map out a place for themselves in Hegel's state because the philosophical politics Hegel offered was preferable to the ever-receding horizon of possibilities for young Jewish intellectuals in Restoration Prussia. It is important to appreciate, however, that this gray area between real Prussian, and theoretical Hegelian, politics was not a uniquely Jewish space to inhabit. Toews analyzes Gans together with other young intellectuals who embraced Hegelianism between 1817 and 1823: Johannes Schulze, Friedrich Förster, Leopold Henning, Heinrich Leo, and Friedrich Wilhelm Carové. These Hegelian disciples' political orientations varied widely in their relation to the Restoration Prussian state, yet each of them interpreted the political landscape in Prussia through the lens of Hegelian theory. Two aspects of this wider group's engagement with Hegel cast light on the *Vereinler*'s uses of the master thinker. First, Hegelian theory profoundly inflected how several members in this group understood the nature and significance of the work in which they were engaged. Second, the group was ideologically diverse; there was no unified political tendency among 1820s "Hegelians."

Until the Lex Gans of August 1822, the Hegelian *Vereinler* could continue to believe—although it became increasingly difficult for them to do so—that the academy would be a key institution through which Jews would become fully integrated into the state. The Hegelian significance that several *Vereinler* attached to their activities as teachers and researchers lies on a continuum with the self-interpretations of their non-Jewish Hegelian academic counterparts. Schulze provides an especially illuminating comparison. He remained a close friend of Hegel and understood his reorganizing of Prussia's system of higher education as contributing to the realization of Hegel's vision of the modern state. Rather than as the Prussian civil servant that he was, Schulze preferred to see himself in the role of the civil servant of Hegel's political theory. Like Förster and Henning, Schulze had welcomed Prussia's progressive reforms and turned to Hegel after Restoration Prussia's reactionary orientation had become clear. It was Hegelian theory that lent Schulze's work in the Prussian government's educational bureaucracy in the early 1820s "historical and metaphysical justification and significance," in Toews's formulation.[76] The *Vereinler* were thus by no means alone in projecting themselves into the role of Hegelian civil servants.

The apologetic stance that Schulze and, eventually, Förster and Henning adopted toward the Prussian state was bound up with their desire to preserve their own Hegelian self-image.[77] Only if they could see Restoration Prussia as consistent with Hegel's theory of the state as the embodiment of realized freedom could they maintain their ideal image of themselves as the universal bureaucrats of Hegelian theory.[78] Paradoxically, they protected their self-image at the cost of supporting the retrograde Prussian political realities from which they sought to protect their self-image in the first place. It makes perfect sense that, as Toews notes, to the extent that Hegelianism made inroads into the Prussian state, it appealed to civil servants and the educated elite[79]—precisely to the bureaucrats and academics whose importance Hegel so exalts. The *Vereinler*'s tendency to exaggerate Prussia's similarity to Hegel's state was part of this wider tendency, though arguably more was at stake for the would-be civil servants of the Verein than for their non-Jewish counterparts. The *Vereinler*'s Hegelian self-interpretation provided them not with a preferable vision of the service they were actually rendering to the state, but with the vision of performing state service at all.

The range of political orientations among Hegelians shows how various and malleable Hegelian assessments of the Prussian state could be: Hegelians construed Prussia, apologetically, as the embodiment of Hegel's theory of the state (Schulze and, eventually, Förster and Henning) or viewed it, critically, as falling short (Leo and Gans, after the Lex Gans).[80] Moreover, Hegelians in the early 1820s sometimes used seemingly apologetic remarks to in fact criticize Prussian policies. For example, Förster stated that the new journal to which he and Henning contributed, *Neue Berliner Monatsschrift für Philosophie, Geschichte, Literatur, und Kunst*, would "ally itself completely with the spirit of the Prussian government."[81] Yet what Förster identified as the essence of the Prussian state clearly challenged the Prussian status quo. In 1820–21 Förster and Henning envisioned the Prussian state as part of an epochal historical shift. Although they allied themselves with the Prussian state, they held that Prussia had not yet comprehended its own significance or profoundest reality; and although they identified their positions as "Protestant," they opposed "all forms of religious faith" as forms of retrogressive subjectivism based on sentiment rather than reason.[82] The politicized critique of religious subjectivity that characterized Henning's and Förster's Protestantism was, as we will see, likewise at the heart of the *Vereinler*'s Hegelian project of a *Wissenschaft des Judentums*, and in the early 1820s the *Vereinler* and Henning and Förster had a similarly exuberant faith in the power of thought to complete the world-historical trajectory toward freedom. Förster's and Henning's rhetorical strategy in 1820–21 of critiquing the shortcomings of Restoration Prussia in terms that superficially might appear apologetic was one that Gans also deployed in his presidential addresses.

The amenability of Hegelian theory to various political orientations helps us appreciate how *Vereinler* like Gans and Moser could remain within a Hegelian idiom even as they reversed their positions, as I discuss in chapter 3, on key issues such as the lessons to derive from the Verein's failure to achieve its ambitious goals, or the acceptability of conversion to Christianity. Hegel provided the *Vereinler* with a conceptual apparatus to use in understanding and justifying the positions they took, but it did not determine those positions. Here, too, a comparison with how the *Vereinler*'s non-Jewish counterparts negotiated their identities and relationships to visions and realities of the state is illuminating. Toews argues that "like his non-Jewish contemporaries who joined the 'magic circle' of Hegel's disciples during the early 1820's, Gans was drawn toward Hegel by the need to resolve the frustrating, debilitating dichotomy between a subjective vision of communal integration and the social and political reality of postwar Germany."[83] Hegel's narratives initially inspired Gans and the other Hegelian *Vereinler* to believe they would achieve their "vision of communal integration" despite the shortcomings they perceived in both the Jewish community and the Prussian government. Eventually they drew on Hegel to come to terms with the impossibility of achieving their goals. In this movement from flush optimism to perplexity and dismay, the *Vereinler* had to reassess both their historical roles as Jewish intellectuals and the nature of the Prussian state. The fact that Gans and his colleagues remained in a conceptually and rhetorically Hegelian framework should not obscure the real shifts in their thinking. Gans articulated his ultimate exasperation with Prussia and the Jewish community, for example, in an idiom every bit as Hegelian as the one in which he had earlier elaborated a sanguine view of Prussia's trajectory and the possibilities for Jewish integration. Hegelian thought provided the pliant conceptual medium through which Gans negotiated a changing historical and personal situation. In the late 1810s and early 1820s Hegel himself was trying to negotiate the widening gulf between his vision of the state and Prussian realities, and the same was true of Schulze, his bureaucratically well-positioned disciple.[84] Gans, however, was theorizing at a professionally and personally more treacherous fault line—between an imagined progressive Prussia and the Prussia that eventually, with the Lex Gans, expressly excluded him.

The Performativity of Hegelian Discourse

What about Hegel's thought could encourage the young intellectuals of the Verein to attribute such power and agency to theoretical endeavors? It is evident enough why they were attracted to Hegel's vision of politics, but why were they so ebulliently hopeful that their efforts to reconceptualize Jewish history with *wissenschaftlich* rigor would actively help realize, and integrate Jews into, Hegel's state? How did Hegelian discourse help sustain the *Vereinler*'s vision that their modest work as researchers and part-time teachers was politically transformative? Whence came such overvaluation of the power of thought? To answer these questions requires an analysis of both performative and substantive aspects of an array of Hegelian texts. Although these elements are thoroughly intertwined, I will discuss the performative thrust of Hegel's thinking first, then specific substantive components of Hegel's thought that animated the Verein's project.

Hegel was not considered a dynamic lecturer, yet the lecture was his major genre. Of the four books he published—*Phenomenology of Spirit* (1807), *Science of Logic* (first edition, 1812–16), *Encyclopedia of the Philosophical Sciences in Outline* (first edition, 1817), and *Philosophy of Right* (1821)—the latter two were intended as synopses for Hegel and his students to use in his courses. Significantly, the balance of Hegel's *oeuvre* has come down to us in the form of posthumous reconstructions of his far-ranging lectures, based on his manuscripts and his students' notes and transcripts. Certainly, most philosophers lecture, but the intimate connections Hegel maintained between even his "books" and his verbal performances in the lecture hall were not dictated merely by the exigencies of academic life. Rather, they exemplify part of the performative thrust of Hegel's style of thought.[85]

Ernst Behler remarks on links between Hegel's *Encyclopedia* and his lecture performance: "Through the voice of the lecturer the encyclopedia was supposed to attain a vivid enactment. . . . To see a lively element in these texts, one also should consider that Hegel reworked them until the end of his life and constantly gave them new shape."[86] The fact that Hegel, in the most systematic of his texts, the *Encyclopedia*, explicitly defers to the supplement of oral presentation points up the profound role of performance in Hegelian *Wissenschaft*. Hegel's written deferral to an oral supplement in the preface to the 1817 *Encyclopedia* is of a piece with the philosopher's famous ambivalence toward the genre of the preface and introduction. First and most famously in the preface to the *Phenomenology of Spirit*, and subsequently in the introductions to the *Science of Logic* and the *Encyclopedia*, Hegel negotiates the embarrassment of having to begin a project for which he regards all possible starting points as premature by definition. Unlike other disciplines, whose objects can be assumed to exist outside and prior to their elaboration, philosophy, for Hegel, generates and demonstrates its own subject matter and form (or methodology) in and through the necessary process of its unfolding in consciousness.[87] No grounding propositions can be posited at the outset, and proof can only come at the end: proof, in other words, is immanent in Hegel's intellectual performance itself. In Frederick Beiser's characterization, "Hegel's hermeneutical method leaves us with only a promissory note. There is no a priori guarantee that a system or organized whole will emerge from any dialectic, whether it is that of consciousness or world history. This is a point that Hegel himself . . . stresses. . . . In the end, everything depends upon the specific arguments of the dialectic and whether the philosopher has reported them correctly."[88] Whether in its deferral to the literal oral performance of the lecturer speaking to students, or to the unfolding of an argument that both recounts and enacts a conceptual process, Hegel's style of thinking emerges as intimately tied to its very articulation. In this sense, Hegel is doubtlessly one of the most performative of all philosophers.

The texts and lectures by Hegel with which the *Vereinler* engaged most intensively were *Philosophy of Right*, *Philosophy of History*, *History of Philosophy*, and *Philosophy of Religion*. The relationships between performativity and history that animate Hegel's thought are salient for understanding the *Vereinler*'s theorization of *Wissenschaft des Judentums* as a historical and philosophical discipline and their self-conception vis-à-vis both Jewish history and the state. As Beiser argues, the novelty of Hegel's conception of *Wissenschaft* lay neither in its historicism nor in its systematicity, but in its joining of the two.[89] If "it was Hegel's unique and grand ambition to *historicize* the Kantian ideal of science and to *systematize* historicism,"[90] he viewed this project as feasible because he assumed history to be rational and systematic. Beiser's comment that Hegel's history of philosophy "is a kind of phenomenology, the story of the inner dialectic of philosophical history, the stages of philosophy's self-discovery"[91] applies mutatis mutandis to Hegel's accounts of the evolution of historical formations (religion, law, and world history) generally.

With his historicist bent, Hegel purports to appreciate historical formations on their own terms, yet at the same time to unearth a rational development in the historical evolution of spirit that culminates, significantly, in the ability to perceive and articulate the dialectical trajectory of that very development. In this way, Hegel grandiosely inscribes his own elaboration of the historical evolution of spirit as spirit's culminating coming to consciousness.[92] Hegel fulfills the rational process he discovers and distills. His articulation of the phenomenological drama of *Geist*'s dialectical coming to self-awareness performatively corroborates the truth of the narrative.

The way Hegel understands his thought to participate in the reason it theorizes throws into relief the presentist thrust of his historical discourse. The account of the past that Hegel renders is in a sense always en route to the present of his own utterance: the arc of the *erzählte Zeit* of his historical narrative bends always and ultimately toward the *Erzählzeit* of his narration. It is at the point when Hegel's phenomenological analysis of reason's progress arrives at the present of its articulation in Hegel himself that absolute *Geist* finally becomes fully present to itself. Hegel's phenomenological historicism is both an analysis and the *Aufhebung* of the rational essence of the past. In this way his very utterance becomes the avant-garde of reason's world-historical drama; world history happened as Hegel spoke.

The implications of Hegel's performativity bear crucially on the *Vereinler*'s overestimation of the agency of *Wissenschaft*. If Hegel pulls off his audacious philosophical tightrope act, he does much more than articulate insights into the past. He not only analyzes the drama of reason's historical progression but performs that drama's glorious final act. Performance is, of course, always contingent, and Hegel was frequently experienced as awkward and boring in the lecture hall. Yet the performative dynamics of Hegelian discourse were surely seductive to his most fervent followers, who must have felt they were witnessing absolute *Geist* coming to self-awareness before their eyes.

Hegel's history of philosophy lectures provide a particularly striking example of the intimate connection between performative utterance and substantive analysis in Hegelian discourse. The standard (composite) text of these lectures describes the distillation of the past in the self-consciousness of the present in these terms:[93] "The most recent (*letzte*) philosophy is the result of all the previous ones; nothing is lost, all principles are preserved. This concrete idea is the result of all of the *endeavors of spirit* (*Bemühungen des Geistes*) throughout nearly 2,500 years . . . of its most *earnest work* to become objective to itself, to know itself."[94] Even if slowly and at times obscurely, spirit moves inexorably forward.[95] The endpoint of this millennia-long process of spirit's dialectical advancement culminates in spirit's consciousness of itself as spirit—in Hegel's own discourse:

"This work of the spirit to know itself, this activity to find itself, is spirit, the life of spirit itself. Its result is the concept (*Begriff*) that it grasps of itself: the history of philosophy [is] the clear discernment (*klare Einsicht*) that this is what spirit has wanted throughout its history. This work of the human spirit in the recesses of thought is parallel in all stages of reality. No philosophy oversteps its own time. The history of philosophy is the heart of world history (*das Innerste der Weltgeschichte*)."[96] Given the strict parallel Hegel draws between history and the history of philosophy, his insistence that no philosophy can transcend its moment emphasizes the limitations of earlier historical stages of thought and the realized self-comprehension of Hegel's own.[97] If Hegel can, at last, comprehend *Geist*'s ultimate pattern and goal, then history (and not merely philosophy) must necessarily have progressed to something like its culmination point.

This is not to say that Hegel claims that philosophy or *Wissenschaft* as such drive the historical process. Instead, Hegel's hubris is dialectical and takes the form of what we could call a *List der Demut*, or cunning of humility. Part of his philosophical gambit is to insist on taking himself out of the equation: he claims to speak not as a subjective thinker but rather as (just) the messenger of the *Weltgeist*. Because he rhetorically erases his own contingent agency in the production of his thought, agency is returned to Hegel in absolute terms. Given his insistence on the necessity of spirit's dialectical progress and his claim that spirit achieves its goal of becoming fully conscious of itself as absolute spirit in his own philosophy, the ability to produce Hegelian discourse, although not an agent of world history per se, becomes something so exactly coordinated with history's direction and ultimate aim that the distinction becomes frivolous. The very ability to produce Hegelian *Wissenschaft* demonstrates history's fulfillment of its essential goals, for this is the condition of possibility of Hegel's bringing these goals to conscious in *Wissenschaft*. To speak Hegelian, then, is not to make history happen, exactly, but it is to claim—or rather performatively to demonstrate—that a certain version of history necessarily has already happened. This sense of world history already having reached an apotheosis of *Geist* and now merely awaiting the surface details to fall into place almost exactly describes the messianism of the Verein's *Wissenschaftler*.

If the Hegelian *Vereinler* confused theory and reality and attached secular messianic importance to their practice of *Wissenschaft des Judentums*, their exaggerated faith in the power of *Wissenschaft* is not a wild appropriation of Hegel but is instead inherent in certain moments in Hegel's thought. At the close of his history of philosophy lectures, for example, Hegel casts *Wissenschaft* (a term he frequently uses interchangeably with philosophy to describe his own project) as the apotheosis of historical development in which absolute spirit comes finally to know itself, fulfilling a universal need of both philosophy and the present age:[98]

> To know in unity opposition and in opposition unity, this is *absolute knowledge*; and *Wissenschaft* is this: to know this unity in its whole development by means of itself.
>
> This is then the *need of the universal age* [der allgemeinen Zeit] *and of philosophy*. A new epoch has arisen in the world. It appears that the world-spirit has now succeeded in casting off from itself all alien objective existence and grasping itself at last as absolute spirit, in producing out of itself what becomes objective for it, and in expounding it calmly. . . . The struggle of finite self-consciousness with absolute self-consciousness, the latter appearing to the former as outside itself, now ceases. Finite self-consciousness has ceased to be finite; and in this way absolute self-consciousness . . . has attained the reality it previously lacked. It [absolute self-consciousness] is all of world history until now in general and the history of philosophy in particular, which represents only this struggle [*welche nur diesen Kampf darstellt*]. It [philosophy] appears to have reached its goal at the point when this absolute self-consciousness, which it represents [*dessen Vorstellung sie hat*], has ceased to be something alien, where, that is, spirit, as spirit, really is. For it [spirit] is such only by knowing itself as absolute spirit; and it knows this in *Wissenschaft*. . . . [O]nly in *Wissenschaft* does it know itself as this absolute spirit, and this knowledge alone, spirit, is its true existence.[99]

In Hegelian *Wissenschaft* world spirit comes home to itself and comprehends itself as a differentiated self rather than as opposed to an Other. All otherness becomes integrated into absolute spirit's self-comprehending differentiated unity, and Hegel can thus claim that *Geist* now becomes capable of engendering objectifications (*was ihm gegenständlich wird*) out of itself (*aus sich*). Absolute spirit can calmly propound its own objective products and keep them under its control *(mit Ruhe darlegen, in seiner Gewalt zu behalten*) because, at the culmination point of history, apparent otherness reveals itself to be part of a greater totality. After history's dialectic has run its course, opposition—the historical dialectic's motor—becomes *aufgehoben* in absolute self-consciousness. Productivity no longer requires otherness. In *Wissenschaft*—and only in *Wissenschaft* —absolute spirit now comprehends the place of all its diverse products. The parallel trajectories of history and the history of philosophy now converge in their common goal: both reach their culmination point (*Ziel*) in *Wissenschaft*, which Hegel defines as the site of spirit's profoundest reality (*Wirklichkeit*), as opposed to the accidental realm of mere empirical existence. *Wissenschaft* is where spirit is really manifest as spirit (*Geist als Geist wirklich ist*). *Wissenschaft* is the productive language of absolute world spirit.

At this point of convergence of subject and object, of spirit and history, Hegel declares his lectures provisionally "closed." The passage above continues: "This is the standpoint of the current age, and the series of spiritual formations is therewith for the present concluded. Herewith this history of philosophy is *concluded*."[100] Given the architecture and performative dynamics of his argument, Hegel can be read as concluding not only his lectures on the history of philosophy but indeed the history of philosophy *tout court* with his performative utterance.

State, Religion, and Wissenschaft

In addition to the exhilarating performative power of Hegelian discourse—which, I am arguing, inflated the *Vereinler*'s sense of what their essentially academic pursuits could in fact achieve—specific substantive elements in Hegel's theorization of the interrelationships of religion, state, and *Wissenschaft* inspired and authorized the *Vereinler*'s mission. Hegel's theorizing of these interrelations in texts from the late 1810s and early 1820s like *Philosophy of Right*, lectures on the philosophy of religion and the philosophy of world history, and his 1822 foreword to Hinrich's *Die Religion im Inneren Verhältnisse zur Wissenschaft* further illuminates how Hegel's thought sustained the *Vereinler*'s fantasy that *Wissenschaft* would serve as the means of integrating Jews into the state.

Hegel's theorization of the religion-state-*Wissenschaft* relationship, in the famous § 270 of *Philosophy of Right* and in related passages from his lectures on the topic prior to the book's publication in January 1821, articulate a framework that the *Vereinler* were able to adapt for their own purposes and self-understanding. Hegel's rationalized interpretation of Protestantism and its harmonic relationship with the state offered the *Vereinler* a model of how to reconcile Judaism and the state through a philosophically freighted understanding of the function of a *Wissenschaft des Judentums*.

Even as Hegel privileged Protestantism as the religion most compatible with the state, he understood Protestantism in a highly philosophical way and measured its compatibility with the state in terms of the rationality he understood it to embody. In contrast to Kant's theorization of different spheres of rationality (pure reason, morality, and esthetics), Hegel insists on the proposition, which underlies all his thought, that there exists a single rationality, even if it is expressed in different forms. In insisting that the rational core of Protestantism consists of the same substance,[101] albeit in a less transparently self-conscious form, as the universal reason that is more fully actualized in the rational state, Hegel modeled a critical posture that the *Vereinler* would adapt to their understanding of their relationship—as a new type of Jewish intellectuals—to both Judaism and the state. Defining the essence of religion in terms of a rationality essentially identical to, albeit more fully realized in, *Wissenschaft* and the state lent great political consequence to the *Vereinler*'s redefinition of Judaism in terms of its philosophical essence, as well as to their vision of a *Wissenschaft des Judentums* in which the rational unity between subject and object, particular and universal—Judaism and the state—becomes manifest to consciousness. Rather than aligning the Verein with the restoration Prussian state, moreover, Hegel's theorization of the religion-state-*Wissenschaft* triad offered a philosophical politics that the *Vereinler* deployed in defiant opposition to Prussian political realities.

Hegel lectured on the philosophy of right three times prior to publishing the book version in January 1821 (and four times thereafter). He first lectured on the topic in Heidelberg in winter 1817–18 and then in Berlin, where members of the Verein attended, in winter 1818–19 and winter 1819–20.[102] Moser made his often-cited remark at the inaugural Verein meeting on November 7, 1819, that "the sense in which I here use the word ["state"] requires no explanation,"[103] more than a year before the publication of the *Philosophy of Right*. Clearly, Moser and his colleagues owed their enthusiastic familiarity with Hegel's philosophy of the state to the Berlin lectures of 1818–19 and 1819–20; the latter course had begun on October 25, 1819, just two weeks before Moser made this remark. Indeed, the *Vereinler* shuttled between Hegel's lecture hall and their own meetings during the eighteen months that they devoted to planning and theorizing the Verein, and they continued to read, hear, discuss, and appropriate Hegel throughout the Verein's existence.

In Hegel's first Berlin lectures on *Staatswissenschaft* in 1818–19, Moser and his colleagues would have heard this formulation—which anticipates § 270 of the *Philosophy of Right*[104]—of the relations between religion, state (or ethical spirit), and philosophy:

> Ethical spirit as real, manifest (*wirkliches, daseyendes*).—That which is religious (*Das Religiöse*) positions itself (*stellt sich*) . . . as something higher vis-à-vis ethical life, and philosophy mediates between (*[macht] <zeigt> den Übergang*) by showing the identity of both. What is recognized (*erkannt*) in philosophy is in religion only felt through imagination (*nur vorgestellt gefühlt*), it has a subjective, limited form compared to philosophy.—What are

only different forms of the same spirit thus manifest themselves in religion as different things (*Daher fällt in der Religion als verschiedenes auseinander, was nur verschiedne Form desselben Geistes ist*).[105]

From its limited subjective perspective, religion wrongly imagines itself to be substantially different from—and higher than—ethical life ("ethical spirit as real, manifest,"—that is, as the state). Philosophy, however, mediates between religion and ethical spirit by showing them to be substantially the same. Hegel argues further that religion wrongly opposes outward action to its own inner spiritual life (he alludes to the retreat from political life by monks and Quakers). For the state, such piety (*Gotteseligkeit*) and the "retreat of the individual into himself" is not sufficient, for "the state is not concerned with the salvation, the interiority of the individual, but rather with his actions (*Tun*)." Hegel now articulates one of his formulations of the need for religion to serve as a foundation for the state: "The state must be built upon religion, the latter founded on substantial spirit (*diese gegründet auf den Geist, der der wesentliche ist*).—On the other hand, religion must acknowledge (*zugeben*) that the other form is just as essential, not the degradation but rather the realization, animation of spirit."[106] The state must be founded on religion, but only insofar as religion, in turn, is founded on substantial (*wesentlich*) spirit; only, in other words, to the extent that religion already embodies the rationality that philosophy identifies as religion's essence. To serve as a foundation for the state, moreover, religion must acknowledge that the state is not the degradation but the realization of this spirit.

The fact that religion and philosophy are different articulations of a common rational substance is a major theme in Hegel's philosophy of history and religion. *Philosophy of Right* § 270 and the corresponding passages in the lectures underscore the political import of both the continuity of and the distinction between religion and *Wissenschaft*. In the necessary but potentially fraught relation between state and religion, *Wissenschaft* acts as intermediary and arbiter. Closely aligned with the state, *Wissenschaft* distinguishes between the wrong (subjective, polemical) and the right sort of rational religion that must serve as a foundation for the state. Hegel acknowledges that at times in history, the church has been the bastion of higher spirituality while the secular powers embodied pure barbarism, yet he sees the historical trajectory of the principle of universal freedom as tending toward the actualization and self-consciousness of rationality in the form of the state, not the church.[107] "In contrast with the *faith* and *authority* of the Church in relation to ethics, right, laws, and institutions, and with its *subjective conviction*," he writes, "the state possesses *knowledge*. Within its principle, the content is no longer essentially confined to the form of feeling and faith, but belongs to determinate thought."[108] And more explicitly still: "Since the essential principle of the form of the state as a universal is thought, it was in fact *from the state* that *freedom of thought and science* first emerged. . . . Thus, *science*, too, is to be found on the side of the state, for it has the same element of form as the state, and its end is *cognition*, by means of thought, of *objective* truth and rationality."[109] The fact that the secular, law-governed state is the matrix out of which "*freedom of thought and science* first emerged" is not a matter of historical accident but of rational affinity, for science and the state embody the same—express, objective, "determinate"—form of rational cognition. Both *Wissenschaft* and law embody thought as the "essential principle of the form of the state as a universal." Just as the state becomes explicit to itself in expressly articulated thought (law, constitution), *Wissenschaft* overcomes religion's merely subjective feelings and convictions by grasping and articulating objective determinate truths. In Hegel's more expansive conception of the state (incorporating religion, art, and science), *Wissenschaft* takes on crucial political functions.

Hegel's emphasis on "*cognition* . . . of *objective* truth and rationality" as the nexus where science and the state converge illustrates what Paul Franco aptly describes as "the essentially cognitive, nonvoluntaristic, character of Hegel's model of political participation."[110] The importance of Hegel's politicization of cognition itself—his view of rational thought's constitutive role in realizing ethical spirit—can scarcely be overstated for an understanding of the *Vereinler*'s self-conception. It allowed and encouraged them to imagine that by articulating knowledge (by engaging in *Wissenschaft*), they were participating in the state. As a form of determinate thought, scientific discourse distills thought and renders it explicit, in seductive analogy to how free rationality becomes objectified (that is, becomes what Hegel calls an Idea) in the state. The strong analogy Hegel draws between determinate thought and actualized reason (objective spirit) opened the door wide to the *Vereinler*'s fantasies that they could indeed do something quite substantial—help actualize the rationality of the state—by producing *Wissenschaft*. This parallel between law and *Wissenschaft* as related forms of self-conscious rational articulation goes far in explaining the Verein's emphasis on elaborating formal statutes and bylaws and gaining state recognition for them. The prolonged effort this required seemed warranted because of the theoretical and symbolic importance the *Vereinler* ascribed to the express articulation of rational principles, and because of the modicum of real integration into the state that such recognition would have bestowed on the Verein.

In *Philosophy of Right* § 270 Hegel theorizes the same relationship between the actual and the real that is at stake in the famous *Doppelsatz* of the book's preface ("what is rational is actual; what is actual is rational"). The focus, however, falls on the distinction between the actuality of the rational state (in which the particular embodies the universal) and the mere existence of a state lacking such unity. Hegel posits rational totality as the principle of the truly actual state and attenuates the reality of the merely existing state. Such an ontological hierarchy gave the *Vereinler* license to attribute substance to their theoretical vision of the state—their philosophical politics—and, at times (for example, in Gans's final presidential address, as I discuss in the following chapter) to derealize Restoration Prussia as merely existing. Hegel writes:

> Actuality is always the unity of universality and particularity, the resolution of universality into particularity; the latter then appears to be self-sufficient, although it is sustained and supported only by the whole. If this unity is not present, nothing can be actual, even if it may be assumed to have existence (*Existenz*). A bad state is one which merely exists; a sick body also exists, but it has no true reality. A hand which has been cut off still looks like a hand and exists, but it has no actuality. . . . An essential part of the fully developed state is consciousness or thought; the state accordingly knows what it wills and knows this as an object of thought (*ein Gedachtes*). Since, then, the seat of knowledge is within the state, science also has its seat *here* and not within the Church.[111]

The theoretical distinction between the true and the merely existing state permitted the *Vereinler* to maintain a highly ambiguous relationship to "the state," which was anything but synonymous with Prussia. Systematic scientific thought grasps the organic whole, which is what lends the parts true actuality. In the absence of totalizing scientific insight, severed parts merely exist, devoid of essential reality. In this way scientific self-knowledge participates in and completes the state.

In Hegel's view, the foundation in universal determinate reason that the state and science share guarantees their harmony. Conversely, religious orientations defined in opposition to reason must conflict with the state. One can legitimately perceive a threat to particularist identities and commitments (including forms of Judaism and Jewish identity) in Hegel's discounting of particular religious elements purportedly incapable of being subsumed under the universal. Franco rightly cautions against the anachronism of reading Hegel's support for Jewish civil rights in *Philosophy of Right* § 270 as a celebration of cultural pluralism. Hegel's explicit hope, rather, is that equal rights will lead to greater assimilation.[112] It is nonetheless crucial to appreciate that Hegel's litmus test for a religion's salubriousness was not its self-proclaimed Christianity but its "objective" rationality. Far from arguing for a "Christian state," Hegel polemicizes ardently against the idea of "unity of state and Church."[113] The rational state can establish itself "as the *self-knowing* ethical actuality of spirit" only by transcending religious authority and faith. "Only then, [when it stands] above the *particular* churches, can the state attain *universality* of thought as its formal principle and bring it into existence (*Existenz*)." Hegel's sustained polemic against Fries's religiously tinged ethics of subjective conviction goes to the heart of the fundamental distinction that Hegel makes between religiously inspired subjective ethics and the universal ethics of the state articulated in law. As long as "the Christian religion" (that is, Protestantism) embodies the principle of freedom that Hegel considers its true essence, it offers a powerful way to experience such freedom, and thus it encourages rather than hinders respect for the freedom that is actualized and self-consciously comprehended in the state. Yet harmony between the state and Protestantism is possible only insofar as Protestantism embodies a spirit of freedom, which the state actualizes and self-consciously comprehends without submitting to religious authority. Hegel makes clear that "philosophical insight" is the best way to achieve respect for the state and to appreciate one's place in it. In the absence of such philosophical penetration, religion inculcates such respect in a beneficial, albeit intellectually less profound, way: "If it is meant that human beings should have respect for the state as that whole of which they are the branches, the best way of achieving this is, of course, through philosophical insight into its essence. But if this insight is lacking, the religious disposition may lead to the same result. Consequently, the state may have need of religion and faith. But the state remains essentially different from religion."[114] Whenever Protestantism's spirit of freedom becomes "perverted into unfreedom under the influence of superstition," a conflict arises between religion's subjective conviction and the state's objective knowledge. Religion then fosters "a *polemical* kind of piety."[115] Rather than advocating the fusion of state and religion into a totalizing "Christian state" that would tolerate no difference or particularity, then, Hegel underscores the danger of substituting religious piety, authority, and conviction for the rule of rational law. He argues vigorously that the ethical totality of the state must protect diversity and determinate particularity from the threat of religious fanaticism that would destroy them: "And if this [religious (my addition)] totality sought to take over all the relations [*Beziehungen*] of the state, it would become fanaticism; it would wish to find the whole in every particular, and could accomplish this only by destroying the particular, for fanaticism is simply the refusal to admit particular differences."[116]

The manifestations of religion that Hegel considered narrowly subjective—and thus polemical vis-à-vis the state—were, overwhelmingly, forms of Christianity. The danger he saw in Catholic thinkers like Friedrich Schlegel and Protestant thinkers like Friedrich Schleiermacher, Fries, and Friedrich Heinrich Jacobi is that they privilege forms of Christian subjectivity and faith over universal rationality. Even as Hegel can rightly be said to equate the state with the actualization of the principle of rationalized Protestantism to which he subscribed, he considered many forms of Protestantism (and, more vehemently, Catholicism) willfully uninformed, irrational, and politically corrosive.[117] It is indeed only a highly philosophical and secularized form of Protestantism—that is, the essence of Protestantism as understood by philosophy or *Wissenschaft*—that is contiguous with the rational freedom actualized in the state.

By making compatibility with rational totality the principle that distinguishes true religions from polemically subjective ones, Hegel leaves open the possibility that non-Christian religions can likewise harmonize with the state, provided they can be reconciled with the state's actualized ethical freedom. A Hegelian Judaism seemed possible to the *Vereinler* as long as *Wissenschaft* could discover in it an abiding rational principle that would integrate Judaism into the broader ethical unity.

In their aspirations to harmonize Jews and Judaism with the state by explaining Judaism to itself from the objective vantage point of science, the *Vereinler* probably also drew encouragement from Hegel's theorization of the role of pedagogy in inculcating rational freedom in the minds of individuals. In his 1819–20 lectures on the philosophy of right, Hegel remarks: "To the extent that the state has laws that bear on the reality of freedom, and to the extent that it is its concern that the universal manifest itself in the consciousness and will of individuals, pedagogy also falls within its realm. Religion, if it remains of a genuine nature, cannot come into conflict with the state. Religion can, however, cling to its principle according to a one-sided form and consider the form of subjectivity to be the essential one. It thereby enters into opposition and contradiction with the state."[118] In aligning the pedagogical enterprise (*das Lehrgeschäft*) with the state, in contrast to narrowly subjective forms of religion that oppose and contradict the state, Hegel insists that education not be left to religious authorities. He can furthermore be read to suggest that a *Lehrgeschäft* founded on the rational principles of the state could serve as a corrective to religion's polemical excesses by explaining to religion what constitutes genuine religion (*echter Art*). Such a reading of a *Lehrgeschäft* as an extension of the state and a corrective to religion squares perfectly with how the *Vereinler* understood their pedagogical mission. By discovering as Judaism's essence the principle of unity and totality, they sought to inculcate in the consciousness of their fellow Jews the principle that would bring them into harmony with the Hegelian state.

Let us return to Moser's famous remark that the Verein should strive to assume the role of, or act in the place of, the state, and his comment that "the sense in which I am here using the word [that is, *Staat*] surely requires no explanation." Although his fellow Hegelians may not have needed an explanation, the contemporary reader likely requires some elaboration.[119] The wider context of Moser's lines throws light on how he envisioned Hegel's state and the place of Judaism in it. Moser invokes Hegel's version of the state as one into which Jews can integrate as Jews, without converting. In fact, he considers conversion to Christianity incompatible with entry into Hegel's state.[120] Rather than converting by embracing dogmas that could only be obnoxious to the state, Jews must bring their religious culture into harmony with the state. Judaism, like nondogmatic Christianity, could and should be a part of the national culture.

As they attempt to effect an *Aufhebung* of the opposition "between Jewish culture and general European or, if you prefer, Christian culture," Moser admonishes his colleagues to comprehend the destination to which they wish to lead Judaism within a broader vision of the ultimate goal of humanity itself.[121] Thinking of Judaism as part of this broader humanistic aim—as embodied in Hegel's state—precludes the option of conversion. To strive for a complete *Aufhebung* of the opposition between Jewish and Christian culture

> would amount to nothing other than adopting the view of many contemporaries who regard conversion to Christianity as our only salvation and pronounce a condemnation on every other endeavor. This way of thinking is not ours. We do not deny that the achievement of this aim would in many ways mean a significant step forward for the nation (which would thereupon cease to be one), but with that higher aim in mind a different orientation (*Richtung*) is enjoined upon us (*uns . . . vorgeschrieben*), which demands greater efforts. Only to the extent that these two paths (*Richtungen*) converge is the resolution (*Aufhebung*) of the opposition appropriate (*geboten*).[122]

Moser admits that conversion would "improve" the situation of Jews by opening up opportunities from which they are barred, albeit at the cost of ending the collective nature of the Jewish nation, a goal he explicitly disavows.[123] Significantly, this "easier" way to civil improvement through conversion would be incompatible with the "higher aim" of humanity, to which, Moser insists, any transformation of Judaism must remain true. The *Vereinler* must therefore follow a more demanding path toward harmony between Christian and Jewish culture, involving a noncoercive *Zusammenlaufen* rather than an *Übergang*. For Moser, Hegel's state is the site where such a coexistence with shared ultimate goals can occur.

Moser specifies that Jewish and European, or Christian, culture converge (*laufen zusammen*)

> insofar as the disparity between the cultural condition of our nation and the state (the sense in which I use the word surely needs no explanation) can be overcome (*aufzuheben ist*); and they again diverge insofar as national religious education, on the one hand, confronts (*gegenübersteht*) ecclesiastical religious education, on the other. In other words: the ideal Judaism (*Judenthum*) must appear to us (*muß uns erscheinen*) as completely reconciled with the state, insofar as it is conditioned by civic culture (*bürgerliche Kultur*), but in decided opposition to the prevailing church as such (*mit der herrschenden Kirche als solcher*), and with regard to her dogmas. This idea [is] the foundation of our entire endeavors.[124]

Moser evokes the Hegelian state as the entity into which Jews can be fully integrated, in contrast to a state allied with the Christian church and its dogmas. In Moser's opposition between *national-religiöse* and *kirchlich-religiöse Bildung* we see a version of Hegel's rational versus polemical religion. Moser does not oppose Jewish national culture to the religious culture of the church; rather, he opposes religious culture that is compatible with the state with dogmatic religion, which is not compatible. According to this interpretation, Moser is proposing that Judaism can and should be integrated into *national-religiöse Bildung* along with salubrious forms of Christianity. Whether Jewish or Christian, religion should be integrated into the organic cultural fabric of the state; in Hegel's idiom, it should be a foundation for the state, not a corrosive, polemical force. Dogmatic religious culture remains detrimental to the state, and Judaism must remain firmly opposed to it. Since conversion can happen only by confirming Christian dogmas, it must ultimately be at cross-purposes with the highest goals of humanity. Conversion would thus not bring Judaism into harmony with the organic rationality of the state but only with the narrow, subjective, oppositional posture of dogmatic Christianity. Instead, Judaism must be reconceived and reorganized so that it, while remaining Judaism, can be part of the confluence that is Hegelian ethical totality.

Moser returns to his vision of what it would entail to replace (*ersetzen*) the state near the end of the memorandum he read at the Verein's inaugural meeting. The context is important because it shows how Moser mobilizes the Hegelian state in order to critique Prussia's policy toward the Jews:

> In view of the sad neglect on the part of the state to which the Jews are subject and which remains very prejudiced (*befangen*) toward this segment of

its subjects, who need its wise paternal care the most, the highest guiding idea from which we must set out (*von der . . . ausgegangen werden muß*), particularly in matters concerning outward culture, is to stand in for this state (*diesen zu ersetzen*), and thereby simultaneously make a useful contribution to it. (A circumstance, which, by the way, would be an incentive [*Rücksicht*] for the state to encourage apostasy less zealously.) Directing our united energies toward lending the abundance of *nationaliers* here a more beneficent (*segenreicheren*) result, and attaching to them a more illustrious aim than the empty, vain, pitiful one they pursued to their own detriment, is worthy of the striving of noble men. Indeed, if there were enough centrifugal force it would not be too bold an idea to establish a school for the fine sciences (*schönen Wissenschaften*), in which every decided talent would find an arena for laudable activity, and would neither be inhibited in his initial development by the most deplorable resistance, nor have to succumb in the difficult struggle to dedicate his own life's purpose to the cause of the nation (*dem schweren Kampf, der Sache der Nation seine eigene Lebensbestimmung aufzuopfern unterliegen müsste*); a school that could produce the preachers and teachers who would spread out to all regions, and everywhere disperse the darkness of prejudice with the torch of truth, so that we too could finally work ourselves out of our Middle Ages and [so that] our condition would no longer present the concerned humanitarian (*Menschenfreund*) with such a bleak sight but [it] would rather be a heartwarming joy to see how we help work, with courage and vigor, on the great edifice of humanity.[125]

Moser's hope of standing in for the Prussian state, which continues to prolong rather than ameliorate the Jews' disadvantages, is oppositional, not conformist. His vision of establishing a school under the Verein's auspices imagines the Verein as a sort of Jewish ministry for education in a state that it would help move from present Prussian realities in the direction of Hegel's vision. Such a school would train Jewish preachers and educators, who would, in turn, bring Jews throughout Germany into harmony with the "great edifice of humanity," which, as Moser has already made clear, he virtually equates with Hegel's vision of the state. In this way making a "useful contribution" to the Prussian state by standing in for it in matters pertaining to Jews would entail actively transforming the state and its misbegotten policies concerning Jews. The fact that Moser indeed proposes a version of Hegel's state as a corrective to Prussian policies and their deleterious consequences for Jews is evident in Moser's remarks about the *nationaliers*' ill-fated goals. Given the context, Moser can only be referring to Jewish *nationaliers*. As I read him, Moser means the many Jews who fought patriotically for Germany against Napoleon "to their own detriment," because Napoleonic law was far more progressive toward Jews and in general than any German legislation, and because Germany's victory brought with it both antisemitic nationalism and retrograde Restoration policies. Thus the meaning of the French word *nationaliers* is richly layered. Moser designates this cause as "empty," "vain," and "pitiful" in its own right, not only (though doubly) for the Jews who devoted themselves to it. Moser's lofty hope, then, is to transform the Prussian state in ways that would give Jews a more progressive political model to strive for than the illusory project of German nationalism fueled by crude Christian-German chauvinism. By establishing itself as a sort of Hegelian ministry for Jewish education, the Verein would both check Prussia's encouragement of Jewish conversion and open up possibilities for talented Jews to develop their gifts. In Moser's vision of the emerging Hegelian state, Jewish quasi-civil servants would enlighten the Jewish nation and also provide Jews with a patriotic alternative to the post-Napoleonic German nationalist cause. Moser's hope is that Jews will raise their level of culture and knowledge and be able to participate fully, as Jews and not as converts, in a more perfect state. Hegel's vision of the state lent the *Vereinler* a vantage point from which to critique Prussian policies and German nationalist movements, and to imagine a Jewish place in a differentiated universal political culture.

Hegel's Lectures on the Philosophy of Religion

Other lectures by Hegel reinforced the lessons the *Vereinler* had derived from his lectures and book on the philosophy of right for conceptualizing Judaism, their work as Jewish *Wissenschaftler*, and the relationship of both to the state. The subject and timing of Hegel's lectures on the philosophy of religion—first delivered summer 1821—made them a key text for the *Vereinler* as they theorized their central aims. These lectures elaborate on the relationship between religion and the state explored by Hegel in *Philosophy of Right* (published as a book in January 1821). Just as *Philosophy of Right* made clear the political necessity of a scientific engagement with religion, these lectures present a philosophy of religion as politically urgent lest the definition of religion be ceded to contemporary epistemological and religious subjectivists, in whom Hegel discerned a pernicious threat.

One of the terms by which Hegel—early in the introduction to the 1821 philosophy of religion lectures—designates the task of articulating the objective truth of religion is *Wissenschaft der Religion* (science of religion). The University of Berlin's 1821 summer semester began on April 30.[126] The timing is significant because Gans first used the term *Wissenschaft des Judentums* at a meeting on May 27, 1821, when he suggested the association adopt the name "Verein zur Beförderung der Kultur unter den Juden und der Wissenschaft des Judentums."[127] In other words, Gans and his associates would have attended the first month of Hegel's philosophy of religion lectures immediately before he proposed this now-famous phrase. In contrast to the ample attention scholars have paid to the inspiration that Zunz's teachers Friedrich August Wolf and August Wilhelm Böck provided for his conception of *Wissenschaft des Judentums*, the inspiration that Hegel's theorization of a new, politically urgent *Wissenschaft der Religion* provided for Gans's conception of—and name for—a *Wissenschaft des Judentums* has been relatively neglected.[128] Although Zunz's philological version of *Wissenschaft des Judentums* bore real fruit in the form of a substantial program of research that is widely viewed as one crucial origin of modern Jewish scholarship, the Hegelian version of the new Jewish science has more to tell us about the *Vereinler*'s political aspirations and self-understanding. Analyzing key passages from the philosophy of religion lectures will illuminate how the *Vereinler* appropriated Hegel's politicized conception of the new *Wissenschaft der Religion* for a vision of a *Wissenschaft des Judentums* intended to reconcile Jewish particularity with the universality of the state.

Hegel maintains that his cognitive approach to religion had never been so important or necessary as exactly then, in 1821: "I wanted to make this cognitive knowledge [of God and religion] the object of my lectures because, <in the first place,> I believe it has never been so important and so necessary that this cognition should be taken seriously once more. <The special interest and importance of the philosophy of religion for our time lies here.> For the doctrine that we can know nothing of God, that we cannot cognitively apprehend him, has become in our time a universally acknowledged truth, a settled thing, a kind of prejudice."[129] Hegel presents his work as a corrective to two harmful misunderstandings of religion and its relation to rational thought: the epistemological limits of Kantian subjectivism and religious subjectivism as theorized by post-Kantian thinkers. He bemoans the Kantian "doctrine that we can know nothing of God, that we cannot cognitively apprehend him," characterizing this view as "the last step in the degradation of humanity" since it places ultimate knowledge of the nature of the world beyond human cognition.[130] Hegel bemoans the fact that "humanity [has reached] the conclusion through cognition itself [that] its cognition grasps everything else *except* the true. . . . This [is] the more specific concern of the science of religion [*Wissenschaft der Religion* (my addition)] in our time, which has been handed [to us]."[131] As Peter Hodgson and others have noted, one of Hegel's prime motivations for introducing this course in summer 1821 was his wish to get out in front of his rival Schleiermacher, who was preparing to publish *Der christliche Glaube*, in which he maintains that "the essence of piety is . . . that we are conscious of ourselves as absolutely dependent, that is, that we feel dependent on God."[132] Such a view was anathema to Hegel, of course, and the need to combat it was what lent such urgency to the *Wissenschaft der Religion* that he propounded. With characteristic humility, Hegel declared at the outset of his 1821 course: "these lectures . . . have . . . the purpose of knowing God."[133] Since, according to Hegel, God could be objectively known, it was obscurantist and politically pernicious to insist on subjective feeling as a foundation for religion. With his religiosity of sentiment Schleiermacher, like Jacobi before him, had responded to Kant's insistence on the impossibility of grasping God cognitively with a theory of extrarational experience: the God who could not be known could be intuitively felt. Hegel viewed bracketing rational knowledge and giving religion a foundation of affect privileged religious subjectivity as defined in opposition to reason, precisely the sort of subjectivity wont to assume polemical postures vis-à-vis the rational state. A chief purpose of the new science of religion, then, was to combat this politically unacceptable definition of religion. Although the rational state could tolerate a certain number of recalcitrant religious subjects, defining religion as a form of subjective sentiment essentially opposed to, rather than a foundation for, the state's objectively knowable rationality could not be tolerated. Clarity on this point was crucial to Hegel's entire political project.

Early in part 1 of the 1821 lectures, "The Concept of Religion," Hegel elaborates his understanding of how the state must rest on religion, which he had already broached in his lectures and book on the philosophy of right. Understanding how Hegel thought the state should rest on religion, and what role *Wissenschaft der Religion* should play in mediating between religion and the state, is crucial for grasping how the *Vereinler* understood themselves in relation to the state as practitioners of *Wissenschaft des Judentums*:[134]

> The practice of righteousness attains stability {W2 adds: and the fulfillment of duty is secured} only when religion forms its basis, when its most inward [mode], namely conscience, first finds in religion its absolutely genuine sense of duty, an absolute security regarding its obligation. . . . *The state must rest essentially on religion; the security of attitudes and duties vis-à-vis the state becomes for the first time absolute in religion.* Against every other mode of obligation one can supply excuses, exceptions, counter reasons. If one knows how to disparage the laws, the regulations, and the individuals who govern and are in authority, to regard them from a point of view from which they are no longer worthy of respect, [one can do this]. For all these objects {W2 alter-

native: For all these characteristics are not simply what they are implicitly and inwardly; rather they} have at the same time a contemporary, finite existence. They are so constituted as to invite reflection and investigation with a view to justifying them or criticizing them, etc.; [in short,] they invite *subjective consideration. It is only religion that suppresses all of this, nullifies it, and thereby introduces an infinite, absolute obligation.* <To sum up:> reverence for God or the gods secures and preserves individuals, families, states; contempt for God or the gods dissolves rights and duties, the bonds of families and states, and leads to their destruction.[135]

This passage articulates the distinctly political thrust of the philosophy (or science) of religion's task of reasserting the human capacity to know God. Subversive religious subjectivity finds its counterpart in political irreverence. Even the realm of objective ethical spirit (involving regulations, laws, government officials, and the state) has its "contemporary, finite aspect" that is susceptible to "subjective consideration" and criticism. Although a certain intellectual elite may identify with the objective spirit embodied in the state through self-conscious cognition and scientific discourse, this is not available to everyone. The state thus needs religion—properly understood—to check intractable forms of subjectivity and instill a sense of duty and respect for authority. Precisely because religion is vitally necessary to the smooth workings of the Hegelian state, the political task of a *Wissenschaft der Religion* is not to overcome religion but to rehabilitate and rationally stabilize religious subjectivity so as to "suppress" and "nullify" (polemically) "subjective consideration" of the "contemporary, finite" aspect of laws and civic obligations. True religion's corrective to self-asserting subjectivity carries over into the political realm: religious subjects' respect for the absolute encourages political subjects to see the state also in its absolute (rather than "contemporary, finite") aspect. Citizens duly prepared by the right sort of religion, I read Hegel as saying, will not be quick to question or criticize this particular, fallible government official, or the questionable application of a law in a given case, but will grasp and revere the totality and necessity of the state's entire rational architecture. Yet religion can fulfill this politically stabilizing function only if it indeed lifts individuals out of themselves into respectful contemplation of a higher rationality. In Hegel's view, Schleiermacher's religion of subjective sentiment short-circuits precisely this politically crucial religious transcendence of subjectivity. Defining religion in terms of subjective feeling rather than as a form of knowledge of the absolute (though not yet absolute knowledge) disrupts the dialectical evolution and continuity of rational consciousness. Religion then ceases to be an essential foundation for the rational state and becomes oppositional to it. It falls to the new science of religion to demonstrate the continuity between religion, the higher rationality of science, and the state by coming to know religion's determinate content. A fragment almost certainly stemming from a transcript of the 1821 religion lectures records this statement: "Spirit may have something in its possession without having a developed consciousness of it."[136] To remain in Hegel's idiom, the urgent task of *Wissenschaft der Religion* is to explain to religious spirit what it has in its possession yet lacks developed consciousness of.

The urgent political function of Hegel's project of philosophy of religion, then, is to check finite—and promote infinite—subjectivity, the better to reconcile particular subjects with the totality of *Sittlichkeit*. True religion would serve as a foundation for Hegel's rational ethical state by providing a capillary extension of rationality into particular subjectivities. True religion moves rationality inside, sutures the individual into a rational totality that, though not yet the state itself, is a kind of prerequisite for integration into it. The reason Hegel takes so seriously the contest between his conception of religion's rational, knowable content and Schleiermacher's religiosity of sentiment is that subjectivity, and religious subjectivity in particular, is vital yet highly problematic for Hegel's conception of how to overcome abstraction in the state.

A mark of the actualized state is that its subjects both know and feel themselves to be meaningful parts of a rational order. The complex mediations Hegel theorizes between individuals and the state are meant to insure that individuals achieve this sort of deep identification with the state. Properly functioning religion ensures a foundation of what we might call proto-rational sentiment. When religious subjects overcome their atomizing subjective abstraction, the state likewise sheds its abstraction; its rational totality becomes embodied in individual subjectivities. Although mere subjectivity is an obstacle to the realization of objective spirit, universal subjectivity is an indispensable site where the rational becomes actual.

Religious subjectivity, then, becomes for Hegel the site of a contest between abstract and universal subjectivity, with high political stakes. The new project of a science of religion must demonstrate religious subjectivity to be a universal relation to absolute spirit, rationality, and truth. Religion must be the site where mere subjectivity transcends itself:

> Precisely God should be for [Spirit] something different from its subjectivity and finitude. . . . Religious sensibility should contain just this, being set free from its subjectivity and possessing within itself what is substantial, as against the accidental character of our opinions, preferences, inclinations,

> etc. . . . [T]he drawing of lines, merely being oriented [toward God], does not reach this genuine, unifying, self-subsistent object. It does not achieve a true and actual renunciation of itself. For this acknowledgment of something higher and wholly indeterminate, these lines that are drawn toward it, have no hold on, determination by, or connection to this object itself; they are and remain *our* doing *our* lines, *our* goal—something subjective. . . . [A]ll worship shrivels into mere feeling. . . . What remains the foundation is only subjective sensibility.[137]

Insofar as it competes with, substitutes for, or obscures the pursuit of objective knowledge and civic engagement, Hegel considers subjectivity a politically pernicious force.[138] True religion is what sets us free from our subjective limitations and allows us to identify with determinate rational truth.

Hegel's *Wissenschaft der Religion* was at once academic and preeminently political, as it provided the conceptual basis for bringing potentially polemical religious subjectivity into harmony with the state. This is the background against which we can see the theorists of early *Wissenschaft des Judentums*—Gans, Wolf, and Moser, in contrast to the primary practitioner of the new Jewish science, Zunz—as "state Jews" of the Hegelian state. By pursuing their new academic practice, they understood themselves to be taking up positions in the rational state as Hegel theorized it. They hoped to mediate between the wider Jewish community and the state and to integrate the former into the rationality of the latter.

Finally, Hegel's religion lectures probably bolstered the *Vereinler*'s faith in the agency of thinking. Hegel characterizes the progress from abstract to universal subjectivity in both religion and ethical life as an activity of thought: "Thought is intrinsically activity; [that is,] thought as such [is activity], not thought as subjectivity."[139] By participating in universal thought, subjects transcend their abstraction and isolation, a necessary step toward eventual integration into the substantive totality realized most fully in the state. This movement of thought from abstract particular to concrete universal is for Hegel analogous in religion and ethical life. In religion it is the relationship to thought that distinguishes universal from merely particular religious subjectivity, as Hegel elaborates at some length.[140] Particular religious subjectivity is and remains affectively determined, whereas "objective, universal subjectivity" is defined by "the externalizing of sentient singularity." I "externalize" determining affect when I make what I feel to be an object of representation to myself, at which point this object ceases to be "immediately identical with me; [I] withdraw myself from the injury and from determinacy in general."[141] Such self-conscious reflection—or, in Hegel's language, such "being-for-myself of subjectivity in relation to objectivity"—distinguishes human beings from animals. For "as sentient, I am something entirely particular, thoroughly immersed in determinacy. . . . I am subjective, only subjective without objectivity and without universality."[142] True religion requires representation, a mode of thought. The immediacy of feeling does not define my relationship to God; rather, God, as active thought, liberates me from my sentient determinacy. Religion that is not a form of thought is not religion at all.[143]

Hegel makes explicit the way thought constitutes the essence of God and the fact that religion has its precise analogue in the way thought constitutes the essence of ethical life (that is, the state). "God *is* only in and for thought," Hegel maintains, against the "usual" contention "that religion is something apart from, independent of, and alien to thought, indeed that thought is opposed to and detrimental to religion."[144] Moreover,

> it is precisely the same [with thought in regard to religion, as (my addition)] with thought in regard to right and ethical life: I have right and ethical life only insofar as I *know* myself to be free and know ethical life [to be] free substance. [I] know myself as this essential, infinite [being]; [I] know this infinitude, universality, [as] the substantiality of [my] will—speaking generally, [as] the rationality of will. All this is not *my* willing, my interest and purpose, as this single, particular individual, but rather simply my universality, my essentiality. Otherwise [there is] only desire, force, free choice, etc. It is one of the gravest and crudest errors of our time that *thought* is not recognized to be the element and essential form in all of this, as well as the sole fundamental content.[145]

Hegel emphatically underscores the idea that participation in true religion and ethical life is cognitive. Universal subjectivity in both its religious and political forms is achieved in a self-recognition that is likewise a self-negation: I know myself as essential, infinite substantiality when I recognize that the rationality of my will is not merely "*my* willing, my interest and purpose" but understand that I am most fully myself in my identification with a substantive rational totality. There is more than an analogy between the agency of thought in religion and in ethical life; coaxing religious subjectivity out of its immediate feeling and harmonizing it with universal rationality is a prerequisite for a viable state. And defining religious subjectivity correctly emerges as the key means of keeping potentially "polemical" religious subjects in check.

Hegel's theorization of the political stakes of a *Wissenschaft der Religion* gave the Hegelians in the Verein every reason to understand their project of a *Wis-*

senschaft des Judentums in highly political terms. Their understanding of *Wissenschaft* was in no way a retreat from the political aspirations that Moser voiced in his memo at the Verein's inaugural meeting and that continued to animate the Verein throughout the first year and a half of its existence, as Gans insisted on working out elaborate statutes and petitioning the government for recognition. On the contrary, *Wissenschaft* itself enacted a Hegelian politics. The *Vereinler*'s ostensible shift from practical to academic pursuits must be read in the context of the agency that Hegelian theory assigns to scientific thought itself. Hegel's rational state would not only admit Jews, but *Wissenschaft des Judentums* would pave the way via which its practitioners, and the wider community they presumed to represent, would enter.

Chapter Three

Locating Themselves in History

Hegel in Key Texts of the Verein

In the previous chapter I analyzed the Hegelian inspiration for the *Vereinler*'s politicized self-understanding. This chapter examines how different *Vereinler* engaged with Hegel in key texts in the Verein's early days, when its members were flush with optimism, the period of its demise, and even its afterlife. These texts—Immanuel Wolf's famous lead essay introducing the Verein's *Zeitschrift*, Eduard Gans's presidential addresses to the Verein, and the post-Verein correspondence between two of its erstwhile members, Wolf and Moses Moser—let us see a rich variety of interpretations of and lived relationships to the Verein project, as well as a range of creative engagements with Hegelian thought. Wolf's essay is a programmatic statement of the scope and meaning of the new discipline of *Wissenschaft des Judentums*. In my close reading I try to unearth ways that Wolf is both thinking with, and also subtly against, Hegel's narrative of the world-historical evolution of spirit culminating in *Wissenschaft* and how the Jews figure into it. Gans was the most systematically Hegelian member of the Verein, and in his presidential addresses he sought to show his colleagues the world-historical significance of the work in which they were engaged, a task that became increasingly vexed as the Prussian authorities pursued reactionary policies rather than the sort of progressive agenda that Hegel had come to Berlin to help usher in, and that had initially filled the young *Vereinler* with such confidence and optimism. In the final section of this chapter I analyze how Hegel and *Wissenschaft* haunt Moser's and Wolf's private letters following the collapse of the Verein as they attempted, in ways ranging from the hilarious to the poignant, to make sense of their personal circumstances and even quotidian existences.

Wolf, Hegel, and Spinoza, or Doing (Wissenschaft) *without Christianity*

Among the most famous of all Verein writings is Wolf's programmatic essay "Über den Begriff einer Wissenschaft des Judenthums" (On the concept of a science of Judaism), which served as the lead essay in the inaugural, spring 1822, issue of the *Zeitschrift für die Wissenschaft des Judenthums*. The essay's conclusion heralds a messianic age of *Wissenschaft*:

> It remains to indicate in a few words that aspect, in the light of which the establishment of a science of Judaism seems to be a necessity of our age. This is the inner world of the Jews themselves This world, too, has in many ways been disturbed and shaken by the unrelenting progress of the spirit and the associated changes in the life of the peoples. It is manifest everywhere that the fundamental principle of Judaism is again in a state of inner ferment, striving to assume a shape in harmony with the spirit of the times. But in accordance with the age this development can only take place through the medium of science. This scientific attitude is the characteristic of our time. But as the formation of a science of Judaism is an essential need for the Jews themselves, it is clear that, although the field of science is open to all men, it is primarily the Jews who are called upon to devote themselves to it. The Jews must once again show their mettle as doughty fellow workers in the common task of mankind. They must raise themselves and their principle to the level of science, for this is the attitude of the European world. This attitude must banish the relationship of strangeness in which Jews and Judaism have hitherto stood in relation to the outside world. And if one day a bond is to join the whole of humanity, then it is the bond of science, the bond of pure reason, the bond of truth.[1]

Read against the background of Hegel's account in 1821 of the necessity of a philosophy (or science) of religion as a means of integrating inwardly focused religious subjectivity into universal rational totality, this passage makes unmistakable the extent to which Wolf adapts of a distinctly Hegelian project of a science of religion for a science of Judaism.

In a text composed only shortly after Wolf wrote his essay, Hegel distills key themes of his own 1821 religion lectures in ways that strikingly parallel Wolf's conclusion.[2] In the foreword Hegel penned for Hermann Friedrich Wilhelm Hinrichs's *Die Religion im Inneren Verhältnisse zur Wissenschaft* (Religion in its inner relationship to science, published in 1822), Hegel reiterates (now for a reading audience) his diagnosis of the malady of the age (*das Übel der Zeit*) that he had used to highlight the urgency of his 1821 *Lectures on the Philosophy of Religion*. In his foreword to Hinrichs's book, Hegel characterizes this ill as "the *contingency* and *arbitrary will* of *subjective* feeling and its opining, combined with the *culture of reflection* which claims that spirit is *incapable* of the *knowledge of truth*."[3] The malady of subjective religiosity encouraged by the Kantian spirit of epistemological limits also defined the need of the age (*das Bedürfnis der Zeit*). Regarding this requirement Hegel remarks that "the *common* requirement of *religion* and *philosophy* is *directed* toward a *substantial, objective content of truth*."[4] Religion has its own tasks to perform to meet this need (distinct from those of philosophy proper): it must counter arbitrary opinion, enhance respect for religion's content, and establish itself as a bond [*Band*] of objective belief, doctrine, and worship.[5] Although religion and philosophy have distinct spheres and tasks, they coincide to the extent that it has become a need of the age to know what it believes:[6] "When . . . the element of rational principles [*Grundsätze*] has infiltrated the religious requirement, then that requirement is no longer separate from the requirement and activity of thought, and religion demands, according to this aspect, a science of religion [*Wissenschaft der Religion*]—a theology."[7]

Hegel defines the convergence between religion and philosophy as the sphere where religion itself has come to require cognitive knowledge, and he calls the religious and philosophical project that will satisfy this need (a "need of the age," which will overcome the subjectivist malady of the age) *Wissenschaft der Religion*. Wolf, in the passage quoted above, characterizes *Wissenschaft des Judentums*, too, as an urgent need of the age (*nothwendiges Erforderniß unserer Zeit*) that arises, as in Hegel's description, out of a religious group's (the Jews') inner need ("the formation of a science of Judaism is an essential need for the Jews themselves"). Insofar as a science of Judaism has become an essential need of the Jews, they are on their way to overcoming their strangeness vis-à-vis the surrounding world, Wolf claims. Just as, in Hegel, it falls to *Wissenschaft der Religion* to help combat self-isolating religious subjectivity, so Wolf posits *Wissenschaft des Judentums* as the means by which Jews and Judaism will overcome their isolation and strangeness and enter a universal human communion. On this reading it appears as though Wolf concludes his essay with an almost dutiful application to the Jews of Hegel's *wissenschaftlich* program to combat the political ills of deleterious religious subjectivity. Here, however, I will try to show how creatively and at times subversively Wolf draws on Hegel's thought for his own purposes.

Wolf's essay is rightly seen as shot through with Hegelian borrowings.[8] The first sentence already betrays Hegel's profound influence on the conception of the new *Wissenschaft des Judentums*: "If we are to talk of a science of Judaism, then it is self-evident that the word 'Judaism' is here being taken in its comprehensive sense—as the essence of all the circumstances, characteristics, and achievements of the Jews in relation to religion, philosophy, history, law, literature in general, civil life and all the affairs of man—and not in that more limited sense in which it only means the religion of the Jews."[9] The various fields of cultural achievement Wolf signals as relevant for the new Jewish science are the precise topics he and his fellow *Vereinler* had been listening to Hegel lecture on during the past few years. By the time Wolf wrote these words (published in March 1822), the *Vereinler* had had occasion to hear their teacher lecture on the philosophy of right or law [*Recht*] in three different versions prior to the publication of Hegel's *Philosophy of Right*, on the history of philosophy (1819 and 1820–21), and the philosophy of religion (1821); and they would soon hear his lectures on the philosophy of history (1822–23). It is, thus, all the more significant that Wolf's definition of Judaism's essential idea contradicts Hegel's characterization of Judaism in lectures the *Vereinler* would have heard.

In his 1821 philosophy of religion lectures Hegel still clung to a dismal interpretation of Judaism that accorded with his characterization of Jews in his posthumously published *Early Theological Writings*. Jews are externally determined, alienated, isolated, obstinate egos, essentially slaves to God rather than divinely inspired free moral beings. In the same spirit, in his introduction to his first philosophy of history lectures, delivered October 1822–February 1823,[10] Hegel defines Judaism (together with Islam) as a religion of diremption (*Religion der Trennung*) in which there is no mediation between God and singular consciousness—that is, no true spirit:

> In general there occur in religion two cases, such that one is the religion of diremption, in which . . . God is exterior as an abstract being, in which particular consciousness [*die Einzelheit des Bewußtseins*] is thus not posited, so that this [being] may perhaps be called Spirit, but is only called so—an empty name. Thus religion has been as Judaism, and Islam is even now.[11] . . . This is the religion of diremption, which can further take different forms, in that something universal can be envisaged [*vorgestellt*] as a natural entity in natural, elemental fashion, as air, fire, etc. It can, however, also be envisaged as universal, as thought, as in Judaism, etc.[12]

On the other side of Hegel's schematic bifurcation of religious principles—on the side of "the unity of the infinite and the finite, the unity of God and the world"—lie Indian incarnation, Greek art, which "represents the divine in human form,"[13] and Christianity: "in Christ appears [*erscheint*] the unity of divine and human nature, which has the God appear in his son [*welche den Gott in seinem Sohn erscheinen läßt*], and thus brings the unity to people's consciousness. This anthropomorphic nature is not represented [*dargestellt*] in an unworthy manner, however, but rather in a way that leads to the true Idea of God. Inherent in the true Idea of God is that it is not a beyond, remote from consciousness [*gegen das das Bewußtsein draußen und drüber steht*]."[14] Throughout the Verein's formative years, then, Hegel disparaged Judaism's historical contribution to the dialectic of spirit and located Judaism, nearly without qualification, on the wrong side of the dyadic typology of religions of unity and religions of diremption. Wolf's famous definition of Judaism's central principle as the "the idea of unlimited unity in the all" ["Idee der unbedingten Einheit im All"] and as "the living unity of all being in eternity, the absolute being outside defined time and space" evokes Hegel's conception of unity and totality.[15] But it also contests Hegel's assessment of Judaism as structurally ("sublimely") incapable of grasping the essence of the unity of God and world. Wolf's insistence on the relevance of the Jewish idea of unity beyond space and time, moreover, makes no concessions to Hegel's critique of the purported deficiencies of this sublime, unmediated idea. On the contrary, Wolf holds up as a standard of spiritual and intellectual purity the idea that Hegel finds so wanting. Wolf's definition of Judaism implies a very different narrative of the development of human spirit and, crucially, a different path to *Wissenschaft* than Hegel's.

The key figure in Wolf's account of the route to Jewish *Wissenschaft* is Spinoza, in whose philosophy Wolf sees the quintessential expression, in the premodern world, of the Jewish idea of unity. Noting Spinoza's ostracism from his seventeenth-century Amsterdam Jewish community and his renunciation of Judaism, Michael Meyer remarks aptly: "That [Wolf] could see Spinoza as a great representative of 'pure' Judaism is the best indication of the degree to which Jewish history was for Wolf the history of a concept, one not even necessarily present at all times in the consciousness of the people."[16] As Meyer notes further it is in Wolf's "conception of the substance of Jewish history" that his "debt to German idealist philosophy is most apparent."[17] Yet even as it would be unthinkable without the key Hegelian texts on which it draws (*Lectures on the Philosophy of Religion*, *The Philosophy of Right*, *Lectures on the History of Philosophy*, and *Lectures on the Philosophy of History*), Wolf's interpretation of Jewish history, and of Spinoza as the quintessential expression of its "idea," significantly revises the Hegelian script from which it works. In asserting that Judaism shares with *Wissenschaft* the essential principles of unity and totality, and that these Jewish and *wissenschaftlich* principles converge in Spinoza, Wolf subverts Hegel's narrative of world history, in which Jews play a bit part, and casts them in a leading role.[18]

Albeit brief, Wolf's remarks on Spinoza are of great consequence. Embedded as they are in a discourse that owes so much to Hegel, they must be read alongside, and against, Hegel's own assessment of Spinoza. Hegel's engagement with Spinoza dates from his Jena period, and there is much continuity between Hegel's critique of propositional argumentation and mathematical truth in the preface to the *Phenomenology of Spirit* (1807) and his critique in *Lectures on the History of Philosophy* of Spinoza's propensity for formal, propositional exposition.[19] The *Vereinler* would have been familiar with Hegel's critique of Spinoza from the Berlin lectures on the history of philosophy of summer 1819 and winter 1820–21 as well as from *Science of Logic*, both volume 1 (1812–13) and 2 (1816). Indeed, it is because Hegel had already had so much to say about Spinoza that Wolf could say so much about Hegel by saying relatively little about Spinoza. Hegel's critique of Spinoza condenses his narrative of philosophical supersessionism and posits an implicit analogy between his relationship to the Jewish philosopher from Amsterdam and Christianity's relationship to Judaism. By proposing a different vision of Spinoza's philosophical relevance Wolf significantly revises the supersessionist thrust of Hegel's narrative of the dialectic of spirit and the place of Jews—and Hegel—within it.

In *Lectures on the History of Philosophy* Hegel emphasizes Spinoza's Judaism and sees in his concept of unity a Europeanized version of Eastern thought.[20] Like Judaism, Spinoza conceives of the absolute but removes it from the concrete world. In this way the charge of "acosmism" that Hegel levels at Spinoza rehearses his diagnosis of Jewish remoteness from an infinitely distant God.[21] Hegel interprets Christianity as responding dialectically to Judaism's alienation from the absolute, grasped only as abstract unity. In Hegel's philosophical allegory of Christianity, the absolute achieves mediated self-differentiation in the trinity, and actualization in Christ. Although one can hardly read an entire critique into Wolf's brief remark, he is clearly having none of this. Wolf sees Spinoza as articulating the essence of the Jewish idea—unity—and, in this, anticipating Hegel and *Wissenschaft*.

The status of subjectivity is a key concern in Hegel's treatment of Spinoza, as well as of thinkers Hegel considered vulgar critics of Spinoza, such as Friedrich Heinrich Jacobi. If what Hegel faults in Spinoza is a deficit of universal subjectivity and concretion (the inability of substance to differentiate itself into the particular forms of spirit capable of propelling spirit's dialectic), what he faults in Spinoza's vulgar critics is a surfeit of narrow subjectivity. Hegel charges that Jacobi and others critique Spinoza for the wrong reasons, and that their particular criticisms of Spinoza reveal more about themselves than about the sage from Amsterdam: those like Jacobi who accuse Spinoza of atheism are not out to protect God but rather themselves, in all their narrow subjective finitude.[22]

Hegel sees in Spinoza not atheism but rather "too much God": only God has true existence, the world none (the charge of acosmism). Spinozan substance thus leaves no room for subjectivity defined as the unity of the finite and infinite. What those who charge Spinoza with atheism in fact "cannot forgive Spinoza for" is annihilating nature and, more to the point, themselves.[23] The subjectivity Jacobi and, mutatis mutandis, Friedrich Schleiermacher are out to preserve is not the universal subjectivity that Hegel deems to be missing from Spinoza's substance (which does not descend into self-differentiation) but, rather, the sort of narrow subjectivity that fails to ascend to the universal at all.

Hegel is battling on two fronts: against what he sees as Spinoza's abstract universal substance, which cannot differentiate itself into particular forms and thus preempts subjectivity altogether, and against Jacobi's (and, by extension, Schleiermacher's) privileging of irrational finite subjectivity—which likewise, if in a different way, forecloses on mediation between the finite and infinite. Wolf deploys Spinoza in an equally complex way to position the *Vereinler* both against forms of finite subjectivity that are incommensurable with spirit's rational development and against the secularized Christian supersessionism that undergirds Hegel's genealogy of the actualized free subject in the modern rational state.

Hegel's positioning of Spinoza (in contrast to his own completion of philosophy) as the secular analogue to Judaism (in contrast to Christianity) is thoroughgoing in his discussions of Spinoza and could scarcely have escaped the notice of Wolf and his colleagues. Much as, in his philosophy of religion lectures, Hegel appreciated Jewish monotheism as essentially true yet abstract, incomplete and in need of being mediated through the Christian trinity and incarnation, he sees Spinoza's monistic understanding of substance as abstractly true but incapable of actively differentiating itself into concrete spirit. It is in this sense that Spinoza is the "foundation" and "commencement" of all philosophy (which finds its completion in Hegel himself):

> This Idea of Spinoza's we must allow to be in the main true and well-grounded; absolute substance is the truth, but it is not the whole truth; in order to be this it must also be thought of as in itself active and living, and by that very means it must determine itself as mind. But substance with Spinoza is only the universal and consequently the abstract determination of mind; it may undoubtedly be said that this thought is the foundation of all true views—not, however, as their absolutely fixed and permanent basis, but as the abstract unity which mind is in itself. It is therefore worthy of note that thought must begin by placing itself at the standpoint of Spinozism; to be a follower of Spinoza is the essential commencement of all Philosophy.[24]

Hegel associates Spinoza with the Eleatics (who also stressed the unity of all being) and explicitly contrasts the undifferentiated unity of Spinozan-Eleatic philosophy with mediation and concretion in Christianity: "Through the agency of Christianity concrete individuality is in the modern world present throughout in spirit. But in spite of the infinite demands on the part of the concrete, substance with Spinoza is not yet determined as in itself concrete."[25] The temporal inscription signaled by Hegel's "yet" exemplifies the supersessionary logic that structures his reading of Spinoza throughout. Just as Judaism is "not yet" Christianity, Spinoza is "not yet" Hegel.[26]

Faulting Spinoza for starting from formal definitions instead of deducing the truth of his claims, Hegel aligns Spinoza with Jewish abstraction and formalism in contrast to Christian and Hegelian concrete universal determination: "The last three moments [substance, attribute, and mode (my addition)] Spinoza ought not merely to have established in this way as conceptions, he ought to have deduced them; they . . . correspond with what we . . . distinguish as universal, particular and individual. They must not, however, be taken as formal, but in their true concrete sense; the concrete universal is substance, the concrete particular is the concrete species; *the Father and Son in the Christian dogma are similarly particular, but each of them contains the whole nature of God, only under a different form*."[27] Hegel reads Spinoza's mode, the individual and finite form of substance, as substance *manqué* rather than as a true self-division and mediation of universal substance with the concrete. Instead of differentiating itself and taking on the the form of concrete manifestations, substance—in the form of the Spinozan mode—"only descends to a lower stage, the mode is only the foregoing [that is, substance] warped and stunted. Spinoza's defect is therefore this, that he takes the third moment as mode alone, as a false individuality."[28] In contrast to the false individuality and subjectivity of Spinoza's mode, which is "a mere retreat from the universal," the true individuality and subjectivity is "at the same time Being-for-itself, determined by itself alone." Such particularity is "the return to the universal and in that it is at home with itself, it is itself the universal. . . . [T]o this return Spinoza did not attain. Rigid substantiality is the last point he reached, not infinite form."[29] Hegel's remarks are replete with Christian overtones: Spinoza cannot overcome quintessentially Jewish unhappy consciousness and alienation. With the notion of substance at its core, Spinoza's is a philosophy of sublimity that awaits completion in Hegel's philosophical mediation.

At other moments Hegel contrasts Spinozan with Christian subjectivity even more explicitly, contending that Spinoza understands God only as substance and not, in contrast to Christianity, as spirit and subject.[30] In Spinoza's philosophy "it may with justice be objected that God is conceived only as Substance, and not as Spirit, as concrete. The independence of the human soul is therein also denied, while in the Christian religion every individual appears as determined to salvation. Here, on the contrary, the individual spirit is only a mode, an accident, but not anything substantial."[31] If, for Hegel, Jacobi and Schleiermacher privilege an irrational form of subjectivity, Spinoza's abstract rationalism leaves no room for self-conscious subjectivity at all. In Spinoza "thoughts form the content, but they are not self-conscious thoughts or Notions: the content signifies thought, as pure abstract self-consciousness, but an unreasoning knowledge, into which the individual does not enter: the content has not the signification of 'I.'"[32] Because Hegel's Spinoza permits no mediation with the absolute, there is "an utter blotting out of the principle of subjectivity, individuality, personality, the moment of self-consciousness in Being."[33]

Hegel links Spinoza's purported inability to think particularity, including human subjectivity, as anything but negation of the one substance with Spinoza's mathematical method of argumentation, which merely postulates claims without deducing them.[34] The implication is that Hegel's own method, in contrast, performs the very kinds of mediations it theorizes, and thereby manifests the dynamism of spirit that evades Spinoza in both his conception of substance and his geometric method of demonstration. Spinoza's substance is unable to self-differentiate into dynamic spirit in the way the God of Christianity differentiates itself in the trinity: "His philosophy has only a rigid and unyielding substance, and not yet spirit; in it we are not at home with ourselves. But the reason that God is not spirit is that He is not the Three in One. Substance remains rigid and petrified."[35]

In the concluding passage of the section on Spinoza in *History of Philosophy* Hegel nicely condenses the way he has set himself up as the secular Christian fulfillment, in both method and content, of the secular Jewish philosopher. Hegel contends that his philosophy yields two related forms of self-consciousness lacking in Spinoza. First, the absolute differentiates itself and obtains an object of self-consciousness, with two consequences that mirror each other: the absolute acquires objectivity, and objective reality immanently participates in—is imbued with—the absolute. Second, there emerges a related new form and appreciation of self-conscious free subjectivity that, precisely in its self-consciousness, participates in—is returned to—the absolute or universal. Once again, we see how Hegel understands subjectivity in Spinoza—subjectivity as negation of substance, incapable of reflecting or recognizing itself in substance—as a variant of Jewish unhappy consciousness. Such deficient Spinozan subjectivity stands in a relation of exteriority and radical dependency vis-à-vis the absolute. It is wholly dependent on—as Hegel says, born from the "ocean" of—absolute substance.[36] With Christian mediation, and Hegel's speculative philosophy, self-consciousness achieves active independence. Such speculative self-consciousness is an act of cognitive mirroring whereby the self overcomes alienation and restores itself to the absolute by recognizing itself in, and recognizing its identity with, its own objects. (Indeed, the subject's grasping of its identity with the object of its self-consciousness is what self-consciousness is.) In self-conscious thought (and, most perfectly, in *Wissenschaft*), the undifferentiated absolute obtains, and recognizes itself as, differentiated unity. Thus with the advent of Hegelian self-consciousness, Spinoza's ("mere") modes attain true existence ("the existent as such"):[37] they become part of a dynamic differentiated speculative unity. In Hegel, Spinoza's infinitely distant God becomes mediated, differentiated, manifest; the Christian differentiated unity of Hegelian science fulfills Spinoza's Jewish abstract unity.

Such was the image—and allegory—of Spinoza that the Verein Hegelians took away from Hegel's lectures and his various published remarks on Spinoza. Wolf theorizes the fundamental Jewish idea of unity not, like Hegel, in terms of abstraction in need of mediation by Christianity and its secularized spiritual manifestations, but, much more affirmatively, in terms of conceptual purity. Following, it would seem, a Maimonidean tradition, Wolf argues that the conceptual purity of the Jewish idea has had to make certain concessions to limited stages of human understanding:

> This concept is revealed to the Jewish people, i.e., posited as a datum. But this took place at a time when man's mind was far from ready to grasp it in all its universality. For man needs time in order to raise himself from the world of the physical and the many to that of the universal unity, the all-embracing and all-existing Monas. Thus the idea of the unity of God, as taught by Judaism, could only gradually be comprehended and recognized by a people which had not yet raised itself from the physical world. At first, therefore, the idea of God had to be conveyed in personal and individual shape and could only gradually be revealed in is full universality. Therefore the idea of God, if it was to continue and develop among mankind, had to be clothed in a body and thus brought nearer to human understanding. In this way Judaism intimately united the world of the spiritual and the divine with the world of human life. But it depicted the divine in its first revelation as a living, spiritual entity, incommensurable with the world of matter and incapable of physical representation. But the body surrounding the divine idea, in which its gradual unfolding and development proceeded, was Mosaic theocracy. Thus the Jewish people became a nation of priests in the sense of guardian of the idea of God—a people of God.[38]

Wolf's idealist reinvention of Judaism contests Hegel's supercessionist narrative. In the face of Hegel's critique of Judaism's and Spinoza's conception of unity as flawed, removed from or lacking mediation with the world, Wolf presents the Jewish idea of unity not as deficient and abstract in Hegel's sense but as enduring, demanding, and awaiting ultimate human comprehension. The idea of unity revealed in Judaism was beyond humanity's limited grasp, and—in Wolf's account—humanity spends the next several millennia catching up with the original Jewish idea of this "living, spiritual entity, incommensurable with the world of matter and incapable of physical representation." Concrete mediation of the Jewish idea of unity here fulfills a decidedly different need than does actualization in the Hegelian dialectic of spirit. Rather than fulfilling the function of *Geist*'s necessary apprenticeship in the real world, as actualization does in Hegel's speculative bildungsroman, concretization, in Wolf's conception, is a concession to those who cannot grasp the idea in its purity; it is Judaism's idea dressed up in more tangible garb for imperfect intellects. In this way much of Judaism—and, by extension, virtually all of Christianity—becomes a sort of primer for limited human understanding but not the indispensable dialectical progress of the idea itself. Yet if the Jewish idea of unity has, since its revelation, awaited the human capacity to grasp it in its purity, this is precisely what *Wissenschaft des Judentums* finally achieves. In Wolf's narrative, Judaism's purported lack of concrete mediation is less a deficit than a kind of spiritual precociousness that the world spirit, as it unfolds in history, is only ever catching up to. This changes Judaism from the Hegelian religion of arrested development in need of being perfected (*vollendet*) in Christianity to an idea to which religion can do justice only at its point of convergence with science: it is the Jewish idea in its purest form that the world spirit realizes in *Wissenschaft*.

Wolf stages Spinoza in a way that draws on yet subverts Hegel's dialectic of world spirit. Wolf credits Spinoza with having, long before Hegel, grasped Judaism's idea of unity *wissenschaftlich*, and he clearly understands the *Vereinler* to be carrying on Spinoza's legacy:

> In the inner family life of the Jews there were preserved, together with old customs and habits, ineradicable traces of a nobler human nature and an active mind. But what is of the highest importance is this: that Judaism, in succumbing, so to speak, beneath the weight of years and external violence into a debilitating lethargy, was yet depicted in accordance with its unique, vital, and eternal idea, in the latter's highest degree of definition, consistency, and freedom—as though this were the last, exhausting act of its manifestation—in

the manner of the pure speculative thinking, i.e., purely scientifically. This was in the system of Benedict de Spinoza, a man whose subtlety and profundity were centuries in advance of his time, whose highly significant influence on the more consistent and profound philosophies of the present day is unmistakable, who did indeed renounce the external rites of Judaism, but who had understood all the more its inner spirit.[39]

One of the central tenets of Wolf's essay is that throughout their existence, Jews—contra Hegel—have exercised a profound influence on the human spirit.[40] The fact that even at the purported nadir of Jewish historical development, Judaism's "unique, vital, and eternal idea" could be articulated so purely, freely, and with such scientific rigor bears witness to its power and abiding relevance. Indeed, Spinoza's articulation of the Jewish idea has profoundly influenced Hegel (creator of the most salient among "the more consistent and profound philosophies of the present day").[41]

The relationship between a remark that Heinrich Heine, some twenty years after the fact, recalled Hegel having made, and a passage in Wolf's *Zeitschrift* essay immediately following his remark on Spinoza presents us with an intriguing puzzle that bears on how we understand the relationship Wolf establishes, via Spinoza, between the Verein's *Wissenschaft des Judentums* and Hegel. In an essay on Michelet in *Lutezia* (1843), Heine relates this anecdote: "My great teacher, the blessed Hegel, once said to me: if the dreams that people had dreamed during a given epoch had been recorded, a very true image of the spirit of that epoch would emerge from reading these collected dreams."[42] No one has been able to link Heine's anecdote to a passage in any text by Hegel, and Heine's language ("*sagte mir einst*,"or "said to me") suggests that he is recalling a comment that Hegel made orally.[43]

The existence of a parallel passage in Wolf's essay, just after his remark on Spinoza, however, complicates the question of what comment by Hegel Heine might be referring to—and it even raises the question of whether he is referring to Hegel at all. Wolf takes issue with those who measure historical development only in external events, without perceiving the inner workings of *Geist*. Only this error, he maintains, could lead one to the erroneous view that Judaism has not made a profound contribution to world history, for Judaism's contributions have played out in the realm of spirit, not of battle and conquest. Wolf contends that the dreams of the greatest men of each age would be as fully indicative of its *Geist* as would their deeds:

Thus Judaism shows itself to be for most of the history of the world an important and influential factor in the development of the human spirit. The only person who can fail to recognize this is the man who looks at history, as he looks at everything else, with preconceived notions; or the man who only sees in the history of the world an aggregate of individual events, to whom the random succession of diverse events is a mere source of amusement, and for whom only bloody battles, bold conquests, and miraculous coincidences of fate are of importance. . . . But events are only manifestations of the moving and developing spirit and it is indeed the gradual unfolding of the living spirit which constitutes the instructive element in world history, which alone makes possible a true understanding of the past and the present. History, considered from this point of view, would be just as instructive and as meaningful if it were to give us a complete record of the dreams of the greatest men of every age, as these could tell us just as much as their actions about the development of the spirit.

An idea, such as Judaism, which has developed and remained in existence for so many centuries, which has been alive and productive for such a long period in the history of the world must for this very reason be founded on the essence of humanity itself and thus be of the greatest significance and importance for the thinking spirit.[44]

Wolf's passages and Heine's anecdote are evidently linked, but one can only speculate as to the nature of the link. Does each passage have a common source in a never published remark made by Hegel at a lecture that Heine and Wolf both attended? Or that one attended and told the other about? Or that a third party attended and told one or both of them about?

Another intriguing possibility is that what Heine remembers as a remark by Hegel is in fact this passage by Wolf. It is noteworthy that Wolf does not refer to Hegel to support his thesis about the world-historical significance of dreams. Had Wolf been inspired directly by a remark by Hegel, we might expect him to nod to his teacher.[45] However we interpret it, the relationship between Wolf's defense of Judaism's world-historical significance via an interpretation of dreams and Heine's recollection of Hegel's purported remark illuminates aspects of the *Vereinler*'s Hegelianism. If we heuristically assume the remark to stem from Wolf and not Hegel (a proposition for which there is admittedly only weak support), then Heine would in 1843 have been remembering Wolf as Hegel, suggesting that Heine remembered Hegel's discourse and that of the Verein as so similar that he could conflate them.

If, alternatively, we suppose Wolf's passage and Heine's anecdote to have a common source in an oral remark by Hegel, Wolf's use of this remark is also revealing. On this interpretation, Wolf's silent appropriation of Hegel's comment as a way to explain the Jews' contribution to world spirit would certainly have been a creative use of Hegel for Wolf's own purposes. Heine's use of the remark in his 1843 essay on Michelet would then become more complex, too. If Heine did not get the quote (unconsciously) from Wolf, but rather (with Wolf) from Hegel, then Heine would presumably have known from reading Wolf's essay that Wolf had also used Hegel's remark to help theorize the Jewish contribution to world history. It is likely that Heine would have been aware of the resonances that Hegel's remark had for the Verein, and Heine's invocation of it in his Michelet essay could be said to carry with it the memory of Wolf's version of Judaism as a sort of spiritual *Traumbild* of world history.

Heine invokes Hegel's purported remark in order to describe Michelet's French history as just the sort of "collection of dreams" or "dream book" (*Traumbuch*) that Hegel had signaled would be able to capture the spirit of an age.[46] It is interesting to note, however, that the wider context of Heine's invocation of Hegel's remark, and what is centrally at issue in Heine's thoughts on Michelet, is Michelet's position in a dispute between clerical and secular factions over what was being taught at universities. "The true meaning of this quarrel," Heine concluded, "is none other than the age-old opposition between philosophy and religion."[47] The relationship between philosophy and religion, as we have seen, is what was centrally—and politically—at stake in Hegel's elaboration of his *Wissenschaft der Religion*, and in the *Vereinler*'s invention of *Wissenschaft des Judentums*. Even if Wolf is paraphrasing Hegel with his remark on spirit and dreams, he is using Hegel against Hegel to the extent that he deploys the remark to stress the importance of Judaism's principle of unity in diversity: Judaism has borne witness to this idea, and history has, in effect, been a process of catching up to it. The Jewish idea of unity is the dream that has always been in advance of actions on the ground, a thought that flies in the face of Hegel's Christian-centric emphasis on the need for concretization, particularization, and subjectivization of the absolute in active spirit. Whether Wolf is using Hegel creatively or inventing an original image to counter Hegel (which Heine then remembers as being Hegel's image), the tension with Hegel remains significant: Wolf's dream remark challenges the place of Christianity as an indispensable stage for world spirit to pass through in order to remain relevant and, eventually, to move beyond religion into science.

Especially as a continuation of his remark about Spinoza, Wolf's interpretation of dreams aligns Judaism with Hegelian *Wissenschaft* even as it revises Hegel. Wolf's remark, or adaptation of Hegel's remark, inscribes dreaming Jews or Jewish dreamers into the narrative of the world spirit, which we can be fairly certain was not Hegel's intent when he uttered it—if he did. In downplaying deeds (*Handlungen*), Wolf prepares the gesture of transcending history in cerebral *Wissenschaft*, which, as the secularly messianic culmination of his essay would have it, is destined to unite all humanity. In Wolf it is the Jewish idea of unity, the Jewish ur-idea, that reaches its apotheosis in *Wissenschaft*, and Spinoza, who first articulated the Jewish idea *wissenschaftlich*, proves both this idea's modern relevance and its ability to do without the mediation of Christianity. Far from being insignificant for the progress of world history, Judaism's essential idea as first unlocked scientifically by Spinoza and now, differently, by the new *Wissenschaft des Judentums* has always been the *telos* toward which world history was moving.[48] Wolf pushes theoretical possibilities that Hegel's account of historical progress opens up for the interpretation of Jewish history in directions that contest Hegel's Christian-centric version of the Jewish contribution to world history. In other words, Wolf is not merely repeating after Hegel but writing Hegelian history in a Jewish key, elaborating not only a Jewish *Hegelianism* but also a *Jewish* Hegelianism.

Here Hegel's version of Judaism—the religion of division that must be overcome by Christianity's unifying thrust—unravels. Although Hegel's Spinoza very much needs Hegel, Wolf's Spinoza does not. By affirming Spinoza as the purest, *wissenschaftlich* articulation of the essential Jewish idea, and not immediately calling for this idea to be perfected, mediated, dialectically overcome, or anything of the sort, Wolf deploys a Hegelianized Spinoza against both Hegel's version of Spinoza and Hegel himself. Wolf's alternative interpretation and emplotment of Spinoza contest Hegel's supercessionary logic precisely because Hegel had set himself up as the Christian fulfillment of Spinoza's abstract Jewish philosophy. Wolf's programmatic vision of *Wissenschaft des Judentums* grasps not only Judaism as a *wissenschaftlich* concept but also *Wissenschaft* as a Jewish one. It is in *Wissenschaft* that Judaism's "inner spirit" finds its most perfect expression, as Spinoza demonstrated "centuries in advance of his time," and as the new Jewish *Wissenschaftler* now aimed to demonstrate to their contemporaries. Wolf rejects Hegel's itinerary that routes spirit's path to science necessarily through Christianity, even as he borrows from Hegel the performative discursive mode whereby the elaboration of a scientific argument about history itself becomes historic, makes history. The note of *wissenschaftlich* messianism on which Wolf concludes does not embrace Hegel's secularized Protestantism but fulfills the original Jewish idea of unity. Like Judaism's core idea of living unity, science unites diverse phenomena under the sign of their fundamental concept.[49] The essay ends in an unmistakably Hegelian apotheosis of *Wissenschaft* as the fulfillment of absolute spirit, but Wolf's embrace of Hegel is not straightforward. Rather, Wolf theorizes *Wissenschaft* as Judaism's ultimate homecoming. Wolf's Spinoza shows the way to do (*Wissenschaft*) without Christianity.

Gans's Addresses: Wissenschaft *between Triumphalism and* Ressentiment

In addition to the numerous papers Gans presented as one of the most active members of the Verein's academic seminar, he made addresses as the Verein's secretary on March 11, 1820, and subsequently as president on five occasions between November 1820 and May 1823, when the Verein was already in decline.[50] In these addresses Gans elaborates the most sustained Hegelian interpretation of the association's sociopolitical mission as well as the meaning of its inner organization, its conceptual architecture. Although Gans's framework remains Hegelian throughout the various addresses, his positions evolve in relation to an increasingly reactionary Prussian state and a Jewish community that took precious little interest in the Verein. I am concerned here chiefly with two focal points of Gans's theoretical elaboration. The first is his conception of the relationship between theory and reality. The early speeches brim with confidence that the Prussian fatherland is en route to becoming something akin to Hegel's state and that the Verein is at the vanguard of a Jewish community in the process of bringing itself into harmony with this state. By the time of his last speech before the Verein, delivered, notably, after the so-called Lex Gans had been decreed, it was no longer possible to sustain this vision. Seeing the Verein left with only the most tenuous grounding in reality, Gans revised his initial position on the relationship between theory and historical reality.

The second of Gans's preoccupations I will analyze is the role of the Verein and its vision of *Wissenschaft* as a political instrument in the project of reconstituting the Jewish community as a collective harmonic with the ethical totality of the Hegelian state. In the course of theorizing this political and ethical reorganization, Gans draws on Hegel's political philosophy and philosophy of history, in particular his critique of subjectivism and the Enlightenment. Gans also creatively deploys Hegel's conception of the family and corporations as proto-ethical moments in an extended metaphorics that seeks to redefine Jewish communal bonds in ways that harmonize with Hegelian ethical totality.

Gans's remarks on *Wissenschaft* and the state must be understood in the context of his efforts to gain an academic appointment.[51] He had studied in Heidelberg with Anton Friedrich Julius Thebaut (1771–1840), an opponent of the historical school of law, graduating in 1819. In the same year he published two monographs and submitted an application to the Prussian minister of education for an academic appointment in the law faculty of the University of Berlin; however, Friedrich Carl von Savigny and his colleagues in the historical school rejected his application. This faculty's letter to the ministry of education advising against Gans's appointment explicitly raised the question of whether or not Gans, as a Jew, was eligible for public service.[52] Although Gans would eventually convert in 1825 to gain the appointment he sought, during his years at the head of the Verein, in Terry Pinkard's words, he "defiantly continued to apply for a position on the juristic faculty."[53] From 1819, when he applied for the privilege to lecture in the law faculty, until the ruling in August 1822 definitively denied him this privilege—that is, during most of the Verein's existence and throughout what was certainly its most optimistic and productive period—Gans was fighting to be granted an appointment to a university that Hegel envisioned would play a key role in shaping the future of the state.[54] Throughout the Verein's productive existence Gans was a Jewish *Wissenschaftler* peering into the state, very much hoping that it was indeed moving toward Hegel's vision and would let him in. If Gans at times elides *Wissenschaft* and the state, this is in part because he imagined, and not entirely implausibly, that he was on the verge of entering the state as a Jew on the basis of *wissenschaftlich* achievement.

At the Verein's inception Gans drew on Hegel to theorize how Jews would be integrated into a wider ethical totality. As time and circumstances belied this hopeful prognostication, Hegelian theory came increasingly to provide a fragile alternative to the reality that it was meant to grasp and transform. The effort Gans led to enact a Jewish Hegelian politics resulted in failure, but it illuminates what the possibilities and limitations were for ambitious Jewish intellectuals in Germany around 1820, positioned as they were on the periphery of German social, political, and academic life but on the cutting edge of one of the most productive currents within what contemporary critical discourse refers to with a hypostatizing capital letter: Theory.[55]

Gans closes his first address as the Verein's president, on November 2, 1820—almost exactly one year after the organization's founding—with a self-assessment that expresses contempt for popularly elected Jewish leaders and hubristically equates the *Vereinler*'s own superior intelligence with absolute power:

> Representatives of Israel, who have not been elected by meaningless [*nichtssagende*] popular votes [*Volksstimmen*] but rather called together here by virtue of higher intelligence and a deeply felt need, and by virtue of an absolute power to which you are entitled [*und aus einer euch zustehenden Machtvollkommenheit*], fulfill the task that you have taken upon yourself; let our actions in the future consist not only of words, and let our future disputes

be nothing more than indefatigable rivalry. No revolution is more difficult than the reconstruction and radical change of dispositions. Here no external power or movement will do; the psychic malady requires a psychic cure. You will effect it. It will be my joy and my pride that I was once the president of this honorable assembly.[56]

In a move he would repeat in subsequent addresses, Gans establishes superior intelligence rather than "meaningless" popular support as the basis of the *Vereinler*'s rightful authority, and ability, to reshape the Jewish community. Gans presents the Verein's task of integrating the Jews into the state as both a "revolution" and a "cure" for a sick Jewish *Gesinnung*. Thus he casts the Verein as a quasi-political assembly whose authority, however, derives from its members' cognitive prowess and whose mission it is to convert bad Jewish subjects into good rational ones. Confident that he has discerned the *telos* toward which history is advancing, Gans even speaks from a temporally doubled—a proleptically retrospective—vantage point. So surely was the Verein destined in Gans's mind to rationalize the Jewish spirit that he looks forward to being able to look back, with joy and pride, at his role at the helm of the association that will have ushered in this epochal change.

In his next presidential address, on April 1, 1821, Gans locates the Verein at a crossroads. The Verein's formal preliminaries (*Vorarbeiten*)—that is, the work on the statutes—are now over, and its members have arrived at a moment of truth when they will discover whether all their conceptual labor over the previous eighteen months will bear practical fruit.[57] Ever the Hegelian, Gans insists that there is no strict distinction between comprehending (*Erfassen, Auffassen*) and executing (*Ausführen*) an idea; on the contrary, "the correct comprehension and execution are one."[58] Yet the broader point Gans makes is that, given this basic equation between the accurate comprehension and the execution of an idea, the *Vereinler* will have no alibi should their theoretical vision fail to corroborate itself in tangible transformation (Gans's jaunty confidence that history will bear his and his colleagues' vision out was not merely a momentary posture, moreover; as we shall see, he will refer back to and reiterate this position six months later):

> If we return to what was said earlier—that we find ourselves at a crossroads between willing and executing—it should not be understood in such a way—should we fail, and take home, instead of the glory of the accomplished deed, the shame of the failed one—that we would then, I say, be allowed to think [*meinen*] that we had willed and grasped what was right and only an external obstacle completely independent of us and impossible to conquer had

inhibited and hindered us. Rather, it will then be revealed that we did not will and grasp what was right, or, what amounts to the same thing, that we did not approach it in the right way, [*nicht auf die rechte Weise in dasselbe eingegangen sind*], and, to remain within the previous metaphor [*Bild*], if the Idea, which we all seemed to revere, proves itself, at the moment we would seize control of it utterly and completely [*da wir uns ganz und gar ihrer bemeistern wollen*], to be the noli me tangere, then this surely occurs not because it has once and for all conspired against all contact, but rather because *we* lack the fingers to touch it, because in us there is, instead of a higher sense of touch, blind groping and, instead of fine antennae, coarser tools.[59]

Precisely because of his brimming confidence that their conceptual labor portends ineluctable empirical transformation—that their *Auffassen* of the idea is essentially identical with its eventual *Aufführen*—Gans is eager to insist that failed execution would necessarily indicate a flawed conception.

In his insistence that the Verein's (still hypothetical) failure would bespeak intellectual shortcomings on the part of its members, Gans links the two related problematics with which I am chiefly concerned: the relation of theory and reality and the project of refashioning Jewish subjectivity so as to harmonize with a "scientifically" comprehended structure of ethical totality. Should reality belie, not fulfill, the Verein's theoretical vision, Gans reasons that the failure must be attributed to personal flaws, and in a sense to the flaw of personality (or bad subjectivity) itself. These links become clearer in the remarks with which Gans closes this speech:

No cause, I've often said in this assembly, requires more true enthusiasm than ours: whoever allows personality to prevail here, or places personal aims over ours, acts not only traitorously vis-à-vis our cause but also nonsensically and inconsistently; for since joining with us precisely demonstrates [*beweist*] that each personality has been relinquished and removed [*aufgegeben und beseitigt*], he must be called shallow and empty who, having the great wide world beyond us at his disposal for his ego, intrudes into our circle in order to install it here [*um es hier gelten(d) zu machen*]. . . . We do not need forces but rather one living force, and this has never been made up of the mere aggregate of individuals.[60]

Gans defines the Verein's success as contingent on the suspension of personality. His call to leave personality at the door and to devote oneself to the Verein's cause echoes Hegel's theorization of how civil servants overcome their subjective interests in the service of the universal interests of the state.[61] If the Verein is to integrate Jews into the state by "curing" problematic Jewish subjectivity, the Verein must itself model such self-transcendence. The *Vereinler* saw in their own superior intelligence, their universal *Wissen* and *Wissenschaft*, the corrective to oppositional subjectivity; and in so doing they understood their conceptual talents and pursuits not only in academic but also in decidedly political terms.

Gans's subsequent addresses remain steeped in Hegel's political philosophy and philosophy of history, the latter of which Hegel sketched out at the end of *Philosophy of Right* and began lecturing on in winter 1822–23.[62] In theorizing the Verein's mission and significance Gans draws heavily on Hegel's idealization of the bureaucracy and his theorization of the family, corporation, and the state as different institutional embodiments of ethical community. On October 28, 1821, Gans assures his audience that history is progressing ineluctably from separation to unity, from particularity to universality, despite certain recent phenomena that might suggest atavistic backsliding. Echoing Hegel's iteration of a prevalent orientalist geographical notation in the section on world history at the end of *Philosophy of Right*, Gans locates humanity's childhood in the Orient and its culmination in the present age, which, unmistakably, is a version of Hegel's state. This age puts an end to medieval social divisions and, for Jews, oppression and exclusion. Gans tells his colleagues that doors will open to their coreligionists, as long as they spare no effort to open them.[63] The opponents of historical progress are powerless: "they would like to obstruct the spokes of the wheel of the world [*Weltrad*], and the rattling and creaking would not kill them?"[64] Gans's effusive praise for the *Vaterland* shows the extent to which he at this stage saw Prussia as the—emerging—embodiment of Hegel's state:

> We have a fatherland and may rejoice over this fatherland. We are citizens [*Bürger*] of a state, subjects [*Unterthanen*] of a gentle ruler, and we may rejoice over this. As we are gathered here, we have the educational institutions and the various benevolent provisions and facilities of our state to thank for the level of insight that we have attained, as well as for the knowledge we have come to posses [*die unser Eigenthum geworden*]; and so grateful loyalty to this fatherland and its ruler, the most devout fulfillment of our duty, is written on our hearts in a never-extinguishing script of flame [*mit nie zu erlöschender Flammenschrift*].[65]

The question Gans goes on to raise for the *Vereinler* is how to reconcile their fierce loyalty to the fatherland with their fealty to their fellow Jews, an iteration of the Verein's central question of how to harmonize the Jewish community and the state.

Here Gans reimagines the nature of Jewish communal bonds in a distinctly

Hegelian key. Before analyzing the dynamics of this reimagining, it bears underscoring that it is indeed Jewish *communal* bonds that Gans undertakes to theorize. However drastically Gans's Hegelian paradigm led, or enabled, him to rethink traditional Jewish ties, this paradigm not only allows, but in fact requires, that Jews be thought as a collectivity and not merely as so many individuals. Working within a Kantian conceptual framework, Bendavid, as we saw in chapter 1, located the malady of Judaism in its collective character and the cure for this malady in the moral autonomization of Jewish subjects. Hegel's intersubjective conception of ethical community and corresponding critique of epistemological and ethical subjectivism, in contrast, allowed the Verein Hegelians to imagine ways of being woven into the ethical fabric as a collectivity. My point is not that the particular ways Hegel privileges the political and ethical salience of extrasubjective loyalties and identifications make his thought attractive (or unattractive) for theorizing Jewish community, only that Hegelian theory in fact allows and requires Jewish identity to be thought in collective terms. Rather than demanding the radical depoliticizing and confessionalizing of Judaism or the dissolution of Jewry into so many autonomous individuals, Hegel opens up ways to grant the collective aspect of Jewishness political significance.[66]

Gans attempts to reconcile the dual loyalty felt by Verein members—to their Jewish brethren and to the state—by presenting it as analogous to the dual loyalty of someone who is both a *Bürger* and a *Familienvater*. One's loyalties as citizen and paterfamilias are so compatible and mutually reinforcing, Gans claims, that, as a rule, only the good *Familienvater* is a good *Bürger* and vice versa:

> Just as the loyal citizen reverently devoted to his duty is nearly always also the better, more loving paterfamilias; just as vigorous zeal and devotion for the state, which is the greater family [*die größere Familie*], cannot cancel the particular [zeal and devotion for] wife and children and for the welfare of every individual [*und jedes Einzelnen Wohlfahrt*]; just as enthusiasm for the whole is grounded in love of the particular and vice versa; so we could not be called genuine sons of the fatherland, loyal citizens of the state, if we lacked a loving disposition toward our coreligionists who lag far behind; if we did not endeavor to make this newly won fatherland the homeland of their yearning, and also procure for the fatherland a not insignificant number of loyal citizens and reverent subjects [*fromme Untertanen*], including insofar as their inward journey and cultivation [*Bildung*] are concerned.[67]

Norbert Waszek notes how in this passage state and family are correlated in a Hegelian sense.[68] Indeed, Gans here borders on paraphrasing Hegel's theorization of the family in *Philosophy of Right*. Hegel sees a crucial symmetry and an important distinction between familial bonds and the substantial ethical ties of the state. The family is based on natural ties of love and feeling, whereas the state is based on law and articulated thought. Still, the family parallels the state in its ethically vital function of drawing individuals out of the egoistic self-sufficiency that defines them as members of civil society and allowing them to become part of a greater unity, even as that unity substantiates and confirms their particular selves.[69] As Hegel describes it, "the disposition [appropriate to the family] is to have self-consciousness of one's individuality within this unity as essentiality which has being in and for itself, so that one is present in it not as an independent person [*eine Person für sich*] but as a member."[70] In its substantive unity, marriage transcends the sort of abstract subjectivity characteristic of the legalistic personalities of civil society (the realm of commerce and contracts): "For the precise nature of marriage is to begin from the point of view of contract—that is, that of individual personality as a self-sufficient unit—*in order to supersede it* [*ihn aufzuheben*]."[71]

We have already seen in the previous chapter that what makes religion a foundation for the state is its capacity to pull individuals beyond themselves and to instill a sense of piety before a higher totality. Indeed, overcoming narrow subjectivity is the defining aspect of all the institutions Hegel characterizes as foundations for the state. In addition to families, Hegel places corporations in this category.

> The *family* is the first *ethical* root of the state; the *corporation* is the second, and it is based in civil society. The former contains the moments of subjective particularity and objective universality in *substantial* unity; but in the latter, these moments, which in civil society are at first divided into the *internally reflected* particularity of need and satisfaction and abstract legal [*rechtlichen*] universality, are inwardly united in such a way that particular welfare is present as a right and is actualized within this union.
>
> The sanctity of marriage and the honor attaching to the corporation are the two moments round which the disorganization of civil society revolves.[72]

When Gans theorizes the Jewish community as a kind of family and imagines the Verein as something between a corporation and the civil service, he draws on Hegel's symmetrical stacking of family, corporation, and state.[73] Rethought as a family, the Jewish community can be reconciled with the state, "the greater family," in Gans's paraphrase of Hegel. Construing the Jewish community as a family—with the Hegelian *Vereinler* as its *Familienväter*—allows Gans to reconcile the Verein's particular and universal commitments, for in the family, as in the state, the particular and the universal do not cancel but reflect and sustain each other. In their concern for their fellow Jews, the *Vereinler* help render them "loyal citizens and reverent subjects, including insofar as their inward journey and cultivation are concerned"—that is, model subjects of Hegelian political theory, possessing a profound inward sense of piety before the greater ethical totality. Hegel enables Gans to redefine loyalty to fellow Jews, widely maligned as a stubborn form of particularism pernicious to the state, as a kind of altruistic devotion and a necessary prerequisite for the individual's full integration into the state's higher substantive unity.

Gans goes on to evoke and reconfirm the position he had articulated six months earlier—namely, that in the event of failure, the *Vereinler* could not claim they had grasped and willed the right thing and had been inhibited only by "an external obstacle completely independent of us and impossible to conquer." A hypothetical failure would show, on the contrary, that they had not grasped and willed the right thing (*das Rechte*), or, "what amounts to the same thing, that we did not approach it in the right way."[74] Gans closes this address on a messianic note that extends his reconceptualization of the Jewish community in terms of a Hegelian metaphorics of the family in complex ways:

> In our circle, devoted to a noble cause, where only the holy and pure may have a place, we must above all diligently guard against letting morbid apathy, vicious ill will, and capricious temperament—these internal mortal enemies of every better pursuit—arise in any of us. Let the purity of thought that every ethical brotherhood represents, the highest being the state, also imbue every individual soul. No longer is there a column of fire in Israel by night, but clouds aplenty by day. Disperse these clouds. . . . [O]ne has idolized the crusaders, and the first followers of Mohammed—because they indeed made sacrifices for an idea, which none of these idolizers could comprehend [*begreifen*]. We have chosen the better part. We honor the purest and highest thought, without means that dishonor it. Onward, then, all of you who are of more noble spirit; onward, those whom the hundredfold shackles and their incisions could not enslave; onward, you who place your *Wissenschaft* and love of your own and good will above all; attach yourselves to this noble society, and I see in the firm manifestation of brotherhood [*festen Verbrüderung*] between such good souls the dawning of the messianic age of which the prophets speak, and which alone the perpetual depravity of the race [*des Geschlechtes jederzeitige Verderbtheit*] has reduced to a fairy tale.[75]

Gans makes a number of significant conceptual and performative moves in this rich passage. He admonishes the *Vereinler* in terms that echo Hegel's high praise for civil servants. Just prior to ending his address on this note, Gans asks what action would be appropriate to their outlook [*Gessinung*] and (conveniently) finds the answer to lie in the very existence [*Daseyn*] of the Verein and the concept [*Gedanke*] it is realizing.[76] In Hegel's idealization of the bureaucracy, civil servants embody precisely the sort of universal rationality to which Gans alludes with the phrase "purity of thought' [*Reinheit des Gedankens*]. Hegel's *Beamtentum* is an elite, selfless, universally oriented group that mediates between private interests—including the sentimental ties of the family—and the true universality of the state. Because their work embodies selfless altruism, moreover, "the work of a civil servant . . . is as such a value in and for itself."[77] The way Hegel imbues bureaucratic work with universal ethical value opens the door wide to the *Vereinler*'s own exalted self-interpretation: by adopting the posture and habitus of civil servants, they could construe their activity as of the highest value in and for itself.[78]

The irreverence of Gans's closing remarks tends to distract from the subtlety with which they extend his reconceptualization of the Jewish collective according to a Hegelian metaphorics of the family. The image of a column of fire (by night) and a cloud (by day) by which God made his presence known to the Israelites as Moses led them on their peregrinations occurs a few places in the Bible, notably Exodus 40:38. In recasting the mark of divine guidance as a source of befuddlement to be dispersed by reason and *Wissenschaft*, Gans replaces Moses with Hegel as the prophet who will lead the way into the state, the new promised land. The phrase "perpetual depravity of the race," moreover, redefines the traditional ties that bind the Jewish people as subethical. Gans continues the ethical recoding of Jewish communal ties he began when he cast the *Vereinler* in the role of Hegelian *Familienväter* of the reconceptualized Jewish family. Now the Verein appears as an ethical fraternity (*Verbrüderung*) parallel to the ultimate ethical fraternity of the state. As particularist attachments, the Jewish community's traditional ties bind together a pseudo-ethical community that is deficient and, by definition, perpetually depraved. The Verein introduces a central, universal orientation around which the *Vereinler* hoped the Jewish community would reconceive itself as an ethical collective in Hegel's sense. As the embodiment of rational selfless altruism—a universal brotherhood bound by purity of thought and devotion to a noble cause—the Verein was to mediate between this reconstructed Jewish community and the ethical universality of the state. In this way, Gans theorized the Verein as the corrective to the perennial *Verderbtheit* of the Jewish *Geschlecht*: the Verein's embodiment of universal ethical substance heralds, at long last, the "messianic age." Gans claims not only a place, but a privileged place, for Jews within a Hegelian *Beamtentum* when he contrasts Judaism's manner of honoring "the purest and highest thought" with the admixture of idolatry that has marred Christian and Muslim devotion to an exalted idea. Those who idolize the crusaders and first followers of Mohammed do so because they are unable to comprehend [*begreifen*] the idea for which the crusaders and early Muslims made sacrifices. The "we" that Gans distinguishes from those who commit such Christian and Muslim errors when he says "We have chosen the better part. We honor the purest and highest thought, without means that dishonor it" inhabits a locus at which the purity of Hegelian reason and that of Jewish thought intersect: it is a "we" of Jewish Hegelian civil servants.

As will have become apparent, Gans's ethical redefinition of the Jews proceeds largely by way of a recoding of the matrilineal ties that traditionally define inclusion in the Jewish community. Just as Hegel explicitly defines the modern ethical family as patriarchal, so Gans writes "subethical" matrilineal bonds out of the picture as he reconstitutes the community as a rational and distinctly patriarchal subunit of the *Vaterland*.[79] The Jews' *Verderbtheit* inheres in their status as *Geschlecht*, understood not in a modern racial sense but as a subrational, subethical ordering principle. Gans parallels Hegel's distinction between the bourgeois family and older familial arrangements such as the largely economic unit of the medieval family, the tribe [*Stamm*], or the Greek *oikos*. As he incorporates Jews into the Hegelian paradigm, Gans assigns the *Vereinler* the role of masculinizing, rationalizing, and rendering ethical an older *verdorben* form of subethical and maternally mediated community. Hegel argues that each newly formed modern family assumes autonomy vis-à-vis the wider kinship network that had defined premodern families (*Stämme*, *Häuser*): "When a marriage takes place, a new family is constituted, and this is self-sufficient for itself in relation to the kinship groups or houses from which it originated; its links with the latter are based on the natural blood relationship, but the new family is based on ethical love."[80] In Hegel's interpretation every marriage reenacts the historical leap from older familial models to the modern family by severing ties with the extended family and establishing a new unity through bonds of ethical love. The *Vereinler* should enact a comparable messianic leap out of the *Geschlecht*'s maternal ties of "natural blood relationship" into the *Vaterland*. As would-be *Familienväter* the *Vereinler* are bound to their fellow Jews by ties of ethical quasi-familial love that are continuous with those of the politicized fraternity (*Verbrüderung*) of the Verein itself and, ultimately, with the *Sittlichkeit* of the state.

Gans returns to this line of thinking in his final address to the Verein, on May 4, 1823. Adapting the critique of Enlightenment subjectivism that Hegel had recently articulated (for example, in his history of philosophy and his philosophy of religion lectures), Gans contrasts the superficial bonds of the Berlin Jewish community with the sort of ethical collectivity the Verein aspired to embody and cultivate. He points to the "rupture in the hitherto purity of Jewish life" [*Bruch in die bisherige Gediegenheit des jüdischen Lebens*] that Mendelssohn and the Haskalah had effected fifty years previously, which had dissolved the old Jewish community into so many individuals devoid of the "authenticity of the old way of life" [*Innigkeit des alten Seyns*].[81] In Gans's dialectical historical schema, however, the Enlightenment's atomizing effects and emphasis on the rational individual were a necessary step toward a new, more profound ethical totality to which Jews should now aspire, for "this return . . . is what matters."[82] In this context Gans again deploys a metaphorics of the family: "The individual who has grown beyond his family in turn becomes the progenitor of a new family; that which has truly liberated itself and become truly independent celebrates this liberation by binding itself once again and returning to the substance from which it detached itself. However, that which does not return, after its individuality is sufficiently strengthened, perishes in this isolation . . . : like the willful bachelor [*Hagestolz*], who, indeed, maintains his individuality most steadfastly and longest, yet perishes unmourned, unpitied, and unremembered."[83] The unresponsive Berlin Jewish community has not embraced the Verein's scientifically sanctioned ethical orientation, so that, regrettably, "the more profound return to this authenticity has not occurred."[84] The Jewish community's failure to respond to the Verein's efforts serves Gans as the "explanation [*Erklärungsgrund*] . . . for the still too-slow progress of this society."[85] The apparent symmetry between the old and new families in the dialectical progression from family to individual to new family should not obscure the fundamental reorganization of the Jewish community Gans is proposing. The Jewish progenitor (or the progenitor of Jewishness), again, is the Jewish mother; and the traditional ties that bind the Jewish people are—not only, but certainly also—a system of the sort of *Blutverwandschaft* that Hegel associates with preethical kinship systems. The "individual who has grown beyond his family" has extracted himself from the kinship ties that Gans earlier associated with the Jews' ethical shortcomings. The new—male—progenitor will not extend the Jewish *Geschlecht* but found an ethical unit within the totality of the state.

Yet if the post-*Aufklärung* Berlin Jews are so many atomized *Hagestolze* who resist reintegration into the new family of which the Verein would be the hub, what then is the status of Gans and his fellow *Vereinler*? Instead of the productive *Familienväter* they had hoped to become, they appear now like so many stranded individuals, bachelors despite themselves, hapless *Hagestolze* on the outside of both the Jewish community and the state—the two entities they had hoped to mediate between. When Gans delivered his angry final address, the failure of the Verein's mission had become manifest. The association had virtually no financial backing and had generated scant interest on the part of the Jewish community. Moreover, its own unapologetic intellectual elitism had left its journal not only unread but, as noted in chapter 2, virtually incomprehensible to even the likes of Heine.[86] The Verein's death knell however, came only when Gans was refused an appointment to the Berlin University law faculty—that is, when he was literally excluded from participation in the state because he was a Jew.

Gans's scathing diagnosis of the Berlin Jewish community as bad subjects par excellence—unproductive, isolated bachelors fated to live out an irrelevant existence and die unreconciled to the organic movement of world history—thus dramatizes his own crisis in the aftermath of the Lex Gans. The Verein's central objective had been to reconcile Jewish particularity with a Hegelian version of rational universality, to integrate Jewish consciousness and institutional life into the ethical totality of the state. Although the ire Gans directs at the perceived shortcomings of the Jewish community is surely sincere, his crisis was precipitated by the *Vaterland*'s definition of him as an unintegratable Jewish subject. Below I will analyze the ways that Gans responded to this changed status in his theorization of the Verein in his final presidential address. First, however, it is necessary to scrutinize Gans's penultimate address, of April 28, 1822, which contains his most elaborate vision of Jewish integration into the state, even as it also shows signs of marginalization and, correspondingly, more pronounced political defiance on Gans's part.

Gans's opening gambit in this address is to impugn the either-or logic of the debate about the political nature of the Jews that had been going on since the end of the anti-Napoleonic German campaign (*Freiheitskampf*).[87] Both those who oppose the Jews, frequently evoking "philosophy" in the process (this is presumably an allusion to Jakob Fries and others), and those who counter by listing the Jews' moral virtues fall prey to what we could call a subjectivist fallacy: "The fallacy of both these kinds of hubbub [*Treiben*] lies in the basic view that world history moves according to the standpoint of the freedom of the individual; as if one could say of world history that it too must accomplish good and avoid evil."[88] Few have avoided this for-or-against logic, which stems from an inability to transcend an individualistic conception of freedom, yet the prerequisite for grasping—and by correctly grasping, taking part in, rather than merely ineffectually indicting—the movement of world history is that one transcend precisely the sort of subjective parameters that have structured the positions in the debate.[89] This requires that one think of freedom not merely as an individual but, above all, as a collective achievement, and that one always theorize the place of the Jews in the context of a wider social and political life.

Gans effectively summarizes Hegel's characterization in *Philosophy of Right* of the achievement of modern society as having harmonized particular freedom with organic totality and also follows his mentor in characterizing "today's Europe" as the necessary product of a many-millennia-long "effort of rational Spirit, which manifests itself in world history."[90] Contemporary Europe's concept (*Begriff*) is "the plurality whose unity exists only in the whole," and its distinctiveness [*Eigentümlichkeit*] rests chiefly on "the wealth of its many-limbed organism."[91] "There is here [*da*] no thought that has not come into being or found its shape; there is here no tendency and no activity that has not achieved its [full] dimensions. Everywhere are manifest the most fertile variety of social classes and conditions, the work of spirit moving ever closer to its perfection. Each of these classes is a self-contained unit, complete in itself, and yet it does not gain its meaning from itself [*von sich*], but only from Another; each limb has its own particular life, and yet lives only in the organic whole."[92] Ostensibly following Hegel's periodization at the end of *Philosophy of Right*, Gans claims that in order to call forth this totality, the Orient contributed monotheism, Hellas beauty and ideal freedom, the Roman world the gravity of the state vis-à-vis the individual, Christendom the treasures of universal human life, and the Middle Ages its differentiation into sharply delimited estates and segregations (*Abteilungen*). The contribution of the modern world has been its philosophy, in which all the previous stages reappear as moments, after their temporal hegemony has ended. "Europe" is the *Gesamtproduct* of this dialectical process: "This is the happiness and significance of the European: that he may freely choose his own class from among the manifold classes [*Stände*] of civil society, and yet feel all other classes of society in the one he has chosen. Take this freedom away from him, and you have deprived him of his foundation and his meaning [*Begriff*]."[93]

Although the general world-historical development has culminated in harmony in contemporary European life between subjective freedom and organic totality, Gans maintains that Jews have remained largely aloof from the trajectory leading to Europe's differentiated unity. If Europe represents the "plurality that achieves unity only in the whole," *Judentum* is "the unity that still has not become a plurality."[94] Gans echoes Hegel's characterization of Judaism (in his philosophy of religion lectures and elsewhere) when he identifies the Jews' defining feature as "the fertile creativity [*Bildsamkeit*] by which they gave birth to a new world without themselves being able to partake of this world [*ohne selbst dieser*

Welt theilhaftig zu werden]."[95] In other words, with monotheism, the Jews engendered the world that would follow, but they did so through what we could call an act of immaculate estrangement that left no Jewish residue.[96] Instead of taking part in the new world of which it was the matrix, *Judentum* sustained a certain unity through concentration in a commercial estate (*Handelsstand*). Though effectively closed off from others, as a commercial class Jews were also potentially open to all other estates (*Stände*).

Gans somewhat normalizes the Jews' purported failure to realize their potential for integration when he notes that premodern corporate society was, after all, characterized by an *Auseinander* of different groups.[97] Social isolation was the rule, not the exception. Given the harmony between the particular and the universal in contemporary Europe, however—with its open, noncoercive possibility of exercising freedom as a particularity within a broader organic unity—it has become incumbent on the Jews to overcome their vestiges of bad particularity and to bring themselves into harmony with the diversified unity of modern European life. Refusal to integrate into contemporary Europe becomes increasingly obnoxious. Gans locates Jews at a historical crossroad: they must define themselves in concert with the historical evolution of freedom taking shape in "Europe" (Hegel's state) or define themselves in increasingly intolerable opposition to Europe's differentiated whole. The memorable metaphors Gans uses to refer to the process of Jewish integration into European totality can be, and have been, variously understood. On the one hand, one can read Gans as advocating a coercively assimilationist position. On the other hand, Gans's vision is not a demand for Jewish capitulation, but an argument that history has advanced and will now allow Jews to take up a place in a noncoercive totality of European life. Gans offers this vision, I would argue, very much in defiance of reactionaries who would define the state and the Jews as mutually incompatible:

> The issues that have been articulated in the last decades regarding the cause of the Jews and that have emerged as an important concern, . . . these find their resolution in the concept of contemporary Europe given above. . . . The fewer unintegrated particulars [*Einzelheiten*] there are, the more disturbing these few become, and the compelling drive [*Drang*] of the age, one that cannot be refused, is to integrate these remaining formations into the harmonious unity. Where the organism requires a wavy line, a straight line is anathema [to it]. Thus the demand of present-day Europe—that the Jews should completely incorporate themselves [into Europe]—is one that issues from the necessity of its concept [*seines Begriffes*]. If it [this demand] were not made,

it [contemporary Europe] would be denying itself and its concept. The time for this demand, and its fulfillment, has come. What, then, to many, who do not go beyond the surface of daily phenomena, looks like the age of atavistic and incomprehensible hatred, as an age of resurfaced barbarism, is nothing but the manifestation [*Aeußerung*] of the struggle that issues from the need for unity, and that must occur before this unity can ensue. The true triumph of the necessity of world-historical development is that those who believe they could impede or indeed destroy it serve the ineluctable course of events no less than its so-called supporters.[98]

It is crucial to grasp the double-edged nature of Gans's recourse to a version of Hegel's *List der Vernunft*. On the one hand, Gans insists that Jews must remake themselves in accord with the ineluctable advance of world history. On the other hand, he asserts that history is indeed ineluctably advancing, and that those who try to obstruct it will be crushed. Phenomena that seem to reveal the age as one of recrudescent hatred and barbarism (an ostensible allusion to the Hep-Hep pogroms) will be powerless to halt the necessity of freedom's progress; indeed, they are but epiphenomena of such progress. So although Gans is calling, in very stark terms, for Jewish self-transformation and integration, he is also insisting—against mounting evidence—that there will in fact be an organic unity (a version of Hegel's state) for the Jews to integrate into. What is easy to miss in Gans's call for Jews to bring themselves into harmony with Europe is the political defiance in his vision of the Hegelian state (here, Europe): history *is* advancing toward greater freedom, including for Jews, reactionaries notwithstanding.[99]

It is in this context that Gans deploys his most vivid language about the future of Judaism in the new Europe, including his famous metaphor of *Judentum* flowing into European life like a stream into the sea:

How such a merging of the Jewish into the European world must be thought follows, once again, from the concept invoked above. To merge is not to perish [*Aufgehen ist nicht untergehen*]. Only the independence that is disruptive and self-preoccupied [*Nur die störende bloß auf sich reflectirende Selbstständigkeit*] shall be destroyed, not that which is subordinated to the whole; since it serves the totality [the latter] shall not need to lose its substance [*sein Substantielles*]. That into which it merges shall become that much richer for what has merged with it, not merely that much poorer for the opposition that has been lost.... What was characteristic of Europe was after all the fullness and richness of its particularities. It cannot reject the very thing in which its vitality [*Kraft*] consists, nor can it ever have enough of it. No particularity harms it [Europe]; all that must cease is its [a particularity's] autocracy

> [*Alleinherrschaft*], its exclusive right; it must become a dependent element [*Moment*] among the many others. Those have understood their age and the entire question very poorly for whom no third alternative exists between destruction and pronounced demarcation [*Abmarkung*]; who hold the eternal substrate of the Idea to be more ephemeral than that of matter; who do not see in *each* particularity the truth of the whole [and] in the whole the truth of each and every particularity, but for whom, rather, their momentary standpoint [*ihr jedesmaliger Standpunkt*] is the Absolute and the opposing one [*der andere*] is a lie. This, however, is the consoling lesson of history properly understood: that everything wanes [*vorübergeht*] without vanishing [*vergehen*], and that everything remains, even when said to be long past. For that reason the Jews can neither perish, not can Jewry [*das Judenthum*] disintegrate [*sich auflösen*]; in the great movement of the whole it will seem to have disappeared, and nevertheless live on, as the current [*Strom*] lives on in the ocean. Recall, gentlemen and friends, recall on this occasion the words of one of the most noble men of the German fatherland, one of the greatest theologians and poets; they express concisely what I have said more ramblingly: "There will come a time in Europe when one will no longer ask who is a Jew and who a Christian."[100]

Whether we read Gans's vision of Jewish integration into Hegel's state as a disturbing call for total Jewish assimilation, a defense of cultural pluralism and the right to be different, or something in between, we must not overlook how Gans's call for Jewish *Aufgehen* into European life arrives at two addresses.[101] There is no question that for Gans the Jews must transform themselves; such a transformation had been at the heart of the Verein's project from its inception. Insofar as *Judentum*'s self-definition or consciousness is anchored in what Gans, along with Hegel, views as bad subjectivity ("disruptive and self-preoccupied" independence), it must be transcended. But some version of Jewish particularity will have a place in the new substantial totality. In giving voice to this vision, Gans defiantly, if only implicitly, insists that the Prussian state, too, will have to come around to the principle of European life as grasped by Hegel; willingly or not, it must become the sort of entity into which Jews will be able to flow like a current into the ocean. Some scholars see a subtle contestation of Hegel in Gans's use of "Europe" rather than "the state" or "the Germanic Empire," the latter a term by which Hegel designates the modern state's geographical matrix.[102] Since by "*das germanische Reich*" Hegel meant France, England, and Germany, however, it is odd to interpret Gans's use of "Europe" as a jab at Hegel. Gans is not subtly contesting Hegel's vision of the state in order to find a place in it for Jews, but rather leaning heavily on Hegel's state—which, as Gans understands it, has a place for Jews—in order to contest the emerging Christian-German state, which emphatically does not. He is thinking Jewish with, not against, Hegel.

As the Verein's estrangement from both the Prussian state and the Jewish community became evident, Hegelian theory was all the *Vereinler* had left to sustain their self-image and claim to authority and agency. In this sense, Hegelian theory sustained the *Vereinle*r by sustaining their illusions (which, as Leopold Zunz, Heine, and others, looking back, concurred were what the Verein had actually consisted of). Hegelian thought generated a place for a secular investigation and theorization of Judaism by giving the Verein an institutional locus, at a critical remove from both the Jewish *Gemeinde* and the Prussian state apparatus, in a "state" that existed nowhere but in Hegelian theory. Hegel's state, and only Hegel's state, gave the Verein a home. A remark by Gans anticipating skepticism that the *Vereinler* would likely encounter regarding the authority on which they presumed to speak and act illustrates to what extent Hegelian theory was ultimately all the *Vereinler* possessed to legitimize themselves. "There will be people," Gans remarks,

> those who, unable to marshal any objection to the conception [*Gedanke*] of your association, will ask . . . about your license [*Patent*] and your credentials [*Ausweisung*] for your vocation [*Beruf*]. Should you bother to answer the petty souls who inquire about your qualifications [*Competenz*] when it is substance [*die Sache*] that matters; who, when collective enthusiasm is propelling everyone toward the desired goal, still have not been able to break through the layer of ice of their personal concerns? What you are doing you owe as human beings to humanity, as brothers to your coreligionists, and as citizens to your king and your fatherland: it is a debt of gratitude that you are repaying.[103]

In an evolution of the sentiment Gans had voiced in his first presidential address—that the Verein was elected to represent the Jewish community by virtue of its superior intelligence rather than by popular vote—he here dismisses questions regarding the *Vereinler*'s credentials and authority with an appeal to theoretical expertise. Though Hegel is not named explicitly, it is unmistakable that it is Hegelian historical and political theory that gives the *Vereinler* purchase on *die Sache*, gives them the true competence that trumps their lack of official credentials or authority. In contrast to the triumphalism and exuberance of the early Verein vision, here we begin to see the *Vereinler* as exposed and defensive, retreating into the refuge of Hegelian theory rather than drawing on it to conquer the world at will.[104] Just as it is Hegel who allows them to dismiss their hypothetical skeptics as trapped in the perspective of narrow subjectivity ("the layer of ice of their personal concerns"), it is also Hegel—and only Hegel—who allows them conceptually to overcome such subjectivity and grasp humanity, their coreligionists, and the fatherland as thoroughly compatible ethical collectivities. Certainly neither their coreligionists nor their king, to whom the *Vereinler* claimed to be repaying a debt of gratitude, recognized the the propinquity of these entities or the Verein's capacity to mediate between them.[105] Instead of finding itself confirmed in history's ineluctable progress, Hegelian theory had begun to compensate for reality's lack of cooperation.

After being expressly and legally excluded from the state in August 1822, Gans had to revise his initial views on the relation of theory to reality more dramatically still. In his final address of May 4, 1823 (the familial metaphorics of which I discussed above), Gans reverses the position he had articulated in his address of April 1, 1821, and reiterated on October 28, 1821, regarding how the *Vereinler* would have to interpret their eventual hypothetical failure. As we have seen, Gans's earlier caution against seeking out external alibis in the event of failure issued from his confidence in the rightness and agency of his historical conception; in a manner of speaking, Gans was playing chicken with world history, daring it to try to prove him wrong. Presuming to speak from the vanguard of the triumphalist march of reason, Gans had hewn closely to Hegel's famous *Doppelsatz* in the preface to *Philosophy of Right*: "what is rational is actual; what is actual is rational."[106] What was not rational, however, had now become actual and had thrown into crisis Gans's already strained identification of himself and the Verein with the state. This turn of events required a dramatic rethinking of the relation of theory to actuality and of the Verein's relationship to the movement of world history.

The opening rhetorical gambits of Gans's final address enact the acute problem of the status of the *Vereinler*'s subject position in the face of their failure and explicit exclusion from the state. The thrust of their political project, after all, had been to model and promote a rationalized Jewish particularity that could be woven into the differentiated fabric of the Hegelian state, whose hallmark is the mutual penetration of the particular and the universal, of subjective freedom and universal ethical substance. Now the Prussian state had defined Gans as a sort of Jewish *Fremdkörper*, unfit to hold an official state position regardless of his cognitive prowess and other talents. Gans responds to this predicament with various attempts to evade the vexed position of his *Ich*. He begins with a metacommentary on the duty of the historian to become transparent and let events speak for themselves: "The highest demand made of the historian is to annihilate and abandon himself [*sich zu vernichten und aufzugeben*] to understand himself as the passive instrument [*das leidende Werkzeug*] that affords the deed, in its quest to become word, passage through a neutral region; in short, to watch how events manage to find the expression appropriate to them by themselves and without aid."[107] Gans's desire to annihilate his subject position in order to become a neutral observer and a passive instrument of a historiographical operation, whereby events write themselves, accords with a nineteenth-century ideal of scholarly objectivity, but in Gans's case the will to transparency and objectivity is overdetermined by the crisis of the status of his Jewish subjectivity. In the foreword to "Etwas über die rabbinische Literatur," Zunz adopts the first person only long enough to banish it from his discourse proper.[108] But if Zunz in 1818 sought to retreat into the pure objectivity of *Wissenschaft*, Gans in 1823 finds himself in the thornier predicament of wishing to coincide with a Hegelian version of necessary rational historical process while also needing to render an account of the Verein's historical failure.

As Gans tries to negotiate the hazard his subject position has become, he enacts something akin to what Freud theorizes as the "splitting of the ego in the process of defense" to account for the Verein's failure.[109] Gans narrates this failure, that is, from a bifurcated enunciatory position that seeks self-confirmation through a strategy of self-circumvention: "I have many severe things to say today, and it is not I who says them; I must lay bare the ultimate causes of a miserable vegetative existence, and it is not I who lays them bare. I must speak of weakness and poverty of spirit, of half-heartedness and paucity of love; and I wish I were able to speak of so many virtues. . . . Would that I could bar the door against this subject [*Gegenstand*], so that it would choose a different instrument to divulge itself! Long have I tried . . . [and] fought against it and refused it entry, but its superior power has finally prevailed and insists on asserting itself."[110] Gans clearly is loath to see himself and his colleagues as so many stranded subjects who have misjudged the course of history. His strategy of self-abnegation is both ingenious and poignant, as it allows him to speak in the negated first person: no *Ich* but rather a *nicht-Ich* enunciates the account of the Verein's failure. The enunciating *nicht-Ich* finds its counterpart in the *nicht-Sie* it addresses: "Is it we, I hear it being asked, the members of this association, to whom these words of incrimination are directed? Is it we, who, with sacrificing love, are dedicated to a collective purpose, at whom this load [*Last*] of such strong reproofs is being hurled? . . . And I answer: it is not you whom I mean [*nicht Sie sind es, die ich meine*]."[111] Despite certain shortcomings on the part of the *Vereinler*, Gans says, they are not the real problem. In fact, Gans remarks that it would be better if the fault could indeed be located in the *Vereinler*, because then they could redouble their efforts and correct their course. The real culprit, though, is the unresponsive coreligionists with whom the *Vereinler* have had to contend: "The ground in which it [the perversion of the Verein's efforts] is rooted is, alas, the life of our coreligionists in general. I am, however, justified, indeed obligated, to speak of it, because we have devoted our most vigorous activity to the cultivation of this ground, because in its character [*Beschaffenheit*] and receptivity we await the first condition of the success of so much endeavor and effort!"[112] This sort of looking for insurmountable obstacles outside themselves in order to salvage their vision of history is exactly what Gans had repeatedly insisted his colleagues must never do. Gans blames not the *Vereinler*'s understanding of the necessary movement of history, but rather the incorrigible mediocrity of their fellow Jews. In his earlier exuberance Gans had insisted that the evolution of events would reveal the rightness or error of the *Vereinler*'s theoretical vision, but he now has little choice but to reverse himself and assert the essential reality of the Verein's conception over against the merely accidental nature of contemporary circumstances. Gans confesses a certain tedium and exhaustion at having, semiannually or annually, to reiterate the conceptual architecture of the Verein, to so little avail. Not only the uneducated masses, but even the "better" social strata (hopelessly infatuated as they are with passé *Aufklärung*) fail, year after year, to grasp or help realize the Verein's *Gedanke*.[113] Gans does not, however, express doubt in the rightness of his grasp of the Verein's concept; he only bemoans its not having been understood.

Evidently inspired by Hegel's lectures on the philosophy of history that would have been fresh in Gans's mind (Hegel gave them for the first time in winter 1822–23), Gans defines the highest achievement of the "history of the human race" as the reconciliation of subjectivity and objective conditions in self-consciousness, which occurs when consciousness recognizes itself in the world while also knowing that world to be the necessary culmination of the rational historical process. Such reconciliation is "the highest stage that can ever be attained" and therefore also provides the "greatest calm," for consciousness is finally at home in the world; it "knows itself to be at home in the phenomena of life to the same degree as these find in consciousness their justification and explanation."[114]

As a sort of mirror image of the function Gans had earlier assigned to reality as the judge of theory, reconciled consciousness (absolute knowledge) now assumes the power to judge reality:

> Since consciousness has reconciled itself with the phenomena [*Erscheinungen*] and knows itself to be one with them, it presses with greater vigor than before for this justification and accounting of things before its Judg-

ment [*Richterstuhl*]:[115] it wants to penetrate them, to know itself in them; and the possibility of this penetration is nothing other than this justification. If it [consciousness] cannot penetrate a particular phenomenon, if it cannot know itself in it, oh, then the phenomenon's death sentence has been declared; it is not at all real but its existence is rather only an ephemeral one, temporary and trifling.[116]

The critical utility of absolute consciousness here lies in its availability as a *Richterstuhl* apparently in advance of the eventual reconciliation of subjectivity and objectivity in the objective Idea, the state, or what have you.[117] Even prior to the achievement of the state in objective spirit, consciousness reconciled with the world can serve as a lens to train on historical phenomena to evaluate whether they possess true or merely accidental existence. Because reason knows itself in part of the world, or in the fundamental movement of the historical process, it can diagnose the circumstances and phenomena in which it cannot recognize itself as insubstantial and ephemeral. If Gans's earlier hubristic prognostications that reality would substantiate the Verein's conception of Judaism's central idea took the form of *wissenschaftlich* triumphalism, his flight into defensive intellectual elitism takes the form of *wissenschaftliches Ressentiment*: seeing the values and prognoses of *Wissenschaft* contradicted by reality, Gans insists that reality in truth does harmonize with *Wissenschaft* and that facts contradicting *Wissenschaft* have only an accidental, ephemeral, and vacated existence.[118]

Faced with the Verein's objective failure to translate its *Gedanke* into practical success, Gans does not discern a flaw in the *Gedanke* (the conclusion he had earlier insisted would be inescapable in this circumstance) but rather gives voice to one of the most recurrent laments of the modern intellectual: the horror of banality. It is not conceptual opposition that worries Gans, for the Hegelian concept would emerge victorious, and merely dialectically enriched, out of any conceptual conflict. Rather, it is the subconceptual quotidian world that presents the real challenge. The obstacles that have opposed the will (*Wollen*) of the Verein "consist in that which has always proven to be the most irreconcilable enemy of thought because it is precisely that which has remained devoid of any thought, namely the pure externality and materiality of everyday life and the life of idle pleasure [*des Alltags- und Schlaraffenleben*]."[119] Everything has a double nature, Gans submits, both a universal and a particular aspect. In pursuing the universal, the Verein has not been able completely to detach itself from its own particular *Boden*—which is to say, from the simply incorrigible mediocrity of the Jews.

The conflict Gans sets up between the Hegelian philosophical reality of the

Jews and the mundane sociological reality of the Jewish community pivots on which reality is essentially, and which is only apparently, real. Gans attempts to maintain a purchase on reality and authority in the face of irrelevance and exclusion. The self-transformation that Jews must undertake hinges on achieving self-consciousness as an ethical unity within a broader totality. The Verein's task was and remains "to bring Jewry, as the object to which it [the Verein] is solely committed, to self-consciousness, to make the Jewish world apparent to itself [*das Judenthum als den Gegenstand, auf den er ausschließlich angewiesen ist, zum Bewußtseyn zu bringen, die jüdische Welt sich selbst vorstellig zu machen*]."[120] Since true reality lies in the organic unity toward which world history is ineluctably progressing, what is paramount is not pragmatism and remediation on the local level.[121] Rather, it is a new conscious knowledge among Jews of this "higher unity" structuring their existence: "what appears in the most varied expressions of a still merely naive vegetable life, what wilts and dies through its isolation devoid of context, to this we want to provide a central point toward which to steer its life [*wohin es sein Leben hinzuleiten habe*] and from which it can once again deduce itself [*von dem es sich wieder herleiten kann*]: it is this higher unity on which we had our eye, not any particular *this* [*irgend ein bestimmtes* Dieses] with which one might like to saddle us. This unity, however, is the consciousness of all that occurs, or becomes phenomenon [*zur Erscheinung wird*], the knowledge of Judaism and of the Jews."[122] It is only *Wissenschaft des Judentums* (or *das Wissen vom Judenthum und von den Juden*) that can provide the needed consciousness of Judaism and the Jews as a rationally coherent ethical totality (which, as such, is integratable into the state) rather than as the mere aggregate of atomized individuals and local concerns. It is this totality of conception that constitutes the indispensable political function of the Verein's version of *Wissenschaft des Judentums*.

Gans can attribute such agency to ideas, knowledge, and *Wissenschaft* precisely because access to Hegel's state is, arguably, primarily cognitive. Without the requisite knowledge and consciousness, all local practical interventions will amount to nothing. It is precisely in absolute consciousness, when one knows oneself in the world, that one overcomes the subject-object split and becomes truly at home in the world's differentiated unity (the modern state). This is why the Verein's central task becomes "to bring Jewry . . . to self-consciousness, to make the Jewish world apparent to itself." Having put forward his rationale for why the *Vereinler*'s activity is and must be a quintessentially *wissenschaftlich* one, *Wissenschaft* being "the purest consciousness of things," Gans turns to the question of how far the *Vereinler*'s practical activity should extend.[123] He argues that what is truly practical is precisely what is *wissenschaftlich*:

> That which cannot answer for and justify itself before consciousness has above[124] been identified as the trivial and ephemeral, with which time dispenses. Whatever in Judaism is incapable of accounting for itself before *Wissenschaft* in its contemporary form will not fall away or require a special act to be overthrown. Rather, it has already fallen away and been overthrown by virtue of the fact that it could offer no justification for itself to *Wissenschaft*. Since you recognize and honor existence as such [*das Seyende als solches*], any particular phenomenon that makes no claim to such recognition has vanished and quit the very circle of life. What is scientific in you is also what is practical in you. What is untenable flees like smoke as soon as you attempt to hold the torch of knowledge up to it, but what earlier had an utterly inconspicuous existence develops with giant advances and becomes a mighty edifice by virtue of having science and knowledge on its side.[125]

Gans's *wissenschaftliches Ressentiment* approaches a form of magical thinking. The Hegelian intellectual declares what exists but that, according to his knowledge of the essential structure and trajectory of the historical process, lacks justification for existing to be essentially nonexistent, devoid of "existence as such." Gans's Hegelian insistence on the agency of the idea, of the practical force of a conceptual architecture, emerges as a fantasy of power compensating for weakness and exclusion. In Gans's description the *Vereinler* become superheroes of *Wissenschaft*. They can fix their scientific gaze on nonessential objects and virtually vaporize them. They can disperse the degradations of an idiotic world like so much smoke. Moreover, Gans predicts dramatic reversals of fortune: what appears powerful can crumble almost instantaneously, and what appears weak can grow swiftly into a mighty edifice.

As in his penultimate address, however, Gans's assertion of scientific power is directed at two targets. If it is the Jews' unbearable banality that Gans points to explicitly as the obstacle to the realization of the Verein's version of *Wissenschaft des Judentums* as a political project, the other, implicit object of his critique is the Prussian government, which had demonstrated so emphatically, and with such personal consequence for Gans, that it was not Hegel's state. The problem for Gans was not only a Jewish community that, marked by Enlightenment epistemology, subjectivism, and sheer banality, refused to be brought to a unifying scientific consciousness of itself. Even more intractable, arguably, was a state that had barred access even to the most qualified *Wissenschaftsjuden*. One can view Gans's fantasy of scientific power as ludicrous or poignant, or some combination of the two, and one can view his harsh critique of the maddeningly un-Hegelian Jewish community as reckless. To see in either of these a gesture of acquiescence to the Christian state, however, would be a mistake.

Gans's insistence that the Jews and the state can be reconciled is not a gesture of state conformism but one of political defiance. It is a fantasy, on the part of the marginalized Jewish Hegelian intellectual, of triumphing not only over his incorrigible coreligionists but also over the reactionary Prussian state. In raising *Wissenschaft* to the position of the *Richterstuhl* of history and reality, Gans assumes, however ineffectually, a vantage point from which he can declare the essential nullity of existing Prussian realities. Gans insists that there is no essential flaw in the *Vereinler*'s understanding of *Judentum*, the state, or the reconcilability of the two. True, Jews as they actually exist, and the state as it actually exists, fail to grasp their true natures; but the banal Jewish community and the reactionary Prussian state are ephemeral and not really real. *Wissenschaftsjuden* and Hegel's state are.

If the Verein disintegrated in a very real sense as a result of Prussia's ruling to exclude Gans and all Jews from state positions, it is because the ruling strained to the breaking point the *Vereinler*'s guiding illusion of an essential equivalence between reason, science, the state, Europe, and the age, and relegated the Verein to a position of rude exteriority. Try as they might to think their way across it, a chasm yawned between Restoration realpolitik and the *Vereinler*'s Hegelian ideals and fantasies. In June 1823 the Prussian government offered Gans a travel stipend, and, needing money badly and having no other good options, he took it. After accepting what could be seen as hush money, Gans's credibility as Verein president was irreparably compromised, and there was no one else with his charisma and skill to take over.[126] Gans went to Paris but failed to find a niche or meaningful employment there. He had himself baptized in Paris in December 1825 and was subsequently given the position on the law faculty of the University of Berlin from which he had been barred.

The arc of the Verein's Hegelianism stretched from confidence to delusion, from triumphalism to *ressentiment*, but we should not be too hasty to condemn or lament Hegel's effect on the *Vereinler*'s thought, or to dismiss their Hegelianism as an unnecessary distraction or an intellectual seduction. It is true that by the time of Gans's final address to the Verein he had nothing but Hegelian theory with which to legitimize and substantiate the Verein's project of politicized *Wissenschaft*, which had manifestly failed. Only recourse to a Hegelian fantasy of conceptual agency that inverted an intolerable reality could sustain the vision that *Wissenschaft* would provide a bridge into a political universalism with a place for Jews. The *Vereinler* could continue to embody Hegelian universal subjectivity only through contorted strategies of self-evacuation: a *nicht-Ich* addressing an audience of *nicht-Sie*. Only such games of conceptual and rhetorical hide-and-seek enabled the *Vereinler* to evade both the banality they perceived in the Jewish community and the status of excluded Jewish subjects that the Prussian state had imposed on them. Still, without the home that Hegel provided for the *Vereinler*—however equivocal, fragile, or delusional it may have been—they would have had no home at all. There was never any real place in the Jewish community, the Prussian bureaucracy, or the Prussian academy for the Verein's version of *Wissenschaft des Judentums* as a political project. From the Verein's inception to its demise, Hegelian *Wissenschaft* provided the *Vereinler* with a place from which to articulate a vision of Jewish integration into the state. Even if their feelings about this vision moved from hope and confidence to defiance and delusion, we must realize that the problem was not finally that the *Vereinler* were excluded from Hegel's state, but rather that it was only Hegel's state to which they could gain access.

The Moser-Wohlwill Correspondence

In the previous two chapters I explored how the Hegelian conception of *Wissenschaft* served as the vehicle for the *Vereinler*'s bold, sometimes defiant, and frequently chimerical political and metaphysical aspirations. Just as he was the most serious Jewish scholar within the Verein, Zunz is the primary figure who continued to develop *Wissenschaft des Judentums* as a scholarly practice beyond the group's demise. The best source in which to follow the afterlife of the Verein's peculiarly freighted Hegelian version of *Wissenschaft*, however, is the correspondence between two Verein members who produced virtually no scholarship: Moser and Wolf, who adopted the name Wohlwill in 1822.

Klaus Briegleb has dealt extensively with the Hegelian elements in this rich correspondence, which ensued when Wohlwill moved to Hamburg in late 1822 with great expectations of finding fertile ground there for spreading the Verein's vision of transforming Jewish society.[127] The circumstances, however, proved inauspicious for the envoy of Jewish Hegelianism. The Berlin Verein began to decline at this time, and its relationship with the *Specialverein* established by members of the Hamburg Reform Temple was never productive. The young Berlin *Vereinler* looked on the Hamburg crowd as so many Philistines, while the Hamburgers must have viewed as simply laughable the Berlin upstarts' repeated insistence that they define their association and its activities in strict accordance with the Berlin Verein's abstruse and self-aggrandizing conception.[128]

It is remarkable to what extent Hegel permeates this correspondence between close friends: Hegel informs how they understand their aspirations and disappointments, and even their jokes. Briegleb notes Wohlwill's tendency to assert himself through what we could call minor declarations of independence from Hegel, while Moser typically strives ascetically to subordinate individual concerns to a higher cause for which *Wissenschaft* frequently does shorthand.[129] The opposition between *Wissenschaft* and the private self emerges as a recurrent motif that mirrors and structures the way Moser and Wohlwill grapple with how to understand themselves in the bleak political landscape in the wake of the failure of the Verein's grand synthetic project.

Moser's first letter to Wohlwill (of February 2, 1823) exemplifies how closely the *Vereinler* associated their mission with Hegelian philosophy. Moser writes that he appreciates Wohlwill's vow not to write for three months (that is, until he had established himself in Hamburg), yet he wonders: "How is it, though, that one hears absolutely nothing about you by indirect channels? Is the Schlachterstrasse and its environs such unreceptive ground for Hegelian philosophy?"[130] If nothing had gotten back to him about the impression Wohlwill was making in Hamburg, Moser reasons, this could only mean that the Hegelian philosophy it was Wohlwill's mission to spread had not found fertile ground there.

In an undated letter of early April 1823 Moser contrasts the grandiosity of the movement of the *Weltgeist* with the banality of his own quotidian existence: "My life . . . is virtually nothing more than the movement of the hand on the clock, of which nothing more can be said than at which point it stands on the clock face; and this clock face is not the world spirit in its great circumference [*Umfassung*], as it really should be, but only the smallest of all the interlocked circles in the epicyclical system."[131] The same opposition between Hegelian philosophy of history and banality could also, however, offer a refuge from the superficiality of the age. Moser writes of the "urgent need" he feels to improve his grasp of history by delving into its "primordial ground," Egypt and the Orient. He also hopes "to find there a refuge from the insubstantiality and vacuous reasoning of the present age insofar as it has not yet pushed through to a cultivated form of consciousness, of which I find the preliminary stage prepared in Hegelian philosophy, which I likewise strive to penetrate."[132] Characteristically, Moser dismisses the dissatisfaction he feels with the meaninglessness of his existence as a personal failure and momentary self-indulgent caprice: "I am dissatisfied at most only with myself, and even this is merely the whim of isolated moments."[133]

Wohlwill expresses a different sort of self-dissatisfaction in his reply. Whereas Moser dismissed his dissatisfaction with the world and his place in it as an indulgence of a momentary mood, Wohlwill asserts his right, in his self-disappointment, to be concerned with himself: "For my part, dear friend, I am less dissatisfied with the world than with myself. The *Weltgeist* can take care of the world and its operations [*Getriebe*]; it has kept order this long, it will also see how it can continue to be done. Whatever is, is right [sentence in English in the original]. But with myself I am quite dissatisfied. I don't make many demands of the world, of myself, however, great ones."[134] The *Welt* and *Weltgeist*, we could paraphrase Wohlwill as saying, can take care of themselves; it is *me* I am worried about. Wohlwill goes on to put considerable ironic distance between himself and Hegel. In a letter to Moser of April 15, 1823, Wohlwill, feeling homesick for Berlin, evokes Hegel's mockery of those who can muster amazement for the starry sky (that is, Berlin) but not for nearer-to-hand phenomena like the circulation of the blood (that is, Hamburg). "However," Wolf adds, "I don't want to parrot [*nachbeten*] Hegel—he can't pray [*beten*]."[135] A similar irony toward Hegel is visible in Wohlwill's letter to Moser of May 6, 1826. The recently solvent Wohlwill sends money and asks Moser to pay the debts he still owed from his student days in Berlin, including one to Hegel for allowing him to defer paying the fee for attending lectures. Wolf jokingly asks Moser also to extend a greeting to "the Absolute": "Prof. Hegel gets 3 Louis d'or for lectures that student Im. Wolf took with him on credit 1821 & 22, with the obligation to pay him or his heirs within 5 years. While you're at it, my greetings to the Absolute."[136]

Wohlwill's and Moser's letters of spring 1823 reflect a shift in the Verein's self-understanding, an acknowledgement of its extremely slim prospects for real intervention in the face of Prussia's staunch opposition to progressive change. In a letter of late April or May 1823, Wohlwill complains to Moser that he, a Verein ambassador, is hearing nothing about its Berlin activities.[137] Moser's reply makes clear that there simply was not much to tell. He gives colorful expression to the *Vereinler*'s frustration with the Berlin Jewish community: "There is nothing more annoying than speaking about things Jewish [*Judensachen*], which explains my silence. If *Weißbier* is the image of the character of Berlin, then the Jews are that which has gone flat in it. Who can even stand to look at that insipid drink. We others must let it turn to vinegar, that's the only way it can become palatable."[138] If the perceived flatness of the Berlin Jewish community was one source of grief for the *Vereinler*, the Prussian state was another. Moser articulates a more restricted definition of the Verein's project in the face of state restrictions. He notes that the censor had denied permission to publish a work recommending "improvements" in the Jewish prayer service on the ground that this would lead to a "new sect, which the state could not abide," although the same censor granted permission to launch a journal to a society dedicated to the conversion of Jews. Given the realities of the Jewish community and the Prussian state, Moser writes, the Verein has had to retreat into the realm of thought and word: "The Verein is confined to thought and word; it must pull back from all other endeavors and put all its energies into these. The second volume of the *Zeitschrift* will strike a different tone than the first. We are getting ever closer within ourselves to deciding what we want, and that is: to say what we feel [*wie es uns ums Herz ist*], and nothing more. There are no obstacles in this regard, other than, say, the censor."[139] What is perhaps most striking about Moser's realization that the Verein had been reduced to thought and word is its belatedness (his letter is dated May 31, 1823). The change Moser describes is one in the *Vereinler*'s self-understanding rather than their practice, for despite their elaborate plans for "productivizing" Jews and other practical interventions, they had never really ventured beyond the realm of thought and word. Moser's remark reveals, however, the extent to which they had previously equated their intellectual labors with a form of practical intervention. It was this faith that could no longer be sustained.

Moser repeatedly admonishes Wohlwill to turn to *Wissenschaft* as an antidote to indulging in subjective melancholy. Given the bleak circumstances and the Verein's correspondingly pessimistic self-assessment, Moser's call to *Wissenschaft* has shed most of the political freight it once carried. It now appears as merely a preferable and more honorable disposition than the sort of sulking in which he believes Wohlwill is engaging. In a letter of April 23, 1823, Moser recalls Wohlwill's inability to reconcile himself with Hamburg and hopes spring will chase away his friend's dark mood and, above all, will bring about "a *wissenschaftliche* activity, such as your intellect is capable of."[140] Moser will repeatedly propose *Wissenschaft* as the best medicine for self-indulgence.

In a letter of June 6, 1823, Wohlwill refers to an earlier moment in their correspondence when Moser believed that Wohlwill had overreacted to an ironic remark and suggested that Wohlwill might indeed profit by mocking his own pedantry. Wohlwill responds with a performance of intricate Hegelian humor. He first declines to mock his own pedantry because, he explains, Moser, with his Argus eyes, would detect the pedantry at work in the attempt to mock the very pedantry itself, which, instead of purging himself of his shortcomings, would only expose new ones. Wohlwill goes on to describe, hilariously, the Hegelian cast that such an unwittingly pedantic mockery of his own pedantry would take, were he to pursue it:

> I would manage at best to offer a broad deduction of the essence of pedantry along with a few side digs [*Seitenhiebe*]; to examine to what extent certain expressions of the totality of my soul could be susceptible to attack from individual *qualitates occultae* of this essence, to what extent, namely, I don't exist merely insofar as I am a human being, but *this* human being, with a particular developmental history [*Bildungsgeschichte*] (cf. Gans's third report

> and Hegel's Logic); how a certain pedantic strain need not be damaging, and can even be beneficial, to a man's character; how a real outbreak of this moral Saint Vitus's dance is not to be feared in a person who has the requisite power to abstract with ease away from life, with all its idolized miseries [*angebeteten Armseligkeit[en]*], and to lift himself effortlessly above the entire realm of form and appearance.
>
> Give Gans my best. The Jews have probably never before received such philosophical instruction as in his report for this year. It pleases me to have seen *en passant* how intensively our Hegel has been studied this year.—A pity that the Jews, who here could *in specula intueri*, don't understand the presentation. One of the leading local luminaries confessed to me "the reading made his head spin."[141]

The layers of irony here include self-parody, a spoof of Hegel, and swipes at Moser and Gans. Wohlwill's protest that he wishes to avoid further exposing rather than purging himself of his pedantic leanings is itself self-mockingly pedantic. In detailing why he prefers not to follow Moser's advice to mock his own pedantry, he does precisely that. At the same time Wohlwill's self-mockery mocks its own Hegelian idiom. Ludic self-mockery shades into pointed critique as Wohlwill identifies pedantry, for which Hegelian *Wissenschaft* has only contempt, as the very quality that makes him a real, embodied person. The reference to Gans's recent (final) presidential address and to Hegel's *Logic* serve as footnotes of sorts in this pedantic Hegelian spoof of (his own) Hegelian pedantry, but they also turn Gans's and Hegel's critiques of subjectivity on their heads. However ironically articulated, Wohlwill's argument is that he would be susceptible to being attacked by strains of pedantry to the extent that he is not a generic but rather a particular person, with a particular *Bildungsgeschichte*. And so the defense of pedantry begins: a bit of it is a good thing insofar as it individualizes a person. The person who is not susceptible to pedantry embodies the greater danger, since he all too easily abstracts away from the banality and self-indulgent misery that, after all, define so much of real life. In getting off these promised "side digs" against Hegel, Gans, and, to be sure, Moser, Wohlwill converts his own humorous self-mockery as a hopelessly Hegelian pedant into the sarcastically articulated but substantive charge that Moser equates particular subjectivity with mere pedantry. Through his intricate comedy Moser finally embraces an identity as an ironic "pedant," but in a transformed sense of someone who, rather than lose himself in soothing abstractions, chooses to concern himself with something so "shallow" as lived experience.

The above passage's second paragraph seems unresolved. Wohlwill praises

Gans for giving the Jews such a philosophy lesson in his 1823 presidential address, even as he remarks (passively aggressively) that it was nice to learn from Gans's address—no one had been keeping him in the loop—how intensively the *Vereinler* had been studying "our" Hegel. Yet Wohlwill voices his lament that Gans's sophistication is wasted on the Jews, even the supposed intellectuals among them, seemingly with a forked tongue that impugns both the Hamburg crowd's intellectual mediocrity and Gans's ineffectual elitism.

Moser responded that, when he suggested that Wohlwill make light of his own pedantic streak, he did not have in mind being given such short shrift as he had received in Wohlwill's letter—yet he would generously leave Wohlwill's cocky [*übermütig*] joke to one side. Moser assures his friend that he is not one to moan and groan about unfulfilled youthful dreams and adds that he has no time for the "slavery of eudemonism" [*Knechtschaft der Glückseligkeits-Philosophie*]."[142] In this letter Moser twice reiterates his call for Wohlwill to put an end to his hypochondria and self-indulgent doldrums through concerted *wissenschaftlich* labor.[143]

Wohlwill's response to Moser of July 18, 1823, persists in resisting Moser's *wissenschaftlich* cure for his private disappointments. He starkly, if only implicitly, contests the position Gans had taken in his final presidential address, that only awareness of the total conceptual architecture of the historical process and the place of Jews and Judaism in it could lend local interventions true practical value. Wohlwill questions the value of thought and consciousness, especially for young people, who might be far better served by acting, even if such action were naive and not conscious of its own sources:

> One thing is becoming ever clearer to me: it is neither natural nor beneficial for youth to direct all its energy into pure thought, for the element of pure thought is *unity*; in turbulence and confusion it [pure thought] bewilders and ruins its author [*Schöpfer*]. Is turbulent, restless youth really made for finding the way to this unity?—The *free* act: even as it is something *singular,* it is something *whole*; and even if, in its greatest liveliness and energy, it must be the product of a rigorous conceptual unity, it still does not require consciousness of this source; and certainly the greatest actions have flowed from the naive immediacy of life's driving forces.[144]

In a clear retort to Hegel and the evolution of the Verein under Gans's leadership, Wohlwill insists that the naive act is more beneficial for youth than pure, self-conscious, and unified (or systematic) thought. Young people's lives lack the unity that such thought requires, and it thus only bewilders and ruins young minds. To be effective, action must accord with, but does not require conscious awareness of, an underlying conceptual unity (*Gedankeneinheit*). On the contrary, acts are often of the greatest consequence when performed naively. The Hegelian *wissenschaftlich* ideal of spirit self-consciously knowing itself is not all it is cracked up to be.

Wohlwill elaborates further on his psychic state as he tries to make the transition from youth to adulthood and social integration. He writes a good deal about the dissolution of youthful *Traumleben*, *Phantasie*, and so forth, and how difficult it is to come to terms with something more solid. His allegorical description of this process would seem to be largely (though not only) a reckoning with the Verein and its Hegelian dreams:

> Soon we tread nearer the bustle of social intercourse; the sun of life no longer shines in a reflection, its rays no longer fall on us obliquely; they burn at the zenith. We hold our dream images [*Traumbilder*] up to the so-called real ones in the midday sky: they no longer correspond; the representation does not resemble the model [*das Abbild will dem Vorbilde nicht gleichen*]: we pull out our instructions for life and its joys [*ziehen unsere Anweisung an das Leben und die Lebensfreude hervor*]; no one comes to us and wants to hear and recognize our most ponderous demands. It is no longer enough that our imagination [*die Phantasie*] be engaged, will and vigor demand their right. Spirit seeks, since nothing was realized [*weil ihm nichts geworden*], all the more eagerly to comprehend and appropriate [*sich aneignen*] the whole, or at any rate to find a place in the universe [*im All*] from which it might survey the Other [*das Andere*]. It searches for unity and truth; who finds these and holds on to them? The age's complex [*verworrene*] and demanding conditions and unfortunate, unpleasant individual circumstances proliferate the bleakness and bitterness of this view of the world and of life.[145]

As Wohlwill struggles to find a viable professional and social position, he realizes that the fantasy life in which he had been living corresponds to no available reality. He describes spirit's attempt to comprehend unity and truth as an essentially defensive action: because it has not been able to realize itself (*weil ihm nichts geworden*), spirit tries to compensate by comprehending the whole, by searching for unity and truth. This attempt is doomed to fail, however, and indeed seems only to repeat the *Traumleben* to which the world has already given the lie. The grasp of the whole that spirit achieves is not Hegel's ideal of the identity of spirit and world but rather an alienated perspective on the world as Other. The age does not correspond to the image that sprit would like to make of it.

Wohlwill describes feeling torn (*zerrissen*) by the impossible wish to hold onto the dream life of youth, and he sees no way out of this impasse.[146] One nonpossibility would be an unexpected ordeal (*Unglück*) that would interrupt one's accustomed life and force one to summon new strength and achieve "the solidity and unity of one's own self."[147] But why then, Wohlwill wonders, wait for a violent disruption from without? Why not simply pursue the escape (*Ausweg*) of this desired strong, unified self? Because, he confesses, he cannot summon the requisite strength. And *Wissenschaft*, he notes, is of no help: "This would require at least a less lame arm than mine now is, a bolder self-confidence than I for now generally possess.—You refer me to *Wissenschaft*, but it cannot stand beneath life if it is to raise [one] up above life; it must be embraced completely, with free and unadulterated mind and soul, if it is to exercise its beneficial sovereignty. With what else would I be spending my hours other than scientific pursuits; these, however, are too lacking in a unifying orientation to have the right effect on my life-constitution."[148] Science's ability to lift its practitioner up is contingent on the enthusiasm and energy he or she can muster to pursue it. In fact, science can have a positive and unifying effect on individuals only if psychological and material circumstances permit them to devote themselves in a concerted way to its pursuit (they must bring an *einheitliche Richtung* to their *wissenschaftliche Beschäftigung*). No *deus ex machina*, science can transcend life only through the concrete individuals who practice it. To the person mired in the exigencies of life, *Wissenschaft* is essentially impotent: it is subject to life and thus cannot be called on to lift one above life's discouraging circumstances. For Wohlwill, grappling with how to establish a self capable of living and acting in a world that rudely fails to correspond to one's dreams, *Wissenschaft* is useless.[149]

Moser does not mince words as he becomes more adamant in his diagnosis of Wohlwill's pathological self-absorption: "You suffer from a morbid self-scrutiny, which never opens itself to the true life and pure happiness."[150] He chastises Wohlwill for his melancholy and apathy and admonishes that "only resignation yields full enjoyment. One's 'I' must renounce itself in order most truly to arrive at itself [*Das Ich muss sich entäussern um zum wahrhaften Insichseyn zu gelangen*]."[151] Moser takes particular offense at Wohlwill's assessment of *Wissenschaft*'s uselessness for life: "What you said about *Wissenschaft* I can't let pass my censure. It is a statement that must have come from your gut [*Unterleib*], not your mind. 'Without certain endowments [*Rüstung*] it is not germane [*nichts Rechtes*] and these certain endowments—have not been given to you'?! So here, too, the roasted dove is supposed to fly into your mouth."[152] Whether by design or accident, Moser's call for Wohlwill to stop complaining and get to work reframes the latter's more subtle lament that *Wissenschaft* is of little existential use to him as so much mere moaning about lacking the requisite gifts to pursue *Wissenschaft*.

Replying on October 16, 1823, Wohlwill refines his comments on the relationship between *Wissenschaft* and the subjectivity of its would-be practitioner. First, where Moser had interpreted him to be making excuses for biding his time, his orientation toward a more auspicious future must not be confused with capitulation; it is "a brooding for the future in a barren and unedifying [*unerquicklichen*] present."[153] Second, he complicates Moser's tendency to cast scientific productivity as a matter of sheer will:

> Even if the scientific activity is very much, indeed thoroughly, a matter of individual freedom, it is nonetheless only true and pure when, at its center, is the whole person. . . . Whoever has only tangential or secantial contact with the circle of *Wissenschaft* touches its inner essence in only a few points and cannot boast of having completely penetrated and grasped it. Now this centrality, the real touchstone of true scientificity [*Wissenschaftlichkeit*], it seems to me—as some lack the capacity for it altogether—is not always something we can freely choose [*wohl nicht immer in unsere Freiheit gegeben*]. For me at least, wherever I am capable of it, it is completely contingent upon the state [*Standpunkt*] of my inner life, my disposition; and this has not yet come close to achieving consistency.[154]

For Wohlwill no will-to-*Wissenschaft* can offer a way out of the subjective predicament of its would-be practitioner, for the simple reason that the pursuit of *Wissenschaft* remains contingent on the spiritual well-being of those who would engage in it. He explains that he can only really do *Wissenschaft* when his *Gemüt* is in balance, which—especially given the bleakness of the age—it generally is not. Whereas Moser calls for the subordination of one's self to the higher cause of *Wissenschaft*, Wohlwill characterizes *Wissenschaft* as a practice carried out by embodied persons who sometimes are, and sometimes are not, up to it for both personal and wider historical reasons. There is simply no stepping beyond the contingencies of one's inner life—or historical realities—in the name of *Wissenschaft*.

In his next letter (of March 14, 1824) Moser remains typically dismissive of Moser's "thoughts about the centrality of the soul, etc." which made him think of the sixteenth-century mystic Jacob Boehm.[155] Moser spins out his associations into a sarcastic parable of how "Immanuel Wohlwill, or, when he was still an author, Wolf" had been transformed into a sigh (*Seufzer*) that drifts down the Elbe by moonlight into the fog with a buxom female sigh as his companion. Moser's sardonic reverie concludes the following morning in the *Freischule* in Hamburg, in which Wohlwill taught, where Moser has Wohlwill lament "how parochial it was for you in Hamb. and how difficult it was there to penetrate to the true center of the soul."[156] Moser would—hilariously, though surely not without some sting—continue to exploit his distinction between the *Wissenschaftler* Wolf and the self-indulgent Romantic Wohlwill in subsequent letters.[157]

Wohlwill's response (March 24, 1824) to Moser's satire is noteworthy for the way Wohlwill links his emotional state, which Moser so ridicules, with the age in general and with his relationship to Judaism in particular. Wohlwill says that he is thankful for the satire but that he does not deserve scorn (*Spott*):

> My entire flaw [*Fehler*] consists in the fact that feeling predominates in me to a great degree. Many things have conspired to make this predominance of feeling, to which I have a natural tendency, ever more oppressive. But I am well aware of my condition—and isn't the sickness of the age, the universal epidemic, of the same kind? The most unfortunate thing is surely that the sensitive nerves of the limb—called Judaism [*Judentum*]—, which was long ago amputated yet still lives on, polyp-like, in a chronically ill partial existence, experience the suffering of the organism, as if the pain of a wound, with doubled intensity.[158]

Wohlwill links his emotional flaw to the age *tout court*: Romanticism is in, and the epidemic of excessive sentiment has become universal. Yet his particular emotional "condition" has everything to do with his embodiment of a violent encounter between Judaism and modernity. Wohlwill makes his own person a locus of this encounter by likening his exaggerated feeling to lingering ghost pains from the amputated limb called Judaism. To remain within Wohlwill's metaphor, *Judentum* has "long ago" been cut off from "the organism," though he does not specify from what organism (world history? the state? Europe?). Strikingly, in Wohlwill's metaphor it is not the organism that feels ghost pains for the lost limb, but the amputated limb—Judaism as it lives on in its polyp-like partial existence—that doubly feels the pain of the suffering of the organism from which it has been severed. On which side of this cut, then, does Wohlwill locate himself? The answer is not simple. Insofar as he offers this metaphor as an explanation of his *Fehler* of exaggerated affect, he locates himself on the side of the excised Jewish limb that doubly feels the pain of the whole. Yet to diagnose Jews as sustaining an only partial existence is to distance oneself from the isolated "polyp" of Judaism; it is indeed only from the perspective of the whole that Judaism can appear to exist as such a severed and isolated entity. Wohlwill would seem to occupy two places at once: he speaks from the point of view of the amputated limb and of the whole from which it has been cut off, or, more precisely, he seems unreconciled to either place and speaks from the u-topia of the wound that constitutes both the distance between the Jewish part and the greater whole and the painful communication between them, the ghost pain. In the wake of the Verein's grand vision—articulated most paradigmatically by Wolf himself in his programmatic *Zeitschrift* essay—of a reconciliation of *Judentum* with the integrated rational totality of the contemporary world (the state, the fatherland, Europe), Wolhwill's metaphor mobilizes an opposed semantics of violence, dismemberment, isolation, and ineffectual suffering. To be sure, the polyp-like partial existence that Wohlwill attributes to *Judentum* corresponds to his own existence in the face of the failure of the Verein's grand synthetic project. He is an individual Jew, excluded from the state and, to a great extent, alienated from the Jewish community. He is the nerve that feels the pain issuing from both sides of the cut.

Moser replies (May 3–4, 1824) with an extended metaphor of Judaism suspended between death and existence. As usual Moser remains in his outlook more devoted to Hegel. The thrust of Moser's letter is to belittle the parochialism of the Hamburg Reform community (with which Wohlwill was not very happily involved as a teacher and preacher). Once again Hegel serves as the universal standard by which to assess the narcissistic flaw that mars the Hamburg crowd's version of progress:

> I hear that [*ein mächtiges Geschwätz*] has begun there [in Hamburg] about us Verein people here [in Berlin]. By all means do not disturb them in this innocent pleasure.—Hegel would never dream of the part his philosophy is curiously playing there. They need, however, only flip through his works and they won't find the Temple [*und sie werden den Tempel so wenig als irgend etwas andres darin finden*]. In his definition of the Absolute that runs through the entire Encyclopedia it after all ultimately says: the Absolute is Spirit, and not the Hamburg Temple, or its preachers, or their audience.[159]

Moser goes on to stress that he has nothing against the efforts of the Hamburg reformers, only that he finds that a "quite curious *Weltanschauung*" issues from this sort of (pseudo-) "universal center of ideas." He forecasts that the Hamburgers' project will remain of merely local significance because it tries to raise Judaism to a universal significance through navel gazing instead of a true (that is, Hegelian) understanding of the wider movement of *Geist*: "For there is nothing left of Judaism than the pain in a few souls [*Gemüthern*]. The mummy crumbles into dust upon contact with the open atmosphere, and the meaningful significance of the hieroglyph it bears is perverted into the latest entry in the family register [*Stammbuch*], just as if Moses had been born and brought up on the Burstah [Der Große Burstah] and had achieved such a level of style that he could contribute to the *Leipziger Literaturzeitung*."[160]

Like Wohlwill, Moser associates what remains of Judaism with a certain pain, though Moser, much less generously than Wohlwill, reduces this pain to subjective sentimentalism (*der Schmerz in einigen Gemüthern*). For Moser, the pseudo-universalism of the Hamburg reformers is so misguided that fossilized Orthodoxy remains truer to Judaism. Moser implies that Judaism is more meaningful in mummified form than as articulated in the clichés to which the reformers had reduced the hieroglyphs this mummy bore. Moser even remarks that a stuffed rabbi in a zoological museum would embody more of Judaism than the living Reform preachers.[161] This is so, he argues, because Judaism is essentially a *Volksreligion* and, as such, incapable of being "modernized" and assigned universal significance once Jews have begun to lose their consciousness of themselves as God's chosen people (it is in this sense that the "mummy" of Judaism can only crumble on contact with modernity's "atmosphere"): "From that point there is no other religion than world religion, as Christ and Mohammed testify to [*zeugen*]."[162] Unlike the Reformers, according to Moser, the *Vereinler* never tried to derive the content of world religion (*Weltreligion*) from the spirit of Judaism. On the contrary, he implies, they assessed Judaism from the perspective of world religion.[163] To Moser, the Reformers are guilty of smugly justifying a particularist spirit with unconvincing universalist trappings. Despite its esthetic beautification, this form of Judaism remains a form of purely subjective sectarian spirit, disguise itself how it might as universal: "The Jewish reflection of the present leaves behind its truth and becomes sectarian spirit, esthetic bric-a-brac [*Kram*], etc. when it adopts the posture of a universal objective principle, as it in fact is a purely subjective one, which merely has to displace [*versetzen*] itself from the ground of folk religion to that of world religion. Hovering in the middle is the necessary manifestation of a certain form of this movement, but it cannot mean anything if it would claim to be the ultimate and highest [stage]."[164]

In the course of this retrospective defense of the Verein and critique of early Reform Judaism, Moser intimates a new position on the acceptability of Jewish conversion that he will return to and elaborate on in his next letter. He writes: "Let it not be viewed as an inconsistency that the Verein is dissolving itself. What we in truth wanted, we still want now, and could want [even] if we had all been baptized."[165] As we saw in chapter 2, Moser's memorandum of November 1819 deployed a Hegelian logic to argue against Jewish conversion as a means of achieving greater civil rights. That early vision of the Hegelian state, however, had presupposed that the state would offer a noncoercive space in which

Jews and Christians could meet on a secular plane of European culture. In the subsequent years the *Weltgeist* seemed at best to have been moving sideways, crablike, and at worst at a backward slant. The original project of cultivating a collective ethical consciousness in the Jewish community that could harmonize with the totality of the state had therefore been reduced to a matter of how each former *Vereinler* individually could best do justice to the Verein's ideals. Free consciousness "will, however,—and this is particularly important—also be articulated through the organ of the individuals."[166] Even Moser's Hegelian apology for Jewish conversion, however, is complex: the former *Vereinler* still want the essence of what they had always wanted, and they could still want it even if they all converted (which, incidentally, neither Moser or Wohlwill would do). This implies that Christianity would no more provide the truth they seek than would Judaism. Moser locates this truth beyond institutionalized forms of both Judaism and Christianity. To be sure, he now draws on Hegel to defend a position—conversion—that he had earlier deployed a Hegelian logic to impugn. The Verein's vision of harmonizing Jews with the state through a transformation of Jewish collective consciousness guided by science had been dashed, in Moser's eyes, both by the Prussian state and the incorrigible bad subjectivity of the Jews. Although Moser came to regard conversion as one available option, however, he did so not because he thought it would represent a philosophical advance but because the question of conversion had for him lost its philosophical and political relevance.

Moser continues to negotiate the personal and political disappointment of Restoration Prussia through recourse to a Hegelian interpretation of history that amplifies the vacuity of the age and individual existence, and the distance of both from the grand design of world spirit, yet also offers a philosophical refuge from just such lived banality. His formulation in a letter of September 11, 1824, implies that the individual can take perverse comfort in the incommensurability between her bleak personal existence and spirit's deeper, distant workings:

> Individual circumstances make precious little difference in the current state of things. It is such that there is everywhere an astonishing incommensurability between one's personal existence and influence [*Wirkens*] and the inner volition of spirit, and no one lives in a really peaceful dwelling. . . . I think . . . that we are living in a very great time, and the authentic transition out of the Middle Ages can be accomplished by returning into them.—That is a lot of nonsense for the Hamburg philosophers, but, as I said, I don't count you among the natives there.—Are you studying Hegel diligently? I have not read in his works for a long time, but his system continuously takes

> shape within me and is confirmed with each new occasional conquest that I make in the sphere of the Idea.[167]

Hegel once again sustains the hope for a supra-individual *Gemeinschaft* that promises to return individuals to substantiality via the same logic by which it underscores the meaninglessness of their isolated and superficial existence:

> I do not belong to those fortunates for whom life takes shape as a substantial [*gediegenes*] and organic whole; for that, the directions of my career [*Thätigkeit*] are too scattered, if I can still call this meandering along [*Hinschlendern*], to which I am damned by my circumstances, a career. How magnificent a collaboration would be in a community of like-minded friends! . . . Everything becomes dispersed in the gaudy, vapid surface appearances in which life consumes its marrow. I long most inwardly to come out of this distraction into a true absorption—concentration—so that all the premises [*Voraussetzungen*] according to which one lives, acts, and suffers would become reality.[168]

Precisely the individual's distance from substantive, ethically meaningful existence, and the palpable incommensurability of the empty superficies of the contemporary landscape with such existence, renders the decision to convert acceptable to Moser. He returns to this issue in response to his friend Daniel Lessmann's recent conversion:

> There was a time when such a step would have meant a breach of friendship for me. Now, however, I don't see anything spiritual in the Jewish community that would merit a noble fight. In this general isolation each individual must see how he will come to terms with the particularities of family ties, etc. that bind him.—It is a great folly on the part of governments that they won't stipulate that the Jews, when they enter into civic life [*sofern sie in das Staatsbürgerleben einschreiten*], therewith have immediately become Christians and [thus] embrace as accomplished what they [governments] try to achieve by so many means—often, however, as fruitless as they are good. The Prussian Jews in particular lack the sort of connection [*Verband*] that could render them a sect able to continue to vegetate for a long period. The general disintegration can also be felt in the provinces. Jewry there continues to live clearly only out of habit. The chimerical nature of all reformation Jews [*Reformations-Juden*] is utterly manifest [*lässt sich doch mit Händen greifen*]. The Hamburgers are sorely deceiving themselves, but it is a deception that one can allow them. Why do they need to know that they are themselves in transition [*im Übergange*]?[169]

The lack of substantive bonds in the Jewish community—Jews' failure to constitute themselves as an ethical collective in a Hegelian sense—renders conversion an individual choice. In the absence of meaningful community and the general isolation (*allgemeine Vereinzelung*) it entails, individuals must come to terms with their circumstances and loyalties as they see fit. As long as it appeared to the *Vereinler* that Jews could constitute themselves as an ethical community (around the central hub of the Verein) that would have a place in a (Hegelian) rational state, they regarded conversion as opportunistic, as a betrayal of the common cause for individual gain. Now Moser sees no ethical substance (*nichts Geistiges*) binding the community and leaves the issue of conversion to each individual to negotiate. Judaism lives on only as habit. The Hamburg reformers are deluded about the ability of Judaism to keep pace with modernity. The deeper transformation that is taking place, Moser's words suggest, will leave both traditional and early Reform Judaism behind.

In a letter of August 1825 Moser returns to the question of conversion one more time, in response to a rumor that Gans had converted (in fact he would do so four months later). Moser rightly doubts the accuracy of the rumor, yet even if it were true, he writes, Gans would "in this simply be following a powerful characteristic of his mind . . . , in which nothing could emerge more naturally than, after the most intense embrace of the substance he presumed Jewry to have, an equally strong aversion to it once it had proved itself to him to be insipid and lacking in spirit [*ungeistig*]."[170] Moser reasons that nothing would be more natural than for Gans to find Judaism disagreeable once it had become clear that it lacked the ethical substance he had presumed it to posses. This "changing of uniforms" would then not be a contradiction but rather a coherent evolution of Gans's character.[171] As Moser had argued in his critique of the Hamburg reformers, for Gans and the Verein it was never a matter of loyalty to Judaism per se but to the trajectory of truth, history, and so forth, with which they believed they could make Judaism harmonize. Since contemporary Judaism had revealed itself to be *ungeistig*, however, Gans would be only consistent to abandon it.

Even as Hegel continues to structure much of the way they grapple with the status and meaning of their own personal existences in the bleak landscape of post-Verein Restoration Germany ("There is a terrible struggle within me between the universal and the individual," as Moser put it in a letter dated May 27, 1825), both Wohlwill and Moser enjoyed using Hegel playfully for comic effect, and both could agree in spring 1825 that Gans's Hegelianism had become fanatical.[172] In a letter of May 28, 1825, Moser writes that Gans "is now properly systematically a fool [*ordentlich systematisch ein Narr*]."[173] Wohlwill, who had just had the unenviable opportunity to spend time with Gans as the latter visited Hamburg en route to Paris, responded on May 25, 1825): "He has translated Hegel not only *in succum et sanguinem, sed etiam in cutem et os*. He says e.g. "*das Heckste*" for *das Höchste* [the highest], can't stand to see any Schiller lying on the table, etc. The local ultra-monists or Unitarians viewed his apology for the triad, which he intentionally pulled out [*seine absichtlich hervorgesuchte Apologie der Trias*], as a predestined *transgressio in partes infidelium*."[174] Whether Gans's Hegelian apology for the triad signaled that he was merely a dyed-in-the-wool Hegelian, already on the way to conversion, or both, Wohlwill wittily suggests that the Unitarians looked on Gans's defense of triadic thought as a regression to heathenism!

Hegel remains a theme of the Moser-Wohlwill correspondence even after the frequency of their letters dropped off substantially in the late 1820s and 1830s. In a letter of November 19, 1832 (now largely unreadable due to deterioration), shortly after Hegel's death, Wohlwill wonders how Hegel had contracted cholera and what his last words were, and asks Moser to inform him "very soon about everything you have learned about our teacher's end."[175] On March 17, 1831, buoyed by what had been happening in France since the revolution of July 1830, Moser remarks that the *Idee* is now becoming real, and that it is as if the *Weltgeist* is finally back in action.[176] Writing to the newly married Wohlwill on November 8, 1831, Moser jokingly approves of his wife's method of keeping him calm by bringing him Hegel's *Encyclopedia* to read (Hegel had revised and greatly expanded the 1817 version in editions of 1827 and 1830): "It is delightful that your wife already knows to bring you Hegel's Encyclopedia when she wants to calm you down. That is far more sensible than if she understood it herself."[177] In the penultimate (undated) letter of their correspondence, Moser writes to Wohlwill about the recent publication of Hegel's lectures as part of the first edition of Hegel's complete works. Praising Karl Ludwig Michelet's work on the *Lectures on the History of Philosophy* as superior to Philipp Konrad Marheineke's on the *Lectures on the Philosophy of Religion*, Moser remarks to his friend: "Hegel's lectures now appearing in print surely will not escape your attention. For you these must also have the special interest of a memory of youth."[178]

As late as May 18, 1828, Moser still understands his existence in the polarized terms of individual existence versus *Wissenschaft*. He shares the following passage with Wohlwill, copied from his diary: "*Wissenschaft* and individual (social, familial) life: my existence stands under the sway of these two powers, and it remains caught in a dim aspiration for unification, which doesn't get realized [*ohne es zur Gestalt und That zu bringen*]. My self [*Die Selbstheit*] is far too *subjected* to these principles instead of taking possession of them to the fullest by generating my own."[179] Moser here ironically echoes a sentiment broadly similar to the one for which he had earlier lambasted Wohlwill. His existence is structured in an unproductive, indeed crippling, way by an irreconcilable opposition between individual life and his will to *Wissenschaft*. As a principle that Moser can at most subjugate himself to but never generate and embody, *Wissenschaft* offers at best a standard by which to measure the fractures of his *Selbstheit*, in which Moser now seems to see *Wissenschaft* itself as profoundly implicated. His irony intact, Moser sees the split between the universality of spirit and the inescapable isolation of the individual as tragicomic. He casts himself as a hapless extra in God's world tragedy, which ham actors are spoiling: "Is it not a misfortune that our spirit [*Geist*] has become so universal yet we still have to kick around in the straitest circumstances? Stand like common extras at the back of the stage, while in the evening actors puff themselves up in front and botch up dear God's world tragedy for him."[180] Although *Wissenschaft* still is the way to connect oneself to the great world-historical drama, to embody and activate *Wissenschaft* in a world-historically meaningful way would require a sort of intellectual heroism that Moser cannot muster.

Even though Moser and Wohlwill did not produce any *Wissenschaft* to speak of, a Hegelian phantasm of *Wissenschaft* had an abiding presence in their lives. If in its most confident phase the *Vereinler* sought in *Wissenschaft* the glue that would bind together *Judentum* and humanity (Europe, the state), it took on the role of a kind of superego in the post-Verein correspondence of the haplessly isolated Jewish Hegelians Moser and Wohlwill. It figured the elusive interface between their private subjectivities and the grand drama of world history. In this way *Wissenschaft* continued to inflect how Moser and Wohlwill understood the world and their individual places in it. Even as non-*Wissenschaftler*, they consistently measured themselves against *Wissenschaft* and sometimes asserted themselves in defiance of it.

Chapter Four

Marx's "Real Jews" between *Volk* and Proletariat

Productivizing Social Abjection and Grounding Radical Social Critique

A War on Abstraction

Karl Marx (1818–83) famously lampooned Bruno Bauer's abstraction in "Zur Judenfrage" (On the Jewish Question; 1843–44), a two-part review essay of works by Bauer, and the first (though far from the last) occasion on which Marx publicly criticized his erstwhile friend and teacher. By the time he took aim at Bauer's abstraction, Marx was varying a theme already well established in Young Hegelian discourse. The critique of abstraction indeed reaches back to Hegel himself. The complex mediations that Hegel theorized in *Philosophy of Right* between the individual and the universal were aimed precisely at overcoming subjective abstraction. For Hegel, the ethical life of the state constituted realized freedom. Yet Hegel's critical followers on the Left saw in the master thinker—and, as the Young Hegelian movement unraveled in the 1840s into a polemical free-for-all, increasingly in each other—an inadmissible degree of lingering abstraction. August von Cieszkowski, Ludwig Feuerbach, Moses Hess, Arnold Ruge, and Marx, among others, would articulate visions of how philosophy should turn from abstraction to reality and deeds, variously conceived.[1] Much of Marx's early work responds to the perceived need to discover a more satisfying basis for the connections between concept and reality than one finds in Hegel's "abstractions," whether about world history consciously comprehending itself in the apotheosis of speculative thought, or freedom realizing itself in the rational state.[2]

It was the wish to reconcile ideas and reality that first brought Marx to Hegel's philosophy and later animated his criticism of Hegel. As Marx related in a long letter to his father of November 1837, he had abandoned the idealism of Kant and Fichte and, *malgré lui*, embraced Hegel's philosophy when he "arrived at the point of seeking the idea in reality itself."[3] Warren Breckman has demonstrated that Marx's disillusionment with Hegel's ability to reconcile the real and the ideal was already at the heart of his doctoral dissertation (written

1839–40) and that Marx saw the political journalism he engaged in throughout 1842 and early 1843 as a form of philosophical praxis, which he frequently contrasted with self-indulgent abstraction.[4]

"Zur Judenfrage" appeared in February 1844 in the only (double) issue of *Deutsch-französische Jahrbücher* [German-French yearbooks], edited by Marx and Ruge. The essay appeared in the guise of a review of two 1843 works by Bauer, *Die Judenfrage* and a shorter subsequent essay, "Die Fähigkeit der heutigen Juden und Christen, frei zu werden" (The capacity of contemporary Jews and Christians to become free).[5] Bauer's and Marx's far-ranging remarks around the issue of Jewish emancipation, the so-called Jewish Question, were part of a wider debate.[6] When Friedrich Wilhelm III died in June 1840, Friedrich Wilhelm IV was greeted as the herald of a new liberal era. Though he would soon surround himself with reactionary aristocrats and orthodox Pietists, the new king's first actions—relaxing censorship and granting amnesty to political prisoners—inspired optimism. Prussia's Jews hoped for reforms in their legal status, which, among other restrictions, barred them from practicing law or holding academic positions and burdened them with unfair taxation.

In late 1841, however, Friedrich Wilhelm IV ordered his minister of the interior, Gustav Adolf Rochus von Rochow, to prepare a law that would create separate corporations for Jews and standardize their status in the various parts of Prussia. Von Rochow published the principles of the new draft law in May 1842. Although presented under the pretext of granting Jews greater independence and authority, the proposed law stated that Jews would not be allowed to have "governmental authority" [*obrigkeitliche Gewalt*] over Christians, and that no rights should be granted to Jews that would encroach on "the Christian polity" [*das christliche Gemeinwesen*]. The proposal to recorporatize Prussian Jewry met with widespread resistance both from Jewish communities and German liberals and set off a far-ranging debate about *die Judenfrage*.[7] Perhaps the most outspoken liberal resistance to the proposal appeared in the pages of the *Rheinische Zeitung*, an organ that featured a number of Young Hegelian contributors and that Marx edited from October 1842 to May 1843.[8] Contributions on this issue in the *Rheinische Zeitung* by Moses Hess and others consistently maintained that the state must grant the same rights to all citizens regardless of religious affiliation.[9] Marx planned to write on the issue in the pages of the *Rheinische Zeitung*, but he never did. In a letter of around August 25, 1842, Marx asked Dagobert Oppenheim—one of the paper's publishers—for "if possible, all Hermes' articles *against the Jews*. I will then send you as soon as possible an article which, even if it does not finally settle the latter question, will nevertheless make it take another course."[10]

Begun in late 1843 and probably finished in early 1844, "Zur Judenfrage" falls within perhaps the most volatile period in Marx's intellectual development. After his editorship of the *Rheinische Zeitung* ended in May 1843 over conflicts with the censor, Marx was at something of a loss, conceptually and rhetorically. Not until *Die deutsche Ideologie* (*The German Ideology*, written in 1845–46), would Marx—in collaboration with Friedrich Engels—first articulate the core analytical tenets of historical materialism (the productive interchange with nature, and social relations structured by labor) to which he would adhere throughout his life.[11]

In the intervening period he was at pains to ground his writings in something "real." What he came up with was a series of rhetorically forceful yet analytically unstable and rapidly changing versions of "reality." By late 1843 Marx had lost faith in liberal politics, and he used Bauer's writings on the Jewish Question as an occasion to critique political rights as the means of achieving human freedom. Marx argued that formal political rights can actually naturalize, by rendering politically irrelevant, the alienation and social fragmentation that competitive commercialism engenders. Genuine human emancipation would require transforming the real world of commercially self-interested civil society.

Scholars have seen "Zur Judenfrage" as pivotal in Marx's intellectual evolution, and Marx's critique of the structural shortcomings of liberal democracy continues to inspire political theorists.[12] Marx's essay is not only famous but also notorious, however, due to the vulgar negative stereotype of Jews to which Marx resorts in part 2.

Many scholars have simply ignored Marx's anti-Jewish language.[13] Other scholars as diverse as Julius Carlebach, Elisabeth de Fontenay, David McLellan and Lawrence Simon—to name only a few—have tried to "rescue" the ideas Marx developed in part 1 from the more troubling rhetoric of part 2, generally by insisting on the latter part's conceptual vacuity and gratuitousness.[14] The majority of scholars who have concerned themselves with Marx's anti-Jewish language per se, including Arnold Künzli, Edmund Silberner, Robert Wistrich, Sander Gilman, and Paul Rose, have interpreted it as a symptom of Marx's own Jewish self-hatred.[15]

My aim, in contrast, is to analyze the relatively neglected function, within Marx's early project, that his anti-Jewish rhetoric performs. I do so by locating Marx's figuration of the Jew as the egoistic embodiment of material interest in the rapid evolution of his thought in the crucial year of 1843.[16] My intention is not to excuse Marx's anti-Jewish statements or deny that the deployment of such ugly stereotypes can have dire consequences for real people.[17] Yet both apologies for and criticisms of Marx's rhetorical abuse of "real Jews" tend to displace attention from what the figure of "the real Jew" does for Marx. Arguments that see in Marx's *Judentum* a mere allegory for capitalistic commerce (*Judentum* had this connotation in Marx's day) fail to account for his rhetorical excesses and choice to privilege anti-Jewish stereotypes as the vehicle for his critique. Arguments from self-hatred on Marx's part understand his anti-Jewish remarks as an attempt to dissociate himself from Jews and Jewishness, and they typically underscore the long line of rabbis on both sides of Marx's family; his conversion to Protestantism at age six; the occasional antisemitic insult Marx endured from adversaries (including Ruge after their break, Mikhail Bakunin, and Eugen Dühring); and the numerous offensive statements Marx made about Jews in his private correspondence and occasionally in published writings.[18] In a classic essay Silberner documents how Marx's published, unpublished, and private remarks about Jews were consistently negative throughout his life.[19] Yet to harbor antisemitic sentiments and to choose to publish them in the service of a polemical philosophical-political project are different things. I seek to redirect the question. Instead of asking what Marx's anti-Jewish remarks in "Zur Judenfrage" can tell us about Marx as a person, I ask what they can tell us about the evolution of his early thought.

This requires an archeology of multiple philosophical and polemical contexts, including the relationship of Marx's evolving project to those of Feuerbach, Bauer, and Hess; his waning faith in liberal politics; and his complex turn from an idealist to a materialist theory of historical agency. Given the densely imbricated nature of this discursive constellation, this chapter traces crucial arguments and strategies of Marx's most important interlocutors before elaborating a reading of "Zur Judenfrage."

In this period what Marx understands to constitute critical bedrock (the foundation on which he bases his critique of politics and society) repeatedly dissolves and is replaced by something ostensibly more basic. What Marx takes to be solid reality in one moment he may come to view as so much abstraction in the next. It is a testimony to the velocity of this trajectory that one finds three distinct and theoretically incompatible articulations by Marx in the pages of the *Deutsch-französische Jahrbücher* of February 1844. In a May 1843 letter to Ruge, Marx used the ideal collective political agent, the *Volk*, as a yardstick with which to measure the abjection of German subjects and petty rulers. Half a year later, in "Zur Judenfrage," he used the figure of the real Jew (*der wirkliche Jude*) to describe the egoistic members of civil society. In the essay he wrote immediately after "Zur Judenfrage," "Zur Kritik der Hegelschen Rechtsphilosophie. Einleitung" ("A Contribution to the Critique of Hegel's Philosophy of Law: Introduction"), the proletariat makes its initial appearance. Marx deploys a rhetoric of abject materiality in relation to each of these three protagonists, yet the relationship Marx entertains to these various figures of abjection changes dramatically.

Grounding Feuerbachian Species-Being in Society

In his evolving critique of Hegelian abstraction Marx was inspired by several contemporaries including Bauer, Hess, and especially Feuerbach. Feuerbach's materialist anthropology offered a critique of abstraction in religion, theology, and speculative philosophy that was exhilarating both in its content and its spirited, earthy idiom. In *The German Ideology* Marx would fundamentally critique the limitations of Feurbach's materialism and replace Feuerbach's natural and static conception of species-being with his own understanding of social labor as the force driving history and leading to eventual human emancipation.[20] Yet Marx's attempts to ground his critique in "reality" began well before he arrived at such a viable theory of historical materialism. Each of the three texts Marx published in the *Deutsch-französische Jahrbücher* has its roots in a substantial Feuerbachian critique of Hegel's theory of the state that Marx composed in Kreuznach between March and August 1843.

In the posthumously published *Zur Kritik der Hegelschen Rechtsphilosophie*, or Kreuznach *Kritik*, Marx drew on Feuerbach's method of grounding religion, theology, and speculative philosophy in a materialist humanism. In his anthropological critique of Christianity (which he considered the essence of religion per se) in *Das Wesen des Christentums* (*The Essence of Christianity*; 1841 and 1843, in a revised edition with a highly influential preface), Feuerbach identified the God of Christianity as the mystified projection of the infinity, transcendence, and perfection that define humanity's *Gattungswesen*, or species-being.[21]

Classic accounts of Marx's appropriation of Feuerbach in the Kreuznach *Kritik*, such as those by Shlomo Avineri and Richard Hunt, focus on Marx's deployment of Feuerbach's transformative method of correcting an inverted subject-object relationship.[22] In his socialization of species-being in the Kreuznach *Kritik*, Marx indeed made a similar move: just as God was the predicate of humanity, not vice versa, so politics was the predicate of society. Marx faults Hegel for assigning to the Idea the role of subject, and to the institutions of the family and civil society the role of predicate. In reality, the relationship is the reverse.[23]

As Breckman has shown, however, Marx also crucially appropriates Feuerbach's critique of Christianity as a profoundly self-oriented religion that, through its emphasis on a personal God and the salvation of individual souls, hypostatizes collective humanity as discrete sovereign persons. Marx brings Feuerbach's transformative method and critique of personal hypostatization to bear on his reading of Hegel's *Philosophie des Rechts*, which he charges with a twofold process of mystification:[24] Hegel both reverses subject and predicate by assuming the agency of the Idea and arbitrarily embodies abstract logical categories in specific persons or groups.[25] The most important of these persons is the monarch—whom, as Marx contends, "Hegel is concerned to present . . . as the real 'God-man,' as the real embodiment of the Idea."[26] However, Marx sees the same dynamic at work in the status Hegel assigns to the estates, the landed gentry, and the bureaucracy. Hegel invests each of these groups with a universality it does not, Marx argues at length, truly embody.

Even as he leaned on Feuerbach to critique Hegel, Marx became preoccupied in 1843 and early 1844 with how to rethink Feuerbach's anthropological conception of human intersubjective ontology (species-being) in more specifically social terms.[27] We can chart the trajectory of Marx's social inflection of species-being by the changing protagonists he privileges as figures of social agency, from *das Volk* of the unpublished 1843 Kreuznach *Kritik* and the letters to Ruge published in the *Deutsch-französische Jahrbücher* to the "real Jews" of "Zur Judenfrage" and then to the proletariat of the "Zur Kritik der Hegelschen Rechtsphilosophie, Einleitung." These texts are intricately related. The second of Marx's letters to Ruge published in the *Deutsch-französische Jahrbücher* dates from May 1843, some two months after he began work on his Kreuznach manuscript on Hegel. He turned to "Zur Judenfrage" immediately after completing the Kreuznach *Kritik* in late summer 1843; and the next essay he wrote was the "Einleitung," which was intended to serve as an introduction to a longer work on Hegel's political philosophy (a reworking of the Kreuznach *Kritik*). Marx's thought was evolving so rapidly in this period, however, that by the time he wrote the "Einleitung" it was no longer compatible with much of the analysis in the *Kritik* (one reason, presumably, that Marx never produced the planned work that the "Einleitung" was to introduce). Any understanding of the role that the Jews of "Zur Judenfrage" play in the evolution of Marx's thought must take into account this broader context of the protagonists that successively advanced Marx's attempts to rethink species-being in social terms. The *Volk*, the Jews, and the proletariat each embody a different theorization of society and of the interrelationships between consciousness and social materiality as these pertain to revolutionary agency or praxis.

In his 1842 journalism as well as the May 1843 letter to Ruge, Marx repeatedly critiques a brute order. This line of Marx's early thought opposes human idealism (a term he frequently uses affirmatively) with animal materialism. Marx's strategy in this idealist period is not to try to ground abstraction in real, empirical conditions but to insist that human rationality and freedom must permeate and shape what is otherwise merely animal reality. While Marx attacks Hegel's abstract spirit, then, what Marx offers as an alternative at this point remains less a form of material social practice than a vaguely socialized version of Feuerbachian human consciousness.

The result of what Marx sees as Hegel's merely allegorical actualization of abstract categories in real persons is that human rationality leaves, brute material circumstances untransformed. In Marx's reading, Hegel's *Philosophy of Right* becomes a political-philosophical allegory arbitrarily superimposed on animal nature. In an appropriation of Feuerbach's transformative method, Marx counters Hegel's abstraction with a "real" social agent, the *Volk*. It is Marx's Feuerbachian critique of Hegelian hypostatization, however, that most effectively reveals how Marx defines the reality of this social agent in opposition to base materiality. Working through a few of the most important examples of Marx's critique of the collusion between abstraction and brute materiality in Hegel's political theory will illustrate the complexity of the relationships between the ideal and the material as Marx deploys them in *Kritik* and prepare us to appreciate the changes in Marx's conception of these relationships that occur in "Zur Judenfrage."

Marx quotes Hegel's defense of the monarchy as "something not deduced but purely self-originating" and retorts: "In a certain sense, every necessary being is 'purely self-originating'; in this respect the monarch's louse is as good as the monarch."[28] In a similar vein, he savages the political importance that Hegel assigns to the estates and landed gentry as exaltation of an essentially animal principle. The constitution based on the estates does not so much transcend the principle of social exclusion and atomization as exemplify it by making "the individual function . . . into a society for itself." "*Estate* is based," Marx continues, "on the supreme law of the *division* of society, but, in addition, it separates man from his universal essence, it transforms him into an animal that is identical with its own immediate determinate nature. The Middle Ages is the *animal history* of mankind, its zoology."[29] In "modernizing" the medieval estates Hegel fails to transcend their basic "zoological" principle of "natural" division; he merely adapts it, through metaphysical sleight of hand, to the modern political context. Whereas Hegel makes much of the nominal continuity between social class and political class (both *Stand* in German), Marx charges that by assigning "the" estates (*Stände*) different meanings in the (real) civil and (abstract) political spheres, Hegel achieves an only apparent synthesis that in fact exemplifies his arbitrary (allegorical) hypostatization:

> The same subject is given different meanings, but the meaning is not that of self-determination, but of an allegory foisted onto it. The same meaning

> could be given a different subject. The meaning of civil class distinctions in the political sphere is not their own meaning, but one derived from the political sphere itself. . . . This is the *uncritical, mystical* way in which to *interpret* an *old view of the world* in terms of a new one. . . . This *uncritical mysticism* is the key both to the riddle of modern constitutions (especially constitutions based on Estates) and also to the mystery of the Hegelian philosophy, above all the *Philosophy of Right* and the *Philosophy of Religion*.[30]

Instead of realizing the universal human essence, Hegel's "uncritical mysticism" legitimates the brute divisions of the status quo by providing it with a metaphysical political alibi.

Marx takes fuller aim at how Hegel's idealism collapses into base materialism in his lengthy analysis of Hegel's assessment of primogeniture, the system whereby property is passed on in full to the eldest son. Where Hegel saw the landed nobility as particularly suited to state service due to the relative security and independence that the institution of primogeniture afforded it, Marx repeatedly contrasts humanity and true idealism with the brute stupidity of the soil. He points up a contradiction in the status Hegel assigns private property in civil versus constitutional law. In the sphere of civil law Hegel sees the ability to alienate property as the measure of one's fullest possession of it, of its having become fully infused with one's will.[31] Regarding primogeniture in the life of the state, however, Hegel extols the virtues of the inalienability of the land, the noble owner's inability to divide his estate even among equally loved children.[32] This Hegel interprets as an admirable reversal of the principle of the family, to which the landed gentry submits for the good of the state in keeping with their "hard sacrifices made for political ends."[33]

Marx views Hegel's interpretation of primogeniture and the role of the landed gentry in civic life as one of the most egregious examples of Hegel's forced interpretations of the status quo to fit a preestablished abstract schema. He argues that primogeniture, far from humanizing private property by submitting it to the higher principle of the state, only installs the principle of private property as the sovereign subject determining human will.[34] In primogeniture private property cannot be alienated because it is not possessed by, but rather possesses, human will: "My will does not possess, it is possessed."[35] Marx frames the contradiction he discerns in Hegel's different assessments of the relation of will to property in civil versus constitutional law as a conflict between (good) idealism and (bad) materialism. "What sort of state is it," Marx asks, "that cannot even tolerate the idealism of its own civil law?"[36]

Marx seeks to expose the qualities Hegel admired in the landed gentry as but the triumph of brute private property itself, devoid of human subjectivity and will.[37] Where Hegel appreciated the role of birth in the institution of primogeniture as a bulwark against the "hazards of election," Marx contrasts the mere physical fact of birth with elections as the expression of human will.[38] Here Marx emphatically contrasts true idealism with Hegel's unacknowledged brute materialism: "At every point Hegel's political spiritualism can be seen to degenerate into the crassest *materialism*. . . . The highest political offices coincide with individuals by way of their birth the same way that an animal's place, its character and mode of life, etc., is something it is immediately born with. The highest offices of the state thus acquire an *animal* reality. Nature takes revenge on Hegel for the contempt he has shown her. If matter is to be shorn of its reality in favor of human will then here human will is left with no reality but that of matter."[39] In these various examples, Marx sees Hegel's arbitrary (allegorical or mystical) abstraction as a philosophical-political legitimation of brute materialism. Of course, Marx continued to decry base, stupid materiality even after he arrived at the basic tenets of historical materialism—for example, in his contempt for German parochialism in *The German Ideology* and in the memorable comment in *The Communist Manifesto* that in creating great cities, the bourgeoisie had "rescued a considerable part of the population from the idiocy of rural life."[40] Yet the salient distinction in these texts is between backward ways of life and the materialist dialectical world historical process from which they remain insulated. In the Kreuznach *Kritik*, in contrast, the active agent defined over against base materialism (animal existence or zoology) remains, essentially, human consciousness. Indeed, Marx virtually equates people's "real participation" in the state—something that in true democracy would be equivalent to their "social existence" itself—with consciousness:

> Deliberation and decision are the means by which the state becomes *effective* as a real concern. It therefore appears to be self-evident that all the members of the state have a *relation* to the state: it is a mater of *real concern* to them. . . . However, if they are a part of the state, it is obvious that their very *social existence* already constitutes their *real participation* in it. Not only do they share in the state, but the state is their share. To be a conscious part of a thing means to take part of it and to take part in it consciously. Without this consciousness the member of the state would be an animal.[41]

Reality ("real concern," "real participation") and consciousness are here nearly synonymous. "Deliberation and decision" are the means by which the state can be effectively realized on the plane of "social existence." What distinguishes human beings from brute animal existence is (quintessentially Feuerbachian) consciousness.[42]

Even as he reconceives of Feuerbachian species-being in terms of social existence, Marx defines the agency of the *Volk*—the real social protagonist beneath Hegel's mystifications—in terms of a collective (or species) consciousness, opposed to abstraction and base materialism equally:

> In monarchy the whole, the people, is subsumed under one of its forms of existence, the political constitution; in democracy the *constitution itself* appears only as *one* determining characteristic of the people, and indeed as its self-determination. In monarchy we have the people of the constitution, in democracy the constitution of the people. Democracy is the solution to the riddle of every constitution. In it we find the constitution founded on its true ground: *real human beings* and the *real people*; not merely implicitly and in essence, but in *existence* and in reality. The constitution is thus posited as the people's *own* creation. The constitution is in appearance what it is in reality: the free creation of man.[43]

For all its rhetoric of the real, in Marx's claim that in true democracy the constitution is "founded on its true ground: *real human beings* and the *real people* . . . in *existence* and in reality," what is most "real" about "*das wirkliche Volk*" remains a form of consciousness. Andrew Chitty maintains that Marx's conception of the essence of the state in his 1842 journalism remains close to Hegel's, even if Marx has a decidedly republican orientation and "suggests that it is the will of the people as a whole that should be the highest authority in the state."[44] As Chitty argues, Marx's various statements to this effect "remain compatible with the underlying Hegelian conception of the state and its essence . . . as long as the will of the people is not defined as whatever majority opinion on a matter is, but as a will that expresses and demands the institutionalisation of the freedom, reason, and equality realised in the people's spirit, and everything Marx says on the subject is consonant with such an 'idealising' conception of the people's will."[45] Chitty's point holds for much of Marx's critique of Hegel's conception of the state in the Kreuznach *Kritik* as well.[46] If Marx charged Hegel with assigning an allegorical status to specific real persons and groups, Marx himself assigns a real status to what remains an idealized group, *das Volk*.[47] Marx follows Feuerbach in conceiving of true humanity in terms of species consciousness. Humanity—or, in political terms, the *Volk*—is little more than a hypostatized substrate of such free consciousness. Despite Marx's assault on Hegel's abstraction, the will of Marx's people remains essentially synonymous with the rational essence of the state.

Even as Marx invokes the *Volk* as the real foundation beneath the abstraction of Hegel's Idea, it is real qua human (ideal, rational, conscious) in contrast to the animal realm that, in Marx's assessment, Hegel's philosophy mystifies without transforming. There is no contradiction per se in Marx's use of different conceptions of (good and bad) materialism and (good and bad) idealism, but it is important to note the double nature of each. As Marx continues his project of rethinking Feuerbachian species-being in social terms, the idealized *Volk* yields to other, more emphatically material signifiers: first to the "real Jews" of "Zur Judenfrage," then to the proletariat of "Einleitung." In the course of this evolution, good and bad reality—kept neatly separate in the Kreuznach *Kritik*—intersect, and it is precisely this intersection that defines the theoretical ambivalence of "Zur Judenfrage," to anticipate my reading of this text.[48]

Marx charges that Hegel "does not allow society to become a truly determining thing because this would require a *real* subject while he has nothing more than an abstract one, a figment of the *imagination*."[49] In the works that immediately followed the Kreuznach *Kritik*, Marx continued to grapple with how to theorize society as the "real subject." Although Marx appropriated Feuerbach to overcome Hegel's abstraction, Marx would soon have to confront what he would come to see—by spring 1845, when he wrote "Theses on Feuerbach"—as Feuerbach's own abstraction. Feuerbach never convincingly integrated his celebration of sensuous existence with his privileging of the agency of species consciousness, and Marx would place the integration of agency and social materiality at the center of his theoretical agenda. His quest to replace Hegel's abstraction of ethical spirit in the state with a real social subject demanded a rethinking of the relationship between social materiality and consciousness as these pertained to revolutionary agency and the closely related role of criticism and the critic.

These questions were at the core of Marx's debate with Bruno Bauer, and it was largely in and through this debate that Marx's theorization of this tangle of issues rapidly evolved. Examining texts by Marx from the *Deutsch-französische Jahrbücher* that exemplify his thinking on these issues before and after "Zur Judenfrage" will bring into focus the conceptually ambivalent and pivotal nature of that text and the work that the figure of "real Jews" performs in it.

Bookends of "Zur Judenfrage"

Marx's pieces in the *Deutsch-französische Jahrbücher* that bookend "Zur Judenfrage"—his letters to Ruge that precede and the "Einleitung" that follow it—dramatize the volatility of Marx's ideas in 1843. The upheaval in his conception of the role of materiality in social agency left a certain theoretical void at the center of Marx's evolving critical project, a conceptual lack for which, I argue, he attempts to compensate in no small part through rhetorical *effets de réel*. At this turning point between idealism and inchoate materialism, Marx's work reveals an abiding preoccupation with abjection. Abject positivity (or animal materialism) had served as a foil for human rationality and autonomous agency in Marx's thinking up to this juncture, but in 1843 it becomes a complex and vexed focal point in its own right.

Three letters that Marx wrote to Ruge while working on the Kreuznach *Kritik* appeared (probably in revised form) in the *Deutsch-französische Jahrbücher* as part of a wider correspondence that served as an introduction of sorts to that new journal.[50] In the first letter (March 1843) Marx savages the stupidity, despotism, and Romantic delusions of Friedrich Wilhelm IV but ends on a hopeful note: the German ship of fools will eventually drift to its own demise in political revolution. Ruge replied pessimistically that Germans are too resigned and docile to make a revolution. In his letter of May 1843 Marx disputes Ruge's pessimism about the political maturity of the German nation and insists that Germany will, eventually, achieve political freedom. Still conceiving of real engagement and change under the banner of politics, Marx faults Ruge's resigned pessimism for not being "political." The political protagonist in whom Marx refuses to abandon hope remains, here, the *Volk*. Ruge's letter was "a fine elegy, a funeral song that takes one's breath away; but there is absolutely nothing political about it. No people wholly despairs [*kein Volk verzweifelt* (my addition)], and even if for a long time it goes on hoping merely out of stupidity, yet one day, after many years, it will suddenly become wise and fulfill all its pious wishes."[51]

Yet Marx combines this broadly optimistic view of the German *Volk*'s political future with a dramatically bleak assessment of its present. He savages the self-confirming "realism" of the philistine Germans, both rulers and ruled, and vividly depicts Germany as a sub-human "politische Tierwelt" (political animal kingdom). Here Marx goes Ruge one further and declares Germany and Germans hopeless, brainless, and utterly abject:

> The Germans are such prudent realists that their desires and loftiest thoughts do not go beyond bare life. And this reality—nothing more—is accepted by those who rule over them. These latter people, too, are realists, they are very far removed from any kind of thoughts and from any human greatness; they are ordinary officers and country squires, but they are not mistaken, they are right; just as they are, they are quite capable of exploiting [*benutzen*

(my addition)] this animal kingdom and ruling over it, for here, as everywhere, ruling and exploiting [*Benutzung* (my addition)] are a *single* concept. And when they have homage paid to themselves and survey the swarming mass of these brainless beings, what is more likely to occur to them than the thought that Napoleon had at the Berezina? It is said of him that he pointed to the crowd of drowning people below and exclaimed to his companion: "Voyez ces crapauds!" This is probably a fabrication, but it is true nonetheless. Despotism's only thought is contempt for humanity, the dehumanized human being, and this thought has the advantage over many others of at the same time being a fact. The despot always sees people as degraded. They drown before his eyes and for his sake in the slime of vulgar life, from which, like toads, they continually reemerge. If such a view obtrudes even upon men who were capable of great aims, such as Napoleon before his dynastic madness, how can a completely ordinary king in such a reality [*in einer solchen Realität* (my addition)] be an idealist?[52]

In labeling the Germans "realists" Marx is not paying them a compliment, but rather assailing their failure to achieve what we could call the "good idealism" of politics. If politics is the Aristotelian measure of man, the Germans remain animals, reduced to the prepolitical concerns of "bare life" (*das kahle Leben*). The collective German failure to achieve political consciousness attenuates (without, to be sure, erasing) the distinction between the ruled and their rulers. Marx's idealist conception of human rationality leads him to focus, above all, on German rulers' incapacity to think of their subjects as human beings. Instead, they regard them with a self-fulfilling dehumanizing contempt. The German toads die and are continuously reborn out of the German muck, and neither these brainless, abjectly dehumanized beings nor "even" the mediocre despots who lord it over them are capable of transcending German animal *Realität* and achieving the consciousness of *homo politicus*. Although Marx refuses to give up on the *Volk* as the collective subject that will eventually realize itself in a democratic republic, real existing Germans remain a sub-*Volk*, a primordial political animal kingdom outside the narrative of modern political history. Marx makes no attempt here to ground his theoretical discourse in, or ally it with, Germany's materiality or "reality." On the contrary, abject German reality is the emphatic Other of democracy and humanity and of "idealists" like Marx and his dissident colleagues "who have the audacity to want to turn men into human beings."[53]

It bears underscoring that even in his "idealist" conception of politics and the state as the realization of human rationality, Marx did not champion the state as a sphere apart. The true state would permeate all aspects of reality.[54] Nonetheless, in this letter the elusive *Volk*—which will, eventually, express itself in a true state—remains the idealized embodiment of rational principles and not the actual *Volk* existing in the real world of German slime.[55]

Marx goes on to portray German dehumanization as the flip side of the monarchical principle: "The monarchical principle in general is the despised, the despicable, *the dehumnised man*."[56] The subjects of the Prussian king are deprived of their humanity because "in Prussia the king is the system. He is the sole political person. In one way or another, his personality determines the system."[57] This dehumanizing principle is inherent in the monarchical system, no matter what the king's personal aspirations might be. Marx champions radical republicanism, the "consequences" [*Folgen*] of the political revolution in France, as the "idealists'" antidote to the monarchical system that monopolizes political personality in the person of the king and reduces all others to subhuman status.[58]

Critics have seen an anticipation of Marx's later understanding of the proletariat in the way out of the German impasse that Marx envisions at the end of this letter. This reading is valid to an extent (not least because Marx's first conception of the proletariat modifies, without radically rethinking, Hegel's idealist dialectic), but it is also indicative of a wish, in hindsight, to read the evolution of Marx's thought as the progressive distillation of later Marxian ideas.[59] Marx explains to Ruge that "if, nevertheless, I do not despair of [the present time], that is only because it is precisely the desperate situation which fills me with hope."[60] Whence will come this reversal? From a convergence between thinking and suffering humanity—"enemies of philistinism," a "new type of humanity"—that the industrial age is producing with unprecedented speed:

> The system of industry and trade, of ownership and exploitation of people . . . leads . . . to a rupture within present-day society. . . . But the existence of suffering human beings, who think, and thinking human beings, who are oppressed, must inevitably become unpalatable and indigestible for the passively and thoughtlessly consuming animal world of philistinism.
>
> For our part, we must expose the old world to the full light of day and shape the new one in a positive way. The longer the time that events allow to thinking humanity for taking stock of its position, and to suffering mankind for mobilising its forces, the more perfect on entering the world will be the product that the present time bears in its womb.[61]

The "product" Marx here envisions is republican democracy, the "consequence" of the French Revolution. Although Marx's theorization of the alliance between thinking and suffering humanity as the force that will eventually effect political revolution indeed anticipates the alliance between critic and proletariat in "Einleitung," there are crucial differences. As we will see shortly, there is a neat division of labor in "Einleitung" between the thinking critic and the suffering proletariat, and the envisioned outcome of this alliance is social—not political—revolution. No clear distinction between the roles of thinkers and sufferers obtains in Marx's May 1843 letter: thinking human beings are oppressed, and suffering human beings think. And even as Marx anticipates the proletariat when he associates this new suffering humanity with the rise of industry and trade and the forms of human exploitation they entail, what defines the new suffering humanity is not that it suffers but that it thinks: it is political consciousness that distinguishes this "new type of humanity"—that is, political animals—from its passive, brainless German counterpart. It is thought—political or human consciousness—that renders ineffectual passive suffering active.

This, surely, is one reason why Marx expends no energy depicting the suffering of this new group, in contrast to his considerable investment in depicting the animality of subpolitical Germans. Their suffering is not productive per se but is rather a force that serves as a yardstick for and galvanizes active conscious thought. Marx can allude to the suffering of this emerging humanity on German soil, but to elaborate on or depict the nature of its suffering as extreme would erode its status as an active, productive political agent in contradistinction to the essentially passive subpolitical animal order. Even as he enlists a new kind of suffering humanity in the cause of creating a political revolution in Germany, Marx continues to privilege thought and consciousness as the active agent in this political (human) transformation.

By the end of the period reflected in the one double issue of *Deutsch-französische Jahrbücher*, Marx's investment in abjection had shifted from bemoaning the stupidity of toady German philistines to his first theorization of the proletariat. Although thought remains an—arguably the primary—active force in Marx's new conception of the proletariat, the proletariat's abject suffering becomes a productive force in its own right. One of the chief innovations of "Zur Judenfrage" is that Marx abandons faith in politics per se and in the political protagonist, the *Volk*. The endpoint of this trajectory in the abject, but potentially active and redemptive, proletariat helps bring into focus the conceptual strain of "Zur Judenfrage," the fractured late 1843 text that mediates between these two theoretical positions.

The first half of Marx's "Einleitung," written in late 1843 and early 1844—immediately after, and possibly concurrently with portions of, "Zur Judenfrage"—deals with different aspects of the reality and nonreality of Germany. The opposition of philosophy to reality largely misses the point in the German context, Marx contends, because it is only in the philosophy it has produced that Germany has achieved reality; only in its thinkers—above all, Hegel and Marx's fellow Young Hegelians—is Germany the contemporary of modern society (France) and politics (England).

In "Zur Judenfrage" Marx radicalizes the critique he began in the Kreuznach *Kritik* of the state as an illusory realm that offers only a fiction of universal equality and dignity while perpetuating real social injustice. In "Einleitung" he tries to envision a possibility of true human emancipation via social, not political, revolution, and he introduces the proletariat as the hero of this drama. His invention of the proletariat fulfills two key functions. First, it serves as the hopelessly backward German *Volk*'s saving grace, and second, it is the German theorist's practical partner and legitimating foundation: "As philosophy finds its *material* weapons in the proletariat, so the proletariat finds its *spiritual* weapons in philosophy. And once the lightning of thought has squarely struck this ingenuous [*naiven* (my addition)] soil of the people the emancipation of the *Germans* into *human beings* will take place."[62]

Marx can envision such a transformation occurring in politically retarded Germany because he now thinks of politics essentially as a detour on the way to true human emancipation. Although there exists no class in German society bold or vigorous enough to appear (however temporarily or falsely) to embody the universal interests of all of society and thus to carry out a political revolution (as the bourgeoisie had done in France), this apparent weakness could be a strength. Marx's hope is that Germany will be able to leapfrog over the illusory stage of political emancipation and achieve human emancipation through social revolution instead. Marx no longer calls for an idealist and political transcendence of abject German reality. He now theorizes human emancipation as a possibility of dialectical reversal inherent in the radical abjection of the German proletariat itself. Abjection has become Germany's last best hope as well as the material handmaiden—or perhaps the alibi—of the German theorist. Marx invents the proletariat, *in* theory, as the material partner *of* German theory. And it is difficult to imagine the proletariat being anywhere as utterly abject as in Marx's positing of it, which borders on theoretical sadism. To his own question "So where is the *positive* possibility of German emancipation?" Marx responds:

> Answer: In the formation of a class with *radical chains*, a class of civil society which is not a class of civil society, an estate which is the dissolution of all estates, a sphere which has a universal character by its universal suffering and claims no *particular right* because no *particular wrong* but *wrong generally*

> is perpetrated against it; which can no longer invoke a *historical* but only a *human* title; which does not stand in any one-sided antithesis to the consequences but in an all-round antithesis to the premises of the German state; a sphere, finally, which cannot emancipate itself without emancipating itself from all other spheres of society and thereby emancipating all other spheres of society, which, in a word, is the *complete loss* of man and hence can win itself only through the *complete rewinning of man*. This dissolution of society as a particular estate is the *proletariat*.[63]

The toads living and dying in the German muck, below the threshold of political life, reappear here, but with a dialectical difference. German reality is no longer defined in terms of a political deficit but rather, as embodied in the German proletariat, as a social force for overcoming the illusions and structural shortcomings of politics. The proletariat as the negation of humanity negates the negating force, agonistic civil society, and ushers in true human emancipation. This—Marx's first—proletariat figures a way out of civil society defined as a sphere of narrow egoism and self-interest precisely by manifesting the abject dissolution of the very possibility of selfhood. Marx posits the proletariat as the embodiment of "universal suffering"—that is, suffering so general and diffuse that it precludes the consolidation of any self-consciousness or class interest. By speaking for the proletariat Marx can claim to speak from a position at once universal and grounded. Indeed, he constructs his own perfect counterpart: material, the proletariat figures the possibility that Marx's ideas can be realized; mute, it leaves all the thinking and talking to him. The proletariat thus fills the void left by the derealization of politics, the reconception of the political in terms of alienation and illusion.

As ponderous as these questions are, I will bracket both the merits and shortcomings of Marx's particular discrediting of political modernity in order to underscore how Marx, in inserting the proletariat into a theoretical space once occupied by politics and the *Volk*, makes a new, powerful rhetorical strategy possible. In a kind of rhetorical multiplier effect Marx can now deploy the rhetorical force of his description of human suffering in support of his theory of social revolution. Human abjection is no longer the foil of human agency; instead, it is its motor. To the same extent that Marx theoretically abuses the proletariat—to the extent that he reduces them to an abject state beneath all possible self-interest, or selfhood *tout court*—he also enlists them in the service of a universal social revolution against the principles of private property and self-interest. The theoretical violence Marx directed at the German toads was essentially wasted; it served only to establish German animal conditions as the Other of the political agent, the *Volk*. Here, in contrast, Marx recuperates all of the theoretical force with which he obliterates the proletariat's human integrity, for it is their abjection that constitutes their universality, on a material plane beneath civil society rather than in the abstraction of a political heaven above it.[64]

Marx's theorization of, and self-positioning as a theoretician of, social abjection are fundamentally different, and basically incompatible, in his May 1843 letter to Ruge and in "Einleitung," but they are not internally ambivalent. "Zur Judenfrage," published together with these texts in the *Deutsch-französische Jahrbücher*, falls chronologically and conceptually between them and marks a highly ambivalent theoretical crossroad in Marx's evolving theory of social reality.

Marx, Bauer, and the Position of the Radical Critic

Marx's two-part "Zur Judenfrage" appeared in the guise of a review of two works by Bauer. The history of the relationship between Marx and Bauer is a crucial component of the complex nexus at which Marx's essay is situated. Marx heard lectures by Bauer in Berlin, and the two maintained a correspondence and friendship between 1838 and late 1842. Marx hoped through Bauer's influence to obtain a position in Bonn. This hope was dashed, however, when Bauer was dismissed from his position there in March 1842 by the new minister of culture, Johann Albrecht Friedrich von Eichhorn, a conservative anti-Hegelian appointed by Friedrich Wilhelm IV. In 1842 Bauer returned to Berlin and became the central figure of the *Freien* or freethinkers, a group of bohemian radical Young Hegelian intellectuals. Marx assumed the editorship of the *Rheinische Zeitung* on October 15, 1842, a position he held for five months before resigning, on March 17, 1843, in protest over the interference of the censor. As editor of the *Rheinische Zeitung* Marx quickly lost patience with his erstwhile colleagues in Berlin, in whose contributions he saw conceptual vacuity wedded to a self-indulgent extremism that was anything but helpful to Marx in his capacity as the editor of a liberal paper with pragmatic political aims.[65]

Remarks by Marx regarding the *Freien* in two letters from this period—one written some six weeks before, the other some six weeks after, he assumed the editorship of the *Rheinische Zeitung*—illuminate the nature of his understanding of Bauer's abstraction. In a letter from around August 25, 1842, to Oppenheim, Marx opines that the paper had erred in recently publishing a potentially highly controversial article by Edgar Bauer, Bruno Bauer's brother, on "The Juste-Milieu." Marx finds the real risks to the paper of increased censure or complete suppression far too great to warrant running an article whose call for criticism would at any rate have no effect on the powers that be, and would only alienate "the greatest part of freethinking practical men, who have taken on the arduous role of fighting for freedom step by step, within the constitutional frameworks, while we, from our comfortable armchair of abstraction, point out to them their contradictions."[66] Newspapers, Marx argues, are the proper forum for practical questions, which are part of the "real State" (*Fragen des wirklichen Staats, praktische Fragen*).[67] Marx mocks the armchair critic's self-aggrandizing conception of the efficacy of pure critique, which he opposes to practical work, such as the practice of journalism, and he urges Oppenheim to take a clearer editorial stand against contributions like Edgar Bauer's.

As editor of the *Rheinische Zeitung* Marx would eventually stop accepting contributions from the *Freien* altogether. In a letter to Ruge of November 30, 1842, he related demands he had recently made to the *Freien* regarding their submissions. He faulted the group for locating freedom in a cheaply shocking but finally comfortable form (*in einer lizentiösen, sanskülottischen und dabei bequemen Form*) rather than in substantive content.[68] Marx already viewed the critique of religion per se as an idle task and had demanded of the *Freien* that they incorporate the critique of religion into an analysis of secular political conditions, "because this approach fits better the nature of a newspaper and the education of the public, for religion has no content of its own and does not live from heaven but from earth and falls automatically with dissolution of the inverted reality whose theory it is."[69] From Marx's vantage point, the *Freien*—abstract and comfortably disengaged—mistook cheap scandal for true freedom and radical critique.[70]

Marx anticipated other aspects of his debate with Bauer in further correspondence with Ruge, most explicitly in a letter of March 13, 1843: "Just now the president of the Israelites here came to see me and asked for my support for a petition to the provincial parliament on behalf of the Jews, and I will give it. Although I find the Israelite faith repugnant, Bauer's opinions still seem to me to be too abstract. The point is to punch as many holes in the Christian state as possible and to smuggle in the rational as far as we can."[71]

Ruge would have been sympathetic to Marx's complaint about Bauer's hostility to pragmatism ("punching as many holes in the Christian state as possible," in Marx's pugnacious phrase). Ruge had mocked Bauer and the *Freien* in a letter of December 12, 1842, to his friend Moritz Fleischer.[72] After visiting them in a Berlin *Kneipe* (pub) that they frequented, Ruge was left with the impression that the group was ludicrously self-important and uncoupled from reality:

> [Bauer] wanted to defend all the both theoretical and practical extravagances, which are decidedly as arbitrary as Romanticism itself, and laid the

> most ridiculous things on me [*heftete mir die lächerlichsten Dinge auf die Nase*], e.g., the state and religion had to be dissolved *in the concept* [im Begriff *aufgelöst werden*], property and the family as well; what was to be done constructively [*positiv*] he [*man*] didn't know, he only knew that everything had to be negated, i.e. make a principle of the negativity of the frivolous world and suspend [*aufheben*] all certainty, all character, all enthusiasm for humanity's historical tasks, which one can never conceive of other than in positive terms. . . . It is sadly only too true that it really is the system of frivolity: not to recognize intellectual certainty as positive, but rather to dissolve each certainty immediately, due to its narrowness, into the laughter of the super-clever [*superklugen*] subject. . . . *Die Freien* are a frivolous and blasé clique.[73]

For a contextualized reading of Marx's "Zur Judenfrage" it is important to appreciate the nature of the inflammatory and emphatically antipragmatic stance Bauer was moving toward in 1842 and the role that his interventions on the Jewish Question played in this evolution. As Douglas Moggach notes, when Marx criticized Bauer and the *Freien* on tactical grounds in autumn 1842 the two nonetheless "shared a republican orientation."[74] Instead of the tactical recklessness of Bauer and the *Freien*, Marx called for a more pragmatic approach to contesting reigning political conditions. He also opposed "real" political conditions to contentless religion. In "Zur Judenfrage," roughly a year later, Marx would dismiss politics as essentially lacking in content. He had come to see religion and politics as different forms of abstraction away from a more fundamental social reality. Thus while Marx consistently sees Bauer as in some sense too abstract, after resigning as editor of the *Rheinische Zeitung* Marx had to rethink radically the nature of the reality he would oppose to Bauer's abstraction. If Marx's polemics with Bauer took shape around essentially tactical questions, they became more urgently implicated in Marx's self-definition as Marx struggled to define himself as a theorist and activist beyond the pale of liberal life and politics. Marx could no longer dismiss Bauer's mode of self-aggrandizing incendiary intellectual elitism with calls for a more pragmatic commitment to causes that Marx had now come to view as also radically insufficient. In "Zur Judenfrage" Marx begins to define his own theory and practice of radical critique in contrast to Bauer's, and to redefine the very ground from which he speaks.

Bauer was the most conspicuous self-styled radical critic on the German scene in 1842–43, precisely when Marx was struggling most acutely to redefine himself as a radical (postliberal) social critic. In the volatile period between Marx's abandoning liberal politics and his working out the precepts of historical materialism, Bauer was an important figure against whom Marx defined himself—both in terms of Bauer's theoretical positions and his posture, or his social self-positioning as a radical intellectual. In addition to working out his conceptual differences with Bauer in response to Bauer's writings on the Jewish Question, Marx was also working out, on a performative register, a counter-model of how socially to position himself as a radical critic. Their works on the Jewish Question were key moments for both Bauer and Marx, through which they changed not only their theoretical positions but also their postures and allegiances as radical intellectuals.

Bauer abruptly changed his critical posture at this moment, and not least in and through his writings on the Jewish Question. Bauer's dismissal from the University of Bonn for heterodoxy in March 1842 became a cause célèbre, and Bauer launched a campaign to mobilize liberal support for, as the title of his book put it, "Die gute Sache der Freiheit und meine eigene Sache" (the good cause of freedom and my own case).[75] It was in part in response to the failure of this campaign that Bauer adopted a more stridently elitist and antiliberal orientation. Moggach notes that the "immediate consequence" of the publication of Bauer's two essays on the Jewish Question "was that Bauer forfeited his leading position in the opposition movement, as he was seen to reject one of its central demands."[76] Bauer's antagonizing of his erstwhile allies was, however, by no means inadvertent.

The version of Bauer's *Die Judenfrage* to which Marx responds in "Zur Judenfrage" was the pamphlet that appeared in 1843, but Bauer had first published the essay in November 1842 in Ruge's *Deutsche Jahrbücher* (except for the conclusion, which the censor suppressed).[77] Bauer's remarks in a letter to Ruge of October 27, 1842, accompanying the manuscript of *Die Judenfrage* merit being quoted at length for the light they shed on his strategic intentions in writing the essay, as well as on his pronounced antipathy for Jews, including baptized Jews. He writes Ruge that the essay is the result of a study with which he has been occupied the entire summer, noting that it is

> complete, exhaustive; everything is new, yet correct—the only solution to the problem about which so much has been written—yet about which not a single accurate word has until now been produced. I've gone through the entire literature from Dohm and Mirabeau that has been written on the topic. They will be astonished, scream mightily, but we will thereby progress infinitely, and be done with the empty, disgusting theories that have circulated even in the *Rheinische Zeitung*. . . . We must break with all half-measures, all hypocrisy or unconsciousness, and on the Jewish Question up to now, only

this marvelous manure has propagated itself. All Jew friends and the Jews have up to now acted as though there were no such thing as *Kritik*. In order to be complete and to put all theology—including theological privilege—out of business, *Kritik* must now direct itself against Judaism [*das Judenthum*], the most disgusting form of privilege and monopoly.[78]

Bauer mentions in this letter that he had submitted the essay to the *Rheinische Zeitung* but that it had been rejected by the censor, which he imagines must have come as a relief to the newspaper's publishers, in particular Oppenheim (a Jewish convert to Protestantism).[79] Bauer continues:

> But Jewishness [*das jüdische*] so forcefully asserts privilege and monopoly that even the baptized ones can't dispense with monopoly. Those dogs want to have a monopoly against *Kritik*—quintessentially Jewish, all monopoly is Jewish—and the stupid Jew friends have all failed to see where the snag is that has got everything caught up. . . . There is only One salvation, only One possibility of progress: the break with all half-measures and all that is illusory! Thoroughgoing *Kritik*. . . . The deeper the concentration and the more austere the objective, the more enemies we will have, the more we will move forward, the clearer the cause will become, the more the friends of the old will stand out as embarrassed, baffled, and helpless, the more possible it will be that the all-deciding hour will arrive, the more we will act on the people [*das Volk*], and the more and better friends we will acquire.[80]

Beyond Bauer's outspoken aversion to *Judentum* (it is the "most disgusting form of privilege and monopoly"; the essential Jewish penchant for monopoly is not altered by conversion; the opponents of Bauer's form of critique are "dogs" and "quintessentially Jewish" because "all monopoly is Jewish"), this passage underscores Bauer's aim to be as provocative as possible. He declares war on any incrementalism that would seek to increase freedoms within the terms set by the Christian state. Referring to this letter, Hans-Martin Sass remarks: "The campaigns of pure *Kritik*, against all the rules of warcraft, aim to involve as many opponents as possible in the most decisive battles possible at the same time."[81] Rather than support Jewish emancipation as a pragmatic step in the right direction (as Marx consistently did) Bauer's *Die Judenfrage* attacks it—from an aggressively antipragmatic position—as an instance of half-measure, a compromise, a step that fails to break radically with the logic of privilege. Bauer's strategy is to polarize maximally, both by arguing against any form of compromise with the logic of privilege and by intentionally provoking the defenders of causes (in particular Jewish emancipation) that, in his eyes, manifested such a spirit of compromise. By exacerbating differences Bauer believed he could force fundamental conflicts to become more sharply defined and force their proponents to embrace their positions more consciously. In this way he believed historical contradictions would more quickly reach a crisis point and be resolved. His tone in the letter accompanying *Die Judenfrage* is at times apocalyptic; by exacerbating oppositions and provoking and proliferating enemies, he hopes to force history to its "all-deciding hour."

In 1841 Bauer had already elaborated a theoretical rejection of compromise in favor of strategic polarization.[82] It was first with his interventions on Jewish civil rights, however, that he put his theory into practice and spoke out against a concrete political demand that enjoyed almost universal support among progressives.[83] In so doing Bauer adopted an elitist posture that derealized—that is, categorized as inessential, illusory, and misguided—liberal politics while claiming for himself, as the voice of "pure critique," a position in the vanguard of world-historical agency.[84] Sass notes how Bauer collapses critique and praxis and privileges the reality of pure critique over a politics of pragmatic "compromise": "Because the model of pure critique in which theory, critique and practice coincide brooks no compromise or pragmatic mediation with existing conditions, the critic is personally thrust into the decisive battle in a completely different manner than when the critique still could comprise [*einkalkulieren*] possibilities for the theory to retreat and winter over [*Rückzugs und Überwinterungsmöglichkeiten*]. . . . The substance of absolute critique is ultimately incarnated in the critic himself."[85] The propositional content of pure critique, in other words, becomes inseparable from the strategic performance of the critic, Bauer, who articulates it. It is the predominance of the critic's utterance over the substance of his theoretical argument that renders it impossible to compromise or wait for a more auspicious season. In a double gesture Bauer derealizes his opponents—who are all beholden to "the old," the superseded—and casts the now of his own performative critical praxis as the cutting edge of world-historical consciousness's teleological advancement.

An integral part of Bauer's evolving self-definition as a "pure" critic involved denigrating as *die Masse* those he considered beneath his level of critical consciousness. During the same transitional period, as we have seen, Marx was moving away from his idealized conception of the *Volk* toward an alliance with emphatic "massiness" in the form of the proletariat, understood as the embodiment of revolutionary agency. These opposite trajectories away from (Bauer) and toward (Marx) social materiality have a common point of departure in a basically shared conception of the *Volk*, one that became untenable for each thinker with their divergent turns to postliberal radicalism. Moggach notes how Bauer's conception of the *Volk* as a unified revolutionary subject begins, in late 1843, to share the scene with and define itself against *die Masse*, a new category Bauer would go on to deploy expansively to refer, chiefly, to the liberal bourgeoisie but also to the working classes.[86] In an 1842 book review (which Marx found "exquisite [*köstlich*]"), Bauer equated *das Volk* with *Wahrheit*.[87] In and apropos of his writings on the Jewish Question, however, he begins to distinguish between a more restricted authentic *Volk* and *die Masse*, a pliant category under which he would come to subsume all the changing groups he deemed to be driven by particular interest rather than universal self-consciousness. In *Die Judenfrage* Bauer distinguishes between the universal *Volk* and particularistic *Masse* in the context of his critique of the illegitimacy and socially corrosive effects of the Christian state. His analysis of the pseudo-mediating instances in Hegel's model of the state has many parallels with Marx's Kreuznach *Kritik*. Because the sovereign powers are uncoupled from the authentic people, they require hordes of intermediaries to represent them for what is thus a "nonpeople . . . inauthentic people . . . minors [*die Unmündigen*]."[88] The "estate of intermediaries" is a prerogative awarded on the basis of birth or other arbitrary criteria having nothing to do with the mediatory function. The internally compartmentalized and segregated "inauthentic *Volk*," represented by the arbitrary appointees of the powers that be, "is precisely only the mass, which has no universal rights and is not permitted to have any universal consciousness."[89] Such "particular circles, constructed and determined by chance, which distinguish themselves according to their interests, particular passions and prejudices . . . receive, as a privilege, the permission to close themselves off one from another. They have—can and may have—no universal concern; so that they never so much as think about having universal concerns, autonomy and a private authority is granted them in the management of their particular affairs."[90] Bauer blames the state for disrupting the authentic *Volk*'s universal consciousness (*allgemeines Bewußtsein*) and reducing it to a "mass of the inauthentic people" (*Masse des uneigentlichen Volks*). By denying the authentic *Volk* universal rights and fracturing its universal consciousness, the illegitimate, privilege-based state divides the authentic *Volk* into a mass of particular interests.

Bauer here blames the Christian state for the diremption of the authentic *Volk* into the "mass" of competing interest groups. In his first response (of December 1843) to critics of his interventions on the Jewish Question, however, he—in an intentionally polarizing gesture—extends the category of the particularist *Masse* to include the liberal bourgeoisie.[91] Bauer's reply to critics of *Die Judenfrage* was the lead essay of the first issue of the *Allgemeine Literatur Zeitung*, which Bruno and Edgar Bauer launched and edited (and which Marx and Engels savage in *Die heilige Familie*). The text—and with it the new journal—opens with a broadside against the historical irrelevance of the German liberal bourgeoisie, whom Bruno Bauer now subsumes under the derogatory label "*die Masse*," and then addresses specific non-Jewish and Jewish critics of his provocative positions. Bauer now deems the German liberal bourgeoisie to be complicitous with the state for making compromises with, rather than radically opposing, its principle of privilege—notably, in the bourgeoisie's support of Jewish emancipation.[92]

Bauer proceeded via a critique of the purported pure particularity of the Jews to a notion of "massiness" that redefined and displaced his earlier understanding of the *Volk*. In contrast, Marx deployed the Jews as a middle term between the *Volk* and the proletariat. Bauer's conceptual realignment renders explicit the ideal quality of the *Volk* as he—and Marx—had been using it. This was not a problem for Bauer, since his turn to postliberal radicalism proceeded via a supercilious and self-aggrandizing posture that set his own critical practice (characterized by true reality and revolutionary agency) emphatically against the only apparent reality of the institutions and opponents he subsumed under the protean category of massiness. For Marx, who was striving to overcome the sort of abstraction and theoretical solipsism he saw Bauer embracing and to position his analysis on a solid basis in social reality, the loss of the *Volk* as a viable theoretical and political protagonist was more problematic. Although Bauer set himself apart from the mass, Marx needed a massy social counterpart to legitimize his antiphilosophy. It was on the way to the massy protagonist—the proletariat—that Marx had his brief encounter with the massy antagonist, real Jews.

Bauer's Secular Salvation History

A full account of Bauer's writings on Jewish rights exceeds the scope of this chapter. Since these are the texts to which Marx responds in "Zur Judenfrage," however, and because they provide much of the very language Marx uses by both direct and indirect citation, some familiarity with Bauer's argument is indispensable for understanding how Marx uses Bauer's discourse as a conceptual and performative foil. Bauer insists that meaningful liberation requires overcoming particularistic identity—the logic of monopoly and privilege that divides and enslaves humanity. In demanding emancipation, Jews make a particularistic appeal (they appeal as Jews) for rights, a universal category. Bauer thus sees any Jewish appeal to rights as caught in a self-disqualifying enunciatory paradox.[93] In appealing to the Christian state, moreover, Jews make demands of an entity that is structurally incapable of fulfilling them. Supporters of Jewish emancipation willy-nilly support the cause's particularistic framework instead of opposing the very principle of division and privilege, which Bauer sees as the fundamental obstacle to universal liberation.

David Leopold underscores the inconsistency in Bauer's treatment of Christianity and its relationship to Judaism in his writings on the Jewish Question. On the one hand, Bauer casts Christianity as superior to and indeed a supersession of Judaism. On the other hand, he considers Christianity as merely one manifestation of the egoistic principle undergirding all religion.[94] Within the framework of a general critique of religious egoism Bauer urges Jews and Christians alike to overcome their religious limitations and embrace universal human self-consciousness. Although he states at the end of "Die Fähigkeit der heutigen Juden und Christen, frei zu werden" that this will be much more difficult for Jews than Christians, he at least appears to consider it possible for Jews as well. However, the thrust of the competing framework—Bauer's secularized Christian supersessionism—defines Jews as essentially unable to achieve free subjectivity and participate in the unfolding drama of infinite self-consciousness.

Moggach has attempted to square Bauer's writings on the Jewish Question with his mode of "republican rigorism," an austere form of republicanism that demands that citizens accord with (an essentially Kantian model of) universal moral principles—not only outwardly, in their actions, but also inwardly, in their interests and motivations.[95] Bauer's demand to transcend religious consciousness inwardly does indeed appear to apply to all potential citizens. Jews, it is true, would have to stop being Jews, but Christians would likewise have to stop being Christians. Bauer's more pernicious strain, however, reveals the parallelism in his treatment of Jews and Christians to be only apparent. As I read Bauer, he understands the enunciatory Catch-22 in which he sees Jews caught whenever they demand civil rights to be, finally, ontologically determined and inescapable. He argues not only that Jews need to do more work than Christians to achieve human freedom, but also that they are incapable of doing precisely this work. This strain in Bauer excludes Jews from humanity and makes his position on Jewish emancipation incompatible with any republican model worthy of the name.

As Moggach points out, the key to Bauer's version of the Hegelian unity of concept and being lies in a teleology of human freedom, an understanding of human history as in constant development toward greater freedom and self-determination. By fusing ontology and history in defining human essence as the historical development of free self-consciousness, Bauer defines people, such as Jews, whom he deems to have outlived their contribution to this teleological development as having exhausted their very humanity.[96] Bauer does not advance the thesis that Jews are merely unhistorical—outside the flow of human *Entwicklung* but potentially able to rejoin and participate in it. He argues, rather, that Jews are fundamentally antihistorical: they oppose free human development merely by virtue of their continued existence, and they prolong their pseudo-existence only insofar as they oppose such development.[97]

In this way Bauer prefigures his later opposition between *Kritik* and *die Masse* with his distinction in *Die Judenfrage* between authentic historical *Völker*, who advance free self-consciousness, and the chimerical Jewish people qua historical dead weight and inert particularity, precisely the qualities Bauer would soon subsume under the rubric of massiness. The *Volk-Masse* dichotomy that redefines Bauer's earlier and more broadly affirmative conception of the *Volk* (and his own self-positioning as a critic), in other words, emerges in large part through his opposition between the authentic historical *Volk* and the chimerical Jewish *Volk*:

> We were all excluded through our limitations; everyone was limited, and upon the Jewish quarter border the quarters in which we are pigeonholed [*rubricirt*].
>
> Not only the Jews, but we too no longer want to be satisfied with a chimera; we too wish to become a real people, real peoples.
>
> If the Jews wish to become a real people—however, they cannot do this in their chimerical nationality, but rather only in the nations of our age that are historical and capable of participating in history [*geschichtsfähigen und geschichtlichen*]—then they must give up the chimerical prerogatives that will, as long as they cling to them, always separate them from the nations [*Völkern*] and alienate them from history. They must sacrifice their unbelief in the nations and their exclusive belief in their groundless nationality before they will even in the slightest be able to put themselves in the position to take part in real affairs of the state and the people.
>
> We, however, must give up our unbelief in the world in general and in the right of the human being—and must thus give up our exclusive faith in monopoly and minority—before we can think about being and remaining real peoples, and true human beings within the life of the people [*des Volkslebens*].[98]

Bauer insists that all of "us" are just as oppressed as the Jews, even as he emphasizes an implicit ontological distinction between Jews and "us." Whereas Jews are essentially limited, "we" have wrongly been confined to particularistic categories. Typically, while Bauer calls for both Jews and Christians to become historical peoples, he insists that only Christians and not Jews can accomplish this task. Christians need only an attitude adjustment; Jews need a complete ontological makeover. Christians need only shed their erroneous belief in the unreality of the world and in their immaturity [*Unmündigkeit*] and affirm the historical existence that they already, essentially, possess. In Bauer's historical ontology Jews must sacrifice themselves *to* historical development.[99] Jews must realize that, as a people, they have no real historical existence, and try to become incorporated into a people that does. Bauer's historicized conception of human agency, however, renders this reentry into history essentially parasitic and thus impossible. As Bauer repeatedly makes clear, since humanity is constituted in active participation in the historical unfolding of human freedom, Jews cannot receive human freedom as a gift.[100] Bauer's dialectical conception of human development as the historicized unity of concept and being equates possessing historical reality with actively contributing to historical development. Since Christians, according to Bauer, have actively contributed to the development of free self-consciousness, they will ultimately be able to discover the true human core of their theologically misapprehended agency. Jews, however, are essentially inert and thus can only obstruct free humanity's advance. They possess no human essence that could be liberated from its theological shell.

If Bauer deems the task of becoming real historical peoples so achievable for Christians, it is because his concept of free human consciousness amounts to a secularized version of Christian spirit, defined over against a conception of Judaism as an inert positivity. Bauer casts Jews' very being as a kind of doing, a culpable act. This negative agency retains no positive content of its own, because any positive content Judaism historically possessed has been *aufgehoben* in Christianity. Judaism remains only as dead weight, a kind of unproductive refuse. It merely stands in the way, in and through its stubborn insistence on persisting beyond all possible rationales for existence. In this way Bauer contests the idea that the Jews could have suffered innocently. He gives the Jews backhanded credit for their historical persecution, arguing that they, in their very being (*Sein*), have caused it themselves: "[The Jews] were . . . themselves to blame for the oppression they suffered, because they provoked it by their adherence to their law, their language, to their whole essence. A nothing cannot be oppressed. Whatever is oppressed must have caused the oppression by virtue of its entire being and the nature of that being."[101] Bauer's construction of Judaism's ontological guilt becomes clearer in his description of the nature of Judaism's opposition to historical progress. He deems the Jewish *Volksgeist* consistent in its inconsistency, for "it does not really progress in its progress, does not really develop in its development,"[102] despite the higher ideas that Judaism (especially the Prophets) may contain. To the extent that Judaism contains a kernel of universal truth, Jews must paradoxically evade it in order to continue to exist, for the truth of (their own) history is that there is no longer any historical justification for their continuing existence. Since Jews can neither participate in history nor prevent history from progressing, they can only deny (*verläugnen*) history.[103] In defining Jewish existence as an active denial of the historical truth of the nullity of that very existence, Bauer inscribes guilt in Jews' very being. Continued Jewish existence becomes a crime against history and, given Bauer's definition of humanity in terms of free self-consciousness's historical unfolding, against humanity itself. At a fateful dialectical fork in the road, Jews opted for particular existence over truth and so lost their historical innocence; they have become *geschichtswidrig*: "Under these circumstances, he [the Jew] is, however, no longer what he was: (the Jew capable of this particular development, who had it before him and necessarily had to posit [*setzten*] it): after that development and after he has denied it, he is instead the Jew who exists contra the intention of his history, thus also despite his history, the Jew who exists in opposition to his determination—in short the history-transgressing [*geschichtswidrige*] Jew."[104] Bauer places Jews in a dialectical double bind: if the Jew realizes (*verwirklichen*) the ideas to which his history and faith lead (that is, his historical truth), then he cannot remain "the real Jew" (*der wirkliche Jude*). Jews are not merely stubborn; they owe their very existence to their stubbornness. Their existence is thus so wrongheaded as to constitute a wrong (*Unrecht*): "The fact that he [the Jew] must be so stubborn and groundless [*haltlos*]—because he could no longer be the lawful [*gesetzliche*] and exclusive, i.e. the real, Jew [*der wirkliche Jude*] if he realized [*verwirklichte*] the ideas to which his history and his faith led him of themselves—makes his entire essence a contradiction, his existence a sickly one, indeed even a wrong [*Unrecht*]."[105] Jews can preserve their existence only by evading the truth of their essential nonexistence through the "chimerical" and "hypocritical" midrashic and Talmudic reinterpretation of Jewish law.[106] Thus the Jews' historical-ontological guilt is inescapable; the measure of their *Unrecht* is their continued existence itself.

Albeit in the name of a radically atheistic interpretation of history, Bauer only secularizes, without fundamentally rethinking, Christian triumphalism and Christian Jew-hatred.[107] He rehearses secularized versions of the Christian theological bias that deems Jews stubborn and interprets Jewish suffering as bearing witness to a divine curse (*Fluch*). In his secularization of the latter idea, Bauer interprets the *Fluch* under which Jews suffer as the consequence of the contradictory relationship they maintain to history: "What one calls the divine curse is nothing but the natural consequence of a law, that, in itself already chimerical and unable to build the soul of a real life of a people [*eines wirklichen Volkslebens*], contradicts the development that alone could lend it a certain support [*Halt*], and wishes to preserve itself uncoupled from it. The supposed divine curse consists in nothing else than the natural consequences of the contradiction into which the Jews have brought themselves with history at large and with their law."[108] Bauer substitutes his secular dialectic of infinite human consciousness for the Christian theology of a *Fluch*. Divine judgment disappears, and Bauer locates Christians simply on the right, and Jews on the wrong, side of history. Constituted in heteronymous (and eventually perfectly chimerical) law rather than the historical law of autonomous *Entwicklung*, Jews can only be mangled, never improved, by the workings of the historical dialectic. Thus while history propels Christians in the right direction eventually, Jews remain barred from true historical participation.

The same secularized Christian supercessionism structures "Die Fähigkeit," Bauer's second, shorter contribution to the debate around the Jewish Question. In this philosophy of history Christians appear as cryptohumans: they contain, within their alienated consciousness, a true human core that needs only to be liberated. Jews, in contrast, are defined by their historical-ontological *Unrecht*: they are nothing but the husk that history, with the advent of Christianity, has sloughed off. Although it has become incumbent on Christians—in the wake of the Enlightenment, the French Revolution, and Bauer's (in his own assessment) epochal brand of *Kritik*—to overcome their theological narrowness, they possess the necessary force to do so. Antithetical to human *Entwicklung*, Jews, however, cannot develop a human core that, Bauer insists, they radically lack. Instead they must cease to exist. Here, too, Bauer simultaneously calls on Jews to transcend their particularity and defines Jews as incapable of such self-transcendence.[109] In "Die Fähigkeit," the main intertext of the second part of Marx's "Zur Judenfrage," Bauer contrasts, perhaps still more emphatically than in *Die Judenfrage*, Christian universal spirit with the Jewish orientation to material practice and need. He presents the base materiality of Jewish practice as evidence of Jews' lack of true human spirit and historical agency, a contrast that will largely structure Marx's strategy of exploiting Jewish materiality in his attempt to counter Bauer's overvaluation of the agency of autonomous self-consciousness with an inchoate theory of materialist praxis.

Bauer contends Christianity has a human core that enables it to contest itself. Since according to Bauer "the full human being," "developed consciousness," and the "spirit that nowhere sees a limit that contains it" are nowhere to be found in Judaism, it has no resources at its disposal for such a struggle.[110] Instead of participating in the development of free human consciousness, Judaism remains limited to the satisfaction of natural needs:

> The struggle against Christianity was . . . only possible on the part of Christians, because it itself, and it alone, had grasped the human being, consciousness, as the essence of all things, and it was only a matter of dissolving this religious representation [*Vorstellung*] of the human being, a representation that actually destroyed [*vernichtete*] all humanity, since according to it only One is Everything. The Jew, on the other hand, was far too preoccupied with the satisfaction of his still natural needs—which required of him his physical [*sinnlich*], religious tasks, his ablutions, purifications, his religious selection and purification of daily foods—to be able to think about what a human being is per se. He could not struggle against Christianity because he did not even know what was at stake in this contest.[111]

Although Christian spirit need only be secularly *aufgehoben* to become infinite self-consciousness, Jews are too preoccupied with their practical cult even to think about *den Menschen überhaupt*. Echoing Feuerbach's characterization of Judaism in *Das Wesen des Christentums* as a cult involving no more than the satisfaction of base needs, and remarks of his own in *Die Judenfrage*, Bauer characterizes Judaism as a set of rites concerned with earthy, bodily tasks.[112] Bauer continues this line of argument by distinguishing between Christian and Jewish casuistry. Although all religions are by their nature "Jesuitical," Christian casuistry is a confused, religious pursuit of real, universal human values, whereas Jewish casuistry is pure material egoism, a self-serving hypocrisy devoid of intellectual content: "Jewish Jesuitism is merely the slyness of sensual egoism, common cleverness, and . . . because it always has to do with totally natural, physical needs, is brute, crass hypocrisy. It is so crass and repulsive that one can only turn away from it in disgust, but cannot even seriously contest [*bestreiten*] it."[113] For Bauer Jewish practice is "animal cunning" and a "slyness of empirical egoism" that, in its natural, sensual orientation, is repulsive (*widerlich*) and fills the rational observer with disgust (*Ekel*).[114] Marx will try to harness the force of the repulsiveness of Jewish material egoism for his own purposes in the second half of his polemical response to Bauer.

Marx's "Zur Judenfrage": Overview

In his polemic response to Bauer, Marx gives notoriously short shrift to the finer points of Bauer's arguments and exploits formulations from Bauer's text that do not accurately represent the balance of Bauer's position. In particular, Marx's central claim—that Bauer calls only for political emancipation but not real human emancipation—seriously misrepresents the thrust of much of

Bauer's argument, which is precisely that citizens must—in reality and not just formally—overcome their religious attitudes and all other forms of particularist privilege and consciousness as a prerequisite for meaningfully realizing a universal state.[115] Only with this prerequisite would political emancipation have a chance to become true human emancipation, to paraphrase Bauer's position in Marx's idiom.

At the heart of Marx's emerging polemic against his erstwhile friend and colleague, however, is Marx's inchoate attempt to theorize historical agency in social and material terms. Marx could so closely associate Bauer's methodology with the limitations he perceived in political emancipation, I argue, not because Bauer collapses political and human freedom but because Marx now sees in politics the sort of problematic abstraction he had long objected to in Bauer. Marx now sees Bauerian self-consciousness, political liberation, and religious salvation as structurally analogous and as far too abstract agents of transformation. Yet although Marx contended—against the overvaluation of human consciousness in various guises (theological, political, critical)—that the motor of human liberation must be grounded in social reality, his grounding of his social critique could be little more than rhetorical until he developed the materialist theory of labor and production that offered a satisfying alternative to the idealist theory of agency he was struggling to overcome.[116]

Even as Bauer's and Marx's changing assessments of politics—and the social critic's self-definition in relation to politics—are at the heart of Marx's emerging disagreement with Bauer, the fact that each thinker, albeit differently, derealizes politics renders the terms of Marx's polemic against Bauer unstable. Bauer derealizes pragmatic political causes with *Die Judenfrage* and begins megomaniacally to consolidate "real" historical agency in his own pure critical activity. In "Zur Judenfrage," Marx sharpens the diagnosis he had begun in his 1843 Kreuznach *Kritik* of politics as an ineffectual, essentially theological abstraction. Marx's disparagement of the substance of politics gives him a new tool to attack Bauer's abstraction from a locus purportedly more grounded in reality than is Bauer's mode of criticism (which Marx now closely associates with the limitations—or abstraction—of political emancipation), yet it also ambiguates this very "reality." In his jab at Bauer's position as "too abstract" in his letter to Ruge of March 13, 1843, Marx, as a political journalist, had aligned himself with the liberal task of punching holes in the authoritarian Christian state. Even as Marx in "Zur Judenfrage" continues to recognize "actual, practical" political emancipation as "a great step forward," he could no longer appeal to a pragmatic political agenda as a counterweight to Bauer's abstraction.[117] Politics becomes at this moment a slippery category for Marx; although he defines his own critical practice—over against Bauer's "theological" orientation—as the critique of emphatically secular politics, the innovative thrust of his critique of politics is to expose its lack of substantive reality, its essentially theological nature. Thus Marx's attempt to ground his critique solidly in reality paradoxically erodes the solidity of the very reality—the world of secular politics—to which he lays claim.

Ironically, at the precise moment at which it becomes more urgent for Marx to distinguish his theory and praxis from Bauer's, it also becomes more difficult to do so. By diagnosing the secular state as the completion or consummation of the Christian state (*die Vollendung des christlichen Staats*),[118] Marx becomes trapped in a certain circularity: he insists both that secular politics represents the true basis of the religious epiphenomena on which Bauer remains narrowly focused *and* that secular politics is inherently more theological than religion per se could ever be. Secular political conditions are the foundation of religious consciousness, but a foundation that eventually morphs into its own theological antithesis. Lacking a pragmatic engagement (journalism) and faith in political pragmatism, Marx—at the moment of his pivoting to radicalism—seemed, like Bauer, to have little more to fall back on than critique itself.

The insufficiency of Marx's finally circular attempt to ground his analysis in empirical conditions in part 1 of his "Zur Judenfrage" (hereafter ZJ1) is a crucial preamble to the markedly different tone, strategy, and analytic model he adopts in part 2 (hereafter ZJ2), where he leans heavily on the emphatic reality of "real Jews." Although Marx does not ultimately remedy the circularity of his argumentation in ZJ1, he clearly strives to unearth the driving forces of secular reality. He attempts to anchor his analysis more emphatically in social reality. Society now becomes the active agent of which politics is the effect. This move is a crucial step in Marx's attempt to wed his critical practice to a social reality below the heaven of politics rather than, as was the case with Bauer, above the bourgeois *Masse*. I have argued that Marx's treatment of the proletariat in "Einleitung" is an attempt to think beyond the agency of pure consciousness by attributing productivity to social abjection itself. This process begins, however, in a more inchoate and ambivalent form, in Marx's treatment of the figure of the real Jew (*den wirklichen weltlichen Juden, [das] real[e] Judentum*) in ZJ2.

Marx's real Jews are antagonists and not protagonists, agents of humanity's alienation and not its emancipation; but real Jews are nonetheless also the first agents whose agency Marx theorizes as emphatically tied to their materiality, not their free or human consciousness. In this way Marx's construction of real Jews forms a bridge between the agency of the *Volk* as collective will and the construction of the proletariat as the agent of human liberation, or between his political and his postpolitical theoretical heroes. Marx's infamous anti-Jewish rhetoric allows him to lay claim to a grounding in emphatically—indeed, obscenely—real social conditions. His emphasis on real rather than "sabbath Jews" advances Marx's inchoate attempt to relocate agency from the abstract realm of consciousness into social materiality. Given Marx's analytical and polemical need to ground his social critique in "reality," and his lack of theoretical tools to satisfy this need, his rhetorical strategies necessarily become freighted. Marx's anti-Jewish rhetoric both serves his polemical needs and embodies a new theory of social agency that he can as yet articulate only obscurely.

Atomized Society as the Product of Theological Politics

Marx wrote "Zur Judenfrage" at an exceedingly fecund and volatile moment in his development. The text explodes with ideas that are still in movement; certain arguments and strategies are at cross-purposes with others. Most crucial for the way ZJ1 illuminates how and why Marx resorts to his notorious characterization of real Jews in ZJ2 is the tension, throughout ZJ1, between Marx's attempt to ground his discourse in conditions of secular reality and the way he erodes that very ground by insisting that secular conditions are governed by the structure and dynamics of Christianity. (I will call the secularized "Christian" structures and dynamics that Marx sees governing political modernity—dualism, alienation, and atomization—"structural Christianity," as distinct from the beliefs and practices of self-identified Christians.) If in 1842 and early 1843 Marx could appeal to political pragmatism as the corrective to Bauer's and the *Freien*'s abstraction, excessive focus on religion, and counterproductive tactics, he had now come to view political democracy as essentially an iteration of religious abstraction and alienation. Marx, it bears underscoring, supported Jewish emancipation and acknowledged that political emancipation was meaningful as "real, practical emancipation."[119] However, the thrust of Marx's argument is that political emancipation remains ineffectual because what passes as secular politics is still governed by a quintessentially religious dualism: the political state in which citizens are free and equal (one could say redeemed) amounts to a secular analogue of Christian heaven. An illusory realm of equality, it presupposes and perpetuates social fragmentation and competition.

This shift in Marx's view of the substantiality of politics obviously changes the terms of his assessment of Bauer: pragmatic engagement in liberal politics could no longer serve as the solid basis from which Marx could critique Bauer's abstraction. In "Zur Judenfrage" Marx asserts that his critique of secular politics is more basic than Bauer's still theological orientation. Yet Marx's attempt to analyze religion no longer as the "basis" [*Grund*] but as merely a "phenomenon"

[*Phänomen*] of secular political narrowness, and to "reduce" the bifurcations of religious consciousness to the antagonisms that structure the world of secular politics is vitiated by his own critique of politics, the thrust of which is to drain the political of real substance and to define it as, in essence, a form of religion.[120]

As a consequence of his derealization of politics, Marx abandons faith in the political collective, the *Volk*, which he had championed during his republican phase and which he still upheld as the real ground beneath the abstraction of Hegel's state in his Kreuznach *Kritik*. Although Marx would almost immediately begin to reconceive revolutionary agency and his relation to it as a theorist via the proletariat, in "Zur Judenfrage" he tries to theorize radical social change while lacking a clear revolutionary protagonist. The resulting instability of Marx's conceptions of agency at this juncture causes him to oscillate between a lingering idealist line of argument that privileges Christianity as a stage in human development culminating in the state-society dualism of the modern secular world (the dominant perspective in ZJ1) and a competing argument that more emphatically privileges social materiality—the base materiality of civil society—as the active agent propelling history and producing the state in what we can recognize as an inchoate base-superstructure vector (the predominant position of ZJ2). In the framework of the first argument Jews figure as but one group among others haplessly limited, particularized, and rendered egoistic by the reigning structure of secularized, perfected Christianity. In the terms of the second argument, however, Jews become the privileged signifier of the base materiality and self-interest of civil society as an active principle.

Despite Marx's claim that "we do not turn secular questions into theological questions. We turn theological questions into secular ones,"[121] he had as yet none of the tools for secular analysis that would become the backbone of his historical materialism.[122] Marx insists that "only the criticism of political emancipation itself would have been the conclusive criticism of the Jewish Question and its real merging in the 'general question of the time,'" yet since he defines politics in strict analogy to religion, the critique of secular politics only displaces the critique of religion without fundamentally changing its terms.[123] Indeed, Marx relies on tools developed by Feuerbach and Bauer precisely in their critiques of religion. Marx's reliance on insights cribbed from radical theological critique leaves his argument circular and unstable. Marx "turn[s] theological questions into secular ones" only by discovering theological structures at the core of the secular world.

Feuerbach provides the main model for Marx's critique of political democracy in "Zur Judenfrage."[124] The democratic state—political heaven—atomizes and alienates species-being in the precise ways that Christian heaven does in

Feuerbach's analysis. The democratic state declares the sovereignty of each individual, with the twofold Feuerbachian effect of alienating collective species-being from itself (it is projected into political heaven) and atomizing it into so many monads (the political analogue of Christian souls). This hypostatization of the individual as sovereign is so socially corrosive because it allows egoistic individuals fictitiously to transcend their limitations without providing a framework for true social transformation, true realization of species-being. Modern politics merely declares the sovereignty of individuals in all their brute, untransformed positivity: "Political democracy is Christian since in it man, not merely one man but every man, ranks as *sovereign*, as the highest being, but it is man in his uncivilised, unsocial form, man in his fortuitous existence, man just as he is, man as he has been corrupted by the whole organisation of our society, who has lost himself, been alienated, and handed over to the rule of inhuman conditions and elements—in short, man who is not yet a *real* species-being."[125] Although Feuerbach's critique of projection and hypostatization provided a key model for Marx's analysis of liberal democracy, aspects of "Zur Judenfrage," possibly despite Marx's intentions, also mirror typically Bauerian perspectives. Though polemical, "Zur Judenfrage" is not the sort of broadside against Bauer that Marx would elaborate in *Die heilige Familie* and *The German Ideology*. More important than whether or not Marx in "Zur Judenfrage" wanted to go for Bauer's jugular, however, is the fact that he lacked the theoretical wherewithal to do so.[126] However tendentiously, Marx misidentifies Bauer's fundamental theoretical flaw as the assumption that achieving a secular state beyond narrow theological interests would in itself constitute true emancipation.[127] Marx faults Bauer for directing criticism only at theological limitations and not at the limitations of the secular political state.[128] Marx clearly wishes to be more grounded in reality than Bauer, but since he defines secular political reality in analogy to theology he does not so much offer an alternative to Bauer's mode of critique as extend it to the secular state, in which Marx now sees the completion of Christianity.

After passing swiftly over the incompletely secularized Christian-German state, Marx describes the completely secularized democratic state in ways that point up the circularity of his manner of grounding his critique in secular phenomena, and his continuing proximity *malgré lui* to Bauer.

> But . . . the religious spirit cannot be *really* secularised, for what is it in itself but the *non-secular* form of a stage in the development of the human mind? The religious spirit can only be secularised insofar as the stage of development of the human mind of which it is the religious expression makes its appearance and becomes constituted in its *secular* form. This takes place in the

democratic state. Not Christianity, but the *human basis* of Christianity is the basis of this state. Religion remains the ideal, non-secular consciousness of its members, because religion is the ideal form of the *stage of human development* achieved in this state.[129]

Notwithstanding his emphatic claims to base his analysis in empirical history, Marx espouses a model of history in which successive stages of human consciousness unfold teleologically. Behind both "religious spirit" and the realm of secular politics in which Marx would resolve questions of religion lies the "human basis of Christianity." What is this foundation of foundations common to religion and secular politics alike? It is a "stage of development of the human mind" (*Entwicklungsstufe des menschlichen Geistes*). This stage of human spirit can express itself in a secular guise (in democratic politics) or in the guise of religion proper. Marx argues that this spirit cannot really be secularized because it is not really secular. It can only be secularized in the sense that, or to the limited extent (*insofern*) that, it can be expressed in secular form in the democratic state. Whatever is erected on this spiritual human foundation—whether the secular state or religion proper—will reflect its dualistic structure. The realization of the "human basis" of religion cannot be more secular than the basis itself. The realization of the human basis of religion in the secular state remains religious because—beyond the nominal distinction between secular and religious—all manifestations of the current stage of development of the human spirit remain dualistic (structurally Christian). Breckman distills the circularity of Marx's argument when he notes that "at the same time as [Marx] resolved to turn 'theological questions into secular ones,' he metaphorically converted secular phenomena into theology. His intention to explain religion as a manifestation of secular narrowness in fact exposed the 'theological' structure of that secular base."[130]

Marx's claim to be able to resolve the Jewish Question and questions of religion in general into questions of secular politics rests on the concomitant claim that the dualism of modern secular politics—the society-state dichotomy—is more basic than the mere epiphenomena of religion. Yet the structuring dualism of secular politics is more basic insofar as it is a more universal expression of the current structurally Christian stage of human development. Secular political modernity is the foundation of religion, in other words, by virtue of being a more perfect or universal expression of religious mentality than religion itself could ever be. The secular world in which Marx wishes to ground his argument turns out to be an expression of the religious essence beyond religion. "The human basis of Christianity" understood as a "stage of development of the human mind" or spirit manifests itself only imperfectly in religion proper and is most fully expressed in its super-Christian, secular political form.

Whereas Bauer wanted to propel human autonomy forward through the ruthless critique of religion, Marx one-ups Bauer and calls not for a critique of religion generally, or of the universal religion, Christianity, but of the super-Christianity of the secular democratic state. Such criticism will enable human spirit to take the decisive step forward toward true emancipation. Even as Marx is obviously straining toward a theory of ideology according to which religious consciousness reflects secular reality, he is unable to conceive of reality as anything but a secular version of precisely the Christian dualistic consciousness he is tying to ground. As already noted, Marx would eventually locate a more satisfying historical motor in the means and relations of production, social relations that he would see reflected in ideology. In "Zur Judenfrage" he begins with the structure of dualistic theological consciousness and merely rediscovers this structure in a series of increasingly empirical iterations: religious consciousness reappears in political consciousness (in ZJ1) and, as we will see, in consciousness structured by a fetishized relationship to money (in ZJ2). As much as Marx wants to secularize what he attacks as Bauer's theological conception of agency, he cannot theorize a compelling alternative. Throughout ZJ1 the secularized theological principle of super-Christian politics remains the active force that alienates species consciousness and thereby engenders social atomization. The corrective that Marx proposes to both theological politics and to Bauer's still theological critique of theological consciousness comes down to a critique of yet another layer of theological (secular, super-Christian) consciousness.

Marx's view of political modernity as the ultimate manifestation of structural Christianity determines his treatment of Jews and Judaism in ZJ1. Given how heavily he leans on the figure of the real Jew in ZJ2, it is striking how unimportant Jews remain—and must remain—within ZJ1's conceptual architecture. Marx never argues that Jews embody egoism in an exemplary way, and he even repeatedly rebuts Bauer's claims that they do. Marx treats Jews as no more than one group among others that inevitably become caught in political modernity's super-Christian dualism: it is Christianity's dualistic structure—not any Jewish quality—that determines the Jews' contradictory relation to the state:

> We do not say to the Jews as Bauer does: You cannot be emancipated politically without emancipating yourselves radically from Judaism. On the contrary, we tell them: Because you can be emancipated politically without renouncing Judaism completely and incontrovertibly, *political emancipation* itself is not human emancipation. If you Jews want to be emancipated po-

litically without emancipating yourselves humanly, the half-hearted approach and contradiction is not in you alone, it is inherent in the *nature* and *category* of political emancipation. If you find yourself within the confines of this category, you share in a general confinement. Just as the state *evangelises* when, although it is a state, it adopts a Christian attitude towards the Jews, so the Jew *acts politically* when, although a Jew, he demands civic rights.[131]

Marx's rhetorical moves are certainly objectionable. As Bauer is so wont to do, Marx interprets the truth of Jews for Jews (who clearly need such assistance).[132] Marx's patronizing apostrophe tells Jews that if *even they* can be politically emancipated, political emancipation clearly has serious limitations. Marx's larger point, nonetheless, is that the contradiction between wishing to maintain particular interests and demanding political emancipation—a contradiction that Bauer derives from the quintessential egoism of Jews—is in fact determined by the Christian logic of the political state. Jews remain one particular social group (and so many egoistic individuals) vis-à-vis the political state in precisely the same way as do other social groups and individuals of civil society. Jews share in a general confinement (*Befangenheit*) determined by the essence and category of political emancipation itself. When Marx says the state "evangelizes" the Jew, he does not mean the Christian state, but rather the secular state that remains (secretly, structurally) Christian "although it is a state." As his analogy between *evangelisieren* and *politisieren* makes clear, Marx considers "acting politically" to entail a necessary submission to what he considers the deep logic of Christian dualism. In demanding emancipation while remaining Jewish, Jews only submit to the evangelizing logic of the super-Christian state with its promise of abstract salvation. Marx rebuts Bauer's argument about the incorrigible particularity and egoism of the Jews with the contention that Jewish particularity is determined by the deep logic of Christianity as perfected in the secular state, which grants political freedoms, and even human rights, only to atomized individuals (secularized Christian souls).[133] Political emancipation naturalizes individuals in society in their brute positivity and redeems only their secular souls as citizens of the state. When Jews demand political rights, they do not express their corrosive Jewish particularism but rather, ineluctably, behave like (structural) Christians! Whatever egoism Jews may embody is analogous to the private interests of other groups differentiated by both material (private property) and spiritual factors (*Bildung* and religion).[134] Christianity's dualistic logic—understood properly as humanity's arrested stage of development, its secularly Christian spirit—governs all of humanity: Jews, Christians, atheists, everyone.

Jews are central neither to Marx's critique of political emancipation nor to the polemical strategies by which he tries to distinguish his position from Bauer's. Jews, quite simply, perform no essential work for Marx in ZJ1.[135] In ZJ2, in contrast, Marx deploys the figure of real Jews to distinguish his conception of social agency from what he considers Bauer's privileging of the agency of consciousness. Real Jews fill the role into which Marx presses them only ambiguously and ambivalently, but his turning to this figure at all is a result, I argue, of the void left by the demise of the *Volk* as a protagonist capable of embodying agency and effecting self-liberation. The *Volk*'s exit creates the space that Marx briefly fills with real Jews before turning to the (arguably equally figural) proletariat. Examining how the *Volk* falls out as a viable agent of liberation in ZJ1, then, will set the stage for the appearance of real Jews in ZJ2.

One of the most revealing indices of Marx's abandoning of the *Volk* is his reticence to discuss the *Volk* even when the *Volk* figures centrally in passages by Bauer that Marx cites. In a passage I have already discussed, Bauer criticizes how, in the Christian-German state, the monarch and his intermediaries reduce the authentic *Volk* to an inauthentic *Nicht-Volk* or *Masse*. Bauer's critique of the illegitimacy and atomizing effects of the monarch and his intermediaries generally aligns with the position Marx articulates in his Kreuznach *Kritik* regarding Hegel's theorization of the monarch and his intermediaries. Yet when Marx engages this passage, he gives Bauer's critique of the Christian German state conspicuously short shrift:

> Bauer then explains that the people of a Christian state is only a non-people, no longer having a will of its own, but whose true existence lies in the leader to whom it is subjected, although this leader by his origin and nature is alien to it, i.e., given by God and imposed on the people without any co-operation on its part. Bauer declares that the laws of such a people are not its own creation, but are actual revelations, that its supreme chief needs privileged intermediaries with the people in the strict sense, with the masses, and that the masses themselves are divided into a multitude of particular groupings which are formed and determined by chance, which are differentiated by their interests, their particular passions and prejudices, and obtain permission, as a privilege, to isolate themselves from one another, etc. (P. 56.)[136]

Marx rebuts Bauer's analysis here of how the Christian state atomizes the *Volk* by directing a further passage from Bauer's *Die Judenfrage*—in which Bauer tries to demonstrate the Jews' inability to separate the public from the religious and, by extension, to demonstrate the incompatibility between Judaism and republican citizenship—against Bauer himself: "However, Bauer himself says: 'Politics, if it is to be nothing but religion, ought not to be politics, just as the cleaning of saucepans, if it is to be accepted as a religious matter, ought not to be regarded as a matter of domestic economy.' (P. 108.) In the Christian-German state, however, religion is an 'economic matter' just as 'economic matters' belong to the sphere of religion. The domination of religion in the Christian-German state is the religion of domination."[137] In the passage Marx quotes, Bauer purports to refute, through *Kritik*, what he belittles as the Parisian Sanhedrin's merely apologetic assertion of compatibility between Judaism and French citizenship. Jewish claims of being able to participate in public life ring hypocritical to Bauer, for whom in Judaism everything is religion and religion everything. Since it is really religion (egoism, privilege), Jewish "politics" should not be considered politics at all, and Jews should not receive political rights until they cease being Jews.[138] Marx turns Bauer's point against him to vitiate his critique of the Christian-German state: since that state remains rooted in religion it does not embody secular politics, and Bauer's critique of it does not constitute true political analysis. Even so, Marx could still—but emphatically and revealingly does not—follow or redirect to his own ends Bauer's distinction between the "authentic *Volk*" and the *Masse* into which the Christian-German state has divided this *Volk*. Instead, Marx, in keeping with his second *Deutsch-französische Jahrbücher* letter to Ruge, refers to the basis of the Christian state simply as "human rubbish [*Menschenkehricht*]."[139] The concept of the *Volk*—at least in the German context—had evidently lost all analytical validity for Marx.

Marx refuses to speak in the name of an authentic German *Volk* (even a latent one) and instead points up Germany's abject human refuse. He effectively dismisses the republican *Volk* as a viable agent of social revolution without, significantly, appealing to the demos of "true democracy" as a corrective. Toward the end of ZJ1 Marx underscores how "enigmatic" [*rätselhaft*] it is that the French people, even in the vital stages of constituting itself in the modern political sense, and while emphasizing devotion to the nation as paramount, nonetheless equated "the human being" with the atomized, "egoistic" member of civil society rather than with the intersubjectively constituted member of the wider community:[140]

> It is puzzling enough that a people which is just beginning to liberate itself, to tear down all the barriers between its various sections, and to establish a political community, that such a people solemnly proclaims (Declaration of 1791) the rights of egoistic man separated from his fellow men and from the community, and that indeed it repeats this proclamation at a moment when only the most heroic devotion can save the nation, and is therefore imperatively called for, at a moment when the sacrifice of all the interests of civil so-

ciety must be the order of the day, and egoism must be punished as a crime. (Declaration of the Rights of Man, etc., of 1793.) This fact becomes still more puzzling when we see that the political emancipators go so far as to reduce citizenship, and the *political community*, to a mere *means* for maintaining these so-called rights of man, that therefore the *citoyen* is declared to be the servant of egoistic *homme*, that the sphere in which man acts as a communal being is degraded to a level below the sphere in which he acts as a partial being, and that, finally, it is not man as *citoyen*, but man as *bourgeois* who is considered to be the *essential* and *true* man.[141]

Marx solves this enigma with the argument that, in establishing the political state as a realm apart, the French Revolution removed political significance from actual, lived experience and thereby naturalized egoistic civil society, the only palpable reality left.[142] He substantiates this claim by contrasting the *Volk*-state relationship in feudalism with that in political modernity. In feudal society one could claim no universal political status apart from, or above, one's particular social station, or corporation. The relationship of one's particular corporation to the state also determined one's general relationship to the life of the people [*allgemeines Verhältnis zum Volksleben*]. Marx echoes elements of his critique of the monarch in the Kreuznach *Kritik* of spring 1843 when he concludes that the feudal dispersal of political status gave rise to the false perception that political unity could only reside with the sovereign and his servants.[143] In the Kreuznach *Kritik*, however, Marx still retained faith in the true *Volk*'s capacity to embody the consciousness, unity, and active will of the state, which had been illegitimately appropriated by the monarch. In contrast, the *Volk* has now lost its status as the agent of emancipation. Marx no longer invests hope in the demos implied in his earlier notion of true democracy and focuses solely on the *Volk*'s paradoxical, self-canceling function in the process of political emancipation:

> The political revolution which overthrew this sovereign power and raised state affairs to become affairs of the people [*Volksangelegenheiten*], which constituted the political state as a matter of *general* concern, that is, as a real state, necessarily smashed all estates, corporations, guilds, and privileges, since they were all manifestations of the separation of the people from the community [*Trennung des Volkes von seinem Gemeinwesen*]. The political revolution thereby *abolished* the *political character of civil society*. It broke up civil society into its simple component parts; on the one hand, the *individuals*; on the other hand, the *material* and *spiritual elements* constituting the content of the life and social position of these individuals. It set free the political spirit, which had been, as it were, split up, partitioned and dispersed

in the various blind alleys of feudal society. It gathered the dispersed parts of the political spirit, freed it from its intermixture with civil life, and established it as the sphere of the community, the *general* concern of the nation [*der allgemeinen Volksangelegenheit*], ideally independent of those *particular* elements of civil life.[144]

The paradox of the *Volk* as Marx theorizes it is that its consolidation in the modern political sense is coextensive with its alienation and derealization. The modern state finally unifies feudalism's fractured and disrupted *Volksleben*—it consolidates the political spirit that had been scattered across so many feudal "blind alleys" into a "general concern of the nation"—but only as a sphere apart, independent of the concrete particulars of social existence. The *Volk* seems to harbor potential only so long as illegitimate authority proscribes its consolidation, yet it becomes derealized through the very process of its political self-constitution. Although Marx does not explicitly discount the *Volk* as a potential emancipatory agent, he theorizes the (political) *Volk* as so implicated in the process of political self-estrangement that it loses all viability as an agent for overcoming that estrangement. In relegating all communality to the new political heaven, the "enigmatic" revolution in modern politics bestows on the dog-eat-dog world of civil society the status of a natural foundation (*Naturbasis*). The abstractly constituted *Volk* could not be called upon to revolutionize that naturalized social foundation.

Real Jews as the Abjection of Christian Spirit

In ZJ2 Marx responds chiefly to Bauer's "Die Fähigkeit," in which Bauer locates Christians, in their theological universalism, at one remove from free, secular, universal human consciousness and Jews, in their theological particularism, at two removes. Marx conspicuously shifts the style and thrust of his argument from ZJ1 and more pugnaciously challenges Bauer's ladder-of-consciousness model (in which consciousness successively transcends its particularist limits in a triumphalist upward trajectory to unfettered self-realization) with an emphatic downward descent from the lofty illusions of secular Christian spirit into the materiality of "Jewish" civil society. The opening sentences of ZJ2 attack Bauer for using proximity or distance from Bauer's brand of *Kritik* as the measure of Judaism's and Christianity's capacity to become free. For Marx, Bauer's historical teleology merely secularizes salvation history: "The theological problem as to who has the better chance of gaining salvation—Jew or Christian—is here repeated in a more enlightened form: who is the more *capable of emancipation*."[145]

The form of *Kritik* Bauer touts as free human activity par excellence remains, in Marx's assessment, within the logic of confession (*Bekenntnis*): "For the Jew it is still a matter of a profession of faith [*Bekenntnis*], though no longer faith in Christianity but rather in Christianity in dissolution."[146]

Marx prepares his shift toward social reality with his dismissal, at the end of ZJ1, of the political act (*Tat*). In the course of his critique of the illusory universality of the French Revolution—the great political revolution—Marx comments: "The *rights of man* appear to be *natural rights* because *self-conscious activity* is concentrated on the *political act*."[147] The political act had undergone a process of derealization in Marx's eyes since he wrote his Kreuznach *Kritik* only a few months previously. The orientation of self-conscious activity toward the political act does not liberate human beings but only installs as human rights what are in fact the rights of egoistic private persons. As heaven naturalizes unjust earthly social conditions while promising a fictitious ultimate refuge from them, political heaven also lends the inhuman conditions of egoistic civil society the appearance of a natural condition. Since the political state and egoistic civil society in this way produce each other mutually and carry the structure of Christian dualism into secular modernity, political emancipation offers no solution. Instead, it is fragmented, egoistic society—the pseudo-natural ground above which the abstractly universal political sphere hovers—that must be "revolutionized."[148]

Marx intensifies his critique of Bauer's model of historical agency in ZJ2. Near the beginning of it he charges Bauer with transforming the emancipation of the Jews into "a philosophical-theological act."[149] Marx states his goal in this essay to be to displace emancipatory agency from the plane of theological, philosophical, and political pseudo-action into real social practice: "We are trying to break with the theological formulation of the question. For us, the question of the Jew's capacity for emancipation becomes the question: What particular *social* element has to be overcome in order to abolish Judaism?"[150]

In late 1843, however, Marx still lacked the tools for socioeconomic analysis that this ambitious project demanded. He developed a compelling theory of production through intensive reading in economics in 1844; his friendship with Engels, whose firsthand knowledge of factory conditions in England pushed Marx in a more empirical direction; and a series of increasingly vituperative polemics against erstwhile Young Hegelian colleagues, culminating in *The German Ideology*, the first articulation of the principles of dialectical materialism. Marx's relative ignorance of economics and inchoate conception of production in "Zur Judenfrage" only increase the burden his rhetoric of the real had to bear at this moment. Marx has a polemical and theoretical need to anchor his critique in social reality, yet he can access that reality only by conjuring it in gritty rhetoric.

The following quote conveys ZJ2's timbre:

> Let us consider the real secular Jew—not the *sabbath Jew*, as Bauer does, but the *everyday Jew*.
>
> Let us not look for the Jew's secret in his religion: rather let us look for the secret of religion in the real Jew.
>
> What is the secular basis of Judaism? *Practical* need, self-interest.
>
> What is the secular cult of the Jew? *Haggling*. What is his secular God? *Money*.
>
> Well then! Emancipation from *haggling* and from *money*, i.e. from practical, real Judaism, would be the same as the self-emancipation of our age.[151]

Marx creates the effect of speaking from the locus of reality itself by conjuring an image of a hyper-real Jew—here, the "*everyday Jew*," "the real Jew," "practical, real Judaism." To take but one further example, toward the end of ZJ2 Marx characterizes the "essence of the contemporary Jew not as an abstract, but rather as a supremely empirical being."[152] In ZJ1 Marx sought to lay bare how the cause for Jewish civil rights was ultimately determined by the logic of structural Christianity as perfected in the secular state. He now proposes to derive religion—not just Judaism, but religion *tout court*—from the real Jew.

Marx further universalizes Judaism by claiming that all of civil society has become crassly egoistic, "Jewish": "The Jew has emancipated himself in a Jewish way not only by acquiring financial power but also because, with and without him, *money* has become a world power, and the practical Jewish spirit has become the practical spirit of Christian nations. The Jews have emancipated themselves insofar as the Christians have become Jews."[153] Unlike in ZJ1, Jews and Judaism here wield real, practical, empirical power that easily overwhelms ethereal Christian spirit. Jewish power is dehumanizing rather than redemptive, but it is real. Although Jews have thoroughly negative connotations in ZJ2, they have the virtue, we could say, of embodying the real problem rather than illusory solutions (Christian salvation, political rights, and so forth). Although obviously a figure—a phantasm, even—Marx's real Jew is a phantasm of the real. It has the quasi-generative power to spread realness itself. This transitive power of Jewish realness—the way it spreads and transforms the entire Christian population into so many Jews—represents at once the ultimate human degradation and the necessary precondition to a real solution. The universal spread of Jewish realness gives the lie to Christian salvation in religion and in politics and prepares the stage for the coming human emancipation, which will not look to such abstract solutions but will rather transform relations among real embodied people, not Christian souls in their various guises.

It is of course not possible to account fully for why Marx shifted his line of argumentation so dramatically—and his rhetoric so bewilderingly—between ZJ1 and ZJ2. It seems likely, however, that Marx found useful analytical and rhetorical tools in "Über das Geldwesen" ("On the Essence of Money"), an essay Moses Hess submitted to Marx for publication in the *Deutsch-französische Jahrbücher*. Whether or not Marx had completed his own essay before he received Hess's, and thus how much Marx may have taken from Hess, is a matter of some dispute; but Marx most likely read Hess's essay after writing ZJ1 but before writing ZJ2.[154] Hess's main theses are that human essence consists in "life activity," and that this life activity is alienated in money. Hess's title self-consciously evokes Feuerbach's *Das Wesen des Christentums*, and indeed Hess analyzes money as operating according to the logic of religion as Feuerbach understands it, albeit on an emphatically social and commercial plane. If Christianity is a mystified projection of man's empirical collective essence, it does in theory what money does in reality—for money, in Hess's view, is precisely the repository of man's alienated essence, his "life activity." Hess furthermore uses some quite gruesome imagery: he writes of money as congealed blood, for example, and describes atomized social relations organized by money as a form of cannibalism. In addition, he characterizes money as a form of waste or trash [*Plunder*].[155] Although Hess derives the world of isolated, alienated individuals in religion, politics, and commerce overwhelmingly from Christian dualism, he sometimes refers to Judaism and Jews as also implicated in religious alienation and its secular realization in the world of commerce. For example, he writes: "The mystery of Judaism and Christianity is revealed in the modern Jewish-Christian world of shopkeepers."[156] Importing Feuerbach's critique of alienation and personalism to the plane of social relations, Hess—already a committed communist—argues that under relations of private property, collective species-being is perverted into agonistic competition among alienated individuals.[157]

Hess's essay modeled new ways to think about money's dehumanizing effects as a mediator of social relations, as well as vivid, unsettling ways to use rhetoric to evoke such human degradation. Hess was probably one inspiration for Marx's shift in argument and rhetoric, but Marx put the elements he found in Hess's work to his own conceptual and polemical purposes. Marx deployed the figure of the huckstering real Jew to lend rhetorical mass to his claim to be engaging in analysis of hard social reality—in contrast to Bauer, who never got beyond the question of Jewish religious or theological consciousness. Marx's rhetorical excesses in ZJ2 serve a function that is in part compensatory: with his turn to coarse rhetoric Marx is clearly trying to finesse an inchoate materialist argument in the absence of a coherent generative theory. Enzo Traverso notes the immaturity of Marx's economic conceptions in ZJ2 and how Marx's equation of Judaism, trade, and bourgeois society tends "to see in commerce and circulation, rather than in production, the characteristic traits and the fundamental structure of the capitalist system."[158] Rather than oppose "Jewish" circulation and (proletarian) production, I argue that we should look at Marx's early conception of circulation *as* his inchoate—highly rhetorical and conceptually weak—theory of production. Marx is attempting to explain historical agency in material terms and to theorize a material substrate that engenders forms of religious and political alienation before he has the conceptual tools to theorize production in a satisfying way. In ZJ2 Marx is no longer content to expose the structural dualism, the structural Christianity, of the secular world, and he now posits material social relations as more fundamental than the secularized Christian spirit he sees behind Bauer's exalted critical consciousness. Financial power (*Geldmacht*) has become a world power (*Weltmacht*). Money (*Geld*) and the Jewish money man (*Geldmensch*) have become the true driving force (*Weltmacht*) of which religion is a mere epiphenomenon.

In the absence of a viable theory of production, however, Marx can construct his critique only on the dubious foundation of a rhetoric of the real, a predicament that leads to the notorious slippage in ZJ2 between registers of the figural and the real. The more emphatically Marx can conjure the reality of the real Jew as the embodiment of social reality under the conditions of modern commerce—the more obscene the reality that accrues to this figure—the more Marx can believe he is anchoring his analysis in a solid substratum beneath the "Christian" abstraction of Bauer's self-consciousness and political liberalism alike. This, however, renders Marx's debasement of the real Jew extremely ambivalent. Marx marshals the real Jew's obscene reality even as precisely the obscenity of the Jew's reality simultaneously renders the Jew a material agent with whom the radical social critic could not possibly partner. Marx's real Jews become both more and less useful to Marx's project the more abject they become.

Even as Marx takes an important step toward grounding historical agency in the materiality of society, he continues to work largely within—or at the very least he as yet has no viable alternative to—an idealist conception of the agency of consciousness.[159] To understand the intense ambivalence the figure of the real Jew embodies for Marx it is important to appreciate that he takes his first inchoate steps toward articulating a theory of material agency or productivity essentially *within* a conceptual and rhetorical framework that continues to denigrate materiality as the base and disgusting foil of human freedom. This fundamental ambivalence is evident in Marx's figuration of material productivity in terms of the paradigmatic processes of the quintessentially ambivalent phenomenon of abjection: birth and, more insistently, evacuation.

Marx associates Jews with the production of excrement, an obscene mode of material production, and ascribes to "Jewish" civil society the ability to deliver itself of the political state. As noted, Hess had equated money with excrement. But whereas Hess casts money as a purely negative force that vampirically drains, sacrifices, and cannibalizes human life activity, Marx has a use for precisely the human detritus that remains, stripped of its human essence. In an emphatic rebuttal to Bauer's conception of history as the progress of Christian and post-Christian consciousness and his assessment of the Jews as *geschichtswidrig*—as a dead, spiritless, but stubborn obstruction to humanity's historical advancement—Marx insists that "Judaism has not sustained itself despite but rather through history."[160] History's driving force is not the Christian spirit that needs only to be secularized in the form of universal self-consciousness, as Bauer maintains; rather, the force pushing history is "Jewish" bowels, intestines, and entrails. To capture the at once humanly negating yet also—in contrast to the impotent illusions of Christian spirit (however secularized)—productive quality of this material historical motor, Marx employs the apt metaphor of defecation. History advances according to a cycle in which "out of its own entrails [*Eingeweiden*], civil society ceaselessly produces [*erzeugt*] the Jew."[161] As this passage continues, Marx associates base Jewish concerns with defecation in further ways, and he likens modernity's strict bifurcation of state and civil society to a far-from-immaculate process whereby (Jewish) society "births the political state out of itself": "What actually was the foundation of the Jewish religion? Practical need, egoism. Hence, the Jew's monotheism is actually the polytheism of many needs, a polytheism that makes even the toilet an object of divine law. *Practical need, egoism* is the principle of *civil society* and appears purely as such as soon as civil society has fully birthed the political state out of itself [*sobald die bürgerliche Gesellschaft den politischen Staat vollständig aus sich herausgeboren* (my interpellation)]. The god of *practical need and self-interest* is *money*."[162] Marx follows Feuerbach (*Wesen*) and Bauer ("Die Fähigkeit") in deploying practical "need" (*Bedürfnis*) as a key term to characterize the essence of Jewish religion. However, when he characterizes Judaism as a polytheism of many needs, extending even to the toilet, Marx puns on *Bedürfnis* (need) as a (now antiquated) synonym for "*Notdurft*" or "call of nature." He identifies the foundation (*Grundlage*) of Judaism as practical need and deploys the "need" of defecation as the privileged synecdoche for Judaism's whole system of needs. Judaism as a polytheism of vulgarly practical needs not only extends to the toilet (*Abtritt*), but this *Bedürfnis* signifies the essence of all others. As though

Midas's obscene twin, Judaism transforms all that it touches into excrement, and it touches everything:[163]

> Money is the jealous god of Israel, before which no other god may exist. Money degrades all the gods of human beings [*des Menschen*]—and turns them into a commodity. . . . Money is the alienated essence of man's labor and existence, and this alien essence dominates him, and he worships it.
>
> The god of the Jews has become worldly; he has become the god of the world [*Weltgott*].[164]

Money is the god of Judaism's base needs, and it is filthy money indeed. Marx exploits the strong psychic link between money and feces and insinuates that in the alienated form of money, humanity's true essence is transformed into a fetishized waste product.[165]

Marx's association of Jews and Judaism with the toilet echoes thinkers before him such as Voltaire and Hegel, who made the same association. In his lectures on the philosophy of religion, Hegel refers to a remark in which Voltaire ridicules Judaism for the way it makes even latrines part of religious practice, even as the Pentateuch lacks any explicit mention of the eternality of the soul. In a witticism he quotes from the English deist Anthony Collins, Voltaire maintains that the Jewish God cares more about the Jews' derrières than their souls.[166] Hegel uses Voltaire to distinguish between merely formal faith in contingent content and events (for example, the specific miracles Christ is said to have performed, or whether the Jewish houses in Egypt really were marked with red as a sign to God's angel) and authentic faith, which is a matter of spirit. If literalist fundamentalism defines faith, Hegel argues, then no cultivated person can have faith. He evokes Voltaire's critique of literalist belief approvingly:

> Voltaire's bitterest attacks are directed against the demand for this sort of belief. He says, among other things, that it would have been better if God had given the Jews instruction about the immortality of the soul rather than teaching them how to go to the privy [*Abtritt*] (*aller à la selle*). This is to make latrines part of the content of faith.
>
> What is unspiritual, by its nature, cannot be part of the content of faith [*kein Inhalt des Glaubens*]. When God speaks, what he says is spiritual, for spirit reveals itself only to spirit.[167]

Presumably picking up on these remarks by Hegel and Voltaire, Marx deploys the association of Jews and defecation to very different ends. Both Hegel and Voltaire see in Deuteronomy 23:13–15 evidence of Judaism's inability to distinguish between base material content and genuine faith and spirit. The biblical text commands Israelites to relieve themselves outside the boundaries of their camp and to bury their waste, "for the Lord thy God walketh in the midst of thy camp."[168] However removed Voltaire and Hegel both, differently, were from Christian orthodoxy (Protestant Orthodoxy's dogmatic literalism is one of Hegel's targets in this passage), they both adapt without fundamentally subverting a well-worn Christian theological opposition between Jew (body, letter, and so on) and Christian (soul, spirit, and so on). In contrast to Bauer, and both like and in contrast to Feuerbach, however, Marx is trying to overcome the privileging of the agency of Christian spirit in its various secular guises. Far from recommending a focus on authentic spirituality, Marx is out to reveal Bauer's theological assumptions and expose the Christian illusion of the immortality of the soul as the secret and fundamental flaw of modern secular politics. In other words, Marx is privileging, however obscurely, material social reality and material productivity over misplaced faith in the agency of secular Christian spirit.

Feuerbach devoted a chapter of *Das Wesen des Christentums* to critiquing the Jewish God as merely the Jewish people's egoistic projection of a provider of its material needs; the Feurbachian Jew relates to God strictly through his stomach.[169] Marx goes Feuerbach one better and associates Jews with bowels and the worship of money as a form of excrement. Marx counters what he sees as Bauer's exaltation of Christian spirit (however secularized) with the Jewish anus as the obscene model of material production in society. The new Jewish world power (*Weltmacht*) is a fetishized process of excretion; it transforms human essence into abject matter devoid of spirit. One of the fundamental insights of Julia Kristeva's study of the power of the abject in Western culture is the threat that the abject poses to subjectivity. Abject matter confuses the distinction between life and death and between the "I" and the "not-I"; neither subject nor object, it is what is a part of me yet what I cannot possibly be.[170] Marx deploys the phantasm of the real Jew aggressively to subvert the forms of subjectivity and spirit he is trying to move beyond, chiefly political rights and Bauer's model of critical self-consciousness. Marx mobilizes the dichotomy privileging Christian spirit over Jewish matter, but to the aggressive end of rubbing Christian spirit in Jewish filth.

In *Anti-Judaism*, David Nirenberg notes how Marx remains within a Pauline (and, more broadly, Western) semantics that opposes Christian spirit and Jewish body and literalism, even as he critiques Bauer's Christian paradigm of critique. Nirenberg notes further that Marx deploys this opposition in a way that goes beyond mere convenient semantic shorthand. What sets Marx's use of this trope apart is, in Nirenberg's phrase, "the centrality of the 'real.'" Marx, he observes, "requires the reality of his Jews and his Judaism."[171] Nirenberg features Marx's "Zur Judenfrage" prominently in his book's introduction and returns to it in a later chapter "because it provides such a powerful example of the phenomenon this book is about."[172] What makes Marx's essay a key text for Nirenberg is the slippage it exhibits between the figurative and the real. Marx clearly seems to have insight into how the stereotypical figure of the "Jew" is produced by a social semantics that has nothing to do with actual Jews; "Jews" are not real. Because Marx does have this insight, Nirenberg finds it all the more unforgivable that he nonetheless creates a "new and powerful confusion of the figural and the real" by so emphatically insisting that "Jews" are real.[173] Nirenberg aptly poses the question that Marx's essay presents to us: "What led Marx to embrace these confusions and amplify them?"[174] Nirenberg, however, essentially sidesteps his own question instead of trying to answer it.[175] His chief interest lies not in contextual analysis but rather in locating Marx's essay in a long history of anti-Jewish structures of thought. Yet the question of why Marx insists on the reality of "Jews" demands a more precise answer than that it participates in a long tradition of "habits of thought that understood human life and history in terms of the struggle to achieve the proper relation between law and love, thing and person, letter and spirit, and the failure to achieve that ideal 'Judaism.'"[176] It is obvious enough that Marx's discourse is thoroughly indebted to this tradition of thought, but this tells us little about how and why Marx deploys elements of this tradition of anti-Jewish discourse in particular ways in an attempt to arrive at new theoretical insights and a new critical posture.

Read against a Pauline master semantics of spirit versus matter, what is most striking is indeed the way Marx so emphatically (exuberantly, violently, even hysterically) insists on the denigrated reality of real Jews not as a foil to validate Christian spirit, but to expose as an impotent illusion belief in the agency of Christian spirit in its various forms. Marx insists that Jews are real not only or primarily to denigrate Jews, but to be able to lay claim to the real itself, which he could—and in essence could only—evoke through his rhetorical abuse of the despised figure of the bodily, material, venal Jew. Marx's violent rhetorical excess, his assault on the real Jew, is not simply a rejection but in fact an abusive embrace of this figure.

Marx's ambivalent relationship to abject real Jews falls chronologically and conceptually between his relationship to the subpolitical German toads of his May 1843 letter to Ruge and his mobilization of the proletariat's abjection as a universally emancipating force in "Einleitung." In his pivoting away from the *Volk*, Marx was able to avail himself of stereotypes of Jews as, on the one hand, material and dirty and, on the other hand, ubiquitous and international. Jews are both obscenely *there* and everywhere, a quality that permits Marx to use

Jews as figures of a civil society that spans the Christian nations he explores (Germany, France, and the United States). Marx's turn to the proletariat continues, and further productivizes, this wedding of the material and the universal.

Marx's phantasmatic realism—the figure of the obscenely empirical Jew and the obscure model of material production as the production of waste—is a rhetorical gambit that exploits the very disgust it provokes to suggest having critically unearthed a real motor driving history and generating religion and the political state. Marx's relationship (as a radical critic) to real Jews, however, remains irreducibly ambivalent.Real Jews authorize his radical social critique to the extent that they embody—but offer few means of resolving—the problem of base egoism that he deems social revolution necessary to overcome. As figures of the abject, Jews are objects of both disgust and desire. They embody humanity's universal denigration but therefore are also a necessary step in its liberation from the illusions of Christian and post-Christian abstraction. The path to humanity's freedom runs through the Jewish muck, not through Christian heaven or its secular political analogue. Marx's obscenely real Jews make clear that human redemption must pass through material degradation, yet the obscure forms of productivity Marx ascribes to Jews only proliferate the excremental materiality of "Jewish" society without revolutionizing it. To get out of this impasse—Marx's own Jewish problem, if you will—Marx would have to theorize a class more basic than civil society itself; a class of civil society that is not of civil society; a manifestly material class whose abjection would nonetheless render impossible the *Leibegoismus* that the real Jews, even in their obscene fecundity, embody and consolidate. After his inchoate and insolubly ambivalent attempt to productivize the abject in "Zur Judenfrage," Marx would have to invent the proletariat.[177]

Coda: A Thesis on Marx's "Theses on Feuerbach"

Marx's condensed remarks on Feuerbach of spring 1845 are widely read as one of the earliest articulations of the dialectical conception of historical materialist praxis—humanity's collective self-creation out of historically specific forms of productive interchange with nature, which also structure social relations in classes. Marx would soon elaborate these ideas more fully in *The German Ideology* and is not "there yet" in his conception or, perforce, his exposition in the brief "Theses on Feuerbach." To my knowledge it has gone unnoticed how Marx, as part of the breakthrough this text makes in the theorization of historical materialism, reckons, however obliquely, with his earlier conception of "Jewish" materiality.

The thrust of Marx's critique of Feuerbach's materialism in the "Theses" is that Feuerbach conceives of the material world chiefly as an object of perception and reflection, while continuing to understand theoretical—not practical—activity the only essentially human activity. Aside from some passing remarks on work as species activity, Feuerbach consistently focuses on species-being as a form of consciousness. In contrast, Marx insists on seeing "sensuous human activity, practice" in terms of agency, or "subjectively." In other words, social agency as what Marx here calls "objective activity" signals a definitive break from an idealist conception of the subject-object binary that aligns human agency with a semantic field including rationality, ideality, and consciousness as opposed to materiality, reality, and practice. For all Feuerbach's emphasis, in Marx's words, on "the thing, reality, sensuousness," Feuerbach could not conceive of human agency in material terms. Instead, "in *Das Wesen des Christentums* he regards the theoretical attitude as the only genuinely human attitude, while practice is conceived and fixed only in its dirty-Jewish manifestation. Hence he does not grasp the significance of 'revolutionary,' of 'practical-critical,' activity."[178]

In light of the preceding analysis of Marx's "Zur Judenfrage," we can see in Marx's remark on Feuerbach's arrested conception of practical material agency also the *Selbstkritik* of an erstwhile Feuerbachian. Marx seems to have in mind the opening of part 2 of Feuerbach's *Das Wesen des Christentums*, which draws a contrast between pure theoretical and vulgar practical reflection [*Anschauung*].[179] For Feuerbach the material world is important chiefly as the object of disinterested reflection for theoretical consciousness (of which species consciousness is a form). Religion short-circuits human theoretical reflection by providing an easy all-purpose answer. As a provider of human needs, moreover, God transforms our drive for disinterested theoretical reflection into a merely practical interest in egoistic needs. Whereas theoretical reflection is man's essential activity, Feuerbach argues, "practical reflection is a dirty reflection, besmirched by egoism [*eine schmutzige, vom Egoismus befleckte Anschauung*]."[180] Feuerbach calls practical reflection that concerns itself with material needs "*schmutzig*," but not Jewish. In the chapter of *Das Wesen des Christentums* that he devotes to Jews, Feuerbach sees base materialism at the heart of the antitheoretical Jewish conception of creation: God as the provider of the Jews' bodily needs. Not even in this chapter, however, does Feuerbach use the term "*schmutzig-jüdisch*." "*Jüdisch*" is Marx's addition.

What does it tell us that, in this reckoning with the theoretical limitations of Feuerbachian materialism, Marx uses "Jewish" as shorthand for Feuerbach's denigrating conception of practical reflection and material existence? In trying to move beyond Feuerbach's dismissal of practical materiality as a realm beneath true human agency, Marx is reckoning not only with Feuerbach but also with his own Feuerbachian attempts to move beyond philosophical abstraction. Marx's criticism of Feuerbach is valid for his own attempt to confront Hegel's abstract philosophical state with a real social agent, the *Volk*, and in his attempt to extend Feuerbach's critique of religion and speculative philosophy into the realm of society and politics in his Kreuznach *Kritik*. Even as Marx tried to ground Feuerbach's anthropology in a social locus (the *Volk*), he continued to align agency with human consciousness, defined in opposition to brute materiality or animal nature. It was with ZJ2 that Marx first emphatically situated his analysis on the level of practical needs. This is the beginning of his move beyond Feuerbach into a theory of material agency. As we have seen, whatever theoretical advance this represented for Marx was rendered equivocal by the fact that he chose the figure of obscene reality, the real Jew, to expose the lingering idealism (the theological antitheology) in Bauer's (and Feuerbach's) conception of historical agency. The real Jew could indeed figure only a "dirty Jewish" materiality. Although *Judentum* could briefly and ambivalently provide Marx with a partner in his attempt to overcome abstraction, it "could not create a new world."[181] Marx would need, and he immediately invented, a more viable partner to carry forward a theory of material agency and to reenvision his own emerging role as a radical social critic in terms of "practical-critical activity." With his remark in "Theses on Feuerbach" about the limitations of conceiving material reality in "dirty-Jewish," rather than revolutionary, practical-critical terms, Marx is referring less to Feuerbach than to himself.

Chapter Five

Patriotic Pantheism

Spinoza in Berthold Auerbach's Early Career

Berthold Auerbach (1812–82) and Moses Hess (1812–75) were intimate friends for a number of years in the late 1830s and early 1840s, a period during which both young men were trying to establish themselves within German culture and politics. As they sought to situate themselves on the German scene Auerbach and Hess both engaged intensively with the philosophy of Baruch Spinoza, in whom they both found inspiration for their progressively divergent, and ultimately mutually hostile, cultural and political orientations. This tale of two Spinozas is the subject of this chapter and the following one.

Literary scholars remember Auerbach chiefly as the author of the *Schwarzwälder Dorfgeschichten* (*Black Forest Village Stories*), which catapulted him to literary stardom in 1843. Before his unlikely rise to fame as a German *Volkschriftsteller* Auerbach was a poor, unknown erstwhile rabbinical aspirant trying, through various genres, styles, and subjects, to break into the literary market. Hess has a secure place in two different intellectual contexts: as the author of the 1862 proto-Zionist epistolary treatise *Rome and Jerusalem* and as a pioneering socialist theoretician and activist who made his most influential contributions in the 1840s. Auerbach made his novelistic debut in 1837 with *Spinoza: Ein historischer Roman* (Spinoza: a historical novel), and in 1841 he published a five-volume German translation of Spinoza's works, prefaced with an original biography of the philosopher.[1] Hess also published his first book in 1837: *Die Heilige Geschichte der Menschheit* (The Holy History of Mankind), which inscribes Spinoza as the avatar of the modern age and appeared anonymously, "by a disciple of Spinoza." One of the rare contemporary mentions of this work by Hess came, in fact, in a review of the *Spinoza* novel by Auerbach, whom the reviewer mistakenly assumed also to be the author of Hess's anonymous book.[2]

Against the background of wide-ranging debates about the role of subjectivity, egoism, and personality in religion, literary culture, philosophy, and politics in Germany in the 1830s and 1840s—some key moments of which I explored in the previous chapter—Hess and Auerbach each drew on Spinoza to try to resolve the challenges subjectivity presented to their (differing) visions of social collectivity. Like the majority of the figures in this book, Auerbach engaged in philosophical politics by drawing creatively on a major philosopher to think his way into the polity. This chapter looks especially at the criticism and literary production of Auerbach's early years to see how his conceptions of Jewish and German identity and community and his engagement with Spinoza shaped one another. My exploration uncovers a pervasive and anxious concern on the early Auerbach's part with being seen as un-German due to his Jewishness and thereby revises David Sorkin's important assessment of the early Auerbach as naively blind to the ways his contributions to German culture could be perceived by non-Jews as not fully German. Auerbach's abiding anxiety is especially evident in the way he was constantly at pains to distance himself and Jews in general from Heinrich Heine, who served as a privileged target for ideologically varied fulminations against purportedly nefarious, egoistic, and Jewish currents in German society. Auerbach deployed Spinoza to negotiate the specter of such purportedly Jewish and un-German flaws and to imagine a liberal patriotism that would have a place for Jews like him.

Auerbach's Early Career

Auerbach was born in the Black Forest hamlet of Nordstetten in 1812 and grew up in its rural Jewish community, attending a traditional *heder* (elementary school) from age six to nine. From age nine until his bar mitzvah he went to an innovative community school whose curriculum included secular subjects. It was here that Auerbach learned to read and write German. Directly after his bar mitzvah, Auerbach's parents, who wished to see him become a rabbi, sent him to attend a traditional yeshiva in nearby Hechingen; but Auerbach did not thrive in the two years he spent there. In 1827 his parents, whose finances had so deteriorated that they could no longer afford the boarding fees, sent him to Karlsruhe. There, with support from his paternal uncle, Auerbach continued to receive tutoring in Talmud while also auditing classes at the Lyceum.[3]

Auerbach discovered Spinoza on his own while, at age eighteen, he was in Stuttgart preparing for gymnasium admission exams.[4] An 1828 Württemberg law had made a university degree obligatory for entrance to the rabbinate. Auerbach passed the gymnasium's entrance exams on his second attempt and, after two years of study, *Abitur* in hand, enrolled in the University of Tübingen in 1832.

After having abandoned his study of theology and law at Tübingen (the two faculties in which he was alternately enrolled), Auerbach felt drawn to philosophy, largely through the lectures he heard David Friedrich Strauss deliver in winter 1832–33.[5] While studying (and attending lectures by Friedrich Schelling) in Munich in summer 1833, Auerbach was arrested for his involvement in the Tübingen *Burschenschaft*. Due to his arrest he was stripped of the scholarship he had enjoyed and expelled from Tübingen, whereupon he continued his studies at Heidelberg. It is unclear to what extent Auerbach retained his earlier desire to become a Reform rabbi, but his criminal record definitively blocked this career path: Auerbach learned in late 1835 that he would be barred from sitting for the theology exams required of rabbinical candidates by the 1828 Württemberg law. It was while studying in Heidelberg that Auerbach first turned to writing as a means of generating much-needed income.[6] He landed a good position as a literary critic for August Lewald's important journal *Europa: Chronik der gebildeten Welt* (Europe: chronicle of the educated world).

Auerbach debuted in 1836 with the essay *Das Judenthum und die neueste Literatur* (Jewry and the most recent literature), and his first significant literary work appeared in August 1836, a substantial sketch of the life of the German-Jewish epigrammatist Ephraim Moses Kuh, a contemporary of Moses Mendelssohn and the first Jewish poet to publish verse in German.[7] Auerbach would later expand this sketch and turn it into his second novel, *Dichter und Kaufmann: Ein Lebensgemälde aus der Zeit Moses Mendelssohns* (Poet and merchant: a picture of life from the times of Moses Mendelssohn; 1840). As Auerbach recounts in at least two places, however, his passionate interest in Spinoza "pushed itself forward" (*drängte sich vor*), and fleshing out the Kuh sketch had to wait.[8] Auerbach began work on his Spinoza novel in autumn 1836. After the conclusion of the criminal investigation into his *Burschenschaft* activity, Auerbach was interned at the Hohenasperg Fortress near Stuttgart from January 8 until March 8, 1837.[9] After his release he continued to research and write his Spinoza novel day and night.[10] It was published in November 1837.

Auerbach's second period of intensive engagement with Spinoza began two and a half years later, when the peripatetic author moved to Bonn at the end of May 1840 (where he made the acquaintance of Moses Hess). Believing his literary activity was over and planning to become a lecturer in philosophy, he began work on his translation of Spinoza's complete works, a project that consumed his energies until the end of August 1841.[11] In the period between his novelistic debut and his work on the Spinoza edition, Auerbach continued literary projects he had begun before writing his novel about Spinoza. His novel about Kuh, expanded from his early biographical sketch, appeared in 1840. He also continued to write literary reviews for *Europa* and edited and wrote for a publication devoted to Jewish biographies, *Gallerie der ausgezeichnetsten Israeliten aller*

Jahrhunderte, ihre Portraits und Biographien (Gallery of the most outstanding Israelites of all centuries, their portraits and biographies).

After completing his Spinoza edition Auerbach tried in various genres to harmonize Spinozan ideas, both explicitly and implicitly, with a liberal vision of the German *Volk*. He hoped to publish his Spinoza biography in *Europa* as a separate piece prior to its appearance in his Spinoza edition, but Lewald, *Europa*'s editor, rejected it on August 16, 1841, as unsuitable for the journal. Shortly after completing the Spinoza edition Auerbach also embarked on what he planned as a cycle of "philosophical stories" (*philosophische Novellen*) intended to highlight in popular form "particular questions [*Aufgaben*] of speculative ethics."[12] Auerbach describes his project of Spinoza-inspired stories in the short preface, dated 1850, to his 1851 story collection *Deutsche Abende* (German evenings), which included the only two stories from the planned Spinoza cycle that came to fruition.[13]

In the preface to *Deutsche Abende* Auerbach recalls further stories he had planned for the Spinoza cycle and remarks that he abandoned the project when he came to have a different view of life.[14] The other "*Fassung des Lebens*" Auerbach embraced is the one for which he would become famous and for which he is remembered today: politically, it entailed faith in an idealized conception of the German *Volk*; esthetically, it manifested itself in Auerbach's turn to what would become his wildly popular *Black Forest Village Stories*. Although Auerbach's explanation that he abandoned his planned Spinoza cycle due to a changed worldview suggests a neat shift from a concern with Spinoza to a preoccupation with the *Volk*, attention to these sources reveals not only cesurae but also surprising continuities between Spinozan philosophy and German *Volkstümlichkeit*, as Auerbach conceived them.

Auerbach was at work on his Spinoza stories and earliest *Dorfgeschichten* simultaneously, in late 1841 and early 1842.[15] He completed his first *Dorfgeschichte*, "Der Tolpatsch" (The bumpkin), on December 1, 1841, and a fortnight later wrote to Rudolf Kausler that he was at work on both *Deutsche Abende* and his *Dorfgeschichten*.[16] Auerbach's Spinoza stories and village stories overlapped in in their venues of publication as well as in the chronology of their composition. The journal that rejected Auerbach's Spinoza biography, *Europa*, in September 1842 published "Der Tolpatsch." In March 1843 it published Joseph Braun's highly favorable discussion of Auerbach's new genre, well before the appearance of *Schwarzwälder Dorfgeschichten* in book form in October of that year.[17] To take another example, the appearance of the Spinozan story "Liebe Menschen" in *Der Freihafen* in April 1842 was followed by the *Dorfgeschichte* "Tonele mit der gebissenen Wange" (Tonele with the bitten cheek) in the same journal four months later.

Tracing Auerbach's engagement with Spinoza and his changing visions of German community from his first novel through his abortive cycle of Spinozan stories to the verge of his literary breakthrough as the author of village stories reveals the extent to which Spinoza inspired Auerbach's particular liberal invention of the German *Volk*. The title Auerbach chose for his planned Spinozan cycle—*Deutsche Abende*—attests to his attempt to situate Spinoza at the heart of a vision of Germanness. In the period between the height of his engagement with Spinoza's thought in 1840–41 and his emergence as a phenomenally popular *Volksschriftsteller* in 1843, Auerbach's vision of Spinozan philosophy and his vision of German community would continue to inform each other in striking ways. Even as the *Volk* displaces Spinoza, and the *Dorfgeschichte* the *philosophische Novelle*, as the focus of Auerbach's literary ambitions, Auerbach's understanding of Spinoza continued to undergird his idealized liberal vision of the *Volk*.[18]

Auerbach and the Anxiety of German-Jewish Identity

David Sorkin's epochal *The Transformation of German Jewry, 1780–1840* (originally published in 1987) challenged the paradigm of German-Jewish assimilation by unearthing a distinct German-Jewish subculture. As Scott Spector notes, however, Sorkin did so not by investigating subjective experience as a complex historical phenomenon, but through a structuralist analysis that tends to short-circuit questions about German Jews' own awareness of their situation and predicament.[19] In Sorkin's ingenious interpretation, acculturating nineteenth-century German Jews constituted "a community invisible to itself."[20] An irony lies at the heart of Sorkin's analysis of German Jewry's acculturation process: while Jews in Germany thought they were doing German, Sorkin reveals how they were unwittingly doing German-Jewish. Sorkin defines this irony as structural and therefore not experiential.[21] The subculture's irony *is* its invisibility to itself; it is a kind of dramatic irony born of the fact that Sorkin recognizes something in the situation of the historical actors that they were not equipped to see themselves.

Sorkin devotes an important chapter of *Transformation* to Auerbach as an avatar of the German-Jewish subculture in the realm of secular culture, reading him as a paradigmatic embodiment of the subculture's blindness to its particular situatedness vis-à-vis German culture.[22] Auerbach, however, was not naively blind to acculturating German Jews' discernible Jewishness; rather, he was haunted by anxiety that the Jewishness of his Germanness might indeed be visible. The irony of Auerbach's identity that I would underscore is not the structural irony of self-blindness but an anxious irony of double consciousness. Due to differences in social position and the liminality of Jewish visibility, this form of double consciousness is both similar to and distinct from W. E. B. Du Bois's classic theorization of the divided self-consciousness of *fin de siècle* African Americans.[23] Whereas Du Bois described American blacks' attempt to overcome this painful self-division and achieve a more authentic and unified self-consciousness, Auerbach was more inclined to postulate, idealize, and create forms of German culture in which Jews could see themselves as unproblematically German and no longer subject to double consciousness. Auerbach's pronounced antipathy for any esthetic or political orientation emphasizing social fracture or subjective doubling, non-self-correspondence, wit, or irony is not born of naive freedom from, but rather an anxious disavowal of, double consciousness.

Auerbach's desire to inhabit a unified, quintessentially unironic locus within German culture is perhaps nowhere more evident than in his vexation over Heine and Heinean irony. Auerbach's attack on divided subjectivity and irony and his eschewal, in particular, of a cultural discourse linking irony and Jewishness suggests that the irony of the subculture's situation did not remain neatly in that subculture's own blind spot but haunted its self-image. The linkages between Jewishness and problematic, fissured, or ironic subjectivity that Heine dramatized both as a provocative agent and as an excoriated target converged in the specter of unreconciled Jewish particularity that Auerbach could not blithely or blindly ignore but rather had, anxiously, to try to disavow and neutralize. Both implicitly, in Auerbach's literary criticism, and explicitly, in his novelistic and biographical portraits of the philosopher, Auerbach found in Spinoza's ontology and ethics support for understanding shared human qualities, rather than subjective idiosyncrasy, as embodying true virtue and freedom.

Heine and the Specter of Jewish Egoism

Warren Breckman has demonstrated that, at the latest after David Friedrich Strauss's epochal 1835 *Das Leben Jesu* (Life of Jesus), Young Hegelian theological debates became deeply politicized.[24] The key targets of the Young Hegelian assault on Christian personalism were Restoration Germany's sovereign and aristocratic privileges, which Young Hegelians understood to be theological personalism's political analogues. As it became more radical, the German Left extended its critique from theological to increasingly liberal models of the self until, in Breckman's words, "by the time Marx described political democracy as 'Christian since in it man, not merely one man but every man, ranks as sovereign, as the highest being,' the Left's identification of theological and 'secular' liberal notions of personhood was essentially complete."[25]

In equivocal conjunction with their assault on Christian personalism and its legacy in the egoism of modern society and the ideology of the sovereign liberal self, Young Hegelian intellectuals also frequently pilloried Judaism as a particularly narrow and basely material form of egoism. The problem Auerbach faced had less to do with the German Left's critique of Christian personalism than with how to negotiate the partly overlapping discourse of egoism as a peculiarly Jewish trait. The career of this anti-Jewish sentiment in German Idealism has philosophical roots in Hegel's construction of Judaism as a religion of sublimity that bars mediation with the Absolute: infinitely removed from God, Hegel's Jews are unable to advance the dialectical progress of spirit as subject, and their deficit of spiritual subjectivity manifests itself in a surfeit of brute materiality and egoism. As I discussed in chapter 4, the association of Judaism with narrow egoism became pronounced in Left Hegelian works such as Feuerbach's 1840 *The Essence of Christianity*, Bruno Bauer's 1843 *Die Judenfrage* (The Jewish Question) and Marx's critique of political liberalism by way of response to Bauer. Nor was the protean discourse of Jewish egoism limited to Hegelian sophisticates: it was deployed from both the Left and the Right in politicized literary and philosophical discourse of different registers. In an overdrawn yet still illuminating argument, Paul Rose maintains that egoism was not merely one among many negative traits in the *Vormärz* image of the Jew but was widely seen, even by progressives such as Karl Gutzkow, as the originary Jewish defect from which all others issued.[26]

Heine—the most popular, controversial, and flamboyantly subjective writer of Jewish origin of the period (he had converted to Protestantism in 1825)—served as a lightning rod for attacks on base, deleterious, and indulgent subjectivity, whether understood as liberal, Romantic, French, or (most commonly) Jewish. As the privileged embodiment of problematic subjectivity, especially a despised "Jewish" subjectivity, Heine haunted Auerbach's early career as both an explicit and implicit referent.[27]

Politically opposed constructions of Heine's subjectivity make clear how similar images of Heine could be deployed in the service of divergent projects, and how pervasive critiques of Heinean subjectivity were in the cultural landscape in which Auerbach began his literary career. In summer 1828 the Munich circle around the ultraconservative Catholic journal *Eos*—which is to say, the center of political Catholicism in southern Germany—made Heine a target in its antiliberal campaign when the Catholic theologian Ignaz von Döllinger took aim at him in an attack on the liberalism of Heine's publisher, Johann Friedrich von Cotta.[28] The *Eos* campaign against Heine, which unfolded with interruptions over the next several years, by no means created the image of Heine as egoistic, frivolous, insincere, or witty but lacking in substance, for, as George Peters has shown, this litany of Heinean flaws had become widespread by the late 1820s.[29] The campaign was novel, however, in associating these traits with Heine's Jewishness in an emphatic and sustained way.[30] Döllinger conflated Protestant liberals with morally decrepit and venal Jewish journalists à la Heine and underscored Heine's self-indulgent subjectivity.[31] In an 1831 review of the fourth volume of Heine's *Reisebilder* Döllinger dismisses the "Freiheit" for which Heine calls in *Englische Fragmente* as a passing fad and so much aping of the French.[32] Neither Heine nor the crowd (*Menge*) understands what true freedom is, in Döllinger's view. Heine's book is a "most despicable product of the most depraved Jewish impudence [*Judenfrechheit*]."[33] What Heine and the liberals understand as freedom is really "detachment from mores and morality [*Sitte und Sittlichkeit*]."[34] In a word, liberal freedom is depraved (Jewish, French) egoism, as opposed to wholesome German Catholic communal solidarity.

In 1831, in response to the first volume of Ludwig Börne's *Briefe aus Paris* (Letters from Paris; 1830), Eduard Meyer, a Hamburg gymnasium teacher, published *Gegen L. Börne, den Wahrheit-, Recht- und Ehrvergeßenen Briefsteller aus Paris* (Against L. Börne, the letter writer from Paris oblivious of truth, right, and honor). Directed chiefly against Börne, Meyer's pamphlet also attacked Heine and the Jewish-born satirist Moritz Saphir. Though all three writers had converted to Protestantism, Meyer contended that the name "Jew"

> denotes not only the religion, but also the entire nationality, and so stands in relation to Germans, Slavs, and Greeks, not only Moslems [*Muhammedanern*] or Christians. It is not the Jews' faith that we hate, as they would like to exculpate themselves by having us believe, but rather the many ugly peculiarities of these Asiatics [*Eigenthümlichkeiten dieser Asiaten*], which cannot so easily be cast off with baptism: the insolence and overbearance so common among them, the immorality and insouciance, their cheeky character and their frequently so mean fundamental disposition.[35]

Meyer further characterized Börne and Heine as the most "significant Jewish political literati" whose "ultrarevolutionary orientation" had its "chief cause in the exasperating, misguided [*verkehrten*] nature of their disposition, which is closely linked with their Jewishness [*Jüdischheit*] and which harbors not a bit of love and respect for that which has been historically achieved and cultivated by the German people."[36] In response to Meyer's polemic, the stalwart Jewish rights activist Gabriel Riesser contested the purported Jewishness of Börne and

Heine as well as of their readership, reviewers, epigones, and the character of the age. Regarding Heine, Riesser wrote: "Work yourselves up as much as you want over Heine's flippancy and frivolity; but, in the devil's name, leave the Jews out of it."[37]

Auerbach's first published essay, *Das Judenthum und die neueste Literatur*, included a rebuttal to the influential literary critic Wolfgang Menzel, who had recently concluded an essay called "Unmoralische Literatur" (Immoral literature), in which he attacked the anti-Christian bent of the Young German writers Karl Gutzkow and Ludolf Wienbarg, with the dark question of what Jewry hoped to gain from such "literary lackies" in the struggle for emancipation, "since one hears everywhere that the so-called Young Germany is really a 'Young Palestine,' and since public opinion already generally holds Judaism responsible for all that is obnoxious in the boundless importunacy, the enthusiasm for the French [*Franzosensucht*], and the spiteful impotent hatred toward Germans and Christians" that characterizes Young German propaganda.[38] As Jeffrey Sammons aptly describes it, though, Auerbach's point "is not to defend Young Germany against association with Jewishness, but rather to defend Jewishness from association with Young Germany."[39] Auerbach seeks above all to save Jewishness from association with Heine. He endorses the criticism of Young Germany as promoting a "sensualist radicalism" that "threatened to poison the healthy parts of German national life" and sees Heine as someone who, having realized the insufficiency of the resources of his personality [*Persönlichkeit*], has adopted the laughable [*lächerlich*] posture of a servent of a higher idea—namely, the pseudo-principle of "uninspired sensualism."[40] Auerbach merely wishes to disassociate these tendencies from Jews and Judaism and, clearly, from himself as an aspiring Jewish writer.[41] Auerbach is careful to point out that Heine's Saint-Simonian "*réhabilitation de la chair*," his "new cult," has no use for either Christians or Jews.[42] In this essay Auerbach embraces a version of Judaism consistent with early Reform and insists, repeatedly, that nothing in Judaism in its current historical development is incompatible with belonging to the German national community.

In a postscript Auerbach responds to two essays blaming the Jews for Young Germany's ills, both of which had appeared after he had completed *Das Judenthum und die neueste Literatur*. One was an anonymous pamphlet attacking "Die jeune Allemagne in Deutschland," which characterizes Jews as "homeless hermaphrodites" (*heimathscheuen Zwitter*), "devoid of a fatherland" and unable "to denationalize themselves, no longer to be that which their history, their religion, their innermost nature, their *future* demand—*Jews*."[43] The author asserts an affinity between the Jews and the French, grounded in a shared negating character, and deploys further nasty anti-Jewish stereotypes to hold up Jews as the insidious hucksters of the French culture that he believes is poisoning the pure German *Gemüth*. The other was a subsequent essay that Menzel had penned against Young Germany, "Die junge Literatur." In it Menzel identifies Heine and Heine's Jewishness as the chief source of the ills of the Young German movement.[44] Auerbach does not object to the warning that the essay sounds about the perils of the French (above all, Saint-Simonian) ideas that *jeune Allemagne* was importing from across the Rhine.[45] What he objects to is the fact that the essay pursues these serious issues only as a means of heaping anathema on the Jews and "their supposed leader, the fashionable H. Heine."[46] Combating Menzel's branding of Heine and Gutzkow as the "prototype of Judaism and the Jews," Auerbach asks: "Where is a stroke of Heine's pen that can be attributed to Jewishness per se [*Judenthum an sich*], where a single word that he could not also have uttered as a born Christian?"[47] In a *cri de coeur* Auerbach exclaims: "We [German Jews] respect and love German morality and German heart [*Herz*] because it is also our morality, our heart. I am of the happy, confident conviction that I express the sentiments of the entire young generation of Jews when I add: Test us in the crucible of danger [*Feuerprobe der Gefahr*], and you will find us pure, pure of all dross [*Schlacken*] of egoism and cunning vice [*raffinierter Unsitte*]."[48]

Although Spinoza makes only fleeting appearances in Auerbach's debut essay, the philosopher's legacy is a significant subtext of the aspiring writer's vigorous dissociation of himself and Jewishness from Heinean self-indulgence. One of the key texts with which Auerbach takes issue is Heine's *Zur Geschichte der Religion und Philosophie in Deutschland* (On the history of religion and philosophy in Germany), which had appeared roughly a year earlier. Heine had attempted, Auerbach writes, "a historical justification for his sensualistic revolts. As the encyclopedists did to church history in order to negate it, he, in his opposition, has recast the history of philosophy as a *chronique scandaleuse*."[49] Auerbach claimed that at the heart of Heine's project was a desire to establish a new religion, "so-called pantheism, i.e. [Heine and Co.] wish to make an idol of the beloved ego [*das liebe Ich*], with all its dependencies and contingencies."[50] Beyond the immediate problem of disputing the purportedly Jewish nature of Heinean subjectivity, Auerbach is particularly exercised by what he considered Heine's egoistic perversion of pantheism: his subversive inscription of Spinoza into the history of German philosophy with the aim of justifying wantonly sensualist subjective pleasures.[51] Auerbach, who was beginning work on his novelistic portrayal of Spinoza as a transcendent figure, would have been distressed indeed by what he saw as Heine's deployment of Spinoza.[52] Heine famously said in *Zur Geschichte der Religion und Philosophie in Deutschland* that pantheism was Germany's secret religion; Spinoza was also a secret subtext of Auerbach's polemic against Heine.[53]

Attacks on the Jewish origins of Heine's frivolity, caustic wit, and self-indulgence continued to shape the context in which Auerbach produced his earliest work. Riesser's sustained attention to the discourse of Heine as the embodiment of a caustically witty and purportedly Jewish subjectivity provides an important index of the extent to which this image of Heine was a political problem with which German Jews had to contend. In 1838 the poet and critic Gustav Pfizer published an eighty-page study of "Heine's Schriften und Tendenz."[54] Riesser devoted the third of his *Jüdische Briefe* (Jewish letters)—in volume 1, published in 1840—to refuting Pfizer, and a significant portion of this important work (all of letters 4, 5, and 7, and part of letter 6) to refuting statements by Menzel, Pfizer, Herman Marggraff, and others who in various ways held up Heine's perceived negative qualities as representative of "Jewish" intellectual currents.[55] Riesser argued that Heine's *Zerrissenheit*, *Witz*, and egoism were functions of his *not* identifying with the Jewish community and its struggles: "Egoism may be cold, flippant, contemptuous, frivolous; empathy is warm and serious. This is the point that distances us, the proponents of the Jewish cause, so infinitely from Heine so that starker contrasts could scarcely be found in the entire field of literature than between him and us." Riesser concurs with Pfizer and his many predecessors that Heine is motivated by "self-interested talent" (*Selbstsucht des Talents*) and that "Heine's subjects [*Stoffe*] merely allow him to practice his wit, his rare talent of speech; he does not serve the cause he treats, he merely wants to make it serve his talents."[56] Proponents of the Jewish cause, in contrast, "have generally been devoid of precisely the quality that Herr Pfizer has the beneficence to designate as characteristic of the Jew, namely wit. The light, flighty, unrestrained nature of wit is not terribly compatible with unconditional devotion to one's cause, with the dogged striving for a particular, serious objective."[57]

In the critique of Heine to which Riesser felt compelled to respond at length, Pfizer, like almost everyone, acknowledges Heine's poetic gifts but bemoans how Heine has inspired so many imitators to take "wit, which kills genuine poetry," as their guiding principle [*Lebensprinzip*].[58] Heine's poetry, moreover, was popular among "frivolous, bored and blasé cosmopolitans [*Weltleute*]" because of the *Witz*, irony, nastiness, unbelief [*Unglauben*], and immorality it contained.[59] Heine's esthetic and moral flaws become only more pronounced in his prose. He is capable of writing good prose when he, only ever briefly, holds back his subjectivity [*seine Subjektivität zurückhält*] and something objective makes him briefly forget "the fundamental theme of his entire authorship, his sublime and ingenious ego." This, however, lasts only as long "as a fish can remain flying above water: he always quickly plops back down into his natural element, his authorial egoism [*Autoregoismus*], his frivolous addiction to wit [*Witzsucht*]."[60] "To take up a lasting, honorable place in German literature," Pfizer contends, it would not suffice for Heine to break particular bad habits; rather, he "would have to cease to be who he is."[61]

Pfizer moreover fantasizes that the proponents of Jewish emancipation "secretly" regard Heine as "one of their own." Even as, with their words, they deplore Heine's rashness, they applaud his blasphemy "with gestures"; and "Christians would have to be quite deaf and dumb not to discern from the hissing and whispering that those ones [*jene*] are proud of their ally [*Bundesgenossen*] Heine."[62] Pfizer warns darkly that it could only damage the cause were the advocates of Jewish emancipation to "move in the intimate company of open enemies of Christianity, and defiantly and arrogantly make a spectacle of their friendship with them."[63] He raises the question of whether Heine, "a Jew by descent if not by confession, has inherited in his essence and character individual traits peculiar to his people [*Züge von der Eigenthümlichkeit seines Volkes*], e.g. wit, audacity, etc."[64] Pfizer further warns Jews that it would only feed the hateful sentiment against them should they follow Heine in behaving tactlessly and polemically, instead of peacefully cultivating the ground that has been yielded to them. Jews should "avoid even the appearance of being in cahoots with a Heine," and eschew his "modish [*eingerissene*] literary Judaizing."[65]

Heine's un-German egoism was not only a target of the Catholic Right and of liberals like Pfizer. As the radical Left in the 1830s took up and extended in its own directions the Catholic Right's earlier critique of Protestant egoism, Heine continued to serve as a privileged bête noire, as the Heine criticism by the Young Hegelian Arnold Ruge attests.[66] In *Jüdische Briefe* Riesser notes Ruge's lengthy 1838 essay on Heine as a rare critique that refrains from associating Heine's flaws with his Jewishness.[67] Although Ruge portrays Heine as essentially un-German and at times smears him with antisemitic associations, indeed Ruge does not exploit Jewishness as a central component in his Heine critique.[68] As Breckman notes, until his engagement with Feurbach's 1841 *Das Wesen des Christentums*, Ruge saw the incursion of Catholic irrationality and arbitrary authority as the main threat to political progress in Prussia.[69] In the manifesto he coauthored with Theodor Echtermeyer, for example, "Der Protestantismus und die Romantik" (Protestantism and Romanticism; 1839), Ruge assails Romanticism's overvaluation of "das geniale Ich," which he deems of a piece with the Catholic dualism of God and world and its concomitant arrogant disregard of humanity.[70] Under Feuerbach's influence, Ruge changed his views and identified Protestant freedom as the pseudofreedom of abstract, antisocial, and politically ineffectual individuals—in a word, as the problem rather than the solution. Even after he had shed his optimism about the political viability of secularized Protestantism, however, Ruge continued to hold up Heinean *Witz* as the embodiment of the asocial subjectivity that he now associated chiefly with Protestantism. Bad subjectivity was now Catholic, now Protestant, but it was consistently Heine.[71]

In "Der Protestantismus und die Romantik," Ruge dismisses the Young German writers collectively as the latest incarnation of the Romantic cultural tendencies between 1770 and 1830, although he does not single out Heine. In both his 1838 Heine essay and much of his subsequent Heine criticism, however, Ruge holds up Heine as a symptom of the age and the embodiment of the kind of subjectivity he at that time associated with Catholicism.[72] In his 1838 Heine essay, the still-patriotic Prussian Ruge characterizes Heine as more loyal to France than Germany and contends that Heine's *Witz* prevents him from penetrating Germany's religious and philosophical life.[73] Whereas Fichte and others had sought to liberate the state, the uncommitted Heinean *Genie* wants only to revel in his own impertinence and pseudofreedom.[74] For Heine, "fun and wit are ends in themselves, the only ends."[75] Ruge changed precious little in his critique of Heine as the embodiment of pernicious egoism, even as he came to associate egoism, frivolity, and pseudofreedom chiefly with Protestantism. In his substantial review "Die Frivolität: Erinnerungen an Heine" (Frivolity: memories of Heine; January 1843), for example, Ruge equates "real" with "political" freedom and warns against the "siren song of Protestantism," which is "not to be trusted when it points up [*uns vorspiegelt*] our spiritual freedom within an unfree political life [*Staatsleben*]."[76]

There was, then, a widespread discourse that held Heine up as the embodiment of a corrosive and decidedly un-German form of subjectivity. This image of Heine was remarkably stable even as very different sorts of critics—sophisticated Hegelians and more vulgar intellectuals, archconservatives, liberals, and left-wing radicals, Catholics and Protestants—pressed it into the service of their disparate cultural political agendas. Heine was always implicitly, and not infrequently explicitly, held up as a negative example from whom German Jews should distance themselves. Even though Auerbach saw the weakness of arguments like Pfizer's and, indeed, articulately disputed the association of Jewishness with Heine on which they rested, the *Vormärz* anti-Heine discourse still profoundly shaped the way Auerbach approached his entry into the German literary culture of the 1830s and 1840s. Although Auerbach's distaste for Heine was surely genuine, the call to prove oneself a good German Jew by showing oneself to be the opposite of Heine added urgency to Auerbach's critiques of Heine and the cultural currents for which Heine, however unjustly, was widely held responsible.

Attacks on egoism, indulgent subjectivity, *Zerrissenheit*, *Ichspoeten*, *Selbstbespiegelung*, and so forth were mainstays of the literary criticism Auerbach published in the late 1830s in the journal *Europa*. His pronounced antipathy to literature that drew attention to the joys, torments, contradictions, and ironies of subjective experience is overdetermined by the wider characterization of indulgent subjectivity as socially corrosive and typically Jewish.[77] As Auerbach distanced himself from the specter of Heine and Jewish subjectivity in his literary criticism, the alternative cultural vision he articulated drew implicitly on his conception of Spinozan totality. More than any other figures during his early career, Heine and Spinoza would embody for Auerbach, respectively, the cultural political problem of the widespread perception of an un-German Jewish egoism and its possible resolution.

Auerbach's Early Literary Criticism: Spinoza against Heine

In an 1838 review of Ernst Willkomm's novel *Die Europamüden: Modernes Lebensbild* (The Europe weary: a portrait of modern life), Auerbach justifies the relatively extensive critique to which he subjects this novel with the claim that it is emblematic of contemporary literary culture.[78] He objects to Willkomm's failure esthetically to transform the *Lebensschmerzen* he depicts. Typically, Auerbach takes particular aim at Willkomm's staging of the problematic subjectivity that experiences such woes. He dismisses the book as "nothing but theatrical trappings and coquettish self-reflection" and finds its "coquetting with itself . . . offensive and unnatural."[79]

In Auerbach's view, contemporary literature's prodigal concern with the problematic modern self stems from a fundamental misunderstanding of the nature of historical agency. Against the prevailing pathos of the battered and torn modern subject, Auerbach frames modernity as what we could call a postheroic age. Auerbach's conception of modernity as postheroic tends to strip individuals of their status as historical agents and to assign historical agency, instead, to a collectivity or distilled Everyman. Auerbach welcomes literature that depicts the "wrestling and struggles of our age," but he insists:

> Real or poetic truth must assert its right; no one who desires what is better will be able to befriend manufactured confusions and turpitude; despairing

> about the present and reveling in the future accomplish nothing. Performing a world-historical deed [*eine Weltthat*] is something only a few heroes in human history have succeeded in doing. The nations have ceased to be place-holding zeros that derive value only from the preceding denominator of a hero; peoples' history [*Völkergeschichte*] has thus not died, even if its moments [*Momente*] are not very conspicuous.[80]

Auerbach praises literature that engages the present, yet he insists it must distill a "poetic truth" (*poetische Wahrheit*) from the present age that transcends its confusions and turpitude. The present must not be seen as a hopeless imbroglio that only a radically different future might disentangle and redeem. Auerbach implies, moreover, that such an erroneous view of the present stems from the equally erroneous view that history is (still) made by great men or heroes. In the modern world the nations have come of age as collective agents and no longer need a national hero to lend them worth. Instead of a "heroic" history of great individuals Auerbach insists on the importance of a collective *Völkergeschichte*, even if its *Momente* have become inconspicuous and their authors anonymous. Contra the tormented moderns (*modernen Schmerzenreichen*), Auerbach deems the present to be as full of promise as any other time in history. To believe otherwise, he insists, is to forfeit "ourselves" (*uns selber*). The self Auerbach is at pains to preserve clearly is collective; he "solves" the problem of problematic subjectivity with an idealization of anonymous community.[81]

Auerbach's assessment of his age as postheroic was a widely shared sentiment. The title of Karl Immermann's voluminous *Die Epigonen* (1836), the most important German novel of the mid-1830s, attests to a sense of living in the shadow of the cultural and political giants of the preceding age. Yet Auerbach welcomes this perceived historical situation as progress. He expresses his faith in the *Volk*'s collective ability to steer history on a healthy course. Auerbach implies that the modern subject can contribute to healing the historical rupture and fragmentation that modernity has wrought precisely by avoiding excessive self-reflection, which only exacerbates the crisis it strives to ameliorate.

Auerbach held up Ferdinand Freiligrath's *Gedichte* (1838) as a laudable model for appreciating the relationships among literature, history, and subjectivity. Commending a turn in Freiligrath's poetry from exotic fantasies of faraway places (*Ausländereien*) to historical portraits (*historischen Bildern*), Auerbach writes:

> In what has historically gone before, the purely human once manifested itself in a particular form; the poetic understanding of the past affords the possibility either to depict the contemporary moment [*das Zeitgenossische*],

> from a historical point of view, as something objective, or to grant subjectivity a breakthrough and elevate the suffering and hopes of the individual—as resonant in the revelation of the age—to a higher universality. Freiligrath can in many respects be seen as the diametric opposite of the *Ichspoeten* who can never get beyond their contingent experiences [*Begebnisse*]; he keeps his subjectivity mostly to himself. He strives with laudable energy after an objectivity in which he can maneuver freely [*in der er frei schalten könne*].[82]

Auerbach locates the strength of the historical portrait in its ability to put subjectivity into a universal perspective. The *Ichspoeten* indulge in the contingencies of subjectivity, but a "poetic" gaze on history distills its higher "objective" truth. Such a perspective on the past also offers a model for how to look at the subjective vicissitudes of the present, whereby these, too, reveal the age's "purely human" essence.

In Auerbach's appreciative assessment, Freiligrath's poetry deploys historical distance and perspective to look at subjectivity and contemporaneity (*das Zeitgenossische*) in a manner that approaches the Spinozan ideal of regarding events *sub specie aeternitatis*. Such a view approaches timeless rational truth and reveals subjective problems as the ephemeral, illusory product of a limited perspective. Freiligrath's historical perspective, in other words, offers a way to grasp not only what has been universal and objective in subjective experience in a past moment, but it also offers a corrective to understanding the present in terms of contingency and subjective experience. Freiligrath's poetic historical perspective offers a way to look at contemporaneity as though from a historical remove. It is in this sense that Auerbach sees Freiligrath's perspective as the opposite of that of the despised *Ichspoeten*. Such a perspective is the vanishing point of subjects into humankind, particularities into generality, and contemporaneity into the revelation (*Offenbarung*) of history. Auerbach's linking of Freiligrath's pursuit of objectivity to the exercise of free agency (*in der er frei schalten könne*) likewise jibes with Spinoza's conception of virtue and true freedom, which is achieved by overcoming subjective passions and acting in unity with the objective world. The implicit Spinozist subtext for Auerbach's literary criticism emerges more starkly in view of how, in both his novelistic portrait and biography of Spinoza (which I will examine in a moment), Auerbach identifies the sage's most profound ethical legacy to be having shown that what human beings have in common embodies more rationality, virtue, and freedom than whatever might be peculiar to individuals.

In another 1838 *Europa* review, "Bemerkungen über Titel und Vorreden in der neuesten schönen Literatur" (Remarks on titles and prefaces in the most recent literature), Auerbach castigates broad contemporary literary trends and offers a programmatic vision of the purposes that literature and literary criticism should serve. Literature should act as "a powerful lever for the higher cultivation [*Bildung*] of the age" and, to do so, must assume the form of "clear, unadorned simplicity," which Auerbach opposes, once again, to the literature of indulgent subjectivity, self-reflexivity, irony, and inner turmoil.[83] In this review Auerbach bemoans the wave of travel writings initiated by Heine's *Reisebilder* (1830). He disparages Heine's "*Selbstironisirung*" and expresses the hope that with Heinrich Laube's multivolume *Reisenovellen* (1834–37), "subjective, niggling [*subjective räsonirende*] travel literature has . . . been put to rest."[84] Auerbach emphatically rejects self-conscious writerly postures, which isolate a clique of literati from the broad public.

Auerbach's meditation on the prefaces—the most subjective form of paratext—to recent books amounts to his own preface of sorts to the literary criticism on which he was embarking at *Europa*:

> Among the ancients a preface was an appeal to the muses; for us it is an appeal to the critics. Among the ancients the poet retreated with his personality [*Persönlichkeit*] completely into the work; among the moderns we find "I" or the modest royal "we" on nearly every page. Börne was the first to have the courage truly to say "I." This is acceptable for discussion [*für die Discussion*], but not in higher poetic composition. . . . Critics, for their part, should avoid this self delight [*Ichslust*] most of all, and vigilantly guard against appraising new literary publications with reference to their own literary positions.
>
> These individual observations may then be regarded as a preface to critical reviews that we are here beginning anew. "I" and "we," which have become so commonplace, will not appear here in this personal sense. Henceforth all of the significant publications of contemporary literature of all casts shall be evaluated here with scrupulous impartiality, far from all cliques; and we hope that our readership [*das Publicum*] will not deny us amicable interest [*freundliche Theilnahme*].[85]

In Auerbach's contest between the ancients and the moderns, the emergence of the ego into literary (or public) culture represents modernity's defining feature. In contradistinction to a temporally vague group of premodern authors (ostensibly it reaches back to antiquity and ends definitively only with Börne's emphatic *Ich*), modern authors are marked by and stage their subjectivities. In place of the ancient continuity between muse, poet, and (implicitly) audience, modern writers take up positions in a conflictual cultural field and confront critics in metatexts.

After such reflection on the nature and dangers of the authorial "I," how Auerbach negotiates his own voice in what he characterizes as a preface to his activity as a literary critic for *Europa* becomes especially interesting. He delays his own pronomial appearance until after he has emphatically denied critics the right (and pleasure: *Ichslust*) of writing from a subjective position. Auerbach's "*wir*" finally appears, then, in already negated form. He assures readers he will studiously eschew the prevailing trend of deploying a personal *ich* or *wir*. Yet the status of the final "*wir*" in the passage quoted above ("we hope that our readership will not deny us amicable interest") remains enigmatic. Does it or does it not refer to Auerbach as the subject of a desire to be accepted? In rendering this question undecidable, Auerbach both abdicates a particular subject position and performatively produces a literary community into which he can be amicably received.

Auerbach continued to critique and dissociate himself from Heine and the excessively subjective cultural trends for which Heine rightly or wrongly served as the emblem.[86] His antipathy toward Heine finds its most vigorous expression in his scathing review of Heine's (scandalous and almost unanimously condemned) 1840 book *Heine über Börne*. Auerbach's review appeared on October 25 and 27, 1840, when he was intensively at work on translating Spinoza, and—if read carefully—it points in subtle ways to a Spinozan ethos as a curative to Heine's egoistic pathology. Auerbach evokes the well-worn criticisms of Heine's attention-grabbing antics, *Keckheit*, fascination with himself, and so on. He also joins the chorus of those who hold Heine responsible for the sort of ephemeral writing, sustained by spectacle and personality, that they thought was compromising literature in middle-class society (*in der bürgerlichen Gesellschaft*).[87] Because "Heine remained reduced to his personality," he had squandered his poetic genius and made no abiding contribution to literature.[88]

Auerbach cites a passage in which Heine derides the common notion of character (the quality routinely denied him) as merely a mirror in which philistines admire their own conformity and insists that great spirits (like himself) transcend character as it is understood by the mediocre majority (*die Menge*). Auerbach counters by pitting what he sees as Heine's lack of *Charakter* (and surfeit of *Persönlichkeit*) against a concept of character clearly indebted to Spinoza:

> Heine [considers] his a great life; thus he will relegate to the common masses all who deny him character in the higher sense. Actually every thing has character, every person, even the most volatile, changeable, as nothing can step

> out of its nature and sever all its inner connections [*allen innern Zusammenhang abschneiden*]. In this sense even the one most lacking in character can be ascribed that as his character; but character as dispositional consistency [*Gesinnungstreue*], as unity between appearance and essence [*Schein und Sein*], this is something that very few indeed have achieved.[89]

In Auerbach's view, "nearly everything Heine has written emanates from his *Ich*; everything clusters and pivots around this *Ich*; he can make no claim to objective judgment."[90] In both his poetry and his politics, Heine appears "now in this, now in that guise with his *Ich*," whereas true character comes from grasping the objective truth that subjectivity's vicissitudes obscure, thereby achieving unity between one's inner and outer life.[91] Auerbach's acknowledgement that everything has a particular character and cannot step outside its nature echoes Spinoza's ontology. More important, Spinoza's understanding of virtue informs Auerbach's ideal of character as unity between *Schein* and *Sein*. Spinoza defines virtuous individuals as people who come to understand themselves (or their bodies' ideas) "under a species of eternity." They thereby become self-determined rather than determined from without. Through greater, more powerful understanding, the virtuous overcome obscure imagination, illusion, and their enslavement to passions (*Schein*). Guided by eternal reason, they achieve unity between the self and the eternal world (God, or nature).[92] Spinoza is the implicit standard against which Auerbach measures Heine's immoderate *Ich*.

However we assess Auerbach's strategies for dealing with the minefield he faced as a young, unknown Jewish writer, we can appreciate his quandary: How was one to enter the scene as a Jewish writer, when any marker of Jewishness tended to expose one to the protean charge of Jewish egoism? Auerbach's ambivalent engagement with Jewish biography reflects this predicament. His construction of Spinoza's life models a way to reconcile Jewish particularity with unassailable universality. For Auerbach, Spinoza embodied everything Heine was not.

Auerbach's Jewish Biographical Portraits

Just as the discourse of Jewish subjectivity was a crucial subtext of Auerbach's literary criticism of the 1830s and 1840s, it also inevitably complicated his forays into Jewish biography as editor of the *Gallerie der ausgezeichnetsten Israeliten aller Jahrhunderte, ihre Portraits und Biographien* [Gallery of the most outstanding Israelites of all centuries, their portraits and biographies] and as author of "Das Leben Spinoza's" (The life of Spinoza). Auerbach is notably ambivalent about the genre of Jewish biography, and his aims in undertaking these projects indeed pull him in opposite directions. Even as he presents prominent Jewish personalities, Auerbach tries to uncouple Jewishness from its associations with the fraught image of egoistic and caustic personality that was the object of so much contemporary criticism.

In June 1836 Auerbach and Naphtali Frankfurter assumed the coeditorship of the Stuttgart-based *Gallerie* (Auerbach edited the fifth and last volume by himself in 1838).[93] Under its prior editors, Gustav Schlesier and a certain Count Breza, the first three issues of the *Gallerie* had featured a promiscuous mixture of "outstanding Jews" from Moses to Spinoza to David Friedländer, and from Maimonides to Heine to Rahel Varnhagen.[94] Auerbach and Frankfurter changed the editorial orientation markedly.

The preface to the 1836 *Gallerie* is unsigned but, given its tone and content, was almost certainly written by Auerbach.[95] He strains, not very successfully, to reconcile the demands of a publication whose very title promises to profile the most outstanding "Israelites" of all ages with his desire to dissociate Jewishness from the vexed category of personality and, indeed, to downplay the role of heroic personalities in history altogether.

Auerbach vigorously rejects the approach earlier employed in the *Gallerie*, which, in Auerbach's description, had been to "portray, through the cases of particular individuals, the undeniable existence of great human refinement in the Jew—in order to demonstrate the duty of humanity . . . and of *raison d'état* . . . to remove these obstacles and let those innate human capacities [*menschlich(e) Uranlagen*] develop freely." The changed appreciation of the convert encapsulates the new editorial departure. It had made sense for the former editors to include converts in the *Gallerie*, given their emphasis on the Jew's innate capacity for human refinement, "since surely no one would maintain in earnest that a radical rebirth has taken place through the mere act of conversion."[96] Auerbach announces, however, that the new editors will be discontinuing this practice.

The new editorial point of departure is that Judaism—now defined narrowly as a particular religion—harbors no impediment to human development and is thus actually irrelevant in the calculus of personal greatness. Above all, Jewishness must not be considered a character trait: "A dogmatic particularity as such can never be regarded as a definite obstacle to the attainment of universal human or civil purpose so long as the foundational elements contain no such obstacle. The fact that Judaism harbors no such obstacle, even if not yet recognized universally in theory, has, however, been demonstrated in actuality. The attribute Israelite or Jew may no longer be considered a character trait [*Charakteristicum*]."[97] The problem with this argument, of course, is that it erodes the entire conception of a gallery of "outstanding Israelites," which willy-nilly inscribes Jewishness as a characteristic of the great personalities it profiles. The preface directly broaches its central contradiction, yet the attempted resolution of this paradox only underscores its thorniness: "But what, then, is the point of a Gallery of the Most Outstanding Israelites? Precisely because we hope, and confidently work to bring about, that in the appraisal of a prominent personality one will nevermore inquire into the accident of a person's birth within a given religion—precisely therefore it is now the time to sketch the figures who are still viewed under the aspect of this outlook."[98] Auerbach's contorted and temporally vertiginous motivation for the continued need to feature the all stars of Jewish history postulates the immanence of an era in which the question of a person's birth into a given religion will have been rendered moot. In this future, the present approach to the Jewish past—which still sees Jewishness as a significant component in a Jew's biography—will seem so strange that it is worth prolonging for the moment, if only to document it for posterity. Auerbach's aim is to deploy the *Gallerie* in such a way that its presentation of the great figures of Jewish history will undo not only the rationale for including apostates, but the very logic on which the *Gallerie* is founded.

As it continues, the preface displaces the focus on Jewish personalities into the realms of culture and science, in which the contributions of Jews should not be seen as related to their Jewishness. In looking back at the Jewish past, Auerbach asserts, it is imperative to focus not on Jewish individuals per se but on individuals only as vehicles of significant cultural achievement. Jewish cultural history is destined to be appreciated merely as one component of universal culture. Auerbach announces, furthermore, a shift from *Culturgeschichte* to *Wissenschaftshistorie*, which downplays not only the Jewishness of an individual but the individual *tout court*. Although the realm of culture, as Auerbach and his age understood it, remained inherently indebted to the categories of personality, genius, and greatness, the correlation between individual personalities and their contributions to the history of *Wissenschaft* is far more tenuous. Thus in analogy to how the history of science is obliged to "foreground persons whose greatness per se significantly pales in comparison to their work [*Wirksamkeit*]," the new "scientific" editorial policy will give due attention to "apparent anomalies in the developmental history of Jewry [*Judenthum*]"—that is, to achievements by persons whose personality is unremarkable and irrelevant.[99]

As Auerbach turns his attention from the past to the present, he continues to sever the connection between Jewishness and personality by reducing Judaism to a narrow question of faith, and to promote the resolution of Jewish particularity into cultural universality: "When we look around in the present, our aim must be [*so gilt es*] to demonstrate through the cases of particular individuals how Jews everywhere strive to be able to pursue unimpeded, as here and there it is already granted them to do in full measure, their yearning for the true and the great; and how they strive, while retaining their independence of faith, to let their particularities be resolved totally into the service of advancing the general good."[100] The new editorial preface announces the aim to portray not particular Jewish individuals but to demonstrate, through the depiction of Jewish individuals, the Jews' will to universality. Jews everywhere wish completely to resolve their Jewish particularity (*Specialitäten*) into the cause of the common weal. Auerbach's editorial vision was to make the *Gallerie* the swan song of Jewish personality as an operative cultural category, to feature Jewish personality at its vanishing point.

Auerbach contributed four essays to the *Gallerie*. He profiled Gabriel Riesser in the fourth volume and wrote all three portraits in the fifth—on "Rothschild and the Jews," Gotthold Salomon, and Michael Beer.[101] The essay on Beer is arguably the richest with regard to Auerbach's uncoupling of Jewishness and personality.[102] A playwright who in his short life (1800–1833) produced three plays, Beer achieved greatest success with the one-act *Der Paria* (1823), a work in indirect support of Jewish emancipation. Early in the essay Auerbach hails, in Beer's example, the advent in Jewish history of a certain normality in the education process that will repay the losses it entails in "great personalities" (*großartige Persönlichkeiten*) with what Auerbach characterizes (in a phrase he would repeat in various contexts) as "an even temperature of education" (*eine gleichmäßige Temperatur der Bildung*). Auerbach upholds such evenness as the ultimate goal of intellectual endeavor:

> It is gratifying finally to come upon, in the history of the Jews, an educational trajectory with the regularity and consistency that spares individuals from having to work their way through a series of obstacles to [achieve] their natural development. While this entails that far fewer great personalities emerge, an even temperature of education radiates in all directions, and this must indeed remain the aim of all intellectual striving [*geistigen Strebens*]. We mustn't bewail the demise of Jewish poetry and philosophy in our age; poetry and philosophy must rest upon a purely human foundation. When built upon dogmas and confessional beliefs, they have always a merely subordinate value, and only when they open onto universality do they attain their true significance.[103]

Regularity and an "even temperature" of education is preferable to the idiosyncratic greatness of earlier autodidacts, who had to struggle mightily to gain access to European culture. The resolution of specifically Jewish into universal culture, moreover, is to be celebrated, not bemoaned.[104]

Beer's indirect portrayal of Jews through the pariah class in India elicits intriguing remarks from Auerbach regarding the viability of representing the "humanity" of Jews through direct portrayal of them as Jews. Auerbach opines that it surely was not a coincidence that Beer wrote *Der Paria*—in which "the poet tried to mollify the laments of his brothers and to erect an eternal memorial to their pain"[105]—in 1823, a year that witnessed the definitive repeal of many of the civil rights extended to Prussian Jews during the era of reform following Napoleon's defeat of Prussia in 1806: "Yet he could not thematize Jews and Jewish life directly, since, aside from the fact that ill-wishers here trumpet as animosity much that is only a cry of pain from a tortured breast, tragic pathos could have easily been redrawn here as comic derision. Hostile critics would have dragged in a Jew from any old street corner with all his ridiculous junk, motley neckerchiefs, worn trousers and copper kettles; and one single: 'No business to do?' [*Nichts zu handeln?*] would have destroyed the entire illusion among the broad public, which sticks so fondly to externals."[106] Auerbach's meditation on Beer's predicament speaks volumes about his own. He suggests that the indirection by which Beer engages Jewish concerns is necessary for any portrayal of the injustice with which Jews contend. Had Beer approached his subject head on, his play would have been taken by many as an act of hostility. Even more inescapably, it would have forfeited its moral and political force because recognizable signifiers of Jewishness needed only the slightest nudge—if indeed they needed any at all—to cross over into despised and risible stereotypes in the eyes of the broad public. Thus the Jewishness of Jewish experience had to be rendered invisible.

Finally, the Beer essay exemplifies the intimacy between Auerbach's persistent efforts to attack and distance himself from what were perceived as corrosive modes of subjectivity and his anxiety that any mark of Jewishness might signify such subjectivity:

> [Michael Beer's] decided talent and his propensity for the theater protected him . . . from the prevailing ego poetry [*Ichspoesie*], which collapses utterly if one extracts from it the personality of the author. These ego poets [*Ichspoeten*], who speak endlessly of their interesting persons, their true and fabricated sympathies and antipathies, and regard phenomena outside themselves [*eine fremde Erscheinung*] at most through a critical lorgnette. . . . M. B. cannot be placed in the first tier of German poets . . . , but M. B's name will still be named when the much-admired and oft-discussed ego he-

roes [*Ichsheroen*] are long gone, along with the age whose capricious moods they indulged and which thus coddled them.[107]

The poets who are extravagantly concerned with their own subjectivity, the "*Ichsheroen*" to whom Auerbach strenuously opposes Beer, are capable of regarding a phenomenon other than themselves at best only "through a critical lorgnette" (*mit kritischem Lorgnett*), an image and phrase that evoke the "Frenchness" and captiousness of Auerbach's literary adversaries. In distancing Beer from the overly critical and foreign subjectivity of the *Ichspoeten*, Auerbach seeks to safeguard him from the same anti-Jewish stereotype conflating the unwelcome Other within with the enemy across the Rhein that he had challenged in his debut essay, in which he disputed the linkage between "*la jeune Allemagne*" and Jewishness. Moreover, it eventually becomes clear that Auerbach is at pains to defend Beer from the charge of extravagant subjectivity as a Jewish characteristic: "It has rightly been noted that M. B. is an example that can serve to expose the spuriousness of those allegations that aim to instill in the Jews a bad conscience for all the extravagances of Christian authors, and that descry every free expression of life by a Jewish author as an anti-Christian tendency."[108] Echoing his argument in "Das Judentum und die neueste Literatur," Auerbach holds Beer up as evidence of the spuriousness of Menzel's and others' attempt to derive the "extravagances" of even Christian authors from a pernicious quality of Jewishness.

Auerbach's Biography of Spinoza

Much of Auerbach's biography of Spinoza is metabiography. Auerbach reflects at length on the relationship between Spinoza the person and Spinoza the *oeuvre*. Auerbach's meditations furthermore recall his engagement, in his editorial introduction to the *Gallerie* some five years earlier, with the question of the relationship between cultural history (*Culturgeschichte*) and the history of *Wissenschaft*, and the personalities who make contributions to them. He opens the biography by distinguishing between the different ways that "heroes and statesmen" versus "poets and philosophers" are personally implicated in the actions for which history remembers them. The acts these two categories of protagonist perform can be dichotomized into the contingent historical *Tat* (deed) and the timeless *Geistestat* (intellectual or creative act). Although the person of the historical hero is integral to an understanding of the deeds he or she performs, the works of philosophers and poets possess an eternal truth of their own, independent of their—frequently anonymous or indeed mythical—"authors."[109]

Compared to historical heroes, poets and philosophers leave a faint personal imprint on their (intellectual) deeds. Auerbach, however, draws a distinction between the poet and the philosopher. Since poets deal with particular human beings and situations, they necessarily draw on their own experience and that of their age. Philosophers, in contrast, deal with universal truths that have no necessary basis in their particular existence.[110]

Auerbach places Spinoza, however, in a special subcategory of philosopher that defies, in a peculiar way, the general rule of the nonrelationship between a philosopher's *Individualität* and work. The philosopher who belongs to this exceptional category manages to shed all subjective idiosyncrasies and become one with his universal thought. As the exceptional convergence between philosopher and philosophical work, Spinoza embodies the human freedom he theorizes: Spinoza the person embodies his philosophy.[111]

Later in the biography Auerbach refers to Spinoza's critique of anthropocentrism to cast Spinoza as the anti-egoist par excellence: "Spinoza's life and teaching are the diametric opposite of all egoism in the broadest sense. 'All prejudice,' he understood, 'stems from the fact that people view themselves as the center of the universe and wish to comprehend everything only in relation to themselves.' Thus elevated above all particularities he treated the workings of the human soul so freely and independently, so objectively, 'as if it were a question of lines, planes and bodies.'"[112] Spinoza's displacement of the human subject from the center of the universe prepares Spinoza's movement, in Auerbach's portrait of him, beyond the confines of subjectivity. The events of Spinoza's life—the ban pronounced against him by Amsterdam's Jewish community, his break with community and family, and so forth—uprooted him and rendered him the ultimate modern individual, disentangled from familial and communal bonds. Even more important, Auerbach sees Spinoza as embodying his own principle that "the more decisively and consciously one displaces oneself out of the subjective and individual [and] into eternal and infinite life, the more the infinite and the finite are reunited, the more one lives in eternity, in immortality, in God."[113] Spinoza's existential freedom did not lead him to luxuriate in selfhood's pleasures or wallow in its miseries but was essentially synonymous with the harmony he achieved between his particularity and God's timeless universality.

Auerbach concludes his biography with a caution against two perilous extremes of misinterpretation of Spinoza's pantheistic philosophy. The one extreme sees in Spinoza cause for total resignation. Auerbach takes issue with Goethe's interpretation of Spinoza along these lines.[114] If it is wrong to infer from Spinoza's pantheism that the self lacks agency, however, the other extreme, which Auerbach calls "unconditional libertinage," is infinitely more insidious.

This view holds that, since God is everywhere and everything, whatever one desires must, by definition, issue from God and be good. Auerbach castigates this position vehemently as destroying "the world's entire moral foundation": "Pantheism was forced . . . to endure that the most wanton subjective tendencies took refuge at its altar and now even wished to be pronounced holy; the monstrosity of a concept of a free divine subjectivity pompously entered with all its unbridled pretensions."[115] Auerbach objects to the interpretation of Spinoza's pantheism as incompatible with individual freedom because he follows Spinoza in believing that individuals realize freedom not in their idiosyncrasies but in their movement from idiosyncrasy to universality, a trajectory that Spinoza's life had paradigmatically traced. Auerbach leans on Spinoza's famous refutation of the divine origin of miracles in the *Theological-Political Treatise* to argue that pantheism shows that our highest, most holy, and freest nature lies not in our uniquely distinguishing subjective qualities but in the universal qualities common to all: "To consider what is distinguishing and peculiar in subjective nature as higher is the same error as if one were, in objective nature, to consider a miracle a higher revelation than the constant, universal, law-governed course of things. And herein—that what is universal and common to all is what is higher—lies the holy calling of pantheism's moral and its freedom-giving power."[116]

Auerbach's interpretation of Spinozan pantheism as the ultimate guarantor of community provided the ethical standard by which Auerbach critiqued the dangers of excessive subjectivity. The community that Auerbach drew on Spinoza to envision became increasingly patriotic and culminated in the work that made Auerbach famous as a German *Volksschriftsteller*, the *Black Forest Village Stories*. The final sentence of Auerbach's Spinoza biography sums up the essence of Spinoza's philosophy in terms that equally characterize the ethos and esthetic of the village tales, to which Auerbach turned shortly after publishing his Spinoza edition: "to subordinate the particular to the general, yet still to portray the former in the latter . . . this is the essence of active [*tätigen*] pantheism."[117] Auerbach's attempts to use Spinoza to imagine an inclusive German *Volk* took several forms, however, beginning with his first novel.

Auerbach's Jewish Novels

In addition to the biographical entries in the *Gallerie*, Auerbach published a sketch of Kuh in 1836, which—as noted above—he later expanded into his second novel, *Dichter und Kaufmann* (1840).[118] Between the sketch and completion of his novel about Kuh, Auerbach made his novelistic debut with *Spinoza*. Spinoza and Kuh are opposites, the successful and unsuccessful Jewish negotiation of modern subjectivity. Circumstances conspire to unmoor both figures from the social context of their youth and to leave them isolated individuals. Yet they handle their fate as orphaned subjects very differently: Kuh tragically fails in his attempts to inhabit different social roles and milieus. Like Auerbach's parents, Kuh's wished their son to become a rabbi, but Kuh—like Auerbach—became a German writer instead. Finding no viable social locus or identity, he finally succumbs to insanity. He experiences modern subjectivity ultimately as brute isolation.

If Auerbach's Kuh succumbs to the perils of modern subjectivity, his Spinoza transcends them. In a reminiscence written on the occasion of the unveiling of the Spinoza memorial in The Hague in 1880, Auerbach remembers how difficult it was to render as a vibrant literary character a "philosopher who is not moved by affects and passions but rather regards all life *sub specie aeterni* [*sic*], for whom the temporal and the eternal are one."[119] Yet if Spinoza's view from eternity made him an awkward novelistic hero, it also made him attractive to Auerbach as an archetypical modern individual: "the first and possibly most perfect *homo liber*, which he held up as the purest ideal. Spinoza relocated the ideal human being from the clouds of myth to the daylight of knowledge as *homo liber*, the free individual. Spinoza was the first self-made man in the most eminent sense, and that has become the signature of the modern world."[120] Although in Auerbach's novel Spinoza's progressive estrangement from Jewish tradition and community leave him socially isolated, the kind of isolated individuality he embodies is the diametrical opposite of the widely deployed stereotype of the Jew as an egoistic and nefarious foreign element within German society. Even as an individual outside the Jewish community, Auerbach's Spinoza continues to contest the discourse of Jewish egoism with which Auerbach had contended in "Das Judentum und die neueste Literatur." Spinoza's embodiment of individuality and universality, moreover, points ultimately to the possibility of collective harmony. At its culmination Auerbach's novel stages Spinoza in the role of a rational secular messiah, the harbinger of a secular humanism into which both Judaism and Christianity are destined to evolve.

Critics have interpreted Auerbach's portrait of Spinoza differently. Jacob Katz reads Auerbach's *Spinoza* as a "utopia of total assimilation."[121] In a nuanced reconstruction of the position of *Spinoza* between works by Gutzkow and Goethe, Jonathan Skolnik sees Auerbach's novel within a nineteenth-century tradition of Jewish-German historical novels that sought to create "usable fictional pasts" for a secularizing German Jewry. In Skolnik's reading, *Spinoza*—though not devoid of inner ambivalence—remains basically consistent with the universalizing, denationalizing thrust of the nascent Jewish Reform movement, and optimistic about the prospects for a German-Jewish synthesis.[122] In a study of Spinoza as a secular Jewish icon, Daniel Schwartz reads the relationship between Auerbach's debut essay and debut novel as ambivalent and helpfully identifies the status of the modern Jewish individual as the central vexing question posed by the relationship between these two texts. Schwartz points to an exchange in *Spinoza* between the philosopher and another character, da Silva, who (anachronistically) articulates the project of Reform Judaism. Spinoza rejects this project and opts for what Schwartz characterizes as "categorical individualism."[123]

Yet even as Schwartz nicely draws attention to an unresolved conflict in *Spinoza* between Auerbach's support for a Reform institutional religious framework for modern Jewish collective existence and a radical individualism that breaks with Jewish collectivity, he leaves underexplored how Auerbach's project was to envision and forge a German community in which Jews would have a place.[124] Auerbach's central preoccupation was less the tension between Jewish collective commitments and radical individualism than the place Jews could inhabit, whether as individuals or as a collective, within the German *Volk*. Auerbach's argument in "Das Judentum und die neueste Literatur" that a reformed Judaism is capable of sustaining a modern Jewish community cannot be isolated from his insistence, with which it is entwined, that Jews are Germans, and that Germanness and Jewishness in no way conflict. Auerbach's creative use of Spinoza to imagine inclusive versions of the German *Volk* and *Vaterland* go well beyond his explicit depictions and discussions of the philosopher. Indeed, even as Spinoza recedes from view as an icon in Auerbach's work, he continues to inform Auerbach's conception of Germany.

For exploring Auerbach's anxious self-image as a budding Jewish author in Germany, there is no richer text than the preface he attached to *Spinoza*. Since each of Auerbach's two Jewish novels in a sense precedes the other, it is fitting that this preface, titled "Das Ghetto," announced a "*series* of historical portraits of periods and customs from the life of the Jews . . ., of which the present work makes up *the first part*."[125] Here Auerbach has relatively little to say about Spinoza per se, but the way Auerbach imagines speaking to a literary community and the vexed way he stages the reception that awaits his work illuminate the ambiguities and anxieties that accompanied his appearance on the German literary scene with a novel about the Jewish sage from Amsterdam.

Auerbach writes that he would have liked to have placed *Spinoza* at the end of his envisioned cycle of Jewish historical novels, since the Jewish ghetto "in the higher sense ends with Spinoza," but was unable to resist the "force of the idea after it had taken hold of me."[126] Despite numerous abortive plans in his later years, Auerbach never wrote another Jewish-themed work after *Spinoza* and

Dichter und Kaufmann.[127] "Das Ghetto" is a preface to an envisioned career as a writer of Jewish historical novels that Auerbach did not ultimately pursue.

"Das Ghetto" differs markedly from Auerbach's demarcation of the acceptable limits of authorial subjectivity in his 1838 *Europa* essay on prefaces, analyzed above. His authorial position in "Das Ghetto" is divided in a number of ways, and he is hyperaware of writing—or, at any rate, of being read—as a Jewish author. His motivation for undertaking the projected Jewish historical novel cycle is strongly reminiscent of his apology for the biographical portraits in the *Gallerie*. Auerbach appeals to the need to record for posterity images of a rapidly vanishing Jewish life:[128] "Jewish life is gradually disintegrating; one piece after the other breaks off. Therefore it seems to me to be time to let poetry and history and both united preserve its movements in a picture."[129] Unlike in the *Gallerie* preface, however, Auerbach here turns a nostalgic eye toward the inner coherence and self-sufficiency of premodern Jewish life, even as he regards it as having been founded on a distorted worldview:

> One could perhaps designate our age in general as the age of poetic justice; what the previous century and the period of Enlightenment derisively castigated as superstition and folly and had to ridicule and brand with scorn appears to us with awe-inspiring dignity, and even in its distortions we recognize the inner consistency of a hermetic disposition since its sad consequences for life are far removed from us. We are seized by nostalgia [*Wehmuth*] when we contemplate this past: we have lost the old intimacy [*das alte Innige*] and only piecemeal achieved a new one.[130]

As it approaches its vanishing point, and thus no longer needs to be opposed in the spirit of Enlightenment, Jewish life can be granted "poetic" justice in the cycle Auerbach announces with "Das Ghetto." Yet the "*wir/uns*" that bestows such poetic justice is highly ambiguous. The "*wir*" that has lost "the old intimacy" of Jewish life is implicitly Jewish, yet what this collective Jewish subject has lost seems to be distinctly Jewish life itself. Thus does the "*wir*" that has only "piecemeal" achieved a new intimacy coincide with the collective Jewish "*wir*" that has suffered the loss? Or, with the loss of "Jewish life," does the distinction between Jew and non-Jew become so attenuated that this "*wir*" becomes all-inclusive? How useful is this nostalgia for consolidating and sustaining new modes of German-Jewish identity?

A range of possibilities for German-Jewish authorship would emerge in the decades following Auerbach's novelistic debut that were not yet on the cultural landscape he surveyed in 1837. The most influential nineteenth-century German-Jewish journal, the *Allgemeine Zeitung des Judentums* was founded in

1837. As Jonathan Hess has shown in *Middlebrow Literature and the Making of German-Jewish Identity*, this and several other Jewish cultural institutions disseminated a steady diet of middlebrow Jewish fiction to German-Jewish reading audiences. Jewish authors writing for a Jewish audience found ways to reconstruct "usable" pasts, and certain Jewish authors succeeded in depicting usable Jewish pasts also for non-Jewish audiences, as the case of Leopold Kompert, the popular author of ghetto fiction, attests. Kompert began publishing in this genre in 1848 using, ironically, Auerbach's *Black Forest Village Stories* as one of his models.[131] Whereas, in Hess's apt characterization, Kompert's "texts mobilize nostalgia to create new forms of identity for an upwardly mobile, increasingly German-identified Jewish readership,"[132] the operation of nostalgia in *Spinoza* is less viable; and the usability of this Jewish past remains dubious.

Nostalgia is a powerful means of binding a community in relation to an imagined past. Supremely malleable, it can both mark an emphatic break with the past (the object of nostalgia has, by definition, been lost) and offer up an idealized image of the past for enjoyment, identification, and pride.[133] The above passage from "Das Ghetto" tries to construct a nostalgic bridge between the premodern and modern "*wirs*" it puts into play, yet the attempt to deploy nostalgia foregrounds more discontinuities than it smooths over. Auerbach's sarcastic tone provides an important measure of the dividedness and insecurity of his enunciatory position vis-à-vis an uncertain audience. This stance is especially significant because of the extreme rarity of sarcasm in Auerbach's *oeuvre*. The main thrust of his early literary criticism is to attack irony and all forms of enunciative duplicity, and he generally practiced what he preached: utter earnestness. Roughly half of "Das Ghetto," however, is devoted to a spoof of recent Jewish novels and the models—or "recipe"—they offer to the aspiring Jewish writer: "Our belletristic literature is rife with Jewish novels. I want here to give a schema of them and test whether I, too, might have been able to put myself in circulation in this popular way."[134] Auerbach deploys this conceit to parody contemporary Jewish novels and their popular and critical success.

Here is the "recipe" for successful Jewish novels that Auerbach lampoons: A wealthy father who loves nothing but money, save for his beautiful daughter Rahel, "since this and nothing else, or just possibly Judith, is what she has to be called."[135] Rahel, who is as beautiful as an "oriental gazelle" and speaks "as beautifully as the Bible," could never love a "dirty Jew" (*schmutzigen Juden*). (The conscientious writer, Auerbach winks, will consult the Old Testament and find a description of Rahel's beauty in the *Song of Solomon*.) No, Rahel's heart belongs to the Knight Hugo von Hostenthal, though it is a pure, not lascivious, love ("Clauren and Heine had not yet found an audience"). High time, Auerbach writes, for a pogrom! Hugo saves Rahel, who confesses her love to him. Poetic license, Auerbach quips, permits Rahel (who would not have been able to write German) and Hugo (who would not have been able to write) to exchange the most tender of letters: "Philomela's strains are no more tender in *Werther* than in these letters." Alas, however, Knight Hugo grows weary of and abandons the beautiful Jewess and joins a crusade to the Holy Land. Rahel wanders barefoot in the *Judengasse*. Her father has died of grief, and no one gives her refuge.

As he weighs his options for concluding the narrative, Auerbach apostrophizes imaginary readers and imagines how Menzel would react: "Weep, weep with me, you tender-hearted *grisettes*, Friederikas, Emilias, Katharinas, where shall I accommodate my Rahel? I can let her wander about as a harlot, kill herself. But you turn away from me; I have ruined your Sunday reading; I am declared a French *Kraftgenie*; and Herr Menzel hurls his lightning bolt at me. Thus stay just a moment, I have a better alternative. Rahel enters a convent." Rahel, now Ursula, spends her nights bewailing her sorrows and her days tending sick knights. One day she dresses the wounds of—"Help! Help! Bring eau de cologne; she's fainting"—her beloved Hugo. Auerbach considers letting Rahel die before regaining consciousness but dismisses this ending as too hard on the nerves, and instead he has Hugo awaken her with kisses. Rather than running off together, Hugo and Rahel renounce each other: "They speak so beautifully that one must weep. Rahel dies of a broken heart. As Knight Hugo leads his bride to the church he hears the bells from the convent. Rahel is being laid to rest."

Despite the near horror he feels in the face of wit and irony, and his consistent calls for authorial straightforwardness, Auerbach here speaks from anything but a single and stable position. Why this resort to irony? In presenting himself to a reading public, Auerbach feels himself already interpolated as a Jew. Alienated from himself by the imagined gaze of an Other, neither subjective unity nor self-invisibility is an option. Instead, Auerbach tries to subvert through parody the fantasy he imagines his audience has of him as a Jewish writer. Thus the sustained tongue-in-cheek staging of himself as a purveyor of a falsified, exoticized, and eroticized version of Jewish life that was in demand.[136]

Auerbach presents the ready-made authorial role the literary market proffers to the Jewish writer as something between that of a pimp and that of a prostitute. The Rahel whom Auerbach trots out would feed the voracious readerly appetite of Gentile *grisettes* (interestingly, but not surprisingly, women readers are held to blame for the titillating Rahel). Auerbach imagines that this mode of Jewish writing would also find favor with critics like Menzel, whose labeling of the Young German writers as "Young Palestine" had so vexed Auerbach in his

1836 debut essay: "So have I done well? May I not be proud that old *Hofrath* Th[eodor] Hell ranks me beside Wachsmann, and Menzel pats me amicably on the shoulder, only warning me about Frau Therese Huber's novel of renunciation? Now you will be so kind, gentle *grisetttes,* as to recommend me, and next year I will be among Penelope's suitors and will bring you beautiful, beautiful pictures."[137] Though Menzel might think Auerbach is treading too closely to Therese Huber, the former wife of the revolutionary Georg Forster, the Jewish novel that Auerbach parodies would still strike a balance between female and male, popular and critical success.

Auerbach now brings to a close his two-tongued pastiche and invokes his superior knowledge, as a Jew, of things Jewish in order to contest the inaccuracy and mendacity informing the clichés of the "Jewish" novel. In claiming this authority Auerbach continues to address (and imagine himself from the perspective of) a non-Jewish audience. Even as he claims the authority, as a Jew, to point up the melodramatization and exoticization of Jewish life, Auerbach still contends with his interpellation from without as a "Jew" by the vaguely hostile audience he anticipates, and before whom he feels the need to justify himself:

> In this way I might be able to make a decent literary name for myself, but all these hack works are lies, lies from A to Z. Jewish girls were surely as obedient at heart in every age as your blond privy councilor's daughters; they resembled in every age, mutatis mutandis, our beautiful bankers' daughters in Vienna, Frankfurt, and Berlin. They don't fall in love, generally speaking, even with a Jew, an esthetically cultivated clerk [*Commis*], say. They love whomever their fathers permit or command. People make Jewish girls far too interesting. Where, historically, in the Middle Ages, do you find Jewish girls who fall in love by the dozens with Christian knights?
>
> . . . It will not be interpreted as insolence if I maintain that it is infinitely difficult for a Christian to enter completely into the intimacy and the details of Jewish life. There is much that can be experienced only through upbringing, habit, and tradition. We who come from it have the calling to depict it for the world. There is a rich treasure of legends, miracle tales, etc. in the mouth of the people [*im Munde des Volkes*]; we wish to salvage of this whatever can be salvaged.[138]

Auerbach asserts the authority to speak about things Jewish, yet this does not grant him a stable authorial position. The prolixity of Auerbach's profession of unconcern actually attests to how preoccupied he is with the reception he will receive—specifically as a Jewish writer—from Menzel. Auerbach admits it is not without apprehensive hesitation (*Zagen*) that he sends his first major work into the world.[139] However, he insists this feeling has nothing to do with how Menzel will receive him: "Just as little was I concerned that a literary police would plant thoughts in my mind. I consider it the duty of every writer who takes the honor of German literature to heart to speak out openly and frankly about the activities of Hrn. *Menzel*."[140] Auerbach claims not to fear how a "literary police"—that is, Menzel—might plant thoughts in his mind, or fill out his *Seele* with a "Jewish" character. Appearing in a passage devoted to Menzel stretching to some five hundred words, Auerbach's statement that "Hr. M. may consider me a later-born member of Young Germany or place me under a rubric of Jewish writers; it is a matter of indifference to me" is a classic case of protesting too much.[141]

In the midst of so much authorial insecurity, ambiguous relationships to potentially divergent audiences, willed or unwilled dramatization of the ironies of an 1830s German-Jewish writerly self, and intricate defensive strategies on Auerbach's part, it is surprising to come upon the following statement: "I tried to approach that original form of story telling [*Erzählung*] that has nothing but the word. I didn't think of myself even as reading aloud and thus inserted some questions from listeners."[142] Everything in "Das Ghetto" bespeaks an apprehensive hyperawareness of a textualized literary culture and a commodified literary economy that trade in stereotype and cliché. Yet Auerbach wants to imagine himself as a pure *Erzähler*, an oral storyteller, very much in Walter Benjamin's sense of a community-binding transmitter of experience.[143] In this fantasy, no text disrupts the flow of the spoken word between *Erzähler* and *Zuhörer*.

Of course, precious little in *Spinoza* bears out Auerbach's fantasy of immediate oral narration or, more important, the imagined community of readers that such an idealized speech situation would consolidate. Yet it is highly significant that Auerbach emulates this narrative effect, in fantasy, already in *Spinoza*. Auerbach's preface to *Schwarzwälder Dorfgeschichten* echoes his description of his oral narration in "Das Ghetto" in striking ways.[144] He states in the later text: "I almost always thought of myself as narrating orally; the events are like historical facts [*stehen als geschichtliche Thatsachen da*]. Therefore every so often [the narration] had to be sprinkled with rules of life and general observations."[145] Auerbach's self-stylization as an *Erzähler* offering a community-binding mode of oral narration to a listening audience is not the only thing that links his Spinoza novel to his village tales of the 1840s. Recall Auerbach's wish to preserve the treasure of folklore before it vanishes from the mouth of the *Volk*: "There is a rich treasure of legends, miracle tales, etc. in the mouth of the people; we wish to salvage of this whatever can be salvaged." Taken out of context, this sounds like a folklore collection project à la Brothers Grimm, and in many ways it is. The *Volk* in this case, however, is Jewish, and the *Sagen* and *Wundergeschichten* are the remnants of fast-dissolving traditional Jewish life. Auerbach's rendering of Hebrew locutions in provincial dialect further exemplifies his desire to assimilate the Jewish to the German *Volk*: "I have rendered certain Hebrew expressions with German provincialisms, as High German seemed to me not to offer anything that corresponded perfectly."[146] Auerbach's strategies for presenting local Jewish culture and later for rendering the local culture of Black Forest village life are remarkably continuous. The German *Volk* figured as Schwarzwald peasants moves into a literary space that Auerbach had first envisioned for the Jewish *Volk* of his planned Ghetto cycle. In each case, Auerbach provides frequent ethnographic glosses, parenthetically and in footnotes, of exotic customs and locutions for the uninitiated reader. Many of the key characteristics of Auerbach's village tales—the stylized orality of narration and the oral folk culture being narrated, the evocation of locality and regionalism, and the attention to local customs—are already important elements of Auerbach's Jewish novel cycle *Spinoza*.

Auerbach's success in rendering a nostalgic image of a usable Jewish past is, however, very limited in *Spinoza*, for several reasons. Noting the influence of Auerbach's *Schwarzwälder Dorfgeschichten* on Kompert's ghetto fiction, Hess instructively contrasts the two writers' projects: whereas Auerbach "seeks to build bridges . . . between provincial life and a future German political state," Kompert, writing in the Austrian Empire, seeks to harmonize "traditional Judaism and German culture in the most far-reaching sense of the term."[147] It is revealing that Kompert could draw inspiration for his nostalgic portrayals of ghetto life from Auerbach's village tales but not from Auerbach's abortive Ghetto cycle, which—in its programmatic formulation, if much less in its execution—shared many of the goals of Kompert's work. If Kompert aspired to render the recent Jewish past as an esthetic object that could bestow middle-class respectability on acculturating Jews in the German cultural orbit, Auerbach's thrust was indeed more political, even in his early Jewish phase before his popular breakthrough with *Dorfgeschichten*. As a liberal German patriot—indeed, an erstwhile *Burschenschaftler*—Auerbach sought to create a space for Jews not only in the sphere of middle-class German culture but also in an idealized German polity. The most urgent aim of his debut essay, as we have seen, was to contest Menzel's deployment of the label "Jewish" as shorthand for un-German in his attack on the subversive Young German writers and to insist that German Jews are patriotic members of the *Vaterland*. The cultural and political were intimately enmeshed for nineteenth-century German liberals. It is nonetheless possible to identify in Auerbach's envisioned Ghetto cycle a more nostalgia-filled, culturally oriented project of doing poetic justice to the Jewish past, and a more politically motivated interest in Spinoza as a figure who transcends Jewish particularity and points the way to an inclusive liberal politics.

The projects of rendering a culturally usable Jewish past and of rendering a past leading to a liberal German political future pull in different directions that are not successfully harmonized in *Spinoza*. As Nitsa Ben-Ari has noted, the early German-Jewish historical novel (beginning in the 1830s) struggled to balance the not easily reconcilable aims of both disowning the national element in Judaism and looking to Jewish history as a source of pride.[148] Extending to the Jewish past the German fascination with the historical novel that had begun in the 1820s with frenetic translations of Walter Scott and others (who subsequently found native imitators aplenty) was no simple undertaking. Looking back in 1880 on his first novel and the projected cycle it was to launch, Auerbach remarked: "I had read the novels of Walter Scott with great fondness, and even today I am full of admiration for the master of the historical novel. I can say that I have never in my life imitated anyone. . . . I didn't have the slightest intention of imitating Walter Scott; the thought simply entered my mind that it was possible, indeed necessary, poetically to depict Jewish life in its intimacies in a manner similar to how Walter Scott depicted Scottish life."[149] Much in Scott, as a regional Scottish author chronicling the history of a rapidly disappearing minority culture, would have seemed suggestive indeed to the young Auerbach. Edward McInnes notes that the great favor Scott's novels found among German critics was "intimately bound up with the general respect of German critics for his unique position as a regional writer."[150] Yet, as McInnes also stresses, the German appreciation for Scott, the necrologist of Scotland, was only half the story. In contradistinction to the Jewish past that Auerbach in "Das Ghetto" clearly wants to record but not to perpetuate, the Scottish past was one with a national future. Scott's Scottish past was an object of such powerful identification for nineteenth-century Germans because it figured simultaneously the ineluctable loss of a way of life and the resilience of the national subject despite the loss suffered.[151] Auerbach's *Spinoza* could not respond to this double challenge. An unbridgeable chasm separates the Jewish past being narrated from the idealized German national community of *Zuhöher*, whom the act of narration is intended to bind. Auerbach's attempt to create a viable voice in German cultural politics with a Jewish historical novel was fundamentally fraught with contradiction.

Auerbach sought to finesse the tensions inherent in trying to fuse Jewish history and German patriotism by pinning his hopes on the all-resolving figure of Spinoza. The ambiguities regarding the novel's audience—a would-be intimate community, but consisting of whom?—contributed to its failure to find any readership to speak of. Despite the great hopes and fears Auerbach entertained about the reception his debut as a German and a Jewish author would receive, it had little reception at all.[152]

Spinoza would continue for years to shape Auerbach's evolving vision of a German culture and politics, though Spinoza's place in Auerbach's fiction would become less direct. The philosopher appears as an explicit topic of conversation in one of the stories of Auerbach's abortive Spinozan novella cycle, *Deutsche Abende*, but it is only implicit in the other. Even as he continued to envision the reconciliation of particularity and universality in a liberal Germany according to ontological and ethical ideas he considered Spinozan, Auerbach found it most effective to efface Spinoza as a historical Jewish figure. With Auerbach's eventual achievement of a politically and commercially viable form of literary nostalgia, directed toward the idealized provincialism of the Black Forest village, Spinoza recedes from view almost completely and remains detectable only in the shape of the cultural and political space that Auerbach's various attempts at Spinozan patriotism had prepared.

Auerbach's Abortive Spinoza Cycle

In a letter to his cousin Jakob Auerbach on February 27, 1842, the day before his thirtieth birthday, Auerbach related the projects on which he recently had been working: "I've written 'German Evenings,' a sort of new Platonic dialogue. In Kuranda's journal 'Grenzboten,' in this year's November issue, you will find the first: 'Who Is Happy?' In 'Europa' soon the second, called 'Liebe Menschen.' I've also written *Schwarzwälder Dorfgeschichten* (three so far), which are giving me a lot of pleasure. I'm working now on a popular philosophy for the common man [*für den schlichten Bürgersmann*]."[153] *Schwarzwälder Dorfgeschichten* would eventually prove to be Auerbach's ticket to literary success. An adaptation to the German context, according to Auerbach's own cultural and political proclivities, of the American Unitarian preacher William Ellery Channing's *Self-Culture*—the "popular philosophy" to which Auerbach refers—would appear as *Der Gebildete Bürger: Buch für den denkenden Mittelstand* (The cultivated citizen: book for the thinking middle class) in 1843. Auerbach's description of the third project, *Deutsche Abende*, as "a sort of new Platonic dialogue" aptly conveys the cycle's philosophical thrust but omits that it is Spinoza, not Plato, whose ideas Auerbach projects onto his vision of Germany. Auerbach's letter gives no indication that he saw these various projects as incompatible, or that the first village stories dramatically broke with the concerns of his Spinoza cycle. Rather, these appear to have been parallel projects on which Auerbach worked after he completed his Spinoza translation and before the *Dorfgeschichten* took on a career-defining life of their own. Well into his work on the *Schwarzwälder Dorfgeschichten*, Auerbach continued to look to Spinoza as a model for liberal German cultural and political values. For Auerbach, Spinoza's ethics could advance the liberal ideal of the *Vaterland* above all by encouraging individuals to move beyond egoistic pursuits and dedicate themselves to the common weal.

I have argued that two prominent aims of Auerbach's *Spinoza* novel—recovering a usable past for German Jews through nostalgic depiction of traditional Jewish life, and depicting Spinoza as an all-reconciling figure and a model for an inclusive liberal Germany—worked largely at cross-purposes. In his abortive Spinoza cycle Auerbach sheds the former aim and retains only the latter. He displaces Spinoza entirely from the historical milieu of traditional Jewish life and into contemporary German middle-class culture. Spinoza appears in these stories, whether explicitly ("Deutsche Abende: Wer ist glücklich?") or implicitly ("Liebe Menschen"), only as a set of philosophical teachings that Auerbach would clearly like to see shape liberal German self-understanding.

"Deutsche Abende: Wer ist glücklich?" stages a social conflict not between Jews and non-Jews but between different members of the German middle class. The story opens as Edmund, a young lawyer fresh from the university, has just finished reading Clemens Brentano's novella "Die Geschichte vom braven Kasperl und dem schönen Annerl" (The story of brave Kasperl and the fair Annerl; 1817, republished 1838) to a salon at the home of Hofrat and Hofrätin Romann. Brentano's now-classic story of the maid Annerl and Corporal Kasperl is a tragedy less of love than of the savage consequences of social codes of honor.[154] Brentano's theme of honor sets the stage for Auerbach's plot, in which the Hofrat and Hofrätin Romann cruelly thwart the love between Edmund and Antonie, their daughter, because they deem Edmund a disadvantageous match. Edmund is arrested for alleged involvement in the publication of radical literature in Switzerland and spends several months in jail. Let out in 1840, when Friedrich Wilhelm IV, at the start of his reign, grants amnesty to political prisoners, Edmund learns that Antonie is to be married to the widower Regierungsrath Meißner and has fallen gravely ill. Edmund rushes to her, and they embrace in a tearful scene before Antonie dies.

What fills out this meager plot and constitutes the real substance of the story is the extended conversation among the society at the Romanns' salon concerning the nature of happiness. The conversation touches on familiar Auerbachian themes, including egoism versus community; the differing roles of the poet, statesman, and philosopher; and romantic versus intellectual love. One of the guests, a professor, introduces Spinoza's definition of happiness into the discussion, and Spinoza remains the chief philosophical touchstone throughout, even for characters who can claim no direct knowledge of the sage's ideas. Edmund, for example, arrives at the following view of happiness: "Joy in existence, knowledge of one's existence elevated into pleasure, is the root and crown of happiness," a paraphrase of Spinoza's conception of intellectual love.[155] The professor's view of freedom is also evidently borrowed from Spinoza: "Nature's endowments, internal and external, impose a necessity upon us that we cannot suspend but that we can elevate ourselves above through consciousness and knowledge, by conforming to it out of self-determination. We become free not by suspending the laws of the universe or of our own nature but by fulfilling them, for natural necessity and order is freedom's essential form."[156] Such intellectual love, a wider participation in nature achieved through greater knowledge—that is, Spinozan virtue—lifts us out of our illusory pursuits of egoistic pleasure and grants true happiness, the professor argues.[157]

How wedded Spinozan happiness is to patriotic dedication to a just German *Vaterland* becomes evident in the story's closing lines. Despite the personal sadness Edmund has endured, he has redoubled his commitment to the common good. True (Spinozan) happiness, readers are to understand, lies in personal renunciation and altruistic dedication to the higher cause of the community of the *Vaterland*:

> Edmund is loved and honored as a champion of the fatherland and a devotee of justice by all those who support the fatherland and justice; all his love is for [*gilt*] the common weal, and all his striving. He devoted himself to it when he still had reason to hope for personal happiness; he has only remained true to it. His happiness now consists only in the welfare of others.
>
> Who is happy?[158]

Spinoza's presence in Auerbach's 1842 story "Liebe Menschen" is only implicit, though no less pervasive. The story's Christian protagonist, Rudolph, travels to Cologne to pay a visit to his university friend Karl, whom he has not seen in years. When Rudolf arrives Karl has not yet returned home from work. Rudolf is therefore greeted by his friend's sister Elisabetha, with whom he immediately falls in love, and by their mother, in whom Rudolf finds a new "*Herzensheimath*."[159] Auerbach's original title for the story, "Intellectuale Liebe," works on two levels.[160] It refers to the key Spinozan concept of intellectual love and to the story's romantic plot, in which Rudolph and Elisabetha quickly grow attached to each other through a series of intellectual conversations with unmistakable Spinozistic themes. Philosophical dialogue both displaces, and serves as the medium of, romance. This Spinozan romance ends more happily than is the case in "Deutsche Abende: Wer ist glücklich?" The love between Rudolph and Elisabetha grows primarily through intellectual dialogue and *Erkenntnis*, not confused passion. Rudolph sheds his preconceived notions about women's inferior intellect and comes to respect Elisabetha as his equal. When he becomes sure of the strength of their love, Rudolph exclaims to Elisabetha: "You are spirit of my spirit!" (*Du bist Geist von meinem Geiste!*).[161] This ultimate harmonization of love and intellect is consistent with Rudolph's evocation, in the course of the two lovers' growing bond, of Spinoza's concept of intellectual love, or happiness achieved through knowledge. In Rudolph's reflection, Spinozan intellectual love emerges as a viable, indeed superior, form of romance:

> Is it true that the calmly blissful sanctity of love ends if one wants to think and know it? That is the same [as saying] that one can only believe in, but not think and know, God; no, knowledge is God and God is love, and in knowledge devotion and love are no longer exuberant fleeting moments, it [knowledge] is steady and constant. Love no longer hovers unrecognizably and unfathomably above life as a supernatural revelation, poured out over it as the miracle of the Holy Spirit. It is the immanent transfiguration [*innewohnende Verklärung*] of every particular point out of which the circle of life, infinite yet ever closed, is composed.[162]

As charming and seductive as algebra, Spinozan intellectual love nevertheless provides the model for Auerbach's vision of a new sort of courtship and domestic bond.

If Spinozan philosophy acts as the unlikely medium of romance, Spinoza also remains the unifying force in Auerbach's vision of liberal German pluralism. As unmistakable as Spinoza's presence in "Liebe Menschen" is, unlike in "Deutsche Abende: Wer ist glücklich?," it remains unspoken. In an intriguing instance of what we could call self-reflexive silence, however, Auerbach (silently) remarks on Spinoza's absence from the text. Rudolph relates his idea to Elisabetha of instituting a form of secular worship honoring great intellects of the past.[163] When Elisabetha asks why he does not pursue the idea, Rudolph replies that government authorities would not allow many of the most worthy names to be honored, but he adds that such a ceremony is not really necessary: "Monuments need not stand selfishly [*egoistisch*] in the open air; they must become pillars of a great edifice, with no further demands than to help support the vault. . . . If the thought, the feeling, the life of a great intellect [*eines großen Geistes*] infuses the life and spirit of contemporaries and posterity, then he lives for all ages: every breast he causes to swell, every heart he strengthens praises him, even if they do not say or know his name."[164] Rudolph's general reflection on the virtue of anonymously contributing to a cultural edifice (and the superfluous if not deleterious nature of "egoistic" personal recognition) also comments—silently—on the absence of any explicit mention of Spinoza in "Liebe Menschen." Auerbach might indeed be able to use Spinoza most effectively to aid the liberal German cause by studiously avoiding any explicit reference to the philosopher.

Rudolph, the patriotic self-identified pantheist, silently draws on Spinoza to theorize the relationship of part to whole in what he views as Germany's higher freedom and genuine harmony. The Spinozan underpinnings of Rudolph's conception of German provincial and national life gain in importance when we consider the crucial role that an idealized (nationalized) provincialism plays in Auerbach's *Schwarzwälder Dorfgeschichten*. In conversation with Karl, Elisabetha, and their mother, Rudolph declares: "It is delightful . . . that the German nation is beginning to cast off its provincial spirit, its *Cantönligeist*, as the Swiss call it. . . . North and South, East and West, all of us are one, all must recognize the affairs of a particular province or state as that of the fatherland in its totality [*des Gesammtsvaterlandes*]."[165] As this conversation about German pluralism unfolds, Rudolph advances a critique of toleration, which he views as dependent on feeling (*Gemüth, Gefühl*) and therefore unstable and susceptible to being rescinded with the next change in *Gemüthstimmung*. What provides a solid foundation for a viable and harmonious German pluralism is, once again, a version of Spinoza's concept of intellectual love ("the knowledge that becomes love"):

> The mere peaceable sentiment [*Stimmung*], *human tolerance* [humane Nachsicht], lags far behind the insight and the knowledge that becomes love; in the former one allows differences to obtain because one recognizes something of universal relevance therein, but one still regards the particular as erroneous or deficient. In the latter one learns to recognize and love the entire particularity with all its peculiarities as valid and necessary. . . . In the perception and thorough knowledge of particularities *lies harmony; the essence of harmony is not that everything has one tone* [daß Alles Einen Klang habe], *but that everything has consonance* [daß Alles Einklang habe], that the tones persevere in their difference, yet that they cultivate their particular nature unto purity. In this purity they then join, by the power of their innermost nature, the total chorus [*Gesammtklange*]; free and independent, they nonetheless merge into the whole. In my view that is the higher German freedom and genuine harmony.[166]

To highlight the Spinozan nature of Auerbach's vision of the German *Vaterland* and its pluralistic *Volk*, we need only recall Auerbach's definition in his Spinoza biography of "the essence of active [*tätigen*] pantheism" as being "to subordinate the particular to the general, yet still to portray the former in the latter."[167] The patriotic liberal German pantheist Rudolph is the voice of Auerbach's Spinozan *Vaterland*.[168] Spinoza would recede further into silence in Auerbach's *Schwarzwälder Dorfgeschichten*, but it was Auerbach's Spinozan vision of the German *Volk* that prepared the space the peasants of Nordstetten would come to fill.

Chapter Six

Moses Hess

Beyond the Politics of Self-Possession

Auerbach and Hess: Parting Ways

The correspondence between Moses Hess and Berthold Auerbach—of which we have only Hess's letters—was at its most intensive during 1840 and 1841, roughly when Hess was at work on his second major work, *Die Europäische Triarchie* (The European triarchy), and Auerbach on his edition of Spinoza. Hess's letters to Auerbach of 1842 document the unraveling of their friendship as they took their engagements with Spinoza in disparate directions.

Both Auerbach and Hess drew on a version of Spinoza to attack egoism (subjectivity, individualism, and personality) and to imagine inclusive wider communities, but they did so in different ways and for different ends. Spinoza modeled for Auerbach a way to circumvent association with the specter of Jewish subjectivity and all that this concept connoted in the German cultural politics of the late 1830s and early 1840s. Hess read Spinoza as authorizing a more fundamental critique of individualism and the position it occupied at the center of modern identity, religion, philosophy, politics, and commercialized society. Auerbach sought to construct an idealized German *Volk* as a suprasubjective ethical collectivity to which he, too, could belong. Hess drew inspiration from Spinoza, whom he held up (sometimes more and sometimes less) as the quintessence of an idiosyncratic Jewish tradition, to critique individualism as a Christian legacy and the chief obstacle to the realization of modernity's liberating potential.

Hess would move to the vanguard of German radicals, who increasingly saw Germany as irredeemably narrow-minded, *spießbürgerlich* (philistine and conformist), and politically retarded. (In Marx and Engels's *The German Ideology*, their 1845–46 savage reckoning with their erstwhile colleagues in the Young Hegelian movement, "German" is very much as a term of abuse.) Auerbach, in contrast, embraced a moderate liberal national position. His chief focus, beginning in late 1841, became his *Schwarzwälder Dorfgeschichten*. Though Auerbach had difficulty finding a publisher for the first volume of *Dorfgeschichten*, when they finally appeared in October 1843, they were hailed as a major literary event, and Auerbach was transformed overnight from an obscure author of Jewish novels to the authentic voice of the German *Volk*. Hess devoted his energies in the second half of 1841 to launching the *Rheinische Zeitung*, among the most liberal papers in Germany from its appearance in January 1842 until—under its last editor, Marx—it was terminated by the Prussian government in March 1843. Hess encouraged Auerbach to write for the paper but repeatedly had to defend accepting his friend's contributions, which were out of step with the paper's political orientation, to members of the editorial board. In a letter of March 12, 1842, Hess asks Auerbach to contribute more regularly and, above all, to be more oppositional. In a letter of March 27, 1842, he complains that Auerbach's contributions "smell like modern *Deutschtum*" and goes on to vent his exasperation at Germany's political backwardness and cowardice in a scathing assessment of the *Vaterland*. Hess insists that one must not any longer flatter Germany and that only "bitter medicine à la Börne" will help, and he explicitly rejects the strategy of Germany's "apologists."[1] Roughly two weeks after receiving this letter, Auerbach's first *Dorfgeschichte* ("Des Schloßbauers Vefele") appeared in print.

In November 1843 the poet Ferdinand Freiligrath lionized Auerbach for his achievement in a twelve-verse poem, "Dorfgeschichten," in the *Kölnische Zeitung* —the *Rheinische Zeitung*'s archadversary—and Auerbach became a much-sought-after literary celebrity in 1844 and 1845. Whereas Hess would spend 1844 in Paris with Heine, Marx, Engels, and other exiled radicals, Auerbach would spend the year in Karlsruhe editing and writing German *Volkskalender* (popular almanacs) and further *Dorfgeschichten*.[2] In fall 1844 he began a celebrated tour throughout Germany following his many invitations from writers and socialites—whom, according to the influential novelist and literary critic Gustav Freytag's memoirs, he frequently struck as a character who had stepped out of one of his own *Black Forest Village Stories*.[3]

Auerbach looked to Spinoza for a model for negotiating the charge of egoism in general and Jewish egoism in particular, and Auerbach constructed an idealized, liberal-humanistic version of the German *Volk* as the higher totality into which the problematic, divided modern self should be resolved. Hess attacked modern society's commitment—or enslavement—to the institution of the sovereign self and saw in Spinoza the key to liberation. The fact that Hess at least at times saw his ethical project as a Jewish obligation and viewed Auerbach's more conservative political and esthetic adherence to the German *Vaterland* as a betrayal of a Jewish ethical responsibility is evident from a remarkable passage in a letter Hess sent Auerbach in February 1845, on the back of the prospectus for a new socialist journal he was launching (and would edit with Friedrich Engels).[4]

The once intimate friendship between Hess and Auerbach had effectively dissolved under the strain of their political differences over the course of 1842–43, and when Hess wrote these lines, the two had not corresponded in over a year. Hess laments to Auerbach:

> O, if we had stuck together, then you wouldn't have become the sentimental esthetician of the Black Forest and the asshole [*Podex*] of salon literature in this clique of Honeks and Andrés! You would not have retreated from the misery of life back into your foreskin in order to coquet with your own *Gemütlichkeit* [comfort, congeniality] while people are reduced to animal existence, become destitute, and starve. You would have with me entered the hovels of the unfortunate and discovered the terrible secrets of depraved humanity, and depicted them perhaps better than [Eugène] Sue, the French bourgeois, and thus lent your hand to the liberation of humanity, whereas you now, like Honek, write another sort of fairy tale for winter evenings to chase away the terrible boredom of idlers who, for variety's sake, wish for once to call on the *lower* strata, as long as the Ciceros beautify the paths with flowers and whitewash so that they needn't feel ill at ease![5]

The clique of "Andrés and Honeks" requires clarification. "André" was Karl Andree, who became the editor of the *Kölnische Zeitung* shortly before the paper published Freiligrath's paean to Auerbach's *Dorfgeschichten* in November 1843. "Honek" was the pen name of Auerbach's friend Max Cohen, editor of a popular *Volkskalender* with the title *Das Buch für Winterabende* (Book for winter evenings).[6] What surely stung Auerbach most was Hess's charge that he had "retreated into his foreskin" in adopting his new folksy and widely celebrated literary persona, since Auerbach obviously wanted to understand his successful turn to all things *volkstümlich* precisely as proof of an essential harmony between *Judentum* and *Deutschtum*.[7] Whether we view Hess's remark as cruel or apt, ungenerous or hilarious, or some mixture of these, it is important to understand the double aspect of the retreat or retraction it signals: it is at once to play the goy and to shirk an ethical obligation—one Hess here understands as Jewish—by luxuriating in idyllic pseudorealism that apologizes for the status quo instead of advancing the cause of the most needy.

In this chapter, I analyze some of Hess's varied—and sometimes obscure—attempts to draw on Spinoza to critique the autonomous individual as an epistemological error with harmful ethical consequences. Spinoza also provided Hess with inspiration and tools to think human individuality otherwise than according to the logic of Cartesian dualism. Hess's abiding critique of the illusions and human cost of sovereign subjectivity took different forms at different times in his career and drew not only on Spinoza but on many other conceptual models as well, most notably Ludwig Feuerbach's theory of species-being.[8] Yet Hess is at his most original, and strange, when he thinks most closely with Spinoza, for it is then that he attempts not simply to negate the individual or to sublate individuality in, say, the concept of species-being, but rather to conceive of mutually constitutive relations between human individuality and totality in monistic terms. Hess's ambitious and elusive project of imagining a supra-individual Spinozan humanism took vastly different forms over the course of his career, but the history of this preoccupation allows us to see not only a rupture but also a great deal of continuity between Hess's socialist writings of the late 1830s and 1840s and his turn to Jewish nationalism in the 1860s.[9]

The fact that Hess could derive inspiration from Spinoza from his first through his last writings underscores how Hess saw in Spinoza not so much a philosopher as a prophet of a coming age of supra-individual humanistic cooperation. This allowed Hess to continue to embrace Spinoza even as Hess's Young Hegelian contemporaries were scrambling to leave behind and "realize" philosophy. Feuerbach served Marx for a period as a model antiphilosopher, but when Marx came to see Feuerbach as, alas, also a philosopher stuck in the German ideology and incapable of theorizing material praxis, there was no next antiphilosopher to turn to. For Hess, Spinoza was this antiphilosopher from beginning to end; for him, Spinozism ultimately implied a revolution in ethical life.

Spinoza allowed Hess to critique the abstraction of philosophy and the philosophical subject from Descartes through Hegel and the Young Hegelians, "the latest philosophers," to quote the title of Hess's 1845 polemic against Bruno Bauer and Max Stirner. The central target of Hess's critique of philosophy was the abstraction and dualistic subjectivity at its heart. He extended his critique beyond philosophy and theology to attack subjective dualism and abstraction in its political and economic guises. In all its various forms, dualism represented for Hess the legacy of Christianity. He was at times more and at times less explicit about viewing Spinoza as the quintessential distillation of the essence of Judaism, yet he consistently saw Spinoza as the liberating, spiritually and materially unified alternative to Christian and post-Christian dualism and abstraction, even as his vision of the form that Spinozan ethical unity would take changed dramatically.

The Holy History of Mankind

Hess's first book, *The Holy History of Mankind* (*Die heilige Geschichte der Menschheit*), appeared anonymously in 1837 as the work of a "disciple of Spinoza."

As he would in his more famous *Rome and Jerusalem* (1862), Hess here inscribes Spinoza as a profoundly Jewish thinker who ushers in the modern age by showing the way beyond the conceptual and political limitations of Christian dualism.

Heine played a key role in Auerbach's first publication as the specter of Jewish irony and egoism. Heine likewise played an important role in Hess's early development, but for Hess he was a source of philosophical inspiration. Hess admired Heine's *Zur Geschichte der Religion und Philosophie in Deutschland* (*On the History of Religion and Philosophy in Germany*) and, in a letter to Heine accompanying a copy of his *Holy History*, wrote, in a characteristically histrionic idiom: "Without you I would not have become what I am—without you I could not have continued my spiritual life."[10]

Heine saw Spinoza as an avatar of the modern age and also ventured a comparison between the saintly Spinoza and Christ.[11] Hess took both of these points further and proposed an idiosyncratic tripartition of "the holy history of mankind" in which Adam inaugurates the first era ("the history of revelation of God, the father"), Christ the second ("the history of revelation of God, the son"), and Spinoza the third and ultimate ("the history of revelation of God, the Holy Spirit"). Hess sees Christianity's great achievement in its universalism: Christian universalism will leave its mark on the holy state to come, which will no longer be the possession of one people but of all humanity, no longer a particular state but a universal empire. Yet, as Shlomo Avineri has underscored, the denouement of Hess's *Holy History* reinscribes the unity between German thought and French politics, which it sees history working toward, emphatically within a Jewish frame of reference.[12] Hess repeatedly refers to the ancient Jewish state, however universalized through Christianity, as the model for the new society he prophesies. For Hess the contribution of Christian universalism was marred by Christianity's dualism, which disrupted the unity of religion and politics that had defined the ancient Jewish commonwealth. In its dualism, Christianity rights the wrongs of the world only in an abstract, highly spiritualized way, not in reality. The new age Hess envisions would overcome Christian abstraction and reestablish concrete ethical politics. Spinoza thus inaugurates a sort of secular Jewish supersession of the Christian era:

> In the second revelation [that is, Christ's] the old Law was lost; the third will introduce a new one. The time approaches in which the unity, which has been destroyed in the Whole, will be restored, when the state will become holy once more. . . . The old Law was crucified together with Christ only insofar as it had been external, existing in time and space; but its divine

> content, its eternal spirit, continued to live, conquered the world, triumphed over death. This spirit has won! The old Law, whose body had been buried with Christ, has been clarified and resurrected in Spinoza. The kernel of a new covenant resides in the Master's [that is, Spinoza's] teaching of salvation. Just as the ancients had a constitution of a holy state [*Staatsverfassung*], so we shall receive a constitution of a holy empire [*Reichsverfassung*], because Christ has triumphed![13]

Spinozan universalism was not mystified or abstract but rational and encompassed the concrete world. Drawing on Spinoza's definition of the most fundamental good as that which promotes "the knowledge of God," Hess locates human essence in sociability and social equality, since knowledge is best pursued as a collective enterprise.[14] In this way, in the first socialist work written in Germany, Hess mobilizes Spinoza's pantheism against possessive individualism and the related and equally atomizing institutions of heritability (*Erblichkeit*), money, and property: "The reign of full equality comes into being only where there exists communal ownership . . . in all goods, internal as well as external, where the treasures of society are open to all and nothing is tied to a person as exclusive property."[15] If property was a prime target of Hess's Spinozan communism, it was suspect above all because it was tied to the ontologically false and socially deleterious category of personality. More fundamental for Hess than the negation of property, in other words, was the negation of the sovereign personality that could lay exclusive claim to it.[16] Warren Breckman notes the Spinozan inspiration for Hess's radical critique of personality and distinguishes between Heine's interpretation of pantheism in *History of Religion and Philosophy in Germany* and Hess's more rigorously Spinozist views: "Because Hess believed human society to be one divine substance, he hypostatized humanity in the form of one unitary 'individual.' Where Heine envisioned a future democracy of 'terrestrial gods,' Hess imagined the realization of *Gesammtmenschheit*, collective humanity, in a future of perfect unity and equality. In the grammatical difference between Heine's plural and Hess's singular, we see reflected the philosophical difference between a vision of harmony that contains a notion of individuality and one that depends on its erasure."[17] Breckman sees Hess's Spinozism as obliterating any notion of individuality. In contrast, I argue that Hess draws on Spinoza not to erase individuality but to redefine it and rescue it from the illusion of autonomous subjectivity that he sees as a pernicious threat to true individuality and freedom.

Because Hess has been of greatest interest to scholars concerned with the origins and history of Marxist thought—who have often written from within that tradition—there has been a pronounced tendency to belittle and dismiss Hess's peculiarity vis-à-vis his Young Hegelian radical contemporaries. There is certainly truth in the charges frequently leveled at Hess that his thought was idiosyncratic, unsystematic, often self-contradictory, or simply naive. Hess was an autodidact and tended to use terms and concepts strategically rather than systematically. Yet a significant part of what has made him appear to his detractors as both strange and incoherent is that he approaches a constellation of questions about subjectivity, property, religion, and politics via Spinoza, in a decidedly different way than his Hegelian contemporaries or later readers did. Whether Hess got Spinoza "right" is less important than the fact that his reading of Spinoza, in a thoroughly Hegelian discursive climate, significantly distinguishes his social theory from that of his contemporaries. Given Hess's explicit identification with Spinoza, some nod to his Spinozism is common, yet scholars have generally ignored how Hess's engagement with Spinoza extends beyond the vague admiration of the self-proclaimed disciple to the creative deployment of identifiable concepts and moments in Spinoza. Hess says that Spinoza could not have seen the ramifications or implications that he claimed to derive from Spinoza's thought.[18] He is aware that he is elaborating his own vision of Spinoza's contemporary relevance. I argue that Hess's Spinozan idiosyncrasies are not grounds to dismiss Hess but the very reason why we should pay attention to him, for they are what make him such a singular thinker on the periphery of the Young Hegelian movement. Like Bendavid, the *Vereinler*, and Auerbach, he creatively uses philosophy to reimagine a more inclusive polity. Yet whereas Bendavid and the *Vereinler* draw on German philosophers, and Auerbach on Spinoza, to imagine a place for Jews in the German polity, Hess sees Spinoza as a quintessentially Jewish philosopher who shows the way to realizing a cosmopolitan "human" community. For Hess the main point is not that philosophy can be mobilized to reshape both the polity and Jewry so as to reconcile the two. Instead, it is that Judaism, particularly as distilled in Spinoza, holds the key to a nondualistic, supra-individualistic mode of existence that can liberate everyone.

Hess was doubtless the most radical of all his contemporaries in his assault on what he considered false conceptions of the autonomous individual. His position in *The Holy History* differs not only from Heine's but also from August von Cieszkowski's elaboration of a philosophy of the deed in his influential "Prolegomena to a Historiosophy" of 1838. Breckman contends that Cieszkowski preserves a tension between divine process in history and human consciousness and agency—a gap between "freedom and necessity"—but that Hess collapses this distinction entirely: "Hess envisioned action as an extrusion of humanity's identity with God necessarily pressing toward its full realization in the external world. Here, the narrow gap between freedom and necessity vanishes: 'The freedom of humans exists not in their arbitrariness, but in conscious obedience to the divine law. Obedience is the virtue of the pure human.'"[19] Breckman's interpretation of Hess's conception of activity—which, influenced by Cieszkowski, Hess, would soon take up as a central concern—as mere passive obedience to divine necessity is plausible, yet it ignores Hess's own arguments for why activating human freedom required overcoming what he viewed as the detrimental illusion of subjective freedom. Hess embraced Spinoza's proposition that we are active to the extent that we have adequate ideas and passive to the extent that we have inadequate ones.[20] Since Hess views individual autonomy as an epistemological error, he is consistent, as paradoxical as it may seem, in insisting that we actually limit our freedom and action to the extent that we conceive of our ability to act as part and parcel of our being free individuals.

Breckman illuminates the vehemence and originality of Hess's attack on personality when he notes that in *The Holy History* Hess motivates his argument for abolishing the institutions of private property and inheritance not, primarily, by appealing to economic justice but by assailing the dependence of property and inheritance on "the personalist theology of monotheism."[21] For Hess, "inheritance depends . . . on the belief in personal immortality, on the belief in the eternal integrity of the person who may thus rule over his property equally in life and death."[22] Hess sees possessive individualism, modeled on personalist theology and sustained by the institutions of property and heritability, as a form of false consciousness that impedes human activity. He saw his age as moving beyond this limiting form of self-conception and the property relations in which it is thoroughly implicated: "Our age has become aware that it is to eternal God—the great Whole—that the eternal law of inheritance belongs; that, by contrast, nothing can be possessed by individuals and nations in perpetuity since they are fleeting and limited."[23] Hess points to how the universe reclaims the "capital" it has loaned to the individual (that is, her body) to illustrate the justness of the state's reclaiming from its members, upon their death, the capital "which in principal [*im Grunde*] is its property."[24] Here, as elsewhere in *The Holy History* and in other texts, Hess holds up the ancient Jewish state as a sort of blueprint for a state operating according to the principle that no property can be appropriated eternally by individuals or nations: "[The old holy covenant] stipulated that all property should revert after fifty years to its original owner (to whom it had fallen during the original, just distribution of property). Because the divine legislator considered all land as the property of the invisible national God."[25] Although the Jewish state—as both a national rather than a universal state, and an agrarian rather than a modern one—cannot serve as a model for modern politics, it does crucially embody a politics beyond possessive individualism and self-possession. When discussing the ancient Jewish state and Spinoza, Hess consistently associates Judaism with the sort of nonpersonalist ethics he sees as key to achieving human freedom.

Die Europäische Triarchie

Hess's 1837 debut publication articulated many of the concerns that would continue to preoccupy him as his political thought evolved in the 1840s and even in his proto-Zionist treatise *Rome and Jerusalem*: his conception of the individual and self-consciousness in relation to a Spinozan conception of universal substance; the nature of human freedom and activity in relation to divine determination; and his interpretation of Judaism in the grand drama of world history and human liberation. In *The Holy History*, Hess identified monotheism's personalist theology as a problem per se that, in turn, wrought sociopolitical damage. He would continue to see the ideology of the sovereign individual as a central impediment to free human activity as he undertook to critique shortcomings of German philosophy and to develop his own counterphilosophy of the deed in his more widely read next book, *Die europäische Triarchie* (The European triarchy; 1841) and in subsequent writings, notably the essay "Die Philosphie der Tat" (The philosophy of the deed; 1843).[26]

Die europäische Triarchie articulates a tripartite philosophy of history and socialist critique of egoistic individualism broadly similar to that of *The Holy History*, yet it reflects Hess's extensive reading in French socialism, Hegel, and Young Hegelian discourse (Cieszkowski's "Prolegomena to a Historiosophy" and Feuerbach's recently published anthropological critique of religion, *The Essence of Christianity*, are among the work's important intertexts), and a greater knowledge, as well, of European politics. Hess's vision here is once again of a vaguely conceived socialist cosmopolitan order that will combine the freedom manifested in the German Reformation and German philosophy with French political activism. Hess now joins these to the pragmatic prowess of England, the third member of the "European triarchy."[27] Hess's Spinoza-inspired cosmopolitanism contrasts markedly with Auerbach's embrace of the German *Volk*. As Hess stresses, "it is here no longer a matter only of German, but of European, independence."[28] (Even in his vaguely adumbrated political vision, however, Hess is careful to stress that the cultural and religious particularity and diversity of the three integral parts of Western Europe—Germany, France, and England—have not been and will not be negated by the unity the three countries constitute.)[29] Hess's *Europäische Triarchie* is centrally concerned with critiquing subjectivism and narrow particularism in its various iterations: philosophical, political, social, and national. Against what Hess sees as the epistemological errors and negative ethical and political consequences of narrow self-assertion, he proposes an alternative, Spinoza-inspired way to think of the relationship of parts to wholes. He continues, explicitly, to understand the movement of his philosophy of history toward his vision of European unity in terms of the realization of truths revealed in Spinoza's *Ethics*.[30] Although Hess understood *Die Europäische Triarchie* in political terms, the balance of the book is quite abstract. This is in keeping with the lingering abstraction of the various Young Hegelian calls for a shift from abstraction to action, but it also stems from Hess's Spinozan understanding of thought *as* a kind of action. For Hess, thought does not need to become something that it is not in order to become activity; rather, it must come to see itself as the intregal part of free human activity that it already is. Intellectual freedom—free intellectual activity—is for Hess the key to achieving social, ethical, and political freedom: "Ethical and social bondage ensue only from spiritual bondage. Conversely, the emancipation of laws and of morals is likewise a necessary consequence of the emancipation of the spirit. This conclusion must either be reached or the premise, spiritual freedom, denied. Freedom is an organism that cannot be missing even one limb without being maimed. The three emancipations that have been elaborated here [Germany, France, and England] are merely different emanations of one and the same essence, human independence."[31] As abstract as Hess's Spinozan political vision was, Hess, however naively, understood it to have the highest possible practical stakes. The chief obstacle Hess sees to the realization of freedom is our enthrallment to false and deleterious understandings of subjectivity.[32] Though Hess does not refer here (and only infrequently refers anywhere) to specific propositions or arguments in Spinoza, it is clear enough that in *Die Europäische Triarchie* he has in mind Spinoza's contention that as knowledge, power, and virtue—which are all essentially synonymous for Spinoza—increase, so does social cooperation, and simultaneously strife, born of unfreedom and bondage to the passions, decreases. As Spinoza states in *Ethics*, for example, "men, in so far as they live in accordance with the guidance of reason, to that extent alone necessarily do those things that are necessarily good for human nature, and consequently for each man."[33]

In the substantial introduction to *Die Europäische Triarchie* Hess refers repeatedly to Cieszkowski's "Prolegomena to a Historiosophy."[34] Hess follows Cieszkowski in calling for a move from contemplative philosophy to a philosophy of the deed.[35] And, again like Cieszkowski, Hess critiques Hegel's philosophy for its orientation to the past and neglect of the future, which, both claim, diminishes Hegel's political relevance. As Hess puts it, "the Hegelian concept trails behind the facts of history but in no way underlies them [*liegt ihnen . . . zu Grunde*], neither prophetically, mystically nor speculatively."[36] (Hess's three modes of perceiving the workings of holy history—prophetic, mystical, and speculative—correspond to the three stages of his tripartite philosophy of history.) Since Hegelian thought can identify the spirit's trajectory only in retrospect, so this critique went, it could never actively shape history, never become what Cieszkowski was the first to call praxis. Hess is obviously indebted to Cieszkowski, yet their visions for concretizing abstract subjectivity differ in crucial ways that go to the heart of the specifically Spinozist cast of Hess's understanding of the deed, subjectivity, and socialist politics.[37] Hess affirms Cieszkowski's charge that Hegel privileges consciousness over activity. As Cieszkowski writes, "in Hegel consciousness is the Alpha and Omega, and in general he derives the entire system of his philosophy from consciousness and he subordinates the entire process of world history to consciousness."[38] Hegelian thought thus amounts to a reflection on "facts" that cannot generate "acts."

Hess likewise follows Cieszkowski in identifying their contemporary moment as a threshold in world history at which human consciousness can transform its passive relation to facts into an active one. In Cieszkowski's words, "we are . . . at a world-historical turning point in the conversion of facts into acts. That is, consciousness occupies a distinct place in the true system of philosophy; thus the universe is not therefore closed with it. What lies before it (according to thought) is unconscious, i.e. fact, but what follows from it must develop itself consciously, and that is the deed."[39] Cieszkowski assigns the apogee of consciousness in Hegelian philosophy a place "within" philosophy and thereby subverts its claim to have brought history or "the universe" to a close. Cieszkowski's ingenious strategy of historicizing Hegel brings Hegel's assessment of art to bear on Hegel's own philosophy. Hegel considered art to have reached its perfection in classical Greece. Modern art (Romanticism) brought conceptual advances but entailed a loss of the perfect harmony between idea and material being. In its very perfection, art reveals its limitation; and in the modern age, art becomes spiritually subordinated to the all-synthesizing discourse of philosophy. Cieszkowski historicizes the purportedly "absolute" nature of Hegel's synthesis of thought and being by praising it as the perfection of philosophy (or philosophical consciousness). Just as art's limitation becomes evident in its own perfection, philosophy's limitation emerges in its apogee in Hegel. The nature of Hegel's shortcomings, moreover, revindicate the superseded realm of the esthetic: "Just as art, when it had attained the classic form, proceeded beyond itself and dissolved itself in the romantic form of art, but also at the same time ceded world dominion to philosophy, so also has philosophy itself attained such a classic point where it must go beyond itself and thereby at the same time must cede true world dominion to another."[40] This "other," postphilosophical force poised to claim world dominion is praxis. It will go beyond philosophy by overcoming the opposition between philosophy and art—that is, by embodying absolute thought once again in an actual substrate. The identity that Hegel claimed to have achieved between thought and being—this is at the center of both Cieszkowski's and Hess's critique of Hegel—in fact remained within thought.[41] The "new demand" for a synthesis of thought and being in the deed, in contrast, is a demand "to develop a substantial identity from the formal one."[42] Resolving this contradiction "is the destiny of the highest, practical, social life"; "being and thought must . . . dissolve in action, art and philosophy in social life."[43]

Cieszkowski critiques Hegelian philosophy as a secularized Christian mode of thought that remains more like theology than it acknowledges. Through speculation, philosophy replaces belief with thought as the highest form of truth, yet the synthesis this thought achieves remains confined to abstract subjective consciousness, in the religious and political guises of Protestantism and liberalism, respectively, which "are merely the peaks of abstract subjectivity."[44] Hess agrees with Cieszkowski that Hegel's synthesis of thought and being remains one-sided (within thought), abstract, and subjective, and also agrees that world history is moving toward a more profound synthesis of thought and being in deeds or sociopolitical praxis.[45]

Hess emphatically parts ways with Cieszkowski, however, regarding the role of property. Cieszkowski sees in proprietorship the path by which modern subjects can overcome the abstraction of Protestant and liberal subjectivity and achieve real ethical agency: "Only as proprietor is man a particular and real man. This is the most immediate stage of his concreteness, which we take here not at all in the abstractly legal sense, but rather in the highest moral sense."[46] Instead of seeking to concretize the abstract self through proprietorship, Hess tries to expose the discrete self as an epistemologically and morally insidious error that both perpetuates and is perpetuated by the socially atomizing institution of private property.

Whereas Cieszkowski deployed Hegel's historicization of art to historicize Hegel's own philosophy of consciousness, and to expose it as lacking in precisely the concretion that was art's chief virtue, Hess turns the tables on Hegel in a different way, by deploying Hegel's critique of Spinoza against Hegel. As noted in chapter 3, Hegel deemed Spinozan substance incapable of becoming an active, conscious, or differentiated subject. In his view the awesome unity of

Spinozan substance left no room for dynamism or particularity.[47] Hess reverses the Hegelian charge and argues that Hegel never manages to move beyond the bubble of subjectivity and consciousness to achieve the unity of Spinozan substance.[48] Hess repeatedly characterizes Hegel's philosophy as subjective thought that, in insisting on its own absoluteness, suffers from a sort of delusion of grandeur: "As absolute, Hegelian philosophy would see no alienation of itself in the substantial act. However, because this philosophy is merely the highest manifestation of the thinking spirit, it thinks it loses itself in substance [*in der Substanz*], and it will never admit that the absolute subject . . . can be exceeded."[49] Hess charges that, in understanding his own limited and subjective philosophy as absolute, Hegel was guilty of philosophical hubris:

> Hegelian philosophy cannot be faulted for anything but illegitimately encroaching upon foreign territories. It does not know its *limits*, does not know when to make self-*sacrifice* [weiß sich nicht *aufzuopfern*]. Hegelian philosophy gives the thinking spirit the most concrete, most correct concept of itself, but it [Hegelian philosophy] expects too much from the same (from itself) if it demands from it [thinking spirit] anything more than that it comprehend its own self (the absolute subject). For all genuine knowledge is only a knowledge of self [*ein Wissen von sich*]. However, to the extent that Hegelianism wishes to grasp more than its concept [*Begriff*], it blunders [*macht er Mißgriffe*].[50]

Hegel's philosophy of consciousness selfishly refuses to acknowledge its own limits, to sacrifice itself in the service of the truly absolute unity that it errs in identifying with itself.

Hegel, the diagnostician of bad subjectivity, remains, according to Hess's critique, within the confines of subjective consciousness. Instead of following Cieszkowski in finding a post-theoretical synthesis in proprietary subjectivity, however, Hess appeals to Spinoza's understanding of the parallelism of thought and extension as different attributes of the same single substance to reveal the errors of the subjective mindset. Hess faults Hegel for believing that, because human consciousness progresses through mediation, substance itself requires mediation. Hegel had faulted Spinozan substance for not engaging in the drama of mediation that animates world history; Hess counters that Hegel's concept of mediation presumes and perpetuates the false dualistic hierarchy that is Hess's consistent target:

> Not only God, as the unity of nature and spirit, is above every mediation, but the eternal attributes of God are too. Hegelianism places spirit over nature

> because spirit must struggle to raise itself up to the highest through its own activity. Against this one could however object: if by nature, as well as by world spirit, one understands not merely this or that stage of its totality but rather this totality itself, then both are equivalent in their verity. . . . Indeed spirit and nature are one and the same entity, which manifests itself now in this, now in that form, yet "ordo et connexio idearum idem est ac orde et connexio rerum."[51]

Hegel's absolute reconciliation of spirit and nature is necessary only because it misconstrues them in the conventionally dualistic and hierarchical terms to which Spinoza, not Hegel, offers a true alternative. In this way Hegelian mediation presumes and perpetuates the divisions it purports to overcome.

For Hess, modern philosophy—including Hegel—engages in an egoistic practice insofar as it strives to separate itself from, and assert itself over, nature while also refusing to acknowledge its own limitations. Hess sees in the Spinozan concept of intellectual love an intellectually and practically superior orientation. A philosophy of intellectual love does not jealously guard or hubristically overestimate its own limited sphere. Rather, even as philosophy, it understands itself to be a part of and a participant in nature; it goes beyond itself, "offers up" (*aufopfern*) its neat contours qua philosophy, and joyfully knows itself to be part of the universe's dynamic activity:

> Hegel quite correctly defines fanaticism as the enthusiasm for an abstract idea, which has no relationship to or consideration for existing conditions. The opposite of this is the indifferentism, which, mired in relationships and considerations, cannot engage in free acts [*nicht zur freien That kommen kann*]. Between these aberrations stands genuine enthusiasm, which has as much love as logic. Only intellectual love engenders something good and useful in philosophy as in art, in spirit as in life. Yet philosophy has until now remained without love and therefore sterile. If it had had love, it would not have remained within itself [*wäre sie nicht bei sich selber stehen geblieben*] but would have sacrificed itself and passed over into deed.[52]

German philosophy, including Hegel, misunderstands its role and egoistically shuts its eyes to its limitations. Intellectual love, for Hess, is joyful. Indeed, we could say it is a form of epistemological and ontological "ecstasy": a knowledge of participation in being beyond oneself. The jealously guarded self poses an obstacle to greater knowledge and activity. The most perfect understanding explodes egoistic limitation; this joyful epistemological traversing of one's limited self is what intellectual love is.[53] If Hegelian thought had been animated by such "love" it would have "offered itself up" and progressed to activity. In intellectual love, self-possessed subjectivity opens or sacrifices itself and participates in, and joyfully knows itself to be participating in, dynamic processes greater than any it can claim as its "own."

Does Hess's conception of human freedom really negate individuals, as Breckman's critique of Hess's Spinozism has it? Hess, at any rate, does not think so and elaborates an argument to the contrary. His aim is not simply to level individuality but to rethink it with Spinoza and to draw out the ethical (sociopolitical) implications of such a rethinking. Later in *Die Europäische Triarchie* Hess explicitly refutes Hegel's reading of Spinozan substance as a kind of ontological hoarder that negates all particularities (or subjects). Against Hegel's charge of acosmism, Hess insists that in Spinozan ethics human beings partake of substance only as the particular entities (minds and bodies) that we are; substance, insofar as we partake of it, has no residence beyond its immanent manifestation in us. Spinozan substance thus in no way levels particular individualities:

> Hegel said, and many repeated after him, that in Spinoza the world vanishes in God, diversity in unity, the subject in the substance. . . . You believe you discern contempt for the world and for life in Spinoza's ethics, and see corroborated therein [the argument]: everything for substance, nothing for the subject [*Alles der Substanz, Nichts dem Subject darin vindicirt zu sehen*]. But the last (5th) chapter of the *Ethics* consists almost exclusively of propositions in which the divinity and eternity of the subject, the person, or as you like to express yourselves, the "personality of God" is deduced. Now tell me then, how is your understanding of Spinoza's *Ethics* compatible with its statements that place so much weight on the preservation of life that even a proposition like this can appear there: "An idea which excludes the existence of our body cannot exist in our mind, but is contrary to it."—A proposition that brands "letting oneself merge with God" or, in a word, acosmism, as a form of insanity? This proposition, however, follows completely logically from the principles of the *Ethics*. For what constitutes the true life of the human being, according to these principles, is not the substance, as you seem to believe, not God as such, but God insofar as He lives in *us*, forms the essence of *our* existence. Precisely contrary than you think, we do not partake of the divine life insofar as God is substance and inheres in everything, but only insofar as He is subject and inheres in us. In his metaphysics Spinoza recognizes only substance; in his ethics, however, only the subject. Our idealists seem

here, as everywhere, to have studied the metaphysics at the expense of the ethics.[54]

Hess could not be more explicit or adamant in his rejection of the widespread Hegelian reading of Spinozan monism as entailing the negation of particularities.[55]

The stakes of Hess's defense of a different reading of Spinoza entail his ability to redefine individuality and the relation between individuals and society. He vehemently rejects the view that Spinozan substance negates human individuality or subjectivity. He first paraphrases, then contests, the argument that Spinoza negates all particularities. In his paraphrase, "destruction of oppositions is destruction of life. Individuals, families, classes [*Stände*], tribes, nations, races are concrete organizations. If you destroy these natural oppositions, you destroy concrete creations of which human society consists, etc."[56] The counterargument Hess offers stresses repeatedly that the system of relationships, in which particularities participate, in no way negates those particularities: "Through sublation [*Aufhebung*] of oppositions the lower organizations [*Organisationen*] of love indeed become sublated, not destroyed, however, but rather raised up out of raw, natural life to cultivated, spiritual life. When husband and wife unite in love, two individuals form one essence, the family; but the original two are not destroyed in this One. And when one day tribes, nations, races unite in love, form One big family, pursue One interest, these earlier organizations of love will not thereby be destroyed."[57] With Spinoza, Hess argues that subjects become more, not less, free, and more, not less, active and powerful when they come to understand themselves as part of the wider totality to which they owe their particular existences. Selves are not negated by, but rather exist only by virtue of, their wider contexts. To activate themselves, then, subjects must come to know their true relationship to the material world, which, in turn, requires that they move beyond their illusory self-definition as sovereign selves in opposition to the merely material world. Such one-sided, dualistic thinking can arrive only at a negative freedom, never at the synthesis of mind and matter required for positive activity.

What is striking about Hess's Spinozan conception of freedom—and startling to our Cartesian sensibilities—is his contention that freedom and activity necessarily exceed the claims that any given subject can make on them. Freedom and activity are not things that subjects can possess; subjects can only participate in them in a manner that necessarily exceeds subjective self-delimitation. For Hess, paradoxically, subjects remain incapable of knowing and participating in true freedom unless they move beyond themselves. Subjective freedom per se can only ever be negative freedom, freedom from "outside" forces. True freedom, however, is positive and takes the form of conscious activity, or deeds. Rather than merely providing a defense against negative external threats to subjective integrity, true freedom permits the fullest possible participation in the world. The achievement of true freedom involves overcoming the dualism—the self-world dichotomy in its various guises—to which the self owes the illusion of its sovereignty: "Only in its organic union with active and real freedom does the freedom of the spirit become a positive one. Freedom is always of a merely negative nature wherever it appears one-sidedly, be it in extrasensual abstract spirit or in undetermined, unlimited will, or, finally, in bad reality [*schlechten Wirklichkeit*], severed from spirit and soul."[58] The dynamic movement of the universe constantly generates and destroys particularities. True activity and freedom derive from an understanding of one's participation in that broader dynamic process, not from the delusion that one remains immune to it.

Again, however, this does not imply that particularities lack positivity or purpose. They have these, yet not by virtue of an illusory autonomy but rather to the extent that they participate in the wider dynamic process:

> Just as the speculative consciousness must not rest with freedom of spirit [*Geistesfreiheit*] but must proceed out of it to the free deed, to ethical freedom, it likewise cannot rest with this freedom. It is true that the ethical deed is an end in itself and gratifies and delights [*beseligt*] wholly irrespective of its results. But freedom of spirit is also an end in itself, as everything has its positive side. A thing's positive side cannot, however, ward off its destruction. Thus we see at every moment, in nature as in spirit, positive creations, which manifest the divinity of their origin as truth or beauty, appear and perish. Yet it is not what is positive, but only its one-sidedness and particularity, thus only the negative, that is negated in these manifestations of God. We see this process, in which reason [*Vernunft*] sits in judgment of one-sided understanding [*Verständniß*] in matters from the smallest to the largest. The all-encompassing, the unitary always holds up to what is one-sided and peculiar their opposite and thus causes collisions, contradictions, and doubts that finite understanding [*Verstand*] cannot, but only eternal reason [*Vernunft*] can, engender and resolve.[59]

From Hess's Spinozan vantage point, the relationship of subjectivity and freedom results in a paradox of the nonfreedom of the individual who imagines himself or herself free. Hess addresses the issue of fatalism and loss of subjective freedom directly:

> The autonomous person [*Der Selbständige*] knows that, as an individual, he is serving part of a higher life, a greater whole, and precisely because he consciously and voluntarily submits to the higher will, makes it his own, he only needs to obey himself. In contrast the person who imagines himself free qua individual, who is, however, no less serving part of a higher unity yet acknowledges no higher will that determines his arbitrariness, must for precisely that reason obey a different master, an external God. Rationalism has long striven against the assumption of an eternal, necessary law of life and defended bad freedom [*die schlechte Freiheit*], arbitrariness. . . . It was indeed its [rationalism's] calling to negate the mere belief in a Providence in order to prepare a clear insight into the divine governance of the world. If it, however, even now continues to raise its thin voice and cry out about fatalism, undermining of morals, destruction of all freedom and energy of human action, then one can dispatch it quickly and with ease. The will by the power of which the truly free person acts is not the pygmy will of an isolated individual, who can neither inhibit nor further the course of world history; rather, it is the will of God. The energy, vigor, and joy in action of one who recognizes God's will, far from being inhibited by this recognition, raises himself to the level of creative genius.[60]

Hess contends that the freedom that individuals perceive as threatened is mere caprice, *Willkür*. True freedom cannot be contained within subjectivity, and subjectivity thus becomes a serious impediment to achieving freedom. Moreover, Hess deems fears about the loss of human freedom and agency as symptomatic of the very dualistic paradigm that, in Hess's view, Spinoza overcomes. To Hess, the necessity that governs the world is not a limitation imposed by an external Providence (given Spinozan immanence, there is no such external position for the divine to inhabit). On the contrary, the recognition of necessity amounts to a joyful discovery of powers in which one certainly participates but cannot claim *to possess*; it is an act of intellectual love. Indeed, one can tap into real power and agency only if one relinquishes and ceases jealously to guard a paltry, minuscule reserve of power as one's own.[61]

"Philosophie der Tat"

Hess's critique of individualism is at the heart of his more theoretical socialist writings throughout the 1840s. Arguably the most influential of these is "Philosophie der Tat" (Philosophy of action; 1843), in which Hess further elaborates the call to move philosophy from abstraction to action that he, following Cieszkowski, had issued in *Die Europäische Triarchie*.[62] Hess opens "Philosophie der Tat" with a Spinozan critique of contemplative subjectivity as modeled in the Cartesian *cogito*. His critique of the self-contained Cartesian subject remains crucial throughout.

As noted in chapter 4, Feuerbach's "Provisional Theses for the Reformation of Philosophy" (1842) and *Principles of the Philosophy of the Future* (1843) strongly influenced Hess's and Marx's evolving attempts in late 1843 and 1844 to "realize" philosophy by acting to transform society. In these works Feuerbach takes aim at what he saw as the lingering theological thrust of philosophy from Descartes (and Spinoza) to Hegel.[63] Hess's and Feuerbach's critiques of modern philosophical subjectivity, though coeval, move in different directions. Where Feuerbach sees a way to overcome the dualism of thought and being by inverting the theological hierarchy and assigning primacy to the objective world, Hess—following Spinoza—views thought and material existence as parallel phenomena, neither of which is prior to or more fundamental than the other. Within a Spinozan conception of monistic immanence, the whole question of grounding being simply cannot arise in the form that was such an abiding preoccupation for Feuerbach.

For Feuerbach modern philosophy continues to err in assigning primacy to thought and consciousness because concrete being resides in the natural object, which can be perceived immediately through the senses. The hallmark of the natural object is its irreducible singularity, which defies translation into the abstract philosophical categories and concepts that make up speculative philosophy's hermetic bubble. In vigorously privileging sensual perception of the concrete natural object in this way, Feuerbach's voice became the most incisive and influential in the chorus critiquing Hegel's reconciliation of thought and being as in fact one-sided and remaining within speculative thought, this side of concrete reality.[64] But Feuerbach's particular way of coming at Hegel—and the philosophical tradition he saw culminating in Hegel—preserves a subject-object dualism, even as Feuerbach subverts the subject-object hierarchy: now the material object and its immediate sensuous perception are primary, and "abstract" reflection and consciousness, privileged since Descartes as the guarantor of the subject's being, is secondary.[65] For Feuerbach objective being is independent of and prior to thought; man does not exist because he thinks, but rather because he exists in flesh and blood and perceives through the senses:

> Modern philosophy proceeded from theology; it is indeed nothing other than theology dissolved and transformed into philosophy. . . . In order to transform God into reason, reason itself had to assume the quality of an

> abstract, divine being. The senses, says Descartes, give neither true reality, being, nor certainty; only mind separated from the senses gives truth. Whence this cleavage between the mind and the senses? It is derived only from theology. God is not a sensuous being; he is, rather, the negation of all sensuous determinations and is only known through the abstraction from sensation. . . . Descartes transforms this objective being into a subjective one and the ontological proof into a psychological one; he transforms the proposition, "because God is thinkable, therefore he exists," into the proposition, "I think, therefore I am."[66]

For Feuerbach, Hegel is the "culmination of modern philosophy," inaugurated by Descartes.[67] The entire philosophical tradition since Descartes, including Hegel, in fact perpetuated the theology it displaced insofar as it continued ontologically to privilege abstract thought over immediate sensuous objectivity.[68] The "new philosophy"—Feuerbach's own—"is the realization of the Hegelian philosophy or, generally, of the philosophy that prevailed until now."[69]

There are many broad similarities between Feuerbach and Hess at this moment, especially regarding their conceptions of man's social essence. As Feuerbach writes near the end of *Principles of the Philosophy of the Future*, "the single man for himself possesses the essence of man neither in himself as a moral being nor in himself as a thinking being. The essence of man is contained only in the community and unity of man with man; it is a unity, however, which rests only on the reality of the distinction between I and thou."[70] Rather than trying to provide a new ground for being, however, Hess assesses the costs of our investments in counterproductive notions of being, self-contained subjectivity chief among them. Even at the point where Hess is closest to Feuerbach, in his vision of human essence as social rather than individual, crucial differences in emphasis are evident. Feuerbach's theory of love, dependency, community, and the intersubjective I-thou relation "rests," as Feuerbach puts it in the passage quoted above, "only on the reality of the distinction between I and thou." Feuerbachian totality is assembled, as it were, out of the building blocks of unique human beings. For all their radical incompletion and lack as individuals, Feurbach's human beings are still the foundation on which the greater human totality "rests." There is an evident tension between Feuerbach's social ontology, on the one hand, which denies full human being to discrete individuals, and his emphasis on the ontological primacy of concretely existing singularities, including human beings, on the other hand.

Feuerbach's critique of the *cogito* proceeds by pointing up the theological nature and ontological nullity of the I's abstract consciousness and inverting the subject-object hierarchy so that now sensual objectivity, rather than thought and consciousness, provides the ground of being. In contrast, Hess attacks the *cogito* by emphasizing how much productive activity, how much dynamic movement, is arrested in our obsessive quest to lay possession to, or capture, being. Such an orientation only limits our understanding of ourselves and our individuality, for it is paradoxically only by understanding the wider whole in which we are embedded that we fully grasp what constitutes us as individuals. We understand ourselves most accurately and most productively, in other words, when we move beyond our obsession with possessing being as discreet selves.

Genevieve Lloyd distills the crucial distinction between Descartes's and Spinoza's conceptions of individuality:

> The Cartesian mind rightly prides itself on its god-like self-completeness. For Spinoza we are not individual substances, either as bodies or as minds. But we are nonetheless individuals. In withdrawing the status of substance from the human mind, Spinoza does not deny its individuality. And the concept of substance continues to have moral significance for human life, though in a very different way. Spinoza calls into question the traditional links between individuality and the concept of substance. And it cannot be denied that this gives his treatment of individuality a paradoxical character. But he certainly does not present individuality as an illusion. There is a false, distorted way in which a mind can think of itself and of other things as individuals—a source of error that must be transcended by a mind pursuing freedom and virtue. But in that pursuit the mind comes to a true understanding of its own individuality.[71]

For Spinoza, thinking of oneself as a discrete entity is both an epistemological error and an error that impedes the exercise of power and freedom. As idiosyncratic a thinker as Hess was, his variations on this theme have a firm basis in Spinoza's understanding of individuals as constituted by their place in a wider immanent context. As Lloyd aptly remarks, "to be a Spinozistic individual body is precisely to be part of wider wholes. It is being thus inserted into a totality that constitutes a thing's individuality."[72] Hess is not simply calling for a politics that negates individuality, but for a Spinozan politics that conceives of individuality in non-Cartesian ways.

Reflecting on the messianic element in Hess's political thought, Erich Thier characterizes Hess as an "ecstatic" thinker.[73] It is useful to think of Hess's as an "ecstatic" understanding of the self, albeit in a particular way. He understands human beings as always in excess of the narrow conceptions we have of our selves, yet his is a Spinozan ecstasy of immanence: we simply are (part of) what is outside ourselves. It is not that Hess wants to move beyond the self, because it is not real or true, into some transcendent beyond that is; rather, Hess understands our selves as part of a wider environment that our dualistic, theological notions of subjectivity keep us from grasping and participating in with freedom and power. Lloyd's formulation of how Spinoza understands thought to extend beyond the self-contained individual is helpful: "Self-awareness is not awareness of something whose limits can be independently circumscribed."[74] The Spinozan self is constituted relationally and only ever perceived from a more or less incomplete and confused perspective; it is not a clearly delineated, self-contained substance. To understand my mind's individuality in Spinozan terms requires that I understand it as a site and source of ideas and equally that I understand that my ideas exist only by virtue of their relationships to other ideas. To turn once again to Lloyd's apt formulation, "we must both think of ourselves as knowing subjects, with particular perspectives on the world, and place ourselves outside that perspective, to think of relationships among ideas that include ourselves."[75] By getting beyond our narrow selves, we more fully become ourselves; we participate more extensively and powerfully in the universe. Hess's critique of "theological" subjectivity (Descartes and after), as well as of politics and religion, is rooted in a Spinozan rejection of dualism. Hess sees the division between inner and outer, self and other, as issuing from the mistaken metaphysical distinction between God and the universe. Spinoza recognizes no seat of the divine beyond the universe—no place, given God's omnipresence in the universe, for a personalist God to be. For Hess, analogously, there is no place beyond other people and the world where humanity's freedom can be said to reside, be it heaven, the political state, or the theological self. There is no transcendent mental sphere beyond or external to oneself where one is essentially and pristinely oneself. Such a narrow conception of the self, moreover, does not transcend the material world but only narrows one's possibilities for participating in it.

Hess's critique of the *cogito*—"Whoever says: I am I, or: I know that I am—he knows nothing. He simply believes in a mathematical point; he's staring into the dark and sees only what is not real, namely the distinction of the thinking from the thought, the subject from the object, not their identity"—proposes, with Spinoza, that we are what we are not.[76] Not because we melt into cosmic unity with all that is, but because the wider totality in which our bodies and minds are embedded is what constitutes us in our very individuality. To construe myself as a subjective being is to miss the opportunity to discover the wider conceptual and material contexts and the dynamic relationships by virtue of which I am constituted as me. Only by letting go of my being can I gain greater knowledge, freedom, and power to act. To bank on one's being in the form of an abstracted consciousness—or thinking divided from content, the "thought about"—is to believe obscurely and ignorantly in one's I instead of gaining the empowering knowledge of how the world works, the world of which I am a part. In this way, the belief in one's self—subjectivity—is for Hess of a piece with belief in other abstract religious and political categories that dominate and deactivate us as individuals and collectivities, such as God, heaven, and the state.

Hess's intervention at bottom faults Descartes for attempting to derive something as paltry and closed as subjective being from as dynamic and open-ended an activity as thinking: "Only the first word of the Cartesian philosophy is true . . . I know that I think . . . that I am *active*, not, however, that I *am*."[77] Hess's point is not only that trying to derive "I am" from "I think" results in an abstract "I" devoid of content, but, more consequentially, that the preoccupation with consolidating subjectivity actually impedes the vital act of thinking that it tries, as it were, to contain within narrow ontological parameters—"being."

> The simple "I," the thinking in distinction from the thought-about, is empty, has no content. . . . Only the "I think" amounts to anything, that is, the likeness to itself of the one in the other. What the "I"-sayer believes, the "I," the identity, here becomes the imminent content of the act—In contrast to which [*wogegen*] the mathematical point, the black nothingness that calls itself Being, reveals itself to be the frozen act of self-consciousness, arrested in its activity. The act thus becomes only half-realized, the thinking becomes arrested in the process of differentiation from the thought-about, which is really itself, so that the spirit runs its head against the wall, against the barrier that it has created and not broken through; it runs itself into a dead end. The act becomes frozen. . . . Living Becoming is turned into dead Being, and self-consciousness into theological consciousness, which now must lie its way out of black nothingness into pallid Being.[78]

Hess objects to a conception of being constituted through an act of fixing or arresting dynamic activity in a thinking subject sealed off from its thought objects. In Hess's conception the act of thinking traverses the limit that separates thinking subject from thought object, the very limit, that is, that constitutes the subject of the *cogito*. For Hess, the "fixed and frozen act of self-consciousness" of the transcendent and contentless "I" is merely a crippled and poorly understood version of dynamic, active spirit; it is spirit uselessly suspended in opposition to itself. The wall that this divided spirit runs up against and cannot break through, then, *is* the discrete self. The Cartesian subject, Hess seems to argue, can only run its head against a wall, but not break through, because this dividing wall—the false distinction between self and other, subject and object—is what constitutes the Cartesian self in the first place. In Hess's view the price we pay in order to lay claim to such paltry being is exorbitant. A clearer and more empowering understanding of ourselves, conversely, would involve relinquishing our epistemologically and ethically misguided insistence on self-possession.[79]

Hess draws on Spinoza to theorize individuality and particularity otherwise than as dualistic subjectivity and self-possessed being, which he sees as such a drag on our intellectual and ethico-political potential. Hess's understanding of individuality (whether the individual person or an individual people) is unconventional but by no means consists in mere negation.[80] On the contrary, Hess argues that the universal has no existence other than as it immanently manifests itself in individuals:

> The universal is thus unreal, merely an abstraction of the individual, which reflects the idea to which it belongs yet to which it understands itself in opposition instead of as its [the idea's] reality. The life idea [*Lebensidee*] in general, the eternal law, "absolute spirit," "world spirit," "God," or however one may properly or improperly [*eigentlich oder uneigentlich*] call the universal and eternal, is only *real* in fluctuation, in becoming-other [*Sichanderswerden*], in diversity, in the individual or, more accurately, in an infinite series of individuals, in an infinite becoming-other or self-generation [*Sichselbsterzeugen*]. The universal, in other words, comes to its self-consciousness through individuals [*aus den Individuen*], and the person who recognizes the life idea, the universal, as his life is its [the universal's] highest or most perfect reality.[81]

With Spinoza, Hess understands ideas and bodies as different modes of the same substance. Given the correspondence between idea and individual body, it is erroneous to construe their relationship dualistically and oppositionally. The misconception of the individual in terms of a mind-body opposition—the already abstract individual or theological subject—engenders, in turn, the abstraction of *das Allgemeine* (the universal, absolute, God, and so forth) in opposition to the world. In fact, the universal just is the totality of the universe in flux, constantly constituting itself as different, ever-changing particularities or individualities. This would seem to be why Hess moves from "the individual" to an infinite series of "individuals," constantly becoming themselves by becoming other than themselves. The discrete individual has no purchase on being and cannot suspend the dynamic set of relations in which it participates and that constitute it as an individual. The person who recognizes the universal as his life understands himself, then, as not merely himself but as part of this much greater totality.

A parallelism runs through Hess's critique of religious, philosophical, political, commercial, and subjective forms of dualism. The way our individuality is dominated by our "I's" (a sort of external sovereign within) is structurally analogous to and crucially interlinked with how we are dominated and deactivated by external illegitimate religious and political authorities and institutions. One's "I," conventionally understood, is for Hess born of the misguided attempt to usurp being, and it results in the enslavement, not freedom, of the individual. The attempt to understand our true situation, in a plane of immanence, in the false terms of dualistic hierarchy (mind versus body, self versus other, God versus humanity, ruler versus subject) serves to deprive us of our reality and liberty. Hess, then, does not call for the negation of individuality in the name of collective ontology. Rather, he wants to overthrow dualistic conceptions of the self, religion, and politics in order to activate free individuals, who can be seen only as part of, not constituted in opposition to, the whole that indeed constitutes them as individuals.

Hess argues that the modern subject does not overcome but rather continues the individuality-leveling dualistic principle that culminated, religiously, in Christianity and, politically, in monarchy. Religious and political absolutism could advance no further and so gave rise to revolution—the political revolution in France and the Young Hegelian critical revolution in Germany.[82] Anticipating and likely influencing Marx's "Zur Judenfrage," Hess critiques both these revolutions as marred by latent, secularized Christian dualism, which they have only displaced and disseminated in the form of modern philosophical subjectivity and modern political subjectivity, rooted in the dualistic and abstract conception of human rights that emerged from the French Revolution. In place of a single tyrant, modern subjects are so many tyrants, and also slaves. Thus the modern alienated subject is constituted in an ontological elsewhere, which it constantly strives to reclaim by identifying with abstractions (such as self, God, and state) and by laying claim to or dominating the material world (for example, property, money, and other people).

The crucial prerequisite for ethical progress is to overcome, by identifying with creative action, our obsession with possessing being. In a draft manuscript of "The Philosophy of the Act," Hess writes: "I *am* only what I engender out of myself. My act is my life. Whatever is *created* through my power, potency, vigor, that *alone* bears witness to, that alone convinces me of my I. The *products* [*Erzeugnisse*] of [one's] vigor are so many testimonials [*Zeugnisse*] to it. I am as much as I do, without holding on to any scrap [*einen Rest*] for myself."[83] There can be no guarantor of being beyond the plane of one's immanent activity. One's being is synonymous with one's doing; there is no being unresolved into immanent activity that one could retain for oneself. From this vantage point, it seems worth noting, the question of free will is badly posed, for it presupposes the self-world dichotomy that Spinoza disputes. Our individuality is part of the universe. Since we are not separate from the universe (or God) there is no separate, distinct agency—opposed to or wholly different from us—that could use us as a means. In a world of immanence, there is no final residence for an agency (Providence) that could pursue strategies of instrumentality, rendering our actions unfree in a conventional sense. By the same token, this conception of the universe and the individual as constituted by the wider whole is incompatible with conventionally conceived free subjectivity: in an immanently conceived universe, everything is determined. One is always situated in a web of causal factors and constituted and reconstituted by their changing relationships. There is no place, no refuge beyond immanent causality, to be.

Hess identifies the construal of activity as a means to an end—rather than its own immanent reward—as humanity's ur-curse and points to Spinoza's notion of activity as inherently pleasurable and its own reward as the liberating alternative.[84] As Hess theorizes it, the deed or act (*Tat*, *Selbsttat*, or *Geistesthat*) constitutes the heart of modernity's accomplishments and future promise by uniting conceptual and material action in free praxis: "The free thought-action [*Geistestat*] is the center point, from which all of modernity's endeavors have issued and into which they all return. It is therefore necessary to explore its law, structure [*Organismus*], and consequences. The basis of the free act is the *Ethics* of Spinoza, and the present 'Philosophy of the Act' is only intended as a further development of that work."[85] Hess sees in Spinoza's philosophy of unity of spirit and world the all-important bridge between thought and praxis, and thus a sort of blueprint for the communist unity that Hess sees Europe advancing toward through the meeting of German philosophy and French social and political activism.

If Auerbach's Spinozism authorized his embrace of the imagined ethical community of the German *Volk*, Hess's stressed a radical activist version of Spinoza's ethics that saw the free exercise of thought and the radical reshaping of social institutions as indissolubly wedded: "The centerpiece of social and intellectual freedom is ethics [*die Sittlichkeit*], the highest good, the 'recognition of God,' as Spinoza calls it, or the self-consciousness of the 'absolute Spirit,' as the Hegelians, inexactly, put it. It is the spirit's consciousness of its self-identity in its becoming different from itself, the overcoming of alterity as something fixed, the transformation of natural determination into self-determination. Without this, no equality and no liberty are possible."[86] Hess leverages a version of Spinozan variegated unity as the vantage point from which to critique false authority and how institutions of power, privilege, and private property fix unjust social relations under the sway of a false ontological premise. In a striking neologism, Hess calls this "*Seinsucht*": "It is precisely *Seinsucht*, the obsession with continued existence as a particular individuality, as a limited I, as a finite being—that leads to *Habsucht*."[87] *Seinsucht*—ontological obsession or addiction to being—precedes and animates *Habsucht* (avarice or, literally, addiction to having). Our fateful confusion of what we have with what we are rests on our deeper need—or addiction—to having being in the first place. Only because we fail to see the products of our labor as part of us through our productive activity—and regard them instead as foreign objects—do we feel the need to lay claim to them, and to our own being through ownership of them. If we identify with our productive activity itself, however, we do not enter into this false subject-object dualism and do not become addicted to being and owning. The institutions of money and private property perpetuate alienation and inequality. We become weighed down—alienated and enslaved—by so much accumulated baggage, through which we try to secure our being. Our egos insidiously limit us even as we mistake them for the condition of possibility of our existence. We imagine that we are confirming ourselves in our individuality when we grasp at and try to own our being, but—Hess argues, following Spinoza—we fail to understand our individuality when we fail to grasp the context that constitutes and sustains it. In committing the error of possessing ourselves, we relinquish the greater power and freedom to which only self-knowledge beyond the self can give access.[88] Hess sees the truest freedom decidedly not in possessive individualism and the social institutions that it supports and that are supported by it, but rather in the endlessly dynamic principle of action or deed (*Tat*), a never-ending intellectual and material creative process and an end in itself.

Rome and Jerusalem

Hess was a highly eclectic thinker who drew significantly, at various moments, on Hegel, Feuerbach, and Marx, among others. Throughout his varied career, however, Spinoza remained for Hess, as Francesco Tomasoni notes, "the most important point of reference . . . in interpreting his own identity and understanding the modern world."[89] If Spinoza was Hess's most enduring intellectual inspiration, his most consistent object of critique was the atomized egoistic individual and the conceptual structures and religious, political, and commercial institutions that perpetuated it and that it perpetuated. Spinoza's presence in Hess's critiques of the causes and disastrous effects of modern individualism is sometimes explicit, as in his important 1843 essay "Socialismus und Communismus" ("Socialism and Communism") and at times only implicit or even conceptually faint, as in his more Feuerbachian "Über das Geldwesen" ("On the Essence of Money"; 1843). In his major socialist essays Hess certainly became more reticent about presenting Spinoza as the quintessential articulation of a specifically Jewish idea of unity, or suggesting, as he had in *The Holy History*, that the fulfillment of human freedom would involve a renewal of a unified mode of existence first achieved by the Jews in their ancient state.

Both of these themes—the Jews as the ultimate redeemers of humanity and Spinoza as the ultimate articulation of the Jewish tradition—return to prominence in Hess's meditation on Jewish nationalism, *Rome and Jerusalem* (1862). Hess's embrace of nations as humanity's vital organic units, and thus as crucial if humanitarian socialism is to have real existence, marks a major departure from his earlier socialistic thought as well as from contemporary socialist trends. Yet there are also strong continuities between his Spinozan socialism of the 1840s and his vision of Jewish nationalism two decades later.

Throughout the different phases of his intellectual evolution, Hess relentlessly identified Christianity and its secular outgrowths as responsible for the apotheosis of the sovereign individual and modern society's associated and widely ramified ills. Even as Hess moved away from holding up the resources of the Jewish tradition as the necessary corrective to the problem of modern egoism, and even as he occasionally implicated Jews in it—as in "Über das Geldwesen"—his identification of Christian dualism as the force inhibiting the realization of ethical communal existence was sustained and fierce. In "Die letzten Philosophen" (The latest philosophers; 1845), for example, Hess characterizes Bruno Bauer and Max Stirner as thoroughly Christian "philosophers" (now a term of abuse signifying ineffectual abstraction), in spite of their strident atheism, because they celebrate the conscious and the material self, respectively. Here and in general in this period, Hess faults Christian dualism for the socially atomizing thrust of religious, political, commercial, and philosophical institutions and structures. Like Marx in "Zur Judenfrage" (who, in fairness to Hess, had cribbed a good deal from Hess in that essay), Hess sees the citizens of the modern secular state as secularized Christian souls. Unlike Marx, however, Hess also sees the base materialism of civil society as a thoroughly Christian, not a Jewish, product. Alongside the bodiless spirits of the Christian heaven and the post-Christian state there also exists "the spiritless materialism of the Christian world; it exists in civil society."[90] Hess also uses a distinctly Christian metaphorics to evoke the harmful role that money plays in secular society: "The money-hungry possessive animal consumes not only its alienated theoretical essence—its God—but above all it consumes its estranged practical essence:

money. To satisfy its egotistical needs, it not only attends its Holy Mass [heilige *Messe* (my addition)], but above all attends to the profane Mass (the Mercenary Mass) [*Krämermesse* (my addition)] held in the market place. And if this world knows how to revere the Church and God as its *Sunday meal*, so must it also take into account the stock-market and the cult of wealth (money making) as its *daily bread*."[91] The extent to which Hess continued in this period to understand his socialism as rooted in Judaism can only be a matter of speculation. He certainly kept up no meaningful ties to the Jewish community, and in 1842 he even looked favorably on the prospect of the disappearnce of the "national" and all "separatistic" character among the Jews through intermarriage with Christians.[92] Nonetheless, even in his socialist writings he saw socialism as destined to overcome the limitations of secularized Christian culture and institutions, and he continued to see Spinoza as the figure who showed the way to this messianic, post-Christian future.

The most profound continuity between Hess's Spinozan communism of the 1840s and his Spinozan Jewish nationalism of twenty years later lies precisely in his critique of the religion, philosophy, politics, and competitive commerce of the autonomous individual.[93] Indeed the most characteristic quality and chief virtue that Hess sees in the Jewish nation are the extra-individual ties that bind its members. Hess's Jews hold the key to ushering in humanity's final redemption ("the Sabbath of History") because they embody human existence otherwise than as discrete individuals.[94] Hess projected onto the Jewish nation his Spinoza-inspired ideal of a monistic human totality that united spiritual energies and a natural substrate and that constituted the individuals it comprised and exceeded: "We are on the eve of the Sabbath of History and should prepare for our last mission through a thorough understanding of our historical religion." As a prolegomena to such a historical understanding, Hess adds:

> We cannot understand a single word of the Holy Scriptures, so long as we do not possess the point of view of the genius of the Jewish nation which produced these writings. Nothing is more foreign to the spirit of Judaism than the idea of the salvation of the individual which, according to the modern conception, is the cornerstone of religion. Judaism has never drawn any line of separation between the individual and the family, the family and the nation, the nation and humanity as a whole, humanity and the cosmos, nor between creation and the Creator. Judaism has no other dogma but the teaching of the Unity.[95]

It goes without saying that Hess presents an idiosyncratic version of the Jewish tradition (nothing in the spirit of Judaism distinguishes between creation and

Creator?), the thrust of which is to install supra-individualism at the heart of the Jewish nation. Well-known themes from *Rome and Jerusalem* such as Jewish —particularly maternal—love, which is never exhausted in individual sexual desire or romantic sentimentality but rather is profoundly oriented toward children and the future; Hess's praise of Jewish patriotism and trenchant critique of Reform Judaism for reducing a national religion to a matter of individual faith; his embrace of an ineluctable racial component in Judaism that ties even apostates and their offspring to the Jewish totality and has sustained itself for millennia—all these exemplify the supra-individuality that for Hess is the Jews' defining characteristic, their genius.[96]

When Hess holds up Jewish collective sensibilities and life practices, and Spinoza, as the antidote to the ills of Christian dualism and the spiritual and materialistic individualism it engenders, we recognize a variation on familiar Hessian themes:[97]

> It is the Jewish conception of the family which gave rise to the vivid belief in the continuity of the spirit in human history. . . . When modern dualism of spirit and matter, the result of the separation of Christianity from Judaism, had found its highest expression in the works of the last Christian philosopher, Descartes, and had threatened to kill all unity of life, there arose again out of Judaism the belief in the existence of one eternal force in Nature and history. This belief acted as a bulwark against spiritual egoism, on the one hand, and materialistic individualism on the other. Just as Christian dualism received its mortal blow from the teachings of Spinoza, so does the existence of the ancient Jewish people, with its model family life, act as an antidote against this disease of dualism in practical life.[98]

A confluence of factors—including the anthropology and biology that Hess devoted himself to in the late 1850s, mid-nineteenth-century race discourse, and the contemporary phenomenon of Italian nationalism—allowed Hess to see in the Jewish race the promise of a living, monistic, human totality unencumbered by the limitations of egoism and its attendant ills:[99] "Judaism does not allow either spiritualistic or materialistic sects to exist in its midst. Jewish life, like its divine ideal and goal, is undivided, and it is this Monism of Jewish life which is only the reverse side of Christian spiritualism. I do not speak here of philosophical systems or of religious dogmas, or of life conceptions, but of life itself."[100]

Hess sent a copy of *Rome and Jerusalem* in advance of its publication to his old friend Auerbach. If he hoped his book might mend the long-standing rift in their friendship, he was mistaken. Auerbach put down Hess's work in disgust without having finished it.[101] Hess's national and racial understanding of Judaism and trenchant critique of what he considered the delusions of German Jews who denationalized their Judaism and identified with the German people were wholly out of step with mainstream German-Jewish sensibilities and more than Auerbach could countenance. In the late 1830s and 1840s both friends set out with Spinoza to try to reimagine the polity and the nature of community, but the paths down which they followed Spinoza led in radically different directions.

Concluding Remarks

Moses Hess's Spinozan Jewish nationalism—his celebration of the monism of Jewish life as opposed to the dualism and egoistic spiritualism of secularized Christian thought and institutions—brings us full circle. Lazarus Bendavid hoped to slay the monstrous collective Jewish body and awaken Kantian moral will in postcollective Jewish individuals. Hess leans on Spinoza to insist that there is such a thing as a Jewish national body at a time when secularization and acculturation, liberalism and Reform had made this a questionable (and to many German Jews, including Berthold Auerbach, an infuriating) proposition.

Hess's 1862 *Rome and Jerusalem* takes us well beyond 1848, which ushered in a new political sensibility among German Jews as well as, however briefly, highly prominent Jewish participation in German politics. (Auerbach, for example, served in the Frankfurt *Vorparlament*, although he was not elected to the National Assembly.) The events of 1848–49 did not ultimately advance the cause of Jewish emancipation. Indeed they probably impeded that cause.[1] Yet 1848 did mark a significant change in German-Jewish political self-understanding. The emergence of prominent Jewish politicians and activists, the nearly unanimous support among German liberals for Jewish emancipation, and the widespread popular antisemitic violence that erupted in German lands in March and April 1848 strongly consolidated the Jewish identification with liberalism that leading Jewish political activists like Gabriel Riesser had been fostering since the early 1830s.[2] The liberal cause now won over even the members of the old Orthodox community, among whom—up to the eve of the revolutionary events—there could still be found significant resistance to the project of emancipation and the denationalization of Jewish identity that it entailed.[3] Despite the reactionary backlash of the immediate postrevolutionary years, this political orientation proved resilient, and it grew stronger as liberalism found new energy after 1858 and Jewish emancipation made significant gains in the course of the 1860s. The Jewish community's internal religious diversity notwithstanding, the overwhelming majority of Jews in Germany had come to identify as German Jews and to see their political hopes as thoroughly entwined and largely identical with those of their non-Jewish countrymen across the liberal spectrum.[4]

The role that philosophy played in political theory and strategy in Germany also diminished markedly in the 1840s. Over the course of that decade the radical, highly philosophical antiphilosophy of the Young Hegelians yielded to more economically grounded analytic models, such as Marx's "scientific" theory, and to more palpable forms of political activism and party organization. In the decades following 1848, industrialization, rising economic prosperity, liberalism, and positivism predominated, and little remained of the vibrancy, innovation, and political urgency that had characterized German philosophical culture in the period between Kant and the Young Hegelians. Both the key negative and key positive inspiration for the intellectuals whose work I have explored in this book to invest tremendous faith in the political efficacy of philosophical thought—the relative lack of possibilities for political participation for Jews, and the spectacular developments in German Idealism, respectively—had lost their force.

Hess's meditation, in the theoretically abstruse epilogue to *Rome and Jerusalem*, on what he characterizes as the "last antagonism"—that between "labor and speculation"—underscores how far he had moved from his Spinozan communism of the 1840s.[5] He now opposes "speculation," on the economic and industrial plane, to labor, which it exploits for capitalist profit. On the theoretical plane, he opposes "speculation" to conceptual productivity via investigation and experimentation. The idiom of Hess's understanding of both economic and epistemological productivity would be out of place in his essays of the early 1840s. Yet the fact that Spinoza is still the lens through which Hess ultimately understands the movement and meanings of modern European and Jewish history and politics reveals the extent to which his early theorizing established a scaffolding on which he could later hang ideas inspired by subsequent economic realities, nationalist movements, discourses of race, and developments in the empirical sciences. Even though in the 1860s he no longer articulates his messianic hopes through a critique of the *cogito*, for example, his earlier Spinoza-inspired assault on the philosophical subject still provides an indispensable window onto the preoccupations that animate his proto-Zionism.

The question of the afterlife of Hess's early philosophical politics in his later theorizing of Jewish nationalism can open onto the broader question of the resonance of Jewish philosophical politics in Germany between 1789 and 1848 with intellectual and historical dynamics of other moments animated by highly politicized theory. What can the channeling of political aspirations through the needle of philosophical discourse by German-Jewish intellectuals of the late eighteenth and early nineteenth centuries help us discover about the efficacy and limitations of politicized theory in the late twentieth and early twenty-first centuries, including strains of deconstruction, postcolonial theory, and feminism? A longer view of the dynamics—in particular, the willed and unwilled performativity—of theoretical politics (not political theory, but politicized theory) could reveal much about the position of intellectuals in general, and of intellectuals in minority groups in particular, vis-à-vis institutions of political power, and their aspirations and predicaments as they engage in the irreducibly ambivalent project of thinking politics.

Abbreviations

AF	Friedlander, Albert. "The Wohlwill-Moser Correspondence." *Leo Baeck Institute Yearbook* 11 (1966): 262–99.
BA	Bettelheim, Anton. *Berthold Auerbach: Der Mann, sein Werk, sein Nachlaß*. Stuttgart: Cotta, 1907.
BS	Hegel, Georg Wilhelm Friedrich. *Berliner Schriften: (1818–1831), voran gehen Heidelberger Schriften (1816–1818)*. Edited and with an introduction by Walter Jaeschke. Hamburg: Meiner, 1997.
DHA	Heine, Heinrich. *Historisch-kritische Gesamtausgabe der Werke*. Edited by Manfred Windfuhr. 16 vols. Hamburg: Hoffmann and Campe, 1973–97. This edition is known as the Düsseldorfer Heine-Ausgabe.
DS	Breckman, Warren. *Marx, the Young Hegelians, and the Origins of Radical Social Theory: Dethroning the Self*. Cambridge: Cambridge University Press, 1999.
ECJ	Bendavid, Lazarus. *Etwas zur Charackteristick der Juden*. Leipzig: J. Stahel, 1793.
EPW	Marx, Karl. *Marx: Early Political Writings*. Translated and edited by Joseph O'Malley with Richard A. Davis. Cambridge: Cambridge University Press, 1994.
HHM	Hess, Moses. *The Holy History of Mankind and Other Writings*. Edited by Shlomo Avineri. Cambridge: Cambridge University Press, 2004.
HHS	Von der Luft, Eric, ed. and trans. *Hegel, Hinrichs, and Schleiermacher on Feeling and Reason in Religion: The Texts of Their 1821–22 Debate*. Lewiston, NY: Edwin Mellen, 1987.
IKW	Kant, Immanuel. *Immanuel Kant Werkausgabe*. Edited by Wilhelm Weischedel. 12 vols. Frankfurt: Suhrkamp, 1968.
JF	Bauer, Bruno. *Die Judenfrage*. Braunschweig, Germany: Friedrich Otto, 1843.
KMEW	Marx, Karl. *Karl Marx: Early Writings*. Translated by Gregor Benton and Rodney Livingstone. Introduction by Lucio Colletti. New York: Vintage, 1975.
KMSW	Marx, Karl. *Selected Writings*. Edited by Lawrence H. Simon. Indianapolis, IN: Hackett, 1994.
LHP	Hegel, Georg Wilhelm Friedrich. *Lectures on the History of Philosophy*. Translated by E. S. Haldane and Frances H. Simson. 3 vols. Lincoln: University of Nebraska Press, 1995.
LPR	Hegel, Georg Wilhelm Friedrich. *Lectures on the Philosophy of Religion*. Edited by Peter C. Hodgson. Translated by R. F. Brown, Peter C. Hodgson, and J. M. Stewart, with the assistance of H. S. Harris. 3 vols. Reprint. Oxford: Oxford University Press, 2007.
MECW	Marx, Karl, and Friedrich Engels. *Collected Works*. 47 vols. New York: International, 1975–2004.

MEGA	Marx, Karl, and Friedrich Engels. *Gesamtausgabe*. Edited by the Institut für Marxismus-Leninismus beim Zentralkomitee der Kommunistischen Partei der Sowjetunion and the Institut für Marxismus-Leninismus beim Zentralkomitee der Sozialistischen Einheitspartei Deutschlands. Berlin: Dietz, 1972–.
MEW	Marx, Karl, and Friedrich Engels. *Werke*. 43 vols. Berlin: Dietz, 1956–90.
PN	Lloyd, Genevieve. *Part of Nature: Self-Knowledge in Spinoza's "Ethics."* Ithaca, NY: Cornell University Press, 1994.
PP	Moggach, Douglas. *The Philosophy and Politics of Bruno Bauer*. New York: Cambridge University Press, 2003.
PR	Hegel, Georg Wilhelm Friedrich. *Elements of the Philosophy of Right*. Edited by Allen Wood. Translated by H. B. Nisbet. Cambridge: Cambridge University Press, 1991. Cited by paragraph (§), except for "Preface," which is cited by page number. Page references for the "Preface" ("Vorrede") in German are to TWA, volume 7.
PSS	Hess, Moses. *Philosophische und sozialistische Schriften 1837–1850: Eine Auswahl*. Edited by Auguste Cornu and Wolfgang Mönke. Expanded ed. Vaduz, Liechtenstein: Topos, 1980.
RA	Rose, Paul Lawrence. *Revolutionary Antisemitism in Germany from Kant to Wagner*. Princeton: Princeton University Press, 1990.
RRT	Kant, Immanuel. *Religion and Rational Theology*. Translated and edited by Allen Wood and George di Giovanni. New York: Cambridge University Press, 1996.
SA 1 and SA 2	Auerbach, Berthold. "Spinoza-Arbeiten: Ein Stück aus meinem Leben." *Neue Freie Presse* (Vienna), September 14 and 15, 1880. SA 1 is September 14; SA 2 is September 15.
TC	Schorsch, Ismar. *From Text to Context: The Turn to History in Modern Judaism*. Hanover, NH: Published for Brandeis University Press by University Press of New England, 1994.
TWA	Hegel, Georg Wilhelm Friedrich. *Werke in 20 Bänden mit Registerband*. Edited by Eva Moldenhauer and Karl Markus Michel. Frankfurt: Suhrkamp, 1986.
VPW	Hegel, Georg Wilhelm Friedrich. *Vorlesungen über die Philosophie der Weltgeschichte, Berlin 1822/1823*. Edited by Karl-Heinz Ilting, Karl Brehmer, and Hoo Nam Seelmann. Vol. 12 of G. W. F. Hegel, *Vorlesungen: ausgewählte Nachschriften und Manuskripte*. Hamburg: Meiner, 1996.
WL	Hegel, Georg Wilhelm Friedrich. *Wissenschaft der Logik*. Edited by Friedrich Hogemann and Walter Jaeschke. Vols. 11 and 12 of *Gesammelte Werke*. Hamburg: Meiner, 1978 and 1981.
WM	Correspondence between Moses Moser and Immanual Wolf-Wohlwill. Typescript, Leo Baeck Foundation, New York.
YHKM	McLellan, David. *The Young Hegelians and Karl Marx*. London: Macmillan, 1969.

Notes

Introduction

1. For a detailed account, see Jacob Toury, *Die politischen Orientierungen der Juden in Deutschland*. For a briefer overview, see Michael A. Meyer and Michael Brenner, *German-Jewish History in Modern Times*, 2:262–67, 280–91.

2. See Bernard Yack, *The Longing for Total Revolution*.

3. Classic studies of the treatment of Jews and Judaism in German philosophy include Nathan Rotenstreich, *Jews and German Philosophy: The Polemics of Emancipation*, and Emil Fackenheim, *Encounters between Judaism and Modern Philosophy*. More recent studies include Francesco Tomasoni, *Modernity and the Final Aim of History*, and Andrée Leroussseau, *Le judaïsme dans la philosophie allemande, 1770–1850*.

4. See Michael Mack, *German Idealism and the Jew*, and Paul Rose, *Revolutionary Antisemitism in Germany from Kant to Wagner*.

5. See Mack, *German Idealism and the Jew*, 4, 10.

6. To be clear, Rose is nuanced in his assessment of Hegel's treatment of Judaism and the Jews (see P. Rose, *Revolutionary Antisemitism in Germany*, 109–16.) He sees the roots of "revolutionary antisemitism" much more in Kant and Fichte. Mack reads Jews as the Other of Kantian transcendental philosophy and Hegelian dialectics alike.

7. For an excellent study of Maimon, see Abraham Socher, *The Radical Enlightenment of Solomon Maimon*.

8. Hess's letter to Auerbach of September 2, 1841, appears in Moses Hess, *Moses Hess Briefwechsel*, 79–80.

9. See Warren Breckman, *Marx, the Young Hegelians, and the Origins of Radical Social Theory*.

10. On Germany, see, for example, Lenore O'Boyle, "The Problem of an Excess of Educated Men in Western Europe (1800–1850)," 473–78. O'Boyle cites a wide range of observers who commented on the perceived surfeit of university-educated men in Germany in the 1820s, 1830s, and 1840s.

11. On the Young Hegelians' exclusion from the academy and its impact on the movement, see Wolfgang Eßbach, *Die Junghegelianer*, 124–31.

12. Although Marcus Herz (1747–1803) studied and eventually carried on an important correspondence with Kant well before Bendavid (1762–1832) began lecturing and publishing on Kant's critiques in the 1790s, Herz never meaningfully engaged with Kant's thought after his critical turn.

13. See Scott Spector, "Beyond Assimilation."

14. "Subjectivity refers to the intricate, complex, and self-contradictory ways in which subjects experience their place in the world, *in contrast to* how they are perceived by others, how they are ordered within relatively rigid external systems" (ibid., 97).

15. See Jonathan Hess, "Beyond Subversion."
16. See Susannah Heschel, *Abraham Geiger and the Jewish Jesus*, 1.
17. See Hess, "Beyond Subversion," 318.

1. *Off with Their Heads?*

Epigraphs: Johann G. Fichte, *Beitrag zur Berichtigung der Urteile des Publikums über die französische Revolution*, 115; Lazarus Bendavid, ECJ, 55.

1. Allen Wood hopes that collecting all of Kant's ethical writings, especially the often-neglected *Metaphysics of Morals*, in one volume "will help correct the false (often grotesque) images of [Kant's] ethical theory that have been formed by reading only the foundational works (the *Groundwork* and second *Critique*)" ("General Introduction," xxxiii). When Bendavid published *Etwas zur Charackteristick der Juden* (hereafter ECJ) in 1793, of course, only the *Groundwork of the Metaphysics of Morals* and second *Critique* (*Critique of Practical Reason*), but not the *Metaphysics of Morals* (1797), had appeared. I have found no evidence of a direct connection between Bendavid's and Fichte's fantasies of Jewish decapitation, though to judge from the timing of publication, it is possible that Fichte could have read Bendavid before publishing *Beitrag zur Berichtigung der Urteile des Publikums über die französische Revolution* (Contribution toward the correction of the public's assessment of the French Revolution). Bendavid's preface to ECJ is dated March 1793; the first part of Fichte's *Beitrag* (containing his fantasy of Jewish emancipation through decapitation) appeared at the *Jubilatenmesse* (that is, in mid-May, *Jubilate* being the third Sunday after Easter) of that year.

2. For Fichte's remarks on Jews in *Beitrag*, see 114–16; for his use of the phrase "Staat im Staat" (state within a state) with regard to the Jews, see 115.

3. My labeling of Fichte's *Beitrag* as a discourse of emergent nationalism requires qualification. Strictly speaking, in *Beitrag* Fichte does not write as a nationalist. As we shall see later in this section of my text, his argument is about the state and is anchored in the autonomy of human beings as such rather than in the particular character or rights of an ethnic nation. Nor does Fichte support his antisemitism with the nationalist opposition of German and Jew; rather, he relies on the opposition of Jew and *Mensch*. With the admittedly dubious aid of hindsight, however, I am tempted to call this opposition "protonationalist" for the reason that Fichte's Jews of *Beitrag* can already be said to embody (quite literally) an incompatibility with the state, into which they can be incorporated only through a fantasy of corporal mutilation. Precisely when imagining the Jews, Fichte does come close to an ethnic essentialism. Paul Rose makes a similar point in *Revolutionary Antisemitism in Germany from Kant to Wagner* (hereafter RA), 124. For Rose's assessment of Fichte's originary role in the development of "revolutionary antisemitism" in Germany, see ibid, chapter 8. For a critique of Rose's reading of Fichte as dubious, see Anthony La Vopa, "Jews and Germans," 680–81.

4. Baron coined the term in his seminal essay "Ghetto and Emancipation," which he ends with a call to "break with the lachrymose theory of pre-Revolutionary woe and to adopt a view more in accord with historic truth" (526). See also Salo Baron, *History and Jewish Historians*, 64, 88, 96.

5. Joseph II issued a series of edicts—known as the Edicts of Toleration—pertaining to Jews in different parts of the Habsburg Empire: for the Jews of Bohemia, there was an edict in October 1781; for Austrian Silesia, December 1781; for Vienna and Lower Austria, January

1782; for Moravia, February 1782; for Hungary, March 1783; and, finally, for Galicia, 1789. See Michael Graetz, "The Jewish Enlightenment," 1:337–41.

6. David Sorkin, *The Berlin Haskalah and German Religious Thought*, 111.

7. As Edward Breuer and Sorkin have shown, the early Haskalah program of cultural renewal not only did not draw on but in fact strongly opposed the historicization of religion as practiced by the German Neologists, who had come to dominate German religious thought by about 1760. In contrast, the later turn to social and political issues by those on the radical fringe of *maskilim* was thoroughly implicated in attempts to reconceive Jewish history. See Breuer, *The Limits of Enlightenment*; and Sorkin, *The Berlin Haskalah* and *Moses Mendelssohn and the Religious Enlightenment*. On the Neologists and the importance of history in eighteenth-century German religious thought, see Peter Hanns Reill, *The German Enlightenment and the Rise of Historicism*, 43–45.

8. For an early defensive response to Bendavid, see Jacob Guttmann, "Lazarus Bendavid: Seine Stellung zum Judentum und seine literarische Wirksamkeit." Brief treatments of Bendavid's treatise can also be found in Hans-Joachim Becker, *Fichtes Idee der Nation und das Judentum*, 57–60; Shmuel Feiner, *Cultural Revolution in Berlin*, 70–72, *The Jewish Enlightenment*, 308–10, and *The Origins of Jewish Secularization in Eighteenth-Century Europe*, 232–33; Jonathan Hess, *Germans, Jews, and the Claims of Modernity*, 157; Jacob Katz, *Out of the Ghetto*, 132; Michael Meyer, *Response to Modernity*, 20–21; Paul Reitter, *On the Origins of Jewish Self-Hatred*, 17–18, 133–34; Hans Joachim Schoeps, *Geschichte der jüdischen Religionsphilosophie in der Neuzeit*, 40–41; Sorkin, *The Berlin Haskalah*, 122–23; and Max Wiener, *Jüdische Religion im Zeitalter der Emanzipation*, 42. Ephraim Navon has written incisively on the Kantian framework of Bendavid's *Etwas zur Charackteristick der Juden* "The Encounter of German Idealists and Jewish Enlighteners: 1760–1800."

9. Dominique Bourel, "Eine Generation später," 379.

10. The Itzig family was the first—and only—Jewish family to receive, in 1791, the right of hereditary citizenship. See Steven Lowenstein, "Jewish Upper Crust and Berlin Jewish Enlightenment."

11. Bourel, "Eine Generation später," 376.

12. Mendelssohn's relationship to traditional Judaism has been the subject of debate, in particular between Allan Arkush and David Sorkin. Arkush argues that the mature Mendelssohn had in fact become a deist and remained outwardly observant for essentially strategic reasons (*Moses Mendelssohn and the Enlightenment*). Sorkin, in a study of Mendelssohn's entire German-Hebrew *oeuvre* (*Moses Mendelssohn and the Religious Enlightenment*), argues that Mendelssohn's position as a theological Wolffian was and remained harmonic with his observance of Jewish law. For an incisive interpretation of Ascher, see Jonathan Hess, *Germans, Jews, and the Claims of Modernity*, 137–67. Brief discussions of Ascher (and especially of his *Leviathan*) can also be found in Schoeps, *Geschichte der jüdischen Religionsphilosophie*, 39–56; M. Meyer, *Response to Modernity*, 21–23; and Sorkin, *The Berlin Haskalah*, 122–23. For a more extensive reading of Ascher's *Leviathan*, see Christoph Schulte, "Saul Ascher's *Leviathan*." Schulte highlights the Kantian rupture in Haskalah ideology (ibid., 25–26). On the importance of Kant for Bendavid's generation of *maskilim*, see M. Graetz, "The Jewish Enlightenment," 1:352–53.

13. Bendavid, ECJ, 65. Throughout this book all translations not otherwise attributed are my own.

14. As Stephen Burnett has remarked ("Distorted Mirrors," 276–77), Margaritha's account represents an especially important moment in the tradition of early modern theological ethnographies of Jews through the influence it had on Johann Buxtorf the Elder's *Juden Schul*. See also R. Po-chia Hsia, "Christian Ethnographies of Jews in Early Modern Germany."

15. For an analysis of Buxtorf's *Juden Schul* in the context of early modern theological polemics, see Stephen Burnett, *From Christian Hebraism to Jewish Studies*, chapter 3.

16. See Menassah ben Israel, *Humble Addresses* (1655) and *Vindiciae Judaeorum* (1656), both in *Menasseh ben Israel's Mission to Oliver Cromwell.*

17. Bendavid, ECJ, 65.

18. On the temporalization of medicine and the sciences generally since the eighteenth century, see Wolf Lepenies, *Das Ende der Naturgeschichte* and "Historisierung der Natur und Entmoralisierung der Wissenschaften seit dem 18. Jahrhundert."

19. Volker Roelcke, *Krankheit und Kulturkritik*, 11–17.

20. Ibid., 16.

21. Martin Davies, "Karl Philipp Moritz's *Erfahrungseelenkunde*," 20.

22. Quoted in ibid., 23.

23. Moritz wrote: "The real happiness of our life depends on our being as little as possible jealous, avaricious, vain, slothful, lascivious, vengeful, etc.; because these are all diseases of the psyche, which can often spoil the days of our lives more than physical disease" ("Revision der ersten drei Bände dieses Magazins," 3).

24. Ernst-Peter Wieckenberg, "Juden als Autoren des *Magazins zur Erfahrungsseelenkunde*," 137.

25. Lazarus Bendavid, "Selbstmord aus Rechtschaffenheit und Lebensüberdruß," 4. Although Bendavid does not refer expressly to the "patient" in this case study as Jewish, Jewish contributors to *Magazin zur Erfahrungsseelenkunde* wrote overwhelmingly about Jews; this was their social context. There is very little likelihood that Bendavid would have reported about a Christian. For the journal's readers, moreover, Jews were arguably the outsiders par excellence, which was one of the reasons Moritz readily published stories about Jews. I thank Liliane Weissberg for her insights on this point. Weissberg also identifies the figure in this case history as Jewish ("Fußnoten," 236).

26. Lazarus Bendavid, "Sonderbare Art des Trübsinnes," 80.

27. I thank Michael Meyer for pointing me to an anonymous manuscript now attributed to Sabbatai Joseph Wolff (1757–1832). Written and revised in 1812–23, it takes up and modifies Bendavid's four-part social typology of contemporary Jews. See Meyer, "The Orthodox and the Enlightened."

28. I thank Christoph Schulte for the opportunity to present my ideas on the affinity between Nietzsche's genealogy of morals and Bendavid's rewriting of the Jewish *Leidensgeschichte* as a *Krankheitsgeschichte* in his 1999 seminar on Kant and the Haskalah. In a subsequent book, Schulte advances a similar thesis in the section titled "Eine Genealogie der jüdischen Moral: Lazarus Bendavid" (*Die Jüdische Aufklärung*, 107–14).

29. Bendavid's and Nietzsche's narratives thus follow different timelines. The crucial turning point for Nietzsche is the experience of powerlessness in the Babylonian Exile, to which priestly Judaism emerged as a moral and psychological response. Bendavid derives the moral *Sklavensinn* of the Jews from the loss of the Jewish state in 70 CE.

30. Bendavid, ECJ, 12–13. See also Nietzsche's remarks on the invention of the idea of free moral will and the reinterpretation of defeat as *Gehorsam* (*Jenseits von Gut und Böse; Zur Genealogie der Moral*, 280–81), on the derivation of "bad conscience" (ibid., 332–36), and on how the ascetic ideal provides a meaning for suffering (ibid., 411–12).

31. See also Nietzsche, *Jenseits von Gut und Böse; Zur Genealogie der Moral*, 281–83.

32. Similarly, Nietzsche sees morality as a form of "spiritual revenge" ("ein Akt der geistigen Rache") and "the most fundamental of all declarations of war" ("dies[e] grundsätzlichtst[e] aller Kriegserklärungen") (*Jenseits von Gut und Böse; Zur Genealogie der Moral*, 267). It is this conception of the moral valorization of weakness as the last resort of the defeated, as a displaced but still essentially martial strategy, that constitutes the substantive conceptual link between Bendavid and Nietzsche. Bendavid's characterization of traditional Judaism as the "slave mentality of past centuries" ("Sklavensinn voriger Jahrhunderte") is not novel rhetorically (ECJ, 65). In *Religion within the Boundaries of Mere Reason,* for example, which appeared on Easter 1793, and thus virtually concurrently with Bendavid's ECJ, Kant contrasts the Greek spirit of freedom—and, especially, the new form of moral freedom ushered in with Jesus's advent—with the "slavish mind" (*Sklavensinn*) of the Jews (*Religion and Rational Theology* [hereafter RRT], 119). Yet Kant defines the Jews' slave mentality in terms of the this-worldly orientation of Jewish law and ceremonial observance and the external compulsion with which it was enforced, in contrast to the pure autonomy of true morality. Unlike Kant, Bendavid does not see the Jew's *Sklavensinn* as inherent in the material and external orientation of Jewish theocracy, but rather theorizes it as a psychological and moral response to the loss of sovereignty. In this, Bendavid's conception of Judaism as the "slave mentality of past centuries" indeed anticipates Nietzsche's memorable characterization in *Beyond Good and Evil* of a Jewish "slave uprising in morality" ("Sklaven-Aufstand in der Moral"; *Jenseits von Gut und Böse; Zur Genealogie der Moral*, 116–17).

33. Bendavid, ECJ, 14.

34. Ibid., 14–17. See also Nietzsche on *ressentiment*, *Jenseits von Gut und Böse; Zur Genealogie der Morale*, 270–74.

35. Bendavid, ECJ, 21–22.

36. For studies from the early twentieth century that posit strong affinities if not identity between Judaism and Kantian moral philosophy, see Hermann Cohen, "Innere Beziehungen der Kantischen Philosophie zum Judentum"; Julius Guttmann, "Kant und das Judentum"; and David Neumark, "Historical and Systematic Relations of Judaism to Kant." Heinz Mosche Graupe surveys the Jewish engagement with Kant as a "chapter in German and Jewish intellectual history of the 150 years between 1780 and 1930" ("Kant und das Judentum," 309). For an analysis of *fin de siècle* appropriations of Kant by Orthodox Jewish thinkers, see David Ellenson, "German Orthodoxy, Jewish Law, and the Uses of Kant."

37. Schulte, *Die jüdische Aufklärung*, 170.

38. Friedrich Niewöhner, "'Primat der Ethik' oder 'erkenntnistheoretische Begründung der Ethik'?"

39. See the note by Andreas Kennecke, the editor and translator of this essay, in Isaak Abraham Euchel, *Vom Nutzen der Aufklärung*, 32. For analyses of Euchel's essay, see Kennecke, *Isaac Euchel*, chapter 9; Schulte, *Die Jüdische Aufklärung*, 162.

40. Schulte, *Die Jüdische Aufklärung*, 167. Bendavid was the first person to deliver public lectures on Kant in Vienna (from 1794 to 1797), where he moved in 1791 and where he wrote

ECJ (see Bourel, "Eine Generation später," 371). Three volumes of Bendavid's (abridged) lectures on the three Kantian critiques, one volume devoted to each, appeared in 1795–96. Bendavid would remain philosophically a Kantian throughout his life. Heinrich Heine, who met Bendavid in the early 1820s, when they were both associated with the Verein für Cultur und Wissenschaft der Juden in Berlin, described Bendavid, somewhat derisively and with characteristic irony, as "ein eingefleischter Kantianer" (a Kantian to the bone; *Historisch-kritische Gesamtausgabe der Werke* [hereafter DHA], 14 (part 1): 268.

41. Niewöhner, "'Primat der Ethik,'" 126.

42. Ibid., 136. Niewöhner discusses the Orthodox Kantian Isaac Breuer, who found in Kant's first critique a philosophical basis for understanding Torah as noumenal. In his chapter on Breuer and other Orthodox Kantians, Ellenson does not include Niewöhner's study in a list of "six major articles on the relationship between Immanuel Kant and Judaism [that] have appeared in the twentieth century" ("German Orthodoxy," 15).

43. Solomon Maimon, *Versuch über die Transcendentalphilosophie* (*Essay on Transcendental Philosophy*). On Maimon's "Maimonidean interpretation" of Kant, see Abraham Socher, *The Radical Enlightenment of Solomon Maimon*, chapter 3.

44. Saul Ascher, *Eisenmenger der Zweite*, 36, 80.

45. Significantly, in remarks on Kant's ethics in his 1794 *Versuch über das Vergnügen* (236–48), Bendavid admits his confusion about the apparent absence of any norm underpinning moral authority in Kant, a problem he illuminates but does not resolve via a comparison with the political authority of the legislator (*Gesetzgeber*). Yet the problem of how to identify the boundary between political and moral authority—the crucial problem that animates Bendavid's ECJ—does not lead him to mount a serious challenge to Kant, and—in his 1796 *Vorlesungen über die Critik der practischen Vernunft*—he seems no longer perplexed and faithfully explicates Kant's theory.

46. Gillian Rose, *Judaism and Modernity*, 122.

47. See, for example, Michael Mack, *German Idealism and the Jew*, especially 34–41.

48. Both Bendavid and Fichte followed the events in France closely. As Fichte's title suggests, his *Beitrag zur Berichtigung der Urteile des Publikums über die französische Revolution* (Contribution toward the correction of the public's assessment of the French Revolution) is a prolonged, if indirect, apology for the French Revolution. And Bendavid, together with David Friedländer, quickly translated into German the petitions that had led to the French National Assembly's 1791 resolution to grant Jews full civil rights. See M. Graetz, "The Jewish Enlightenment," 1:344.

49. Immanuel Kant, *Immanuel Kant Werkausgabe* (hereafter IKW), 3:267–68.

50. For a more elaborate exploration of the problem of universalization and violence in Kantian morality, see Berel Lang, *Act and Idea in the Nazi Genocide*, chapter 7. Lang underscores how, because Kant's formal principle of universalization attains the status of substantive ethical content, his moral conception provides no guidance as to how to engage—morally—with those who fall outside any given delineation of the universal domain: the formal criteria for moral judgment "do not provide the substantive basis which judgment requires in order to make the decision to exclude or include certain groups. . . . [A]n intrinsic opening is left for arbitrariness. The consequences of this opening reach their full force when an individual or group is alleged to cross the boundary by which the universal domain has been defined: the principles originally articulated within the sphere of the universalist

ideal no longer apply. A radically different moral universe becomes possible, one that can nonetheless be held to be compatible with the first, since in each case its members as well as its principles have changed" (ibid., 182–83; see also 187). My claim that Bendavid's and Fichte's metaphors of Jewish decapitation are symptomatic of the violence—the effacement of alterity—inherent in Kant's equation of morality with the formal principle of universalization is more limited than Lang's argument for an "affiliation" (ibid., chapter 7)—something weaker than causal connection, but stronger than mere structural analogy—between Kant's conception of the subject and humanity, and the logic of the perpetrators of the Nazi genocide. For an interpretation of Jewish morality in terms of a triadic relation between the human being, God, and other human beings that cannot be contained within Kant's autonomous-heteronymous dichotomy, see Emil Fackenheim, *Encounters Between Judaism and Modern Philosophy*, chapter 2. Emanuel Levinas's *oeuvre* elaborates a sustained, emphatically post-Kantian ethics that takes radical obligation rather than autonomous reason as its starting point.

51. Immanuel Kant, *Critique of Pure Reason*, 93.

52. "Infinite" in the sense that it sustains faith in the Kantian postulates of God, providence, and the immortality of the soul. The subjective infinity of the "moral law within" indeed provides the counterpart to the "starry heavens above," in Kant's famous phrase (IKW, 7:300).

53. In certain formulations Kant rather confusingly uses *Wille* to designate both practical reason and its perversion by external forces (*gewisse Triebfeder*), which requires the correction of *Nötigung*. See, for example, Kant, IKW, 7:41.

54. Ibid., 7:143. See also Kant, *Practical Philosophy*, 165–66.

55. In his 1793 *Religion within the Boundaries of Mere Reason*, Kant opines that "strictly speaking, Judaism is not a religion at all but simply the union of a number of individuals who, since they belonged to a particular stock, established themselves into a community under purely political laws." In the ancient Jewish theocracy, "God's name was . . . honored . . . only as a secular regent with absolutely no rights over, or claims upon, conscience" (RRT, 154–55). Yirmiyahu Yovel notes Kant's refusal to acknowledge any moral (that is, any truly religious) content in Judaism (*Dark Riddle*, 7). See also Ascher's incisive critique of Kant's remarks on Judaism (*Eisenmenger der Zweite*, 55–79).

56. Nietzsche, *Jenseits von Gut und Böse; Zur Genealogie der Moral*, 300. Jonathan Strauss presents an elegant critique of "the full negative force of sublime freedom" in Kant's aesthetic theory (*Subjects of Terror*, 7–12, especially 9). Strauss also refers to Kant's moral philosophy (ibid., 300, note 33).

57. Bendavid, ECJ, 41 and 60.

58. Ibid., 66.

59. Ibid., 45. Navon points to this passage as evidence of a new *Staatsbewußtsein* among Jews and paraphrases it aptly: "For if the state, Ben David argues, in its goodness tries to absorb you, how dare you, Jews, stand in the way? If you refuse to take the necessary steps, you do so at your own peril" ("The Encounter of German Idealists," 231).

60. Bendavid, ECJ, 41.

61. Ibid., 41–42. Bendavid makes this point repeatedly. See also ibid., 61–63, and the cautionary tale (or mini-case study) of the tragic Jewish convert in ibid., 63–64, footnote.

62. Ibid., 54–55.

63. Of course, the relationship between the subjective interiority of the practicing Jew and the exteriority of the state undergoes an uncanny reversal insofar as the particular interiority of the Jew is by definition exterior to what I have described as the "absolute interiority" of the universal Kantian moral *Mensch,* which Bendavid sees as essentially coterminous with the citizen, or *Bürger*.

64. Bendavid, ECJ, 59–60.

65. Whereas the perceived essential identity between the moral and political led Fichte to attenuate the role and authority of the state sharply, Bendavid attempts to enlist the state's support for a general abolition of Jewish ritual (*allgemeine Abschaffung des Ceremonialgesetzes*). If politics, at bottom, is ethics by other means, then the state can be called on to enforce morality. Fichte would later theorize a regime of ethically oriented compulsion, the *Notstaat* (*Das System der Sittenlehre nach den Principien der Wissenschaftslehre*, 238–44).

66. Daniel Arasse, *The Guillotine and the Terror*, 36.

67. Paul Rose notes Fichte's politicization of Kant's construction of the Jew as the negation of free moral autonomy: "Relying on Kant's a priori ethical definition of the Jew as the negation of freedom and morality, Fichte in 1793 constructed a political definition of the Jew as a being inherently unsuitable for citizenship and civil rights" (RA, 121).

68. Following Fichte's own graphic of four concentric circles representing—from largest to smallest—the spheres of moral conscience, natural rights, contracts *tout court*, and civil contracts in particular (that is, states), one could represent a plurality of states as so many nonoverlapping circles (polka dots, if you will) within the sphere of possible contractual arrangements (Fichte, *Beitrag*, 97). In such a Fichtian schematic, states within states would look no different from the larger states within which they were geographically situated. This is worth emphasizing: if represented in Fichte's own schematic, states within states are indistinguishable from other states. The intersection of states—in this case, the location of a smaller state within a larger one—is purely spatial and, though raising a host of practical issues, is philosophically irrelevant within Fichte's framework. Different civil contracts, philosophically speaking, cannot overlap and are mutually exclusive. There is, then, an interesting tension between the rhetorical power of Fichte's antisemitic slogan and his analytic framework, which actually strips the formulation of any philosophical integrity. Moreover, the labeling of Jews as a state within a state seems curiously able to weather not only its own philosophical vacuity (from Fichte's point of view) but also its own utter inaptness as an image. As Fichte points out in his highly alarmist way, Jews formed a community across a great number of disparate states (ibid., 114). Thus, if they—as Jews—constitute a state, then they certainly do not constitute a state within any state, either philosophically or geographically.

69. As Wood writes, Kant's "Formula of Autonomy" in the *Grundwerk* "leads naturally to the thought of all rational beings as constituting a moral community under a common legislation, whose source is the rational volition they all share" ("General Introduction," xxix).

70. On the history of this slogan, see Jacob Katz, "A State within a State: The History of an Anti-Semitic Slogan." On Fichte, see ibid., 59–64.

71. Ascher critiqued this structural exclusion of Jews from humanity in Fichte and Kant directly (*Eisenmenger der Zweite*, 77–78). On Ascher as a critic of Kant and Fichte, see J. Hess, *Germans, Jews, and the Claims of Modernity*, 137–67.

72. Fichte, *Beitrag*, 115. Anthony La Vopa aptly characterizes Fichte's distinction between the Jewish and the human community: "The language virtually equates the human with the Christian. In the face of the Jewish presence, Fichte's Kantian reverence for 'humanity' provides a new sanction for his ethnocentrism. The Jews, he implies, have no one but themselves to blame for their pariah status; they have placed themselves beyond the pale of human love. That implication stands oddly juxtaposed to his acknowledgment that the Jews, though undeserving of 'civil rights,' cannot be deprived of 'human rights'" (*Fichte*, 146–47). La Vopa's reconstruction of the historical, biographical, and discursive contexts of Fichte's antisemitic remarks is rich and nuanced (ibid., 131–49).

73. Immanuel Kant, *Political Writings*, 54.

74. Bendavid, ECJ, 32–34, and 56.

75. Ibid., 65. Even Bendavid's sense of "natural religion" is thoroughly Kantian. Meyer criticizes the fact that, in ECJ, "Bendavid had simply rejected what Mendelssohn had posited as the differentiating element of Judaism—its ritual laws—while giving a Jewish coloring to what Mendelssohn had determined were its universal components" (*Response to Modernity*, 21). Although Meyer is certainly right to point out the disingenuousness of Bendavid's appropriation of Mendelssohn, this disingenuousness may be even more comprehensive than Meyer suggests. Given the implicit Kantian paradigm within which Bendavid is working, not even the tenets of "natural religion" to which Bendavid would reduce Judaism are consistent with the "universal components" of natural religion as Mendelssohn understood them. Even though Bendavid clearly wishes to smooth over this fact in order to bring Mendelssohn into his own camp, the tenets of his "natural religion" are in fact Kantian postulates. This is clear not only from the general Kantian cast of Bendavid's thought but also from the way in which he describes the members of his fourth category of Jews, the "proponents of genuine natural religion," who "feel the necessity of the duty to believe" (Bendavid, ECJ, 51). These select few enlightened Jews understand the tenets of natural religion not as objective and demonstrable truths (as did the philosophical Wolffian Mendelssohn) but rather as Kantian postulates, or as consequences of one's subjective moral reason in which it is one's subjective duty to believe. When admonishing Jews to adopt the pure religion of Moses, Bendavid not only recreates Moses, the biblical prophet, in the guise of Moses the Enlightenment philosopher, but he also uses Mendelssohn as a Jewish stand-in for Kant.

76. It is apt that Bourel ("Eine Generation später," 379) has pointed to the quasi-messianic tone of Bendavid's discourse. One suspects that this Ben David, this son of David, is (already in ECJ) playing ironically off of his name, as he would do even more unmistakably three decades later in the *Zeitschrift für die Wissenschaft des Judenthums* . In the first of his two contributions to that journal, Bendavid tries to contest the centrality in Judaism of the belief in a messiah, and he ends with the emphatic assertion that the only messiah the Jews require is political emancipation ("Über den Glauben der Juden an einen künftigen Messias (Nach Maimonides und den Kabbalisten)" [On the Jews' belief in a future messiah (according to Maimonides and the Cabbalists]).

77. Bendavid, EJC, 53, 62–63, and 63–64, footnote. Thus, as many scholars have pointed out (for example, Bourel, " Eine Generation später," 378; Feiner, *The Jewish Enlightenment*, 310; Yovel, *Dark Riddle*, 20), Kant is mistaken when he claims in *Streit der Fakultäten* (IKW, 11:320–21) that his own suggestion that Jews publicly accept Christianity, as a step toward purely rational religion, was first proposed by Bendavid. On the contrary, Bendavid's argu-

ment seems more consistent with Kant's opposition to encouraging insincere professions of faith. In 1790 an edict was passed in Prussia under the reactionary Friedrich Wilhelm II and his minister of education and religious affairs, Johann Christoph Wöllner, requiring that candidates for university degrees in theology make a formal profession of orthodox faith. For a concise account of the historical background to Kant's writings on religion in the 1790s, see Wood "General Introduction." In his *Schlußanmerkung* (concluding remark) to his 1791 "Über das Mißlingen aller philosophischen Versuche in der Theodicee" (On the failure of all philosophical attempts in theodicy) Kant writes that "blind and external *professions* (which can very easily be reconciled with an internal profession just as false) can, if they yield *means of gain*, bring about a certain falsehood in a community's very way of thinking" (RRT, 35). See also Kant, IKW, 11:122. Bendavid deploys a related argument. In his view, the Jewish convert's faith in Christianity would inevitably remain hypocritical and would therefore provide no solution to—and could even exacerbate—the essential moral deficit of the Jew. Although Bendavid and Kant disagree on the moral efficacy of conversion to Christianity, they nonetheless agree about the goal of overcoming revealed religion altogether, through purely rational morality. Kant sees conversion as a step in establishing "die reine moralische Religion" (pure moral religion), something that would entail what he disturbingly calls the "Euthanasie des Judentums" (euthanasia of Judaism) (Kant, IKW, 11:321). Bendavid would rather sever the heads of the Jewish hydra in a single moment.

78. See, for example, Bendavid, *Über die Religion der Ebräer vor Moses* and *Zur Berechnung und Geschichte des jüdischen Kalenders*. The later was a radical departure from the usual treatment of the subject and received an outraged rejoinder from Meyer ben Moses Kornrik (*Dabar Be'itto*).

79. Heinrich Heine, *Säkularausgabe* 20:103.

80. Ibid.

81. Ibid., 20:240.

82. Of course, Friedländer made a famous (or notorious) proposal to Propst Teller in 1799 that Jews convert en masse in order to gain access to the polity. However, Friedländer proposed conversion not so much to Christianity as to rational religion in Kant's sense. On the essentially Kantian conception of religion underlying Friedländer's proposal, see Nathan Rotenstreich, *Jews and German Philosophy*, 30–33.

83. Heine, *Säkularausgabe*, 20:240.

84. Heine, DHA, 14 (part 1): 268. Looking back, Heine also praises Bendavid's essay in the *Zeitschrift für die Wissenschaft des Judenthums* contesting the centrality of the Messiah in Judaism (see note 77), although at the time he had dismissed Bendavid's contributions to the journal as outdated. Heine's friend and colleague in the Verein, Moses Moser, wrote to his and Heine's mutual friend Immanuel Wohlwill on March 28, 1832, about Bendavid's death in tones that combined—as would Heine's homage a dozen years later—respect for Bendavid with irony over his unyielding devotion to Enlightenment rationality: "Bendavid died this morning from the effects of dropsy in his chest, for which he stubbornly refused any aid from doctors or nurses. He demonstrated to a visiting friend a priori that it was merely a rheumatic malady, and after he had been overcome by a fainting spell, he calculated, upon awaking, how long he must have lain on the floor unconscious. He reached the age of 70, perhaps the last Jew of the Kantian school" (correspondence between Moses Moser and Immanuel Wolf-Wohlwill, typescript, Leo Baeck Foundation, New York, 128). The Moser-

Wohlwill (to use the name Wolf later adopted) correspondence is the subject of the final section of chapter 3.

2. *Becoming Citizens of Hegel's State*

1. Hanns Reissner, *Eduard Gans*, 50. Five of the seven founding members had belonged to a seminar (*Wissenschaftszirkel*) that Moses Moser, Immanuel Wolf, and Eduard Gans started in fall 1816 to discuss Plato's *Dialogues* and other classics. Within a year, the *Wissenschaftszirkel* had grown to twenty-three members, nearly all Jews, who met regularly to present and discuss papers on a range of subjects, almost none of them Jewish. See Ismar Schorsch, *From Text to Context* (hereafter TC), 206. When the group was reconstituted as the Verein, its orientation was no longer merely academic but also sociopolitical, as its new name conveys.

2. Friedrich Rühs published *Über die Ansprüche der Juden an das deutsche Bürgerrecht* in 1816, which prompted Jacob Fries to publish his review essay *Über die Gefährdung des Wohlstandes und Characters der Deutschen durch die Juden*. Rühs followed up with a second pamphlet, *Die Rechte des Christenthums und des deutschen Volkes*. On writings by Rühs and Fries's about the Jews, see Jonathan Karp, *The Politics of Jewish Commerce*, 190–200. On Rühs's anti-Jewish writings as an impetus for Leopold Zunz's formulation of a new academic approach to Jewish history in "Etwas über die rabbinische Literatur" (first published in 1818), see Schorsch, TC, 219–21. In 1817 Rühs attacked the business practices of Eduard Gans's father, Abraham, during the recent war as an example of war profiteering and Jewish usury. In his refutation of Rühs's charges (reproduced in Ludwig Geiger, "Aus Eduard Gans' Frühzeit [1817]"), Gans rooted ethics in the rule of objective laws that apply equally to all members of society. In this way Gans opposed, in the words of John Toews, "the Christian-German revival in his immediate environment" and "continued to defend the conception of a secular state based on universal rational principles that he saw embodied in the ideals and activities of the Prussian reform movement" (*Hegelianism*, 110). On Rühs and Gans on Gans's father, see also Reissner, *Eduard Gans*, 42–44. Though Abraham Gans had been a well-to-do banker and Court Jew, when he died in 1813 he left the family in debt.

3. See Breckman, "Eduard Gans and the Crisis of Hegelianism," 556. On the Lex Gans, see Johann Braun, " Die 'Lex Gans'"; and Waszek, "Vorwort," 15–18.

4. Michael Meyer, *Response to Modernity*, 67.

5. Todd Presner writes: "World history has a direction and finality, which, at its telos, is also the last judgment of the world. For Hegel the end of history is the truth of the European, Christian state" (*Mobile Modernity*, 127). In his "General Introduction" to *G. W. F. Hegel: Political Writings*, Laurence Dickey reminds us that "one of the great shortcomings of Hegel scholarship is that it has been so convinced that *Sittlichkeit* is an anti-liberal conception that it has forgotten the challenge which the philosophy of *Sittlichkeit* posed to that reactionary alliance of throne and altar that dominated Prussian public policy during the Restoration" (ix).

6. Paul Franco notes that the view of Hegel as a progressive liberal "has long become the consensus view of Hegel's political philosophy, shared, as Allen Wood notes, by 'virtually every responsible scholar in the past generation'" (*Hegel's Philosophy of Freedom*, 364, note 10). Franco also lists the most salient scholarship on Hegel's liberalism (ibid.). The degree

to which Hegel obfuscated his political views in his preface to *Elements of the Philosophy of Right* (hereafter PR) out of fear of the consequences remains contested. Karl-Heinz Ilting argues at length that Hegel's political philosophy was more boldly liberal in his lectures on the philosophy of right than in the book ("Die 'Rechsphilosophie' von 1820 und Hegels Vorlesungen über Rechtsphilosophie" and "Hegel's Concept of the State and Marx's Early Critique"). Franco, in contrast, finds claims about this discrepancy "highly exaggerated" (*Hegel's Philosophy of Freedom*, 123). Toews agrees with Ilting that Hegel's "fear of persecution and desire for peace . . . led him to modify and mystify some of his positions in the 1820s," in particular in his infamously ambiguous *Doppelsatz* in the preface to PR—"what is rational is actual; what is actual is rational"—which was immediately widely criticized "as a philosophical justification of the recently instituted political repression" (Toews, *Hegelianism*, 96). Gans would vigorously argue that this interpretation was misguided (Preface), yet in Toews's view "Hegel himself had contributed to this misunderstanding to a not inconsiderable degree by failing to provide adequate or obvious guidelines for the interpretation of some of his more cryptic and ambiguous phrases and by attacking some of the recent victims of repression with excessive ardor" (*Hegelianism*, 96). It is important to note, however, that the "victims" whom Hegel attacked in the preface to PR included Fries, an outspoken antisemite. This sort of accommodation to the state probably looked very different to the *Vereinler* than to non-Jewish liberals and academics. See also note 38 in this chapter.

7. For selections of Krochmal's posthumously published *Guide of the Perplexed of the Time* with introductory remarks, see Krochmal, "A Philosophy of Jewish History." See also Krokhmal [Krochmal], "Selections from *Guide to the Perplexed of our Time*." On Krochmal's relation to Hegel and (possibly) Giambattista Vico, see Nathan Rotenstreich, *Jews and German Philosophy*, 143–51; *Jewish Philosophy in Modern Times*, 136–48; and *Tradition and Reality*, 37–48.

8. Noah H. Rosenbloom, "The 'Nineteen Letters of Ben Uziel'—A Hegelian Exposition."

9. For selections from Samuel Hirsch's magnum opus, *Das System der religiösen Anschauungen der Juden* (1842), in English, see Samuel Hirsch, "Selections from *The System of the Religious Perceptions of Jews and its Relationship to Paganism, Christianity and to Absolute Philosophy*." On Hirsch and his relationship to Hegel, see, for example, Emil Fackenheim,"Samuel Hirsch and Hegel"; Gershon Greenberg, "Samuel Hirsch: Jewish Hegelian" and "Religion and History According to Samuel Hirsch"; and Rotenstreich, *Jewish Philosophy in Modern Times*, 120–36. For selections from Formstecher's magnum opus, *Die Religion des Geistes* (1841), in English, see Formstecher, "Selections from *Religion of the Mind/Spirit*." On Formstecher and Hirsch, see also Meyer, *Response to Modernity*, 70–74, and "Reform Jewish Thinkers in Their German Intellectual Context."

10. Toews, *Hegelianism*, 119.

11. See Georg Wilhelm Friedrich Hegel, *Frühe Schriften*, vol. 1 of *Werke in 20 Bänden mit Registerband* (hereafter TWA) and *Early Theological Writings*. In his 1795 "The Positivity of the Christian Religion," Hegel, philosophically still essentially a Kantian, attacked Judaism along with Christianity as examples of positive religions—that is, religions based on coercion and heteronymous law rather than the exercise of free practical rationality. Hegel's ugliest assessment of Judaism comes in the section "The Spirit of Judaism" in "The Spirit of Christianity and its Fate" (1798–99). By then Hegel had broken with Kantian moral philosophy and now contrasted Christianity, as the religion of love and community, with Judaism,

as the religion of egoistic self-separation from the human community—a character portrait Hegel sketches out largely through an interpretation of Abraham.

12. Peter Hodgson, for example, sees Hegel moving toward a far more positive view of Judaism in his lectures on the philosophy of religion in 1824 and, even more so, 1827 ("The Metamorphosis of Judaism in Hegel's Philosophy of Religion"). Steven Smith likewise contends that "Hegel's writings on the Jewish Question underwent a considerable change—one could almost say a paradigm shift" (*Spinoza, Liberalism, and the Question of Jewish Identity*, 186) Smith, however, does not privilege the *Philosophy of Religion* among Hegel's later writings; instead, he argues that Hegel's "later writings, especially the *Philosophy of History* and the *Philosophy of Right*, are attempts to remove from Judaism the stigma of a purely 'statutory' or 'positive' religion and to situate it within a larger dialectic of history and culture" (ibid.). Yirmiyahu Yovel finds that Hodgson "exaggerates [the] pro-Jewish content" of Hegel's 1827 *Philosophy of Religion* lectures (*Dark Riddle*, 208, note 1). Unlike Hodgson, who sees a significant change in Hegel's interpretation of Judaism between the 1821 manuscript and the 1824 lectures, Yovel groups the 1821 and 1824 lectures together as giving "a harsher, but also a richer and more complete, account of Judaism" than the 1827 lectures (ibid., 70). Other fundamental contributions to the literature on Hegel's interpretation of Judaism and/or the Jews include Nathan Rotenstreich, "Hegel's Image of Judaism"; *The Recurring Pattern*, chapter 3; and *Jews and German Philosophy*, part 2. Shlomo Avineri highlights the distinction between Hegel's interpretation of Jewish theology and his views on Jewish emancipation in "A Note on Hegel's Views on Jewish Emancipation." See also Lars Fischer's reconstruction of Hegel's support of Jewish emancipation in Heidelberg in 1817–18 as a deliberate intervention on behalf of the universalistic, antinationionalistic minority within the Burschenschaft movement ("Hegel in Support of Jewish Emancipation"). See also Otto Pöggeler, "L'interprétation hégelienne du Judaïsme." On the problem that Judaism poses for Hegelian mediation, see Emil Fackenheim, "Hegel and Judaism" and *Encounters between Judaism and Modern Philosophy*, chapter 3.

13. Heinrich Graetz helped establish the hostile reading of Hegel's influence on the *Vereinler*. He describes Hegel as a "church and court philosopher" who led the naive *Vereinler* astray with abstruse sophistry (*Vom Beginn der Mendelssohn'schen Zeit [1750] bis in die neueste Zeit [1848]*, 439–41). Norbert Waszek observes that many scholars who touch on the Verein's Hegelianism are not Hegel scholars, get their (generally very negative) image of Hegel secondhand, and neglect to analyze what the *Vereinler* do with the Hegelian theory they deploy ("'Wissenschaft und Liebe zu den Seinen,'" 92–93). In a seminal 1935 article on the Verein, Sinai (Siegfried) Ucko downplays Hegel's influence on the Verein ("Geistesgeschichtliche Grundlagen der Wissenschaft des Judentums," 321).

14. As Michael Graetz argues, Zunz and Jost provide the only possible argument for continuity between the Verein and Jewish scholars of the 1840s and 1850s ("Renaissance des Judentums im 19. Jahrhundert," 212). Nils Roemer points out that Jost and Zunz "functioned as mentors to younger university-trained scholars like Abraham Geiger, Zacharias Frankel, Michael Sachs, and Moritz Steinschneider during the 1830s and 1840s, mainly through elaborate correspondences" (*Jewish Scholarship and Culture in Nineteenth-Century Germany*, 34). Nahum Glatzer's analysis of the first generation of modern Jewish scholars in "The Beginnings of Modern Jewish Studies" also understandably focuses on Zunz.

15. A Dr. G. Adersbach notes that "Jost ist ausgetreten" ("Secretarialbericht über die

Sitzungen von Mai und Juny [*sic*], 1820," 3, ARC 4° 792/B11, Archive of the "Association for the Culture and Science of the Jews," Zunz Archive, National Library of Israel, Jerusalem (henceforth Zunz Archive). (Most items in the Zunz Archive are available online at http://www.jewish-archives.org/.) Reissner indicates that Jost quit on May 14, 1820. Roemer mistakenly states that Jost left the Verein in 1822 (*Jewish Scholarship*, 32).

16. Rachel Livné-Freudenthal draws on her extensive knowledge of the Verein documents in the Zunz Archive to interpret the Verein's political philosophy and *Weltanschauung* in several highly illuminating essays, including "Der 'Verein für Cultur und Wissenschaft der Juden,'" "Kultur als Weltanschauung," and "From a Nation Dwelling Alone to a Nation Among the Nations." She acknowledges the origin of the *Vereinler*'s conception of the state and society in Hegel's PR, yet she reads the *Vereinler*—to my mind, unconvincingly—as opposing Hegel's vision of the state from within a liberal conception of an oppositional public sphere (see, for example, "Der 'Verein für Cultur und Wissenschaft der Juden,'" 114). I see this interpretation as subtended by the assumption that Hegel was an apologist for the Prussian state, which leads Livné-Freudenthal to see in the *Vereinler*'s criticism of the Prussian state distance from or opposition to Hegel. In contrast, I read the *Vereinler* as using Hegel as the yardstick by which they measure and critique the Prussian state. The arguably illiberal elements of Hegel's theory of the state—in particular, his intellectual elitism and consequent wish to contain, rather than cultivate, the open expression of subjective opinion—are in fact mirrored, not contested, in the Verein's orientation. In "From 'A Nation Dwelling Alone' to 'A Nation among the Nations,'" Livné-Freudenthal, as I read her, aligns the *Vereinler*'s vision of the state more decisively with Hegel's, against that of their common adversaries, Friedrich Carl von Savigny and the historical school.

17. Yerushalmi writes: "Modern Jewish historiography . . . originated not as scholarly curiosity, but as ideology, one of a gamut of responses to the crisis of Jewish emancipation and the struggle to attain it" (*Zakhor*, 85). See also, for example, Max Wiener, "The Ideology of the Founders of Jewish Scientific Research."

18. Other scholars who look to the Verein primarily as an origin of modern Jewish scholarship include Michael Graetz ("Renaissance des Judentums im 19. Jahrhundert," 213), who sketches a trajectory from the Verein to Fränkel's Jewish Theological Seminary (founded in Breslau in 1854) to the Hochschule für die Wissenschafte des Judentums (Berlin, 1872) to the Akademie für die Wissenschaft des Judentums (Berlin, 1919) to the Freie Jüdische Lehrhaus (Frankfurt, 1920) and to the Jewish studies department that was at the core of the Hebrew University when it was founded in 1925. David Myers likewise begins his narrative of the intellectual and institutional antecedents of the Jerusalem school historians with a brief discussion of the Verein (*Re-Inventing the Jewish Past*, 16–19). As an example of the extent to which some contemporary Jewish studies scholars see their scholarly pursuits as part of the legacy of the epochal program articulated in Wolf's programmatic *Zeitschrift* essay and exemplified in the *Zeitschrift* itself, see Christoph Schulte, "Über den Begriff einer Wissenschaft des Judentums," 279 and 284.

19. Yerushalmi, *Zakhor*, 83.

20. Ibid., 81.

21. Schorsch, TC, 6. In *Jewish Scholarship*, Roemer examines the popular pedagogical uses of *Wissenschaft des Judentums* and illuminates a history of trying to mediate Jewish memory through Jewish historical consciousness. In "Two Persistent Tensions within *Wis-*

senschaft des Judentums," Meyer examines the persistence of religion in *Wissenschaft des Judentums*, especially in the hands of its nineteenth-century practitioners.

22. Schorsch, TC, 219.

23. Zunz's major works include *Die gottesdienstlichen Vorträge der Juden* (1832), *Die synagogale Poesie des Mittelalters* (1855), *Die Ritus des synagogalen Gottesdienstes, geschichtlich entwickelt* (1859), and *Literaturgeschichte der synagogalen Poesie* (1865).

24. Zunz's most influential academic inspirations were the philologist and antiquarian Friedrich August Wolf and Wolf's student August Wilhelm Böck. On the influence of Wolf and Böck on Zunz's conception of *Wissenschaft*, see Giuseppe Veltri, "Altertumswissenschaft und Wissenschaft des Judentums: Leopold Zunz und seine Lehrer F. A. Wolf und A. Böckh"; Leon Wieseltier, "*Etwas über die jüdische Historik*," 137–39 and 148; Schorsch, TC, 222–23, and Michael Meyer, *The Origins of the Modern Jew*, 159–60.

25. Adolf Strodtmann indicates that Zunz's remarks are from a letter to Wohlwill of summer 1824 (*H. Heine's Leben und Werke*, 274).

26. Quoted in ibid., 274–75.

27. A certain reading of Zunz's remarks has contributed powerfully to the "Zunzification" of assessments of the Verein's importance. After quoting this letter (from Strodtmann) Heinrich Graetz comments: "Und wenn der Culturverein, der so hochstrebend begann und so kläglich endete, auch nur dieses Eine erwirkt hätte, die Liebe zur Wissenschaft des Judenthums zu erwecken, so ist sein Träumen und Treiben doch nicht vergeblich gewesen" (*Vom Beginn der Mendelssohn'schen Zeit (1750) bis in die neueste Zeit (1848)*, 447). The editorial notes in *The Jew in the Modern World* to Gans's presidential address to the Verein of April 1822 echo Graetz's sentiment, even as they too, albeit silently, evoke Zunz's letter to Wohlwill: "In addition to the loss of their president and driving spirit [Gans (my addition)], the demise of the society can be attributed to the lack of support from the Jewish community. Yet, in the last analysis, the society was not a total debacle, for emerging from its ruins was the Science of Judaism, thanks largely to the Promethean efforts of its vice president and the editor of its journal, Leopold Zunz" (221).

28. Heinrich Heine, *Historisch-kritische Gesamtausgabe der Werke* [hereafter DHA], 14 (part 1: 270). On Heine's appreciation of the Verein in his eulogy, see Norbert Waszek, "Hegel, Mendelssohn, Spinoza," 187–93.

29. Heine, DHA, 14 (part 1): 270. Scholars of early *Wissenschaft des Judentums* have variously assessed the hopes for sociopolitical transformation that its first practitioners and ideologues invested in it. Referring to the biography of Rashi that Zunz published in the Verein's *Zeitschrift* in 1823, Meyer points subtly to how the new standard of academic rigor always contained an implicit apologetic component: "the apologetic element—far from disappearing—has simply moved from the results to the method" (*The Origins of the Modern Jew*, 178). In Glatzer's description of this apologetic dimension, "scholarship was expected to serve as the most honest method of appeal, as the best possible proof of the Jews' right to be counted" ("The Beginnings of Modern Jewish Studies," 39). In Rotenstreich's view, the early proponents of *Wissenschaft des Judentums* held that "a new basis for civilization was being created by science, and the Jew who participated in this grand and noble undertaking was no less deserving than anyone else. The Science of Judaism . . . would reveal the Jews in their reality and determine their ability to live on the same level as other citizens" (*Tradition and Reality*, 35). David Myers focuses on the tension between scientific

objectivity and its paradoxical instrumentalization in "The Ideology of Wissenschaft des Judentums."

30. Eduard Gans, "Verein für Cultur und Wissenschaft der Juden. Rechenschaftsbericht," Berlin, March 11, 1820, 1, ARC 4792/B11–32, Zunz Archive.

31. Ibid.

32. Reissner, *Eduard Gans*, 59.

33. Hegel also lectured on the history of philosophy in winter 1823–24 and on the philosophy of religion in summer 1824, but by this time the Verein was already in decline.

34. Georg Wilhelm Friedrich Hegel, foreword. The foreword was dated Easter 1822, which was April 7.

35. Hegel's other two previously published books, the *Phenomenology of Spirit* (1807) and *The Science of Logic* (1812–16), were also available to the *Vereinler*.

36. Laurence Dickey, "General Introduction," xxiv.

37. Terry Pinkard, *Hegel*, 430–31. On Hegel's aspirations for his move to Berlin and his negotiation of the changing political climate in his first years there, see ibid., 418–68.

38. See note 2, in this chapter. Hegel polemicized against Fries in the preface to PR and at two points in § 270. He refers to Fries both explicitly, when arguing that the Christian religion can assume a polemical stance vis-à-vis the state, and implicitly, in the footnote advocating Jewish civil rights (see § 270, note 5 by the editor, Allen Wood). As Fischer points out, Hegel had spoken out in Heidelberg for Jewish emancipation shortly after Fries had thrown his weight behind *Burschenschaft* nationalism at the Wartburg festival in October 1817 ("Hegel in Support of Jewish Emancipation," 142). The circumstances under which Hegel attacked Fries in PR contributed significantly to the perception of the book as an apologetic for the authoritarian Restoration Prussian state. Karl Sand, August von Kotzebue's assassin, was a student of Fries. Fries was unfairly condemned for conspiracy with Sand and deprived of his professorship. Even though Hegel's feud with Fries predated the Kotzebue assassination, his sharp attack was widely seen as an endorsement of the purge of an academic colleague. The *Vereinler*, however, would have seen Fries as a virulent antisemite, not a liberal brother in arms, and they presumably approved of Hegel's position. Waszek argues ("'Wissenschaft und Liebe zu den Seinen,'" 89) that Hegel's attack on Fries in PR contributed to the book's impact on Gans, which—in the introduction to *Das Erbrecht in Weltgeschichtlicher Entwicklung*, dated March 23, 1823—he memorably described as follows: "*Hegel* und seinen Schriften habe ich, der ich im Zwiespalt, zwischen meinem abstracten Denken und meiner Wissenschaft begriffen war, die vollere Versöhnung mit der letzteren zu danken; namentlich ist mir seit dem Erscheinen der Rechtsphilosophie zuerst ein heller Tag geworden, wo ich mir nur eines dunklen Herumtappens bewußt war" (*Eduard Gans (1797–1839)*, 101).

39. Klaus Briegleb writes that Moser "very obviously had heard" Hegel's address ("'Jeder Reiche ist ein Judas Ischariot!,'" 126, note 25).

40. Dickey, "General Introduction," xxiii.

41. That is, worthier than that of the Enlightenment and Kantian philosophy, which had considered the human mind incapable of knowing the eternal and divine.

42. Georg Wilhelm Friedrich Hegel, *Political Writings*, 185. For the German original, see Hegel, *Berliner Schriften*, 47–48.

43. These figures are from Schorsch, TC, 206–7. Roemer (citing Reissner, *Eduard Gans*, 174–85) says the Verein had 81 members (*Jewish Scholarship*, 32).

44. See Norbert Waszek, "Vorwort," 26; and Waszek "Hegel, Mendelssohn, Spinoza," 195.

45. On the depth of the Verein's Hegelianism, see Waszek, "Vorwort," 11–26; "Hegel, Mendelssohn, Spinoza," 201; and "'Wissenschaft und Liebe zu den Seinen,'" 89–92.

46. Livné-Freudenthal quotes the protocol of the meeting of 13 June 1820: "Everyone was adamant (*von der Idee durchdrungen*) that without the approval of the state they absolutely did not wish, nor had ever wished, to found a Verein. . . . Their meetings currently are merely the elaboration of their respective ideas about a future Verein, to be founded with state approval" (quoted. in "Der 'Verein für Cultur und Wissenschaft der Juden,'" 111).

47. See Schorsch, TC, 207. Hostile to projects of religious reform (they would ban the Beer Temple in September 1823), yet apparently also unable to fathom a connection between Jews and a notion of secular *Cultur*, the Prussian authorities misread *Cultur* (in the name Verein für Cultur und Wissenschaft der Juden) as *Cultus*. Gans promptly clarified the point, but the Verein was still denied permission to become incorporated (ibid.).

48. Quoted in Reissner, *Eduard Gans*, 65.

49. On the process of formulating and submitting the Verien's formal statutes for government approval, see ibid.

50. My account of Jewish relations to the state in this section is greatly indebted to Cohen's essay.

51. The fact that Gans's father had been a Court Jew may have contributed to Gans's readiness to imagine himself in a position of being able to negotiate with the state on behalf of Jews.

52. On Joseph II's Edicts of Toleration, see chapter 1, note 7.

53. On Wessely's tract and the reaction it provoked, see Shmuel Feiner, *The Jewish Enlightenment*, 87–104.

54. See ibid., 271–83.

55. As Richard Cohen notes, "maskilim seldom envisaged political allies within the broader Gentile or Jewish society. Whether it was for assistance in publishing Enlightenment books . . . , setting up a new educational structure . . . or transforming the economic structure of the Jews . . . , maskilim turned to the rulers, believing that only an imposed solution could bring about the desired results" ("Jews and the State: The Historical Context," 12).

56. Sorkin, *The Berlin Haskalah*, 103.

57. Ibid., 95 and 104.

58. See Thomas Nipperdey, "Verein als soziale Struktur im späten 18. und frühen 19. Jahrhundert," 10. On Jewish associational life in this period, see Sorkin, *The Transformation of German Jewry*, chapter 5.

59. Nipperdey, "Verein als soziale Struktur," 3–4 and 27.

60. Ibid., 34. Nipperdey illuminates how the state-sanctioned *Vereine* were the place where civil society and state bureaucracy, each sharing an interest in the dissolution of corporatist feudal society, met in a spirit of cooperation.

61. As Warren Breckman notes, Hegel and Hegelianism were anathema to the Restoration Prussian political theology of thinkers like the later Friedrich Schelling and Friedrich Julius Stahl, who each subordinate the autonomy of reason to the sovereign will of a finally unknowable personalist God. On Schelling's positive philosophy as conceptually and politically opposed to Hegel's dialectical rationalism, see Breckman, *Marx, the Young Hegelians,*

and the Origins of Radical Social Theory: Dethroning the Self (hereafter DS), 54–62; on Stahl's anti-Hegelian political theology, see ibid., 80–89.

62. Schorsch, TC, 206.

63. On Hegel's admiration for Prussian bureaucrats, see James Sheehan, *German History*, 431–32. One anonymous author's positive response, published in the Verein's *Zeitschrift*, to the news of Alexander I's January 1822 decision to suspend the autonomous Jewish communities (*kahals*) and to put Russian *Beamten* in the place of Jewish community leaders (*Gemeindevorstände*) is ostensibly colored by Hegel's image of civil servants ("Aus dem Archiv für die Correspondenz," 533). Heinrich Graetz attributes this text to Gans (*Vom Beginn der Mendelssohn'schen Zeit [1750] bis in die neueste Zeit [1848]*, 439).

64. As Richard Hunt remarks, "Hegel was much impressed with the achievements of the Stein-Hardenberg civil service and regarded these highly educated and dedicated men as fitting guardians of the common weal. They had renounced the egoism of civil society to devote themselves unselfishly to the service of the whole" (55).

65. "Between an individual and his office there is no immediate natural link. Hence individuals are not appointed to office on account of their birth or native personal gifts. The *objective* factor in their appointment is knowledge and proof of ability. Such proof guarantees that the state will get what it requires; and since it is the sole condition of appointment, it also guarantees to every citizen the chance of joining the class of civil servants" (Hegel, PR § 291).

66. Livné-Freudenthal aptly characterizes the *Vereinler*'s early posture vis-à-vis the Jewish community and the state: "The founders of the Verein no longer conceived of themselves as representatives of the Jews vis-à-vis the state but understood themselves instead as representatives of the state vis-à-vis the Jews" ("Der 'Verein für Cultur und Wissenschaft der Juden,'" 110.

67. At a meeting on March 11, 1820, Gans was charged with drafting the Verein's application for recognition by the state (*staatliche Genehmigung*). The Verein's first president, Josef Hillmar, withdrew from the organization the same day; Jost quit two months later, on May 14, 1820. See Reissner, *Eduard Gans*, 60; and Waszek, "'Wissenschaft und Liebe zu den Seinen,'" 77.

68. Quoted in Nahum Glatzer, *Leopold and Adelheid Zunz*, 34. Jost was more evenhanded in his assessment of the Verein in *Culturgeschichte zur neueren Geschichte der Israeliten von 1815 bis 1845*, 29–34.

69. Quoted in Glatzer, *Leopold and Adelheid Zunz*, 34.

70. Moser reports in a letter to Wohlwill (who had changed his name from Wolf by this point) of September 5, 1823, that Jost's anger at the *Vereinler* only increased after Gans publicly insulted him: "His [Jost's] rage against all Verein members seems to be particularly great since Gans, in the garden of the *Gesellschaft der Freunde* [Society of Friends] called his nonsensical and vehement carping (*Raisonnierrereien*) against us 'idiocies' (*Eseleien*). That really blemished his reputation in this society" (correspondence between Moses Moser and Immanuel Wolf-Wohlwill, typescript, Leo Baeck Foundation, New York, 41–42; also in Albert Friedlander, "The Wohlwill-Moser Correspondence," 294).

71. Reissner understands Moser's comment this way: "Moser probably meant—or implied—that Jews must complete on their own what Napoleon had initiated with his convocation of a Grand Sanhedrin in 1807, i.e. to raise the community to the level of civilization then generally prevailing and desired in Europe" ("Rebellious Dilemma," 180; see also 185).

Ucko interprets Moser's remark as expressing a more modest ambition: "The expression merely sounds overbold (*tollkühn*). Little more was meant by it than that the work of educating the Jews (*der Juden*) had to be organized by Jews (*von jüdischer Seite*); but with regard to the . . . conceptualization of the secularized work on the Jews (*Arbeit am Judentum*) that the perceived substantiality [of the Jews] demanded, this expression is very significant" ("Geistesgeschichtliche Grundlagen," 327).

72. Verein für Cultur und Wissenschaft der Juden, *Entwurf von Statuten des Vereins für Cultur und Wissenschaft der Juden*, 3.

73. Ibid., 4.

74. Joseph McCarney, *Hegel on History*, 157. Merold Westphal likewise notes the distinction in Hegel's use of "state" between a "'strictly political state'"—that is, "the state as a people's system of government"—and the state "as the whole of their life together, including in the broadest sense, their culture" ("Hegel's Radical Idealism," 89).

75. Verein für Cultur und Wissenschaft der Juden, *Entwurf von Statuten*, 5.

76. Toews, *Hegelianism*, 112.

77. On Henning's and Förster's different paths toward accommodation of the Restoration Prussian state, see ibid., 118–22.

78. "For Förster, Henning, and Schulze, the political task of creating a vital community of reborn Germans had been transformed into a pedagogical task of teaching their contemporaries to recognize the reality of that community in the existing state" (ibid., 120).

79. Ibid., 114.

80. Carové assessed the state in yet another way. He viewed not only the Prussian state but the state in general as incapable of achieving the ultimate manifestation of reason, and therefore as a form destined to be transcended in the universal ethical community of a fraternal "church," a "Kingdom of God on this Earth" (ibid., 139). On Carové's vision, see ibid., 134–140.

81. Quoted in ibid., 116.

82. Ibid., 117.

83. Ibid., 111.

84. Although Prussia was Hegel's model of "the modern state of actualized Reason," Toews writes, "the Prussia comprehended in Hegel's political philosophy, however, was not the Prussia of the reactionary repressions of 1819–20 but a 'progressive' state—the Prussia of Stein, Hardenberg, and Humboldt, the Prussia of the Reform Era. . . . [However,] the Prussia of the 1820s was no longer the Prussia of 1807–19, . . . the Prussia Hegel comprehended could not be simply identified with the Prussia in which Hegel lived, for the latter was inwardly divided between progressive principle and a somewhat less than progressive practice" (ibid., 96–97).

85. Hegel remarks in the preface to the 1817 *Encyclopedia*: "The title should suggest partly the scope of the whole, and partly the intent to leave the details for oral delivery" (*Encyclopedia of the Philosophical Sciences in Outline*, 46; the German original is in *Enzyklopädie der philosophischen Wissenschaften im Grundrisses*, 5). Duncan Forbes's remarks on Hegel's orality and what I am calling Hegel's performativity are illuminating: "It is wrong . . . to think of the dialectic as functioning as a process of logical demonstration or deduction in a closed system. . . . It was the result of Hegel's desire 'to think life'; it is a way of thinking concretely and seeing things whole, whose conclusions cannot be proved or disproved, but

which can be seen to be more or less true to life; its purpose is to provide insight. The only way to appreciate it or understand what it is is to watch it at work" (introduction, xiii). Forbes also observed: "Although Hegel insisted that 'Science' was wholly public and a discipline of thinking . . . , nevertheless his philosophy is best approached in the spirit of Plato's, as something that is in danger of being destroyed or distorted if it is written down. Hegel in fact was extremely reluctant to publish; he only published two books, because the *Encyclopaedia* and the *Philosophy of Right* are compendia for courses of lectures" (ibid., xiv). Similarly, Hodgson makes the point that oral exposition was perfectly suited to Hegel's always evolving lectures on the philosophy of religion, which he reworked dramatically each time he gave them (in 1821, 1824, 1827, and 1831): "[Hegel] is not offering empirical descriptions but imaginative constructions. For this purpose the medium of oral lectures was ideally suited, and it is notable that Hegel was reluctant to constrain the fluidity of speech through publication" ("Hegel's Philosophy of Religion," 232).

86. Ernst Behler, "Note on the Texts," xxv.

87. Hegel argues in the introduction to *The Science of Logic* (1831): "To establish or explain the Notion of science ratiocinatively can at most achieve this, that a general idea of the Notion is presented to our thinking and a historical knowledge of it is produced; but a definition of science—or more precisely of logic—has its proof solely in the already mentioned necessity of its emergence in consciousness" (*Hegel's Science of Logic*, 48–49).

88. Frederick Beiser, introduction, xvii.

89. Ibid., xiii.

90. Ibid., xv.

91. Ibid., xvii. Hegel assumed that a historicist interpretation of reason at its various historical stages would finally be (become) systematic: "Both ideals [systematic unity and internal understanding] are satisfied by simply describing the inner logic or self-organization of its subject matter; what Hegel calls its 'concept' or 'notion' (*der Begriff*)" (ibid., xvi).

92. The first lectures on the philosophy of world history paradigmatically exemplify Hegel's tendency to perform the truth of his insight: "Aber die philosophische Weltgeschichte ist mehr ein Aufweisen als ein Beweisen des Gesagten. Der eigentliche *Beweis liegt in der Erkenntnis der Vernunft selbst*. . . . Die Weltgeschichte selbst ist nur eine Weise der Erscheinung dieser einen Vernunft, eine der besonderen Gestalten, in denen die Vernunft sich offenbart" (*Vorlesungen über die Philosophie der Weltgeschichte, Berlin 1822/1823*, edited by Ilting, Brehmer, and Seelmann, 21). The proof of reason (*Vernunft*) in history comes in the form of reason's discovery of itself in history—which happens in Hegel.

93. I quote the text of Hegel's *Vorlesungen über die Geschichte der Philosophie* in TWA, the widely used Suhrkamp edition edited by Eva Moldenhauer and Karl Markus Michel, which is based on the text assembled by Karl Ludwig Michelet for the first, *Freundeskreis* edition of Hegel's works (the history of philosophy lectures appeared in 1833–36 as volumes 13–15). Because he worked from sources that have since been lost—including Hegel's manuscript of his Jena lectures on the history of philosophy in winter 1805–6, which Hegel continued to draw on in his Berlin lectures—Michelet's text is irreplaceable. However, his text is a composite of various sources by Hegel, as well as student transcripts and notes from various years. As yet, no critical edition exists that reconstructs the particular versions of the lectures on the history of philosophy as Hegel presented them. The only specific course of these lectures to have been published is Pierre Garniron's and Walter Jaeschke's

edition of the winter 1825–26 lectures. It is thus impossible to know from published sources whether any given passage from Michelet's composite text was delivered in the same form (or at all) during the years when the *Vereinler* would have heard Hegel lecture on the topic (1819 or 1820–21). On the history of student transcripts from Hegel's lectures on the history of philosophy, see Pierre Garniron and Friedrich Hogemann, "Hegels Vorlesungen zur Geschichte der Philosophie." There are two extant sources for the 1819 lectures, both of which derive from a common source, and one for the 1820–21 lectures (ibid., 115, 117–18). However, there was great thematic continuity over the more than twenty-five-years that Hegel lectured on the history of philosophy (ibid., 111), so we can be fairly certain that auditors in 1819 and 1820–21 would have heard some iteration of the passages I quote here.

94. Hegel, TWA, 20:455. In translating passages from the TWA edition of Hegel's *Vorlesungen über die Geschichte der Philosophie*, I have borrowed from the available English translation by E. S. Haldane and Frances H. Simson (Hegel, *Lectures on the History of Philosophy*). Their translation, however, is of Michelet's shortened second (1840) edition and thus differs from the text of the TWA edition, which is based on the first (see the previous note).

95. Hegel, TWA, 20:456.

96. Ibid.

97. In the 1820 introduction to the history of philosophy lectures, which some of the *Vereinler* surely heard, Hegel states that "the study of the history of philosophy is the study of philosophy itself" (ibid., 20:479).

98. In a similar vein, Hegel characterizes philosophy as "its own time comprehended in thoughts" (PR, "Preface," 21). See also PR, "Vorrede," 26."

99. Hegel, TWA, 20:460.

100. Ibid., 20:461.

101. Hegel expresses this sentiment repeatedly. For example, he writes: "It is philosophical insight which recognizes that Church and state are not opposed to each other as far as their content is concerned, which is truth and rationality, but merely differ in form" (PR § 299).

102. Hegel lectured on the philosophy of right based on the published "Grundriß" in winter 1821–22, 1822–23, and 1824–25. His seventh set of lectures on the philosophy of right, begun in 1831, was cut short by his death. He first published on political philosophy in the "Objective Spirit" section of his 1817 *Encyclopedia of the Philosophical Sciences*. He delivered his Heidelberg and first two Berlin lectures on the topic under the title "Naturrecht und Staatswissenschaft." See Karl-Heinz Ilting's six-volume edition of *Vorlesungen über Rechtsphilosophie* for most of the extant notes and transcripts of Hegel's philosophy of right lectures 1818–31. For transcripts discovered since the publication of Ilting's edition, see Dieter Henrich's edition of *Philosophie des Rechts: Die Vorlesung von 1819/20 in einer Nachschrift*; Emil Angehrn, Martin Bondeli, and Hoo Nam Seelmann's edition of *Philosophie des Rechts, mitgeschrieben von Johann Rudolf Ringier (1819/1820)*; and Hansgeorg Hoppe's edition of *Die Philosophie des Rechts: Vorlesung von 1821/22*.

103. Moses Moser, "Rede vor der Gründungsversammlung des Vereins für Cultur und Wissenschaft der Juden," November 7, 1819, ARC 4 792/B10–2, Zunz Archive. For a substantial excerpt from this memo by Moser, see Ucko, "Geistesgeschichtliche Grundlagen," 328–29 and 330–32.

104. In PR § 270, Hegel states that religion is a foundation for the state only insofar as religion has truth as its content, and that, even then, it is only a foundation (*Grundlage*) and not yet the state's realized *Sittlichkeit*. On Hegel's understanding of religion as a foundation of the state, see Franco, *Hegel's Philosophy of Freedom*, 296–306.

105. Hegel, *Vorlesungen über Rechtsphilosophie* (the Ilting edition), 1:293.

106. Ibid.

107. "On the contrary, the development of this Idea has established the truth [of the proposition] that spirit, as free and rational, is inherently (*an sich*) ethical, that the true Idea is *actual* rationality, and that it is this rationality which exists as the state. It has further emerged just as plainly from this Idea that the ethical *truth* which it embodies is present for *thinking* consciousness as a *content* on which the form of *universality* has been conferred—that is, *law*—and that the state in general *knows* its ends, and recognizes and implements them with a determinate consciousness and in accordance with principles" (Hegel, PR § 270).

108. Ibid. Hegel is here railing not against "polemical" forms of Protestantism but against the illegitimate, irrational authority of the Catholic Church. He adds parenthetically: "In Protestantism, there is no *laity*, so that there is likewise no clergy to act as an exclusive depositary of church doctrine"—in other words, Protestantism does not infantilize its adherents, who are permitted and expected to think for themselves.

109. Ibid.

110. Franco, *Hegel's Philosophy of Freedom*, 328.

111. Hegel, PR § 270. For Hegel, art and religion are also forms of knowing, but not cognitive, scientific knowing, not knowing *als ein Gedachtes*.

112. Hegel's position on Jewish assimilation, however, does not necessarily vitiate the interpretations of those who see Gans's Hegelian vision as striking a balance between integration and the assertion of a form of particularity. (See, for example, Livné-Freudenthal ["Kultur als Weltanschauung," 65], Schorsch [TC, 216], or Waszek ["Hegel, Mendelssohn, Spinoza," 197].) Jewish Hegelians' visions of Jews within a differentiated *Sittlichkeit* should not be assumed to be identical to Hegel's.

113. Hegel, PR § 270. Wood identifies Friedrich Schlegel as the defender of the idea of the "Christian state" whom Hegel "seems to have in mind here" (ibid., editor's footnote 12).

114. Ibid., § 270.

115. Ibid. Hegel also writes: "Instead of mastering one's opinions by the labour of study and subjecting one's volition to discipline so as to elevate it to free obedience, the easiest course is to renounce cognition of objective truth, to nurse a sense of grievance and hence also of self-conceit, and to find in one's own godliness all that is required in order to see through the nature of the laws and of political institution, to pass judgment on them, and to lay down what their character should and must be. And indeed, since these are the findings of a pious heart, they must be infallible and indisputable; for if we make religion the basis of our intentions and assertions, these cannot be faulted on account of either their shallowness or their injustice (*Unrechtlichkeit*)" (ibid.). Wood identifies Fries as the target of Hegel's polemic here (ibid., editor's footnote 5).

116. Ibid, § 270.

117. Laurence Dickey underscores the social thrust of Hegel's Protestantism as a political ideology and shows that Hegel's "Protestantism" was in fact directed against the Orthodox Protestantism of 1820s Prussia, which Hegel saw as mired in narrowly subjectivist faith

and rigid theological doctrine: "As [Hegel's lectures on the philosophy of history] make perfectly clear, there can be no doubt . . . about the social dimension of Hegel's Christianity or about his desire to offer *Sittlichkeit* as a socio-Protestant alternative to the various kinds of anti-social subjectivism that he thought had pervaded the modern world since 1789. . . . Hegel's conception of Protestantism contained a sharp criticism of the kind of anti-social Protestantism that characterized orthodox Lutheranism in the 1820s" ("Religion and Philosophy," 326–27). On Hegel's Protestantism as a "political ideology," see also Dickey, "General Introduction," xxii.

118. Hegel, *Philosophie des Rechts: Die Vorlesung von 1819/20 in einer Nachschrift,* edited by Dieter Henrich, 220–21.

119. Reissner comments: "Moser's friends . . . understood that what was meant was Hegel's conception of the state" (*Eduard Gans*, 52).

120. As I discuss in the final section of chapter 3, Moser later—in his correspondence with Wohlwill, and under very different circumstances—used Hegel to argue that converting had become acceptable, but this was a significant break from his original vision.

121. Moses Moser, "Rede vor der Gründungsversammlung des Vereins für Cultur und Wissenschaft der Juden," November 7, 1819, ARC 4 792/B10-2, Zunz Archive. This passage is quoted in Ucko, "Geistesgeschichtliche Grundlagen," 328.

122. Moser, quoted in Ucko, "Geistesgeschichtliche Grundlagen," 328.

123. Later in his memorandum, Moser argues that, even though many of the customs and laws derived from the Bible are out of step with the current age, some form of them remains necessary to preserve a Jewish national unity as understood within the parameters of the "most correct" (that is, Hegelian) idea: "wir [haben] in der Bibel Vorschriften von Gebräuchen und Gesetzen für einen bestimmten Staat, Zeit und Clima, deren ferneres Bestehen zum Teil in größerem oder geringerem Widerspruch mit den Forderungen der neuen Zeit und neuen Verhältnisse wäre, zum Theil aber auch mehr oder minder wichtig zur Erhaltung einer Nationaleinheit ist, wie diese auch nach der richtigsten Idee gedacht werden möge" ("Rede vor der Gründungsversammlung," 10). This is also quoted in Ucko, "Geistesgeschichtliche Grundlagen," 331.

124. Moser, quoted in Ucko, "Geistesgeschichtliche Grundlagen," 328.

125. Moser, "Rede vor der Gründungsversammlung," 15–16.

126. Hegel's 1821 philosophy of religion lectures lasted seventeen weeks, at four hours per week, from April 30 until August 25. See Peter Hodgson, "Editorial Introduction," 1:4.

127. Gans, quoted in Ucko, "Geistesgeschichtliche Grundlagen," 336. Gans also proposed the names "Verein für Beförderung der Wissenschaft und Kultur unter den Juden" (Association for the Promotion of Science and Culture among the Jews), "Die Maccabäer" (The Maccabees), and "Olympius" on May 27, 1821. The eventual name Verein für Cultur und Wissenschaft der Juden was not adopted until July 5, 1821 (*Protokoll-Buch für d. V. für Cultur und Wissenschaft d. J.* [25 March 1821–14 April 1822], ARC 4° 792/B2, Zunz Archive).

128. For scholarship on the importance of Wolf and Böck for Zunz's conception of *Wissenschaft des Judentums*, see note 24 of this chapter.

129. Georg Wilhelm Friedrich Hegel, *Lectures on the Philosophy of Religion* (hereafter LPR), 1:86. The angle brackets in Hodgson's edition of LPR indicate passages in the margins of Hegel's 1821 manuscript. Square brackets indicate Hodgson's editorial insertions.

130. Ibid., 1:86 and 88.

131. Ibid., 1:88.

132. Friedrich Schleiermacher, *Der christliche Glaube 1821/22*, 1:31.

133. Ibid., 1:89. The passage also appears in Hegel, *Vorlesungen über die Philosophie der Religion*, edited by Jaeschke, 3:7–8.

134. The following passage appears only some fifteen pages into "The Concept of Religion," and Gans and his associates would presumably have heard it before the meeting at which Gans proposed the term *Wissenschaft des Judentums*.

135. Hegel, LPR 1:200. I have interpellated in curly brackets additional and alternative passages from the second (1840) edition of Hegel's *Vorlesungen über die Philosophie der Religion*, edited by Philipp Marheineke and Bruno Bauer, whereas these passages are given in footnotes in Hodgson's edition. The 1840 edition of Hegel's *Werke* draws extensively in its reconstruction of the 1821 *Lectures on the Philosophy of Religion* on a transcript by Leopold von Henning, which has been lost. The only portions of it that have come down to us are those the editors wove together with passages from Hegel's 1821 manuscript in the 1840 edition. Since Marheineke and Bauer may also have drawn on other miscellaneous papers by Hegel to embellish the 1821 manuscript, it is not possible to say with certainty which additions to the manuscript in the 1840 text derive from Henning's transcript and which are, potentially, from Hegel's related papers. According to Hodgson, however, very little of Hegel's miscellaneous papers relate to the 1821 manuscript, and the vast majority of the material that the 1840 edition adds to that manuscript undoubtedly derives from Henning's 1821 transcript—and thus would have been heard by members of the Verein in that year. See Hodgson, "Editorial Introduction," 1:15 and 49.

136. Hegel, LPR 1:187, note 8.

137. Ibid., 1:191–92. The corresponding passage in the 1840 edition (see note 135) includes this formulation: "If the substantial element remains only shut up within the heart, it is not recognized as something higher, and God is only something subjective. The orientation afforded by subjectivity remains at best a drawing of lines into empty space" (quoted in ibid., 1:192, note 20). For this passage in German, see Hegel, *Vorlesungen über die Philosophie der Religion*, edited by Jaeschke, 1:100–101.

138. Hegel's attack on subjectivism as a politically corrosive force in the philosophy of religion lectures continues similar arguments in *Philosophy of Right*, which, as Dickey notes, admonish Protestants to overcome the narrow subjectivism of forms of Protestantism conceived according to feeling and private faith, in order to realize secularized Protestantism's social and ethical potential: "In [the Preface to *Philosophy of Right*], he continues his assault of subjectivism by reiterating the need to shift the focus of philosophy from feeling to thinking. In so doing, however, he adds a religious dimension to the discussion, arguing that, in Protestantism, feeling stands to thinking as an immature Lutheran attitude towards religion stands to a mature Hegelian one. As the Preface reveals, Hegel uses the progression from feeling to thinking to exhort Protestants to turn their inner-directed piety outwards—towards *Sittlichkeit* and civic engagement" ("General Introduction," xxiv).

139. Hegel, LPR, 1:208.

140. See ibid., 1:214–16.

141. Ibid., 1:215.

142. Ibid., 1:216.

143. On religion as representational thought, see ibid., 1:218–19. Hegel clearly directs his

view of religion against Schleiermacher when he says "precisely to the extent that the religious relation is viewed as being only in the mode of sensibility, religion dies away into something devoid of representation and action and loses all determinate content" (ibid., 1:219).

144. Ibid., 1:209.

145. Ibid., 1:209–10.

3. Locating Themselves in History

1. Immanuel Wolf, "On the Concept of a Science of Judaism," 155. For the German original, see Wolf, "Über den Begriff einer Wissenschaft des Judenthums," 23–24.

2. The inaugural number of the *Zeitschrift* (with Wolf's essay) was submitted to the censor's office in March 1822 (Sinai [Siegfried] Ucko, "Geistesgeschichtliche Grundlagen," 336). As noted in chapter 2, Hegel's foreword to Herman Friedrich Wilhelm Hinrichs's *Die Religion im Inneren Verhältnisse zur Wissenschaft* is dated "Easter 1822," which fell on April 7. The chronology makes it impossible for Hegel's foreword to have had any direct influence on Wolf's essay. However, Hegel's work distills ideas that he had presented in his first lectures on the philosophy of religion (begun in April 1821) and nicely exemplifies the blueprint for reconciling faith and reason that the *Vereinler* were absorbing from Hegel in this period.

3. In Eric von der Luft, *Hegel, Hinrichs, and Schleiermacher on Feeling and Reason in Religion* (hereafter HHS, 262). For the German original, see Hegel, *Berliner Schriften* (hereafter BS), 80.

4. Hegel, HHS, 264; and BS, 81.

5. Hegel, HHS, 264; and BS, 81.

6. "The development of the spirit of the times has induced thinking, and the manner of viewing which is associated with thinking, to have grown, for consciousness, into an *unavoidable stipulation* of *what* should be granted and recognized *as true*" (Hegel, HHS, 265; and BS, 81).

7. Hegel, HHS, 265 (original German my addition to von der Luft's translation); and BS, 82.

8. Norbert Waszek ("'Wissenschaft und Liebe zu den Seinen,'" 101) notes the indebtedness of Wolf's conception of *Wissenschaft des Judentums*, with its emphasis on all-encompassing totality, to Hegel's concept of science as articulated in the *Enzyklopädie der philosophischen Wissenschaften im Grundrisse* and elsewhere, and also notes that Wolf draws on the world-historical schema at the end of the *Elements of the Philosophy of Right* (hereafter PR), § 341–60. (Waszek's suggestion that Wolf was also echoing Hegel's *Lectures on the Philosophy of World History: Introduction, Reason in History* is, however, chronologically impossible, as the first issue of the *Zeitschrift* was finished in spring 1822 and Hegel did not begin lecturing on the philosophy of history until winter 1822–23.) Waszek also notes that, in his tripartite division of *Wissenschaft des Judentums*, Wolf follows Hegel in privileging philosophy over philology and history (ibid., 100–101). On Wolf's privileging of philosophy, see also Nils Roemer, *Jewish Scholarship and Culture in Nineteenth-Century Germany*, 29.

9. Wolf, "On the Concept of a Science of Judaism," 143; and "Über den Begriff," 1.

10. Thus, after Wolf had written his essay. Hegel's particular remark on Judaism as a "*Religion der Trennung*" in these lectures had no direct influence on Wolf's definition of Judaism as governed by the core idea of unity, but this remark is consistent with Hegel's view of

Judaism expressed in the 1821 *Lectures on the Philosophy of Religion* and, mutatis mutandis, in Hegel's critique of Spinoza, which I analyze below.

11. Hegel's verb tenses are telling. His supercessionism is evident in his relegation of Judaism to the past: the problem of *Trennung* that Judaism embodied has ostensibly been overcome by Christianity. Islam, by contrast, "still" exists as a religion of diremption, presumably because it is not part of the story of Christian origins.

12. Hegel, *Vorlesungen über die Philosophie der Weltgeschichte* (hereafter VPW), 86.

13. Although Hegel would reverse this hierarchy in his philosophy of religion lectures of 1827, in 1822–23 he still values Greek over Jewish religion, pagan sensual unity over "sublime" Jewish monotheism. On this reversal, see Peter Hodgson, " Editorial Introduction," 1:69–70.

14. Hegel, VPW, 86.

15. Wolf, "On the Concept of a Science of Judaism," 143; and "Über den Begriff," 3. Hegel defines "the universal as such as the identity of what is differentiated" (*Lectures on the Philosophy of Religion* [hereafter LPR], 1:215).

16. Michael Meyer, "Introduction to Immanuel Wolf," in Meyer, *Ideas of Jewish History*, 142.

17. Ibid., 141.

18. Wolf's critical and sometimes ironic distance from Hegel becomes pronounced in his correspondence with Moser, which I explore at the end of this chapter.

19. There is no critical edition of Hegel's *Lectures on the History of Philosophy* (hereafter LHP) that indicates which specific remarks on Spinoza date from which course of lectures (see chapter 2, note 93). Hegel notes, however, that he was involved in Jena with publishing Spinoza (LHP, 3:256). He had probably already worked out his basic take on Spinoza in the Jena lectures, and there is little question that it would have been part of Hegel's first two Berlin series of lectures on the history of philosophy in summer 1819 and winter 1820–21. The following remark regarding Spinoza's propositional rather than phenomenological method exemplifies this aspect of Hegel's critique of Spinoza: "The whole of Spinoza's philosophy is contained in these definitions, which, however, taken as a whole are formal; it is really a weak point in Spinoza that he begins thus with definitions. In mathematics this method is permitted . . . but in Philosophy the content should be known as the absolutely true. It is all well and good to grant the correctness of the name-definition, and acknowledge that the word 'substance' corresponds with the conception which the definition indicates, but it is quite another question to determine whether this content is absolutely true. . . . [E]verything proceeds inwards, and not outwards; the determinations are not developed from substance, it does not resolve itself into these attributes" (LHP, 3:263–64). See also similar remarks by Hegel in ibid., 3:260–61 and, on the distinction between Hegel's philosophical method and propositional demonstration, ibid., 3:283–85.

20. Hegel remarks, for example, that "the dualism of the Cartesian system Spinoza, as a Jew, altogether set aside" (LHP, 3:252).

21. Hegel charges Spinoza with "acosmism" in, for example, LPH, 3:282. In doing so, Hegel means that Spinozan substance has a monopoly, as it were, on true substantiality, thereby draining the finite world of such substantiality; Spinoza's world does not possess substantiality immanently. Hegel borrowed the term "acosmism" from Solomon Maimon, who first used it to describe Spinoza's philosophy (see *Salomon Maimons Lebensgeschichte*,

217). Ze'ev Levy (*Baruch Spinoza*, 82–83) notes this borrowing (and that Friedrich Kuntze already underscored it in 1912). David Biale (*Not in the Heavens*, 32) also notes the origin of the interpretation of Spinoza's "acosmism" in Maimon.

22. See Hegel, LHP, 3:280.

23. Ibid., 3:282.

24. Ibid., 3:257.

25. Ibid., 3:258.

26. In the 1812/13 volume 1 of *Wissenschaft der Logik* (hereafter WL), Hegel faults Spinoza for conceiving of the infinite as absolute affirmation of existence and the finite, in contrast, as negation. In Hegel's view Spinozan substance cannot achieve a speculative relation of identity with the other because differentiation into determinate being, for Spinoza, is mere negation. Hegel sees the advantage of his theory over Spinoza's in its ability to conceive of affirmation of the absolute as a dynamic process of self-differentiation into an Other, and, finally, as a mediated reflection of the Other in the self (universal subjectivity). For Hegel, Spinoza's substance is timeless and inert and fails to achieve subjectivity through dialectical development (WL, 1: 161–62). Hegel also devotes a substantial *Anmerkung* to Spinoza (ibid., 1:376–78), to which he refers back in the in the 1816 second volume (WL, 2:14–15). In identifying Spinoza's purported failure to think dialectical development, Hegel inscribes himself according to a secularized suppercessonist logic as the fulfillment of Spinoza—that is, as the necessary product of the dialectical movement of thought that Spinoza was "not yet" equipped to comprehend. Pierre Macherey analyzes how Hegel constructs Spinoza as a necessary but limited and flawed precursor that he, Hegel, has moved beyond (*Hegel ou Spinoza*, 17–18). On the temporality that Hegel inscribes by repeatedly characterizing Spinoza's substance as "not yet" absolute spirit, see ibid., 18. In addition to Hegel's secularly supersessionist treatment of Spinoza in LHP that I analyze in this chapter, several passages from WL do similar work. In his understanding of negation, for example, Spinoza "stops" (*bleibt . . . stehen*) at the conception of negation as determinacy or quality and does not "proceed" (*geht nicht . . . fort*) to Hegel's insight of absolute or self-negating negation (WL, 1:376). Hegel also faults Spinoza's mode of thinking *sub specie aeternitatis* for its inability to think the finite in terms of becoming (*werdend*) (ibid., 1:377). Hegel's secularized supercessionist stance vis-à-vis Spinoza is likewise unmistakable in another passage, in which he argues that in critiquing Spinoza the goal must not be "*Widerlegung*" but rather sublimation (WL, 2:14).

27. Hegel, LHP, 3:260 (emphasis added).

28. Ibid., 3:260–61.

29. Ibid.

30. "It has been already remarked (pp. 257, 258, 280) that undoubtedly Substance with Spinoza does not perfectly fulfill the conception of God, since it is as Spirit that He is to be conceived" (ibid., 3:281).

31. Ibid., 3:280.

32. Ibid., 3:286. In Spinoza "there is lacking the infinite form, spirituality and liberty" (ibid., 3:287).

33. Ibid., 3:287.

34. Ibid., 3:284–89.

35. Ibid., 3:288. In a similar vein, Hegel repeatedly critiques determination (the particularization of substance) in Spinoza as a form of negation that drains the particular of im-

manent substantiality and freedom and renders it essentially passive. In contrast to Spinoza, who could not progress beyond a nondialectical conception of negation (his purported acosmism), Hegel deploys negation as a dynamic force in the form of subjectivity and the negation of negation.

36. Ibid., 3:289.

37. Ibid.

38. Wolf, "On the Concept of a Science of Judaism," 144; and "Über den Begriff," 3–4.

39. Wolf, Wolf, "On the Concept of a Science of Judaism," 150; and "Über den Begriff," 13–14.

40. This is a major part of Wolf's argument in his *Zeitschrift* essay. In the second paragraph he underscores "that influence on humanity Judaism has exercised, as history incontestably reveals" ("On the Concept of a Science of Judaism," 143; and "Über den Begriff," 2), and he insists, contra Hegel, that Judaism remained vibrant beyond the demise of the ancient Jewish commonwealth: "The Jewish State collapsed but not Judaism" (147 and 9). Wolf sees the period from the expulsion of the Jews from Spain in 1492 until the present as a period of decline (148–49 and 11–12), yet even at the Jewish cultural nadir Spinoza emerged (150 and 14), and Judaism is a still-living principle (151 and 15). In contrast, Hegel, for example in the "Weltgeschichte" section at the end of PR, with which Wolf would have been familiar, contends that each people gets only one chance to make a contribution to *Weltgeschichte* or *Weltgeist*. When natural and geographical factors conspire to make a certain nation hegemonic at a given time, it becomes that nation's task to advance "the self-development of the world spirit's self-consciousness. This nation is the *dominant* one in world history for this epoch, *and only once in history can it have this epoch-making role*. . . . In contrast with this absolute right which it possesses as bearer of the present stage of the world spirit's development, the spirits of other nations are without rights, and they, like those whose epoch has passed, no longer count in world history" (PR § 347). Whereas Hegel theorizes a people's contribution to world spirit in terms of punctuated hegemony, Wolf conceives of contributions to world spirit in terms of sustaining a significant spiritual presence in different moments. Being spiritually significant does not require being hegemonic. For an analysis of how, in his 1822 presidential address to the Verein, Gans also argues—against Christian bias and Hegel alike—for the continuing relevance of Judaism's conception of unity, see Jonathan Karp, *The Politics of Jewish Commerce*, 226–27.

41. Waszek argues that the Verein intellectuals viewed Spinoza and Hegel as "closely related philosophies [*Lehren*], which complement each other as groundwork and execution and are often identified with each other" ("Hegel, Mendelssohn, Spinoza," 192). For his reading of Wolf's image of Spinoza as thoroughly compatible with Hegel's, see ibid., 202–5. I concur that Wolf constructs Spinoza as a precursor to Hegel, but I read Wolf as deploying the perceived conceptual intimacy between the two thinkers to subvert aspects of Hegel's *geschichtsphilosophisch* narrative about the Jews (and Spinoza).

42. Heinrich Heine, *Historisch-kritische Gesamtausgabe der Werke* (hereafter DHA), 14 (part 1): 94.

43. Neither the Düsseldorfer Heine-Ausgabe (DHA, which has extensive apparatus) nor the *Säkularausgabe* can link Heine's anecdote to a passage in any text by Hegel. The DHA states categorically that there is no passage in Hegel to which Heine is directly referring (14 [part 2]: 924), and none of the passages in which Hegel mentions dreams that the editors

suggest (ibid.) Heine might have in mind seems plausible. Thus, if Heine is remembering a comment by Hegel, it must have been made orally, a possibility the editors also entertain.

44. Wolf, "On the Concept of a Science of Judaism," 150–51; and "Über den Begriff," 14–15.

45. Since Wolf makes no direct mention of Hegel, although his essay is deeply indebted to Hegelian concepts about historical periods and progress and the nature of science, one could counter that his lack of attribution of this remark to Hegel is consistent with the silent presence of Hegel throughout. There is a difference, however, between a pervasive debt to a Hegelian conceptual framework and a paraphrase of a specific remark.

46. Heine, DHA, 14 (part 1): 94.

47. Ibid., 90.

48. Hegel's insistence on the circularity of his system and of all truly scientific thought (the endpoint is already inherent in the commencement) makes Wolf's move possible, even if it is not one Hegel would endorse.

49. Wolf, "On the Concept of a Science of Judaism," 154; and "Über den Begriff," 24.

50. Gans assumed the Verein's presidency provisionally after its first president, Joel Abraham List, left Berlin in March 1821. The last three of Gans's presidential addresses were each published shortly after they were delivered and have been republished twice since, first in Salman Rubaschoff, "Erstlinge der Entjudung," and more recently as Gans, "Erste Rede vor dem 'Kulturverein," "Zweite Rede vor dem 'Kulturverein," and "Dritte Rede vor dem 'Kulturverein.'" Part of the second of these three speeches by Gans has also been published as Gans, "A Society to Further Jewish Integration (1822)." Because only these three addresses—of October 28, 1821, April 28, 1822, and May 4, 1823—have been published, they are often referred to (as in Waszek's edited volume) as Gans's first, second, and third presidential addresses. The earlier addresses to which I refer are available in an anonymous typescript, "Transkription einiger Dokumente aus ARC 4 792/B11" (ARC 4° 792/B11–32, Archive of the "Association for the Culture and Science of the Jews," Zunz Archive, National Library of Israel, Jerusalem [henceforth Zunz Archive]). It is a transcription of documents ARC 4° 792/B11–2 through 6; ARC 4° 792/B11–2, 5, and 6 are Gans's addresses, respectively, of March 11, 1820, November 2, 1820, and April 1, 1821.

51. On Gans's efforts to pursue an academic career in the early 1820s, see Hanns Reissner, *Eduard Gans*, 46–117, and Monica Richarz, *Der Eintritt der Juden in die akademischen Berufe*, 206–10. For a sketch in English of Gans's life and intellectual development, see Norbert Waszek, "Eduard Gans on Poverty and on the Constitutional Debate," 24–32.

52. Norbert Waszek ("Vorwort," 16) notes that the Edict Concerning the Civil Status of the Jews in the Prussian State of March 11, 1812, allowed Jews to hold academic appointments but not other state offices. Since members of the law faculty could be called on to serve as appellate judges, whether or not a Jew could be appointed to the law faculty required clarification.

53. Terry Pinkard, *Hegel*, 532.

54. On the relationship between Gans's attempt to gain an academic appointment without converting and his involvement in the Verein, Ismar Schorsch writes: "As his personal campaign dragged on, the cause of the Verein offered Gans consolation, sublimation, and an instrument of battle" (*From Text to Context* [hereafter TC], 208). Gans's oppositional stance (and Isaak Jost's deep dislike of Gans) are clear in Jost's claim that the restriction of Jewish

academic appointments was brought about as an immediate consequence of the sheer obstinacy (*ertrozt ward*) in "the way the famous Gans in his youthful passion [*Feuer*] pursued the issue," something Jost claims to have heard directly from Minister of Culture Karl vom Stein zum Altenstein. See Jost, "Actenmäßige Darstellung," March 14.

55. On Hegel as a prime genitor of Theory, see Jean-Michel Rabaté, *The Future of Theory*, chapter 1.

56. "Transkription einiger Dokumente aus ARC 4 792B11," 5.

57. Ibid.

58. Ibid., 6.

59. Ibid., 7. Later in this address Gans proclaims: "Before you lies the Magna Carta of our institutions, and if no edifice in high style is erected upon this foundation, then it is not the foundation but we who are at fault" (ibid.).

60. Ibid., 7–8.

61. See, in particular, PR § 296, in which Hegel ties the development of disinterested integrity in civil servants to "direct *education in ethics and in thought*," and which ends with the declaration that subjective passions like revenge and hatred "disappear of their own accord in those who are occupied with the larger interests of a major state, for they become accustomed to dealing with universal interests, views, and functions."

62. For a reconstruction of Hegel's 1822–23 lectures on the philosophy of history, based on three separate sets of lecture notes, see VPW.

63. Gans, "Erste Rede vor dem 'Kulturverein,'" 57.

64. Ibid.

65. Ibid., 57–58.

66. Richard Schaeffler's account of "Die Wissenschaft des Judentums in ihrer Bezie hung zur Allgemeinen Gesistesgeschichte im Deutschland des 19. Jahrhunderts" usefully distills aspects of Kantian moral philosophy, Fichtean philosophy of the subject and of history, and Hegel's philosophy of *Geist* that would have been salient for any thinker trying to adapt these philosophical strains for a *Wissenschaft des Judentums*. Yet the links Schaeffler suggests between the wider German intellectual context and actual articulations of Jewish academic scholarship remain generally vague, and the specific examples he highlights are frequently questionable, as when he seems to point to Salomon Maimon and Marcus Herz as the first Jews to draw on Kant's moral philosophy to articulate a Kantian philosophy of Judaism (ibid., 119). Neither Maimon nor Herz did this. Moreover, Schaeffler associates Wolf's *Zeitschrift* essay most closely with Fichte (while acknowledging that Wolf was not "ein schulgetreuer Anhänger Fichtes" [123]) and uses Zunz as an example of a practitioner of a *Wissenschaft des Judentums* who drew inspiration from Hegel (123, 124–25). Nonetheless, Schaeffler is one of the few scholars to note that Hegel's theory of *Geist* allows for a philosophy of Judaism that breaks with the Enlightenment model of the sovereign individual who stands in an unmediated relationship to universal humanity, and that opens up the possibility of thinking of Jews and Judaism as making a contribution to universal spirit as a distinct community (124, 127). This was a possibility that clearly animated the Verein Hegelians. Since he does not engage any of the many moments in Hegel's work that would complicate such an assertion, Giuseppe Veltri's reply to Schaeffler that Hegel's concept of Spirit demands, ultimately, the dissolution of all particularity in the universal, under-

stood as spiritually undifferentiated, seems hasty ("Altertumswissenschaft und Wissenschaft des Judentums," 46). Veltri (ibid.) and David Myers ("The Ideology of Wissenschaft des Judentums," 711) assume their conclusion when they argue that Gans's eventual conversion in 1825 reveals a truth implicit in his Hegelian interpretation of Judaism all along. Leon Wieseltier also closely associates Gans's Hegelianism and his eventual conversion when he describes him as "a devoutly Hegelian historian of law who eventually fled to the font" ("*Etwas über jüdische Historik*," 147).

67. Gans, "Erste Rede vor dem 'Kulturverein,'" 58.

68. Waszek, "Vorwort," 22. Michael Hoffheimer also notes the Hegelian inspiration behind Gans's metaphor of the family (*Eduard Gans and the Hegelian Philosophy of Law*, 111, note 39).

69. Hegel distinguishes the state from civil society in PR § 258. Relations of civil society are "optional" (and thus "external"); relations of the state are substantial. In Merold Westphal's apt description, "marriage as a non-contractual relationship is a double liberation. It frees our self-consciousness from self-centeredness so it can participate in a We which is larger than itself but with which it remains in a relation of identity" ("Hegel's Radical Idealism," 88). Similarly, "I the citizen am who We the people are. Like the family, the state frees self-consciousness from self-centeredness" (ibid., 89). Not only Gans but also Wolf draws on Hegel's theorization of the ethical thrust of the family in his interpretation of Judaism. Typically, however, even as he draws on Hegel, Wolf creatively adapts him to his own purposes. Contesting Hegel's narrative and timeline of the Jewish contribution to spirit, Wolf celebrates the wisdom of the rabbis in displacing erstwhile public culture into the realm of the family life, which he characterizes as "the source and training ground of ethical life" (*die Quelle und Übungschule der Sittlichkeit*) (in "On the Concept of a Science of Judaism," 148; and "Über den Begriff," 10 [translation modified]). Although Wolf's view of the relation between family life and ethical life paraphrases Hegel's remarks to the same effect in *Philosophy of Right*, in contrast to Hegel, Wolf emphasizes the Jewish family as a sustaining force of *Sittlichkeit* after the demise of the Jewish state. In Wolf's narrative of diaspora existence, persecution eventually forced Jews to retreat from the active participation they had for centuries maintained in the cultural and spiritual life of Europe into insular mediocrity, but even under such adverse conditions they were sustained by the institution of the family (150 and 13–14).

70. Hegel, PR § 158.

71. Ibid. § 163.

72. Ibid. § 255.

73. On Hegel's conception of corporations as a sort of family within civil society, see Westphal, "Hegel's Radical Idealism," 82.

74. Gans, "Erste Rede vor dem 'Kulturverein,'" 61.

75. Ibid., 61–62. I understand this passage differently than Schorsch, who renders it: "I see in the close fraternization of such noble people the approach of the messianic era, of which the Prophets speak, and which only the common decadence of our generation has turned into a fairy-tale" (TC, 209). Schorsch translates *Geschlecht* as "generation," which it can mean but not, as I see it, if modified by *jederzeitig* (perpetual or perennial). Thus, whereas Schorsch represents Gans as finding fault only with the present generation of Jews,

Gans actually faults the perpetual depravity of the race or line [*des Geschlechtes jederzeitige Verderbtheit*].

76. Gans, "Erste Rede vor dem 'Kulturverein,'" 58–59.

77. Hegel, PR § 294.

78. Hegel's civil servants are martyrs of sorts, through whose self-sacrifice particular interests become reconciled to universal concerns: "The service of the state requires those who perform it to sacrifice the independent and discretionary satisfaction of their subjective ends, and thereby gives them the right to find their satisfaction in the performance of their duties, and in this alone. It is here that, in the present context, that link is to be found between universal and particular interests which constitutes the concept of the state and its internal stability" (ibid.). The *Vereinler* saw themselves precisely as self-sacrificing Hegelian civil servants, mediating between the particular interests of Jews and the universality of the state. Moreover—in contrast to the agent who is contracted to render a service, a mere means to an end—the civil servant performs work that is valuable in itself. Unlike an external instrumental service, the civil servant's work is fused with his inward character and substantial being (see ibid.): the civil servant's work is his essence, and vice versa. I would suggest that this elision of civil servants' work and being, coupled with Hegel's emphasis on civil servants' comportment (their habit, demeanor, and carriage; see ibid. § 296), allowed the *Vereinler* to equate a certain intellectual and bureaucratic habitus with the actual performance of crucial work. "Being" Hegelian civil servants through performative self-sylization could double as "doing." What to Jost seemed like such a waste of time and resources was in fact a crucial component of the *Vereinler*'s lived Hegelianism.

79. Hegel's claim that "women may well be educated, but they are not made for the higher sciences, for philosophy and certain artistic productions which require a universal element" (PR § 166, Addition) hypermasculinizes the sort of universal reason the *Vereinler* claim to embody. In making that claim, they participate in the ethical substance of the (masculine) state, the *Vaterland*. On Hegel's views on women, see Paul Franco, *Hegel's Philosophy of Freedom*, 243–47.

80. Hegel, PR § 172.

81. Gans, "Dritte Rede vor dem 'Kulturverein,'" 80.

82. ibid.

83. Ibid. Gans's critique of subjective isolation echoes Hegel: "Since the state is spirit objectified, it is only as one of its members that the individual himself has objectivity, genuine individuality, and an ethical life. Unification pure and simple is the true content and aim of the individual, and the individual's destiny is the living of a universal life. His further particular satisfaction, activity, and mode of conduct have this substantive and universally valid life as their starting point and their result" (PR § 258).

84. Gans, "Dritte Rede vor dem 'Kulturverein,'" 80.

85. Ibid.

86. Heine bemoans and ironizes the impenetrable style of the *Zeitschrift* in a letter to Zunz of June 27, 1823. See Heine, *Säkularausgabe*, 20:102–3. Regarding the journal's elitism, see also Zunz's letter to Samuel Meyer Ehrenberg of April 18, 1823, in which an exasperated Zunz declares that the *Zeitschrift* is not a Jewish journal and not intended "to educate the Jews of Braunschweig" (Nahum Glatzer, *Leopold and Adelheid Zunz*, 43).

87. Gans, "Zweite Rede vor dem 'Kulturverein,'" 64.

88. Ibid

89. Ibid.

90. Ibid. Gans would have derived this view from the last section of Hegel's *Philosophy of Right* on world history, as this speech by Gans (delivered, as noted above, on April 28, 1822) preceded Hegel's first course of lectures on world history, in winter 1822–23.

91. Ibid.

92. Gans, "Zweite Rede vor dem 'Kulturverein,'" 64–65. Here I have used, but significantly modified, J. Hessing's translation (Gans, "A Society to Further Jewish Integration (1822)," 215).

93. Gans, "A Society to Further Jewish Integration (1822)," 216 (translation modified), and Gans, "Zweite Rede vor dem 'Kulturverein,'" 65.

94. Gans, "Zweite Rede vor dem 'Kulturverein,'" 65.

95. Ibid.

96. As Yirmiyahu Yovel remarks on Hegel's version of Judaism's role in what Yovel calls "the birth pangs of Christianity," "post-Christian Judaism remains locked outside the gates of the salvation it offers. Judaism's own project is aborted, and the Jews are ejected from history at the moment of their highest achievement" (*Dark Riddle*, 59).

97. Gans, "Zweite Rede vor dem 'Kulturverein,'" 66.

98. Ibid.

99. Todd Presner reads this passage by Gans through the lens of an overly neat opposition between Hegel (whose narrative of history offers no possibility of Judaism surviving as Jewish) and Heine (who heroically deconstructs Hegel's master narrative in the name of Jewish particularity). Consequently, he misses the oppositional thrust of Gans's Hegelian Jewish politics and sees Gans as purely assimilationist: "In this extraordinary passage . . . Gans desires a Judaism that is no longer Jewish in its particularity; he wants a people who have been assimilated into the 'ocean' of Europe and are as historically indistinguishable from other people as one 'current' is from another. In other words, the specificity of Judaism and Jewish history is to be absorbed into the totality of European world history to survive not as Jewish but as European" (*Mobile Modernity*, 129–30). In order to underscore the antisemitic nature of Hegel's narrative of world history, Presner claims that there is "complete accordance" between "Hegel's anti-Semitic description of Judaism in 'The Spirit of Christianity and its Fate' (1798–1800)" and Hegel's mature philosophy of history (ibid., 127). Although there is much to object to in the role(s) that Hegel assigns to the Jews and Judaism in his mature work, his understanding of Judaism's significance in his mature, dialectical historical schema is significantly different from his early, undialectical portrayal of Judaism. Presner's elision of Hegel's treatment of Judaism in "The Spirit of Christianity" and the lectures on world history more than twenty years later might inadvertently leave readers with the erroneous impression that Heine or his colleagues in the Verein would have been aware of Hegel's early texts (Presner nowhere mentions that Hegel's early theological writings remained unpublished in his lifetime). Heine's ironizing of Hegel is not a response to Hegel's early views on Jews, nor does Gans's Hegelianism imply a tacit approval of these early views. Presner's gloss on Heine's ironic presentation of "Systematie" and "ideas" in *Buch le grand* exemplifies his tendency to cast Heine in the role of a Jewish hero doing battle with the alterity-killing Hegelian behemoth: "For Heine the Hegelian concept is complicit with violence because the enclosed logic of any system forces some people into exile, if it does not kill them straight out. Heine's

Reisebilder are, therefore, acts of freedom, defiant and decidedly political acts creating cracks for the survival of a little bit of Jewish alterity" (ibid., 144).

100. Gans, "Zweite Rede vor dem 'Kulturverein,'" 66–67. After the sentence "That into which it merges shall become that much richer for what has merged with it, not merely that much poorer for the opposition that has been lost," Paul Mendes-Flohr and Jehuda Reinharz add a note (*The Jew in the Modern World* 218, note 4) quoting from page 79 of the 1956 Dover edition of Hegel's *Philosophy of History* lectures—lectures that, they point out, Gans was the first to edit and publish in book form. True, but Hegel gave these lectures only after this address by Gans. A chronologically better comparison would be to the *History of Philosophy* lectures, which have the same sentiment—the eternal present of spirit—and were indeed the basis of the *Philosophy of History* lectures. Mendes-Flohr and Reinharz identify the internal quote at the end of the extract I have used from Gans as from Johann Gottfried Herder, *Reflections on the Philosophy of the History of Mankind*, translated by T. O. Churchill, abridged and edited by Frank E. Manuel (Chicago: University of Chicago Press, 1968), 15.

101. Probably the most bewildering aspect of what David Myers characterizes as Gans's "bewildering metaphor" (Myers, "The Ideology of Wissenschaft des Judentums," 711) is that the Jews will "seem" or "appear" to have disappeared yet they will live on—presumably, then, only in invisible ways. But it seems plausible to interpret such a "disappearance" as referring only to Jews understood as a people emphatically apart. If we take nonintegration into the surrounding society to be an essential quality of Jewishness, then the Jews will indeed seem to have disappeared once they have "flowed into" the "ocean" of European life. But we must at the very least assume that organizations like the Verein and the Hamburg Reform Temple, with which the Berlin Verein attempted, not very successfully, to collaborate, were compatible with Gans's vision of integrated Jewish existence. There is no obvious reason not to believe that the vast majority of institutions of American Jewish life—including Reform, Reconstructionist, Conservative, and modern Orthodox Judaism as well as Jewish charities, cultural organizations, or the American Israel Public Affairs Committee—could be accommodated within Gans's vision, mutatis mutandis, of particular currents in the wider sea of American life. Presner's reading of Gans's metaphor (*Mobile Modernity*, 129–30) forecloses the possibility, which Gans's text keeps open, of Jews being not Jewish or European, but both. In his reading of this passage, Emil Fackenheim endorses Heinrich Graetz's view of it as a combination of naiveté and gibberish, and of Gans as having been led astray by Hegel's abstruse sophistry (*Encounters between Judaism and Modern Philosophy*, 127–28). Rachel Livné-Freudenthal ("Kultur als Weltanschauung," 65) and Waszek ("Hegel, Mendelssohn, Spinoza," 197) read Gans's metaphor in a more Jewishly affirmative way, as does Schorsch, who sees in it an emphasis not only on "unity and conformity" but also on "a notion of the right to be different" (TC, 216). Gans's allusion to Herder here also supports a nonradical reading of the ocean metaphor, for in endorsing Herder's vision of a Europe in which no one will any longer ask who is a Jew and who is a Christian, Gans—like Herder—can hardly be hoping or predicting that Jews and Christians will cease to exist, only that there will be a secular sphere of European life in which people will be able to participate without having their participation fundamentally defined by their religious affiliation.

102. Rachel Livné-Freudenthal ("Der 'Verein für Cultur und Wissenschaft der Juden,'" 115, note 54) finds it "*auffallend*" that Gans uses the term "Europe" here but does not specify how she interprets the term's significance. Roemer (*Jewish Scholarship*, 28) also strains to

turn Gans slightly against Hegel by detecting a subversive quality in Gans's use of "Europe" in place of Hegel's "German Reich," even though Hegel uses "German nation," "German Reich," and so forth, to refer to Western Europe, as Waszek ("Hegel, Mendelssohn, Spinoza," 197) and Charles Taylor (*Hegel*, 398), among others, note.

103. Gans, "Zweite Rede vor dem 'Kulturverein,'" 67–68.

104. As quoted in chapter 2, in his first address to the Verein (as its secretary) on March 11, 1820, Gans likened the Verein—organically ordered within—to a state that "has only to look where it wishes to make conquests" (ARC 4° 792/B11, 1, Zunz Archive).

105. Gans ends with grandiose words about the importance of the Verein and the need to devote youthful vigor and manly determination to its task, which the *Vereinler* should hold as the highest cause (*Angelegenheit*) of their lives ("Zweite Rede vor dem 'Kulturverein,'" 74). The success of the Verein depends on such heroic fortitude and on the subordination of the personal to the universal: "Forget divisive strife and all personal discord. Remember the universal; let us, united, pursue the same goal, for humanity's blessing and for the well-being of the fatherland" (ibid.). The personal is corrosive ("personal discord"), whereas the universal is the basis of harmony. Gans's call to pursue the universal for the good of humanity and the German " fatherland" further exemplifies the instability between entities like "Europe," "humanity," and the German "fatherland," an oscillation between philosophical theorems and actual states and governments. Both the *Vereinler*'s inflated self-importance and their orientation toward integration into the state are evident when Gans goes on to apostrophize princes, senates, legislative bodies, and other governmental entities (ibid., 75). Even if it was merely a rhetorical gesture, such apostrophizing is a considerable stretch. Gans had just reported that the Verein now had a handful of letters in its archive, that in the last semester its members had taught twelve students in its *Unterrichtsanstalt*, and that four members had read eleven papers in its Institut für die Wissenschaft des Judentums. This and the *Zeitschrift* (which no one seemed interested in reading) hardly add up to activity likely to command the attention of governments. Gans does say the Verein would be nothing without government support (although the Verein had received no such support!), but he implies that governments likewise have much to gain from the Verein. It is they who will reap the fruit of Jewish integration into the state in the form of "vaterlandsliebende Bürger" (ibid.).

106. Waszek also ("Hegel, Mendelssohn, Spinoza," 199) sees in Gans's position a version of Hegel's famous *Doppelsatz*.

107. Gans, "Dritte Rede vor dem 'Kulturverein,'" 76.

108. Zunz, "Etwas über die rabbinische Literatur," 1–2.

109. In his 1938 "Ichspaltung im Abwehrvorgang," a continuation of his earlier theorization of the fetish as both denial and dramatization of castration, Freud analyzes the way the ego sustains an illusion of integrity not in spite of but, paradoxically, by virtue of, an inner rift (*Gesammelte Werke*, 17:59–60).

110. Gans, "Dritte Rede vor dem 'Kulturverein,'" 76.

111. Ibid.

112. Ibid., 77.

113. Ibid.

114. Ibid. In his first lectures on the philosophy of history Hegel defines the spirit of a people (*Geist des Volkes*) as what unites and binds that people. As a spiritual principle, *Geist* can only be understood intellectually. Spirit does not strive merely to serve particular ends

but also and ultimately to know itself in its noninstrumental essence (VPW, 16–17). The dialectic of spirit culminates when spirit produces itself in and as thought and knowledge: "Dies ist der Zweck des Geistes; er ist dies, sich zu produzieren, zum Gegenstand zu machen, damit er sich als Dasein habe, damit er sich wisse; sein Sein ist, sich zu wissen" (ibid., 45). Gans strongly echoes Hegel when he defines what the age wants (*was die Zeit wolle*) in this way: "sie will das Bewußtseyn von sich erringen, sie will nicht bloß seyn, sondern auch sich wissen" ("Dritte Rede vor dem 'Kulturverein,'" 77). When Gans characterizes subject-object reconciliation in self-consciousness and self-knowledge as the deepest need of the age, the "höchste Stufe . . . die überhaupt errungen werden kann," "das wichtigste Ergebnis für die Geschichte des Menschengeschlechtes," and also the "höchste Beruhigung und die höchste Versöhnung" (ibid., 77–78), he is likewise paraphrasing parallel formulations in Hegel's first *Weltgeschichte* lectures, such as "der Geist also will seine Allgemeinheit wissen, und nur durch dieses Wissen macht er sich eins mit der Seite seiner Objektivität, welche das Allgemeine daran ist. . . . Aber er [der Geist] soll denkend sein, Einheit seines Höchsten und Innersten mit dem Daseienden, und diese Einheit kann nur bestehen, wenn er das Allgemeine seines Werkes und seiner Welt weiß. Dies ist seine höchste Befriedigung, weil das Denken sein Innerstes ist. . . . Auf diesem Punkte weiß der Geist das Allgemeine . . . seiner wirklichen Welt, weiß, was er wesentlich ist" (VPW, 49). In figuring self-knowledge as the moment of reconciliation of (Jewish) subjectivity with the objectivity of circumstances, moreover, Gans follows Hegel's definition of true self-knowledge (*Wissen*) as the thought activity (*Tätigkeit des Gedankens*) through which a *Volksgeist* passes from merely subjective to objective knowledge of itself: "der Volksgeist als Geist muß dazu kommen, sich zu wissen, zu denken, was er ist. Der Volksgeist ist Wissen, und diese Tätigkeit des Gedankens [in bezug] auf die Realität eines Volksgeistes ist, daß er sein Werk als Objektives, als Allgemeines, nicht mehr bloß [als] Subjektives weiß" (ibid., 48).

115. This is a version of Hegel's "Weltgeschichte als Weltgericht" dictum (see PR § 340 and 342), which posits the power of *Vernunft* in history: an optimistic outlook, not a ratification of all forms of brute force. Hegel borrows the phrase "Weltgeschichte als Weltgericht" from Schiller's 1784 poem "Resignation."

116. Gans, "Dritte Rede vor dem 'Kulturverein,'" 78.

117. Hegel's insistence that "prophecy is not the business of the philosopher" is in fact equivocal (*Lectures on the Philosophy of World History: Introduction, Reason in History*, 171; for a similar sentiment, see PR, "Preface," 21, 27–28). Although the philosopher cannot prophesy the future, he grasps substance and truth, which are eternal. So the philosopher can indeed identify what is not reasonable in the past and in the present, and predict that it must disappear. This is the form of philosophical quasi-prophecy that Gans performs here.

118. Although Gans's position vis-à-vis the state was very different from Hegel's, their respective strategies of attenuating the reality of dismaying empirical facts through a hypotrophied faith in the reality of the philosophical *Idee* are variations on a common theme. As John Toews notes of Hegel in 1820–21, "it was during the time when he was most pessimistic about bridging the gap between empirical existence and the philosophical Idea that he appeared to identify them most completely" (*Hegelianism*, 96). The ambiguous relationship between Prussia and the philosophically understood state that is evident in texts like Hegel's 1818 Berlin inaugural address and 1820 preface to *Elements of the Philosophy of Right* issue from Hegel's own negotiation of a political terrain that he first deemed favorable to his vision,

but quickly saw become more treacherous. The philosopher's characterization of the relationship between the empirical state and the idea of the state in his 1822–23 lectures on world history demonstrates, importantly, that this ambiguity continued in statements Hegel made after any illusions of Prussian progressivism had been dispelled. See, for example, Hegel's discussion of the relationship between the people and the government in the state, in "Die Natur des Staats" in VPW, especially 79.

119. Gans, "Dritte Rede vor dem 'Kulturverein,'" 79.

120. Ibid., 78.

121. Ibid.

122. Ibid. Gans here and at the end of his final address has an axe to grind with unnamed people from the Hamburg *Specialverein* who had criticized the Verein for not focusing on specific pragmatic tasks. I am here not interested in the specific quibble but rather in the philosophical argument it elicits from Gans.

123. Ibid.

124. Waszek's edition reads *aber*, whereas the text prepared by Rubaschoff reads *oben* ("Erstlinge der Entjudung," 196). In preparing the text of Gans's addresses, Waszek returned to the original publication of these texts, which I have not been able to consult. He corrects a number of mistakes, and I assume that he simply missed this one. The context militates for *oben*.

125. Gans, "Dritte Rede vor dem 'Kulturverein,'" 78–79.

126. Mendes-Flohr and Reinharz note how Gans's acceptance of the government stipend undermined his moral leadership of the Verein (*The Jew in the Modern World*, 220, note 2). Waszek notes the salient role that Gans's failure to secure an academic appointment played in the dissolution of the Verein and aptly notes: "The integration through *Bildung* and *Wissenschaft* that the Verein had striven after presumed political parameters that did not obtain, or that had revealed themselves to be illusions" ("'Wissenschaft und Liebe zu den Seinen,'" 84). As Waszek notes in another context, the stipendium that Gans accepted was contingent on his agreement, as stipulated by Minister von Altenstein in a letter to Gans of June 6, 1823, to seek a career from which he would not be impeded by his "personal circumstances" (*persönliches Verhältniß*); see Waszek, "Vorwort," 17–18. Gans received this letter from von Altenstein two months after he delivered his final address to the Verein; at that time his Hegelianism was still defiant, not yet compromised.

127. The correspondence continued, eventually only sporadically, until October 1834, shortly before Moser's untimely death. See Klaus Briegleb's illuminating discussions of the correspondence in "'Jeder Reiche ist ein Judas Ischariot!'" and *Bei den Wassern Babels*, 31–47. Adolf Strodtmann's analysis of the Wohlwill-Moser correspondence and Hegel's place in it is still worthwhile, if obviously dated (*H. Heine's Leben und Werke*, 1:263–66). See also Albert Friedlander, "The Wohlwill-Moser Correspondence" (hereafter AF). The typescript of the complete correspondence (correspondence between Moses Moser and Immanuel Wolf-Wohlwill, typescript, Leo Baeck Foundation, New York [hereafter WM]) is less widely available than Friedlander's article, which quotes extensively from it. Thus, in addition to the page number in the typescript, I also give a page number in Friedlander's article whenever the passage in question can be found there.

128. The strained relationship between the Berlin Hegelians and the Hamburg businessmen is evident, for example, in Gans's letters (cosigned by Moser) to Wohlwill of December 23, 1822, and April 22, 1823, and in Gans's final presidential address to the Verein. Briegleb

illuminates the culture clash that ensued when the Berlin Verein tried, via Wohlwill, to send, in Briegelb's subheading, "Hegel nach Hamburg!" ("'Jeder Reiche ist ein Judas Ischariot!'" and *Bei den Wassern Babels*, 31–47). On the Hamburg Temple, see Michael Meyer, *Response to Modernity*, 53–61.

129. Briegleb, *Bei den Wassern Babels*, 36.

130. MW, 3; AF, 286. The Schlachterstrasse was the location of the Hamburg Reform Temple.

131. MW, 16; AF, 289.

132. WM, 17; AF, 289.

133. WM, 16; AF, 289.

134. WM, 20; AF, 292. In the sentence beginning "The *Weltgeist*," I take *sagen* in the typescript to be a typographical error for *sorgen*.

135. WM, 21; AF 292.

136. WM, 96.

137. Ibid., 27. Wohlwill had voiced a similar complaint in a letter of April 13 (ibid., 11).

138. Ibid. 29.

139. Ibid.

140. Ibid., 23.

141. Ibid., 32.

142. Ibid., 33.

143. Ibid.

144. Ibid., 36.

145. Ibid., 37.

146. Ibid., 38.

147. Ibid.

148. Ibid., 37–38.

149. In a frequently cited passage from a letter to Moser of May 23, 1823, Heine describes a related experience of trying to awaken as an individual from Hegelian dreams—or, in this case, a Hegelian nightmare. Heine relates a nightmare in which Moser, much as he admonishes Wohlwill to subordinate his subjectivity to a Hegelian conception of universal spirit, tells Heine not to take his subjective feelings too seriously since he is, after all, only a Hegelian idea. In the dream Moser, Gans, and Marcus marshal Hegelian support for their position, but Heine rages against the terrifying loss of subjective integrity it implies (*Säkularausgabe*, 20:86).

150. WM, 41; AF, 293.

151. WM, 41; AF, 294.

152. WM, 41; AF, 294.

153. WM, 45.

154. Ibid.

155. Ibid., 49.

156. Ibid.

157. For example, Moser's tongue-in-cheek mythology of Wolf/Wolwill's existence—a comical *Lebenslauf* of a Jewish Hegelian—in his letter of May 1825 (dated Berlin, the 40th Omer 5585) (ibid., 67–70): "An old passport says that this mystical being was circumcised in Herzgerode under the name Immanuel Wolf; then I recall frequently having seen him as a pupil [*Klosterschüler*] in the little living room of List's [residence] at Burgstrasse 25; and

when he thereupon had grown up to be a Hegelian he achieved being-other than himself [*da gelangte er zum Andersseyn seiner selbst*] and became Immanuel Wohlwill, teacher at the Freischule, Candidate in Brunnenstrasse Theology [*Candidat der Brunnenstrasssen Theologie*] and well-loved Philistine in Hamburg" (ibid., 68). Moser returns to his Wolf/Wohlwill "mythology" in his letter of July 25, 1825 (ibid., 75–76).

158. Ibid., 55.

159. WM, 57; AF, 296.

160. WM, 57; AF, 296. Der Große Burstah is a street in central Hamburg.

161. WM, 58; AF, 297.

162. WM, 58; AF, 297.

163. WM, 58; AF, 297.

164. WM, 58; AF, 297.

165. WM, 58; AF, 297.

166. WM, 58; AF, 297.

167. WM, 60–61.

168. Ibid., 61.

169. Ibid., 61–62.

170. Ibid., 80.

171. Ibid.

172. In addition to Wohlwill's request in his letter of May 6, 1826, that Moser extend a greeting to "the Absolute," and Moser's Hegel-inspired mythological *Lebenslauf* of Wolf/Wohlwill, Moser's New Year's letter to Wohlwill on December 31, 1831, provides a further instance of Hegelian humor in the correspondence. Moser closes the letter with Hegelian jokes. After the brief hope of the July 1830 Revolution, world history is once again in arrears. The Hegelian accountant, however, does not see world history nearing bankruptcy but predicts that Rothschild will continue lending to it on the power of its *Wechsel*, a double-entendre suggesting both a bill of exchange and the possibility of historical change. Moser also says he is confident that the newly married Wohlwill, given his Hegelian orientation, will not remain mired in "dualism" with his wife—that is, he will instead get busy making babies. See WM, 124.

173. WM, 70.

174. Ibid., 71. The Latin phrases mean: "He has converted Hegel not only into the humors and blood but also into the skin and the mouth," and "transgression in the region of unbelief."

175. Ibid., 122.

176. Ibid., 114.

177. Ibid., 120.

178. Ibid., 137.

179. Ibid., 105.

180. Ibid., 106.

4. Marx's "Real Jews" between Volk *and Proletariat*

1. In his 1838 *Prolegomena to a Historiosophy* (*Prolegomena zur Historiosophie*) August von Cieszkowski sought to redirect Hegelian thought away from Hegel's reflection on the past toward a shaping of the future via social "praxis," a usage of Cieszkowski's coin-

age. Ludwig Feuerbach's anthropological critique of Christianity in his 1841 *The Essence of Christianity*—and especially in the revised 1843 edition with its trenchant preface—was highly influential, as was his critique of speculative abstraction in "Provisional Theses for the Reformation of Philosophy" (1842) and *Principles of the Philosophy of the Future* (1843). The need to move from merely contemplative ideas and concepts to deeds that would actively shape future society and politics are major themes of Moses Hess's *Die Europäische Triarchie* (1841; in *Philosophische und sozialistische Schriften 1837–1850*) and "The Philosophy of the Act" (1843), among other essays. In "A Self-Critique of Liberalism" (January, 1843), Arnold Ruge held that "nothing but critique remains to us for making a beginning of praxis" ("A Self-Critique of Liberalism," 239; for the German original, see "Eine Selbstkritik des Liberalismus," *Deutsche Jahrbücher*, January 2, 1843), and that "theory's purpose is theory's praxis" ("Eine Selbstkritik des Liberalismus," *Deutsche Jahrbücher*, January 4, 1843), among many similar sentiments. Rolland Lutz's wry observation is worth bearing in mind, however, that the Young Hegelian antiphilosophical philosophers "got no further than the transition from a philosophy of contemplation to thoughts about action; 'philosophy of action' would imply too much" ("The 'New Left' of Restoration Germany," 242). The early Marx's most cited articulation of the need to overcome philosophy is in the last of his "Theses on Feuerbach," but the quest to realize philosophy was a recurrent theme in his thought well before that. In a July 1842 *Rheinische Zeitung* article in response to an editorial by Karl Hermes, editor of the conservative *Kölnische Zeitung*—in which Hermes had denounced the *Rheinische Zeitung* as an enemy of the state for attacking Christianity and called on the government to prohibit discussion of religion and philosophy in the press—Marx writes of the need for philosophy to enter "into contact and interaction with the real world not only inwardly, through its content, but also externally, through its appearance [*Erscheinung*]" (Karl Marx and Friedrich Engels, *Werke* [hereafter MEW], 1:98). On Hermes's polemic with the *Rheinische Zeitung*, see Auguste Cornu, *Karl Marx und Friedrich Engels*, 1:277. On Hermes's writings on the Jewish Question and how they set the stage for Bauer's and Marx's contributions to that debate, see Julius Carlebach, *Karl Marx and the Radical Critique of Judaism*, 82–85. For a philosophical analyis of Marx's and Feuerbach's attempt to "leave philosophy," see Daniel Brudney, *Marx's Attempt to Leave Philosophy*.

2. Shlomo Avineri goes so far as to claim that "the various economic, social and historical studies undertaken by Marx are but a corollary of the conclusions he drew from his immanent critique of Hegel's political philosophy" (*The Social and Political Thought of Karl Marx*, 5). Dieter Henrich makes a similar point ("Marx als Schüler Hegels," 199).

3. Karl Marx and Friedrich Engels, *Collected Works* (hereafter MECW), 1:18.

4. Warren Breckman underscores the critique of the limitations of subjective freedom, which contends with the affirmation of free self-consciousness generally seen to be at the heart of Marx's dissertation. He demonstrates Feuerbach's significant influence on Marx even in this early work and highlights how Feuerbach's analysis (in his 1838 "Critique of Positive Philosophy") of "the process of hypostatization, whereby human essence has been given a distorted representation in the form of the atomized, single person," shaped Marx's analysis of atomism (Breckman, *Marx, the Young Hegelians, and the Origins of Radical Social Theory: Dethroning the Self* (hereafter DS), 268).

5. The essay was published in the famous 1843 volume edited by the radical poet Georg Herwegh, *Einundzwanzig Bogen aus der Schweiz* (Twenty-one sheets from Switzerland).

6. For a survey of the many responses to Bauer's writings on the Jewish Question by Jewish and non-Jewish authors, see Nathan Rotenstreich, "For and against Emancipation."

7. On the proposed law to relegate Jews to a separate corporation and the controversy that ensued, see Carlebach, *Karl Marx and the Radical Critique of Judaism*, 67–69; Edmund Silberner, *Moses Hess*, 110; and Karl Marx and Friedrich Engels, *Gesamtausgabe* (hereafter MEGA), section 2, 1 (part 2): 648.

8. See Silberner, *Moses Hess*, 106.

9. Ibid., 100.

10. Marx and Engels, MECW, 1:391–92 As I discuss below, Bauer originally submitted *Die Judenfrage* to the *Rheinische Zeitung*, but it was rejected by the censor. Hermes, editor of the rival *Kölnische Zeitung* (see note 1), had published a number of articles opposing Jewish emancipation.

11. Written in 1845–46 in Brussels, *The German Ideology* was not published until the twentieth century. The chapter on Feuerbach appeared in the 1920s, the work in its entirety in 1932.

12. Wendy Brown, for example, leans heavily on Marx's critique of the depoliticization of social differences and the illusory nature of political rights in *States of Injury*, chapter 5, especially 100–103, and "Rights and Identity in Late Modernity," especially 90–109.

13. Cornu is an important example of this tendency; see *Karl Marx und Friedrich Engels*, 1:462–80).

14. Carlebach (*Karl Marx and the Radical Critique of Judaism*, 165) describes as "the misfortune of the Jews" the fact that the substantive ideas of part 1 of Marx's "Zur Judenfrage" (hereafter ZJ1) were developed under the title "On the Jewish Question," thereby lending credence to the "incomparably weaker and less convincing" part 2 of Marx's "Zur Judenfrage" (hereafter ZJ2). Elisabeth de Fontenay reads ZJ2 as merely the "verification" and "illustration" of the thesis elaborated in ZJ1 (*Les Figures juives de Marx,* 26). See also David McLellan, *Marx before Marxism,* 141–42; and Lawrence Simon's headnote in Marx, *Selected Writings*, 2.

15. See, for example, Sander Gilman, *Jewish Self-Hatred*, 188–208; Arnold Künzli, *Karl Marx: Eine Psychographie*, 207; Hyam Maccoby, *Antisemitism and Modernity*, 63–72; Paul Rose, *Revolutionary Antisemitism in Germany from Kant to Wagner* (hereafter RA), 296–305; Edmund Silberner, "Was Marx an Anti-Semite?"; Robert Wistrich, *Revolutionary Jews from Marx to Trotsky*, chapter 1 (Wistrich refers to Marx's self-hatred on 34, 35, 37, and 43). For two works that each convincingly contest the purported antisemitism of Marx's "Zur Judenfrage," see David Leopold, *The Young Karl Marx*, 163–80; and Thomas Haury's lucid contextualization of Bauer's and Marx's writings on the Jewish Question in "*Zur Judenfrage*."

16. Jay Geller places Marx's rhetoric in "Zur Judenfrage" in a much wider context of rhetorical signifiers in Marx's *oeuvre* that, he argues, bear Jewish connotations (*The Other Jewish Question*, chapter 6).

17. On socialist misreadings and uses and abuses of Marx's "Zur Judenfrage," see chapters 2 and 3, respectively, of Lars Fischer, *The Socialist Response to Antisemitism in Imperial Germany*. Fischer argues compellingly that "Socialists' preconceptions regarding 'the Jews' clearly did shape their understanding of 'Zur Judenfrage,' but 'Zur Judenfrage' in no way shaped their stance *vis-à-vis* 'the Jews,' which would have been no different had 'Zur Judenfrage' never been written" (ibid., 39).

18. See Gilman, *Jewish Self-Hatred*, 188–208.

19. Silberner ("Was Marx an Anti-Semite?") documents Marx's negative remarks about Jews in private correspondence and articles about the banking crisis of the 1850s.

20. On Marx's conception of work as a moral and emancipatory force in history, see Axel Honneth, "Work and Instrumental Action."

21. In two seminal works of 1842 and 1843, "Provisional Theses for the Reformation of Philosophy" and *Principles of the Philosophy of the Future*, Feuerbach forcefully critiqued Hegel's speculative philosophy as the last refuge of theology. David McLellan argues that these texts had an even greater influence on Marx than Feuerbach's *Das Wesen des Christentums* (*The Young Hegelians and Karl Marx* (hereafter YHKM), 101–13).

22. See Avineri, *The Social and Political Thought of Karl Marx*, 31–40; and Richard Hunt, *The Political Ideas of Marx and Engels*, 59–84.

23. Marx writes: "The family and civil society are the preconditions of the state; they are the true agents; but in speculative philosophy it is the reverse. When the Idea is subjectivized the real subjects—civil society, the family, 'circumstances, caprice etc.'—are all transformed into *unreal* objective moments of the Idea referring to different things," (Karl Marx, *Early Writings* (hereafter KMEW), 62; Marx and Engels, MEW, 1:206).

24. On the importance of personal hypostatization in Marx's Kreuznach *Kritik*, see Breckman, DS, 284–91.

25. See Leopold, *The Young Karl Marx*, chapter 2 (especially 47–56 and 74–82) for a lucid account of what Marx considered Hegel's logical mysticism—his method, among other operations, of subsuming empirical entities under a priori logical categories and misidentifying allegorical connections between such categories and their real embodiments as necessary ones.

26. Marx, KMEW, 81; Marx and Engels, MEW, 1:225.

27. In his letter of August 11, 1844, Marx, identifying himself as a socialist and a communist (the distinction between these terms was still very fluid), conveys to Feuerbach how he understands the philosopher's theory of species-being as a theory of society: "[In your *Philosophie der Zukunft* and *Wesen des Glaubens*,] you have provided—I don't know whether intentionally—a philosophical basis for socialism and the Communists have immediately understood them in this way. The unity of man with man, which is based on the real differences between men, the concept of the human species brought down from the heaven of abstraction to the real earth, what is this but the concept of *society*!" (Marx and Engels, MECW, 3:354).

28. Marx, KMEW, 85; Marx and Engels, MEW, 1:229.

29. Marx, KMEW, 148; Marx and Engels, MEW, 1:285.

30. Marx, KMEW, 149; Marx and Engels, MEW, 1:287.

31. See, for example, Georg Wilhelm Friedrich Hegel, *Philosophie des Rechts*, paragraphs (§) 65–66.

32. Ibid., § 306.

33. Ibid., § 307.

34. Marx KMEW, 168–69; Marx and Engels, MEW, 1:305.

35. Marx, KMEW, 169; Marx and Engels, MEW, 1:306.

36. Marx, KMEW, 170; Marx and Engels, MEW,1:306–7.

37. Marx, KMEW, 172–73; Marx and Engels, MEW, 1:308–9.

38. Marx, KMEW, 174; Marx and Engels, MEW, 1:310.

39. Marx, KMEW, 174 (translation modified); Marx and Engels, MEW, 1:310.

40. Karl Marx and Friedrich Engels, *The Communist Manifesto*, 65.

41. Marx, KMEW, 187; Marx and Engels, MEW, 1:323.

42. On Marx's Feuerbachian privileging of the agency of consciousness during the period of the Kreuznach *Kritik*, see Breckman, DS, 285. This privileging of consciousness also underpins Marx's championing of the universal franchise as the way to overcome the split between society and state and realize "true democracy" (see KMEW, 190–91; Marx and Engels, MEW, 1:326–27). Hunt's point that Marx may have had in mind a very active form of political involvement when he envisioned universal suffrage as the cure for the split between society and state is well taken (*The Political Ideas*, 78–84). However, even though Marx obviously means something radically different when he calls for "universal suffrage" than the sort of political participation characteristic of modern liberal democracies such as the United States (in the *Kritik*, Marx sees no essential difference between the latter, "the republic," and Prussian monarchy [KWEW, 88–90; Marx and Engels, MEW, 1:231–33]), this cure nonetheless privileges the deliberative act of voting as the transformative, revolutionary act par excellence.

43. Marx, KMEW 87; Marx and Engels, MEW, 1:231.

44. Andrew Chitty, "The Basis of the State in the Marx of 1842," 233.

45. Ibid.

46. Chitty locates the beginnings of Marx's substantive turn away from Hegel's "expressivist" conception of the state in the "vitalist" moments in his journalism of late 1842, when Marx invokes "life forces" as a productive agent. Provocatively, Chitty sees a structural analogy between Marx's adherence to an expressivist model of the state (that is, the constitution as the articulated expression of the free, rational essence of the state), and Marx's post-1845 theory of social labor and "social relations of production" (quoted in ibid., 237). Thus Chitty sees Marx's late-1842 "vitalist" conception as both the beginning of his materialist turn and as a vantage point from which to discern a lingering Hegelianism in the post-1845 theory. Possibly due to constraints of space, Chitty moves from Marx's use of "life forces" in late 1842 to his theory of social labor in 1845 without commenting on Marx's attempts to conceptualize production in the two years between ("The Basis of the State," 234–39).

47. Marx's analysis of Prussian society as fractured into different interest groups (chiefly the estates) also makes plain the ideality of his conception of the *Volk*, whose universality he opposes to these narrow entities. See, among other articles, Marx, "Verhandlungen des 6. rheinischen Landtags: Debatten über das Holzdiebstahlsgesetz," October–November, 1842 (Marx and Engels, MEW, 1:109–47); "On the Commissions of the Estates in Prussia," December 1842 (Marx and Engels, MECW, 1:292–306); and "Rechtfertigung des Korrespondenten von Mosel," January 1843 (Marx and Engels, MEW, 1:172–99).

48. Ruge ended "A Self-Critique of Liberalism" (1843) with a call to replace liberalism with democratism by raising the people's consciousness. In his 1843 correspondence with Ruge, published in the *Deutsch-französische Jahrbücher*, Marx concurs with him about the primacy of consciousness-raising. In "Zur Judenfrage," and more emphatically in "Einleitung" and his August 1844 polemic against Ruge, "Critical Marginal Notes on the Article 'The King of Prussia and Social Reform. By a Prussian,'" Marx had begun to reverse his strategy of improving human misery through consciousness-raising and had begun to ide-

alize abject groups (for example, the proletariat in "Einleitung" and the Silesian weavers in "Critical Marginal Notes") as showing the way out of impotent philosophical critique toward real social transformation. Consciousness continues to play a role in Marx's theorization of this transformation only as an alternative to—indeed, as a reversal of—what in his 1844 Paris manuscripts Marx lampoons as "the spiritual idolatry of *'self-consciousness'* and *'mind'*" of the "theological critic" (Marx and Engels, *Economic and Philosophic Manuscripts of 1844*, 17). As Hunt aptly observes, "The crucial point is that for Marx, consciousness would come to the proletariat not *only*, or even *necessarily*, from the outside, from intellectuals like himself. It would emerge from the workers' own spontaneous efforts to cope with the conditions in which they found themselves" (*The Political Ideas*, 91). In other words, Marx moves from affirming the need to educate and raise the consciousness of the abject animal masses to exploiting proletarian consciousness as a corrective to the abstract consciousness of the theoretician. The Hegelian and Young Hegelian overprivileging of the agency of consciousness (and pure thought and philosophy) is a significant target of the *Economic and Philosophic Manuscripts of 1844* (see, in particular, "Preface" and "Critique of the Hegelian Dialectic and Philosophy as a Whole"), and a mainstay of Marx and Engels's polemic against Bauer's *kritische Kritik* in *Die heilige Familie*.

49. Marx, KMEW, 192; Marx and Engels, MEW, 1:327.

50. Ruge contributed three letters to this epistolary exchange, and Feuerbach and Mikhail Bakunin wrote one letter each.

51. Marx and Engels, MECW, 3:134; and MEW, 1:338.

52. Marx and Engels, MECW, 3:137–38 (translation modified); and MEW, 1:339–40.

53. Marx and Engels, MECW, 3:140; and MEW, 1:341. It is also crucial to bear in mind that in 1842–43 the authorities made continuing to publish in Germany virtually impossible for these dissidents.

54. Thus Marx's advocacy of politcs here should not be confused with support for the sort of politics as a realm apart that he critiques in the Kreuznach *Kritik* and "Zur Judenfrage." The issue is not a complete reversal but rather of a rethinking of the relationship between materiality and agency. Increasingly, Marx's faith in the expressivist model, in which rationality exists somewhere (for example, in the latent will of the *Volk*) ready to be realized, yields to greater concern for the material agents of social revolution. Marx's December 1842 article "On the Commissions of the Estates in Prussia," for example, demonstrates how he at this point continues to define active agency (and the will of the *Volk*) as spiritual, in contrast to the objective material world. He argues that the state must be the people's active "self-representation" and must permeate all aspects of life (he refers to "nature"); but he also insists that "only spiritual forces" are universal and political, whereas matter and material things are antithetical to the principle of the state (Marx and Engels, MECW, 1:305–6).

55. Marx's contrast between the world of politics and the animal world is consistent with his frequent use of what he termed "animal law" as a foil for true human rationality and justice in his 1842 political journalism. Significant examples of Marx's critique of the reign of brutal, arbitrary "animal law" can be found in his August 1842 broadside against Gustav Hugo as the author of the ur-text of the historical school ("Das philosophische Manifest der historischen Rechtschule," in Marx and Engels, MEW, 1:78–85) and his famous article of October–November 1842 on "Debatten über das Holzdiebstahlsgesetz" in the Rhenish parliament (ibid., 1:109–47), among other essays.

56. Marx and Engels, MECW, 3:138; and MEW, 1:340.

57. Marx and Engels, MECW, 3:139; and MEW, 1:340.

58. Marx and Engels, MECW, 3:140; and MEW, 1:342.

59. Cornu's reading of this letter as Marx's first, if clumsy [*unbeholfen*], articulation of his "Auffasung vom Kommunismus" exemplifies this sort of retrospective smoothing out of Marx's development (*Karl Marx und Friedrich Engels*, 1:448–49).

60. Marx and Engels, MECW, 3:141; and MEW, 1:342.

61. Marx and Engels, MECW, 3:141 (translation modified); and MEW, 1: 342–43.

62. Marx and Engels, MECW, 3:187; and MEW, 1:391.

63. Marx and Engels, MECW, 3:186; and MEW, 1:390.

64. The destitute wood collectors in Marx's "Debatten über das Holzdiebstahlsgesetz" anticipate the structural position of the proletariat of "Einleitung" but also highlight how the latter work breaks with Marx's conceptual model of 1842. Marx locates the wood collectors' social position outside German civil society structured in terms of particular interests—that is, they belong to a class that has no interests. In keeping with his privileging of the agency of human reason in 1842, however, he concentrates on the relationship the destitute have with human rationality and justice. The almost umbilical link that the destitute maintain to cosmic justice—Marx's rather mystical view of how they understand nature to provide a measure of cosmic justice where human justice has failed—is valid, in Marx's view, because it asserts, obscurely, the legitimacy of true human justice waiting to be fulfilled. Thus when the privileged appeal to customary rights, they reason within—appeal to—the animal logic of the reigning system of privilege; when the destitute appeal to their customary rights, in contrast, they glimpse, however instinctually, a truly human justice beyond it. In his empathetic defense of the vulnerable wood collectors, in other words, Marx argues that they obscurely intimate a truer form of human reason and justice than the arbitrary and brutal logic that defines the civil society from which they are excluded. In this, the wood collectors remain squarely within Marx's idealist model of the state as the realization of human reason.

65. On Bauer's contributions to the *Rheinische Zeitung* in the first half of 1842, see Hans-Martin Sass, "Bruno Bauers Idee der 'Rheinischen Zeitung'"; and Douglas Moggach, *The Philosophy and Politics of Bruno Bauer* (hereafter PP), 126–28. Moggach notes how Bauer sought to "crystallize the oppositional consciousness and to undercut the possibility of compromise," and how his stance led to a conflict with Marx in late 1842 over the direction of the *Rheinische Zeitung* (ibid., 127–28). McLellan (YHKM, 74–75) downplays the break between Marx and Bauer at this time. Although Marx continued to read Bauer with interest throughout 1842 and 1843, he took issue with Bauer's intellectual posture beginning in late 1842.

66. Marx and Engels, MEW 27:409–10.

67. Ibid., 27:410.

68. Ibid., 27:412.

69. Ibid.

70. In his letter to Ruge of November 30, 1842, Marx alludes only in passing to Bruno Bauer and does not single him out as an exception to his harsh criticism. Bauer's essay "Die Judenfrage" had just appeared in Ruge's *Deutsche Jahbücher* (November 17–26, 1842).

71. Karl Marx, *Karl Marx: Early Texts*, 60 (translation modified); Marx and Engels, MEW, 27:418.

72. A *Notiz* in the *Rheinische Zeitung* of November 29, 1842 (three days after the last

installment of Bauer's "Die Judenfrage" in *Deutsche Jahrbücher*) alludes to Ruge's and Herwegh's criticism of the *Freien*. It states in part: "*Herwegh* and *Ruge* found that the 'Freien,' through their political romanticism, obsession with genius [*Geniesucht*] and gasconade, compromised the cause and the party of freedom" (Marx and Engels, MEW, 27:665, note 333).

73. Ruge, *Briefwechsel und Tagebuchblätter*, 290–91.

74. Moggach, PP, 165.

75. On Bauer's vision of German republicanism in *Die gute Sache*, see ibid., 120–25.

76. Ibid., 145.

77. Bruno Bauer, *Feldzüge der reinen Kritik*, 271.

78. Quoted in Gustaaf A. van den Bergh van Eysinga, "Het Jodenvraagstuk," 29–30.

79. See ibid., 30.

80. Quoted in ibid.

81. Bauer, *Feldzüge der reinen Kritik*, 255. Sass does not mention that this letter accompanied Bauer's *Die Judenfrage*.

82. In *Die Posaune des jüngsten Gerichts über Hegel: Den Atheisten und Antichristen. Ein Ultimatum* (1841); see Moggach, PP, chapter 5. Moggach notes that Bauer's articles of summer 1842 were particularly devoted to critiquing reformism and exacerbating conflict (ibid., 243, note 72). *Die Judenfrage* was a major part of Bauer's theoretical and tactical antipragmatic turn in this period.

83. Moggach, PP, 146.

84. In his meticulous study of Bauer's *Vormärz* republicanism, Moggach refutes charges that Bauer was interested only in political emancipation and not in social transformation, and that Bauer believed ideas alone could transform the world and so did not theorize the interaction between self-consciousness and objective reality, including social institutions. Maggoch underscores how Bauer's dialectic of infinite self-consciousness involves a relationship between the subjective and objective: from an analysis of the trajectory of history, self-consciousness discerns the trajectory of human freedom and then acts on the world to bring it more into harmony with the dictates of free human rationality. Since no positivity can halt the movement of infinite free self-consciousness, this process is endless in principle (see ibid., especially 112–13). Even in his consistently generous reading of Bauer, however, Moggach acknowledges both the nebulousness of the connection Bauer posits between the subjective and objective sides of his model and the arrogance of his writings of the period, beginning with his works on the Jewish Question and continuing through at least his 1844 contributions to the *Allgemeine Literatur-Zeitung*. Bauer consistently conceives of real social transformation as the realization of the agency of self-consciousness. Historical agency embodied in social reality amounts, for Bauer, to heteronomy. Thus at the heart of his critique of socialism (for example, in "Die Gattung und die Masse" of 1844) is the view that the proletariat pursues not universal but particular, and therefore heteronymous, interests.

85. Hans-Martin Sass, "Nachwort," in Bauer, *Feldzüge der reinen Kritik*, 255–56.

86. On Bauer's oppositional bifurcation of the *Volk* into *Volk* and *Masse* (the brute embodiment of positivity, particularity, materiality), see Moggach, PP, 136 and 151–54. On the evolution of Bauer's concept of "the masses," "massiness," and so forth, see ibid., 158–63.

87. See Bruno Bauer, review of *Die Geschichte des Lebens Jesu*. For Bauer's equation of the *Volk* and truth, see ibid., 185. For Marx's comment that "Bauer on Ammon is exquisite," see his letter to Ruge of March 13, 1843 (Marx and Engels, MEW, 27: 417).

88. Bruno Bauer, *Die Judenfrage* (hereafter JF), 56.

89. Ibid.

90. Ibid.

91. One can only assume that Marx was familiar with Bauer's December 1843 reply to critics of his two essays on the Jewish Question when Marx wrote ZJ2, though he did not engage this text by Bauer explicitly until *Die heilige Familie.*

92. Bauer, "Neueste Schriften über die Judenfrage" (1843). Bauer's letter to Ruge quoted above anticipates this opposition between the *Volk*, which Bauer aspires to galvanize, and the many enemies he wishes merely to antagonize—that is, the intellectually mediocre *Judenfreunde*, whom he would soon relegate to the ranks of *die Masse*. Bauer continued to welcome new enemies. In a further response to critics of his writings on the Jewish Question, he wrote gleefully of Abraham Geiger's criticims of his *Die Judenfrage*: "The number of our opponents has grown. We congratulate ourselves!" ("Neueste Schriften über die Judenfrage" [1844], 14).

93. Bauer, for example, claims that Jewish dietary laws would inevitably belie Jews' "most beautiful words [*Reden*] about equality with others and about humanity" by declaring, in practice, that non-Jews are not the Jew's "equal, not fellow human beings [*Mit-Menschen*]." Yet his characterization of Jewish dietary laws only reinforces his argument about the linguistic impossibity of a Jew's expressing a wish to transcend particularism and join a wider collectivity: dietary practices would betray Jews' irremediable particularism even if the Jew "wished, although this is not possible, to be vigilant in his language and hold at bay all the locutions that give the lie to his assurances—but once again! It is not possible!" (JF, 30).

94. For David Leopold's illuminating commentary on Bauer's two essays on the Jewish Question, see "The Hegelian Antisemitism of Bruno Bauer." On this particular tension in Bauer's argument, see ibid., 192.

95. Douglas Moggach, "Republican Rigorism and Emancipation in Bruno Bauer," 130–33.

96. In Moggach's apt wording, "Bauer fuses teleology and freedom and situates them in the rational subject, in opposition to the sphere of positive, irrational institutions" (PP, 112). Bauer's form of Hegelianized (historicized) Kantian autonomous moral subjectivity indeed defines the rational—that is, the human—subject in terms of its relationship to a perceived teleological development of free self-consciousness in history. Subject positions deemed to embody and propel the teleological development of human freedom possess true human being. Subjectivities deemed to be particular (or "immediate") subordinate free consciousness to matter and thus lack the autonomous universality that is constitutive of humanity itself. Bauer defines rational subjectivity as a fusion of historical teleology and freedom, not only in contrast to "irrational institutions," then, but also to other subjects—such as the "*geschichtswidrigen*" Jews (Bauer, JF, 34).

97. Leopold aptly notes of Bauer's argument: "That the Jews lack 'an ability to develop with history' is no trivial failing for a Hegelian . . . [because] the historical rationale for the existence of an entity is its continued contribution to that progress" ("The Hegelian Antisemitism of Bruno Bauer," 187). For this reason, as Leopold also notes, Bauer deems Jewish tenacity deplorable, not admirable (ibid., 188).

98. Bauer, JF, 61.

99. According to Bauer's logic of sacrifice (see, for example, JF, 34–35 and 61, and "Die Fähigkeit," 64 and 71), Christians must sacrifice the nonhuman part of themselves—the

nonessential part—so that *their* human essence can prevail. In contrast, Jews must sacrifice themselves so that *humanity*—to which Jews do not contribute—can prevail: "[The Jew must] renounce himself utterly and completely and negate the Jew [*sich ganz und gar aufgeben und den Juden verneinen*]" ("Die "Die Fähigkeit der heutigen Juden und Christen," 71). This is also why Bauer says that Christians, when they become secular, give humanity everything (they profer humanity itself), whereas Jews give humanity nothing (they have no humanity to give); see ibid., 65.

100. The thought that Jews could ultimately get something for nothing vexes Bauer considerably. He repeatedly fantasizes about parasitic Jews who take delight (*sich kitzeln*) at the prospect of cashing in on the heroic critical labor of people like him. See, for example, "Die Fähigkeit," 58–59.

101. Bauer, JF, 4.

102. Ibid., 33.

103. Ibid., 34.

104. Ibid.

105. Ibid.

106. For Bauer's assessment of Jewish law as "chimerical" and of the midrashic imagination and Talmud as mere dead sophistry, see ibid., 24–30. For remarks on Jewish practice as hypocritical, see, for example, ibid., 42–43. On this aspect of Bauer's argument, see Leopold, "The Hegelian Antisemitism of Bruno Bauer," 183–84.

107. On Bauer's conceptual indebtedness to Christianity even after he became its radical critic, see Jacob Katz, *From Prejudice to Destruction*, 169–79. Moses Hess attacks Bauer as "Christian" even in his atheism in "Die letzten Philosophen."

108. Bauer, JF, 23.

109. Bauer's Hegelian orientation thus rehearses, in historicized terms, the Kantian aporia regarding how to integrate Jewish heteronomy into a human community defined by its autonomy, which Fichte in 1793 could resolve only through a fantasy of Jewish decapitation. Moggach notes how influential Kantian moral philosophy remained for Bauer's understanding of human autonomy ("Republican Rigorism," 125–27; and PP, 112–13 and 148). Notwithstanding Moggach's valiant defense of Bauer's "republican rigorism," Bauer's "historically" arrived at definition of Jews as antithetical to the quintessentially human work of advancing infinite consciousness remains problematic for even the most rigorist definition of republicanism. Since Bauer defines Judaism as recalcitrance to universal values, the only sufficiently "rigorous" adjustment of Jewish interiority to universal values would be the obliteration of Judaism. The symmetry in Bauer's call for Christians to overcome Christianity is only apparent. To become human, Christians need only liberate the truth of their inner being, which is mystified, but not cancelled, in Christianity. Lacking such an inner human core, Jews are called on to obliterate not merely their misguided Jewishness, but their entire being. Anything that remains in a Jew—be it a (pseudo-)enlightend Jew, who abandons Jewish observance; a Reform Jew, who renounces Jewish peoplehood; or a Jew who understands his demand for rights as part of a universal campaign—remains for Bauer Jewish, and not human. Spinoza is the sole example, in Bauer's two essays on the Jewish Question, of a Jew who managed to leap out of Judaism into humanity. The thrust of Bauer's argument, however, constructs such a transformation as an ontological impossibility.

110. Bauer, "Die Fähigkeit," 59. Bauer's account of Judaism strongly echoes Feuerbach's

portrayal of Judaism as an egoistic cult and his view of the Jewish understanding of the Creation as the projection of a divine provider of natural needs. Judaism makes nature serve its needs but, unlike Christianity, fails to transcend natural limitation.

111. Ibid., 59–60.

112. Bauer asserts that Judaism wrongly imbues the trivial and mundane (*das Willkürliche, Zufällige*) with religious significance. This both evinces and perpetuates an inability to distinguish *Geist* from *Natur*, and the confinement of the Jewish essence [*Wesen*] within the most trivial and vulgarly material mundane objects (pots, household utensils, cloths, and ointment bowls). See JF, 37–38.

113. Bauer, "Die Fähigkeit," 60.

114. Ibid., 61.

115. Marx quotes and exploits Bauer's formulation that if the state ceases to privilege any religion, religion will eventually disappear (for Bauer's wording, see JF 66; Marx cites it Marx and Engels, MEW, 1:350). Yet the thrust of Bauer's argument is that unless individuals root out their particularist proclivities in a rigorous way—and religious egoism is for Bauer the "Urprivilegium" (see, for example, JF, 60)—their egoism will continue to corrode even formally secular and universalistic institutions (as occurred in France after the July Revolution, in Bauer's assessment). Bauer deems real transcendence of religious limitation a prerequisite not merely for narrow, formal political emancipation but also for substantial human emancipation. True human emancipation requires not only that the state, but also that individuals, have overcome religion. (On this point, see Leopold, "The Hegelian Antisemitism of Bruno Bauer," 191–92.) Moggach shows that Bauer frequently (including in JF) stressed the primacy of politics over religion, arguing that religion had lost its real force and was now only being propped up by the state to serve its own particularist interests. On how Bauer, *pace* Marx, also distinguished between political and human emancipation, and deemed not only political but also social transformation necessary, see Maggoch, PP, 145. In McLellan's view, too, Bauer, at the end of *Die Judenfrage*, does "with as much clarity as Marx ever achieved, precisely what Marx criticized him for omitting: he explains 'The religious servitude of citizens by their secular servitude' and 'transforms theological questions into secular ones'" (YHKM, 77). Rudi Waser (*Autonomie des Selbstbewußtseins,* 162–63) rightly notes a contradiction, however: Bauer claims both that secular differences have become more important than religious distinctions (for example, in JF, 96), and that religion is the generative "ur-privilege," of which all subsequent privileges are iterations (for example, in JF, 60).

116. On how Marx still lacked the tools of secular economic analysis he thought he was deploying in "Zur Judenfrage," see Breckman DS, 293–94. McLellan notes that Marx in his Kreuznach *Kritik* repeatedly "crosses out the term 'self-consciousness' which he had originally written and substitutes another term more evocative of practical realities" (YHKM, 75). McLellan interprets this as Marx's attempt to counter Bauer's privileging of self-consciousness.

117. Karl Marx, *Selected Writings* (hereafter KMSW), 10; Marx and Engels, MEW, 1:356.

118. Marx and Engels, MEW, 1:361.

119. Marx and Engels, MECW, 3:155. Implicit in ZJ1, this argument becomes explicit in Marx's revisiting of the Jewish Question (and Bauer's treatment of it) in *Die heilige Familie*. Pierre Birnbaum reads Marx's "Zur Judenfrage" as more antisemitic than Bauer's essays on the Jewish Question (see *Geography of Hope*, 50–61) and argues that Marx takes a stand for

Jewish emancipation only in the *Die heilige Familie*, and then only to score points against Bauer (*Geography of Hope*, 64). In fact, Marx argues expressly in ZJ1 that Jews deserve political emancipation: "If Bauer asks the Jews: Have you from your standpoint the right to want *political emancipation?* we ask the converse question: Does the standpoint of *political* emancipation give the right to demand from the Jew the abolition of Judaism and from man the abolition of religion?" (Marx and Engels, MECW, 3:150). Marx answers his own question with a resounding "no." He writes further of political emancipation that although it is "not the final form of human emancipation in general . . . it is the final form of human emancipation within the hitherto existing world order. It goes without saying that we are speaking here of real, practical emancipation" (ibid., 3:155). Marx says, then, that political emancipation is the highest form of liberation yet achieved in human history, and that Jews fully deserve it and should not have to give up their religion or particular identity as part of a quid pro quo for political rights. Paul Rose claims that "*On the Jewish Question* is in fact the foundation of an entirely secularized form of Jew-hatred far more systematic in its theory than the other revolutionary efforts of Bauer and company" (*Revolutionary Antisemitism in Germany from Kant to Wagner* [hereafter RA], 301–2). Rose refers to the uses a subsequent tradition of antisemitism on the Left made of Marx's text, but his statement also seems (it remains ambiguous) to see Marx's "Zur Judenfrage" itself—and not only its subsequent appropriations—as a "far more systematic" theory of Jew-hatred than Bauer's. On subsequent socialist abuses of Marx's text, see Fischer, *The Socialist Response*. For recent even-handed assessments of the antisemitism of Marx's essay, see Haury, "*Zur Judenfrage*," and Leopold, *The Young Karl Marx*, 163–80.

120. Marx and Engels, MEW, 1:352.

121. Marx and Engels, MECW, 3:151.

122. See Breckman, DS, 293–94.

123. Marx and Engels, MECW, 3:149.

124. Marx wrote in a third letter to Ruge published in the *Deutsch-französische Jahrbücher* (dated September 1843, when Marx was working on ZJ1): "The reform of consciousness consists *only* in making the world aware of its own consciousness, in awakening it out of its dream about itself, in *explaining* to it the meaning of its own actions. Our whole object can only be—as is also the case in Feuerbach's criticism of religion—to give religious and philosophical questions the form corresponding to man who has become conscious of himself" (Marx and Engels, MECW, 3:144; and MEW, 1:346). Marx seeks to reveal to the world the alienation of its consciousness in the political state in strict analogy to how Feuerbach reveals the alienation of consciousness in religion. He draws an ironic, but still telling, analogy between the aims of the *Deutsch-französische Jahrbücher* and Christian confession and mercy: "We can formulate the trend of our journal as being: self-clarification (critical philosophy) to be gained by the present time of its struggles and desires. This is a work for the world and for us. It can be only the work of united forces. It is a matter of a *confession* [*Beichte*], and nothing more. In order to secure remission of its sins, mankind has only to declare them for what they actually are" (Marx and Engels, MECW, 3:145; and MEW, 1:346). If Marx opens ZJ2 by deriding Bauer's model of emancipation as merely a *Bekenntis*—an emancipation of consciousness only—the same criticism is apposite for Marx's model in ZJ1. In Marx's ideological "confession" one comprehends and disavows the errors of mystified consciousness, and by this act freedom almost magically realizes itself: "It will then become evident that the

world has long dreamed of possessing something of which it has only to be conscious in order to possess it in reality" (Marx and Engels, MECW, 3:144; and MEW, 1:346).

125. Marx and Engels, MECW, 3:159; and MEW, 1:360.

126. McLellan (YHKM, 75–81) argues that Bauer's method of critique continued to serve as an important model for Marx in "Zur Judenfrage," "Einleitung," and even the 1844 Paris manuscripts.

127. See note 115 of this chapter.

128. Marx and Engels, MECW, 3:150; and MEW, 1:350–51.

129. Marx and Engels, MECW, 3:158–59; and MEW, 1:360.

130. Breckman, DS, 295.

131. Marx and Engels, MECW, 3:160; and MEW, 1:361.

132. In keeping with his ontological and historical schema, in which Jews engage in sophistry to avoid the dimly grasped knowledge that their existence had become chimerical and lacked all justification, Bauer frequently takes it on himself to explain the Jews' ontological nullity to the Jews themselves, who are inherently incapable of seeing it. For example, Bauer takes aim at "enlightened" Jews who "seem" on the verge of overcoming all that makes them Jews (and thus becoming worthy of citizenship), yet who ultimately betray their egoistic Jewish essence all the more starkly by wanting to be equal as Jews (JF, 28). For Bauer, anything Jews undertake as Jews bears witness to their immutable misanthropic essence. In Fischer's apt formulation, "the very existence of post-Biblical Judaism . . . contradicted the course of historical development. By maintaining its distinct existence, post-Biblical Judaism also amounted to an active revolt against the potential perfection of Biblical Judaism's perfectible elements and thus against its very essence. . . . Consequently, Jewry could not even provide a comprehensive account of its own essence" (*The Socialist Response*, 94). As Fischer discusses, Bauer found a satisfying account of the Jewish essence in Johann Andreas Eisenmenger's *Entdecktes Judenthum*!

133. To appreciate how fully Marx in ZJ1 rejects Bauer's argument that there is anything particularly Jewish about the contradiction between the demand for universal rights and continued particular existence, consider Marx's insistence that "for man as a bourgeois, 'life in the state' is 'only a semblance or a temporary exception to the essential and the rule' ["Die Fähigkeit," 57 (my addition)]. Of course, the *bourgeois* like the Jew, remains only sophistically in the sphere of political life, just as the *citoyen* only sophistically remains a Jew or a *bourgeois*. But this sophistry is not personal. It is the *sophistry of the political state itself.* The difference between the religious man and the citizen is the difference between the merchant and the citizen, between the day-laborer and the citizen, between the landowner and the citizen, between the *living individual* and the *citizen*. The contradiction in which the religious man finds himself with the political man is the same contradiction in which the *bourgeois* finds himself with the *citizen*, and the member of civil society with his *political lion's skin*" (Marx and Engels, MECW, 3:154; and MEW, 1:355). As so often in "Zur Judenfrage," Marx's rhetoric derives from Bauer's, even when Marx does not make this clear. The extent to which Marx disputes Bauer's identification of egoism as a particularly Jewish trait becomes evident when we compare Marx's language to the passage in Bauer's "Die Fähigkeit" to which Marx here responds. Bauer contends that Jews cannot be real citizens because their sensibility and allegiance as Jews will always trump their sensibility and allegiance as citizens. "Only sophistically, in appearance," Bauer argues, "would the Jew be able to remain a Jew in the life of the

state; mere appearance, if he wished to remain a Jew, would thus be the essential thing and carry away the victory, that is, his life in the state would only be appearance or a temporary exception to the essential and the rule" ("Die Fähigkeit," 57). When he quotes Bauer's text, Marx reframes it so that the criticism Bauer directs at Jews specifically illuminates the structural predicament in which Marx sees "man as bourgeois" caught generally. In Bauer's text it is specifically the Jew's "life in the state" that would be "only appearance or a temporary exception to the essential and the rule," the Jews' essence being inveterate egoism. In Marx's appropriation of Bauer's formulation, it is "man as a bourgeois" who for structural, not personal, reasons can maintain only a "sophistical" relation to the state. "Sophistry" is inherent in the dualistic structure of the political state itself. For Marx, there is nothing particularly Jewish about Jewish particularism.

134. Marx and Engels, MECW, 3:154; and MEW, 1:355.

135. Shlomo Na'aman notes that Marx's title "Zur Judenfrage" is accidental, determined only by the title of Bauer's *Die Judenfrage*, and that a title reflecting any of the topics Marx treats—the relationship between state and society, political and human emancipation, or the inherent egoism of human rights—would have been more apt (*Marxismus und Zionismus*, 51).

136. Marx and Engels, MECW, 3:157; and MEW, 1:359. Marx's paraphrase of Bauer (the sentence beginning "Bauer declares") implies that Bauer equates the "*Masse*" with the "*eigentlichen Volk*" ("*mit dem eigentlichen Volke, mit der Masse*"). On the contrary, however, Bauer uses the term "*Masse*" to describe the *uneigentliche Volk*, the *Nicht-Volk*, the *Volk* that has been atomized by the sovereign's illegitimate *Vermittler*, who falsely claim to represent it but in fact only fracture and divide it. At least three widely used English translations mistranslate "*mit dem eigentlichen Volke*" in Marx's faulty paraphrase of Bauer as "with his *own* people": KMSW, 12; Marx, *Marx: Early Political Writings* (hereafter EPW), 40; and *Karl Marx: Early Texts*, 98. (In the last of these three, McLellan adds an 'and' ["with his own people and the masses"] to distinguish "people" from "the masses," which is precisely the distinction that Marx collapses.) Gregor Benton and Rodney Livingstone translate the passage correctly (KMEW, 224). The translation in Marx and Engels, MECW, which I quote from here, makes the point possibly too emphatically ("with the people in the strict sense, with the masses") but correctly preserves Marx's error.

137. Marx and Engels, MECW, 3:157–58; and MEW, 1:359.

138. Bauer, JF, 108.

139. Marx and Engels, MECW, 3:158; and MEW, 1:359.

140. Marx acknowledges that Jacobin practice frequently required the sacrifice of the personal to the communal, but he submits that such practice was the exception and the articulated theoretical formulation of human rights was the rule. And even if one takes the practice as the rule, Marx adds, the question remains why the framers of human rights discourse nonetheless conceived and theorized man to be the egoistic individual (Marx and Engels, MECW, 3:165; and MEW, 1:367).

141. Marx and Engels, MECW, 3:164; and MEW, 1:366.

142. Moses Hess's critique of the limitations of the paradigm of rights to emerge from the French Revolution—in "Philosophie der Tat" and "Socialismus und Communismus" (in Hess, *Philosophische und sozialistische Schriften 1837–1850* [hereafter PSS], 210–26 and 197–209, respectively), both published in *Einundzwanzig Bogen aus der Schweiz* (1843)—was almost certainly an inspiration for Marx.

143. Marx writes: "As a result of this organization, the unity of the state, and also the consciousness, will and activity of this unity, the general power of the state, are likewise bound to appear as the particular affair of a ruler isolated from the people, and of his servants" (Marx and Engels, MECW, 3:166; and MEW, 1:368).

144. Marx and Engels, MECW, 3:166 (my interpellations); and MEW, 1:368.

145. Marx, KMEW, 235; Marx and Engels, MEW, 1:371.

146. Marx and Engels, MEW, 1:371.

147. Marx, KMSW, 20; Marx and Engels, MEW, 1:369.

148. Marx and Engels, MEW, 1:369–70.

149. Ibid, 371.

150. Marx and Engels, MECW, 3:169; and MEW, 1:372.

151. Marx, KMEW, 236; Marx and Engels, MEW, 1:372.

152. Marx and Engels, MEW, 1:376; Marx, EPW, 56 (translation modified).

153. Marx, KMSW, 23; Marx and Engels, MEW, 1:373.

154. It us unclear why Marx did not publish Hess's "Über das Geldwesen" (PSS, 329–48), though he may have been saving it for a later issue, of which there ultimately were none. Carlebach (*Karl Marx and the Radical Critique of Judaism*, 110–24) argues vigorously against the many scholars—including Shlomo Avineri, *Moses Hess*, 115 and 133; Auguste Cornu and Wolfgang Mönke, "Einleitung," xxvi, xxxvii, and xlvi; McLellan, YHKM, 155; Zvi Rosen, *Moses Hess und Karl Marx*, 137–58; Silberner, *Moses Hess*, 192; and Robert Tucker, *Philosophy and Myth in Karl Marx*, 111—who see considerable intellectual and rhetorical borrowing on Marx's part, especially from Hess's "Über das Geldwesen." The timeline at the heart of Carlebach's argument, according to which Marx completed "Zur Judenfrage" before departing for Paris and thus before reading Hess's essay, is belied by Marx and Engels, MEGA, section 2, 1 (part 2): 650–51, which dates Marx's writing of "Zur Judenfrage" to after his move to Paris (between, at the earliest, mid-October and, at the latest, mid-December 1843). As Julius Kovesi ("Moses Hess, Marx, and Money," 178) suggests, it is plausible that Marx could have written the short ZJ2 quickly after reading Hess's essay. Waser (*Autonomie des Selbstbewußtseins*, 190–94) likewise sees no evidence of Hess's influence in ZJ1 but strong evidence thereof in ZJ2, and he rightly contrasts the care (typical for Marx) in the elaboration of the argument and engagement with sources in ZJ1 with the brevity and lack of engagement with sources in ZJ2. Whatever the timing of Marx's reading of Hess's essay in relation to his writing of ZJ2, however, Hess had already articulated key aspects of Marx's argument in "Zur Judenfrage"—including bringing Feuerbach to bear on social life, the critique of a dualistic structure common to religion and politics, and the critique of the rights paradigm of the French Revolution—in "Philosophie der Tat" and "Socialismus und Communismus," both of which Marx had read with admiration before he wrote "Zur Judenfrage."

155. Hess, "On the Essence of Money," 190, 201; " Über das Geldwesen," PSS, 335, 343 On Hess's use of a metaphorics of blood, cannibalism, and human sacrifice, see P. Rose, RA, 313–16.

156. Hess, "On the Essence of Money," 203; " Über das Geldwesen," PSS, 345.

157. I analyze Hess's Spinozan critique of the institution of the modern sovereign individual in chapter 6. Clearly, a great deal in Hess's " Über das Geldwesen" pointed Marx in new directions. Its influence is evident on much of what Marx would soon go on to write,

such as his notes on James Mill and his famous remarks on alienated labor in the 1844 Paris manuscripts. On similarities between Hess's essay and Marx's 1844 manuscripts, see Carlebach, *Karl Marx and the Radical Critique of Judaism*, 120–22.

158. Enzo Traverso, *The Marxists and the Jewish Question*, 20. Breckman (DS, 292) and Hunt (*The Political Ideas*, 66) argue that productive forces and class relations do not become important for Marx until his collaboration with Engels in 1844.

159. For an analysis of the ambivalence regarding the direction of the causal vector Marx envisions in ZJ2 and the uneasy coexistence of materialism and idealism, see Jonathan Karp, *The Politics of Jewish Commerce*, 239–40 and 255–56.

160. Marx and Engels, MEW, 1:374.

161. Marx, KMSW, 24 (my interpellation); Marx and Engels, MEW, 1:374.

162. Marx, KMSW, 24 (translation modified); Marx and Engels, MEW, 1:374.

163. David Nirenberg aptly notes that the Jewish god of money is "commutative, infectious: money, the true god of Israel, makes all of its users Jewish" (*Anti-Judaism*, 437).

164. Marx and Engels, MEW, 1:374–75; Marx, EPW, 54 (translation modified).

165. This is an association that Freud explores in such essays as "Charakter und Analerotik" (Character and anal eroticism, 1908; in Freud, *Gesammelte Werke*, 7:203–9) and "Über Triebumsetzungen, insbesondere der Analerotik" (On the transformations of instinct, as exemplified in anal erotism, 1917; in *Gesammelte Werke*, 10:402–10).

166. In chapter 3 of "L'examen important de Milord Bolimbroke, ou le tombeau du fanatisme" (written in 1736), Voltaire asks: "Is it possible that God could have prescribed to the Jews the manner in which to go to the toilet in the desert yet hid from them the doctrine of a future life?" (*Oeuvres complètes*, 33:19). He adds in a footnote: "Dean Swift has said that according to the Pentateuch God took greater care of the derrière of the Jews than of their souls. See Deuteronomy Chapter XXIII and you will see that the dean indeed was right" (ibid.). Voltaire again quotes Deuteronomy 23 in *La Bible enfin expliqué* (203–4), but in a footnote there he attributes the witticism about God's concern for Jewish derrières to the English deist Anthony Collins: "The order that the Lord himself gives regarding how to answer the call of nature [*la manière de faire ses nécessités*] appeared to the famous Colins [*sic*] to be unworthy of divine majesty. He went so far as to say that God takes greater care with the derrière [*du derrière*] of the Israelites than with their souls; that the words *immortality of the soul* nowhere appear in the Old Testament; and that it is base indeed to care about the manner in which one must go to the toilet. This is said with precious little respect. All that we can say is that the Jewish people was so coarse, and that even into our own days the populace of this nation is so foul and dirty, that its legislators were obliged to descend into the smallest and most vile details" (204, note 11).

167. This passage appears in the first, 1832, edition of Hegel's *Vorlesungen über die Philosophie der Religion*, edited by Philipp Marheineke (1:151), and in Bruno Bauer's second, 1840, edition (1:214) (although Marheineke's name remained as editor, the 1840 edition was really Bauer's). I have modified the English translation of the nearly—but not completely—identical passage as it appears in Hegel, *Lectures on the Philosophy of Religion*, 1:339.

168. Deuteronomy 23:15. Bauer's 1840 edition of Hegel's *Philosophy of Religion* lectures adds an explicit reference to Deuteronomy 23:13–15, which is only implied in Marheineke's 1832 edition. Voltaire, Hegel, and Marx may also have in mind the *asher yatzar* blessing, which praises God for the miraculous combination of openings and cavities with which he

has endowed the human body, and which observant Jews recite either every time they relieve themselves, or just once in the course of early morning blessings.

169. Feuerbach, *Das Wesen des Christentums*, "Die Bedeutung der Kreation im Judentum" (The significance of the creation in Judaism).

170. Julia Kristeva, *The Powers of Horror*. For a discussion of the threats and possibilities that the abject presents to and beyond subjectivity, see Jonathan Strauss, *Human Remains*, chapter 8.

171. Nirenberg, *Anti-Judaism*, 437.

172. Ibid., 433.

173. Ibid., 437.

174. Ibid., 438.

175. Instead of trying to answer his own question through analysis Nirenberg merely refers to certain tendencies among groups of unspecified interpreters of Marx's "Zur Judenfrage" before concluding that Marx's reasons for insisting on the reality of "Jews" surely are "overdetermined" (*Anti-Judaism*, 438).

176. Nirenberg, *Anti-Judaism*, 439.

177. Marx would reproduce a somewhat reworked version of "Zur Judenfrage" in his and Engels's 1844 polemic (directed chiefly against Bruno Bauer), *Die heilige Familie*. Although Marx exploits Jews (and real Jewish critics of Bauer) as, in their "massiness," preferable to Bauer, the critic of *die Masse*, Marx already had more effective "massy" protagonists at his disposal to marshal against Bauer, and he here almost completely omits the rhetoric with which he figures the Jew as the obscene embodiment of the real. Jews would never again figure in a prominent way in his theoretical writings.

178. Marx, KMEW, 421–22 (translation modified); MEW, 3:5-7.

179. Auguste Cornu also identifies this passage in Feuerbach as what Marx is referring to (*Marx' "Thesen über Feuerbach,"* 11, note 14).

180. Feuerbach, *Das Wesen des Christentums*, 120.

181. Marx, EPW, 55; Marx and Engels, MEW, 1:376.

5. *Patriotic Pantheism*

1. Benedict de Spinoza, *B. v. Spinoza's Sämmtliche Werke. Aus dem Lateinischen mit dem Leben Spinoza's von Berthold Auerbach.*

2. *Phönix* (Frankfurt), unsigned review of *Spinoza*.

3. For details about Auerbach's life, I have drawn on Anton Bettelheim's *Berthold Auerbach* (hereafter BA).

4. In a letter to Jakob Auerbach, his cousin and confidant, of June 29, 1830, Berthold Auerbach remarks with evident delight that he and Spinoza share the name Baruch (*Briefe an Seinen Freund Jakob Auerbach*, 5).

5. See Berthold Auerbach, "Spinoza-Arbeiten," September 14 (hereafterSA 1). Auerbach wrote this piece in 1880 for the occasion of the unveiling of the Spinoza monument in The Hague, which he attended.

6. Auerbach's first published piece was a pseudonymous commissioned two-volume biography of Frederick the Great (published in 1834–35).

7. Berthold Auerbach, "Ephraim Moses Kuh." The work was originally serialized in *Zeitung für die elegante Welt.*

8. Auerbach, SA 1 and "Das Ghetto," vii.

9. Auerbach notes that an advance he received for the novel allowed him to pay for better food and the privilege to move freely about the fortress during his confinement (SA 1).

10. Ibid.

11. Auerbach's Spinoza edition and biography appeared in December 1841. He relates that he began the translation "in 1840, when I believed that my writing career was over and that I must prepare to become a lecturer [*Docent*] in philosophy." He remarks that he frequently worked twelve-hour days on the translation ("Spinoza-Arbeiten," September 15 [hereafter SA 2].

12. Berthold Auerbach, *Deutsche Abende*, v.

13. In addition to "Liebe Menschen" and "Deutsche Abende," the two Spinoza-inspired stories written in 1841, the 1851 *Deutsche Abende* included "Des Waldschützen Sohn," which Auerbach had first published in a *Jugendkalender* for 1847. Auerbach continued to add to *Deutsche Abende* in subsequent editions. He changed the title of "Deutsche Abende: Wer ist glücklich?" to "Was ist Glück?" for the 1851 *Deutsche Abende* but did not otherwise revise the stories. "Deutsche Abende: Wer ist glücklich?" was also included in an 1842 anthology, *Novellen-Album*. Page references are to this edition.

14. Berthold Auerbach, *Deutsche Abende*, vi.

15. According to a letter from Auerbach to Rudolf Kausler of December 15, 1841 (see the anonymous chronology of Auerbach's life in Thomas Scheuffelen, "Berthold Auerbach, 1812–1882," 45). In the same letter Auerbach relates his plan to move to London in spring 1842 to start a German newspaper, an indication of how changeable his career plans remained before his success with the village stories.

16. Ibid.

17. Joseph Braun, "Ein Phänomen in der neuesten Literatur" (A phenomenon in the latest literature).

18. The entry on Auerbach in the 1906 *Jewish Encyclopedia* wryly notes: "That an atmosphere of 'Spinozism' breathed through these most artless tales did not materially detract from their charm." ("Auerbach, Berthold [Baruch].")

19. Scott Spector, "Beyond Assimilation," 92.

20. David Sorkin, *The Transformation of German Jewry*, 140.

21. According to Sorkin, the ideologues of emancipation "could neither recognize nor acknowledge that their ideology, designed to foster integration, had become a basis of separation. The bourgeoisie could not see that its acculturation made it not German but German-Jewish. . . . Invisibility was a structural and not a subjective problem. It did not occur because of willful self-denial. To assert such self-denial imputes far too much knowledge to the majority of German Jews, for it assumes that they fully understood the nature of their nascent community and simply chose to deny its existence. This book is not a study of self-denial but of irony—the consequences of the discrepancy between German Jewry's actual and its imagined situation" (*The Transformation of German Jewry*, 7). Sorkin is surely right that the issue is not one of self-denial as he defines it here, yet his either-or opposition between self-denial and self-invisibility is ill equipped to appreciate much of the gray area in between. Anxiety can be (in fact, generally is) based on very partial knowledge. The Jewishness of the German-Jewish subculture was not invisible and unconscious but something acculturating Jews partially and anxiously perceived and negotiated in various ways.

22. Sorkin writes: "The role of the subculture played in both his [Auerbach's] life and his work remained invisible. Auerbach could not see how even the production of secular culture could be conditioned by the subculture. His life presents an exemplary case of how participation in secular culture did not lead to assimilation but to the confirmation, however unwitting, of a new sort of Jewish identity. Thus where towards the end of the century the historian Heinrich von Treitschke accused Auerbach of having created peasants who were little more than 'disguised Jews,' he thought he was merely casting another anti-Semitic aspersion. In fact, he revealed a significant truth not only about Auerbach's literary vision, but also about the nature of German Jewry" (ibid., 155). Sorkin's analytic aperture tends to absolutize a blindness that was never total and effectively removes from historical experience all ironic awareness on the part of Auerbach (and the wider German-Jewish community) of the tenuousness of their claim to unproblematic Germanness. Moreover, Sorkin passes over in silence precisely the moments in which Auerbach's nervousness about not being accepted as German are most apparent, such as his debut essay, *Das Judenthum und die neueste Literatur*, and "Das Ghetto," his jittery preface to his 1837 novel about Spinoza. (Sorkin refers to the revised 1854 version.) He is also silent about Auerbach's Spinoza biography and a number of quasi-ethnographic journalistic essays that dramatize tensions between Auerbach's idealized version of the *Volk* and his experience of social exclusion as a Jew, including "Das Sängerfest zu Frankfurt a. M.," "Tagebuch aus Weilbach," and the unsigned "Schildereien aus dem Taunus." Jeffrey Grossman challenges aspects of Sorkin's interpretation of the central role of *Bildung* in the "invisible" German-Jewish community by analyzing moments in Auerbach's *Schwarzwälder Dorfgeschichten* in which the function of *Bildung* vis-à-vis community appears highly ambivalent, and *Bildung*'s capacity to unite the liberal national community Auerbach envisioned thus become dubious ("Auerbach, Heine, and the Question of Bildung in German and German-Jewish Culture," 85–96).

23. W. E. B. Du Bois, *The Souls of Black Folk*, chapter 1.

24. Warren Breckman, *Marx, the Young Hegelians, and the Origins of Radical Social Theory: Dethroning the Self* (hereafter DS). Auerbach attended two philosophy lecture courses that Strauss, who would become a lifelong friend, gave at Tübingen in winter 1832–33: *Geschichte der Philosophie* and *Scholae Platonico-Aristotelicae* (SA 1). Horton Harris notes that Strauss used the privilege he enjoyed, as a lecturer at the famous Tübingen Seminary, of being able to lecture at Tübingen University in order "to forward the new Hegelian philosophy" (*David Friedrich Strauss and His Theology*, 36). Auerbach also refers to studying Hegel in Tübingen (SA 1). Strauss's epochal *Das Leben Jesu*, which would inaugurate Left Hegelianism, did not appear for two more years, but Auerbach would have been exposed to the more radical Hegelian framing of the ethico-political problem of personality and subjectivity in his study of Hegel and recent German philosophy through the lens of one of the boldest proponents of the new scientific approach. In summer 1832, the semester when Auerbach began studying at Tübingen, Strauss created a stir at the seminary by disputing, in the presence of the seminary's director, Johann Christian Friedrich Steudel, the Lutheran Church's doctrine regarding the Person of Christ (Harris, *David Friedrich Strauss*, 37–38). Auerbach had read Strauss's *Das Leben Jesu* by January 1836 (see the anonymous chronology of Auerbach's life in Thomas Scheuffelen, "Berthold Auerbach, 1812–1882," 36, 40).

25. Breckman, DS, 182–83. The internal quotations are from Marx's "On the Jewish Question."

26. Paul Rose, *Revolutionary Antisemitism in Germany from Kant to Wagner* (hereafter RA), chapter 11 in general and 198 in particular.

27. See Helen Ferstenberg, *Meditations on Jewish Creative Identity*, 77–78.

28. Heinrich Heine, *Historisch-kritische Gesamtausgabe der Werke* (hereafter DHA), 7 (part 2): 1337. In summer 1828 *Eos* changed editorship and became more conservatively Catholic and adamantly antiliberal. The journal adopted as its new motto, "Judeis quidem scandalum, gentibus autem stultitiam," from *Corinthians* 1:23. See the editorial note in *Heinrich Heines Werk im Urteil seiner Zeitgenossen*, edited by Eberhard Galley and Alfred Estermann, 1, "Kommentar," 64.

29. See George Peters, *The Poet as Provocateur*, 23–24.

30. See the editorial note in *Heinrich Heines Werk im Urteil seiner Zeitgenossen*, edited by Galley and Estermann, 1, "Kommentar," 64–65. The campaign culminated in the feud between Heine and August von Platen, who was close to members of the *Eos* circle, including Döllinger. Platen had taken antisemitic swipes at Heine in his 1828 play, *Der romantische Oedipus*. In *The Baths of Lucca* (1829) Heine struck back at Platen by cruelly ridiculing his homosexuality. Widely seen as beyond the pale, Heine's act was nearly universally condemned and seriously damaged his reputation. See Peters, *The Poet as Provocateur*, 26–28.

31. In an 1829 review of Heine's third volume of *Reisebilder*, for example, in which Heine mocks the ignorance and servility of Tyroleans, Döllinger contrasts the Tyroleans' loyalty to *Religion* and *Vaterland* with the "individuality of our ingenious traveler." Whereas this small *Volk* clings to collective traditions, Heine possesses an "excess of self-assurance" (*Übermaß von Selbstgefühl*) and is guided by a liberal overvaluation of "Persönlichkeit" (Ignaz von Döllinger, "Notiz zu Reisebilder Bd 3," 1:354.

32. Döllinger, "Notizen zu *Heines Werke*," 1:548.

33. Ibid., 1:549.

34. Ibid., 1:548.

35. Eduard Meyer, "Notizen zu *Reisebilder*," 1:576–77.

36. Ibid., 1:577.

37. Gabriel Riesser, "Börne und die Juden," 2:77.

38. Auerbach quotes the conclusion of Menzel's "Immoralische Literatur" in *Das Judenthum und die neueste Literatur*, 54.

39. Jeffrey Sammons, "Observations on Berthold Auerbach's Jewish Novels," 66.

40. Auerbach, *Das Judenthum und die neueste Literatur*, 47, 48.

41. Lothar Kahn and Donald Hook locate Auerbach within a group of Jewish writers who, struggling to establish themselves as truly German, sought to dissociate themselves from Heine, whom they saw as "a dire threat to their continued well-being in Germany" ("The Impact of Heine on Nineteenth-Century German-Jewish Writers," 53). Auerbach's *Dichter und Kaufmann* provides further evidence of how Auerbach had to confront wit and ironic subjectivity as specifically Jewish phenomena. Auerbach's Lessing encourages Kuh to dedicate himself to the epigram, which he sees as the ideal genre for the expression of Jewish wit (*Berthold Auerbachs Romane*, 2:86). For Lessing the Jewish propensity for wit derives from the "contrast" or "conflictual" relation in which Jews stand to the wider society (ibid.). As Ferstenberg (*Meditations on Jewish Creative Identity*, 77) points out, however, even as Auerbach's Lessing encourages Kuh to pursue his Jewish talent for wit, he disparages it as ultimately insubstantial (Auerbach, *Berthold Auerbachs Romane*, 2:86). Indeed, Less-

ing suggests that wit is a hollow currency (*Scheidemünze*) in the Jewish nation and that the great Jewish spirits "rather are pathetic or subtle logicians . . . such were Spinoza, Mendelssohn" (ibid.). Later in the novel the narrator expounds on the deleterious effects of wit and locates the origins of Jewish wit in the dynamics of Jewish secularization and acculturation (ibid., 2:150). The narrator echoes Lessing's disdain for wit, which he, too, likens to a cheap currency and even to a kind of "spiritual suicide, which betrays the most profound emotions and turns them into their opposite for momentary attention" (ibid., 2:150–51). The narrator's characterization of wit as superficial, self-indulgent, and unhealthy accords with Auerbach's opposition to irony and witty self-dramatization in his *Europa* reviews and elsewhere.

42. Auerbach, *Das Judenthum und die neueste Literatur*, 49.

43. "Die Jeune Allemagne in Deutschland," 1:161–2. The pamphlet's anonymous author is generally held to be its publisher, Samuel Gottlieb Liesching (see, for example, Jacob Katz, *From Prejudice to Destruction,* 180; Alfred Estermann, *Politische Avantgarde*, 2:659). Paul Rose (RA, 177, note 17) identifies the author as Paul Pfitzer [*sic*], brother of Gustav Pfitzer [*sic*]. I analyze Gustav Pfizer's criticism of Heine below.

44. For example: "Young Germany swears by nothing higher than the name *Heine*, and it is indeed from this ingenious, yet, unfortunately, just as frivolous as ingenious Heine, that the whole mischief has issued. A Jew by birth. . . . He was the first, moved [*verlockt*] by Jewish antipathies and French examples, to make the mocking of Christianity and morality, German nationality and custom [*Sitte*], the proposals to emancipate the flesh . . . the fruitful subject that the Young Germans have since played out in all their variations" (Wolfgang Menzel, "Die junge Literatur," 1:166).

45. For the history and usage of the phrase "Die jeune Allemagne," see Estermann, *Politische Avantgarde*, 2:608, note 5.

46. Auerbach, *Das Judenthum und die neueste Literatur*, 64.

47. Ibid., 66.

48. Ibid., 67–68. Of Auerbach's postscript directed at the pamphlet "Die jeune Allemagne in Deutschland," Paul Rose remarks: "Auerbach had grasped that the main thrust of Jew-hating had become the charge of egoism, whether financial or moral egoism. And he believed that this continuation of Jew-hatred was contaminating the very feeling of Germanness that should eradicate it" (RA, 230).

49. Auerbach, *Das Judenthum und die neueste Literatur*, 13.

50. Ibid., 14.

51. Willi Goetschel has demonstrated how Heine had recently subversively unwritten much of the Hegelian narrative of reason's progress (unto Hegel) by assigning Spinoza a central place in intellectual history in his *Zur Geschichte der Religion und Philosophie in Deutschland* (*Spinoza's Modernity*, 253–64).

52. Another significant immediate response by a Jew to the links Menzel (and the anonymous authors he inspired) posited between Young German morality and politics and Heine's Jewishness was by Jakob Weil in 1836. Weil refuted the charge that Heine's mockery of Christianity was driven by "Jewish antipathies" by insisting that Heine's foremost religious target was Judaism (and Christianity only because of its association with Judaism). In disassociating Heine from Judaism, Weil emphasizes that Heine is not a Jew but a "pantheist," a strategy that underscores the double obstacle Heine posed for Auerbach: Heine was seen as the embodiment of both corrosive "Jewishness" and of "pantheism," a version of

which Auerbach wanted to rehabilitate as a cure for the very *Zerrissenheit* for which Heine, more than any other figure, was the emblem ("Das junge Deutschland und die Juden," 3:514; on Heine's pantheism, see also 3:513). In a March 1836 review of Heine's *History of Philosophy and Religion*, Menzel underscores how, of all the religious thinkers and philosophers he discusses, Heine shows true admiration only for "the Jew" Spinoza. Among the attempts by philosphers to offer something new in the place of religion, Heine finds "that of the Jew Spinoza the most deserving of thanks. To this Jew alone he grants unqualified honor. The Christian philosophers, even when he praises their anti-Christian engagement [*Treiben*], always receive some sort of mocking parting shot" (Menzel, "Rezension zu *Der Salon Bd 2*," 3:566).

53. See Heine, DHA, 8 (part 1): 62.

54. Gustav Pfizer, "Heine's Schriften und Tendenz." The essay was originally published in the inaugural issue of *Deutsche Vierteljahrs Schrift*. As Jonathan Skolnik ("Writing Jewish History between Gutzkow and Goethe," 119, note 10) points out, Auerbach refers in *Das Judenthum und die neueste Literatur* to Pfizer's poem "Der ewige Jude," which appeared in his 1831 *Gedichte* (284–89). Pfizer's poem is also an intertext in the culminating scene of Auerbach's 1837 *Spinoza*, in which he attempts to put the figure of Ahasuerus, as the embodiment of base particularity, literally to rest.

55. For Riesser's *Jüdische Briefe*, see volume 4 of his *Gesammelte Schriften*. The letters pertaining to Heine and his critics are reproduced in Riesser, "Jüdische Briefe."

56. Riesser, "Jüdische Briefe," 5:221.

57. Ibid.

58. Gustav Pfizer, "Heine's Schriften und Tendenz," 4:239.

59. Ibid.

60. Ibid., 4:247.

61. Ibid.

62. Ibid., 4:267.

63. Ibid., 268. Pfizer forgets his own contention a few sentences earlier that Jews show their support for Heine only through secret gestures, a contradiction that was not lost on Riesser. See Riesser, *Gesammelte Schriften*. 4:76.

64. Pfizer, "Heine's Schriften und Tendenz," 4:268.

65. Ibid.

66. On this dynamic, see Breckman, DS, 182–83.

67. Riesser, *Gesammelte Schriften* 4:69.

68. For a passage of Ruge's 1838 Heine essay (originally published in the *Hallische Jahrbücher*) with antisemitic overtones, see Arnold Ruge, "Heinrich Heine, charakterisiert nach seinen Schriften," 4:301–2.

69. Breckman, DS, 252. Ruge makes his change of view explicit in his 1842 essay "The Christian State." In the early 1840s, in such essays as "Hegel's 'Philosophy of Right' and the Politics of Our Times" (1842) and "A Self-Critique of Liberalism" (1843), Ruge emphatically follows Feuerbach.

70. Theodor Echtermeyer and Arnold Ruge, "Der Protestantismus und die Romantik," 258.

71. Heine would finally redeem himself in Ruge's eyes with his politically engaged *Deutschland, ein Wintermärchen* of 1844. After the publication of this text, Ruge—along with Marx; Heinrich Börnstein, editor of the radical German exiles' Paris journal *Vorwärts*;

and others—helped rehabilitate Heine as the leading oppositional writer after the disaster Heine's image had suffered in the wake of his 1840 book on Börne. See Peters, *The Poet as Provocateur*, 58. In part because of Heine's turn to more politically engaged satire, and in part because of Ruge's philosophical development and his own treatment at the hands of the Prussian censors, Ruge had found a Heine he could embrace.

72. For example, Ruge, "Heinrich Heine," 4:308–9. Heine is indeed conspicuously absent from "Protestantismus und Romantik." Echtermeyer and Ruge's politicized assessment of recent German cultural history is obviously indebted to Heine's own account of much of the same territory in *Die Romantische Schule* (1836). Yet Echtermeyer and Ruge disassociate themselves from the Heine who has clear affinities with them.

73. See Ruge, "Heinrich Heine," 4:296–97. On the significant role that the discourse about Jewish *Witz* played in the formation of nineteenth-century German cultural identity, see Jefferson Chase, *Inciting Laughter*.

74. Ruge notes approvingly the continuity between Fichte (of *Reden an die deutsche Nation*), the *Burschenschaft* movement, and the *Befreiungskrieg* before contrasting such positive commitment to freedom with Heine's negative "*Freiheitssucht*" (Ruge, "Heinrich Heine," 4:299–301). Ruge's critique of Heine and romantic subjectivity is greatly indebted to Hegel's critique, in the introduction to *Vorlesungen über die Ästhetik*, of Romantic irony as empty egoism, a delusion of grandeur of sorts on the part of merely formal subjectivity devoid of true substance.

75. Ruge, "Heinrich Heine," 4:303.

76. Arnold Ruge, "Die Frivolität: Erinnerungen an Heine," 7:292.

77. Sorkin notes Auerbach's aversion to "*Weltschmerz*" literature in his *Europa* reviews but does not remark on how, chiefly through Heine, this literature was widely regarded as originating in Jewish subjectivity (*The Transformation of German Jewry*, 142–43).

78. Berthold Auerbach, review of *Die Europamüden*, 567–68.

79. Ibid., 566 and 567.

80. Ibid., 568.

81. Ibid.

82. Berthold Auerbach, review of *Gedichte*, 568.

83. Auerbach, "Bemerkungen über Titel und Vorreden in der neuesten schönen Literatur," 40.

84. Ibid., 38.

85. Ibid., 40.

86. Auerbach's antipathy for Heine was abiding and did not ebb with time. He wrote to Jakob Auerbach, his cousin, on March 2, 1867: "Heine, for whom everything is vendible for a joke, is deeply abhorrent to me, and given my core being I must also be abhorrent to him" (*Briefe an Seinen Freund Jakob Auerbach*, 324). Heine indeed expressed contempt for Auerbach, both privately and publicly. The entirety of Heine's letter of April 5, 1847, to Heinrich Laube reads: "Dear Laube! My condition is still the same—my head is as weak as if I were the author of an Auerbach village story—my stomach as miserably sentimental and religiously and morally insipid as one of those stories—still I plan to visit you around 11 o'clock. Your sick friend H. Heine" (*Säkularausgabe*, 22:247). In a preface to the German translation of Alsatian village tales by Alexandre Weill, dated Good Friday 1847, Heine makes a point of slighting Auerbach's achievement in this genre by relating that "friends" had informed him

that Weill (not Auerbach, whom Heine does not deign to name) published not only the first, but also the best, such stories in German. Heine claims he is unable to confirm this claim due to unfamiliarity with the "masterworks of periodical writing" (*Tagesschrifstellerei*) on the other side of the Rhine ("Vorwort," n.p.).

87. Berthold Auerbach, "Rezension zu *Heinrich Heine über Ludwig Börne*," 6:192.

88. Ibid., 6:193.

89. Ibid., 6:197.

90. Ibid.

91. Ibid.

92. Benedict de Spinoza, *Ethics*, V.

93. Rabbi in the town of Braunsbach, Frankfurter was also the brother of Auerbach's Nordstetten teacher and friend, Bernard Frankfurter.

94. Anton Bettelheim, Auerbach's biographer, relates that Riesser disparaged these issues of the *Gallerie* as "nothing but a failed bookseller's speculation" (Bettelheim, BA, 97). Whether or not Auerbach shared Riesser's assessment of the *Gallerie*, he needed money badly and so was in no position to decline the work.

95. Bettelheim takes this view as well (BA, 97–98).

96. [Berthold Auerbach], "Vorwort."

97. Ibid.

98. Ibid. Bettelheim notes the "similarly dubious motivation" (BA, 98) at work in this passage and in Auerbach's presentation of his Jewish historical novels in "Das Ghetto," which I discuss below.

99. [Auerbach], "Vorwort."

100. Ibid.

101. See Sorkin (*The Transformation of German Jewry*, 144–46) for an analysis of Auerbach's generational relationship to Gotthold Salomon, rabbi at the Reform Temple in Hamburg, and the ideology of emancipation he embodied.

102. The other three figures Auerbach profiled were all still living when he wrote about them.

103. Berthold Auerbach, *Gallerie der ausgezeichnetsten Israeliten aller Jahrhunderte, ihre Portraits und Biographien*, 5:21. Auerbach was fond of the phrase "an even temperature of education" in these years, using it also in "Tagebuch aus Weilbach," 115, and his letter to Alexander Weill of May 12, 1839 (quoted in Bettelheim, BA, 131–32).

104. In "Das Leben Spinoza's" (xvii–xviii) Auerbach elaborates on this view that traditional Jewish culture deindividualizes those who remain within it but also produces, among those who break away from it, highly idiosyncratic individuals.

105. Auerbach, *Gallerie*, 5:24.

106. Ibid.

107. Ibid., 33.

108. Ibid., 34.

109. Auerbach, "Das Leben Spinoza's, xi–xii. Auerbach echoes these thoughts on authorial anonymity some years later in *Schrift und Volk* (85), in which he contrasts the irreducibly subjective nature of Romantic authorship with the essential selflessness of the *Volksdichter*.

110. Auerbach, "Das Leben Spinoza's," xii.

111. Ibid., xii–xiii.

112. Ibid., lxxvii–lxxviii. Auerbach refers to the preface to Spinoza's *Ethics*, III, for the second of his quotations from Spinoza here. The first quote about the error of anthropocentrism seems to be a paraphrase of lines in the Appendix to *Ethics*, I.

113. Auerbach, "Das Leben Spinoza's," lxxix.

114. Ibid., cxxi.

115. Ibid.

116. Ibid., cxxi–cxxii. And see Benedict de Spinoza, *Theological-Political Treatise*, chapter 6.

117. Auerbach, "Das Leben Spinoza's," cxxv.

118. See Auerbach, "Ephraim Moses Kuh." Bettelheim (BA, 97) mentions numerous Jewish biographies that Auerbach had in mind when he began coediting the *Gallerie*, most of which he never pursued.

119. Auerbach, SA 2. Auerbach compensated by building the plot around the Sephardic experience of exile as an important part of the prehistory of Spinoza's residence in Holland and by spinning out an infatuation Spinoza may or may not have felt for the daughter of his teacher, Van den Enden, into a major plot line. In his explanatory notes to *Spinoza*, Auerbach cites Johannes Colerus's early Spinoza biography as the source of his knowledge of Spinoza's love for "Olympia" (the character based on Clara Maria van den Enden), though he acknowledges that there was no reliable corroboration for this (*Spinoza*, part 2, 303). According to Steven Nadler (*Spinoza*, 108–9), the story is probably apocryphal.

120. Auerbach, SA 2.

121. See Jacob Katz, "Spinoza und die Utopie einer totalen Assimilation der Juden."

122. Skolnik, "Writing Jewish History between Gutzkow and Goethe," 104. For Katz's bleaker interpretation of Auerbach's novel, in whose culminating scene the figure of the Wandering Jew, Ahasuerus, visits Spinoza in a dream but proves unable to survive Spinoza's universalist spirit, see "Spinoza und die Utopie einer totalen Assimilation der Juden." For reasons given below, I disagree with Skolnik insofar as I see the Jewish past as Auerbach depicts it in *Spinoza* as not terribly "usable," precisely because of the not easily reconciled uses Auerbach would like to make of it.

123. Daniel Schwartz, *The First Modern Jew*, 75. Schwartz's analysis of the ambivalence in Auerbach conveyed by this scene hinges on the degree to which Auerbach identified with his own figure of Spinoza. Schwartz argues very plausibly that "there is good reason to suspect that, in this scene, Auerbach is airing a very personal ambiguity over modern Jewish identity" (ibid.). In "Spinoza-Arbeiten," Auerbach addresses the nature and limits of his identification, as a Jew, with Spinoza at the time he was writing this novel and confirms what Schwartz suspects: "I felt as a Jew like Spinoza and, like him, could not avow membership in any positive religion. But I can also say I felt more like a Jew than Spinoza, the critical scholar [*Forscher*] and philosopher" (SA 1). Auerbach views Spinoza as far more iconoclastic than he and sees him, despite his purity of soul (*Seelenreinheit*) and independence, as too embittered by his experiences to appreciate the poetry and esthetic beauty (*Kunstschönheit*) of the Bible. Moreover, Spinoza's reclusive nature left him unable to grasp the "gemüthlichen Zusammenhang der Juden und die tiefe Intimität ihres Empfindungslebens" (ibid.). Auerbach believes that he was sufficiently independent as a writer, despite his veneration for Spinoza, to portray the justification for the campaign against him on the part of the Portuguese Jewish community in Amsterdam). In Auerbach's remark that he felt "as

a Jew like Spinoza," but also felt "more like a Jew than Spinoza," we can see that Auerbach was aware of his identification with and admiration for Spinoza, but also of the limits of both. Of course, the context of the antisemitism debate and Auerbach's own painful experience of antisemitism may have inflected his memory of how he felt Jewish and how Jewish he felt in the mid-1830s, but given his position in "Das Judentum und die neueste Literaturm" there is very good reason to take Auerbach's later remarks at face value. Nothing, to be sure, suggests that Auerbach ever identified with a radical Spinoza; on the contrary, he strove consistently to domesticate Spinozan ideas.

124. Schwartz, *The First Modern Jew*, 58.

125. Auerbach, "Das Ghetto," iii.

126. Ibid., vii.

127. The anonymous Auerbach chronology in Scheuffelen's "Berthold Auerbach, 1812–1882" mentions numerous abortive Jewish projects that Auerbach entertained between 1875 and 1881, including a Jewish *Dorfgeschichte*, a Jewish novel, and an essay on Heine and Disraeli. His late "Kindheitserinnerungen aus Nordstetten" contain interesting reflections on the relations between Germans and Jews in the Nordstetten of his childhood.

128. Bettelheim (BA, 98) notes the affinity between the *Gallerie* preface and "Das Ghetto."

129. Auerbach, "Das Ghetto," iii.

130. Ibid.

131. Jonathan Hess, *Middlebrow Literature and the Making of German-Jewish Identity*, 73.

132. Ibid., 80.

133. See Hess (*Middlebrow Literature*, chapter 2) for an analysis of how Kompert's ghetto fiction partly accomplishes this dual function for an upwardly mobile German-Jewish audience while also appealing to a non-Jewish audience.

134. Auerbach, "Das Ghetto," iv.

135. Here and in the following pages I paraphrase and quote from Auerbach's Jewish novel "recipe" in "Das Ghetto," iv–vi.

136. Auerbach's pastiche of the contemporary popular Jewish novel evokes aspects of, among other works, Walter Scott's *Ivanhoe* (1820) and Eugénie Foa's two-volume *La Juive, histoire du temps de la regence* (1835), which was immediately translated into German as *Die Jüdin: Geschichte aus den Zeiten der Regentschaft*. Foa's novel was reviewed in mainstream German literary journals, such as the *Morgenblatt für gebildete Stände* in 1836. Foa's self-exoticization as a Jewish author would have been particularly repellent to Auerbach. On Foa, see Maurice Samuels, *Inventing the Israelite*, chapter 1.

137. Auerbach, "Das Ghetto," vi. Theodor Hell is a pseudonym for Karl Gottlieb Theodor Winkler (1775–1856), author and publicist. *Penelope* (1811–48) was a *Taschenbuch* (a literary prose almanac) published by Theodor Hell. I have been unable to identify the Wachsmann to whom Auerbach refers in this passage.

138. Auerbach, "Das Ghetto," vi–vii.

139. Ibid., viii.

140. Ibid., ix.

141. Ibid.

142. Ibid., vii.

143. See Walter Benjamin, "Der Erzähler," especially 388. On one level, Benjamin is re-

sponding to the incommunicable trauma of World War I, yet he sees this as part of a broader phenomenon whereby modern technologies of the word undermine the communicability of immediate experience. This wider perspective makes Benjamin's argument as relevant for the 1840s as for the 1920s.

144. Auerbach's "preface" to his *Schwarzwälder Dorfgeschichten* appeared belatedly, after the first volume of collected village tales had already appeared in book form. It was published in *Europa* ("An J. E. Braun vom Verfasser der Schwarzwälder Dorfgeschichten") as an open letter to Joseph Braun, a critic who, in early 1843, had written a highly positive review of four of Auerbach's village tales that had appeared in journals but had not yet been collected in book form ("Ein Phänomen in der neuesten Literatur"). Beginning with the 1857 edition, "Vorreden spart Nachreden" was included in all editions of the *Schwarzwälder Dorfgeschichten*.

145. Auerbach, "Vorreden spart Nachreden," 149.

146. Auerbach, *Spinoza*, viii.

147. Hess, *Middlebrow Literature*, 84.

148. Nitsa Ben-Ari, "1834."

149. Auerbach, SA 1.

150. Edward McInnes, "Realism, History and the Nation," 45.

151. Ibid., 46–47.

152. Auerbach greatly revised his Spinoza novel in 1854, and this version achieved considerable success.

153. Auerbach, *Briefe an Seinen Freund Jakob Auerbach*, 47.

154. In a review in *Europa* of an 1838 edition of Brentano's novella, Auerbach praises it as a wholesome alternative to contemporary literature, stressing *Gegensätze* (contradictions) and *Zerrissenheiten* (inner turmoil; review of "Die Geschichte vom braven Kasperl und dem schönen Annerl," 86). Auerbach encourages writers to emulate Brentano's subtle humor, which comes across "without a lot of coquettish narcissism [*Selbstbespiegelung*] . . . even at the risk of being relegated to a lower sphere by those world humorists [*Welthumoristen*]" (ibid.)—that is, by Heine and others like him.

155. Auerbach, "Deutsche Abende: Wer ist glücklich?," 1:13.

156. Ibid., 1:14.

157. Ibid., 1:15.

158. Ibid., 1:26. Edmund's Spinoza-informed dedication to the public cause mirrored Auerbach's own ethos at the time. In his letter to Jakob Auerbach of February 27, 1842, Auerbach—although he clings to dwindling hope of still finding a fulfilling love life—remarks: "For many years I saw my highest calling in life, indeed the fulfillment of my existence, entirely in a rich, full, youthful warm love life, which was supposed to be for me the highest peak of all existence; I have now gained the knowledge that I must devote myself to a broader life of duty, a life for the more universal [*das Allgemeinere*] without egoistical support [*ohne egoistische Rückwand*]" (*Briefe an Seinen Freund Jakob Auerbach*, 46).

159. Auerbach, "Liebe Menschen," 126. The refuge of the domestic sphere that Elisabetha and her mother represent is further thematized in a passage from Friedrich Schleiermacher's *Predigten über den christlichen Hausstand* that the good mother has bookmarked and left by Rudolf's bed. The lengthy passage from Schleiermacher's text that Rudolf reads (quoted in "Liebe Menschen," 140–41) deals with the possibilities of establishing a Christian

spiritual community outward from a domestic sphere, which is to serve as both its model and center. In a richly ironic moment that enfolds Jewish resonances within this German domestic sphere, the Protestant theologian's words elicit from Rudolph a quintessentially Jewish gesture: "he involuntarily kissed the open book" (ibid, 141).

160. Auerbach changed the title only after giving a reading of the manuscript (*Deutsche Abende*, vi).

161. Auerbach, "Liebe Menschen," 168.

162. Ibid., 165–66.

163. Ibid., 122.

164. Ibid., 122–23.

165. Ibid., 131.

166. Ibid., 132–33.

167. Auerbach, "Das Leben Spinoza's," cxxv.

168. One further 1842 text by Auerbach, "Tagebuch aus Weilbach," is noteworthy for the way it also (silently) stages Spinozan intellectual love as the key to consolidating the German *Vaterland*. Published in the first quarterly (spring) issue of *Der Freihafen*, "Tagebuch aus Weilbach" derives from observations Auerbach made about the local culture during a stay at a spa in Weilbach in summer 1842, where he also wrote one of his most famous village tales, "Ivo der Hairle." In an extended passage ("Tagebuch aus Weilbach," 116–18), Auerbach meditates on the possibility of an individual's realizing himself and/in participating in a collective life—in particular, that of the *Vaterland*—that initially seemed foreign. Toward the end of the passage he alludes to Spinozan "intellectual love" (*intellektuelle Liebe*) as the most reliable means of overcoming narrow subjective limitations and realizing a harmonic, inclusive collective existence. Acknowledging that institutional religion can raise individuals to a higher plane of existence through a more or less dogmatic formulation of religious consciousness, Auerbach asks whether love and religion that derive from individual consciousness also can do this. His answer is yes, as long as this love and religion become "intellectual love": "Certainly, if it has become intellectual love, free and pure knowledge [*Erkenntniß*]; knowledge uplifts more surely and unwaveringly than any law that has become external. It offers the most unshakeable support, only we must habituate ourselves to being able to invoke it always, make it independent of our individual circumstances; we then live, in any situation whatsoever, in the eternal life of knowing love [*der erkennenden Liebe*]" (ibid., 117–18). Here too we see that, even as Auerbach was writing his early village tales, he continued to view Spinozan intellectual love as the key to overcoming confessional and regional differences and consolidating a liberal *Vaterland*.

6. Moses Hess

1. Moses Hess, *Moses Hess Briefwechsel*, 95.

2. Auerbach edited *Das Deutsche Familienbuch* for 1844 and single-handedly wrote *Der Gevattersman: Neuer Kalender für Stadt- und Landbürger auf 1845* (1844).

3. Anton Bettelheim mentions Freytag's comment in *Berthold Auerbach* (hereafter BA), 178. The writers and socialites included Heinrich Laube, Karl Gutzkow, and Gustav Freytag (see the anonymous chronology of Auerbach's life in Thomas Scheuffelen, "Berthold Auerbach, 1812–1882," 52).

4. In his prospectus for *Gesellschaftsspiegel: Organ zur Vertretung der besitzlosen Volksklassen und zur Beleuchtung der gesellschaftlichen Zustände der Gegenwart* (Social mirror: organ for representing the propertyless classes and for illuminating the social conditions of the present), Hess announced that its focus would be to advocate for defenseless poor working people. See Edmund Silberner, *Moses Hess*, 214. On the *Gesellschaftsspiegel*, see also Shlomo Na'aman, *Emanzipation und Messianimus*, 152–60.

5. Moses Hess, *Moses Hess Briefwechsel*, 111.

6. In *Der gebildete Bürger* Auerbach (following William Ellery Channing in *Self-Culture*) discusses the greater availability and affordability of books as a promising means of disseminating *Bildung* to classes whose members had not formerly owned or read books. Auerbach warns, however, against the danger of vapid and bad literature (*Nichtiges und Schlechtes*) that also comes with the modern literary market. He remarks that, because many households buy only one annual calendar, certain "men who are concerned about the well-being of their fellow men" have begun to devote attention to this branch of literature, and he recommends especially Honeck's *Volkskalender* with the *Buch für Winterabende* (*Der gebildete Bürger*, 70).

7. In a letter of May 12, 1839, to Jakob Auerbach, his cousin and confidant, Auerbach wrote that he "seems strange to himself when he, a stepson of the Fatherland" (*komme sich selbst komisch vor, wenn er, "ein Stiefsohn des Vaterlandes"*) comes to Germany's defense against the criticism of the Francophile Alexander Weill (quoted in Bettelheim, BA, 132). In a letter thanking Freiligrath for his poem, Auerbach wrote: "I also have to tell you that it gives me special pleasure that I, a Jew, have succeeded in revealing something from the innermost soul of the German people" (*aus dem Innersten des deutschen Volksgeistes*). More darkly, he also acknowledged: "I know if I were to go out among the peasants with goodwill in my heart and on my lips, the single word 'Jew!' would scare them away from me" (quoted in ibid., 161–62).

8. On Hess's relationship to Feuerbach, see Hou Cai, "Moses Heß und Ludwig Feuerbach," and Junji Kanda, "Moses Heß und der gescheiterte Weg von Hegel zu Feuerbach."

9. On the stability throughout his career of Hess's interpretation of Spinoza as both the basis for socialism and as the philosophical foundation of of Judaism, see Shlomo Avineri, *Moses Hess*, 208–9.

10. Quoted in Warren Breckman, *Marx, the Young Hegelians, and the Origins of Radical Social Theory: Dethroning the Self* (hereafter DS), 192.

11. For an argument about Heine's subversive use of Spinoza to unwrite Hegel's grand narrative of dialectical development (unto Hegel), and to give the Judaic tradition a more central place in intellectual history than the marginal one Hegel had ascribed it, see Willi Goetschel, *Spinoza's Modernity*, chapter 7.

12. Avineri, *Moses Hess*, 41–45.

13. Moses Hess, *The Holy History of Mankind and Other Writings* (hereafter HHM), 93; *Philosophische und sozialistische Schriften 1837–1850* (hereafter PSS), 72.

14. Spinoza defines the knowledge of God as the mind's highest virtue in *Ethics*, IV, p28. Hess alludes to the pursuit of knowledge as the primary reason for individuals to enter into society in, for example, Hess, HHM, 64; PSS, 50.

15. Hess, HHM, 65; PSS, 51.

16. On this point, see Breckman, DS, 195.

17. Ibid., 194.

18. See, for example, Hess's remark to this effect in *European Triarchy*, in PSS, 148. For a critique of Hess's appropriation of Spinoza for a philosophy of history, see Nathan Rothenstreich, "Moses Hess—ein ein Jünger Spinoza's?"

19. Breckman, DS, 194; internal quote (translated by Breckman) from Hess, PSS, 45.

20. See Benedict de Spinoza, *Ethics*, III, p1. In Steven Nadler's formulation, "Spinoza's virtue . . . does not lead to an ascetic withdrawal from the world, but rather a more knowledgeable and successful navigation within the world and a more efficient use of things in it" (*Spinoza's Ethics*, 228).

21. Breckman, DS, 195. As Breckman also remarks, "Hess's negation of personality and property contradicted not only the Saint-Simonians but virtually all his German contemporaries as well, including the equally visionary Cieszkowski" (ibid.).

22. Ibid.

23. Hess, HHM, 72–73; PSS 57.

24. Hess, PSS 57.

25. Hess, HHM, 73; PSS, 57.

26. Ken Koltun-Fromm approaches Hess's writings from his 1837 debut to *Rome and Jerusalem* (1862) as a sustained meditation on the self and Jewish identity but largely ignores the crucial context of politically and philosophically freighted conceptions of the self in which Hess formulated his early ideas. Koltun-Fromm characterizes Hess's ideology of the 1830s through the 1850s as based on a relatively uncomplicated "undivided self and whole identity" (*Moses Hess and Modern Jewish Identity*, 30), or an identity that is "complete, unencumbered by ambiguous attachments, and open to philosophical and scientific scrutiny" (ibid., 31). In Koltun-Fromm's account, Hess shifts to an unresolved and contradictory view of the modern self in *Rome and Jerusalem*, which posits the "structure of the self" as "mysterious to historical beings like ourselves" (ibid., 34). It is hard to reconcile Hess's all-out attack on the sovereign self, and insistence that we recognize our identity with the other, and the view of Hess as subscribing to an "undivided self and whole identity."

27. Hess proposed his vision of an Anglo-French-German "European triarchy" in response to Karl Eduard Goldmann's *Die europäische Pentarchie* (1839), which advocated that Prussia ally itself with Europe's reactionary forces (chiefly Austria and Russia) against France. Goldmann worked under Klemens von Metternich in the service of the Habspurgs and later in the service of the Russian government. (Hess, PSS, 493, note 335). For the context of the conflict between reactionaries and liberals (largely Young Hegelians) in which Goldmann and Hess participated, see Auguste Cornu and Wolfgang Mönke, "Einleitung," xix–xx.

28. Hess, PSS, 162.

29. See, for example, ibid., 161.

30. Hess sees Germany's great contribution to modernity, Hegel, as engaged in a contemplative evaluation of the past and sees Claude Henri de Saint-Simon as Hegel's active, future-oriented counterpart in France. Hess locates the common source of both of these modern trajectories in Spinoza, and Spinoza remains the site where they can be effectively united (see ibid., 148.).

31. Ibid., 159.

32. Genevieve Lloyd articulates well how for Spinoza an accurate and empowering understanding of individuality explodes the limits of conventional notions of self-contained subjects: "At the core of this failure to know ourselves is an inadequate understanding of

individuality. The human body cannot exist in isolation from the surrounding totality that provides and sustains its individuality. The isolated body would cease to exist. The mind, likewise, can exist as an individual only in the context of other modes of thought. But the mind, unlike the body, has open to it a false version of individuality. Minds, unlike bodies, can know what they are. And as well as being capable of knowledge they are capable of error. The mind can think of the body, and hence it itself, falsely—it can think of itself as substance" (*Part of Nature* [hereafterPN], 28–29).

33. Spinoza, *Ethics*, IV, p35d. Spinoza also says: "The good which each person who follows virtue seeks for himself he also desires for all other men, and the more so, the more he has a greater knowledge of God" (ibid., IV, p37).

34. See Hess, PSS, 79, 83, and 89.

35. See ibid., 77.

36. Ibid., 86.

37. On how Hess's negation of private property in *The Holy History* differs from Cieszkowski's Hegelian understanding of the necessity of property for actualizing abstract subjectivity in his "Prolegomena to a Historiosophy." see Breckman, DS, 195.

38. Cieszkowski, "Prolegomena to a Historiosophy," 64.

39. Ibid.

40. Ibid., 66.

41. Cieszkowski refers to Karl Ludwig Michelet's characterization of Hegel's project of "uniting idealism with realism" as "absolute idealism," a formulation Cieszkowski sees as both accurate and highly revealing of "the one-sidedness of this [Hegel's] standpoint" (ibid., 67).

42. Ibid., 68.

43. Ibid., 69, 70.

44. Ibid., 82.

45. For Hess, like Cieszkowski, the abstract interiority and subjectivity of Hegelian philosophy keeps it from becoming truly active and productive: "German philosophy does not really get out of this interiority and manage to create. As little as we e.g. can create a tree because we have its concept within us, Hegelian philosophy is as little capable of engendering a historical deed" (PSS, 85).

46. Cieszkowski, "Prolegomena to a Historiosophy," 83.

47. On this aspect of Hegel's reading of Spinoza, see Lloyd, PN, 5–7.

48. Hess writes: "Not only the Phenomenology and Logic, but the entire Hegelian system belongs to the philosophy of the substance becoming subject, the subjectively active, comprehending spirit" (PSS, 80).

49. Ibid., 78.

50. Ibid., 80.

51. Ibid., 81. G. H. R. Parkinson renders the proposition that Hess quotes in Latin from Spinoza this way: "The order and connection of ideas is the same as the order and connection of things" (*Ethics*, II, p7).

52. Hess, PSS, 86.

53. In contrast to the self-exceeding dynamic of love, Hess associates the opponents of love with *Einzelheiten* removed from their wider context; see, for example, PSS, 155 and 157.

54. Ibid., 148–49. I use Parkinson's rendering of Hess's internal quote from Spinoza, *Ethics*, III, p10. Rotenstreich ("Moses Hess—ein Jünger Spinoza's?," 241) finds it a "somewhat

incredible interpretation" of Spinoza when Hess seems to claim here that Spinoza's concept of substance is decisive only for his metaphysics, and that the subject is decisive for his ethics. I read Hess's strategic aim of countering the Hegelian charge that Spinozan substance leaves no room for subjectivity as paramount here, not a desire on Hess's part to relegate substance and the subject rigorously to different spheres.

55. In a letter to Berthold Auerbach of July 6, 1840, Hess refers to Spinoza's *Ethics*, I, p23 as evidence that, according to Spinoza, there exist contingencies (Hess suggests that Auerbach, who was translating Spinoza's works, render "Accidentes" as "Zufälligkeiten" in German) that are also necessary. "What does this mean?," Hess asks. "Well, they [necessary contingencies] are the same things [as contingencies], but insofar as we consider them in relation to their essence, their ground, in brief, in relation to the other in and through which they are *true* [*in bezug auf das andre wodurch und worin sie* wahrhaft *sind*]" (*Moses Hess Briefwechsel*, 62). In Hess's reading, the lesson to be learned from Spinoza is not that greater knowledge negates contingent particularites, but rather that it reveals to us the wider contexts that in fact constitute particularities.

56. Hess, PSS, 151.

57. Ibid.

58. Ibid., 88.

59. Ibid., 94.

60. Ibid., 147.

61. For a further argument by Hess against the view that freedom and order are in conflict, see ibid., 156.

62. The essay appeared in Georg Herwegh's famous *Einundzwanzig Bogen aus der Schweiz* (Twenty-one sheets from Switzerland). Silberner emphasizes differences between Hess's 1843 "philosophy of the act" and the version he had articulated two years earlier in *Die Europäische Triarchie*. In the earlier work Hess followed Cieszkowski in calling for a philosophy that could discern the future from the past and present and still, according to Silberner, opposed thought and action. Moreover, "the human being for him was not an autonomous being but rather a medium through which the absolute spirit realized itself" (*Moses Hess*, 127). In the 1843 philosophy of the act, however, Hess no longer views thinking and acting as opposed but rather sees each as "activity of the self" [*Tätigkeit des Ich*] (ibid.). Silberner attributes this shift in part to Hess's engagement with Johann Gottlieb Fichte but also rightly warns against overestimating Fichte's influence. I read these two articulations of Hess's philosophy of the act as compatible, despite the different emphases Silberner highlights. Hess's opposition between thought and action in *Die Europäische Triarchie* occurs as part of his wider critique of the disempowering effects of this dualistic opposition—that is, of abstracting thought from its implication in immanent action. And Hess's emphasis on the individual *Ich* in the 1843 essay in no way makes individuals immune to his critique of theological subjectivity—on the contrary.

63. Feuerbach wrote "Provisional Theses for the Reformation of Philosophy" in spring 1842, but the censor delayed its publication and it did not appear until fall 1843. Whereas in *Principles of the Philosophy of the Future* Feuerbach describes the still-theological modern philosophical tradition that culminates in Hegel as beginning with Descartes, in "Provisional Theses" (156) he describes it as beginning with Spinoza. Indeed, Feuerbach's opening salvo at Hegel in "Provisional Theses" is to apply Hegel's critique of Spinoza to Hegel himself.

Feuerbach sees in Spinoza and Hegel the same flaw of assigning the true, concretely existing *something* the status of mere predicate of an abstract subject (the absolute for Hegel; substance for Spinoza), thereby insuring that these ways of doing philosophy encounter real being only as part of the hermetically sealed feedback loop of their own projected conceptual categories (ibid., 157).

64. According to Feuerbach, "Hegelian philosophy is the suspension of the contradiction of thinking and being, as in particular Kant had articulated it. But, note well, the suspension of this contradiction is only *within contradiction*, i.e. within the *one* element, *within thinking*. For Hegel *thought* is *being, thought* the *subject, being* the predicate" ("Provisional Theses," 166).

65. Feuerbach writes: "The true relation of thinking and being is simply this. *Being* is *subject* and *thinking* a *predicate*. . . . Thinking comes from being but being does not come from thinking. Being comes from itself and through itself" (ibid., 167).

66. Feuerbach, *Principles of the Philosophy of the Future*, 30–31.

67. Ibid., 31.

68. Feuerbach writes: "The contradiction of modern philosophy . . . is due to the fact that it is the negation of theology from the viewpoint of theology or the negation of theology that itself is again theology; this contradiction characterizes especially the Hegelian philosophy" (ibid., 31); "*whoever fails to give up the Hegelian philosophy, fails to give up theology*" ("Provisional Theses," 167); and "*the Hegelian philosophy is the last place of refuge and the last rational support of theology*" (ibid.).

69. Feuerbach, *Principles of the Philosophy of the Future*, 31.

70. Ibid., 71.

71. Lloyd, PN, 10.

72. Ibid., 11.

73. Erich Thier, *Das Menschenbild des jungen Marx*, 49.

74. Lloyd, PN, 22.

75. Ibid., 21.

76. Hess, "The Philosophy of the Act," 249; PSS, 210.

77. Ibid.

78. Ibid., 249–50 (translation modified); PSS, 210.

79. Lloyd lucidly describes Spinoza's critique of the epistemological and ethical error of false individuality that Hess appropriates to his own context, and the increased freedom and power to be gained through a knowledge that overcomes this error: "The mind is under constant threat of succumbing to a false individuality—of seeing individuals as essentially independent of the rest of the world, as individual substances. This is a metaphysical error that Spinoza sees as breeding moral error. To see interaction with the rest of reality as incidental to a thing's individuality—to see things only as 'wholes'—is the underlying illusion built into obsessive loves and hates. True freedom of mind, and with it true understanding of individuality, is to be attained only through the apprehension of truth involved in the higher forms of knowledge. The mind's active affirmation of reality through adequate knowledge, Spinoza sees as a vulnerable force, with dubious power against the frequently overwhelming external forces that put the mind into bondage—a force, nonetheless, that contains the germ of freedom" (PN, 30–31).

80. In an unpublished draft of "Zur Philosophie der Tat" (probably from 1844), Hess

argues that property and possessive individualism negate true individuality. He follows a recognizably Spinozist line of thought in his critique of the bifurcation of immanent practice, which is its own inherent reward (true *Eigentum*), into a false, dichotomized relation between *Arbeit* and *Lohn*. False property is the external, abstract value assigned to labor (paradigmatically in terms of money). Crucial to note is that it is Spinozan immanence that for Hess accurately recognizes real individuals and allows them to thrive: "The false sense that now attaches to the word 'property' should not prevent us from giving it back its true sense. True property denotes nothing but the specific characteristic of the individual. True property cannot be appropriated without negating the individual [*Man kann das wahre Eigenthum nicht aufheben, ohne das Individuum afuzuheben*]. Our current property is, however, so different from true property that it cancels [*aufhebt*] precisely the life of the individual" ("Zur Philosophie der Tat," 51). In the same paragraph Hess critiques Pierre-Joseph Proudhon and Charles Fourier along similar lines for perpetuating, rather than overcoming, egoism by engaging in a "false and immoral determination of the value [*Wertbestimmung*] of a person's individual activity" in terms of false, external property (*Besitz*) rather than true property intrinsic to the unique individual (ibid.). Hess, then, clearly does not understand his ethico-political project in terms of negating individuals; rather, he is committed to rescuing individuals, as he understands them according to the principles of his Spinozist communism, from their devaluation and deactivation. For Hess ownership can only consist in an individual's active relationship to materials and ideas. To claim ownership beyond such immanent activity presupposes a subject-object dualism that is epistemologically erroneous and ethically detrimental because it impedes productive activity (interdicts relationships that other individuals could have with the social goods one claims to own). The legal self who lays claim to materials beyond the real self's assimilation of them, in other words, is a version of the theological subject that Hess identifies as the chief obstacle to socialism. It is this same fiction of an immortal subject capable of laying claim to property beyond the limits of the real individual at which Hess takes aim in his attack on heritability in *The Holy History*.

81. Hess, PSS, 212.

82. For Hess's understanding of subjectivity as rooted in a false dualism between material individual and abstract universal that also structures religious and political institutions, see, for example, ibid., 216–17.

83. Quoted in Silberner, *Moses Hess*, 128. Silberner does not date the "extant draft manuscript of 'Philosophy of the Act'" from which he quotes this passage, but he identifies the draft as "Hess-Nachlaß, Signatur: B 21 (unveröff., IISG), S. 4f" (ibid.).

84. Hess, PSS, 220. In Spinoza's *Ethics*, see, for example, III, p53; IV, p18S; V, p42.

85. Hess, PSS, 220–21.

86. Ibid., 224. Compare Spinoza's statement: "The highest good of the mind is the knowledge of God, and the highest virtue of the mind is to know God" (*Ethics*, IV, p28). In *The Holy History* Hess makes a similarly provocative point: "We do not belong to those who have such a fear of real equality as of real death because the later, as the former, destroys a phantom to which their life and their spirit are bound, and besides which they know nothing" (HHM, 65; PSS, 51). The sovereign individual, in other words, is essentially a phantom, something to which people cling as to a fetish because they lack an understanding of the wider totality that truly constitutes them.

87. Hess, PSS, 225. Hess expressly rejects a kind of nihilistic pantheism that claims that

all is one. His point is that a more correct conception of individuals and wider wholes can liberate us from our enslavement to our false and destructive conceptions of our selves, property, and so forth: "*Das materielle Eigenthum ist das zur fixen Idee gewordene Fürsichsein des Geistes.* Weil er die Arbeit, das Ausarbeiten oder Hinausarbeiten seiner selbst nicht als seine freie That, als sein eignes Leben geistig begreift, sondern als ein materiell Anderes erfaßt, muß er's auch für sich fest halten, um sich nicht in's Endlose zu verlieren, um zu seinem Fürsichsein zu kommen. Eigenthum hört aber auf, dasjenige dem Geiste zu sein, was es soll, nämlich sein Fürsichsein, wenn nicht die That im Schaffen, sondern das Resultat, die Schöpfung als das Fürsichsein des Geistes—das Phantom, die Vorstellung des Geistes, als sein Begriff, kurz, sein Anderssein als sein Fürsichsein erfaßt und mit beiden Händen fest gehalten wird. Es ist eben die *Seinsucht*, die Sucht nämlich, fortzubestehen als bestimmte Individualität, als beschränktes Ich, als endliches Wesen—die zur *Habsucht* führt" (ibid.).

88. For how, in Spinoza's view, misunderstood individuality limits power and freedom, see Lloyd, PN, 29.

89. Francesco Tomasoni, *Modernity and the Final Aim of History*, 202.

90. Moses Hess, "The Recent Philosophers," 362; translation modified; PSS, 383.

91. Hess, "The Recent Philosophers," 368–69; PSS, 388.

92. See Hess's unsigned and untitled remarks from "Köln, 30. Mai" under the rubric "Deutschland" in *Rheinische Zeitung* of May 31, 1842. On Hess contributions to *Rheinische Zeitung* on the Jewish Question, see Na'aman, *Emanipation und Messianismus*, 117–18.

93. For a discussion of Hess's subversion of the charge of Jewish egoism in *Rome and Jerusalem*, see Paul Rose, *Revolutionary Antisemitism in Germany from Kant to Wagner*, 329–33. On philosophical-historical continuities between Hess's earlier works *The Holy History* and *Die Europäische Trierarchie* and *Rome and Jerusalem*, see Na'aman, *Emanzipation und Messianismus*, 314–17.

94. On Judaism's mission to usher in the regeneration of humanity, see Hess, *Rome and Jerusalem*, 48–49, 62, 83, and 119–20. On Hess's emphasis on the communitarian aspects of Jewish life in *Rome and Jerusalem*, see Avineri, *Moses Hess*, 228–30.

95. Hess, *Rome and Jerusalem*, 48.

96. It seems warranted to see Spinoza's concept of *conatus* behind Hess's celebration of the Jewish race's self-preservation: "Each thing, in so far as it is in itself, endeavors to persevere in its being" (*Ethics*, III, p6). On the role of love in Judaism, see Hess, *Rome and Jerusalem*, 44–45, 65, and 84–88. For Hess's critique of Reform Judaism, see ibid., 58–59, 62, 94–96.

97. Hess contends that "the basic idea of the system of Spinoza, namely, that God is the only substance, the ground and origin of all being, is the fundamental expression of the Jewish genius, which has ever manifested itself in divine revelations from the time of Moses and the Prophets, down to modern days" (*Rome and Jerusalem*, 212). For a critique of Hess's attempt to interpret "Judaism according to Spinoza and Spinoza according to Judaism" in *Rome and Jerusalem*, see Rotenstreich, "Moses Hess—ein Jünger Spinozas?," 242–43; here, 242.

98. Ibid., 65–66.

99. On Hess's anthropological and scientific studies, see Silberner, *Moses Hess*, 332–57; and see Na'aman, *Emanzipation und Messianismus*, 268–76.

100. Hess, *Rome and Jerusalem*, 84.

101. See Hess's letter to Auerbach of November 25, 1862 in Hess, *Briefwechsel*, 417–18, and *Rome and Jerusalem*, 58. On the exchange between Hess and Auerbach about Hess's *Rome and Jerusalem*, see also Silberner, *Moses Hess*, 388–89.

Concluding Remarks

1. See Werner Mosse, "The Revolution of 1848."

2. On the debates about the place of Jews in the German nation as it was being defined by the Frankfurt parliamentarians, see Brian Vick, *Defining Germany*, chapter 3.

3. See Jacob Toury, "Die Revolution von 1848 als innerjüdischer Wendepunkt."

4. See Jacob Toury, "'Deutsche Juden' im Vormärz," 82; Reinhard Rürup, "The European Revolutions of 1848 and Jewish Emancipation," 30–31.

5. Hess, RJ 217. See also ibid., 218–22.

Works Cited

Primary Sources

Ascher, Saul. *Eisenmenger der Zweite: Nebst einem vorangesetzten Sendschreiben an Herrn Professor Fichte in Jena*. Berlin: Hartmann, 1794.

———. *Leviathan oder über Religion in Rücksicht des Judentums*. Berlin: Franck, 1792.

Auerbach, Berthold. "An J. E. Braun vom Verfasser der Schwarzwälder Dorfgeschichten." *Europa: Chronik der gebildeten Welt* 4 (1843): 33–36.

———. "Bemerkungen über Titel und Vorreden in der neuesten schönen Literatur." *Europa* 1 (1838): 37–40.

———. *Berthold Auerbachs Romane*. 12 vols. Stuttgart: Cotta, 1871.

———. *Black Forest Village Stories*. Translated by Charles Goepp. 1869. Reprint. Freeport, NY: Books for Libraries, 1969.

———. *Briefe an Seinen Freund Jakob Auerbach: Ein biographisches Denkmal*. Vol. 1. Frankfurt: Literarische Anstalt Rütten and Loening, 1884.

———. "Das Ghetto." Preface to Berthold Auerbach, *Spinoza: Ein historischer Roman*, iii–x. Stuttgart: Scheible's Buchhandlung, 1837.

———. *Das Judenthum und die neueste Literatur: Kritischer Versuch*. Stuttgart: F. Brodhag, 1836.

———. "Das Leben Spinoza's." In Benedict de Spinoza, *B. v. Spinoza's Sämmtliche Werke*, edited and translated by Berthold Auerbach, 1:ix–cxxv. Stuttgart: J. Scheible, 1841.

———. "Das Sängerfest zu Frankfurt a. M." *Europa: Chronik der gebildeten Welt* 3 (1838): 481–92.

———. *Der gebildete Bürger: Buch für den denkenden Mittelstand*. Karlsruhe, Germany: J. Bielefeld's Verlag, 1843.

———. *Deutsche Abende*. Mannheim, Germany: Friedrich Basserman, 1851.

———. "Deutsche Abende: Wer ist glücklich?" In *Novellen-Album mit Beiträgen von Berthold Auerbach, Lorenz Diessenbach, L. H. Geibler, A. van Hasselt, Heinrich Koenig, J. Kuranda, H. Laube, F. Lebrun, F. Robin. E. von Schcmidt u. s. w.*, 1:1–25. Leipzig: F. L. Herbig, 1842.

———. "Ephraim Moses Kuh: Ein biographisches Gemälde." *Zeitung für die elegante Welt*, August 15, 16, 18–20, 22, 23, 25, and 26, 1836.

———. *Gallerie der ausgezeichnetsten Israeliten aller Jahrhunderte, ihre Portraits und Biographien*. Vol. 5. Stuttgart: Fr. Brodhag, 1838.

———. "Liebe Menschen: Ein Idyll aus der gebildeten Welt." *Der Freihafen* 2 (April 1842): 117–69.

———. Review of *Die Europamüden: Modernes Lebensbild*, by Ernst Willkomm. *Europa: Chronik der gebildeten Welt* 1 (1838): 565–68.

———. Review of "Die Geschichte vom braven Kasperl und dem schönen Annerl," by Clemens Brentano. *Europa: Chronik der gebildeten Welt* 2 (1838), 86–87.

———. Review of *Gedichte*, by Ferdinand Freiligrath. *Europa: Chronik der gebildeten Welt* 3 (1838): 565–69.
———. "Rezension zu *Heinrich Heine über Ludwig Börne*." In *Heinrich Heines Werk im Urteil seiner Zeitgenossen*, edited by Eberhard Galley and Alfred Estermann, 6:192–98. Hamburg: Hoffmann und Campe, 1992.
———. *Sämtliche Schwarzwälder Dorfgeschichten*. 10 vols. Stuttgart: Cotta, 1884.
[———]. "Schildereien aus dem Taunus." *Das Vaterland* (Darmstadt), August 28–29, 1843.
———. *Schrift und Volk: Grundzüge der volksthümlichen Literatur, angeschlossen an eine Charakteristik J. P. Hebel's*. Leipzig: F. A. Brockhaus, 1846.
———. *Spinoza: Ein historischer Roman*. 2 parts. Stuttgart: Scheible, 1837.
———. "Spinoza-Arbeiten: Ein Stück aus meinem Leben." *Neue Freie Presse* (Vienna), September 14 and 15, 1880.
———. "Tagebuch aus Weilbach." *Der Freihafen* 6, no. 1 (1843): 21–41 and 109–34.
———. "Vorreden spart Nachreden." In *Realismus und Gründerzeit: Manifeste und Dokumente zur deutschen Literatur, 1848–1880. Mit einer Einführung in den Problemkreis und einer Quellenbibliographie*, edited by Max Bucher, Werner Hahl, Georg Jäger, and Reinhard Wittmann. 1:149–50. Stuttgart: J. B. Metzler, 1975.
[———]. "Vorwort." In *Gallerie der ausgezeichnetsten Israeliten aller Jahrhunderte, ihre Portraits und Biographien*, edited by Berthold Auerbach and Naphtali Frankfurter, vol. 4, n.p. Stuttgart: Fr. Brodhag, 1836.
Auerbach, Berthold, and Naphtali Frankfurter, eds. *Gallerie der ausgezeichnetsten Israeliten aller Jahrhunderte, ihre Portraits und Biographien*. Vol. 4. Stuttgart: Fr. Brodhag, 1836.
"Auerbach, Berthold (Baruch)." *Jewish Encyclopedia*. 1906. http://www.jewishencyclopedia.com/articles/2112-auerbach-berthold-baruch. Accessed December 29, 2013.
"Aus dem Archiv für die Correspondenz." *Zeitschrift für die Wissenschaft des Judenthums* 1 (1823): 533–39.
Bauer, Bruno. "Die Fähigkeit der heutigen Juden und Christen, frei zu werden." In *Einundzwanzig Bogen aus der Schweiz*, edited by Georg Herwegh, 56–71. Zurich: Verlag des Literarischen Comptoirs, 1843.
———. *Die Judenfrage*. Braunschweig, Germany: Friedrich Otto, 1843.
———. *Feldzüge der reinen Kritik*. Frankfurt: Suhrkamp, 1968.
———. *The Jewish Problem*. Translated by Helen Lederer. Cincinnati, OH: Hebrew Union College, 1958.
———. "Neueste Schriften über die Judenfrage." *Allgemeine Literatur-Zeitung* 1, no. 1 (1843): 1–17.
———. "Neueste Schriften über die Judenfrage." *Allgemeine Literatur-Zeitung* 1, no. 4 (1844): 10–19.
———. Review of *Die Geschichte des Lebens Jesu*, by Christoph Friedrich von Ammon. In *Anekdota zur neuesten deutschen Philosophie und Publizistik*, edited by Arnold Ruge, 2:160–85. Zürich: Verlag des Literarischen Comptoirs, 1843.
Bendavid, Lazarus. *Etwas zur Charackteristick der Juden*. Leipzig: Stabel, 1793.
———. "Selbstmord aus Rechtschaffenheit und Lebensüberdruß." *Magazin zur Erfahrungsseelenkunde* 9, no. 2 (1792): 1–9.
———. "Sonderbare Art des Trübsinnes." *Magazin zur Erfahrungsseelenkunde* 9, no. 3 (1792): 67–85.

———. “Über den Glauben der Juden an einen künftigen Messias (Nach Maimonides und den Kabbalisten).” *Zeitschrift für die Wissenschaft des Judenthums* 1 (1823): 197–230.
———. “Über den Unterricht der Juden.” In Lazarus Bendavid, *Aufsätze verschiedenen Inhalts*, 117–33. Berlin: Heinrich Fröhlich, 1800.
———. *Über die Religion der Ebräer vor Moses*. Berlin: Hitzig, 1812.
———. “Über geschriebenes und mündliches Gesetz.” *Zeitschrift für die Wissenschaft des Judenthums* 1 (1823): 472–500.
———. *Versuch über das Vergnügen*. 2 vols. Vienna: Stahel, 1794.
———. *Vorlesungen über die Critik der practischen Vernunft*. Vienna: Stahel, 1796.
———. *Zur Berechnung und Geschichte des jüdischen Kalenders*. Berlin: Nocolai, 1817.
Braun, Joseph Eduard. “Ein Phänomen in der neuesten Literatur.” *Europa* 1 (1843): 127–34.
Channing, William Ellery. 1838. *Self-Culture*. New York: Arno, 1969.
Cieszkowski, August von. “Prolegomena to a Historiosophy.” In *The Young Hegelians: An Anthology*, edited by Lawrence S. Stepelevich, 57–89. Amherst, NY: Humanity, 1999.
Cohen, Hermann. “Innere Beziehungen der Kantischen Philosophie zum Judentum.” In Hermann Cohen, *Jüdische Schriften*, edited by Bruno Strauss, 1:284–305. Berlin: C. A. Schwetsche, 1924.
“Die jeune Allemagne in Deutschland.” In *Politische Avantgarde 1830–1840: Eine Dokumentation zum “Jungen Deutschland,”* edited by Alfred Estermann, 1:159–64. Frankfurt: Athenäum, 1972.
Dohm, Christian Wilhelm. *Über die bürgerliche Verbesserung der Juden*. 2 vols. Berlin: F. Nicolai, 1781–83.
Döllinger, Ignaz von. “Notizen zu *Heines Werke*.” In *Heinrich Heines Werk im Urteil seiner Zeitgenossen*, edited by Eberhard Galley and Alfred Estermann, 1:545–551. Hamburg: Hoffmann und Campe, 1981.
———. “Notiz zu Reisebilder Bd 3.” In *Heinrich Heines Werk im Urteil seiner Zeitgenossen*, edited by Eberhard Galley and Alfred Estermann, 1:353–56. Hamburg: Hoffmann und Campe, 1981.
Echtermeyer, Theodor, and Arnold Ruge. “Der Protestantismus und die Romantik: zur Verständigung über die Zeit und ihre Gegensätze: ein Manifest.” In *Philosophie und Literatur im Vormärz: der Streit um die Romantik (1820–1854): Quellenband*, edited by Walter Jaeschke, 192–325. Hamburg: Meiner, 1995.
Estermann, Alfred, ed. *Politische Avantgarde 1830–1840: Eine Dokumentation zum “Jungen Deutschland.”* 2 vols. Frankfurt: Athenäum, 1972.
Euchel, Isaak Abraham. *Vom Nutzen der Aufklärung*. Translated and edited by Andreas Kennecke. Düsseldorf: Parerga, 2001.
Feuerbach, Ludwig. *Das Wesen des Christentums*. Edited by Heinrich Schmidt. Leipzig: A. Kröner, 1909.
———. *The Essence of Christianity*. Translated by George Eliot. Buffalo, NY: Prometheus, 1989.
———. *Principles of the Philosophy of the Future*. Translated by Manfred H. Vogel. Indianapolis, IN: Bobbs-Merrill, 1966.
———. “Provisional Theses for the Reformation of Philosophy.” In *The Young Hegelians: An Anthology*, edited by Lawrence S. Stepelevich, 156–71. Amherst, NY: Humanity, 1999.

Fichte, Johann Gottlieb. *Beitrag zur Berichtigung der Urteile des Publikums über die französische Revolution*. Hamburg: Meiner, 1973.

———. *Das System der Sittenlehre nach den Principien der Wissenschaftslehre (1798)*. Edited by Immanuel H. Fichte. Vol. 4 of Johann Gottlieb Fichte, *Sämmtliche Werke*. 1845–46. Berlin: de Gruyter, 1965.

Friedländer, David. *Akten-Stücke die Reform der jüdischen Colonieen in den Preußischen Staaten betreffend*. Berlin: Vossischen Buchhandlung, 1793.

Fries, Jacob. *Über die Gefährdung des Wohlstandes und Charakters der Deutschen durch die Juden. Eine aus den Heidelberger Jahrbüchern der Litteratur besonders abgedruckte Recension der Schrift des Professors Rühs in Berlin: "Über die Ansprüche der Juden an das deutsche Bürgerrecht. Zweyter verbesserter Abdruck &c."* Heidelberg: Mohr and Winter, 1816.

Gans, Eduard. *Das Erbrecht in weltgeschichtlicher Entwicklung*. 4 vols. Berlin: Maurer, 1824–35.

———. "Dritte Rede vor dem 'Kulturverein.'" In *Eduard Gans (1797–1839): Hegelianer-Jude-Europäer: Texte und Dokumente*, edited by Norbert Waszek, 75–85. Frankfurt: Peter Lang, 1991.

———. "Erste Rede vor dem 'Kulturverein.'" In *Eduard Gans (1797–1839): Hegelianer-Jude-Europäer: Texte und Dokumente*, edited by Norbert Waszek, 55–62. Frankfurt: Peter Lang, 1991.

———. "A Society to Further Jewish Integration (1822)." In *The Jew in the Modern World*, edited by Paul Mendes-Flohr and Jehuda Reinharz, 215–19. 2nd ed. New York: Oxford University Press, 1995.

———. "Vorrede zu Hegels Rechtsphilosophie." In *Eduard Gans (1797–1839): Hegelianer-Jude-Europäer: Texte und Dokumente*, 127-133. Edited by Norbert Waszek. Frankfurt: Peter Lang, 1991.

———. "Zweite Rede vor dem 'Kulturverein.'" In *Eduard Gans (1797–1839): Hegelianer-Jude-Europäer: Texte und Dokumente*, edited by Norbert Waszek, 62–75. Frankfurt: Peter Lang, 1991.

Hegel, Georg Wilhelm Friedrich. *Berliner Schriften: (1818–1831), voran gehen Heidelberger Schriften (1816–1818)*. Edited with an introduction by Walter Jaeschke. Hamburg: Meiner, 1997.

———. *Die Philosophie des Rechts: Vorlesung von 1821/22*. Edited by Hansgeorg Hoppe. Frankfurt: Suhrkamp, 2005.

———. *Early Theological Writings*. Translated by T. M. Knox. Chicago: University of Chicago Press, 1948.

———. *Elements of the Philosophy of Right*. Edited by Allen Wood. Translated by H. B. Nisbet. Cambridge: Cambridge University Press, 1991.

———. *Encyclopedia of the Philosophical Sciences in Outline, and Other Philosophical Writings*. Edited by Ernst Behler. Translated by A. V. Miller, Steven A. Taubeneck, and Diana I. Behler. New York: Continuum, 1990.

———. *Enzyklopädie der philosophischen Wissenschaften im Grundrisse (1817)*. Edited by Wolfgang Bonsiepen and Klaus Grotsch. Vol. 13 of Georg Wilhelm Friedrich Hegel, *Gesammelte Werke*. Hamburg: Meiner, 2000.

———. Foreword to Hermann Friedrich Wilhelm Hinrichs, *Religion in Its Internal*

Relationship to Systematic Knowledge. In Eric Von der Luft, ed. and trans., *Hegel, Hinrichs, and Schleiermacher on Feeling and Reason in Religion: The Texts of Their 1821–22 Debate*, 245–68. Lewiston, NY: Edwin Mellen, 1987.

———. *Hegel's Philosophy of Right*. Translated with notes by T. M. Knox. Oxford: Oxford University Press, 1967.

———. *Hegel's Science of Logic*. Translated by A. V. Miller. New York: Allen and Unwin, 1969.

———. *Lectures on the History of Philosophy*. Translated by E. S. Haldane and Frances H. Simson. 3 vols. Lincoln: University of Nebraska Press, 1995.

———. *Lectures on the Philosophy of History*. Translated by J. Sibree. London: G. Bell and Sons, 1902.

———. *Lectures on the Philosophy of Religion*. Edited by Peter C. Hodgson. Translated by R. F. Brown, Peter C. Hodgson, and J. M. Stewart, with the assistance of H. S. Harris. 3 vols. Reprint. Oxford: Oxford University Press, 2007.

———. *Lectures on the Philosophy of World History: Introduction, Reason in History*. Translated by H. B. Nisbet. Introduction by Duncan Forbes. Cambridge: Cambridge University Press, 1975.

———. *Philosophie des Rechts: Die Vorlesung von 1819/20 in einer Nachschrift*. Edited by Dieter Henrich. Frankfurt: Suhrkamp, 1983.

———. *Philosophie des Rechts, mitgeschrieben von Johann Rudolf Ringier (1819/1820)*. Edited by Emil Angehrn, Martin Bondeli, and Hoo Nam Seelmann. Vol. 14 of G. W. F. Hegel, *Vorlesungen: Ausgewählte Nachschriften und Manuskripte*. Hamburg: Meiner, 2000.

———. *The Philosophy of History*. Translated by J. Sibree. New York: Dover, 1956.

———. *Political Writings*. Edited by Laurence Dickey and H. B. Nisbet. Translated by H. B. Nisbet. Cambridge: Cambridge University Press, 1999.

———. *Vorlesungen über die Ästhetik*. Vol. 3. Vol. 15 of G. W. F. Hegel, *Werke in 20 Bänden mit Registerband*, edited by Eva Modenhauer and Karl Markus Michel. Frankfurt: Suhrkamp, 1986.

———. *Vorlesungen über die Geschichte der Philosophie*. Edited by Pierre Garniron and Walter Jaeschke. Hamburg: Meiner, 1986.

———. *Vorlesungen über die Philosophie der Religion*. 2nd improved ed. Edited by Philipp Marheineke. 2 vols. Berlin: Duncker and Humblot, 1840.

———. *Vorlesungen über die Philosophie der Religion*. Vol. 3 of G. W. F. Hegel, *Vorlesungen: ausgewählte Nachschriften und Manuskripte*. Part 1: *Einleitung. Der Begriff der Religion*. Edited by Walter Jaeschke. Hamburg: Meiner, 1983.

———. *Vorlesungen über die Philosophie der Religion, Nebst einer Schrift über die Beweise vom Dasein Gottes*, 2 vols. Edited by Philipp Marheineke. Berlin: Duncker and Humblot, 1832.

———. *Vorlesungen über die Philosophie der Weltgeschichte*. Vol. 1: *Die Vernunft in der Geschichte*. Edited by Johannes Hoffmeister. Hamburg: Meiner, 1955.

———. *Vorlesungen über die Philosophie der Weltgeschichte, Berlin 1822/1823*. Edited by Karl-Heinz Ilting, Karl Brehmer, and Hoo Nam Seelmann. Vol. 12 of G. W. F. Hegel, *Vorlesungen: ausgewählte Nachschriften und Manuskripte*. Hamburg: Meiner, 1996.

———. *Vorlesungen über Rechtsphilosophie, 1818–1831*. Edited by Karl-Heinz Ilting. 6 vols. Stuttgart-Bad Cannstatt, Germany: Frommann-Holzboog, 1973–74.

———. *Werke in 20 Bänden mit Registerband*. Edited by Eva Moldenhauer and Karl Markus Michel. Frankfurt: Suhrkamp, 1986.

———. *Wissenschaft der Logik I: Die Objektive Logik (1812/13)*. Edited by Friedrich Hogemann and Walter Jaeschke. Vol. 11 of Georg Wilhelm Friedrich Hegel, *Gesammelte Werke*. Hamburg: Meiner, 1978.

———. *Wissenschaft der Logik II: Die Subjektive Logik (1816)*. Edited by Friedrich Hogemann and Walter Jaeschke. Vol. 12 of Georg Wilhelm Friedrich Hegel *Gesammelte Werke*. Hamburg: Meiner, 1981.

Heine, Heinrich. *Historisch-kritische Gesamtausgabe der Werke*. Edited by Manfred Windfuhr. 16 vols. Hamburg: Hoffmann and Campe, 1973–97.

———. *On the History of Religion and Philosophy in Germany and Other Writings*. Edited by Terry Pinkard. Translated by Howard Pollack-Milgate. Cambridge: Cambridge University Press, 2007.

———. *Säkularausgabe: Werke, Briefwechsel, Lebenszeugnisse*. Edited by the Nationalen Forschungs- und Gedenkstätten der klassischen deutschen Literatur in Weimar and the Centre national de la recherche scientifique in Paris. Berlin: Akademie-Verlag, 1970–.

———. "Vorwort." In Alexandre Weill, *Sittengemälde aus dem elsässischen Volksleben*, vol. 2, n.p. Stuttgart: Franckh'sche Verlagshandlung, 1847.

Hess, Moses. "Deutschland." *Rheinische Zeitung* May 31, 1842.

———. *The Holy History of Mankind and Other Writings*. Edited by Shlomo Avineri. Cambridge: Cambridge University Press, 2004.

———. *Moses Hess Briefwechsel*. Edited by Edmund Silberner. The Hague: Mouton, 1959.

———. "On the Essence of Money." In Julius Kovesi, *Values and Evaluations: Essays on Ethics and Ideology*, edited by Alan Tapper, 183–207. New York: Peter Lang, 1998.

———. *Philosophische und sozialistische Schriften 1837–1850: Eine Auswahl*. Edited by Auguste Cornu and Wolfgang Mönke. Expanded ed. Vaduz, Liechtenstein: Topos, 1980.

———. "The Philosophy of the Act." In *Socialist Thought: A Documentary History*, edited by Albert Fried and Robert Sanders, 249–75. New York: Columbia University Press, 1992.

———. "The Recent Philosophers." In *The Young Hegelians: An Anthology*, edited by Lawrence S. Stepelevich, 359–75. Amherst, NY: Humanity, 1999.

———. *Rom und Jerusalem: Die letzte Nationalitätenfrage*. 2nd ed. Leipzig: M. W. Kaufmann, 1899.

———. *Rome and Jerusalem: A Study in Jewish Nationalism*. Translated by Meyer Waxman. Whitefish, MT: Kessinger, 2005.

———. "Zur Philosophie der Tat." In *Neue Quellen zur Hess-Forschung: Mit Auszügen aus einem Tagebuch, aus Manuskripten und Briefen aus der Korrespondenz mit Marx, Engels, Weitling, Ewerbeck u.a.*, edited by Wolfgang Mönke, 44–56. Berlin: Akademie-Verlag, 1964.

Hirsch, Samuel. "Selections from *The System of the Religious Perceptions of Jews and its Relationship to Paganism, Christianity and to Absolute Philosophy*." In *Modern Jewish Thinkers: From Mendelssohn to Rosenzweig*, edited by Gershon Greenberg, 171–204. Brighton, MA: Academic Studies, 2011.

Jost, Isaak M. "Actenmäßige Darstellung des kürzen Daseins einer jüdischen Schul-Commission in der Berliner Gemeinde 1826." *Allgemeine Zeitung des Judentums*, March 7 and 14, 1859.

———. *Culturgeschichte zur neueren Geschichte der Israeliten von 1815 bis 1845*. Vol. 10, part 3, of *Geschichte der Israeliten seit der Zeit der Maccabäer bis auf unsre Tage*. Berlin: Schlesinger'sche Buch- und Musikhandlung, 1847.

Kant, Immanuel. *Critique of Pure Reason*. Translated by Norman Kemp Smith. New York: St. Martin's, 1965.

———. *Immanuel Kant Werkausgabe*. Edited by Wilhelm Weischedel. 12 vols. Frankfurt: Suhrkamp, 1968.

———. *Political Writings*. Edited by Hans S. Reiss. Translated by H. B. Nisbet. New York: Cambridge University Press, 1991.

———. *Practical Philosophy*. Edited and translated by Mary J. Gregor. New York: Cambridge University Press, 1996.

———. *Religion and Rational Theology*. Translated and edited by Allen Wood and George di Giovanni. New York: Cambridge University Press, 1996.

Kornrik, Meyer ben Moses. *Dabar Be'itto*. Breslau: Löbel Sulzbach, 1817.

Krochmal, Nahman. "A Philosophy of Jewish History." In *Ideas of Jewish History*, edited by Michael Meyer, 189–214. Detroit, MI: Wayne State University Press, 1987.

Krokhmal [Krochmal], Nahman. "Selections from *Guide to the Perplexed of Our Time*." In *Modern Jewish Thinkers: From Mendelssohn to Rosenzweig*, edited by Gershon Greenberg, 85–118. Brighton, MA: Academic Studies, 2011.

Maimon, Salomon. *Essay on Transcendental Philosophy*. Translated and edited by Alistair Welchman, Henry Somers-Hall, Merten Reglitz, and Nick Midgley, London: Continuum, 2010.

———. *Salomon Maimons Lebensgeschichte, von ihm selbst geschrieben und herausgegeben von Karl Philipp Moritz*. Edited by Zwi Batscha. Frankfurt: Jüdischer Verlag, 1995.

———. *Versuch über die Transzendentalphilosophie*. Edited by Florian Ehrensperger. Hamburg: Felix Meiner, 2004.

Marx, Karl. *Early Texts*. Edited and translated by David McLellan. Cambridge, UK: Blackwell, 1971.

———. *Early Writings*. Translated by Gregor Benton and Rodney Livingstone. Introduction by Lucio Colletti. New York: Vintage, 1975.

———. *Early Political Writings*. Translated and edited by Joseph O'Malley with Richard A. Davis. Cambridge: Cambridge University Press, 1994.

———. *Selected Writings*. Edited by Lawrence H. Simon. Indianapolis: Hackett, 1994.

Marx, Karl, and Friedrich Engels. *Collected Works*. Translated by Richard Dixo et al. 47 vols. New York: International, 1975–2004.

———. *The Communist Manifesto*. Translated by Samuel Moore. Edited by Joseph Katz. New York: Washington Square, 1964.

———. *Economic and Philosophic Manuscripts of 1844, Karl Marx, translated by Martin Milligan, and The Communist Manifesto by Karl Marx and Frederick Engels*. Amherst, NY: Prometheus, 1988.

———. *The German Ideology*. Amherst, NY: Prometheus, 1998.

———. *Gesamtausgabe*. Edited by the Institut für Marxismus-Leninismus beim

Zentralkomitee der Kommunistischen Partei der Sowjetunion and the Institut für Marxismus-Leninismus beim Zentralkomitee der Sozialistischen Einheitspartei Deutschlands. Berlin: Dietz, 1972–.

———. *Werke*. 43 vols. Berlin: Dietz, 1956–90.

Menassah ben Israel. *Menasseh ben Israel's Mission to Oliver Cromwell: Being a Reprint of the Pamphlets published by Menasseh ben Israel to Promote the Re-Admission of the Jews to England, 1649–1655*. Edited by Lucien Wolf. London: Macmillan, 1901.

Mendelssohn, Moses. *Gesammelte Schriften Jubiläumsausgabe*. Edited by Alexander Altmann et al. Stuttgart-Bad Cannstatt, Germany: Frommann, 1971–2011.

Menzel, Wolfgang. "Die junge Literatur." In *Politische Avantgarde 1830–1840: Eine Dokumentation zum "Jungen Deutschland,"* edited by Alfred Estermann, 1:164–85. Frankfurt: Athenäum, 1972.

———. Review of *Schwarzwälder Dorfgeschichten*, by Berthold Auerbach. *Literatur-Blatt zum Morgenblatt für gebildete Stände* 83 (14 August 1844): 330–32.

———. "Rezension zu *Der Salon Bd 2*." In *Heinrich Heines Werk im Urteil seiner Zeitgenossen*, edited by Eberhard Galley and Alfred Estermann, 3:563–71. Hamburg: Hoffmann und Campe, 1987.

———. "Unmoralische Literatur." In *Politische Avantgarde 1830–1840: Eine Dokumentation zum "Jungen Deutschland,"* edited by Alfred Estermann, 1:56–64. Frankfurt: Athenäum, 1972.

Meyer, Eduard. "Notizen zu *Reisebilder*." In *Heinrich Heines Werk im Urteil seiner Zeitgenossen*, edited by Eberhard Galley and Alfred Estermann, 1:576–77. Hamburg: Hoffmann und Campe, 1981.

Moritz, Karl Philipp. "Revision der ersten drei Bände dieses Magazins." *Magazin zur Erfahrungsseelenkunde* 4, no. 1 (1786): 1–56.

Nietzsche, Friedrich. *Jenseits von Gut und Böse; Zur Genealogie der Moral*. Edited by Giorgio Colli and Mazzino Montinari. Vol. 5 of *Friedrich Nietzsche: Sämtliche Werke: Kritische Studienausgabe in 15 Bänden*. Berlin: de Gruyter, 1988.

Pfizer, Gustav. *Gedichte*. Stuttgart: Paul Neff, 1831.

———. "Heine's Schriften und Tendenz." In *Heinrich Heines Werk im Urteil seiner Zeitgenossen*, edited by Eberhard Galley and Alfred Estermann, 4:227–93. Hamburg: Hoffmann and Campe, 1989.

Phönix (Frankfurt). Unsigned review of *Spinoza: Ein historischer Roman*, by Berthold Auerbach. "Aus Stuttgart." January 31, 1838.

Riesser, Gabriel. "Börne und die Juden. Ein Wort der Erwiderung auf die Flugschrift des Herrn Dr. Eduard Meyer gegen Börne." In *Heinrich Heines Werk im Urteil seiner Zeitgenossen*, edited by Eberhard Galley and Alfred Estermann, 2:77–79. Hamburg: Hoffmann and Campe, 1985.

———. *Gesammelte Schriften*. Edited by Meyer Isler. 4 vols. New York: G. Olms, 2001.

———. "Jüdische Briefe. Zur Abwehr und Verständigung." In *Heinrich Heines Werk im Urteil seiner Zeitgenossen*, edited by Eberhard Galley and Alfred Estermann, 5:207–50. Hamburg: Hoffmann and Campe, 1990.

Ruge, Arnold. *Briefwechsel und Tagebuchblätter aus den Jahren 1825–1880*. Vol. 1: 1825–47. Edited by Paul Nerrlich. Berlin: Weidmannsche Buchhandlung, 1886.

———. "Die Frivolität: Erinnerungen an Heine." In *Heinrich Heines Werk im Urteil seiner*

Zeitgenossen, edited Christoph auf der Horst and Sikander Singh, 7:285–93. Stuttgart: Metzler, 2002.
———. "Heinrich Heine, charakterisiert nach seinen Schriften." In *Heinrich Heines Werk im Urteil seiner Zeitgenossen*, edited by Christoph auf der Horst and Sikander Singh, 4:294–322. Stuttgart: Metzler, 1989.
———. "Eine Selbstkritik des Liberalismus." *Deutsche Jahrbücher für Wissenschaft und Kunst*, January 2 and 4, 1843.
———. "A Self-Critique of Liberalism." In *The Young Hegelians: An Anthology*, edited by Lawrence S. Stepelevich, 237–59. Amherst, NY: Humanity, 1999.
Rühs, Friedrich. *Die Rechte des Christenthums und des deutschen Volkes: Vertheidigt gegen die Ansprüche der Juden und ihrer Verfechter*. Berlin: Realschulbuchhandlung, 1816.
———. *Über die Ansprüche der Juden an das deutsche Bürgerrecht: Mit einem Anhange über die Geschichte der Juden in Spanien*. Berlin: Realschulbuchhandlung, 1816.
Schleiermacher, Friedrich. *Der christliche Glaube 1821/22*. 2 vols. Edited by Hermann Peiter. New York: de Gruyter, 1984.
Spinoza, Benedict de. *B. v. Spinoza's Sämmtliche Werke*. Edited and translated by Berthold Auerbach. Stuttgart: J. Scheible, 1841.
———. *Ethics*. Edited and translated by G. H. R. Parkinson. New York: Oxford University Press, 2000.
———. *Theological-Political Treatise*. Translated by Jonathan Israel and Michael Silverthorne. Edited by Jonathan Israel. Cambridge: Cambridge University Press, 2007.
Strodtmann, Adolf. *H. Heine's Leben und Werke*. Vol. 1. Berlin: Duncker, 1867.
Verein für Cultur und Wissenschaft der Juden. *Entwurf von Statuten des Vereins für Cultur und Wissenschaft der Juden*. Berlin: F. Nietack, 1822.
Voltaire. *La Bible enfin expliquée*. 3rd rev. ed. London [Geneva?], 1777.
———. *Oeuvres complètes*. 71 vols. Basel, Switzerland: J. J. Tourneisen, 1784–89.
Weil, Jakob. "Das junge Deutschland und die Juden." In *Heinrich Heines Werk im Urteil seiner Zeitgenossen*, edited by Eberhard Galley and Alfred Estermann, 3:512–14. Hamburg: Hoffmann und Campe, 1987.
Wolf, Immanuel. "Über den Begriff einer Wissenschaft des Judenthums." *Zeitschrift für die Wissenschaft des Judenthums* 1 (1823): 1–24.
———. "On the Concept of a Science of Judaism." In *Ideas of Jewish History*, edited by Michael Meyer, 143–55. Detroit, MI: Wayne State University Press, 1987.
Zunz, Leopold. "Etwas über die rabbinische Literatur." In Leopold Zunz, *Gesammelte Schriften*, 1:1–31. Berlin: L. Gerschel, 1875.

Secondary Sources

Anderson, Benedict. *Imagined Communities: Reflections on the Origin and Spread of Nationalism*. Rev. ed. New York: Verso, 1991.
Arasse, Daniel. *The Guillotine and the Terror*. Translated by Christopher Miller. London: A. Lane, 1989.
Arkush, Allan. *Moses Mendelssohn and the Enlightenment*. Albany: State University of New York Press, 1994.

Avineri, Shlomo. *Moses Hess: Prophet of Communism and Zionism*. New York: New York University Press, 1985.

———. "A Note on Hegel's Views on Jewish Emancipation." *Jewish Social Studies* 25, no. 2 (1963): 145–51.

———. *The Social and Political Thought of Karl Marx*. Cambridge: Cambridge University Press, 1968.

Baron, Salo. "Ghetto and Emancipation." *Menorah Journal* 19 (June 1928): 515–26.

———. *History and Jewish Historians: Essays and Addresses by Salo W. Baron*. Edited by Arthur Hertzberg and Leon A. Feldman. Philadelphia: Jewish Publication Society, 1964.

Becker, Hans-Joachim. *Fichtes Idee der Nation und das Judentum*. Amsterdam: Rodopi, 2000.

Behler, Ernst. "Note on the Texts." In *Encyclopedia of the Philosophical Sciences in Outline, and Other Philosophical Writings*, edited by Ernst Behler and translated by A. V. Miller, Steven A. Taubeneck, and Diana I. Behler, xxi–xxxiii. New York: Continuum, 1990.

Beiser, Frederick C. Introduction to Georg Wilhelm Friedrich Hegel, *Lectures on the History of Philosophy*, translated by E. S. Haldane, 1:xi–xl. Lincoln: University of Nebraska Press, 1995.

Ben-Ari, Nitsa. "1834: The Jewish Historical Novel Helps to Reshape the Historical Consciousness of German Jews." In *Yale Companion to Jewish Writing and Thought in German Culture, 1096–1996*, edited by Sander L. Gilman and Jack Zipes, 143–51. New Haven, CT: Yale University Press, 1997.

Benjamin, Walter. "Der Erzähler." In Walter Benjamin, *Illuminationen*, 385–410. Frankfurt: Suhrkamp, 1977.

Bettelheim, Anton. *Berthold Auerbach: Der Mann, sein Werk, sein Nachlaß*. Stuttgart: Cotta, 1907.

Biale, David. *Not in the Heavens: The Tradition of Jewish Secular Thought*. Princeton, NJ: Princeton University Press, 2011.

Birnbaum, Pierre. *Geography of Hope: Exile, the Enlightenment, Disassimilation*. Translated by Charlotte Mandell. Stanford, CA: Stanford University Press, 2008.

Bourel, Dominique. "A l'origine du kantisme juif: Lazarus Bendavid." In *La philosophie allemande dans la pensée juive*, edited by Gérard Bensussan, 67–79. Paris: Presses universitaires de France, 1997.

———. "Eine Generation später: Lazarus Bendavid (1762–1832)." In *Moses Mendelssohn und die Kreise seiner Wirksamkeit*, edited by Michael Albrecht, Eva J. Engel, and Norbert Hinske, 363–80. Tübingen: De Gruyter, 1994.

Braun, Johann. "Die 'Lex Gans'—ein Kapitel aus der Geschichte der Judenemanzipation in Preußen." In Johann Braun, *Judentum, Jurisprudenz und Philosophie: Bilder aus dem Leben des Juristen Eduard Gans (1797–1839)*, 46–74. Baden-Baden: Nomos, 1997.

Breckman, Warren. "Eduard Gans and the Crisis of Hegelianism." *Journal of the History of Ideas* 62, no. 3 (2001): 543–64.

———. *Marx, the Young Hegelians, and the Origins of Radical Social Theory: Dethroning the Self*. Cambridge: Cambridge University Press, 1999.

Breuer, Edward. *The Limits of Enlightenment: Jews, Germans, and the Eighteenth-Century Study of Scripture*. Cambridge, MA: Harvard University Center for Jewish Studies, 1996.

Briegleb, Klaus. *Bei den Wassern Babels: Heinrich Heine, jüdischer Schriftsteller in der Moderne*. Munich: Deutscher Taschenbuch Verlag, 1997.

———. "'Jeder Reiche ist ein Judas Ischariot!': Vorläufiges über Heinrich Heine und die Juden in Hamburg." In *Die Hamburger Juden in der Emanzipationsphase (1780–1870)*, edited by Peter Freimark and Arno Herzig, 99–128. Hamburg: Hans Christians, 1989.

Brown, Wendy. "Rights and Identity in Late Modernity: Revisiting the 'Jewish Question.'" In *Identities, Politics, and Rights*, edited by Austin Sarat and Thomas R. Kearns, 85–130. Ann Arbor: University of Michigan Press, 1995.

———. *States of Injury: Power and Freedom in Late Modernity*. Princeton, NJ: Princeton University Press, 1995.

Brudney, Daniel. *Marx's Attempt to Leave Philosophy*. Cambridge, MA: Harvard University Press, 1998.

Burnett, Stephen G. "Distorted Mirrors: Antonius Margaritha, Johann Buxtorf and Christian Ethnographies of the Jews." *Sixteenth Century Journal* 25, no. 2 (1994): 275–87.

———. *From Christian Hebraism to Jewish Studies: Johannes Buxtorf (1564–1629) and Hebrew Learning in the Seventeenth Century*. New York: E. J. Brill, 1996.

Cai, Hou. "Moses Heß und Ludwig Feuerbach." In *Ludwig Feuerbach und die Philosophie der Zukunft: Internationale Arbeitsgemeinschaft am ZIF der Universität Bielefeld 1989*, edited by Hans-Jürg Braun et al., 593–615. Berlin: Akademie-Verlag, 1990.

Carlebach, Julius. *Karl Marx and the Radical Critique of Judaism*. Boston: Routledge and Kegan Paul, 1978.

Chase, Jefferson S. *Inciting Laughter: The Development of "Jewish Humor" in 19th Century German Culture*. New York: Walter de Gruyter, 1999.

Chitty, Andrew. "The Basis of the State in the Marx of 1842." In *The New Hegelians: Politics and Philosophy in the Hegelian School*, edited by Douglas Moggach, 220–41. Cambridge: Cambridge University Press, 2006.

Cohen, Richard I. "Jews and the State: The Historical Context." In *Jews and the State: Dangerous Alliances and the Perils of Privilege*, edited by Ezra Mendelsohn, 3–16. Oxford: Oxford University Press, 2003.

Cornu, Auguste. *Karl Marx und Friedrich Engels, Leben und Werk*. 2 vols. Berlin: Aufbau-Verlag, 1954 and 62.

———. *Marx' "Thesen über Feuerbach."* Berlin: Akademie-Verlag, 1963.

Cornu, Auguste, and Wolfgang Mönke. "Einleitung." In *Philosophische und sozialistische Schriften 1837–1850: Eine Auswahl*, edited by Auguste Cornu and Wolfgang Mönke, xiii-lxviv. Expanded ed. Vaduz, Liechtenstein: Topos, 1980.

Davies, Martin. "Karl Philipp Moritz's *Erfahrungseelenkunde*: Its Social and Intellectual Origins." *Oxford German Studies* 16 (1985): 13–35.

Dickey, Laurence. "General Introduction." In G. W. F. Hegel, *Political Writings*, edited by Laurence Dickey and H. B. Nisbet, vii–xli. Translated by H. B. Nisbet. Cambridge: Cambridge University Press, 1999.

———. "Hegel on Religion and Philosophy." In *The Cambridge Companion to Hegel*, edited by Frederick C. Beiser, 301–47. New York: Cambridge University Press, 1993.

Du Bois, W. E. B. *The Souls of Black Folk*. Edited by Henry Louis Gates Jr. and Terri Hume Oliver. New York: W. W. Norton, 1999.

Ellenson, David. "German Orthodoxy, Jewish Law, and the Uses of Kant." In *Between Tradition and Culture: The Dialectics of Modern Jewish Religion and Identity*, edited by David Ellenson, 15–26. Atlanta, GA. Scholars Press, 1994.

Eßbach, Wolfgang. *Die Junghegelianer: Soziologie einer Intellektuellengruppe*. Munich: W. Fink, 1988.

Fackenheim, Emil L. *Encounters between Judaism and Modern Philosophy*. New York: Basic, 1973.

———. "Hegel and Judaism: A Flaw in the Hegelian Mediation." In *The Legacy of Hegel: Proceedings of the Marquette Hegel Symposium 1970*, edited by J. J. O'Malley, K. W. Algozin, H. P. Kainz, and L. C. Rice, 165–85. The Hague: Nijhoff, 1973.

———. "Samuel Hirsch and Hegel: A Study of Hirsch's *Religionsphilosophie Der Juden* (1842)." In *Studies in Nineteenth Century Jewish Intellectual History*, edited by Alexander Altman, 171–201. Cambridge, MA: Harvard University Press, 1964.

Feiner, Shmuel. *Cultural Revolution in Berlin*. Oxford: Bodleian Library, 2011.

———. *The Jewish Enlightenment*. Translated by Chaya Naor. Philadelphia: University of Pennsylvania Press, 2004.

———. *The Origins of Jewish Secularization in Eighteenth-Century Europe*. Translated by Chaya Naor. Philadelphia: University of Pennsylvainia Press, 2011.

Ferstenberg, Helen. *Meditations on Jewish Creative Identity*. New York: Peter Lang, 2004.

Fischer, Lars. "Hegel in Support of Jewish Emancipation: A Deliberate Political Act?" *Owl of Minerva* 37, no. 2 (2006): 127–57.

———. *The Socialist Response to Antisemitism in Imperial Germany*. Cambridge: Cambridge University Press, 2007.

Fontenay, Elisabeth de. *Les Figures juives de Marx: Marx dans l'idéologie allemande*. Paris: Galilée, 1973.

Forbes, Duncan. Introduction to Georg Wilhelm Friedrich Hegel, *Lectures on the Philosophy of World History: Introduction, Reason in History*, translated by H. B. Nisbet, vii–xxxv. Cambridge: Cambridge University Press, 1975.

Formstecher, Salomon. "Selections from *Religion of the Mind/Spirit*." In *Modern Jewish Thinkers: From Mendelssohn to Rosenzweig*, edited by Gershon Greenberg, 139–70. Brighton, MA: Academic Studies, 2011.

Franco, Paul. *Hegel's Philosophy of Freedom*. New Haven, CT: Yale University Press, 1999.

Freud, Sigmund. *Gesammelte Werke, chronologisch geordnet*. Edited by Anna Freud et al. 18 vols. Frankfurt: Fischer, 1968–78.

Friedlander, Albert. "The Wohlwill-Moser Correspondence." *Leo Baeck Institute Yearbook* 11 (1966): 262–99.

Galley, Eberhard, and Alfred Estermann, eds. *Heinrich Heines Werk im Urteil seiner Zeitgenossen*. 13 vols. Hamburg: Hoffmann and Campe, Heinrich Heine Verlag, 1981–2006.

Garniron, Pierre, and Friedrich Hogemann. "Hegels Vorlesungen zur Geschichte der Philosophie." *Hegel-Studien* 26 (1991): 110–19.

Geiger, Ludwig. "Aus Eduard Gans' Frühzeit (1817)." *Zeitschrift für die Geschichte der Juden in Deutschland* 5 (1892): 93–96.

Geller, Jay. *The Other Jewish Question: Identifying the Jew and Making Sense of Modernity*. New York: Fordham University Press, 2011.

Gillman, Sander. *Jewish Self-Hatred: Anti-Semitism and the Hidden Language of the Jews*. Baltimore, MD: Johns Hopkins University Press, 1986.

Glatzer, Nahum N. "The Beginnings of Modern Jewish Studies." In *Studies in Nineteenth-*

Century Jewish Intellectual History, edited by Alexander Altman, 27–45. Cambridge, MA: Harvard University Press, 1964.

———, ed. *Leopold and Adelheid Zunz: An Account in Letters, 1815–1885*. London: Published for the Leo Baeck Institute by the East and West Library, 1958.

Goetschel, Willi. *Spinoza's Modernity: Mendelssohn, Lessing, and Heine*. Madison: University of Wisconsin Press, 2004.

Graetz, Heinrich. *Vom Beginn der Mendelssohn'schen Zeit (1750) bis in die neueste Zeit (1848)*. Vol. 11 of *Geschichte der Juden von den ältesten Zeiten bis auf die Gegenwart*. Leipzig: Robert Friese, 1870.

Graetz, Michael. "The Jewish Enlightenment." In *German-Jewish History in Modern Times*, edited by Michael A. Meyer and Michael Brenner (assistant editor), 1:261–374. New York: Columbia University Press, 1996.

———. "Renaissance des Judentums im 19. Jahrhundert: 'Der Verein für Cultur und Wissenschaft der Juden' 1819 bis 1824." In *Bild und Selbstbild der Juden Berlins zwischen Aufklärung und Romantik*, edited by Marianne Awerbuch and Stefi Jersch-Wenzel, 211–27. Berlin: Colloquium, 1992.

Graupe, Heinz Mosche. "Kant und das Judentum." *Zeitschrift für Religions- und Geistesgeschichte* 13 (1961): 308–33.

Greenberg, Gershon. "Religion and History According to Samuel Hisch." *Hebrew Union College Annual* 43 (1972): 103–24.

———. "Samuel Hirsch: Jewish Hegelian." *Revue des études juives* 129 (1970): 205–15.

Grossman, Jeffrey A. "Auerbach, Heine, and the Question of Bildung in German and German-Jewish Culture." In *Nexus: Essays in German Jewish Studies*, edited by William Collins Donahue and Martha B. Helfer, 85–107. Rochester, NY: Camden House, 2011.

Guttmann, Jacob. "Lazarus Bendavid: Seine Stellung zum Judentum und seine literarische Wirksamkeit." *Monatsschrift für Geschichte und Wissenschaft des Judentums* 61, n.s. 21 (1917): 26–50; 176–211.

Guttmann, Julius. "Kant und das Judentum." In *Schriften: Herausgegeben von der Gesellschaft zur Förderung der Wissenschaft des Judentums*, 41–62. Leipzig: Gustav Fock, 1908.

Harris, Horton. *David Friedrich Strauss and His Theology*. Cambridge: Cambridge University Press, 1973.

Haury, Thomas. "*Zur Judenfrage* (1843/44): Bruno Bauer und Karl Marx—Eine Textgeschichte." In *Kapitalismusdebatten um 1900—Über antisemitisierende Semantiken des Jüdischen*, edited by Nicolas Berg, 141–79. Leipzig: Liepziger Universitätsverlag, 2011.

Henrich, Dieter. "Marx als Schüler Hegels." In Dieter Henrich, *Hegel im Kontext*, 187–207. Frankfurt: Suhrkamp, 1971.

Heschel, Susannah. *Abraham Geiger and the Jewish Jesus*. Chicago: University of Chicago Press, 1998.

Hess, Jonathan M. "Beyond Subversion: German Jewry and the Poetics of Middlebrow Culture." *German Quarterly* 82, no. 3 (2009): 316–35.

———. *Germans, Jews, and the Claims of Modernity*. New Haven, CT: Yale University Press, 2002.

———. *Middlebrow Literature and the Making of German-Jewish Identity*. Stanford, CA: Stanford University Press, 2010.

Hodgson, Peter C. "Editorial Introduction." In Georg Wilhelm Friedrich Hegel, *Lectures on the Philosophy of Religion*, edited by Peter C. Hodgson. Translated by R. F. Brown, Peter C. Hodgson, and J. M. Stewart, with the assistance of H. S. Harris, 1:1–82. Reprint. Oxford: Oxford University Press, 2007.

———. "Hegel's Philosophy of Religion." In *The Cambridge Companion to Hegel and Nineteenth-Century Philosophy*, edited by Frederick C. Beiser, 230–52. Cambridge: Cambridge University Press, 2008.

———. "The Metamorphosis of Judaism in Hegel's Philosophy of Religion." *Owl of Minerva* 19, no. 1 (1987): 41–52.

Hoffheimer, Michael. *Eduard Gans and the Hegelian Philosophy of Law*. Boston: Kluwer, 1995.

Honneth, Axel. "Work and Instrumental Action." *New German Critique* 26 (1982): 31–54.

Hook, Sidney. *From Hegel to Marx*. Ann Arbor: University of Michigan Press, 1962.

Hsia, R. Po-chia. "Christian Ethnographies of Jews in Early Modern Germany." In *The Expulsion of the Jews 1492 and After*, edited by Raymond B. Wuddington and Arthur H. Williamson, 223–35. New York: Garland, 1994.

Hunt, Richard N. *The Political Ideas of Marx and Engels: Marxism and Totalitarian Democracy, 1818–1850*. Vol. 1. Pittsburgh, PA: University of Pittsburgh Press, 1974.

Ilting, Karl-Heinz. "Die 'Rechtsphilosophie' von 1820 und Hegels Vorlesungen über Rechtsphilosophie." In Georg Wilhelm Friedrich Hegel, *Vorlesungen über Rechtsphilosophie*, edited by Karl-Heinz Ilting, 1:25–126. Stuttgart-Bad Cannstatt, Germany: Frommann-Holzboog, 1973.

———. "Hegel's Concept of the State and Marx's Early Critique." In *The State and Civil Society: Studies in Hegel's Political Philosophy*, edited by Z. A. Pelczynski, 93–113. Cambridge: Cambridge University Press, 1984.

Kahn, Lothar, and Donald D. Hook. "The Impact of Heine on Nineteenth-Century German-Jewish Writers." In *The Jewish Reception of Heinrich Heine*, edited by Mark H. Gelber, 53–65. Tübingen: Niemeyer, 1992.

Kanda, Junji. "Moses Heß und der gescheiterte Weg von Hegel zu Feuerbach." In *Ludwig Feuerbach und die Philosophie der Zukunft: Internationale Arbeitsgemeinschaft am ZIF der Universität Bielefeld 1989*, edited by Hans-Jürg Braun, Hans-Martin Sass, W. Schuffenhauer, and Francesco Tomasoni, 617–42. Berlin: Akademie-Verlag, 1990.

Karp, Jonathan. *The Politics of Jewish Commerce: Economic Thought and Emancipation in Europe, 1638–1848*. Cambridge: Cambridge University Press, 2008.

Katz, Jacob. *From Prejudice to Destruction: Anti-Semitism, 1700–1933*. Cambridge, MA: Harvard University Press, 1980.

———. *Out of the Ghetto: The Social Background of Jewish Emancipation, 1770–1870*. New York: Schocken, 1978.

———. "Spinoza und die Utopie einer totalen Assimilation der Juden." In Jacob Katz, *Zur Assimilation und Emanzipation der Juden: Ausgewählte Schriften*, 199–209. Darmstadt: Wissenschaftliche Buchgesellschaft, 1982.

———. "A State within a State: The History of an Anti-Semitic Slogan." In Jacob Katz, *Emancipation and Assimilation: Studies in Modern Jewish History*, 47–76. Farnborough, UK: Gregg, 1972.

Kennecke, Andreas. *Isaac Euchel: Architekt der Haskala*. Göttingen: Wallstein, 2007.
Koltun-Fromm, Ken. *Moses Hess and Modern Jewish Identity*. Bloomington: Indiana University Press, 2001.
Kovesi, Julius. "Moses Hess, Marx, and Money." In Julius Kovesi, *Values and Evaluations: Essays on Ethics and Ideology*, edited by Alan Tapper, 127–82. New York: Peter Lang, 1998.
Künzli, Arnold. *Karl Marx: Eine Psychographie*. Frankfurt: Europa Verlag, 1966.
La Vopa, Anthony J. *Fichte: The Self and the Calling of Philosophy, 1762–1799*. New York: Cambridge University Press, 2001.
———. "Jews and Germans: Old Quarrels, New Departures." *Journal of the History of Ideas* 54, no. 4 (1993): 675–95.
Lang, Berel. *Act and Idea in the Nazi Genocide*. Chicago: University of Chicago Press, 1990.
Leopold, David. "The Hegelian Antisemitism of Bruno Bauer." *History of European Ideas* 25 (1999): 179–206.
———. *The Young Karl Marx: German Philosophy, Modern Politics, and Human Flourishing*. Cambridge: Cambridge University Press, 2007.
Lepenies, Wolf. *Das Ende der Naturgeschichte: Wandel kultureller Selbstverständlichkeiten in den Wissenschaften des 18. und 19. Jahrhunderts*. Munich: C. Hanser, 1976.
———. "Historisierung der Natur und Entmoralisierung der Wissenschaften seit dem 18. Jahrhundert." In Wolf Lepenies, *Gefährliche Wahlverwandtschaften: Essays zur Wissenschaftsgeschichte*, 7–38. Stuttgart: Philipp Reclam, 1989.
Lerousseau, Andrée. *Le judaïsme dans la philosophie allemande, 1770–1850*. Paris: Presses Universitaires de France, 2001.
Levy, Ze'ev. *Baruch Spinoza—Seine Aufnahme durch die Jüdischen Denker in Deutschland*. Stuttgart: Kohlhammer, 2001.
Livné-Freudenthal, Rachel. "Der 'Verein für Cultur und Wissenschaft der Juden' (1819–1924): Zwischen Staatskonformismus und Staatskritik." *Tel Aviver Jahrbuch für deutsche Geschichte* 20 (1991): 103–25.
———. "From 'A Nation Dwelling Alone' to 'A Nation among the Nations' or: 'The Return to History'—Between Universalism and Nationalism." In *Streams into the Sea: Studies in Jewish Culture and Its Context*, edited by Rachel Livneh-Freudenthal and Elchanan Reiner, 153–77. Tel Aviv: Alma College, 2001.
———. "Kultur als Weltanschauung: Der Kulturbegriff der Begründer der 'Wissenschaft des Judentums.'" In *Arche Noah: Die Idee der 'Kultur' im deutsch-jüdischen Diskurs*, edited by Bernhard Greiner and Christoph Schmidt, 59–84. Freiburg: Rombach, 2002.
Lloyd, Genevieve. *Part of Nature: Self-Knowledge in Spinoza's "Ethics."* Ithaca, NY: Cornell University Press, 1994.
Lowenstein, Steven M. "Jewish Upper Crust and Berlin Jewish Enlightenment: The Family of Daniel Itzig." In *From East and West: Jews in a Changing Europe, 1750–1870*, edited by Francis Malino and David Sorkin, 182–201. Oxford: Basil Blackwell, 1990.
Lutz, Rolland. "The 'New Left' of Restoration Germany." *Journal of the History of Ideas* 31, no. 2 (1970): 235–52.
Macherey, Pierre. *Hegel ou Spinoza*. 2nd ed. Paris: Éditions la Découverte, 1990.
Mack, Michael. *German Idealism and the Jew: The Inner Anti-Semitism of Philosophy and German-Jewish Responses*. Chicago: University of Chicago Press, 2003.

Maccoby, Hyam. *Antisemitism and Modernity: Innovation and Continuity*. New York: Routledge, 2006.

McCarney, Joseph. *Hegel on History*. New York: Routledge, 2000.

McInnes, Edward. "Realism, History and the Nation: the Reception of the 'Waverley' Novels in Germany in the 19th Century." *New German Studies* 16, no. 1 (1990–91): 39–51.

McLellan, David. *Marx before Marxism*. New York: Harper and Row, 1970.

———. *The Young Hegelians and Karl Marx*. London: Macmillan, 1969.

Mendes-Flohr, Paul, and Jehuda Reinharz, eds. *The Jew in the Modern World: A Documentary History*. 2nd ed. New York: Oxford University Press, 1995.

Meyer, Michael A., ed. *Ideas of Jewish History*. 2nd ed. 1974. Detroit, MI: Wayne State University Press, 1987.

———. *The Origins of the Modern Jew: Jewish Identity and European Culture in Germany, 1749–1824*. Detroit,MI: Wayne State University Press, 1967.

———. "The Orthodox and the Enlightened: An Unpublished Contemporary Analysis of Berlin Jewry's Spiritual Condition in the Early Nineteenth Century." *Leo Baeck Institute Year Book* 25 (1980): 101–30.

———. "Reform Jewish Thinkers in Their German Intellectual Context." In *The Jewish Response to German Culture: From the Enlightenment to the Second World War*, edited by Jehuda Reinharz and Walter Schatzberg, 64–84. Hanover, NH: University Press of New England, 1985.

———. *Response to Modernity: A History of the Reform Movement in Judaism*. Reprint. Detroit, MI: Wayne State University Press, 1995.

———. "Two Persistent Tensions within *Wissenschaft des Judentums*." In *Modern Judaism and Historical Consciousness: Identities, Encounters, Perspectives*, edited by Andreas Gotzmann and Christian Wiese, 73–92. Boston: Brill, 2007.

Meyer, Michael A., ed., and Michael Brenner, assistant ed. *German-Jewish History in Modern Times*. 4 vols. New York: Columbia University Press, 1996–98.

Moggach, Douglas. *The Philosophy and Politics of Bruno Bauer*. New York: Cambridge University Press, 2003.

———. "Republican Rigorism and Emancipation in Bruno Bauer." In *The New Hegelians: Politics and Philosophy in the Hegelian School*, edited by Douglas Moggach, 114–35. Cambridge: Cambridge University Press, 2006.

Mosse, Werner E. "The Revolution of 1848—Jewish Emancipation in Germany and Its Limits." In *Revolution and Evolution: 1848 in German-Jewish History*, edited by Werner E. Mosse, Arnold Paucker, and Reinhard Rürup, 389–401. Tübingen: Mohr Siebeck, 1981

Myers, David N. "The Ideology of Wissenschaft des Judentums." In *History of Jewish Philosophy*, edited by Daniel H. Frank and Oliver Leaman, 706–21. New York: Routledge, 2003.

———. *Re-Inventing the Jewish Past: European Jewish Intellectuals and the Zionist Return to History*. New York: Oxford University Press, 1995.

Na'aman, Shlomo. *Emanzipation und Messianismus: Leben und Werk des Moses Hess*. Frankfurt: Campus, 1982.

———. *Marxismus und Zionismus*. Gerlingen, Germany: Bleicher, 1997.

Nadler, Steven. *Spinoza: A Life*. Cambridge: Cambridge University Press, 1999.
———. *Spinoza's Ethics: An Introduction*. Cambridge: Cambridge University Press, 2006.
Navon, Ephraim. "The Encounter of German Idealists and Jewish Enlighteners: 1760–1800." *Jahrbuch des Instituts für deutsche Geschichte Beiheft* (1980): 225–41.
Neumark, David. "Historical and Systematic Relations of Judaism to Kant." *Year Book of the Central Conference of American Rabbis* 34 (1924): 203–21.
Niewöhner, Friedrich. "'Primat der Ethik' oder 'erkenntnistheoretische Begründung der Ethik'? Thesen zur Kant-Rezeption in der jüdischen Philosophie." In *Judentum im Zeitalter der Aufklärung*, edited by G. Schulz, 119–61. Wolfenbüttel, Germany: Jacobi, 1977.
Nipperdey, Thomas. "Verein als soziale Struktur im späten 18. und frühen 19. Jahrhundert." In *Geschichtswissenschaft und Vereinswesen im 19. Jahrhundert: Beiträge zur Geschichte historischer Forschung in Deutschland*, 1–44. Göttingen: Vandenhoeck and Ruprecht, 1972.
Nirenberg, David. *Anti-Judaism: The Western Tradition*. New York: W. W. Norton, 2013.
O'Boyle, Lenore. "The Problem of an Excess of Educated Men in Western Europe (1800–1850)." *Journal of Modern History* 42 (1970): 471–95.
Peters, George F. *The Poet as Provocateur: Heinrich Heine and His Critics*. Rochester, NY: Camden House, 2000.
Pinkard, Terry. *Hegel: A Biography*. Cambridge: Cambridge University Press, 2000.
Pöggeler, Otto. "L'interprétation hégelienne du Judaïsme." *Archives de Philosophie* 44 (1981): 189–238.
Presner, Todd S. *Mobile Modernity: Germans, Jews, Trains*. New York: Columbia University Press, 2007.
Rabaté, Jean-Michel. *The Future of Theory*. Oxford: Blackwell, 2002.
Reill, Peter Hanns. *The German Enlightenment and the Rise of Historicism*. Berkeley: University of California Press, 1975.
Reissner, Hanns G. *Eduard Gans: Ein Leben im Vormärz*. Tübingen: Mohr Siebeck, 1965.
———. "Rebellious Dilemma: The Case Histories of Eduard Gans and Some of His Partisans." *Leo Baeck Institute Yearbook* 2 (1957): 179–93.
Reitter, Paul. *On the Origins of Jewish Self-Hatred*. Princeton, NJ: Princeton University Press, 2012.
Richarz, Monica. *Der Eintritt der Juden in die akademischen Berufe: Jüdische Studenten und Akademiker in Deutschland 1678–1848*. Tübingen: J. C. B.Mohr, 1974.
Roelcke, Volker. *Krankheit und Kulturkritik: Psychiatrische Gesellschaftsdeutungen im bürgerlichen Zeitalter (1790–1914)*. Frankfurt: Campus, 1999.
Roemer, Nils H. *Jewish Scholarship and Culture in Nineteenth-Century Germany: Between History and Faith*. Madison: University of Wisconsin Press, 2005.
Rose, Gillian. *Judaism and Modernity: Philosophical Essays*. Oxford: Blackwell, 1993.
Rose, Paul Lawrence. *Revolutionary Antisemitism in Germany from Kant to Wagner*. Princeton, NJ: Princeton University Press, 1990.
Rosen, Zvi. *Moses Hess und Karl Marx: Ein Beitrag zur Entstehung der Marxschen Theorie*. Hamburg: Christians, 1983.
Rosenbloom, Noah H. "The 'Nineteen Letters of Ben Uziel'—A Hegelian Exposition." *Historia Judaica* 22, no. 1 (1960): 23–60.

Rotenstreich, Nathan. "For and against Emancipation: The Bruno Bauer Controversy." *Leo Baeck Institute Yearbook* 4 (1959): 3–36.

———. "Hegel's Image of Judaism." *Jewish Social Studies* 15 (1953): 33–52.

———. *Jewish Philosophy in Modern Times*. New York: Holt, Rinehart, and Winston, 1968.

———. *Jews and German Philosophy: The Polemics of Emancipation*. New York: Schocken, 1984.

———. "Moses Hess—ein Jünger Spinozas?" *Archiv für Geschichte der Philosophie* 71:2 (1989): 231–47.

———. *The Recurring Pattern: Studies in Anti-Judaism in Modern Thought*. New York: Horizon, 1963.

———. *Tradition and Reality: The Impact of History on Modern Jewish Thought*. New York: Random House, 1972.

Rubaschoff, Salman. "Erstlinge der Entjudung: Drei Reden von Eduard Gans im Kulturverein." *Der jüdische Wille* 1 (1918): 30–42, 108–21, 193–203.

Rürup, Reinhard. "The European Revolutions of 1848 and Jewish Emancipation." In *Revolution and Evolution: 1848 in German-Jewish History*, edited by Werner E. Mosse, Arnold Paucker, and Reinhard Rürup, 1–53. Tübingen: Mohr Siebeck, 1981.

Samuels, Maurice. *Inventing the Israelite: Jewish Fiction in Nineteenth-Century France*. Stanford, CA: Stanford University Press, 2010.

Sammons, Jeffrey L. "Observations on Berthold Auerbach's Jewish Novels." *Orim* 1 (spring 1986): 61–74.

Sass, Hans-Martin. "Bruno Bauers Idee der 'Rheinischen Zeitung.'" *Zeitschrift für Religions- und Geistesgeschichte* 19 (1967): 321–32.

Schaeffler, Richard. "Die Wissenschaft des Judentums in ihrer Beziehung zur Allgemeinen Geistesgeschichte im Deutschland des 19. Jahrunderts." In *Wissenschaft des Judentums/Hochmat Yisrael: Anfänge der Judaistik in Europa*, edited by Julius Carlebach, 113–31. Darmstadt, Germany: Wissenschaftliche Buchgesellschaft, 1992.

Scheuffelen, Thomas, ed. "Berthold Auerbach, 1812–1882." Special issue, *Marbacher Magazin* 36 (1985).

Schoeps, Hans Joachim. *Geschichte der jüdischen Religionsphilosophie in der Neuzeit*. Berlin: Vortrupp, 1935.

Schorsch, Ismar. *From Text to Context: the Turn to History in Modern Judaism*. Hanover, NH: Published for Brandeis University Press by University Press of New England, 1994.

Schulte, Christoph. *Die jüdische Aufklärung*. Munich: C. H. Beck, 2002.

———. "Saul Ascher's *Leviathan*, or the Invention of Jewish Orthodoxy in 1792." *Leo Baeck Institute Yearbook* 45 (2000): 25–34.

———. "Über den Begriff einer Wissenschaft des Judentums." *Aschkenas* 7, no. 2 (1997): 277–302.

Schwartz, Daniel B. *The First Modern Jew: Spinoza and the History of an Image*. Princeton, NJ: Princeton University Press, 2012.

Sheehan, James. *German History, 1770–1866*. New York: Oxford University Press, 1989.

Silberner, Edmund. *Moses Hess: Geschichte seines Lebens*. Leiden, the Netherlands: E. J. Brill, 1966.

———. "Was Marx an Anti-Semite?" In *Essential Papers on Jews and the Left*, edited by Ezra Mendelssohn, 361–401. New York: New York University Press, 1997.

Skolnik, Jonathan. "Writing Jewish History between Gutzkow and Goethe: Auerbach's *Spinoza* and the Birth of Modern Jewish Historical Fiction." *Prooftexts* 19 (1999): 101–25.

Smith, Steven B. *Spinoza, Liberalism, and the Question of Jewish Identity*. New Haven, CT: Yale University Press, 1997.

Socher, Abraham P. *The Radical Enlightenment of Solomon Maimon*. Stanford, CA: Stanford University Press, 2006.

Sorkin, David. *The Berlin Haskalah and German Religious Thought: Orphans of Knowledge*. Portland, OR: Vallentine Mitchell, 2000.

———. *Moses Mendelssohn and the Religious Enlightenment*. Berkeley: University of California Press, 1996.

———. *The Transformation of German Jewry, 1780–1840*. 1987. Detroit, MI: Wayne State University Press, 1999.

Spector, Scott. "Beyond Assimilation: Introducing Subjectivity to German-Jewish History." In *Religion or Ethnicity? Jewish Identities in Evolution*, edited by Zvi Gittelman, 90–103. New Brunswick, NJ: Rutgers University Press, 2009.

Strauss, Jonathan. *Human Remains: Medicine, Death, and Desire in Nineteenth-Century Paris*. New York: Fordham University Press, 2012.

———. *Subjects of Terror: Nerval, Hegel, and the Modern Self*. Stanford, CA: Stanford University Press, 1998.

Taylor, Charles. *Hegel*. New York: Cambridge University Press, 1975.

Thier, Erich. *Das Menschenbild des jungen Marx*. Göttingen: Vandenhoeck and Ruprecht, 1961.

Toews, John. *Hegelianism: The Path toward Dialectical Humanism, 1805–1841*. Cambridge: Cambridge University Press, 1980.

Tomasoni, Francesco. *Modernity and the Final Aim of History: The Debate over Judaism from Kant to the Young Hegelians*. Boston: Kluwer, 2003.

Toury, Jacob. "'Deutsche Juden' im Vormärz." *Bulletin des Leo-Baeck-Instituts* 29 (1965): 65–84.

———. *Die politischen Orientierungen der Juden in Deutschland: von Jena bis Weimar*. Tübingen: Mohr Siebeck, 1966.

———. "Die Revolution von 1848 als innerjüdischer Wendepunkt." In *Das Judentum in der deutschen Umwelt 1800–1850: Studien zur Frühgeschichte der Emanzipation*, edited by Hans Liebeschütz and Arnold Paucker, 359–76. Tübingen: Mohr Siebeck, 1977.

Traverso, Enzo. *The Marxists and the Jewish Question: The History of a Debate, 1843–1943*. Atlantic Highlands, NJ: Humanities, 1994.

Tucker, Robert. *Philosophy and Myth in Karl Marx*, 2nd ed. Cambridge: Cambridge University Press, 1972.

Ucko, Sinai (Siegfried). "Geistesgeschichtliche Grundlagen der Wissenschaft des Judentums (Motive des Kulturvereins vom Jahre 1819)." In *Wissenschaft des Judentums im deutschen Sprachbereich: Ein Querschnitt*, edited by Kurt Wilhelm, 1:315–52. Tübingen: Mohr Siebeck, 1967.

Van den Bergh van Eysinga, Gustaaf A. "Het Jodenvraagstuk: Naar aanleiding van Bruno Bauer's opfattingen daromtrent." *Godsdienst-Wetenschappelijke Studiën* 12 (1952): 22–71.

Veltri, Giuseppe. "Altertumswissenschaft und Wissenschaft des Judentums: Leopold Zunz und seine Lehrer F. A. Wolf und A. Böckh." In *Friedrich August Wolf: Studien,*

Dokumente, Bibliographie, edited by Reinhard Markner and Giuseppe Veltri, 32–47. Stuttgart: Steiner, 1999.

Vick, Brian E. *Defining Germany: The 1848 Frankfurt Paliamentarians and National Identity*. Cambridge, MA: Harvard University Press, 2002.

Von der Luft, Eric, ed. and trans. *Hegel, Hinrichs, and Schleiermacher on Feeling and Reason in Religion: The Texts of Their 1821–22 Debate*. Lewiston, NY: Edwin Mellen, 1987.

Waser, Rudi. *Autonomie des Selbstbewußtseins: Eine Untersuchung zum Verhältnis von Bruno Bauer und Karl Marx (1835–1843)*. Tübingen: A. Franke Verlag, 1994.

Waszek, Norbert. "Eduard Gans on Poverty and on the Constitutional Debate." In *The New Hegelians: Politics and Philosophy in the Hegelian School*, edited by Douglas Moggach, 24–49. Cambridge: Cambridge University Press, 2006.

———. "Hegel, Mendelssohn, Spinoza—Beiträge der Philosophie zur 'Wissenschaft des Judentums'? Eduard Gans und die philosophischen Optionen des 'Vereins für Kultur und Wissenschaft der Juden.'" *Menora* 10 (1999): 187–215.

———. "Vorwort." In *Eduard Gans (1797–1839): Hegelianer-Jude-Europäer: Texte und Dokumente*, edited by Norbert Waszek, 9–51. Frankfurt: Peter Lang, 1991.

———. "'Wissenschaft und Liebe zu den Seinen'—Eduard Gans und die hegelianischen Ursprünge der 'Wissenschaft des Judentums.'" In *Eduard Gans (1797–1839): Politischer Professor zwischen Restauration und Vormärz*, edited by Reinhard Blänkner, Gerhard Göhler, and Norbert Waszek, 71–103. Leipzig: Leipziger Universitätsverlag, 2002.

Weissberg, Liliane. "Fußnoten: Zum Ort der ästhetischen Erfahrung in Lazarus Bendavids Selbstbiographie." *Berliner Aufklärung* 1 (1999): 231–53.

Westphal, Merold. "Hegel's Radical Idealism: Family and State as Ethical Communities." In *The State and Civil Society: Studies in Hegel's Political Philosophy*, edited by Z. A. Pelczynski, 77–92. New York: Cambridge University Press, 1984.

Wieckenberg, Ernst-Peter. "Juden als Autoren des *Magazins zur Erfahrungsseelenkunde*: Ein Beitrag zum Thema 'Juden und Aufklärung in Berlin.'" In *Rahel Levin Varnhagen: Die Wiederentdeckung einer Schriftstellerin*, edited by Barbara Hahn and Ursula Isselstein, 128–40. Göttingen: Vandenhoeck and Ruprecht, 1987.

Wiener, Max. "The Ideology of the Founders of Jewish Scientific Research." *Yivo Annual of Jewish Social Science* 5 (1950): 184–96.

———. *Jüdische Religion im Zeitalter der Emanzipation*. Berlin: Philo, 1933.

Wieseltier, Leon. "*Etwas über jüdische Historik*—Leopold Zunz and the Inception of Modern Jewish Historiography." *History and Theory* 20 (1981): 135–149.

Wistrich, Robert. *Revolutionary Jews from Marx to Trotsky*. New York: Barnes and Noble Books, 1976.

Wood, Allen. "General Introduction." In Immanuel Kant, *Practical Philosophy*, edited and translated by Mary J. Gregor, xiii–xxxiii. New York: Cambridge University Press, 1996.

Yack, Bernard. *The Longing for Total Revolution: Philosophic Sources of Social Discontent from Rousseau to Marx and Nietzsche*. Princeton, NJ: Princeton University Press, 1986.

Yerushalmi, Yosef Hayim. *Zakhor: Jewish History and Jewish Memory*. New York: Schocken, 1989.

Yovel, Yirmiyahu. *Dark Riddle: Hegel, Nietzsche, and the Jews*. University Park: Pennsylvania State University Press, 1998.

Index